"It has been said that Reformed theology *is* covenant theology, for *covenant* is not merely a doctrine or theme in the Bible but is the principle that structures all its revelation. Robert Rollock said, 'God speaks nothing to man without the covenant.' Therefore, it is a delight to see this amazing scholarly collaboration by the faculty of Reformed Theological Seminary, which will surely prove to be a sourcebook for future studies of Reformed covenant theology. Here is a gold mine of biblical and historical studies by trusted pastor-theologians of Christ's church."

> **Joel R. Beeke,** President and Professor of Systematic Theology and Homiletics, Puritan Reformed Theological Seminary; author, *Reformed Preaching*; coauthor, *Reformed Systematic Theology*

"The revived interest in covenant theology has sparked rich insights and lively debate. Representing a variety of views and specialties, and united by biblical fidelity and rigorous scholarship, *Covenant Theology* is a very impressive and welcome collection."

> **Michael Horton,** J. Gresham Machen Professor of Systematic Theology and Apologetics, Westminster Seminary California

"*Covenant Theology* is a gift to the church, a grand account of covenant in Scripture and in Christian theology. This work is scholarly and readable, rigorous and complete. Every chapter is thorough, whether it gathers data on familiar themes or explores new territory. The contributors and editors have presented a resource that pastors and scholars will draw from for many years."

> **Daniel Doriani,** Vice President at Large and Professor of Biblical and Systematic Theology, Covenant Theological Seminary

"This rich and learned compendium updates and extends our understanding of God's initiative in, and manner of performing, his signature saving work. With thirteen chapters on covenant and covenants in the Bible, seven on covenant in Christian thought up to today, and seven on topics like covenant in contemporary New Testament scholarship, dispensationalism, and 'new covenant theologies,' no significant stone is left unturned. From Ligon Duncan's foreword to Kevin DeYoung's meaty homiletical summation at the end, this volume artfully defines a nonnegotiable Christian teaching and reaffirms its centrality. The annotated bibliography offers an invaluable listing of covenant studies in (and in some cases against) the Reformed tradition over many centuries. These important essays by a distinguished seminary faculty are a lasting gift to scholarship as well as to the church."

> **Robert W. Yarbrough,** Professor of New Testament, Covenant Theological Seminary

"Breathtaking! I don't know of any work that has the diversity and scope of *Covenant Theology*. Every aspect of the covenant doctrine receives attention from the book's contributors. Each chapter is an urgent invitation. The covenant doctrine is analyzed here with unquestionable scholarship and inalienable commitment to Scripture and Reformed theology. Starting with the exegesis of biblical material, going through the historical development of the theme in the church, contrasting and comparing it with extrabiblical material, and analyzing the concept of the covenant in modern theology, this book offers the most comprehensive exposition of the covenant doctrine available today."

> **Augustus Nicodemus Lopes,** Assistant Pastor, First Presbyterian Church, Recife, Brazil; Vice President, Supreme Council, Presbyterian Church of Brazil; author, *Apostles* and *The Bible and Its Interpreters*

"If *covenant* is the Bible's word for God's relationship with his people, what could be more important than thinking deeply and clearly about covenant theology? This volume is a sure guide to the covenantal thinking that underpins so much of pastoral ministry. Bringing rigorous exegesis into conversation with historic perspectives and modern debates, it is a remarkably comprehensive and thorough work that will help any preacher or student of Scripture."

Jonty Rhodes, Minister, Christ Church Central Leeds, UK; author, *Covenants Made Simple* and *Man of Sorrows, King of Glory*

"In the history of Reformed theology, the biblical teaching of the triune God's sovereign initiative to enter into covenant union and communion with his people, before and after the fall into sin, has been a central focus, and some say it even defines Reformed theology. For this reason, the contributors to this comprehensive volume, which treats the topic of the covenant or covenants in biblical, historical, and systematic perspectives, provide a wonderful overview of Reformed theology's engagement with Scripture's teaching. Encyclopedic in scope, balanced in tone and temper, sensitive to diversity of expression and formulation—this volume is a model of theological study and an indispensable resource for anyone who has interest in exploring the scriptural witness to God's covenant."

Cornelis P. Venema, President and Professor of Doctrinal Studies, Mid-America Reformed Seminary; author, *Christ and Covenant Theology* and *Chosen in Christ*

"I rarely use the term *magisterial* of any book, but this one deserves it. The faculty of Reformed Theological Seminary have produced an outstanding volume on the biblical doctrine of the covenant. The opening section is marked by superb exegetical studies that ground the whole book in Scripture. The historical section that follows presents material (such as the use of *covenant* in the early church and the medieval period) that is not otherwise easily accessible. Later sections bring the discussions right up to the present time and interact with modern exponents and critics of covenantal theology. This is the volume to which those inquiring into the biblical idea of covenant should be pointed, and its presentation will instruct and challenge, while its annotated bibliography of modern studies will lead to many other sources. Everyone seriously pursuing an interest in this central biblical theme must have this book."

Allan Harman, Research Professor, Presbyterian Theological College, Australia; coauthor, *The Story of the Church*

COVENANT
THEOLOGY

COVENANT THEOLOGY

*Biblical, Theological, and
Historical Perspectives*

Edited by Guy Prentiss Waters,
J. Nicholas Reid, and John R. Muether

Foreword by Ligon Duncan

CROSSWAY®

WHEATON, ILLINOIS

Covenant Theology: Biblical, Theological, and Historical Perspectives

Copyright © 2020 by Guy Prentiss Waters, J. Nicholas Reid, and John R. Muether

Published by Crossway
        1300 Crescent Street
        Wheaton, Illinois 60187

Cover design: Jordan Singer

First printing 2020

Printed in the United States of America

Unless otherwise indicated, Scripture quotations are from the ESV® Bible (The Holy Bible, English Standard Version®), copyright © 2001 by Crossway, a publishing ministry of Good News Publishers. Used by permission. All rights reserved. Some chapters use a different default version, as indicated in those chapters.

Scripture quotations marked KJV are from the *King James Version* of the Bible.

Scripture references marked NAB are from the *New American Bible*, copyright © 1970 by the Confraternity of Christian Doctrine, Washington, DC, and are used by permission. All rights reserved.

Scripture quotations marked NASB are from *The New American Standard Bible®*. Copyright © The Lockman Foundation 1960, 1962, 1963, 1968, 1971, 1972, 1973, 1975, 1977, 1995. Used by permission.

Scripture references marked NEB are from *The New English Bible* © The Delegates of the Oxford University Press and The Syndics of the Cambridge University Press, 1961, 1970.

Scripture references marked NIV are taken from The Holy Bible, New International Version®, NIV®. Copyright © 1973, 1978, 1984, 2011 by Biblica, Inc.™ Used by permission. All rights reserved worldwide.

Scripture references marked NKJV are from *The New King James Version*. Copyright © 1982, Thomas Nelson, Inc. Used by permission.

All emphases in Scripture quotations have been added by the author.

Hardcover ISBN: 978-1-4335-6003-3
ePub ISBN: 978-1-4335-6006-4
PDF ISBN: 978-1-4335-6004-0
Mobipocket ISBN: 978-1-4335-6005-7

Library of Congress Cataloging-in-Publication Data

Names: Waters, Guy Prentiss, 1975– editor.
Title: Covenant theology : biblical, theological, and historical perspectives / edited by Guy Prentiss Waters, J. Nicholas Reid, and John R. Muether ; foreword by Ligon Duncan.
Description: Wheaton : Crossway, 2020. | Includes bibliographical references and index.
Identifiers: LCCN 2019025197 (print) | LCCN 2019025198 (ebook) | ISBN 9781433560033 (hardcover) | ISBN 9781433560040 (pdf) | ISBN 9781433560057 (mobi) | ISBN 9781433560064 (epub)
Subjects: LCSH: Covenant theology.
Classification: LCC BT155 .C73 2020 (print) | LCC BT155 (ebook) | DDC 231.7/6—dc23
LC record available at https://lccn.loc.gov/2019025197
LC ebook record available at https://lccn.loc.gov/2019025198

Crossway is a publishing ministry of Good News Publishers.

SH		29	28	27	26	25	24	23	22	21
15	14	13	12	11	10	9	8	7	6	5	4	3	2

In honor of
O. Palmer Robertson and Douglas F. Kelly

and in memory of
Howard Griffith

CONTENTS

Tables

Abbreviations

AB	Anchor Bible
ABRL	Anchor Bible Reference Library
ACF	*Annuaire du Collège de France*
ACW	Ancient Christian Writers
AnBib	Analecta Biblica
ANE	ancient Near East(ern)
ANES	*Ancient Near Eastern Studies*
ASBT	Acadia Studies in Bible and Theology
AUMSR	Andrews University Monographs, Studies in Religion
AUSS	*Andrews University Seminary Studies*
BA	*Biblical Archaeologist*
BB	Babel und Bibel
BBR	*Bulletin for Biblical Research*
BECNT	Baker Exegetical Commentary on the New Testament
BETS	*Bulletin of the Evangelical Theological Society*
BibInt	Biblical Interpretation Series
BJRL	*Bulletin of the John Rylands University Library of Manchester*
BSac	*Bibliotheca Sacra*
BSS	Barth Studies Series
BTCP	Biblical Theology for Christian Proclamation
BTNT	Biblical Theology of the New Testament
BZNW	Beihefte zur Zeitschrift für die neutestamentliche Wissenschaft
CBQ	*Catholic Biblical Quarterly*
CBQMS	Catholic Biblical Quarterly Monograph Series
CCT	Contours of Christian Theology

CH	*Church History*
CJA	Christianity and Judaism in Antiquity
CNTC	*Calvin's New Testament Commentaries.* Edited by David W. Torrance and Thomas F. Torrance. 12 vols. Grand Rapids, MI: Eerdmans, 1959–1972.
Comm.	*Calvin's Commentaries.* Edited by John King et al. Edinburgh: Calvin Translation Society, 1844–1856.
ConcJ	*Concordia Journal*
ConTJ	*Conservative Theological Journal*
CovQ	*The Covenant Quarterly*
CPSHT	Changing Paradigms in Systematic and Historical Theology
CRT	Classic Reformed Theology
CSCD	Cambridge Studies in Christian Doctrine
CSEMBH	Cambridge Studies in Early Modern British History
CSRT	Columbia Series in Reformed Theology
CTC	Christian Theology in Context
CTJ	*Calvin Theological Journal*
CurBR	*Currents in Biblical Research*
CUSAS	Cornell University Studies in Assyriology and Sumerology
Di	*Dialog*
DJD	Discoveries in the Judean Desert
DS	*Diplomacy and Statecraft*
DSD	*Dead Sea Discoveries*
EBib	Etudes bibliques
EBT	Explorations in Biblical Theology
EPSC	EP Study Commentary
ERT	*Evangelical Review of Theology*
EUSLR	Emory University Studies in Law and Religion
EvQ	*Evangelical Quarterly*
EvT	*Evangelische Theologie*
Exp	*Expositor*
FAT	Forschungen zum Alten Testament
FKD	Forschungen zur Kirchen- und Dogmengeschichte
GSC	Geneva Series of Commentaries

GTJ	*Grace Theological Journal*
HALOT	*Hebrew and Aramaic Lexicon of the Old Testament.* Ludwig Koehler, Walter Baumgartner, and Johann J. Stamm. Translated and edited under the supervision of Mervyn E. J. Richardson. 4 vols. Leiden: Brill, 1994–1999.
HBSt	Herders Biblische Studien
Hist. eccl.	Eusebius, *Ecclesiastical History*
HTR	*Harvard Theological Review*
IBC	Interpretation: A Bible Commentary for Teaching and Preaching
ICC	International Critical Commentary
IJST	*International Journal of Systematic Theology*
Int	*Interpretation*
JAOS	*Journal of the American Oriental Society*
JBL	*Journal of Biblical Literature*
JCS	*Journal of Cuneiform Studies*
JDT	*Jahrbücher für Deutsche Theologie*
JEH	*Journal of Ecclesiastical History*
JETS	*Journal of the Evangelical Theological Society*
JSJ	*Journal for the Study of Judaism in the Persian, Hellenistic, and Roman Periods*
JSJSup	Supplements to the Journal for the Study of Judaism
JSNTSup	Journal for the Study of the New Testament Supplement Series
JSOTSup	Journal for the Study of the Old Testament Supplement Series
JTISup	Journal of Theological Interpretation, Supplements
JTS	*Journal of Theological Studies*
KTC	Peter J. Gentry and Stephen J. Wellum. *Kingdom through Covenant: A Biblical-Theological Understanding of the Covenants.* 2nd ed. Wheaton, IL: Crossway, 2018.
LCC	Library of Christian Classics
LJI	Library of Jewish Ideas
LNTS	Library of New Testament Studies
LRS	Leipziger Rechtswissenschaftliche Studien
LSTS	Library of Second Temple Studies
LTPM	Louvain Theological and Pastoral Monographs

LW	Martin Luther. *Luther's Works*. Edited by Jaroslav Pelikan and Helmut T. Lehman. American ed. 55 vols. Philadelphia: Fortress; Saint Louis, MO: Concordia, 1955–1986.
MC	Mentor Commentary
MEC	Mentor Expository Commentary
MJT	*Mid-America Journal of Theology*
MRS	Mission de Ras Shamra
MSJ	*The Master's Seminary Journal*
NAC	New American Commentary
NACSBT	NAC Studies in Bible and Theology
NAK	*Nederlands Archief voor Kerkgeschiedenis*
NCB	New Century Bible Commentary
NCT	new covenant theology
NHMS	Nag Hammadi and Manichean Studies
NICNT	New International Commentary on the New Testament
NICOT	New International Commentary on the Old Testament
NIDOTTE	*New International Dictionary of Old Testament Theology and Exegesis*. Edited by Willem A. VanGemeren. 5 vols. Grand Rapids, MI: Zondervan, 1997.
NIGTC	New International Greek Testament Commentary
NIVAC	NIV Application Commentary
NovT	*Novum Testamentum*
NSBT	New Studies in Biblical Theology
NSD	New Studies in Dogmatics
NTC	New Testament Commentary
NTL	New Testament Library
NTS	*New Testament Studies*
NTT	New Testament Theology
OECS	Oxford Early Christian Studies
OSHT	Oxford Studies in Historical Theology
OTL	Old Testament Library
OTRM	Oxford Theology and Religion Monographs
OTS	Old Testament Studies
par.	parallel text

PC	progressive covenantalism
PNTC	Pillar New Testament Commentary
Presb	*Presbyterion*
PRJ	*Puritan Reformed Journal*
ProEcclSer	Pro Ecclesia Series
PrTMS	Princeton Theological Monograph Series
PRU	Claude F.-A. Schaeffer, ed. *Le palais royal d'Ugarit*. MRS. Paris: Imprimerie nationale, 1955–1970.
RA	*Revue d'assyriologie et d'archéologie orientale*
RBDS	Reformed Baptist Dissertation Series
REDS	Reformed, Exegetical, and Doctrinal Studies
RefR	*Reformed Review*
RevQ	*Revue de Qumran*
RFP	*Reformed Faith and Practice*
RHT	Reformed Historical Theology
RHTS	Reformed Historical Theological Studies
RIME	Royal Inscriptions of Mesopotamia, Early Periods
RJ	*Reformed Journal*
RRR	*Reformation and Renaissance Review*
RTR	*Reformed Theological Review*
SAA	State Archives of Assyria
SAAB	*State Archives of Assyria Bulletin*
SBET	*Scottish Bulletin of Evangelical Theology*
SBJT	*Southern Baptist Journal of Theology*
SBLDS	Society of Biblical Literature Dissertation Series
SBLMS	Society of Biblical Literature Monograph Series
SBLSS	SBL Symposium Series
SCHT	Studies in Christian History and Thought
SCJ	*Sixteenth Century Journal*
SDST	Studien zur Dogmengeschichte und systematischen Theologie
SHCT	Studies in the History of Christian Thought
SJT	*Scottish Journal of Theology*
SMAL	Studies in Mediterranean Archaeology and Literature

SMRT	Studies in Medieval and Reformation Traditions
SNTSMS	Society for New Testament Studies Monograph Series
SNTW	Studies of the New Testament and Its World
SSBT	Short Studies in Biblical Theology
StBibLit	Studies in Biblical Literature
StPatr	*Studia Patristica*
SwJT	*Southwestern Journal of Theology*
TAPS	Transactions of the American Philosophical Society
TBS	Twin Brooks Series
TCL	Theologians on the Christian Life
TDNT	*Theological Dictionary of the New Testament*. Edited by Gerhard Kittel and Gerhard Friedrich. Translated by Geoffrey W. Bromiley. 10 vols. Grand Rapids, MI: Eerdmans, 1964–1976.
THR	Travaux d'humanisme et Renaissance
TiC	Theology in Community
TJ	*Trinity Journal*
TJT	*Toronto Journal of Theology*
TOTC	Tyndale Old Testament Commentaries
TSAJ	Texte und Studien zum antiken Judentum
TSRPRT	Texts and Studies in Reformation and Post-Reformation Thought
TynBul	*Tyndale Bulletin*
VC	*Vigiliae Christianae*
VR	*Vox Reformata*
VT	*Vetus Testamentum*
WAW	Writings from the Ancient World
WBC	Word Biblical Commentary
WCF	Westminster Confession of Faith. In *The Westminster Confession of Faith and Catechisms: As Adopted by the Presbyterian Church in America*. Lawrenceville, GA: Christian Education and Publications of the PCA, 2007.
WEC	Wycliffe Exegetical Commentary
WLC	Westminster Larger Catechism. In *The Westminster Confession of Faith and Catechisms: As Adopted by the Presbyterian Church in America*. Lawrenceville, GA: Christian Education and Publications of the PCA, 2007.

WSC   Westminster Shorter Catechism. In *The Westminster Confession of
          Faith and Catechisms: As Adopted by the Presbyterian Church in
          America*. Lawrenceville, GA: Christian Education and Publications
          of the PCA, 2007.

WSJ   *Westminster Society Journal*

WTJ   *Westminster Theological Journal*

WUNT   Wissenschaftliche Untersuchungen zum Neuen Testament

ZECNT   Zondervan Exegetical Commentary on the New Testament

ZKG   *Zeitschrift für Kirchengeschichte*

ZNW   *Zeitschrift für die neutestamentliche Wissenschaft und die Kunde der
          älteren Kirche*

Foreword

Ligon Duncan

Reformed theology is covenant theology. Allow me to explain.

Reformed theology, representing the public, ecclesial, doctrinal convictions of a major branch of Protestantism, is a school of historic, orthodox, confessional Christianity that maintains and emphasizes the sovereignty of the triune God, the authority of Scripture, God's grace in salvation, the necessity and significance of the church, and covenant theology. Reformed theology believes that the Bible needs to be studied and understood by employing both biblical theology and systematic theology.

Biblical theology approaches the Bible from a redemptive-historical perspective. That is, biblical theology studies the Bible chronologically, historically, or diachronically. It is the study of special revelation from the standpoint of the history of redemption.[1] As Michael Lawrence puts it, "Biblical theology is the attempt to tell the whole story of the whole Bible as Christian Scripture."[2] Biblical theology is concerned to show that the Bible has one story and to relate all its parts to that one story.

Systematic theology, in comparison, is concerned to show that the Bible has one theology and to relate all its doctrines to one another as part of that one coherent theology. Hence, systematic theology studies the Bible topically, synchronically, and interrelatedly. It works on the collection, summary, interrelation, articulation, and application of what the whole Bible teaches on the major topics that it addresses. Systematic theology is not an enemy of, competitor with, or alternative to biblical theology but is its partner, benefactor, and beneficiary. Biblical theology cannot provide the final assessment offered by systematic theology, but it helps systematic theology make that assessment. Biblical theology and systematic theology, done rightly, are friends. They need each other. They complement one another.

---

1. See Geerhardus Vos, *Biblical Theology: Old and New Testaments* (Grand Rapids, MI: Eerdmans, 1948).
2. Michael Lawrence, *Biblical Theology in the Life of the Church: A Guide for Ministry* (Wheaton, IL: Crossway, 2010), 89.

Covenant theology is a blending of both biblical and systematic theology. If biblical theology is the thematic survey of redemptive history, with an emphasis on the theological development—era to era—of whatever loci is being studied, then covenant theology could rightly be called "biblical biblical theology." That is, covenant theology recognizes that the Bible itself structures the progress of redemptive history through the succession of covenants.

Covenant theology is systematic theology in that it identifies the covenants as a fundamental organizing principle for the Bible's theology. Thus it proceeds to integrate the biblical teaching about the federal headships of Adam and Christ, the covenantal nature of the incarnation and atonement, the continuities and discontinuities in the progress of redemptive history, the relation of the Old and New Testament Scriptures, and law and gospel into a coherent theological system.

So covenant theology is Reformed theology's way of gleaning from and putting together both systematic and biblical theology. Hence, Reformed theology is covenant theology.

No wonder B. B. Warfield called covenant theology the "architectonic principle" of the Westminster Confession of Faith (1647),[3] or James Walker asserted that covenant theology was "the old theology of Scotland."[4] J. I. Packer claims that we cannot understand the gospel, the Bible, or the reality of God without a covenantal framework and that the Bible "forces" covenant theology on us by the covenant story it tells, the place it gives to Jesus Christ in that covenant story, the Adam-Christ parallel in Paul, and the testimony of Jesus to the covenant of redemption in the Gospel of John.[5]

Covenant theology sets the gospel in the context of God's eternal plan of communion with his people and its historical outworking in the covenants of works and grace (as well as in the various progressive stages of the covenant of grace). Covenant theology explains the meaning of Christ's death in light of the biblical teaching on the divine covenants, undergirds our understanding of the nature and use of the sacraments, and provides the fullest possible account of the grounds of our assurance.

To put it another way, covenant theology is the Bible's way of explaining and deepening our understanding of at least four things:

1. The atonement (the meaning and significance of the death of Christ)
2. Assurance (the basis for our confidence of communion with God and our enjoyment of his promises)
3. The sacraments (signs and seals of God's covenant promises—what they are and how they work)
4. The continuity of redemptive history (the unified plan of God's salvation)

---

3. B. B. Warfield, *The Westminster Assembly and Its Work* (Grand Rapids, MI: Baker, 2000), 56.

4. James Walker, *The Theology and the Theologians of Scotland* (Edinburgh: T&T Clark, 1872), 40.

5. J. I. Packer, "Introduction on Covenant Theology," in Herman Witsius, *The Economy of the Covenants between God and Man: Comprehending a Complete Body of Divinity*, trans. William Crookshank, 2 vols. (1677; repr., Grand Rapids, MI: Reformation Heritage Books, 2010), 1:20.

Covenant theology is also a hermeneutic, or an approach to understanding the Scripture, that attempts to biblically explain the unity of biblical revelation.

The Bible's teaching on the covenants is central, not peripheral, to the biblical story. When Jesus wanted to explain the significance of his death to his disciples, he went to the doctrine of the covenants (see Matt. 26; Mark 14; Luke 22; 1 Cor. 11). When God wanted to assure Abraham of the certainty of his word of promise, he went to the covenant (Gen. 12; 15; 17). When God wanted to set apart his people, ingrain his work in their minds, tangibly reveal himself in love and mercy, and confirm their future inheritance, he gave the covenant signs (Gen. 17; Ex. 12; 17; 31; Matt. 28; Luke 22; Acts 2). When Luke wanted to show early Christians that Jesus's life and ministry were the fulfillment of God's ancient purposes for his chosen people, he went to the covenant of grace and quoted Zechariah's prophecy, which shows that believers in the very earliest days of the fledgling Christian church understood Jesus and his messianic work as a fulfillment (not a "plan B") of God's covenant with Abraham (Luke 1:72–73). When the psalmist and the author of Hebrews wanted to show how God's redemptive plan is ordered and on what basis it unfolds in history, they went to the covenants (see Pss. 78; 89; Heb. 6–10).

Covenant theology is not a response to dispensationalism. It existed long before the rudiments of classic dispensationalism were brought together in the nineteenth century. Covenant theology is not sectarian but is an ecumenical Reformed approach to understanding the Bible, developed in the wake of the magisterial Reformation but with roots stretching back to the earliest days of catholic Christianity and historically appreciated in all the various branches of Protestantism under the influence of Reformed theology (Anglican, Baptist, Congregationalist, Independent, Presbyterian, Reformed). As one theologian stated,

> The doctrine of the divine covenant lies at the root of all true theology. It has been said that he who well understands the distinction between the covenant of works and the covenant of grace is a master of divinity. I am persuaded that most of the mistakes which men make concerning the doctrines of Scripture are based upon fundamental errors with regard to the covenant of law and of grace. May God grant us now the power to instruct, and you the grace to receive instruction on this vital subject.[6]

Who said this? C. H. Spurgeon, the great English Baptist preacher! Certainly a man beyond suspicion of secretly purveying a Presbyterian view of the sacraments to the unsuspecting evangelical masses.

What Spurgeon's quote evidences is the influence of covenant theology in the Baptist tradition, and indeed, in our own day there is a revival of what is termed

---

6. C. H. Spurgeon, *The Metropolitan Tabernacle Pulpit*, vol. 58, *Sermons Preached by C. H. Spurgeon during the Year 1912* (Pasadena, TX: Pilgrim Publications, 1978), 517.

"1689 Federalism"—that is, a distinctly Baptist approach to covenant theology derived from the Second London Baptist Confession (1689). Covenant theology, not dispensationalism, is the native soil of not only the Presbyterian, Congregational, and evangelical Anglican traditions but also of historic Baptist biblical theology.

Covenant Theology in the Westminster Confession

Because Reformed Theological Seminary is committed to the inerrancy and authority of Scripture and to confessional Reformed theology, we are committed to covenant theology. The Reformed theology of the Westminster Confession of Faith (WCF) and the Larger and Shorter Catechisms (WLC and WSC, respectively) beautifully summarizes and expresses the main points of covenant theology in chapter 7 of the confession, titled "Of God's Covenant with Man":

> 1. The distance between God and the creature is so great, that although reasonable creatures do owe obedience unto him as their Creator, yet they could never have any fruition of him as their blessedness and reward, but by some voluntary condescension on God's part, which he hath been pleased to express by way of covenant.
>
> 2. The first covenant made with man was a covenant of works, wherein life was promised to Adam; and in him to his posterity, upon condition of perfect and personal obedience.
>
> 3. Man, by his fall, having made himself incapable of life by that covenant, the Lord was pleased to make a second, commonly called the covenant of grace; wherein he freely offereth unto sinners life and salvation by Jesus Christ; requiring of them faith in him, that they may be saved, and promising to give unto all those that are ordained unto eternal life his Holy Spirit, to make them willing, and able to believe.
>
> 4. This covenant of grace is frequently set forth in Scripture by the name of a testament, in reference to the death of Jesus Christ the Testator, and to the everlasting inheritance, with all things belonging to it, therein bequeathed.
>
> 5. This covenant was differently administered in the time of the law, and in the time of the gospel: under the law, it was administered by promises, prophecies, sacrifices, circumcision, the paschal lamb, and other types and ordinances delivered to the people of the Jews, all foresignifying Christ to come; which were, for that time, sufficient and efficacious, through the operation of the Spirit, to instruct and build up the elect in faith in the promised Messiah, by whom they had full remission of sins, and eternal salvation; and is called the Old Testament.
>
> 6. Under the gospel, when Christ, the substance, was exhibited, the ordinances in which this covenant is dispensed are the preaching of the Word, and the administration of the sacraments of Baptism and the Lord's Supper: which, though fewer in number, and administered with more simplicity, and less outward glory, yet, in them, it is held forth in more fullness, evidence and spiritual efficacy, to all nations, both Jews and Gentiles; and is called the New Testament. There are not

therefore two covenants of grace, differing in substance, but one and the same, under various dispensations.

Several things are to be observed here. First, the Westminster Standards set forth a bicovenantal structure of covenant, or federal, theology,[7] with a covenant of works and a covenant of grace providing the theological outline of the biblical story of creation, fall, redemption, and consummation (WCF 7.2–3). That is, even though the chapter heading speaks of God's covenant (singular) with man, the chapter itself makes it clear that there is a fundamental division and distinction between God's covenant relations pre- and postfall. Both covenants, as an expression of his one eternal decree, have in view God's glory and our good, our imaging him and communing with him, to the praise of his glory. But the means by which the covenants of works and grace are secured are distinct, with the covenant of grace dependent on the mediator in the fulfillment of its conditions. To say this yet another way, the Westminster Confession's presentation of covenant theology is not monocovenantal. It explicitly speaks of first and second covenants that are distinct: a covenant of works and a covenant of grace. Indeed, rightly understood, the covenant of works protects the grace of the covenant of grace.

Second, the Westminster Confession explains that God himself is the blessedness and reward of his people but that we could not have enjoyed him as such apart from his "voluntary condescension" (WCF 7.1). This is necessary because of the distance between God and humanity, which is not because of some inherent defect or lack in man but is inherent in the Creator-creature distinction and is because of the greatness of God and the finitude of man (WCF 7.1). The confession identifies God's "voluntary condescension" with covenant in general and with the covenant of works in particular (WCF 7.1–2). For God to covenant is for God to lovingly and generously stoop down, to willingly associate himself with his inferior—that is, with humanity. It should be noted that the confession does not identify this "voluntary condescension" of God as "grace," nor does it speak of "grace" in the context of its presentation of the prefall covenant. While some orthodox covenant theologians have spoken of God's grace or graciousness in the covenant of works, the foregoing point should be borne in mind—it protects against a misuse and misunderstanding of "grace" in relation to the first covenant.

Third, the Westminster Confession identifies and summarizes the covenantal structure of Scripture using the "first" and "second" covenants (or the covenants of works and grace), rather than listing explicitly denominated biblical covenants (e.g., God's covenants with Noah, Abraham, Moses/Israel, David) as ways in which God secures his people's enjoyment of union and communion with him. In doing so, the confession is using the categories of systematic theology. It uses these theological covenants to teach

---

7. In this book, the term *federal theology* is used interchangeably with *covenant theology*, particularly stressing the representative aspect of two great "federal heads," Adam and Jesus. *Federal* derives from the Latin *foedus*, which means "covenant."

that the God of the Bible relates to his creatures covenantally, first in a covenant of works and then through the various administrations of the covenant of grace (WCF 7.5), and it sees all the explicitly designated postfall covenants of Scripture as a part of the one covenant of grace ("the second covenant," WCF 7.3, 5–6). It is right, then, to see the covenant concept as an important architectonic principle of the theology of the confession.

Fourth, the covenant made with humanity before the fall is identified by the Westminster Standards as a covenant of *works* (respecting its terms or conditions; WCF 7.2), a covenant of *life* (respecting its goal or end; WLC 20), a covenant with *Adam* (respecting its party or representative; WLC 22), and the *first* covenant (respecting its chronological priority and indicating that there is a successor; WCF 7.2). All four names are apt descriptors of the same prefall covenant and are aspects essential to it.

Fifth, this first covenant, or the covenant of works, entailed both promises and conditions (WCF 7.2). Furthermore, it comprehended Adam as federal head, or representative, and required of him perfect and personal obedience to the moral law (WCF 19.1–3; WLC 22). When Adam fell, however, he made himself and all his posterity by ordinary generation incapable of life by the covenant of works and plunged all mankind into a condition of sin and misery (WCF 7.3; WLC 22, 23–25). This lays the groundwork for understanding the work of Jesus Christ, the second Adam (WLC 31), the only mediator of the covenant of grace (WLC 36), who satisfied God's justice (WLC 38) and performed obedience unto the law (WLC 39).

Sixth, the Westminster Confession does not equate the instrumentality of faith as it relates to justification in the covenant of grace with the obediential fulfillment of the conditions of the covenant of works (cf. WCF 7.2, "upon condition of perfect and personal obedience," with WCF 7.3, "requiring of them faith in him, that they may be saved"). It carefully distinguishes conditions from requirements, reminds us that even the faith of the elect is the gift of God, and draws a line from the conditions of the covenant of works to the work of Christ, not to the believer's faithfulness or obedience (WLC 32). That is, the conditions that Adam failed to keep under the covenant of works, the second Adam, Jesus, kept on our behalf under the covenant of grace. Our obedience, thus, under the new covenant administration of the covenant of grace is as tied up with and dependent on Christ's fulfillment of the conditions of the covenant, as was Israel's with the sacrificial system under the old covenant (which was necessitated by and remedial of imperfect obedience). To put it yet another way, just as the Mosaic covenant isn't "get in by grace, stay in by works" ("covenantal nomism") but rather "get in by grace, stay in by mediator" (see, e.g., Ex. 19:3–6; 32), so also the new covenant isn't "get in by grace, stay in by works." Our obedience under the new covenant is evangelical obedience (WCF 11.1), obedience that is impossible apart from Christ's active and passive obedience on our behalf, and the Spirit's grace-work in us, and thus it is neither a substitute for nor a supplement to the work of Christ but rather its product in us, the evidence of his grace, and the firstfruits of the whole goal of our creation and redemption, which is that we would be to the praise of God's glory.

Seventh, the terminological distinction between the covenants of works and grace highlights the fullness of the Westminster Confession's usage of the word "grace," which means not simply or merely God's undeserved favor but God's favor to those who deserve disfavor. Grace in its fullness is God's saving blessing to us despite our demerit. Thus there can be no grace (in the fullest sense of the word) without sin, since grace is the love and goodness of God to his people in spite of their sin and their deserving of curse, judgment, and disfavor. Hence, the Standards say, God in his love and mercy (WLC 30) made a second covenant, called the covenant of grace (WCF 7.3), in which he offers salvation to sinners by faith in Jesus Christ and promises to the elect the Holy Spirit (WCF 7.3).

Eighth, the confession indicates that any testamentary themes and terms in Scripture are to be subsumed under the overarching rubric of the covenant of grace (WCF 7.4). This is a unique statement in that it is an observation about the English translation of διαθήκη in certain places in the New Testament ("The covenant of grace is frequently set forth in Scripture by the name of a testament"; cf. the accompanying proof texts, Luke 22:20; 1 Cor. 11:25; Heb. 7:22; 9:15–17). Many modern subscribers to the Westminster Confession take exception to this assertion that "testament" occurs frequently (most scholars today agree that in only two possible places can διαθήκη be translated "testament," Gal. 3:15 and Heb. 9:15–17, though even in these passages there are good reasons to render διαθήκη "covenant").

Ninth, the Westminster Confession affirms that there is one covenant of grace in the Old Testament era ("the time of the law") and the New Testament era ("the time of the gospel") (WCF 7.5). Hence, the confession asserts the unity of the covenant of grace in its various administrations (WCF 7.6), while also affirming its diversity or progress. The confession is clear in its insistence that salvation is by faith in the Messiah, in the Old Testament as in the New (WCF 7.5).

Tenth, the Westminster Larger Catechism goes out of its way to indicate that the covenant of grace is made with the elect, or even more precisely, "with Christ as the second Adam, and in him with all the elect as his seed" (WLC 31). Thus, any attempt to make the covenant of grace apply equally to the elect and reprobate is contraconfessional. Furthermore, it is common in Reformed theology to use the term *covenant of grace* both broadly and narrowly, or externally and internally—that is, to speak of it entailing both everyone who is baptized into the Christ-professing covenant community (broad or external) and those who are elect, members of the invisible church, united to Christ by the Spirit through faith (narrow or internal). Nevertheless, the confession never speaks as if all those who are in the covenant of grace broadly or externally considered (the visible church) are recipients of the substance or saving benefits of the covenant of grace narrowly or internally considered (the invisible church). This is a vital distinction, and so those who deny or confuse it, or who assert that all the benefits of the covenant of grace accrue to all who are baptized, do err and are out of accord with the confession.

Eleventh, though the Westminster Confession does not deploy the term *covenant of redemption*, its teaching comports with such. WLC 31 in its description of the parties of the covenant of grace indicates a belief that is consistent with the idea of a pretemporal *pactum salutis* ("The covenant of grace was made with Christ as the second Adam, and in him with all the elect as his seed"), as does WSC 20 ("God having, out of his mere good pleasure, from all eternity, elected some to everlasting life, did enter into a covenant of grace, to deliver them out of the estate of sin and misery, and to bring them into an estate of salvation by a Redeemer"). As the confession suggests, the doctrine of the covenant of redemption serves to clarify who is included in the parties of the covenant of grace.

Zealous for the Covenant

Sometime in the late second century, Eusebius of Caesarea tells us, Irenaeus (ca. AD 120–202/3) carried a letter to Rome from his fellow Christians in Lugdunum (Lyons), in which they commend him with these words: "We pray, father Eleutherus, that you may rejoice in God in all things and always. We have requested our brother and companion Irenaeus to carry this letter to you, and we ask you to hold him in esteem, *as zealous for the covenant of Christ.*"[8] The expression "zealous for the covenant of Christ" is unique in patristic literature. It is certainly appropriate for Irenaeus, whose *Demonstration of the Apostolic Teaching* reads like a second-century version of O. Palmer Robertson's *Christ of the Covenants.*

As you search the Scriptures, and as you study the contents of this book, may you be so captivated by the truths of God's word about his covenants that you, too, become "zealous for the covenant of Christ."

---

8. Eusebius, *Hist. eccl.* 5.4.2.

INTRODUCTION

Guy Prentiss Waters, J. Nicholas Reid, and John R. Muether

Humanity, as the bearer of the divine image, was created for fellowship with God. But how is a relationship possible between an infinite and all-powerful God and a mere creature? Most religions, Herman Bavinck contends, cannot solve this dilemma. They "either pantheistically pull God down into what is creaturely, or deistically lift him endlessly above it." Fellowship can take place only when religion takes the shape of a covenant, according to Bavinck: "Covenant is the essence of true religion."[1]

Most evangelical Protestants agree that God's way with humanity is covenantal. The Bible often describes our relationship with God, both his promises to us and our duties toward him, in the language of covenant. And so, in this broad sense, they are covenant theologians.

But do we fully understand that term? Is it merely a helpful metaphor to describe the condescension of God in his goodness and faithfulness? Reformed theology believes that Scripture constrains us to go deeper. As we come to see the centrality of covenant to the Christian faith, it provides the foundation for a host of theological doctrines. The covenant of grace drives Christ to the cross in his atoning work, it secures our justification before God, it prompts the ministry of the Spirit in our growth in grace, and it forms our hope of heaven.[2]

This is not all. Sustained study on the covenant theme in Scripture has prompted Reformed theologians to expand beyond a single covenant of grace to a two-covenant scheme (including the covenant of works with Adam in Eden) and even to a three-covenant scheme (including the covenant of redemption, an intra-Trinitarian pact, made before

---

1. Herman Bavinck, *Reformed Dogmatics*, vol. 2, *God and Creation*, ed. John Bolt, trans. John Vriend (Grand Rapids, MI: Baker Academic, 2004), 569–70.
2. This is not to suggest that covenant theology is required to believe in Christ and the benefits he has secured for us, but it is to claim that covenant theology presents those precious truths in the most compelling and coherent way.

time, to establish the salvation of God's people). Together, these covenants help us interpret God's word more clearly and understand his redemption more fully. J. I. Packer goes so far as to assert that the Bible's covenant architecture is "pervasive, arresting, and inescapable."[3]

But many other Protestants have resisted the vocabulary and the categories that are employed in covenant theology. Elaborate covenant schemes appear too detailed and abstract for them. John MacArthur speaks for many when he claims that "theologically derived covenants . . . can alter God's intended revelation."[4] Covenant theology, then, is something unique to the Reformed tradition, and even in Reformed circles some question its value. Norman Harper, one of the early professors at Reformed Theological Seminary, lamented four decades ago that "the doctrine of the covenant of grace has received little emphasis in recent times even from those confessionally committed to covenant theology."[5]

The contributors to this volume, members of the faculty at Reformed Theological Seminary, gladly take on the defense of covenant theology, convinced that it is not a theological abstraction foisted on Scripture but rather the clear teaching of Scripture itself. We present covenant theology through explorations in biblical, systematic, and historical theology, all from a confessional Reformed perspective. In the style of previous Reformed Theological Seminary faculty collaborations,[6] our goal is to address ourselves primarily to the church. This book is a resource for the student in the seminary class, the pastor seeking continuing education, and educated laypeople looking for enrichment in their knowledge of this vital area of biblical doctrine.

What should readers expect to find in the pages of this book? In this introduction, we want to draw attention to several features of our approach to covenant theology.

Covenant Theology Is Exegetical

As a faculty, we submit unwaveringly to the inspiration and authority of the Bible, the infallible rule of faith and practice for the church. We are constrained, then, first and foremost to make a biblical case for covenant theology. Covenant theology mines the Scriptures to find a concrete basis for our relationship with God. Through the "architecture" of the covenant, the purposes and promises of God become increasingly legible on the pages of the Bible.

This book begins, in part 1, "Biblical Covenants," with the biblical revelation of the covenants of redemption and works, which, as we will see, establish the foundation for

---

3. J. I. Packer, "Introduction on Covenant Theology," in Herman Witsius, *The Economy of the Covenants between God and Man: Comprehending a Complete Body of Divinity*, trans. William Crookshank, 2 vols. (Grand Rapids, MI: Reformation Heritage Books, 2010), 1:42.

4. John MacArthur and Richard Mayhue, gen. eds., *Biblical Doctrine: A Systematic Summary of Bible Truth* (Wheaton, IL: Crossway, 2017), 871.

5. Norman E. Harper, *Making Disciples: The Challenge of Christian Education at the End of the 20th Century* (Memphis, TN: Christian Studies Center, 1981), 34.

6. See Miles V. Van Pelt, ed., *A Biblical-Theological Introduction to the Old Testament: The Gospel Promised* (Wheaton, IL: Crossway, 2016); Michael J. Kruger, ed., *A Biblical-Theological Introduction to the New Testament: The Gospel Realized* (Wheaton, IL: Crossway, 2016).

properly understanding the covenant of grace. This may appear as an inauspicious start, because skeptics of covenant theology are generally most doubtful about these covenants. They are right, of course, when they note that neither the covenant of redemption nor the covenant of works is identified in Scripture by these terms. But covenant theology does not emerge from the slim evidence of a proof text or two. Rather, as Guy Richard writes, early covenant theologians derived these covenants from "complex and thoroughgoing examination" of Scripture.[7] Careful exegesis of a variety of texts reveals their covenant features, often by "good and necessary consequences" (WCF 1.6), even when the word itself does not occur.[8]

Covenants are the Bible's way of displaying the grand sweep of redemptive history. Because the covenant of grace—which is "one and the same, under various dispensations" (WCF 7.6)—progresses in its development in the pages of Scripture, it is fitting that this book devote ten chapters to its organic development from promise to fulfillment. In each stage of Old Testament covenantal administration, the picture of the Redeemer to come grows deeper and richer. After the fall of our first parents, God promises that the seed of the woman will destroy the seed of the serpent. That promise is reinforced with the pledge to Noah that common grace will extend throughout redemptive history, guaranteeing the success of the seed. God promises that Abraham will be the father of a great family that will spread God's blessings to the nations. The family is constituted a nation at Sinai, pointing to a new Moses who will lead a new exodus and a true Israel who will obey the Father. When the nation formally comes under the rule of David and his descendants, the promise takes the form of a triumphant Son and an anointed King. Each covenant builds on the previous, all foreshadowing the new covenant that becomes the focus of the message of the prophets. As Michael McKelvey notes, yet another dimension emerges in the prophetic forecast of the new covenant: it will come in the form of a servant, who will fulfill the promises in his suffering.

When the New Testament reveals the Redeemer of God's elect in the person and work of Christ, the language of covenant actually recedes significantly (except in the book of Hebrews). For some interpreters, this is reason enough to dismiss the covenant as a redemptive-historical theme. Two things must be observed in response. First, as Christ is the "substance" of the covenant of grace (WCF 7.6), to exhibit Christ is to reveal the covenant, and to be united to Christ is to be in covenant with him. Thus, covenant theology, far from distracting us from Christ, emphatically drives us to Christ.[9]

---

7. See p. 50 below.

8. John Bolt rightly describes resistance to the biblical covenants as "methodological Biblicism"—that is, a wooden insistence that any implicit or indirect teaching in the Bible is a "theological imposition" on the text. John Bolt, "Why the Covenant of Works Is a Necessary Doctrine: Revisiting the Objections to a Venerable Reformed Doctrine," in *By Faith Alone: Answering the Challenges to the Doctrine of Justification*, ed. Gary L. W. Johnson and Guy P. Waters (Wheaton, IL: Crossway, 2006), 186.

9. Sinclair Ferguson is particularly compelling in arguing this point: "Christ *is* the covenant." Foreword to Cornelis Venema, *Christ and Covenant Theology: Essays on Election, Republication, and the Covenants* (Phillipsburg, NJ: P&R, 2017), xi.

Second, as several contributors observe, the New Testament writers were themselves covenant theologians. Michael Kruger notes that the Gospel writers describe the movement from promise to fulfillment in covenant logic: Christ as the second Adam, the seed of the woman, the new Moses, the true Israel, the greater Son of David, and the suffering servant—all this is covenant-enriched language. As Christ brings the organic development of the old covenant to its intended fulfillment, none of the redemptive plans of God are altered, replaced, or terminated.

Covenant Theology Is Trinitarian

Covenant Theology offers a Trinitarian approach to the covenants. For example, Guy Richard takes note that the mission of God to save his people is based on the uniqueness of the persons of the Trinity, appropriate to the personal properties of each member of the Trinity: "Each person of the Godhead acts in a way that is suited to his own person and mission."[10] In underscoring the finished work of the Son in his death and resurrection and the ongoing work of the Spirit in applying that work to God's elect, we maintain important Trinitarian distinctions.

Similarly, Greg Lanier observes that in the Johannine corpus, "covenantal thinking permeates [John's] description of each divine person."[11] This yields, he goes on to explain, a particularly expansive view of the person and work of the Spirit, who serves as the covenant witness in Revelation. Indeed, the new covenant is particularly the ministry of the Spirit, as Guy Waters explains in his chapter on Paul: all that the second Adam accomplished is for the Spirit to apply.

Covenant Theology Is Eschatological

Yet another feature of this book is the eschatological direction of covenant theology. Robert Cara's study of covenant in Hebrews helpfully highlights that redemptive history is not only horizontal progress (in the movement from the first Adam to the second Adam) but is also a vertical movement from earthly types to heavenly realities. Adam's prefallen communion with God in the garden of Eden was only a provisional arrangement. From the beginning of biblical revelation, the goal of the covenant of works was to bring the people of God into the glorified state of confirmed righteousness in a consummated order of eternal Sabbath rest.

What is the destiny of those united to Christ in his obedience to the covenant of works? We experience not the earthly joy of returning to Eden but the realization of an eternal and heavenly joy. Rather than receiving a recovered innocence, we follow Christ in his consummated glory, the reward that Adam forfeited having been obtained for us by the second Adam. Guy Waters writes, "Christ has not only undone what Adam

---

10. See p. 60 below.
11. See p. 269 below.

did; he has done what Adam failed to do."[12] Indeed, the Scriptures close with a vision of that consummated glory of the new Jerusalem expressed in the very promise of the covenant: "The one who conquers will have this heritage, and I will be his God and he will be my son" (Rev. 21:7).

Eschatological life is a higher life; it is resurrection life of a different order. Moreover, this abundant life does not merely await the believer's entrance into glory. Even now, in the certainty of our entitlement to heaven, we have confidence to serve God in the power of the resurrection.

Covenant Theology Is Historical

To repeat, our case for covenant theology emerges from Scripture, not from Christian antiquity or from church tradition. We trust that readers will find that this book has met that burden. Still, it is incumbent for advocates of covenant theology to demonstrate some continuity of the covenant theme through church history and the benefits of the church's exegesis and theological reflection on the subject. *Covenant Theology* is sensitive to the historical development of covenant theology as it turns, in part 2, to historical studies.

Diverse streams of influence have given shape to covenant theology. The seeds of covenant theology are broad and varied in the early church, as Ligon Duncan demonstrates. While it is not a major feature in medieval theology, Douglas Kelly reveals that covenant theology is still present and assumed.

The first generation of sixteenth-century Reformers began thinking covenantally to reinforce their gospel claims. Howard Griffith demonstrates that the covenant served Huldrych Zwingli and Heinrich Bullinger's desire to stress the unity of God's saving purposes against Anabaptist dismissals of the Old Testament. John Calvin's theology of the covenant emerged as the foundation of both the *historia salutis* (the execution of God's sovereign election in the saving work of Christ) and the *ordo salutis* (the sealing of Christ's benefits by the Spirit). After Calvin, theological reflection on the covenant became increasingly explicit to the point where, by the turn of the seventeenth century, the covenant became an organizing principle in Reformed theological systems.

In complementary studies of the post-Reformation era, Blair Smith (focusing on Puritanism) and Bruce Baugus (focusing on the Dutch Reformed tradition) survey this era of covenant refinement. Far from a departure from the theology of the Reformers, Protestant scholastics established the wider covenantal framework in which to explain Reformation truths such as the imputation of the righteousness of Christ. There is continuity, but there is also expansion and nuance in covenant thinking, especially as new challenges threatened Reformed orthodoxy. These historical pieces, we believe, should put to rest the claim that covenant theology is a Reformed invention. If the

---

12. See p. 88 below.

Reformation was an exercise in retrieval and development, that included the doctrine of the covenants.

Covenant Theology Is Confessional

These historical chapters stress that proponents of covenant theology, as part of an international confessional movement, were churchmen. Diverse formulations of the covenants largely stayed within the confessional standards of Reformed churches. This confessional consensus guarded the development of covenant theology from idiosyncrasy and provincialism.

Like the voices from our Reformed past, the authors of this book are also united in our cordial agreement with historic covenant theology, especially as it finds expression in the Westminster Confession of Faith. As the doctrinal standard for the seminary and the churches we serve, we are duty bound to teach it. Where many theologians in our anticonfessional age might fear doctrinal standards as curtailing freedom in theological reflection, we believe that Scripture and confession promote exegetical reflection and theological creativity, and it is in this context that we approach the subject of covenant theology.

Covenant Theology Is Technical

While it is the desire of this book to communicate accessibly to the church, covenant theology can be a complex subject. Debates in covenant theology wade into deep waters of highly technical matters of difference with competing interpretive theories. Here the readers are also exposed to the rise and fall of particular schools of thought that have held sway in the past: the two traditions of covenant theology (which claimed to identify a divergence between the bilateral covenantal approach of Bullinger and the unilateralism of Calvin), Calvin versus the Calvinists (which drove a wedge between the spirit of the sixteenth-century Reformation and the post-Reformation era on several related topics, including the covenant), and Perry Miller's recasting of Puritanism (where covenant became the means to escape the iron cage of Calvinistic predestinarianism).

Other technical issues are addressed in part 3, "Collateral and Theological Studies." Nicholas Reid, in one of the more challenging essays in the book, takes on ancient Near Eastern parallels to the biblical covenants. This has been a growing field of investigation with recent archaeological discoveries that have raised questions concerning whether similarities between Deuteronomy and ancient Hittite treaties support an early date (and Mosaic authorship) of the book. Reid points to new evidence and constantly changing theories that question earlier assumptions. This reality places limits on the conclusions that comparative studies can draw, and Reid urges caution against relying on extrabiblical evidence at the expense of exegesis. Peter Lee pronounces a similar caution in his look at Second Temple Judaism, another area of contemporary interest. Surveying a wide range of intertestamental literature, he identifies several competing covenantal systems and concludes that popular proposals (such as the "covenantal nomism" of E. P. Sanders) struggle to account for all the traditions of this period.

Covenant Theology Is Charitable

To be sure, covenant theology developed in a polemical age, in the context of intense debates between Reformed theologians and Socinians, Arminians, antinomians, and others. Later, the church faced different challenges. Mark McDowell surveys the particular criticism from Karl Barth and his theological descendants T. F. Torrance and J. B. Torrance. Michael Allen demonstrates why covenant theology has fallen into neglect among modern theologians, though he does highlight the promising work of two notable exceptions. There are competing hermeneutical frameworks today—including dispensationalism, the New Perspective on Paul, and progressive covenantalism. These challenges oblige the contributors to this book to engage their opponents polemically.

Still, it is the desire of the authors to present the case for covenant theology with charity. As Scott Swain reminds us, disagreements can have a sanctifying effect on our theology. If opposition served to sharpen the focus of covenant theology in the past, we hope and expect that new challenges will do the same today. Readers can detect in all the contributors a desire to engage respectfully those with whom they disagree.

Covenant Theology is indebted to a rich tradition of reflection on the covenant. This book does not claim to be the only word—nor to be the last word—on the subject of covenant theology. We lean on the work of others, and names like Calvin, Bavinck, and Geerhardus Vos are frequently invoked. Readers can also find some of the diversity in the Reformed tradition on the covenants in these pages. The faculty of Reformed Theological Seminary are not in complete agreement on all the details of the doctrine of the covenant. The nature of the Noahic covenant, the differences between John Murray and Meredith Kline, and the question of republication in the Mosaic covenant—on these and other areas there are differences among us, all within common confessional commitments. In this way, the book is a window into the faculty of Reformed Theological Seminary, and as editors we have been pleased at the spirit of unity that has characterized work in the project.

Covenant Theology Is Practical

Finally, *Covenant Theology* seeks to be practical. As noted above, the very real purpose of this volume is to help Bible study leaders, pastors, and Christian leaders teach and apply the word of God, with an eye toward edifying God's people as they grow in grace. Kevin DeYoung's afterword, for example, demonstrates how covenant theology and its implications for Christian living can be communicated in simple terms from the pulpit of the church.

Assurance of salvation appears as a recurring theme throughout this book. The eternal covenant of redemption and its historical outworking in the covenant of grace serve to guarantee the salvation of the elect, because what stands behind them is the unchangeable oath of God. We join with Calvin in believing that "we have no reason to be afraid that God will deceive us if we persevere in his covenant."[13] Derek Thomas invites us to grow in the assurance of faith, especially through the God-appointed means of covenant signs and seals. Covenant theology directs us to "improve" (make proper use of) our baptism, especially in times of temptation, and we come to the end of all doubt when we commune with Christ and all his benefits in the Lord's Supper.

All of us at Reformed Theological Seminary want you to be knowledgeable of and passionate about the Bible's teaching on the covenants. This book is designed to give you, our readers, a clearer understanding of the exegetical foundations and theological implications of covenant theology, in the hope that as students of Reformed theology, you will be better equipped to defend and propagate the Reformed faith. More than that, the editors are bold enough to hope that you will emerge encouraged in your understanding of the joy of covenant life.

May this book leave you, the reader, with the great hope and consolation of the gospel: our covenant-making God is a covenant-keeping God. He is "the great and awesome God who keeps covenant and steadfast love with those who love him and keep his commandments," whose ear remains attentive and his eyes open to the prayers of his servants (Neh. 1:5).

———

Three of the contributors to this volume are former faculty members at Reformed Theological Seminary. O. Palmer Robertson, Douglas Kelly, and Howard Griffith were influential and beloved figures in the life of the seminary.

One of the early members of the faculty, Dr. Robertson taught in Jackson from 1967 to 1972 and subsequently at Westminster (Philadelphia), Covenant, and Knox Seminaries, as well as African Bible Colleges in Malawi and Uganda. He has devoted a lifetime to the study of the covenants, especially in his influential *Christ of the Covenants*. His essay "Israel and the Nations in God's Covenants," in this volume, is a fitting convergence of his love for covenant theology and his passion for the worldwide witness of the church.

Dr. Kelly began his career at the Jackson campus (1984–1994) and then taught at the Charlotte campus for over two decades, until his retirement in 2016. He mentored many of the contributors of this book as a professor and as a senior colleague on the faculty, impressing on us all the value of the whole history of Christ's church.

---

13. John Calvin, *Calvin's Commentaries*, 22 vols. (Grand Rapids, MI: Baker, 1979), 4:424 (comm. on Ps. 25:10).

Dr. Griffith's devotion to covenant theology grew in his seminary studies under Meredith G. Kline and Richard B. Gaffin Jr. After pastoring in Richmond, Virginia, for twenty-five years, he joined the faculty at Reformed Theological Seminary, Washington, DC, in 2007, teaching systematic theology and guiding the faculty as academic dean. He finished his contribution to this book only a month before his sudden passing. His mining of Calvin's covenant theology, especially through the Reformer's sermons, testifies to Howard's passion for the preached word in his years of pastoral ministry.

We honor these three faithful instructors, devoted preachers, meticulous scholars, colleagues, and fathers in the faith by dedicating this book to them.

PART 1

BIBLICAL COVENANTS

1

The Covenant of Redemption

Guy M. Richard

Perhaps the most questionable element of historical federal theology is the covenant of redemption—the idea that there is a pretemporal agreement between the persons of the Trinity to plan and carry out the redemption of the elect. Many people today have reservations about the biblical warrant for such an idea.[1] The biblical proof texts employed to support it have come under a fair amount of criticism in recent years. Moreover, there is a sense in which the covenant of redemption feels speculative and unnecessary, because it deals with things happening within the mind of God before the creation of time and because it seems to run counter to the unity of God. If God really is one God with one mind and will, then why would the persons of the Trinity need a covenant to establish agreement between them? Would there not already be agreement by virtue of the fact that all three persons share one and the same mind and will?[2] The covenant of redemption has, for all these reasons, fallen on hard times within the Reformed community at large.

But as we shall see, the covenant of redemption was not always so suspect. It was, in fact, a commonly accepted idea from at least the middle part of the seventeenth century until the early twentieth century. From the moment it was formally expressed in writing, the covenant of redemption was embraced almost universally within the Reformed

---

1. The influence of Karl Barth and, to a lesser degree, John Murray, Herman Hoeksema, O. Palmer Robertson, and Robert Letham helped cultivate many of these reservations regarding the covenant of redemption within the broader Reformed world. See Karl Barth, *Church Dogmatics*, ed. G. W. Bromiley and T. F. Torrance (Edinburgh: T&T Clark, 1956), 4.1:64–66; John Murray, "The Plan of Salvation," in *Collected Writings of John Murray*, vol. 2, *Systematic Theology* (Edinburgh: Banner of Truth, 1977), 130; Herman Hoeksema, *Reformed Dogmatics* (Grand Rapids, MI: Reformed Free Publishing, 1966), 285–336; O. Palmer Robertson, *The Christ of the Covenants* (Phillipsburg, NJ: Presbyterian and Reformed, 1980), 53–54; Robert Letham, "John Owen's Doctrine of the Trinity in Its Catholic Context," in *The Ashgate Research Companion to John Owen's Theology*, ed. Kelly M. Kapic and Mark Jones (Farnham, UK: Ashgate, 2012), 196.

2. Barth offers a similar criticism as this one in *Church Dogmatics*, 4.1:65, as does Letham in "John Owen's Doctrine of the Trinity," 196.

world with a speed that was quite astonishing. What led our forefathers in the post-Reformation period to embrace this doctrine so universally and so quickly? We seek to answer this question by exploring the biblical and theological rationale that made the covenant of redemption a staple within Reformed orthodoxy so quickly and for so long.[3] My hope is that, in doing this, we will all be able to see the beauty that our forefathers saw in this doctrine. In the course of fulfilling my intended goal, this chapter surveys the origins and development of the covenant of redemption, and then it explores the biblical and theological rationale that have been used to support it.

Origins and Development

The precise origin of the covenant of redemption is difficult to pinpoint. David Dickson was apparently the first to speak of it by name in a speech he gave to the General Assembly of the Scottish church in 1638.[4] After that, we see it appear in a good many treatises published in the 1640s.[5] But there are hints that the covenant of redemption may have predated all these occurrences. Johannes Oecolampadius, for instance, specifically referred to a covenant between the Father and the Son in 1525. And it is quite possible that Martin Luther had this same idea in mind as early as 1519.[6] Theodore Beza, too, may well have been speaking of a pretemporal covenant when in 1567 he said, in his translation of Luke 22:29, that the Father had "made a covenant with" the Son, which he linked to the eternal testament of Hebrews 9.[7]

These hints at the existence of a pretemporal intra-Trinitarian covenant continued to be visible to a greater or lesser degree throughout the sixteenth and early seventeenth centuries in the writings of men like Guillaume Budé, John Calvin, Caspar Olevianus, Paul Bayne, William Ames, and Edward Reynolds. Even men from the opposite side of the theological spectrum were willing to speak of a covenant between the Father and the Son. James Arminius did so as early as 1603, and he defined this covenant as a voluntary arrangement to accomplish the salvation of humankind.[8]

It was not until later in the seventeenth century, however, that these hints became expressed much more concretely and the phrase *covenant of redemption* began regularly

---

3. For more on the federal theology of the post-Reformation period, see D. Blair Smith, "Post-Reformation Developments," chap. 17 in this volume.

4. Alexander Peterkin, ed., *Records of the Kirk of Scotland, Containing the Acts and Proceedings of the General Assemblies, from the Year 1638 Downwards* (Edinburgh: John Sutherland, 1838), 158.

5. David Dickson, *Expositio analytica omnium apostolicarum epistolarum* (Glasgow, 1645); Thomas Goodwin, *Encouragements to Faith drawn from several Engagements both of Gods [and] Christs heart* (London, 1645); Edward Fisher, *The Marrow of Modern Divinity* (London, 1645); Peter Bulkeley, *The Gospel-Covenant* (London, 1646); John Owen, *Salus electorum, sanguis Jesu* (London, 1647); Johannes Cocceius, *Summa doctrinae de foedere et testamento Dei* (Leiden, 1648); David Dickson and James Durham, *The Summe of Saving Knowledge* (1648; repr., Edinburgh, 1671).

6. See, e.g., Johannes Oecolampadius, *In Iesaiam prophetam hypomnematon, hoc est, commentariorum, Ioannis Oecolampadii libri vi* (Basel, 1525), 268r (Isa. 55:3); Martin Luther, *Lectures on Galatians* (1519), in *D. Martin Luthers Werke*, Kritische Gesamtausgabe (Weimar: Hermann Böhlaus Nachfolger, 1967), 2:521.

7. Richard A. Muller, "Toward the *Pactum Salutis*: Locating the Origins of a Concept," *MJT* 18 (2007): 40.

8. James Arminius, "Oration 1: The Object of Theology," in *The Works of James Arminius*, ed. James Nichols and William Nichols, 3 vols. (Grand Rapids, MI: Baker, 1991), 1:415–17.

to appear. And within a very short period of time, this covenant secured a standard place in contemporary expressions of federal theology. A survey of the writings of men such as Thomas Blake, Anthony Burgess, Samuel Rutherford, John Bunyan, Patrick Gillespie, Herman Witsius, and James Durham and of confessional documents such as the Savoy Declaration, the Helvetic Consensus (1675), and the Second London Baptist Confession (1689) shows just how widespread the doctrine of the covenant of redemption became in the latter half of the seventeenth century.[9]

The surprising thing is how rapidly this happened and how little opposition there was to this covenant. Richard Muller has argued that "the seemingly sudden appearance of the doctrine as a virtual truism" within a relatively few years in the 1630s and 1640s suggests that the sixteenth-century references were in fact more than merely hints and that the covenant of redemption developed gradually over time from the very beginning of the Reformation. Although the terminology "covenant of redemption" was not used until Dickson's speech in 1638, the groundwork that would later produce the doctrine was in place long before that.[10]

This evidence further suggests that this doctrine was perceived as being overwhelmingly evident to the ministers and theologians of the latter half of the seventeenth century. Rather than seeing the covenant of redemption as unbiblical, speculative, and unnecessary, these men saw it both as biblically and theologically essential and as exceedingly practical. The question is why. What biblical and theological rationale led these men to embrace this doctrine so overwhelmingly?

Biblical Rationale

The people of the sixteenth and seventeenth centuries wholeheartedly embraced the covenant of redemption for one overarching reason: they believed that the Bible taught it. And they believed it did so in three main ways. They argued, first, that the language of Scripture pointed to the covenant of redemption; second, that the recorded dialogues between the Father and the Son also pointed to it; and third, that the teaching of several individual passages proved that it was true.

Language of Scripture

The Bible frequently uses language that is highly suggestive of a pretemporal agreement existing between the Father and the Son. According to Dickson, the Bible does

---

9. Thomas Blake, *Vindiciae foederis* (1653; London, 1658), 14–15; Anthony Burgess, *The True Doctrine of Justification Asserted and Vindicated* (London, 1654), 375–77; Samuel Rutherford, *The Covenant of Life Opened* (Edinburgh, 1655), 282–315; John Bunyan, *The Doctrine of the Law and Grace Unfolded* (1660), in *The Works of John Bunyan*, ed. George Offor, 3 vols. (1854; repr., Edinburgh: Banner of Truth, 1991), 1:522–23, 525–26; Patrick Gillespie, *The Ark of the Covenant Opened, or A Treatise of the Covenant of Redemption between God and Christ, as the Foundation of the Covenant of Grace* (London, 1677); Herman Witsius, *De oeconomia foederum Dei cum hominibus* (Leeuwarden, 1677), trans. as *The Economy of the Covenants between God and Man*, trans. William Crookshank, 2 vols. (London, 1822), 2.2–3; James Durham, *Christ Crucified, or The Marrow of the Gospel* (Edinburgh, 1683), 154–64; Savoy Declaration (1658), 8.1; Helvetic Consensus (1675), 13; Second London Baptist Confession (1689), 8.1.

10. Muller, "Toward the *Pactum Salutis*," 14.

this in three fundamental ways. First, it regularly speaks of the salvation of the elect in terms of buying and selling (e.g., Acts 20:28; 1 Cor. 6:20; Eph. 1:7; 1 Pet. 1:18). But as Dickson pointed out, buying and selling presume that the parties have reached prior agreement regarding the terms of the deal. Second, the titles given to Jesus in the Bible indicate that the Father and the Son must have made some kind of prior agreement. Thus, the fact that Jesus is called our "propitiation" in Romans 3:25 and 1 John 2:2 is evidence that an agreement must have been reached beforehand in which the Son consented to give his life as a propitiatory sacrifice and the Father consented to accept it. Third, Jesus regularly speaks about his mission on earth in terms implying that he and the Father had made an agreement prior to his coming. So we see Jesus talk about the Father "sending" him into the world, "giving" him a specific "work" to do, and investing him with authority to do it, and we also see Jesus "receiving" his Father's "charge," devoting himself to his Father's "business," and accomplishing the specific work he has been given to do (e.g., Luke 2:49 ESV mg.; John 5:36–37; 6:38; 10:18; 17:4).[11] All these things suggest that an agreement was made within the Trinity regarding the salvation of the elect, and this agreement is precisely what the covenant of redemption is meant to embody.

Patrick Gillespie argued that *agreement* is the essential ingredient of all covenants: "The agreement or consent of two or more Parties upon the same thing, maketh a Paction [i.e., a covenant]."[12] In demonstrating this, he turned to Isaiah 28:15—which says,

> We have made a covenant with death,
>   and with Sheol we have an agreement.

He concluded from this that because the two words occur in parallel, they must be synonymous. This meant that all that was required to prove the existence of a covenant between the Father and the Son was to show that there was an agreement between them. And as Dickson's example demonstrates, the Bible shows this in a great variety of ways.

But Scripture also uses language that describes the salvation of the elect as a transaction between the persons of the Trinity. Thus, in the Gospel of John, we see Jesus talk about the elect as those whom the Father "gives" to him (6:37, 39; 17:6–9, 24–25), with the expectation that he will do certain things on their behalf—that is, he will lose none of them (6:37, 39); he will raise them up at the last day (6:39–40); and he will be "lifted up" after the pattern of John 3:14, so that the elect will believe in him and receive eternal life (6:40). We also see Jesus acknowledge that he has come into the world to fulfill his Father's expectations on behalf of the elect (6:38), which again shows the prior agreement of the persons of the Trinity to the conditions and promises of the transaction

11. David Dickson, *Therapeutica sacra* (Edinburgh, 1664), 23–34. See also Durham, *Christ Crucified*, 121–22.

12. Gillespie, *Ark of the Covenant Opened*, 6. Indeed, *agreement* has been the basic definition of covenant from at least Martin Luther in the sixteenth century to Charles Hodge in the nineteenth. See J. V. Fesko, *The Covenant of Redemption: Origins, Development, and Reception*, RHT 35 (Göttingen: Vandenhoeck & Ruprecht, 2016), 172.

of our salvation. For men like Samuel Rutherford, this manner of speaking pointed conclusively to the existence of an intra-Trinitarian covenant in which the Father, Son, and Spirit agreed on the terms of our redemption.[13]

Interestingly enough, this kind of transactional language is reflected in the definition of the covenant of redemption provided by David Dickson and James Durham in their 1648 *Summe of Saving Knowledge*:

> The sum of the Covenant of Redemption is this, God having freely chosen unto life, a certain number of lost mankind, for the glory of his rich Grace did give them before the world began, unto God the Son appointed Redeemer, that upon condition he would humble himself so far as to assume the human nature of a soul and a body, unto personal union with his Divine Nature, and submit himself to the Law as surety for them, and satisfie Justice for them, by giving obedience in their name, even unto the suffering of the cursed death of the Cross, he should ransom and redeem them all from sin and death, and purchase unto them righteousness and eternal life, with all saving graces leading thereunto, to be effectually, by means of his own appointment, applyed in due time to every one of them.[14]

Dickson and Durham even cited John 6:37 on the title page of their treatise as the main text on which their subject matter would be grounded, thereby indicating that this pretemporal arrangement between the persons of the Trinity is the very foundation on which all salvation depends and the source from which it flows.

What is more, several passages of the Bible also use language that describes Christ as being "chosen," "ordained," or "appointed" as mediator for his people (see, in this regard, Ps. 2:7; Isa. 42:1–3 with Matt. 12:15–21; Luke 22:29; Acts 2:23, 36; Eph. 1:4; Heb. 7:22, 28; 1 Pet. 1:19–20). Two of these passages bear further study. The first is Luke 22:29, which has historically been understood as teaching that Christ was "covenantally" appointed by God as King over his mediatorial kingdom.[15] Even as far back as Theodore Beza in the middle of the sixteenth century, scholars within the Reformed tradition recognized that the original Greek word used in this verse (διατίθημι) means "to covenant." They therefore concluded that it was not just true that Christ was "appointed" King, as the Vulgate had previously specified (using the Latin word *dispono*), but that God had actually "made a covenant" with Christ to appoint him King.[16]

The second passage is Psalm 2:7. Here, too, we see reference to a covenantal arrangement existing between the Father and the Son. Patrick Gillespie, for one, argued that

13. Rutherford, *Covenant of Life Opened*, 293.
14. Dickson and Durham, *Summe of Saving Knowledge*, 2.2.
15. See Cocceius, *Summa doctrinae*, 14.34.2; Witsius, *Economy of the Covenants*, 2.2.3; Wilhelmus à Brakel, *The Christian's Reasonable Service*, trans. Bartel Elshout, ed. Joel R. Beeke, 4 vols. (Grand Rapids, MI: Reformation Heritage Books, 1993), 1:255; Francis Turretin, *Institutes of Elenctic Theology*, trans. George Musgrave Giger, ed. James T. Dennison Jr. (Phillipsburg, NJ: P&R, 1992–1997), 12.2.14.
16. Theodore Beza, *Testamentum Novum, sive Nouum foedus Iesu Christi, D.N.* (1567; n.p., 1588), 318 (comm. on Luke 22:29).

the Hebrew word typically translated as "decree" in Psalm 2:7 (חֹק) comes from a root that originally meant, among other things, "to ordain, appoint, or covenant." Citing several exegetical traditions, including the Targums, he pointed out that "most ancient Interpreters" chose the word "covenant" in their translations of this verse. But what was more important for Gillespie was the fact that the same Hebrew word was elsewhere used interchangeably with the word for "covenant" (cf. Jer. 31:35–36 with 33:20; see also Ps. 105:10). That is why Gillespie believed that it was entirely appropriate to take Psalm 2:7 as referring to the same basic thing that Luke 22:29 did, namely, to Christ being appointed "covenantally" as mediator.[17]

The fact that Christ was "appointed" to his role as mediator certainly implies that the persons of the Trinity had made some kind of previous arrangement wherein they agreed on what this role would look like and what conditions and blessings would be attached to it. But the fact that both Luke 22:29 and Psalm 2:7 speak of this appointment in covenantal terms certainly seems to make this arrangement more overt and formal. Christ was not only appointed to be mediator, but this appointment apparently took place within the context of a covenant between the Father and the Son.

Even though the Westminster Confession of Faith does not explicitly mention the covenant of redemption by name, this covenant would appear, nonetheless, to be implicitly reflected in the confession's use of the language of "appointment." Thus, when the confession says that "it pleased God, in his eternal purpose, to choose and ordain the Lord Jesus, his only begotten Son, to be the Mediator between God and man," it is obviously referring to the covenant of redemption, albeit implicitly, by adopting the biblical language of the covenantal appointment of Christ.[18] The Savoy Declaration (1658) and Second London Baptist Confession (1689) both amended the Westminster Confession by adding the phrase "according to a covenant made between them both" to the abovementioned excerpt to make obvious and explicit what was previously obvious but implicit in the Westminster Confession.[19]

Dialogues between Father and Son

The recorded dialogues between the Father and the Son in the Bible also point toward a pretemporal, intra-Trinitarian covenant. One of the clearest examples of this can be seen in Hebrews 10:5–10, which records the words of Psalm 40 and places them on the lips of Christ (Heb. 10:5). The words Christ speaks are directed to God (10:7), and they allude to an agreement between the Father and the Son in the accomplishing of our salvation. Thus, Christ speaks of God's "desires" (10:5), of what gives God "pleasure" (10:6), and of coming into the world to do God's "will" (10:7)—all of which indicate that the Son not only knew about these things before he came into the world (10:5)

---

17. Gillespie, *Ark of the Covenant Opened*, 11–12. More attention is given to Ps. 2:7 below.
18. WCF 8.1.
19. Savoy Declaration 8.1; Second London Baptist Confession 8.1.

but, more importantly, that he also willingly consented to take on the body that God prepared for him, to live according to God's desires, and to do God's will long before he actually did any of these things. These works had already been written down in Scripture (10:7) long before the Son ever took on flesh and dwelt among us, which means that they must have been determined in the counsels of God even before that.

For Patrick Gillespie, the fact that Christ consented to God's proposals was proof positive that there was a covenant of redemption between the Father and the Son.[20] He reasoned that consent showed not only an awareness of the relevant issues involved but also agreement to the conditions and promises of the arrangement. Thus when the Son consented to God's "will," and did so long before the incarnation ever took place, he was demonstrating that something like the covenant of redemption had to have taken place between himself and the Father.

Gillespie then went on to highlight six characteristics of this agreement to which the Son was consenting, all of which further substantiated a covenant of redemption. First, he said, we see the Father asking the Son to do certain things in order to accomplish our salvation and promising that certain blessings and privileges will follow if and when the Son fulfills those commands (Isa. 42:1–4; Mic. 5:4–5; Zech. 6:12–13; John 6:39–40). If commands with promises attached to them amounted to a covenant in the garden of Eden (Gen. 2:17), then commands with promises also constitute a covenant between the Father and the Son.[21] His point is that if we are willing to acknowledge a covenant of works between God and Adam in the Bible (even if we call it by a different name), then we ought to be ready to acknowledge a covenant of redemption between the Father and the Son, because there is just as much evidence for the one as there is for the other.

Second, Gillespie pointed to the presence of promises with conditions attached. Here he cited Isaiah 53:10–12, which presents the unified "will" of the Lord (Yahweh) to "crush" the incarnate Son and put him to "grief" and, in so doing, to account many people righteous, *provided that* the Son "makes [himself] an offering for guilt," pours "out his soul to death," is "numbered with the transgressors," and bears "the sin of many." This, as Gillespie said, is nothing less than a formal covenant with conditions and promises on both sides.[22]

The third and fourth characteristics that Gillespie mentioned in this regard focus on the consent that the Son gives to the Father. As John 10:18 indicates, Jesus not only is "charged" or "commanded" by his Father to lay down his life on behalf of God's people, but he has "received" this charge freely "of [his] own accord." In addition, in John 17:4 Jesus declares that he has "accomplished the work" that the Father gave him to do. And as a result, the Father "highly exalted him and bestowed on him the name that is above

---

20. Gillespie gives five ways that Christ consented to the Father's proposals in Ps. 40. See his *Ark of the Covenant Opened*, 14–16.
21. Gillespie, *Ark of the Covenant Opened*, 17.
22. Gillespie, *Ark of the Covenant Opened*, 17–18.

every name" (Phil. 2:9).[23] This kind of "reciprocation" in the actions of the Father and the Son indicates that something like the covenant of redemption had been established and is now being executed in space and time.

Fifth, there is an "asking and giving" in the dialogues between the Father and the Son in Scripture that reflects the covenant of redemption. So in Psalm 2:8 the Lord invites Christ (his "Anointed," Ps. 2:2),

> Ask of me, and I will make the nations your heritage,
>   and the ends of the earth your possession.

And in John 17:5 Jesus asks the Father, "Glorify me in your own presence with the glory that I had with you before the world existed." In both cases, the requests were answered affirmatively. The Father gave the nations to the Son as his inheritance, and he exalted him to the place that he had prior to his self-emptying (Phil. 2:5–9). This, according to Gillespie, is the language of transaction or of business contracts (*enditio* and *venditio*), either of which would signal some kind of a covenant or agreement.[24]

Finally, Gillespie directed his reader's attention to the language of work and wages in the Bible. This language, Gillespie said, is very similar to the language that is used in covenants that are enacted between the "work-man" and the "work-master" or between the "servant" and "his Lord" in everyday life. It is the kind of language in which one party says, "I give this upon condition you do that," and the other party responds, "I do this upon condition you do that." Gillespie saw this reflected in passages like Isaiah 49:3, 6; 53:11–12; John 10:17; 17:4; Philippians 2:8–9; Hebrews 10:7; and 12:2.[25]

Individual Passages

Thus far we have established that the covenant of redemption was not developed from one or two isolated texts in Scripture but from a complex and thoroughgoing examination of the language that the Bible uses to speak about the relationship between the Father and the Son and the planning and accomplishing of the salvation of God's people. Sadly, much modern discussion of this doctrine has ignored this evidence and focused on isolated proof texts such as Psalm 2:7 and Zechariah 6:13, which are less persuasive when taken by themselves. If we start by looking for the covenant of redemption in these kinds of isolated texts, we will have a good deal more trouble finding it. But if we start by looking at the language of Scripture—which we have done here—and then come to these isolated texts afterward, we will be in a better position to see the covenant of redemption for ourselves.

We can confidently turn our focus to examining a few of these isolated texts and to seeing what they have to say about the covenant of redemption. We will look at three

---

23. Gillespie, *Ark of the Covenant Opened*, 18–19.
24. Gillespie, *Ark of the Covenant Opened*, 19.
25. Gillespie, *Ark of the Covenant Opened*, 19–20.

main texts: Zechariah 6:13; Psalm 110; and Psalm 2. Because of the limits of this chapter, we will be able to give only a cursory examination of each.

Zechariah 6:13

In Zechariah 6:13, we are told about a so-called "counsel of peace" that will be established between two particular people ("them both"). Beginning with Johannes Cocceius and Herman Witsius in the seventeenth century, this verse has often been cited as a proof text for the covenant of redemption. Before we evaluate this assertion, however, it bears mentioning that many earlier treatments of this doctrine did not make any reference to Zechariah 6:13. Men like David Dickson and Peter Bulkeley, for instance, relied exclusively on arguments like those mentioned in the prior two sections of this chapter without ever mentioning the Zechariah passage.[26] This means that regardless of what one makes of the "counsel of peace," the validity of the covenant of redemption is not hanging in the balance. Zechariah 6:13 is not a necessary proof text for this doctrine. But it does add extra weight in support of it, especially when it is placed alongside the abovementioned arguments.

In the context of this passage, Joshua the high priest is a type of Christ. Like Melchizedek before him—and Christ after him—Joshua is going to be both king and priest. John Calvin pointed out that the word "crown" in Zechariah 6:11 is actually plural in the original Hebrew, and he argued that what is going on here is that two crowns are being placed on the one man Joshua. Since both priests and kings wore crowns, Calvin said, this event clearly symbolizes the union of the priestly and kingly offices in one man, which is obviously designed to point ahead to Christ.[27]

Zechariah 6:12 further supports this conclusion. Using an idea common in the Old Testament, Zechariah speaks of the one of whom Joshua is a type by calling him the "Branch." Several key passages describe this Branch: he will be a descendant of David (Isa. 11:1; Jer. 23:5–6; 33:14–18) but will also come from the Lord (Isa. 4:2); he will be an heir to the Davidic throne (Jer. 23:5–6; 33:14–18); he will be full of the Holy Spirit and of wisdom, understanding, and knowledge (Isa. 11:2); he will be called "The Lord is our righteousness" (Jer. 23:5–6; 33:14–18; cf. Isa. 11:4–5); he will be the instrument through which salvation will come to Israel (Jer. 23:5–6; 33:14–18); and he will be a priest who will offer an eternal sacrifice (Jer. 33:14–18). Thus, Zechariah 6:13 is ultimately and most fully about Christ. He is the Branch; he is the one who, according to Wilhelmus à Brakel, will "build the temple of the Lord" and "bear royal honor" and "sit and rule" on the Lord's throne. And therefore, he is also the one who will enter into a "counsel of peace" with the Lord.[28]

---

26. Muller, "Toward the *Pactum Salutis*," 24.

27. John Calvin, *Commentaries on the Twelve Minor Prophets*, vol. 5, *Zechariah and Malachi*, trans. John Owen (Grand Rapids, MI: Baker, 1993), 152–56.

28. Brakel, *Christian's Reasonable Service*, 1:254.

What exactly is this "counsel of peace"? For a couple of reasons, it seems best to conclude that this counsel is an agreement—or, we might even say, a covenant—between the Branch and the Lord (Yahweh) in and by which the peace of God's people will be secured and maintained. In the first place, the prophet Zechariah later states that the Messiah will enter Jerusalem as a king "mounted on . . . the foal of a donkey" and that his kingdom will bring peace for all "the nations." That peace, according to Zechariah, will be secured by "the blood of my covenant with you" (Zech. 9:9–11). In other words, the prophet himself tells us that the chief business of the Branch is to bring peace to the world and redemption "from the waterless pit" (9:11) in and through the offering of a blood sacrifice, and perhaps most significantly, he tells us that this is what the covenant is all about. The fact that Zechariah himself says this indicates that we should understand "counsel of peace" in 6:13 in a complementary way to what Zechariah says about the Messiah in 9:9–11.

In the second place, there are several passages of Scripture that link the ideas of covenant and peace together. The covenant is regularly spoken of as the vehicle that establishes peace, and at the same time, peace is spoken of as the chief consequence of the covenant relationship. So in Joshua 9:15 we read that the Gibeonites deceived Israel into entering into a covenant relationship with them, and despite the premise on which it was established, that covenant secured peace between the two nations. The Gibeonites were after peace, and they knew that the way to achieve it was by entering into a covenant relationship with Israel. They knew that covenant and peace went hand in hand.[29]

Several passages in the Old Testament speak of a "covenant of peace" and describe it as being the vehicle through which God establishes peace for his people. Isaiah 54:10 and Ezekiel 37:26–27 are the most explicit of these. Both passages depict the covenant of peace as an "everlasting" covenant that establishes permanent peace with God (see also Ezek. 34:25). And although these passages do not use the phrase "counsel of peace," it should be obvious that the two phrases are quite similar in their construction and their intention.

The counsel of peace would, therefore, appear to be something that occurs between the Branch (Christ) and the Lord (Yahweh). And it would seem to be an agreement between them to secure an eternal peace for God's people. Herman Witsius helpfully summarized the teaching of Zechariah 6:13:

> The counsel of peace, which is between the man whose name is the Branch, and between Jehovah, whose temple he shall build, and on whose throne he shall sit, Rev. iii.21. And what else can this counsel be, but the mutual will of the Father and the Son, which we said is the nature of the covenant? It is called a counsel, both on ac-

---

29. The idea that covenants establish peace is a well-attested Old Testament principle (see, e.g., Deut. 2:26–34; 20:10–18; Josh. 10:1–4; 2 Sam. 10:19). Peace is also integral to the Messiah's work in the New Testament (see, e.g., Luke 2:14; John 14:27; 16:33; Acts 10:36; Rom. 5:1; Eph. 2:13–18; 6:15; Col. 1:20).

count of the free and liberal good pleasure of both, and of the display of the greatest wisdom manifested therein. And a counsel of peace, not between God and Christ, between whom there never was any enmity; but of peace to be procured to sinful man with God, and to sinners with themselves.[30]

Psalm 110

The second passage that we will consider here is Psalm 110. This psalm, which was written by David, is explicitly messianic. The opening verse tells us quite plainly that David is writing about someone greater than himself, someone he calls "my Lord" (אֲדֹנִי/אָדֹון). This someone will sit at the right hand of God (110:1) and will be both king (110:2–3) and priest (110:4). He will not only be greater than David, but he will also be greater than the angels and the Levitical priesthood, as Hebrews 1:13; 5:5–6; and 7:17–22 make clear. But what is far more significant for us is that, as Calvin said, we have "the testimony of Christ that this psalm was penned in reference to himself," which ought to remove any lingering doubts we might have about it (Matt. 22:41–45).[31]

In this psalm at least two interesting indicators point in the direction of the covenant of redemption. The first is the direct address that Yahweh makes to David's "Lord" in Psalm 110:1, and the second is the oath that Yahweh takes in reference to the same figure in 110:4. In regard to the first, we can say that the address looks ahead to Christ's incarnation and earthly ministry when, in the words of Calvin, he will be "invested with supreme dominion."[32] We know that the Son, as God, already possesses supreme dominion in and of himself; he does not need to be invested with it. But when he humbles himself, takes on human flesh, and places himself in submission to earthly authorities and principalities and to all his Father's will, he does need to be invested with dominion, so that all may know that he really is the Son. These comments in 110:1, therefore, seem to reflect an agreement or arrangement within the Trinity whereby the Son agreed to humble himself and place himself in submission, and the Father agreed to crown the incarnate Son king and to invest him with supreme dominion.[33]

Second, we can say that the language of covenant is reflected in the way that Christ is described as being appointed priest after the order of Melchizedek. The fact that Yahweh swears an oath to do this points clearly to the existence of a covenant relationship. Meredith Kline has argued that in the Bible, "the covenantal commitment is characteristically expressed by an oath sworn in the solemnities of covenant ratification." He has pointed to Genesis 15 and Hebrews 6:17–18 and 7:20–22, in particular, to support his

---

30. Witsius, *Economy of the Covenants*, 2.2.7.

31. John Calvin, *Commentary on the Book of the Psalms*, trans. James Anderson, 4 vols. (Grand Rapids, MI: Baker, 1998), 4:295.

32. Calvin, *Commentary on the Psalms*, 4:299.

33. Psalm 110 is a royal psalm and would most likely have been used at the inauguration of Israel's king. It presents the king as being invested with power and dominion. See Leslie C. Allen, *Psalms 101–150*, WBC 21 (Waco, TX: Word Books, 1983), 83.

claim.[34] O. Palmer Robertson has further argued that this oath does not necessarily have to be part of a "formal oath-taking process." Citing Psalms 89:3, 34–35; 105:8–10; and a whole host of other Scripture passages, Robertson declares that "'oath' so adequately captures the relationship achieved by 'covenant' that the terms may be interchanged."[35] His conclusion is that the Bible teaches not merely that a covenant *contains* an oath but that it actually *is* an oath. If Kline and Robertson are right, Psalm 110:4 is plainly teaching that there is a covenant existing between Yahweh and Christ, one in which the latter is appointed as a priest who will intercede on behalf of God's people forevermore.

Hebrews 7:20–22, moreover, helps us see that the intra-Trinitarian covenant of Psalm 110:4 is a pretemporal covenant. After telling us that Jesus is unique, insofar as he is made priest with an oath, the author of Hebrews cites Psalm 110:4 and concludes by saying, "*This* makes Jesus the guarantor of a better covenant" (Heb. 7:22). In other words, the point is that the oath (of Ps. 110:4) is what has made Jesus the guarantor of the covenant of grace. Now, a guarantor is one that *guarantees* that the promises of the covenant will in fact be carried out.[36] If Jesus is such a guarantor, then this means that the certainty of the covenant of grace is based on him and his role as guarantor. But this role is a result of the oath of Psalm 110:4, which means that there is an oath undergirding or guaranteeing the covenant of grace—an oath between Yahweh and Adonai, or between Father and Son. If Robertson is right that covenant and oath are used interchangeably in Scripture, then Psalm 110 and Hebrews 7 are teaching that a covenant relationship between Father and Son is undergirding or guaranteeing the covenant of grace, which is precisely what Samuel Rutherford said in the mid-seventeenth century: "The Covenant of Suretyship [i.e., redemption] is the cause of the stability and firmnesse of the Covenant of Grace."[37] This covenant relationship must be prior to the covenant of grace not only chronologically in execution but even logically in the stage of conception within the mind of God; otherwise, it could not function as the basis for it. Thus, the intra-Trinitarian covenant of Psalm 110:4 and Hebrews 7 must be pretemporal.

Psalm 2

The third passage that we will examine in this chapter is Psalm 2. This psalm is also obviously messianic, as we know from the New Testament's repeated application of it to

---

34. Meredith G. Kline, *By Oath Consigned: A Reinterpretation of the Covenant Signs of Circumcision and Baptism* (Grand Rapids, MI: Eerdmans, 1968), 16.

35. Robertson, *Christ of the Covenants*, 6n7. Robertson points his readers to G. M. Tucker, "Covenant Forms and Contract Forms," *VT* 15, no. 4 (1965): 487–503, for "a full statement of the evidence that an oath belonged to the essence of covenant" and to Bible passages like Gen. 21:23–31; 31:53; Ex. 6:8; 19:8; 24:3, 7; Deut. 7:8, 12; 29:12–13; 2 Kings 11:4; 1 Chron. 16:16; Pss. 89:3, 34–35; 105:8–10; Ezek. 16:8 for further support of his claims. Robertson, *Christ of the Covenants*, 6–7.

36. The word "guarantor" (ἔγγυος) occurs only here in the New Testament but was commonly used outside the Bible to speak of a "surety or guarantor"—that is, one who "is answerable for the fulfilment of the obligation which he guarantees." F. F. Bruce, *The Epistle to the Hebrews: The English Text with Introduction, Exposition and Notes*, NICNT (Grand Rapids, MI: Eerdmans, 1964), 151n70. Thus, the role of the "guarantor" is to *guarantee*.

37. Rutherford, *Covenant of Life Opened*, 309.

Jesus (see, e.g., Acts 4:25–27; 13:33; Heb. 1:5; 5:5). In examining this psalm, we look chiefly at three sentences that all strongly suggest the covenant of redemption.

The first sentence is found at the beginning of Psalm 2:7, "I will tell of the decree." The significant word in this phrase is "decree," which is also frequently translated "statute" in the Old Testament (חֹק). This word is regularly identified with the idea of covenant, and, as we saw earlier, it is often translated as "covenant." Psalm 50:16 places "statute" (חֹק) and "covenant" in parallel, which indicates that there is at least a great deal of overlap between these two terms, if not outright synonymy. Joshua 24:25 and 2 Kings 17:15 teach us that God's statutes and covenant are so closely identified that keeping his statutes is tantamount to keeping his covenant, and despising his statutes is tantamount to despising his covenant (see also 1 Kings 9:4–5; 2 Chron. 34:31; Neh. 10:29). But perhaps the clearest passage of all in this regard is Psalm 105:8–10 (which is mirrored in 1 Chron. 16:15–17). Here, "covenant," "sworn promise," and "statute" (or "decree") are all used in parallel. The "covenant that [God] made with Abraham" is the same thing as "his sworn promise to Isaac," which "he confirmed to Jacob as a statute, to Israel as an everlasting covenant."

The word "today," which appears at the end of Psalm 2:7, would seem to confirm the idea that the verse's comments should be understood in a covenantal context. Over and over again in Scripture, the word "today" is used to highlight declarations of covenant renewal. One thinks immediately of Deuteronomy 30:15–19 or Joshua 24:15, where the people of Israel are called to renew their covenant with the Lord without delay. They are challenged to choose "this day" whom they will serve and to begin doing so immediately (see also Gen. 15:18; 31:48; 47:23; Deut. 11:2, 8, 13, 26, 28; 19:9; 26:17; Josh. 14:9–12; 22:16, 18, 22, 29; Ps. 95:7–8). For all these reasons, Peter Craigie concludes that "the 'decree' is a document, given to the king during the coronation ceremony (cf. 2 Kings 11:12); it is his personal covenant document, renewing God's covenant commitment to the dynasty of David."[38]

This close identification between "decree" and "covenant" and the use of the word "today" both suggest that the words of Psalm 2:7 should be understood within the context of a covenant relationship between the "Lord" and "me." And since we know that this psalm is ultimately about Christ, the "me" here is ultimately and most fully realized in Christ. That means that Psalm 2:7 is talking about a covenant relationship between Yahweh and Christ, one that is enacted before the foundation of the world and then *renewed* in "the fullness of time" (Gal. 4:4) when the Son becomes incarnate by adding to himself our human nature. This is the covenant of redemption. It is renewed at the incarnation, and that is when Christ is given his "personal covenant document," so to speak. He is invested with power and authority and declared to be Son, as we will see in the very next sentence.

---

38. Peter C. Craigie, *Psalms 1–50*, WBC 19 (Waco, TX: Word Books, 1983), 67.

The second sentence that points to the covenant of redemption is also in Psalm 2:7: "You are my Son; today I have begotten you." This phrase is also part of the coronation ceremony that would apply ultimately and most fully to Christ. It can legitimately be said of David—as can the previous part of the verse—but only insofar as he was a type of Christ. In his capacity as type, David can rightly be said to have been "begotten" when God's choosing him became clearly manifested to the people of Israel. John Calvin put it this way:

> When God says, I have begotten thee, it ought to be understood as referring to men's understanding or knowledge of it; for David was begotten by God when the choice of him to be king was clearly manifested. The words this day, therefore, denote the time of this manifestation; for as soon as it became known that he was made king by divine appointment, he came forth as one who had been lately begotten of God, since so great an honour could not belong to a private person.[39]

And the same explanation would also apply to Christ. As Calvin said, "He is not said to be begotten in any other sense than as the Father bore testimony to him as being his own Son." The verse has nothing to do with the Son's ontological origin. It does not define the nature or timing of his eternal generation. Rather, it refers to "men's understanding or knowledge of it." In other words, it refers to the point in time when the Son's begottenness would be made manifest to the world, or to what the early church understood as Christ's coronation or induction as King of the universe. According to Calvin, this coronation finds its initial fulfillment in the incarnation, when the Son "became flesh and dwelt among us" (John 1:14), but its "principal" fulfillment is found in the "today" of Christ's resurrection (see Acts 13:33; Rom. 1:4). In these two things, Christ is presented to the world as the Son of God in power.[40]

The fact that the Son's coronation occurs within a context of covenant renewal is suggestive of the covenant of redemption. It indicates that a covenant would have been enacted beforehand between the Father and the Son, which would then have been "renewed" at Christ's incarnation and resurrection, because, in order for a covenant to be renewed, it must first be enacted. Moreover, when we view this earlier covenant in light of New Testament passages such as Ephesians 1:11 and 2 Timothy 1:9, we see good evidence for concluding that it must have been enacted "before the ages began" in the "counsel of [God's] will."

The third and final sentence is found in Psalm 2:8:

> Ask of me, and I will make the nations your heritage,
>   and the ends of the earth your possession.

---

39. Calvin, *Commentary on the Psalms*, 1:17–18.
40. Calvin, *Commentary on the Psalms*, 1:18. See also G. K. Beale and D. A. Carson, eds., *Commentary on the New Testament Use of the Old Testament* (Grand Rapids, MI: Baker Academic, 2007), 927–28.

As we mentioned earlier, this verse implies that an agreement had previously been reached between the Father and the Son, which was then carried out in time and space. Conditions are given, and specific promises are attached: if the Son will ask, the Father is promising to give the nations to him as his inheritance and the ends of the earth as his possession. But conditions that have specific promises attached to them indicate that an agreement has been reached beforehand. The Father is not just saying, "If you ask me, I will help you." That is open ended and general and would not necessarily entail prior agreement. The Father is instead saying something more like this: "If you ask me, I will help you in this specific way." That kind of specificity implies that there was agreement between the Father and the Son on the precise terms of the help that would be asked for and then provided. And that kind of agreement is exactly what the covenant of redemption embodies.

Theological Rationale

Thus far we have laid out the biblical rationale in support of the covenant of redemption. We have explored the language of the Bible and looked at the covenantal implications of several individual passages. After reading through this presentation, it should be clear that a strong biblical argument can be made for the existence of the covenant of redemption. We can understand how our post-Reformation forefathers embraced this doctrine so universally and so quickly. The biblical arguments for it are impressive and widespread.

Historically, this argument has not depended wholly on the language of the Bible and the implications of select individual passages. It has also involved certain theological positions that complemented the biblical arguments and even strengthened them. While there is not enough space to explore all these positions fully, we will look more closely at two of them: (1) the covenant of works and covenant of grace and (2) the Trinity.

Covenant of Works and Covenant of Grace

The existence of a covenant of works in the Bible points to the existence of the covenant of redemption. We see this in a number of ways. In the first place, as already mentioned, the same exegetical process that leads someone to embrace the covenant of works will also lead that one to embrace the covenant of redemption. This means that the individual who recognizes the exegetical evidence in support of the one should have little difficulty in also recognizing the exegetical evidence in support of the other.

In the second place, the covenant of works is the theological "mirror image" of the covenant of redemption.[41] This means that the existence of the former covenant—even when it is referred to by a different name—necessarily implies the existence of the latter. There is no mediator in either covenant. Whereas the covenant of redemption is enacted

---

41. J. V. Fesko, *The Trinity and the Covenant of Redemption* (Fearn, Ross-shire, Scotland: Mentor, 2016), 138.

between God (the Father) and the "Son of God," the covenant of works is enacted between God and Adam, who is called "the son of God" in Luke 3:38. What is more, the whole arrangement of Luke 3–4 would seem to be designed to point to Adam and Christ as mirror images. Whereas Matthew's genealogy starts with Abraham and finishes with Jesus, Luke's begins with Jesus and ends with Adam, the son of God. Why would Luke trace his genealogy all the way back to Adam? Why would he not stop with Abraham as Matthew did? Why would he list the names in the reverse order of Matthew's genealogy? And why would he refer to Adam as God's son?

The issue is further complicated when we look at chapter 4 and see that Luke records the three temptations of Christ in a different order than Matthew does. To be precise, the last two temptations are reversed in Luke when compared with Matthew. What could possibly account for this difference?

It would appear that Luke, under the inspiration of the Holy Spirit, is attempting to paint out Adam and Christ as mirror images. The order he gives of the temptations just happens to be the exact same order that we find with Adam in the garden of Eden in Genesis 3: the lust of the flesh, the lust of the eyes, and pride. What we see in Luke 3–4, then, is a genealogy in which Luke goes all the way back to Adam; he does it in such a way that he ends with Adam, whom he calls the "son of God," and then he immediately transitions to the account of the temptations of Christ, in which he records everything in the exact order given in Genesis 3. The point would seem to be that Jesus is the second (and final) Adam, the ultimate Son of God. He came to do exactly what the first Adam failed to do. He came as the "mirror image" of the first Adam to undo the first Adam's failure in the covenant of works.

Because we know that God does everything "according to the counsel of his will" (Eph. 1:11), we know that the failure of Adam did not catch God by surprise but was part of his plan from before the foundation of the world. And this means that God planned to send his Son into the world as the "mirror image" of Adam to succeed where Adam failed and to undo the consequences of his failure as well. If the Bible teaches that the relationship between God and Adam is contained within a covenant, then this implies that there must also be a covenant between God and Christ that establishes Christ as the "mirror image" of Adam, involves agreement between the persons of the Trinity to the particular conditions and promises of the arrangement, and is enacted according to the counsel of God's will before the foundation of the world.

What is more, the existence of the covenant of grace also points to the existence of the covenant of redemption. Because the covenant of grace is enacted in time and because Christ functions as a mediator in this covenant, there must be another covenant that undergirds, establishes, and guarantees the covenant of grace. We will look at these points one at a time. First, that the covenant of grace is enacted in time implies that there must be another covenant enacted before the beginning of time in which the conditions and promises of the covenant of grace are established and agreed to. To be sure, this might not *require* a covenant to do this. It is possible that the agreement between the persons of the Trinity could be represented in another way and that that agreement would then undergird and guarantee the covenant of grace. But as we have already indicated, the Bible speaks of this agreement in terms of an "oath" between the Father and the Son (Heb. 7:20–22), which is widely regarded as being the constitutive ingredient of the covenant relationship.

Second, the fact that Christ functions as a mediator in the covenant of grace suggests that this covenant is not enacted with him personally and that there must be another covenant that is enacted with him personally. We know from Psalm 2; Luke 22:29; and Hebrews 7, along with many other passages, that there is in fact a covenant enacted with Christ personally. If the covenant of grace cannot encompass this, then there must be another covenant that does. This covenant would then undergird, establish, and guarantee the covenant of grace by establishing and guaranteeing Christ's role as mediator in it.

The Trinity

When we admit that there must be some kind of pretemporal intra-Trinitarian covenant that functions as the mirror image of the covenant of works and lays the foundation for the covenant of grace, we immediately raise questions about the implications of such a covenant for our understanding of the Trinity. In particular, how do we avoid the charge that we are separating the three persons of the Trinity by positing three separate wills that must all agree by way of covenant and, thus, that we are guilty of tritheism?

In responding to this objection, the first thing that needs to be said is that the dialogues recorded in Scripture between the Father and the Son suggest that it is quite possible to hold to the covenant of redemption and not be guilty of tritheism. The fact that the triune God has chosen to reveal himself in and through these dialogues indicates that there must be genuine communication between the three persons of the Trinity within the inner life of God. Listen to what Kevin Vanhoozer says on this point:

> Because the way God is in the economy [i.e., in the dialogues that take place between the Father and the Son in time and space] corresponds to the way God is in himself, we may conclude that the Father, Son, and Spirit are merely continuing in history a communicative activity that characterizes their perfect life together.[42]

If we can say that there is genuine communication between the persons of the Trinity within the inner life of God without lapsing into tritheism, then it certainly seems reasonable to say that we can hold to the covenant of redemption—which in one sense is simply a genuine dialogue between the persons of the Trinity regarding the redemption of the elect—without lapsing into it either. The dialogues between the Father and

---

42. Kevin J. Vanhoozer, *Remythologizing Theology: Divine Action, Passion, and Authorship*, CSCD 18 (New York: Cambridge University Press, 2010), 251. See also the helpful discussion in Fred Sanders, *The Triune God*, NSD (Grand Rapids, MI: Zondervan, 2016), 69–75.

the Son in Scripture allow us to say that the covenant of redemption is completely in keeping with the way God has revealed himself in the Bible.

The formula used by the Council of Florence in 1439 to differentiate the oneness of God from his threeness is helpful in understanding this idea further: "[In God] everything is one, where a relation of opposition does not prevent it."[43] This simply means that God is to be considered one everywhere except where a "relation of opposition" obtains—as it does, for instance, in the internal actions of generation and spiration. But relations of opposition must also obtain in regard to the communicative activity of God, if there is to be genuine dialogue between the persons of the Trinity. The Father must stand "over against" the Son, and the Son must stand "over against" the Spirit for there to be genuine dialogue between them.[44] This means that the covenant of redemption in no way requires undoing the unity of God. It simply requires acknowledging that relations of opposition can and do exist. Thus, we cannot say that the covenant of redemption is unnecessary on account of the unity of the divine mind and will. To say this is to overlook the relations of opposition within the Trinity and to lose the threeness of God in his oneness.

The second response to this objection is that because the covenant of redemption deals with the planning and executing of our salvation, we would expect it to be enacted according to the unique mission of each person of the Trinity. The theological maxim *opera ad extra trinitatis indivisa sunt*—which is translated, "the external works of the Trinity are indivisible"—should never be taken to mean that all three persons of the Trinity always do exactly the same tasks. Rather, each person of the Godhead acts in a way that is suited to his own person and mission. The Father does not become incarnate and die on the cross. The Son does those things. The Son does not come at Pentecost and does not apply the finished work of salvation to the elect. The Spirit does those things. Each one acts according to his own person and mission, but all are involved in every external work of the Godhead.[45] Because the mission of each person is unique within God's indivisible work of accomplishing our salvation, we would expect the covenant that plans and executes that salvation to be enacted along the lines of each person's mission.

Geerhardus Vos helpfully differentiates between predestination and the covenant of redemption by pointing out, "In predestination there is one undivided will; [and] in the counsel of peace this will appears as having its own manner of existence in the Persons."[46] Vos is highlighting the fact that predestination simply involves God choosing who will be saved, whereas the covenant of redemption involves planning and executing the details of how that salvation will actually be accomplished. Predestina-

---

43. The Latin reads, *Omniaque sunt unum, ubi non obviat relationis oppositio.* See Norman P. Tanner, ed., *Decrees of the Ecumenical Councils* (Washington, DC: Georgetown University Press, 1990), 1:571.

44. Sanders, *Triune God*, 131.

45. Scott Swain and Michael Allen, "The Obedience of the Eternal Son," *IJST* 15, no. 2 (2013): 117, 127.

46. Geerhardus Vos, *De Verbondsleer in de Gereformeerde Theologie*, quoted in G. C. Berkouwer, *Divine Election*, Studies in Dogmatics (Grand Rapids, MI: Eerdmans, 1960), 164.

tion, therefore, does not involve the unique missions of the persons of the Trinity, but the covenant of redemption does. Therefore, we should expect that, in the covenant of redemption, the will of God "appears as having its own manner of existence in the Persons."

The covenant of redemption, moreover, has historically been understood as an action of the Trinity as a whole. Some have believed that the Father, representing all three persons of the Trinity, entered into this covenant with the Son, while others have believed that all three persons decided the terms of salvation and then commissioned the Father to enter into covenant with the Son on those terms. Both positions are trying to be faithful to the language of Scripture, which consistently portrays the Father as the one who enters into agreement with the Son, but at the same time trying to protect the Trinitarian nature of the covenant of redemption. Both positions see the Father, Son, and Holy Spirit as concurring in the enacting of this covenant agreement.

Why Does This Matter?

Thus far, we have explored the biblical and theological rationale in support of the covenant of redemption. In doing so, we have surveyed the language of Scripture, the dialogues between the Father and the Son, and several key Bible passages. We have also looked at the covenant of works, the covenant of grace, and the doctrine of the Trinity to see how they support the existence of a pretemporal intra-Trinitarian covenant. The only thing that remains is for us to consider how the covenant of redemption is to be used practically in our lives and why it matters that there is such a thing as the covenant of redemption. In his treatment of this covenant, Wilhelmus à Brakel listed five practical uses of this doctrine.[47] We will highlight three.

First, the covenant of redemption guarantees the salvation of the elect and makes it absolutely certain. The "unchangeable" oath of God is standing behind this covenant (or is part and parcel of it), and thus, our salvation is sure (Heb. 6:17–18). Just as it is impossible for God to lie, so it is also impossible for our salvation to be undone. The elect are completely safe and secure because they have all been given by the Father to the Son in the covenant of redemption and because the Son has done everything that he said he would do in this covenant on their behalf.

Second, the covenant of redemption guarantees that all the conditions of our salvation have already been met in full, which is why this doctrine was historically used to fight against Arminianism. The terms of our salvation, which were agreed on before the foundation of the world within the Godhead, have all been accomplished in time and space and will be applied to the elect in the fullness of time. The only thing that remains for us to do is to acknowledge this with our gratitude and to give all praise and glory to God.

---

47. Brakel, *Christian's Reasonable Service*, 1:261–63.

Third, the covenant of redemption reveals the incredible love that God has shown to the elect. We have been chosen as an expression of the love that God has for himself, the mutual delight of the Father in the Son and the Son in the Father forevermore. The covenant of redemption tells us that we are in effect a love gift from the Father to the Son and from the Son back to the Father. As Brakel said,

> Love moved the Father and love moved the Lord Jesus. [The covenant of redemption] is a covenant of love between those whose love proceeds from within themselves, without there being any loveableness in the object of this love. Oh, how blessed is he who is incorporated in this covenant and, being enveloped and irradiated by this eternal love, is stirred up to love in return, exclaiming, "We love Him, because He first loved us" (1 John 4:19).[48]

---

48. Brakel, *Christian's Reasonable Service*, 1:263.

2

THE COVENANT OF WORKS
IN THE OLD TESTAMENT

Richard P. Belcher Jr.

Covenant theology,[1] as expressed in the Westminster Confession of Faith[2] and developed by other theologians, has not always been well received.[3] One of the perceived weak links of covenant theology is the covenant of works. Many argue that there is no evidence of a covenant between God and Adam in Genesis 1–3.[4] Without the covenant of works, the bicovenantal nature of covenant theology crashes to the ground, leaving one covenant to define the relationship between God and humanity (monocovenantalism). The implications of denying the covenant of works can be monumental for theology because the covenant of works lays a foundation for other key doctrines of Scripture, including

---

1. The development of the ideas in this chapter are related to another work on understanding covenant theology that I have been writing for Christian Focus. I thank Christian Focus for allowing me to use many of the ideas developed in that work for this chapter.

2. The Westminster Confession of Faith represents the culmination of the development of covenant theology, so it is emphasized in this chapter. Cornelis P. Venema argues that there is no substantive difference between the Westminster Standards and the Three Forms of Unity on the doctrine of Christ and the covenants. *Christ and Covenant Theology: Essays on Election, Republication, and the Covenants* (Phillipsburg, NJ: P&R, 2017), 16n21. Many Baptists also affirm a covenant theology that has the necessary elements of a covenant of works (e.g., Second London Baptist Confession [1689], 6–7), even though they would differ in their views on the church and baptism.

3. For recent objections to covenant theology, see Ligon Duncan, "Recent Objections to Covenant Theology: A Description, Evaluation, and Response," in *The Westminster Confession into the 21st Century*, ed. Ligon Duncan (Fearn, Ross-shire, Scotland: Mentor, 2009), 3:467–500.

4. Karl Barth, *Church Dogmatics*, ed. G. W. Bromiley and T. F. Torrance (Edinburgh: T&T Clark, 1958), 3.1:231–32, 4.1:56–65; Holmes Rolston III, *John Calvin versus the Westminster Confession* (Richmond, VA: John Knox, 1972); T. F. Torrance, "From John Knox to John McLeod Campbell: A Reading of Scottish Theology," in *Disruption to Diversity: Edinburgh Divinity, 1846–1996*, ed. David F. Wright and Gary D. Badcock (Edinburgh: T&T Clark, 1996); J. B. Torrance, "Covenant or Contract? A Study of the Theological Background of Worship in Seventeenth-Century Scotland," *SJT* 23, no. 1 (1970): 51–76; G. C. Berkouwer, *Sin*, Studies in Dogmatics (Grand Rapids, MI: Eerdmans, 1971). See Mark I. McDowell's treatment of Karl Barth and T. F. and J. B. Torrance in "Covenant Theology in Barth and the Torrances," chap. 19 of this volume.

the obedience of Christ, the relationship between Adam and Christ, and the concept of Christ as a mediator. These ideas are important for a correct view of justification by faith and the imputation of Adam's sin and Christ's righteousness.[5] This chapter presents evidence for a covenant in Genesis 1–3, shows the importance of confirming the covenant of works, and briefly summarizes several views of the relationship between God and Adam in Genesis 1–3 and their implications.

The Evidence for the Covenant of Works in Genesis 1–3

The word "covenant" does not occur in Scripture until the flood account in Genesis 6:18. If the word "covenant" does not occur in Genesis 1–3, what is the evidence that the relationship between God and Adam is a covenant relationship? The absence of the word "covenant" does not necessarily mean that there is no covenant in Genesis 1–3. The word "covenant" does not occur in 2 Samuel 7 or 1 Chronicles 17, where God makes certain promises to David, but other passages refer to this relationship as a covenant (2 Sam. 23:5; Pss. 89:3, 28; 132:11–12). A similar situation occurs with Genesis 1–3. The term "covenant" is not used in the early chapters of Genesis, but later Scripture refers back to Genesis 1–3 and uses the term "covenant" (see the discussion of Hos. 6:7 below). The key is not whether the term "covenant" occurs in Genesis 1–3 but whether the elements of a covenant are present.

Elements of a Covenant Present in Genesis 1–3

Several elements commonly associated with covenants are present in Genesis 1–3.[6] First, the two parties to the covenant are clearly identified. Genesis 1:1 assumes the existence of God, who is "in the beginning." He is the sovereign ruler of the universe as demonstrated in his creation of the world. Special attention is given to his creation of mankind in his image. Human beings have a special place in God's creation. He does not create them "according to its kind" as he does the animals (1:25), but God deliberates with himself before he creates mankind by stating, "Let us make man in our image, after our likeness" (1:26). Human beings are created in God's image and are given a special place of rule over God's creation under his authority (1:26–28). In Genesis 1 the generic term for humanity is used (אָדָם), and in Genesis 2 the specific partners in this covenant are identified as Adam (אָדָם) and Eve. God takes the initiative in creating the world and in entering into a covenant relationship with the first couple.

---

5. The importance of covenant theology in general is stated by Duncan: "Covenant theology explains the meaning of the death of Christ, . . . undergirds our understanding of the nature and use of the sacraments, and provides the fullest possible explanations of the grounds of our assurance." "Recent Objections," 467.

6. The following elements of the covenant of works are discussed in Louis Berkhof, *Systematic Theology* (Grand Rapids, MI: Eerdmans, 1941), 213–17; and more substantially in Herman Witsius, *The Economy of the Covenants Between God and Man: Comprehending a Complete Body of Divinity*, trans. William Crookshank, 2 vols. (1677; Escondido, CA: den Dulk Christian Foundation, 1990), 1:50–103.

Second, covenants have conditions. The condition to this covenant relationship is set forth in the command that God gave to Adam not to eat of the tree of the knowledge of good and evil (2:16–17). God provided everything that Adam needed for life in the garden, including water, work, and companionship in marriage. His abundant goodness was shown in allowing Adam to eat from all the trees in the garden, but he prohibited Adam from eating from the fruit of one tree in the garden. God tested Adam to see if he would disdain his beneficent provision of food to eat from the prohibited tree. No reason is given why Adam cannot eat from the tree of the knowledge of good and evil. This command with a penalty attached to it focuses on the importance of Adam obeying God in everything.[7] It presents Adam a clear choice of obedience or disobedience to God. Adam has the ability to keep this command of God.

Third, covenants have blessings and curses. The relationship between God and Adam and Eve also includes blessings and curses. In Genesis 1:28, God blesses mankind and commands them to multiply and fill the earth, to subdue it, and to have dominion over every living thing that moves on it. God's blessings are experienced in the fulfillment of God's commands. God's blessings are also seen in how God provides everything that Adam needs in the garden for a full and productive life (Gen. 2). The curse is connected to the prohibition that Adam should not eat from the tree of the knowledge of good and evil, for, as God warned Adam, "in the day that you eat of it you shall surely die" (2:17). The penalty for breaking God's command is death. If Adam and Eve disobey God's command, there will be momentous changes in their relationship with God, their relationship with each other, their relationship with creation, and their perception of themselves. Death will include eventual physical death, but it will also have immediate spiritual implications.

Fourth, covenants operate on the basis of a representation principle so that the actions of the covenant representative affect others who are part of the covenant relationship. In every covenant this principle includes descendants (Gen. 17:7; Deut. 5:2–3; 2 Sam. 7:12–16). The penalty clearly states that if Adam eats from the fruit of the tree of the knowledge of good and evil, he will die. The entrance of sin and death into the world affects not only Adam but also creation (Gen. 3:17–18) and Adam's descendants. The triumph of sin in the children of Adam and Eve is shown when Cain murders Abel. There is a separation of the ungodly line from the godly line in Genesis 4, with the intensification of sin in the boast of Lamech (4:23–24). Not even the godly line is exempt from the result of sin, as the genealogy of Adam in Genesis 5 highlights the refrain "and

---

7. Francis Turretin sees the tree of the knowledge of good and evil as a sacrament of trial. *Institutes of Elenctic Theology*, trans. George Musgrave Giger, ed. James T. Dennison Jr. (Phillipsburg, NJ: P&R, 1992), 1:580–82. G. K. Beale understands the tree of the knowledge of good and evil as a probationary judgment tree, where Adam should have discerned between good and evil and thus should have judged the serpent as evil and pronounced judgment on it. *A New Testament Biblical Theology: The Unfolding of the Old Testament in the New* (Grand Rapids, MI: Baker Academic, 2011), 35; see also Meredith G. Kline, *Kingdom Prologue: Genesis Foundations for a Covenantal Worldview* (Overland Park, KS: Two Age, 2000), 103–7.

he died." Adam was the covenant head of the human race, and his sin negatively affected all his natural descendants. Theologically, sin was imputed to every natural descendant of Adam because of Adam's transgression (Rom. 5:12). The implication is that if Adam had obeyed God's command and had passed the test, then he would have experienced further blessings. If disobedience brings death, then it is reasonable to conclude that obedience would mean life enjoyed with greater blessing.[8] Adam was created in a state of positive holiness and was not subject to the law of death, but the possibility of sinning still existed. He did not yet enjoy life in its fullness to the highest degree of perfection.[9]

Fifth, covenants have signs that point to the blessings of the covenant relationship. Scholars have debated how many signs there are in Genesis 1–3, but most agree that the tree of life is a sign of the covenant.[10] The tree of life was a pledge of the covenant of life (WLC 20), the promised reward for obedience. The fruit of this tree should not be seen as having an innate power to prolong life.[11] Rather, it symbolized life so that when Adam forfeited the promise, he was kept from the sign (Gen. 3:22).

Hosea 6:7: Reference to a Covenant with Adam?

It is also significant that another passage in the Old Testament refers to God's relationship with Adam in Genesis 1–3 with the term "covenant." Hosea 6:7 states,

> But like Adam they transgressed the covenant;
>   there they dealt faithlessly with me.

Much discussion centers on whether "Adam" (אָדָם) is a personal name, a generic use referring to humanity, or a place name. Support for the place name "Adam" comes from the use of the adverb "there" (שָׁם) in the next clause. This would refer to some transgression of the covenant that took place at Adam. Yet no scriptural evidence of covenant breaking at Adam exists.[12] Also, this view requires that the preposition before "Adam" be amended from "like" (כ) to "at" (ב). The preposition "like" supports the view that "Adam" is a reference either to the first human being who broke the covenant through

---

8. Andrew A. Woolsey, *Unity and Continuity in Covenantal Thought: A Study in the Reformed Tradition to the Westminster Assembly* (Grand Rapids, MI: Reformation Heritage Books, 2012), 49. See also Beale, *Biblical Theology*, 29–45. There he lays out the evidence from Gen. 1–3 that if Adam had been obedient, he would have experienced even greater blessings than he had before his sin. He argues on the basis of 1 Cor. 15:45–46, where Paul appeals to Adam in his prefall and sinless condition, that even if Adam had never sinned, his prefall existence still needed to be transformed at some climactic point into an irreversible glorious existence. He concludes that "Adam would have been rewarded with a transformed, incorruptible body if he had remained faithful" (45).

9. Berkhof, *Systematic Theology*, 217.

10. Berkhof, *Systematic Theology*, 217. Kline understands both the tree of life and the Sabbath as covenantal signs. *Kingdom Prologue*, 96. Witsius discusses paradise, the tree of life, the tree of the knowledge of good and evil, and the Sabbath as sacraments of the covenant of works, showing what good they signified and sealed to mankind with respect to God. *Economy of the Covenants*, 1:104–17.

11. Turretin, *Institutes*, 1:580–82. He sees the tree of life as a symbol of the reward.

12. James L. Mays argues that this verse refers to a geography of sin in Israel at the three cities of Adam, Gilead, and Shechem. *Hosea: A Commentary*, OTL (Philadelphia: Westminster, 1969), 100–101. Yet Adam is mentioned only in Josh. 3:16, as the place where the waters of the Jordan heaped up prior to Israel's invasion of Canaan. Otherwise, it seems to have no significance. Duane A. Garrett, *Hosea, Joel*, NAC 19A (Nashville: B&H, 1997), 162.

his disobedience[13] or to human beings who "show themselves to be men in violating the covenant."[14] The generic view of "human beings" takes away from the forceful comparison between the Israelites and Adam as covenant breakers.[15] In the context of Hosea 6:6–10, the adverb "there" could be referring to the false worship at Bethel.[16]

Others are persuaded that the adverb "there" is referring to a place name but also believe that Adam is referring to a personal name. In this view the prophet makes a pun on the name of the town and the name of the first transgressor so that the reference is to both.[17] Hosea is well known for his use of wordplays and metaphors.[18] He also refers many times to the stories of Genesis.[19] The least likely view is that Hosea 6:7 is referring only to a geographical location where Israel broke a covenant. Whether "Adam" refers only to the first man or is a pun that refers to both a person and a place, Hosea 6:7 identifies Adam as a covenant breaker to make the point that the Israelites are also covenant breakers and will experience the consequences of breaking the covenant.

Questions Related to the Covenant of Works

The Name of the Covenant

Several questions arise in discussing the covenant of works. The first question concerns the appropriate name for this covenant. Francis Turretin uses the term "covenant of nature." It is considered a natural relationship because it is founded on the nature of mankind as first created by God. Adam and Eve were created in a state of innocence and liberty without the need of a mediator. This relationship was also a legal relationship because the condition was the observance of the law of nature engraved within them. The relationship depended on the obedience that they ought to render to God. Turretin also uses the term "covenant of works" to refer to this relationship.[20]

Geerhardus Vos speaks of Adam standing in a natural relationship to God, to which God added a covenant of works. The distinction between a natural relationship and a

---

13. John L. Mackay, *Hosea*, MC (Fearn, Ross-shire, Scotland: Christian Focus, 2012), 196. He argues that the adverb "there" may function in poetry as an exclamatory particle that means "look" (Pss. 14:5; 36:12; 48:7; 66:5; Zeph. 1:14).

14. John Calvin, *Hosea*, vol. 13 of *Calvin's Commentaries* (Grand Rapids, MI: Baker, 1996), 234–35. He understands the word "there" to refer to their sacrifices. O. Palmer Robertson argues for either Adam or mankind but understands Gen. 1–3 as a covenant. *The Christ of the Covenants* (Phillipsburg, NJ: Presbyterian and Reformed, 1980), 22–25.

15. B. B. Warfield, "Hosea vi.7: Adam or Man?," in *Selected Shorter Writings of Benjamin B. Warfield*, ed. John E. Meeter, 2 vols. (Phillipsburg, NJ: P&R, 2001), 1:127.

16. C. F. Keil and F. Delitzsch, *Minor Prophets*, vol. 10 in *Commentary on the Old Testament in Ten Volumes* (Grand Rapids, MI: Eerdmans, 1978), 100. Hosea 6:6 mentions burnt offerings, a direct cause of the false worship at Bethel, and 6:10 refers to Ephraim's whoredom, a violation of a specific covenant prohibition (Deut. 12:5).

17. Garrett, *Hosea, Joel*, 162–63; Byron G. Curtis, "Hosea 6:7 and Covenant-Breaking like/at Adam," in *The Law Is Not of Faith: Essays on Works and Grace in the Mosaic Covenant*, ed. Bryan D. Estelle, J. V. Fesko, and David VanDrunen (Phillipsburg, NJ: P&R, 2009), 197–99.

18. J. Andrew Dearman, *The Book of Hosea*, NICOT (Grand Rapids, MI: Eerdmans, 2010), 9–16.

19. In "Hosea 6:7 and Covenant-Breaking," Curtis has an extensive discussion of the wordplays in Hosea (198–207) and the many references that Hosea makes to Genesis and to the Pentateuch (188–94).

20. Turretin, *Institutes*, 1:575–86.

covenant relationship is logical and juridical, not temporal. Adam did not for a single moment exist outside the covenant of works. It is through this covenant that Adam received the right to eternal life if he fulfilled its conditions. When the covenant of works served its purpose, the natural relationship stayed in force in all circumstances, including the demands that stem from it.[21]

The discussion of the natural relationship of humanity to God at creation explains to some extent this statement in WCF 7.1:

> The distance between God and the creature is so great, that although reasonable creatures do owe obedience unto Him as their Creator, yet they could never have any fruition of Him as their blessedness and reward, but by some voluntary condescension on God's part, which He hath been pleased to express by way of covenant.

The natural relationship refers to the Creator-creature relationship, in which obedience is required. But for there to be a special relationship that offered mankind a reward for obedience, a covenant relationship was needed. Mankind could not merit anything before God based on the natural relationship alone. In light of this reality, it seems best not to call Adam's relationship with God the covenant of nature.[22]

Some have trouble with the name *covenant of works* because of possible misunderstandings associated with the term. It gives the impression that the relationship was a commercial exchange and that Adam was left entirely on his own in this arrangement.[23] The term "Edenic covenant" has been suggested, but it can be confusing because the covenant of grace also begins in the garden of Eden (Gen. 3:15). Another term for God's relationship with Adam is the "covenant of creation."[24] This term refers to the bond established between God and mankind at creation. It recognizes that there are general aspects of the covenant that relate to the responsibilities of mankind to his Creator and that there are more specific responsibilities of Adam and Eve than just the special point of testing instituted by God.[25] This is a useful term that allows a broad discussion of the issues in Genesis 1–3 as long as the significance of the period of testing for Adam is not overlooked as foundational to the covenant.

The Westminster Standards affirm that the relationship between God and Adam is a covenant relationship. WCF 7.2 calls it a "covenant of works" with "life" offered "upon condition of perfect and personal obedience." WLC 20 and WSC 12 both state that life and death are set forth in the "covenant of life," with the tree of life offered as a

---

21. Geerhardus Vos, *Reformed Dogmatics*, vol. 2, *Anthropology*, ed. Richard B. Gaffin Jr. (Bellingham, WA: Lexham, 2014), 31–36.

22. Berkhof, *Systematic Theology*, 215.

23. John M. Frame, *Systematic Theology: An Introduction to Christian Belief* (Phillipsburg, NJ: P&R, 2013), 62–66. Frame goes on to affirm that the focus is on what Adam does rather than on God's action as the ground of Adam's blessing or curse and that any blessing he received based on his work he would have deserved. These statements answer the objections Frame himself raises concerning the term *covenant of works*.

24. Robertson, *Christ of the Covenants*, 57.

25. Robertson, *Christ of the Covenants*, 67.

"pledge" and the tree of the knowledge of good and evil prohibited on "pain of death."[26] The term *covenant of life* emphasizes that life is the reward for Adam if he would keep the covenant. The term *covenant of works* highlights that the condition of the covenant is perfect obedience. Even after Adam disobeys God's command, the condition of obedience remains a requirement for human beings, even though no one is able to meet it. The obedience of Christ is necessary for this condition to be fulfilled, since he keeps the law as a basis for the imputation of his righteousness to those who have faith. The term *covenant of works* may sound cold and legal, but it expresses what is necessary for salvation,[27] and in light of Christ's obedience, the believer in Christ has great assurance.

The Role of Grace in the Covenant of Works

The legal relationship of the covenant of works and the fact that God condescended to mankind have raised the question of the role of grace during the period before the fall. Some use the term *grace* in a redemptive sense for the prefall situation,[28] but grace in its fullest redemptive sense of unmerited or demerited favor cannot exist before the entrance of sin into the world.[29] It is true, however, that the condescension of God to mankind overcame a great gulf between the creature and the Creator.[30] God could have required obedience without any promised reward, and the covenant relationship does not place God in mankind's debt.[31] God condescends to mankind to enter into a covenant relationship out of grace, defined as the favor of freely bestowing all kinds of gifts and favors, temporal and eternal, on Adam in his condition before the fall.[32]

---

26. Johannes G. Vos, *The Westminster Larger Catechism: A Commentary*, ed. G. I. Williamson (Phillipsburg, NJ: P&R, 2002), 50.

27. Berkhof calls it the preferred name. *Systematic Theology*, 211.

28. An emphasis on redemptive grace in the prefall situation that does not recognize the differences between the prefall and postfall condition of mankind tends to confuse the relationship between faith and works in salvation (discussed below).

29. Duncan, "Recent Objections," 487. Duncan notes that the term "grace" (חֵן) does not appear in the Bible until Gen. 6:8. Sinclair B. Ferguson comments that following *biblical usage*, Puritan theology usually reserved the term *grace* for the activity of God toward *fallen* man. *John Owen on the Christian Life* (Carlisle, PA: Banner of Truth, 1987), 23n6; emphasis original. Venema uses the term "undeserved favor" to refer to the prefall state but clearly distinguishes between the prefall and postfall condition of mankind and argues against obliterating the difference between the two. *Christ and Covenant Theology*, 24–28.

30. Turretin and John Ball use the term "infinite" to refer to God's condescension to mankind. See Turretin, *Institutes*, 1:574; Woolsey, *Covenantal Thought*, 46.

31. Some dispute the use of *merit* in referring to Adam's obedience, but there is nothing wrong with the word *merit* if understood properly. Everything Adam had, he received from God, so that he could not seek anything from God as his own by right. God was also not a debtor to Adam, because the intrinsic value of Adam's obedience was out of proportion to the infinite reward of life. God sovereignly bound himself to the arrangement that Adam's obedience would lead to greater life. Turretin, *Institutes*, 1:578. Some who deny the concept of merit with Adam also deny the use of the term *merit* to refer to Christ's work for us. Rich Lusk, "A Response to 'The Biblical Plan of Salvation,'" in *The Auburn Avenue Theology, Pros and Cons: Debating the Federal Vision*, ed. E. Calvin Beisner (Fort Lauderdale, FL: Knox Theological Seminary, 2004), 136–38. John Murray does not use *merit* to refer to Adam's situation, but he does use *merit* to refer to the work of Christ (see below). It is also possible to avoid the use of *merit* without denying that the covenant of works operates according to a works principle. Guy Prentiss Waters, *The Federal Vision and Covenant Theology: A Comparative Analysis* (Phillipsburg, NJ: P&R, 2006), 41.

32. See the summary of the views of John Ball and James Ussher in Woolsey, *Covenantal Thought*, 46, 48. There can be confusion concerning the prefall relationship of God and Adam if the term *grace* is left undefined or is not defined properly.

The Covenant of Works and the Gospel[33]

The elements of the covenant of works are important because they lay a foundation for the gospel.[34] Adam was given a probationary test to see if he would obey God and keep the terms of the covenant. When Adam broke the covenant, the probationary test of the covenant came to an end, but the obligation to perfectly fulfill the terms of the covenant still remained.[35] This obligation is implied in Genesis 3 and is clearly taught in other passages of Scripture (Gal. 3:10–14). We can make three observations.

First, the punishments of Genesis 3 are passed on to the descendants of Adam. The world of Cain and Abel in Genesis 4 shows the impact of sin that is a result of Adam's transgression. Human beings are held accountable to God and subject to death on the basis of the terms of the original covenant.[36] If the punishment of the broken covenant is extended to all, the covenant and the law are also extended to all.[37] The descendants of Adam are held accountable by God for what Adam did because of the special relationship that Adam had as a representative of his descendants in the covenant of works. Paul makes the point in Romans 5:12–14 that even though the law had not yet been given, death reigned from Adam to Moses. Sin was in the world before the giving of the law, and sin is not counted against anyone without a law. Yet death reigned because of Adam's transgression. The descendants of Adam were held accountable for Adam's sin because he was their representative. When Adam sinned, his sin was imputed to his descendants (see also 1 Cor. 15:22, "In Adam all die").

Second, the continuing obligation to fulfill the covenant requirements is affirmed in later Scripture in the principle "Do this and live." This principle is found in Leviticus 18:5 and is affirmed in Romans 10:5, where Paul writes about a righteousness based on the law over against a righteousness based on faith.[38] Jesus himself refers to this principle in Matthew 19:16–17. The possibility still exists that if someone could keep the law perfectly, he or she could obtain salvation on that basis. The problem is that no human being is able to keep the law perfectly (James 2:10). All people are condemned because they have broken the law.

Third, Christ fulfills the obligations of the covenant for the salvation of his people. The same obligation of personal, perfect, and perpetual obedience that God laid on Adam as the federal representative by the covenant of works is also laid on Christ as the second man and the last Adam (1 Cor. 15:45, 47), who by his obedience accom-

---

33. For more, see Guy Prentiss Waters, "The Covenant of Works in the New Testament," chap. 3 in this volume.
34. For a concise analysis of how the covenant of works is related to justification by faith, see Morton H. Smith, "The Biblical Plan of Salvation with Reference to the Covenant of Works, Imputation, and Justification by Faith," in Beisner, *Auburn Avenue Theology*, 96–117.
35. Robert L. Reymond, *A New Systematic Theology of the Christian Faith* (Nashville: Thomas Nelson, 1998), 439.
36. Reymond, *Systematic Theology*, 439.
37. Turretin, *Institutes*, 1:617.
38. Guy P. Waters, "Romans 10:5 and the Covenant of Works," in Estelle, Fesko, and VanDrunen, *The Law Is Not of Faith*, 210–39.

plished the salvation of the elect, whom he represented.[39] Salvation is by works, not our works but the works of Christ received by faith. Christ kept the law perfectly on behalf of those he represents (those united to him). His righteousness is imputed to his descendants through faith in his person and work.[40] Christ kept the law and died on the cross as the sacrifice for sin, taking on himself the covenant curse that falls on all those who break the law (Gal. 3:12–14). In this way God can justify sinners through faith in Christ. The covenant of works is foundational to the work of Christ as the basis for our salvation.

Various Views concerning the Relationship between God and Adam in Genesis 1–3

Covenant theology is a vast and complex topic. It is easy to get lost in the various approaches and the different emphases of covenant theologians. Part of the confusion comes from the fact that scholars who approach the topic, even from similar viewpoints, use different terminology to describe the components of covenant theology. The purpose of this section is to compare the work of various scholars with the standard Reformed terminology represented by the Westminster Standards to bring clarity to the discussion of covenant theology. Some deviations are minor, but others are more significant and may even affect views of imputation and justification by faith.

O. Palmer Robertson, The Christ of the Covenants

O. Palmer Robertson's book *The Christ of the Covenants* has become a classic and is very helpful in laying out the covenant framework of Scripture, in discussing the relationships of the covenants to each other, and in highlighting the particulars of each of the Old Testament covenants. Robertson, however, uses different terminology than the Westminster Standards do in discussing covenant theology.

Robertson begins by defining a covenant as a "bond in blood sovereignly administered."[41] This definition highlights that God takes the initiative in the covenant relationship and that promises are made through the taking of oaths that are confirmed by the shedding of blood. This definition works with most covenants, especially those covenants between God and his people, but it has limitations. Robertson denies that there is a covenant relationship between the members of the Trinity (usually called the *covenant of redemption*). He affirms that God intended from eternity to redeem a people, but this is not the same thing as proposing the existence of a precreation covenant between the Father and the Son. Such a "covenant," he says, seems artificial, goes beyond

---

39. Reymond, *Systematic Theology*, 439–40.
40. Turretin develops the double imputation of the righteousness of Christ to us and Adam's sin to Christ. *Institutes of Elenctic Theology*, 1:618.
41. Robertson, *Christ of the Covenants*, 4.

the scriptural evidence, and does not fit the definition of a covenant as a sovereignly administered bond.[42]

Robertson acknowledges the difference between a prefall covenant and a postfall covenant and even commends the *covenant of works* and *covenant of grace* terminology. This distinction recognizes the necessity of a prefall probation that required perfect obedience as the meritorious ground of blessing and provided an overarching structure to unite the totality of God in relation to man in his fallen state.[43] Thus Robertson affirms a bicovenantal structure to Scripture. He believes, however, that these terms do not express the whole picture. The term *works* to describe the prefall situation suggests that grace was not operative in the prefall covenant, that works have no place in the covenant of grace, and that the "work" required of Adam is confined to the one command of not eating from the tree of the knowledge of good and evil.[44] Robertson thus opts to call the prefall covenant the "covenant of creation" and to refer to the unfolding covenants in redemptive history as the "covenant of redemption" (instead of the covenant of grace). Although he clearly defines these terms and the reasons for using them, students easily become confused.[45] These minor criticisms, though, should not take away from the value of Robertson's work.

John Murray, "The Adamic Administration"

John Murray calls for a "recasting" of covenant theology to make it more biblically articulated.[46] He does not want to limit covenant theology to the developments that occurred in the seventeenth century. He defines a covenant as a sovereign administration of grace and promise and under this definition includes the Noahic, Abrahamic, Mosaic, Davidic, and new covenants.[47] He does not consider the prefall relationship between God and Adam a covenant relationship because the term "covenant" is not used in Genesis 1–3, and the term, Murray believes, is always used in Scripture in a situation that needs redemption. Also, the term *covenant of works* does not allow for the elements of grace that are present in the prefall relationship between God and Adam. Murray calls the relationship between God and Adam "the Adamic Administration," whereby God, by a special act of providence, established for Adam the provision that would enable him to pass from the state of contingency (able not to sin) to the state of holiness (not able to sin) by means of a probationary test.[48]

---

42. Robertson, *Christ of the Covenants*, 54.

43. Robertson, *Christ of the Covenants*, 55.

44. Robertson, *Christ of the Covenants*, 56.

45. This is especially true if a student adopts Robertson's terminology and then is examined by a church body that adheres to the WCF.

46. John Murray, *The Covenant of Grace: A Biblico-Theological Study* (Phillipsburg, NJ: Presbyterian and Reformed, 1983), 5.

47. Murray uses the covenant with Noah to examine how a covenant should be defined. *Covenant of Grace*, 12.

48. John Murray, "The Adamic Administration," in the *Collected Writings of John Murray*, vol. 2, *Select Lectures in Systematic Theology* (Carlisle, PA: Banner of Truth, 1977), 49.

Although Murray does not call this arrangement a covenant, many of the elements that make up the covenant of works are part of his Adamic administration.[49] It is a sovereign administration whereby Adam acts as a representative for his descendants. The condition of this arrangement was obedience, focused in the command not to eat of the tree of the knowledge of good and evil (Gen. 2:16). The promise held out to Adam, if he obeyed God's command, was everlasting life, symbolized in the tree of life (Gen. 3:22). Murray does not want to associate this promise with the principle "Do this and live" (cf. Lev. 18:5; Rom. 10:5; Gal. 3:12) or with any notion of meritorious reward. If Adam passed the test of obedience, he could only claim the fulfillment of the promise on the basis of God's faithfulness, not on the basis of justice. If Adam failed the test of probation, he and his descendants would experience the full impact of sin and death, which is defined as spiritual (moral and religious), judicial, and psychophysical.

The weakness of Murray's approach is that he does not see the elements of a covenant in Genesis 1–3 and that he does not recognize a continuing principle of works operative throughout redemptive history, highlighted in passages such as Leviticus 18:5 and Romans 10:5. Murray affirms, however, the traditional view of justification by faith, because he is clear on Adam's representative role so that his sin explains why every natural descendant of Adam is born a sinner. Adam's sin was imputed to them.[50] Although Adam failed to keep God's law, Christ obeyed the law and became the vicarious sin bearer in his death on the cross so that the righteousness of Christ could be imputed to those who have faith in him.[51] Murray states, "By Adam sin-condemnation-death, by Christ righteousness-justification-life."[52] Murray confirms that the basic elements of the probationary test for Adam are important, that his disobedience had a far-reaching impact, and that these elements are foundational for the work of Christ, which means they are foundational for understanding justification by faith.

W. J. Dumbrell, Covenant and Creation

W. J. Dumbrell's *Covenant and Creation* is a substantial work on the covenants and presents many beneficial discussions of the various covenants in the Old Testament. Dumbrell, though, denies the existence of a covenant of works because it is argued from biblical inference rather than sufficient biblical content.[53]

---

49. Venema states, "Murray's treatment of the WCF's doctrine of the covenant of works, then, is not so much a repudiation of any of its essential teaching as a revision and refinement of some aspects of the WCF's formulation that he finds objectionable or misleading." *Christ and Covenant Theology*, 22.

50. John Murray, *Redemption Accomplished and Applied* (Grand Rapids, MI: Eerdmans, 1955), 25.

51. Murray, *Redemption*, 123–28. Murray uses the term "merit" to refer to the work of Christ. *Collected Writings*, 2:286–87.

52. Murray, "Adamic Administration," 59.

53. William J. Dumbrell, *Covenant and Creation: A Theology of the Old Testament Covenants* (1984; repr., Grand Rapids, MI: Baker, 1993), 46. This book was first published in 1984 by Thomas Nelson and then was republished in 1993 by Baker.

The first time "covenant" occurs in Scripture is in the context of Noah and the flood. Noah is referred to as "a righteous man," "blameless in his generation," and one who "walked with God" (Gen. 6:9). The word "righteous" (צַדִּיק) refers to conduct arising from a prior relationship that exhibits an attitude toward God of trust and fidelity.[54] Noah's behavior is contrasted with the wickedness of his generation. God instructs Noah to build the ark in preparation for the flood God will send to judge the earth because of the wickedness of humanity (Gen. 6:5, 13–14). God tells Noah, "I will establish my covenant with you, and you shall come into the ark, you, your sons, your wife, and your sons' wives with you" (Gen. 6:18). The normal verb for the inauguration of a covenant is "to cut" (כרת) a covenant. But in Genesis 6:18, the word used is "establish" (קום), which indicates that God is not beginning a covenant relationship with Noah but is continuing a covenant that is already in place. Genesis 9:1–17 presents Noah as a second Adam, armed with the same mandate God gave to Adam, within the context of a fallen world.[55] Genesis 6:18 thus refers to a divine relationship established by creation itself. Therefore, Dumbrell argues, there can be only one divine covenant. Dumbrell rejects the covenant of works because the biblical evidence for it is lacking.[56]

Dumbrell discusses Genesis 1–3 to show its relationship to Genesis 9. He recognizes that God established a condition in his relationship with Adam that prohibited eating from the tree of the knowledge of good and evil (Gen. 2:17). This condition regulated fellowship in the garden, and Adam failed to meet the condition. Adam's failure affected all his descendants, for we were all somehow involved (Rom. 5:19).[57] The difference between the prefall and postfall condition of Adam is that before the fall, Adam was able to determine the course of action to be adopted, but after the fall, he was in the grip of the consequences of the action he chose. By eating the fruit, Adam intruded into an area reserved for God alone and asserted equality with God. Adam's moral defiance of God meant that his life would be full of tension and absolute moral uncertainty.[58] Dumbrell does not discuss further the implications of Adam's failure for his descendants (imputation) or for the obedience of Christ in fulfilling the law (justification). He recognizes the truth of Paul's interpretation of Genesis 15:6 in Romans 4, but he states that Paul "moved this verse into the area of justification."[59] This leaves open the

---

54. Dumbrell, *Covenant and Creation*, 13–14.

55. Dumbrell, *Covenant and Creation*, 26–28. Paul R. Williamson disputes Dumbrell's argument based on the use of the word קום and denies that there is a covenant in Gen. 1–3. *Sealed with an Oath: Covenant in God's Unfolding Purpose*, NSBT 23 (Downers Grove, IL: InterVarsity Press, 2007), 72–76.

56. Dumbrell, *Covenant and Creation*, 32, 44–46.

57. Dumbrell, *Covenant and Creation*, 36–37. In a separate essay, Dumbrell draws a parallel between Adam and Israel. Both were put into sacred space to exercise kingly/priestly roles, both were given laws to maintain the divine space, and both broke the law and were expelled from the divine space. Their continued existence in the divine space was dependent on their obedience to the divine mandate. Dumbrell, "Genesis 2:1–17: A Foreshadowing of the New Creation," in *Biblical Theology: Retrospect and Prospect*, ed. Scott J. Hafemann (Downers Grove, IL: InterVarsity Press, 2002), 62.

58. Dumbrell, *Covenant and Creation*, 37–39.

59. Dumbrell, *Covenant and Creation*, 53.

question whether Genesis 15:6 originally has justification in view. Dumbrell concludes that Genesis 15:6 is Abram's demonstrated example of covenant fidelity, based on his definition that righteousness in the Old Testament indicates behavior consistent with the nature of a relationship already established.[60] Partly on this basis, he also argues that the covenant ceremony of Genesis 15 cannot be the inauguration of the Abrahamic covenant.[61]

The situation in Genesis 1–3 is complex because of how sin affects the original mandate that God gave to Adam and Eve. In standard Reformed theology, there is a distinction between the relationship of God with Adam and Eve before the fall and after the fall. Before the fall, no sin impedes their relationship, but after the fall, sin radically alters all the relationships of Adam and Eve, including their relationship with God. It is impossible for Adam and Eve to have fellowship with God unless God covers their shame and takes care of their guilt. God promises to send someone to do battle with the serpent in order to redeem humanity and restore God's creation (Gen. 3:15). The prefall and postfall relationship between God and humanity cannot be conflated or subsumed under one covenant relationship. They are two different ways Adam and Eve related to God. There was an initial covenant relationship between God and Adam, but that relationship was broken. A different relationship needed to be established so that sinners could have fellowship with God. These two different situations would need to have two different covenants. God's word of judgment to Adam and Eve includes the mandate that God had originally given to them concerning marriage and dominion (Gen. 3:16–19). When Genesis 6:18 refers to a previous covenant, it is referring to the original mandate that God had given to Adam and Eve but not apart from the changes that came with the fall. The instructions related to marriage, dominion, and the image of God continue to be relevant for humanity after sin enters the world. The obligations of the covenant of works continue for humanity because everyone is required to keep the law of God, though now it is impossible to do so.

Federal Vision: From Childhood to Maturity

Federal Vision is a reworking of traditional Reformed covenant theology that gives prominence to vision (or story) over a propositional system of theology. Many of the proponents of Federal Vision stand in the tradition of standard Reformed covenant theology as represented in the WCF, but its adherents are also found in other Reformed denominations, such as the United Reformed Churches in North America (URCNA) and the Communion of Reformed Evangelical Churches (CREC). Their system develops

---

60. Dumbrell has also published a commentary on Romans in which he defines justification primarily in relational, not forensic, terms. Justification expresses covenant membership or covenant identification. He rejects the traditional view of imputation. *Romans: A New Covenant Commentary* (Eugene, OR: Wipf and Stock, 2005), 40–41, 67–68, 102. Williamson argues against reducing righteousness to the realm of relationships. *Sealed with an Oath*, 188.

61. Dumbrell, *Covenant and Creation*, 53–54.

from covenant theology, and they offer a comprehensive vision of an epistemology, a Trinitarian theology, and a doctrine of redemption and its application, as well as a conception of the church, culture, and Christian living in the world.[62] The focus here will be their understanding of Genesis 1–3, how it compares with standard Reformed covenant theology, and the implications for justification by faith. The chapter by James Jordan in a book written by its proponents will be used to present their views.[63]

Jordan sees problems with the traditional Reformed understanding of the covenant of works. He accepts Murray's criticisms of it and takes up his challenge to provide a better systematic construction of the nature of the Adamic covenant. One problem with the covenant of works is the idea of earning eternal life through meritorious works. Jordan calls this arrangement Pelagian in character. The reward earned seems out of proportion to the merits required. Another problem is that the reward earned should not be eternal life but glorification; in other words, the reward should not just be the perpetuation of original life but a new glorified life. He finds confusing and misleading the statement in WCF 19.1 that "God gave to Adam a law . . . by which he bound him and all his posterity, to personal, entire, exact, and perpetual obedience," with the promise of life for fulfilling it and the threat of death for breach of it. He asks, "Where is faith in all of this?"[64]

A better way to understand God's relationship with Adam, Jordan argues, is to see a two-stage process consisting of a stage of human life and a glorified stage that Adam failed to attain. These two stages are found in Paul's discussion of Romans 5 and 1 Corinthians 15. The two stages specifically are a stage of childhood and a stage of maturity. A person does not become a mature adult by earning it through good works. Good behavior prepares a person for mature responsibilities, and bad behavior disqualifies a person from mature responsibilities. Good behavior does not earn points. If Adam had remained faithful to God, he would have matured to the point of being aware that he needed a fuller kind of life from God, which God would have freely given him at the proper time. There is nothing here of merit, but the choice is whether to exercise faith or not. Adam rejected the God-given process of maturation because Adam prematurely seized the privilege that God had held out as the end of that process. Thus, the garden

62. Waters, *Federal Vision and Covenant Theology*, 1–2. For views that agree with or are sympathetic to Federal Vision, see Steve Wilkins and Duane Garner, eds., *The Federal Vision* (Monroe, LA: Athanasius Press, 2004); P. Andrew Sandlin, ed., *Backbone of the Bible: Covenant in Contemporary Perspective* (Nacogdoches, TX: Covenant Media, 2004); Douglas Wilson, *"Reformed" Is Not Enough: Recovering the Objectivity of the Covenant* (Moscow, ID: Canon, 2002); Norman Shepherd, *The Call of Grace: How the Covenant Illuminates Salvation and Evangelism* (Phillipsburg, NJ: P&R, 2000). For a book that interacts with Federal Vision by presenting both sides, see Beisner, *Auburn Avenue Theology*. For negative evaluations, see Waters, *Federal Vision and Covenant Theology*; Venema, *Christ and Covenant Theology*; Brian Schwertley, *Auburn Avenue Theology: A Biblical Analysis* (Saunderstown, RI: American Presbyterian Press, 2005); Jeong Koo Jeon, *Covenant Theology and Justification by Faith: The Shepherd Controversy and Its Impacts* (Eugene, OR: Wipf and Stock, 2006).

63. James B. Jordan, "Merit versus Maturity: What Did Jesus Do for Us?," in Wilkins and Garner, *Federal Vision*, 151–202.

64. Jordan, "Merit versus Maturity," 153–55. An answer to this question is that the covenant of works describes the righteousness based on the law that Adam was capable of obeying.

was a kindergarten, a place where Adam could grow from childhood to kingly maturity, a place of easy life with free food, a place to learn how to cultivate and guard.[65]

This view of Adam in the garden affects Jordan's view of the work of Christ. He does not want to use the term *merit* to speak of Christ's accomplishments because it is a carryover from medieval theology and because it creates the idea that Jesus earned by works his translation into glory.[66] Although he does not disagree with the idea of double imputation (our sins were imputed to Jesus and his glory to us), he rejects the active and passive obedience of Christ. Instead, Jesus became the first mature man, perfect in faith toward the Father and perfect in obedience. He thus became eligible for transformation into glory through death, not because he had earned the right to it but because he had matured to the point of being fit for it. We receive not Jesus's merits but his maturity, his glorification. The reigning paradigm for Adam, for Christ, and for us is growth into maturity instead of the breaking or keeping of the law.[67]

In this view Adam's relationship with God centers on faith, not works or merit. This focus affects Federal Vision proponents' understanding of the work of Christ, who does not fulfill the law on our behalf but becomes the first perfect, mature man through faith, which makes him eligible for transformation into glory. This approach flattens the confessional understanding of the relationship between the covenants by denying the principle of works. It downplays the role of the law as a legal basis for our relationship with God that brings conviction of sin in favor of formulations that stress biblical obligations as "gospel."[68] Imputation is not defined according to the historical definition because it is the glory of Jesus that is imputed to us instead of his righteousness. This approach modifies the traditional understanding of Christ's work as a basis for our justification, which holds that it is his righteousness, derived from the perfect obedience and full satisfaction of his work, imputed to us, whereby God pardons us of our sins (WLC 70–71).[69] A reworking of the covenant of works changes how one understands the work of Christ and the basis of justification by faith.[70]

Conclusion

The covenant of works and the concepts associated with it are very important for understanding our relationship with God. This chapter has laid out the evidence for such a covenant in Genesis 1–3. Those who deny the existence of the covenant of works also tend to argue that the prefall relationship between God and Adam was only of grace. This view flattens the differences between the prefall relationship between God and

65. Jordan, "Merit versus Maturity," 153, 157–60.
66. For the appropriate use of *merit*, see note 31 above.
67. Jordan, "Merit versus Maturity," 193–95.
68. Waters, *Federal Vision and Covenant Theology*, 33. Waters's remarks are made in reference to another Federal Vision proponent, but they apply equally well to Jordan's views.
69. Waters, *Federal Vision and Covenant Theology*, 40.
70. For further analysis of different views of God's relationship with Adam among proponents of Federal Vision, see Waters, *Federal Vision and Covenant Theology*, 30–44.

Adam and their postfall relationship. The principle of works is rejected as a way to speak of God's relationship to Adam before the fall and as a way to describe the work of Christ. Sometimes these views also result in a weakening of the use of the law with a denial of the contrast between the law and the gospel. Such ideas can easily lead to a denial of the traditional view of justification by faith, including the imputation of Christ's righteousness, and a conflation of faith and works as the basis of justification.[71]

Not all who deny the covenant of works get justification by faith wrong, because they affirm certain key scriptural teachings. These teachings include that there is a major difference between the prefall and postfall condition of Adam so that God's relationship to mankind greatly changes after the fall. People are lawbreakers who stand condemned by the law. Faith in Christ over against keeping the law is the way of salvation. The contrast between the righteousness of the law and the righteousness of faith, a contrast between law and gospel, is foundational for a proper view of the work of Christ (Rom. 10:5–6) and our justification.[72] The covenant of works gives the work of Christ a rationale for why he had to come and what he had to accomplish for our salvation (Rom. 5:12–21). The covenant of works is important, but more important is a proper understanding of the gospel, and we should rejoice when people get the gospel right even if they reject the covenant of works.[73]

---

71. Views that do not recognize the differences between the prefall and postfall condition of mankind tend to confuse the relationship between faith and works in salvation. Justifying faith is defined as covenant faithfulness, and justification ultimately takes place at the final judgment, where it is based on performance. Norman Shepherd, "Thirty-Four Theses on Justification in Relation to Faith, Repentance, and Good Works, Presented to the Philadelphia Presbytery of the Orthodox Presbyterian Church, November 18, 1978," thesis 19; N. T. Wright, *The Letter to the Romans*, in *The New Interpreter's Bible*, 12 vols. (Nashville: Abingdon, 2002), 10:440.

72. The contrast between law and gospel leads to a biblical view of justification by faith even without a recognition of a covenant of works, as in much Lutheran theology: "Formula of Concord, Epitome 5," in *The Book of Concord*, trans. and ed. Theodore G. Tappert (Philadelphia: Fortress, 1959), 477–79; John T. Mueller, *Christian Dogmatics* (Saint Louis, MO: Concordia, 1934), 44–47; C. F. W. Walther, *The Proper Distinction between Law and Gospel* (repr., Saint Louis, MO: Concordia, 1929).

73. Two examples of this are John Murray, discussed above, and Paul R. Williamson. The latter denies that Adam's relationship with God, either prefall or postfall, is a covenant relationship, but he affirms the traditional view of justification by faith and the imputation of Christ's righteousness. *Sealed with an Oath*, 52–58, 186–88. It is interesting that Williamson does not discuss Rom. 5:12–21 or 10:5, perhaps because he does not see them as related to the covenant.

3

The Covenant of Works in the New Testament

Guy Prentiss Waters

Few contemporary New Testament scholars acknowledge the presence of the covenant of works in the text of the New Testament.[1] While the phrase "covenant of works" is absent from the New Testament, the concept is very much present.[2] The New Testament writers, and particularly the apostle Paul, understand God to have entered into a covenant with Adam sometime after God created Adam but before Adam first sinned against God. In this covenant, Adam served as a representative man. That is, the fate of Adam's descendants (Jesus excepted) was suspended on Adam's actions in covenant with God. God required of Adam ongoing obedience to the moral commandments that had obliged him since his creation. God also required of Adam obedience to the superadded command not to eat of the tree of the knowledge of good and evil. Had Adam continued in obedience to God, he would have brought himself and his posterity into confirmed, unlosable life. But Adam disobeyed and so plunged himself and his descendants into sin, curse, and death in all its forms. It is this covenantal framework that provides the

---

1. N. T. Wright, one of the most prominent recent advocates for understanding the apostle Paul as a covenant theologian, does not understand Adam's probation and disobedience in terms of a creation covenant. While he sees "what happened to Israel when Torah arrived on Mount Sinai" as "a recapitulation of the primal sin of Adam," referencing Rom. 7:7–12, he refrains from speaking of Adam or Adam's sin in covenantal terms. *Paul and the Faithfulness of God* (Minneapolis: Fortress, 2013), 894; cf. 1010. For Wright, "covenant" properly begins with the Abrahamic narrative. While Abraham's call is a "recapitulation" of Adam's "creation," and the Abrahamic covenant provides "rescue" from Adam's "fall," Wright nevertheless refrains from speaking of an Adamic covenant (784–85). On Wright's understanding of covenant in Paul's theology, see Guy Waters, "Covenant Theology and Recent Interpretation of Paul: Some Reflections," *Confessional Presbyterian* 6 (2010): 167–79.

2. What follows is a summary of the formulation of the doctrine of the covenant of works (also termed the "covenant of life" and the "first covenant") found in the Westminster Standards (WCF 7.1–2; WLC 20–30; WSC 12–20).

context within which the New Testament speaks of the person and redemptive work of the last Adam, Jesus Christ.

In the New Testament, there are two main passages in which the covenant of works is presented at length (1 Cor. 15:20–23, 44–49; Rom. 5:12–21). It is in these verses that the apostle Paul helps us see the sweep and scope of God's purpose to save sinners through his Son. Also, in Galatians 3:1–4:11 and Romans 9:30–10:21, Paul speaks of the Mosaic covenant in ways that have suggested to some Reformed interpreters an association with the covenant of works. When Paul speaks of the condition of the Mosaic covenant as well as its outcome for Israel, they reason, he shows that he understands the Mosaic covenant to be in some sense a republication of the covenant of works.[3] For this reason, we give attention not only to those passages that speak most clearly about the covenant of works (1 Cor. 15; Rom. 5) but also to those passages that have suggested to some readers an association between that covenant and the Mosaic covenant. After reviewing these passages, we address the implications of what Paul says about the covenant of works for our understanding of the Bible and of the Christian life.

Before exploring 1 Corinthians 15 and Romans 5, it is important to offer a brief explanation of why these passages are relevant to the covenant of works.[4] In both these passages, Paul offers a sustained comparison of the persons and actions of Adam and Jesus Christ. Adam and Christ are representative men whose actions have determined the eternal destinies of those whom each represents. Adam's one sin resulted in condemnation and death for his ordinary descendants. Jesus's obedience and death resulted in justification and life for his people. Elsewhere, Paul speaks of Jesus's death for our justification in expressly covenantal terms (cf. 1 Cor. 11:25–26; 2 Cor. 3:4–11). If Paul understands *Jesus's* representative work in covenantal terms, and if Paul understands *Jesus* and *Adam* to be parallel as representative persons, then we are bound to understand *Adam's* representative work in covenantal terms. Paul would therefore have us see both the command that God gave to Adam and Adam's disobedience to that com-

---

3. The most influential republication thesis in recent Reformed exegesis has been that of Meredith G. Kline, "Gospel until the Law: Rom. 5:13–14 and the Old Covenant," *JETS* 34, no. 4 (1991): 433–46; Kline, *Kingdom Prologue: Genesis Foundations for a Covenantal Worldview* (Eugene, OR: Wipf and Stock, 2006), 107–17, 320–23. For those advocating republication in broad sympathy with Kline's project, see Mark W. Karlberg, *Covenant Theology in Reformed Perspective: Collected Essays and Book Reviews in Historical, Biblical, and Systematic Theology* (Eugene, OR: Wipf and Stock, 2000); many (but not all) of the contributors in Bryan D. Estelle, J. V. Fesko, and David VanDrunen, eds., *The Law Is Not of Faith: Essays on Works and Grace in the Mosaic Covenant* (Phillipsburg, NJ: P&R, 2009); David VanDrunen, "Israel's Recapitulation of Adam's Probation under the Law of Moses," *WTJ* 73, no. 2 (2011): 303–24. For critical Reformed engagement with the republication thesis, see, representatively, Cornelis P. Venema, *Christ and Covenant Theology: Essays on Election, Republication, and the Covenants* (Phillipsburg, NJ: P&R, 2017), 3–144; Andrew M. Elam, Robert C. Van Kooten, and Randall A. Bergquist, *Merit and Moses: A Critique of the Klinean Doctrine of Republication* (Eugene, OR: Wipf and Stock, 2014); O. Palmer Robertson, *The Christ of the Prophets* (Phillipsburg, NJ: P&R, 2004), 364–65n6; D. Patrick Ramsey, "In Defense of Moses: A Confessional Critique of Kline and Karlberg," *WTJ* 66, no. 2 (2004): 373–400 (though note the response by Brenton C. Ferry, "Cross-Examining Moses' Defense: An Answer to Ramsey's Critique of Kline and Karlberg," *WTJ* 67 [2005]: 163–68); Rowland S. Ward, *God and Adam: Reformed Theology and the Creation Covenant* (Wantirna, Australia: New Melbourne, 2003), 183–84.

4. I have adapted the following paragraph from Guy Prentiss Waters, *The Lord's Supper as the Sign and Meal of the New Covenant*, SSBT (Wheaton, IL: Crossway, 2019), 33–34. Used by permission of Crossway.

mand in an entirely covenantal framework. For these reasons, we conclude that Paul understood God to have entered into a covenant with Adam as a representative man. The outcome of this covenant was contingent on Adam's works, that is, his obedience or disobedience to God's commands. It is true to Paul, then, to denominate this covenant the "covenant of works." We may now consider what Paul has to say about the nature of this covenant by giving attention to what he says about Adam (and Christ) in 1 Corinthians 15 and Romans 5.

The Covenant of Works

1 Corinthians 15

Paul's earliest formulation of the covenant of works appears in 1 Corinthians 15. He addresses the covenant of works in the context of an extended reflection on the resurrection of Christ. In this chapter, Paul responds to "some" who "say that there is no resurrection of the dead" (15:12). His argument is in three parts. First, in 15:1–11, Paul reminds the Corinthians that the resurrection was an essential element of the gospel. It was this gospel that he preached to them and that they believed for their salvation. Second, in 15:12–34, Paul proves the necessity of the believer's bodily resurrection from the dead. Third, in 15:35–58, Paul treats the "how" of the bodily resurrection.[5] That is, he addresses the nature of the resurrection body and the way we will receive the resurrection body at Christ's return.

In each of the latter two sections of this long argument (15:20–23, 42–49), Paul speaks of the resurrection of Christ in comparison with Adam. Each passage is important in helping us understand what Paul says about the covenant of works. In 1 Corinthians 15:20–23, Paul declares, "As in Adam all die, so also in Christ shall all be made alive" (15:22). Adam and Christ are representative persons. That is, each represents a wide swath of human beings ("all").[6] The action of each representative person carries a corresponding result: "For as by a man came death, by a man has come also the resurrection of the dead" (15:21).[7] The result of the action of the one representative man, Paul clarifies, is determinative of the destinies of the represented: "For as in Adam all die, so also in Christ shall all be made alive" (15:22).

Paul, furthermore, understands a correspondence between each representative person ("as in Adam . . . so also in Christ"). As David Garland summarizes Paul's

5. Herman N. Ridderbos, *Paul: An Outline of His Theology*, trans. John Richard de Witt (Grand Rapids, MI: Eerdmans, 1975), 540.

6. While Paul is not using the term "all" equivalently in 1 Cor. 15:21a and 15:21b, he is not thereby teaching universalism, the doctrine that all human beings are saved in Christ. The "all" in each half of verse 21 means "all who are in Adam" and "all who are in Christ," on which see Gordon D. Fee, *The First Epistle to the Corinthians*, rev. ed., NICNT (Grand Rapids, MI: Eerdmans, 2014), 831, 831n64. For Paul, "all who are in Adam" refers to every ordinary descendant of Adam; "all who are in Christ" refers to each and every person whom the Father has eternally and unchangeably elected in Christ to be saved (Eph. 1:4, 11).

7. In these verses, Paul omits mention of Adam's first sin: "Paul is not interested in making the point that Adam's sin brought death (cf. Rom. 5:12–21), but in showing how Adam's sin had a universal effect on all who came after." David E. Garland, *1 Corinthians*, BECNT (Grand Rapids, MI: Eerdmans, 2003), 706.

point, "Adam leads the way and represents the old order," and "Christ leads the way and represents the new order," in such a way that "the representative determines the fate of the group."[8] In 1 Corinthians 15:21–22, Paul identifies the inception of this new order with the historical resurrection of Christ from the dead. It is in 15:20 and 23 that Paul helps us appreciate the significance and importance of this epoch-making historical event.[9] Paul here describes Jesus as the firstfruits of the resurrection harvest:

> Christ has been raised from the dead, the *firstfruits* of those who have fallen asleep. (15:20)

> But each in his own order: Christ the *firstfruits*, then at his coming those who belong to Christ. (15:23)

As Herman Ridderbos notes, "Here the picture of the harvest is in the background."[10] The context for this image is the considerable number of laws in the Old Testament governing the ingathering of the firstfruits of the harvest.[11] The idea in 1 Corinthians is at least twofold.[12]

First, in his resurrection, Christ has begun the resurrection harvest of the age to come.[13] His resurrection "means the breakthrough of the new aeon in the real, redemptive-historical sense of the word."[14] Paul is thereby calling attention to the temporal priority of Christ's resurrection to believers' resurrection, as he explains in 15:23: "Christ the firstfruits, then at his coming those who belong to Christ."[15] The inbreaking of the age to come, therefore, has already begun but is not yet consummated.

This observation hardly exhausts the significance of Christ as firstfruits of the resurrection harvest in the age to come. There is a second and equally important point that Paul is making here. The "firstfruits" bears an "organic connection and unity" with the remaining harvest, such that there is an "inseparability of the initial quantity with the whole."[16] Paul would have us understand the resurrection of Christ and the resurrection of believers on precisely these terms. As Richard Gaffin puts it, "In the firstfruits, the whole

8. Garland, *1 Corinthians*, 707.

9. The material that follows is substantially drawn from Guy Prentiss Waters, "1–2 Corinthians," in *A Biblical-Theological Introduction to the New Testament: The Gospel Realized*, ed. Michael J. Kruger (Wheaton, IL: Crossway, 2016), 211–14.

10. Ridderbos, *Paul*, 56.

11. See G. Delling, ἀπαρχή, *TDNT*, 1:485; G. M. Burge, "First Fruits, Down Payment," in *Dictionary of Paul and His Letters*, ed. Gerald F. Hawthorne, Ralph P. Martin, and Daniel G. Reid (Downers Grove, IL: InterVarsity Press, 1993), 300–301.

12. Ridderbos, *Paul*, 56.

13. "Paul regards the resurrection of Jesus as the actual beginning of this general epochal event." Geerhardus Vos, *The Pauline Eschatology* (1930; repr., Phillipsburg, NJ: P&R, 1994), 45.

14. Ridderbos, *Paul*, 55.

15. Delling, *TDNT*, 1:486.

16. Richard B. Gaffin Jr., *Resurrection and Redemption: A Study in Paul's Soteriology*, 2nd ed. (Phillipsburg, NJ: Presbyterian and Reformed, 1987), 34.

harvest becomes visible. . . . In [Christ] the resurrection of the dead dawns, his resurrection represents the commencement of the new world of God."[17] For this reason, Gaffin concludes, "Paul views the two resurrections not so much as two events but as two episodes of the same event," even as Paul makes a "temporal distinction" between them.[18]

Paul expands these observations in a second important point that he develops later in the argument of 1 Corinthians 15. In 15:42–49, he compares and contrasts Adam and Christ. As in 15:20–23, both are representative persons. Adam is "the first man Adam" (15:45), "the first man" (15:47). Jesus is "the last Adam" (15:45), "the second man" (15:47). This framework helps us understand Paul's comparing and contrasting the "dead body of the believer and his resurrection body" at 15:42–44a.[19] These two bodies correspond to the two ages overseen by the two representative men, Adam and Christ, and the "two different modes of existence pertaining to them."[20]

What is striking is that Adam is in view in these verses not primarily as the one through whom sin entered the world but as the one whom God created in uprightness and integrity.[21] This perspective is evident from the fact that Paul quotes Genesis 2:7 in 1 Corinthians 15:45 regarding Adam's (prefall) body: "Thus it is written, 'The first man Adam became a living being.'" The Adamic order, in our experience of it, is indelibly characterized by sin, corruption, and death. Paul looks in 15:44b–49, however, to the Adamic order prior to the fall, in its "original state."[22]

What, then, characterizes or distinguishes the eschatological order inaugurated by Christ's resurrection from the preeschatological order inaugurated by the creation of Adam? In 1 Corinthians 15:45b, Paul affirms that whereas Adam "became a living being," the "last Adam became life-giving Spirit" (my trans.; ESV: "a life-giving spirit"). The two words translated "being" (ψυχή) and "Spirit" (πνεῦμα) in 15:45 are cognate with the adjectives translated "natural" (ψυχικός) in 15:44 and "Spiritual" (πνευματικός) in 15:46. These two words in 15:45 therefore reflect the difference between the two Adamic orders that Paul is contrasting in 15:42–49.

How should we understand Paul's phrase "life-giving Spirit?" I have capitalized the noun "Spirit" in my translation because Paul is surely speaking here of the Holy Spirit.[23] The adjective "Spiritual" (πνευματικός) invariably refers, in Paul, to the Holy Spirit.[24] Since two uses of the adjective "Spiritual" (πνευματικός) bracket the cognate noun in 15:45 (πνεῦμα), we should understand that noun to refer to the third person of the Godhead, the Holy Spirit.

---

17. Ridderbos, *Paul*, 56.
18. Gaffin, *Resurrection and Redemption*, 35.
19. Gaffin, *Resurrection and Redemption*, 78.
20. Ridderbos, *Paul*, 542.
21. Vos, *Pauline Eschatology*, 167.
22. Ridderbos, *Paul*, 542n152; cf. Vos, who notes that Paul "widens . . . the representation . . . out to a far more general, even cosmical, one." *Pauline Eschatology*, 167.
23. For the argument that follows, see Gaffin, *Resurrection and Redemption*, 86–87.
24. On which, see Gaffin, *Resurrection and Redemption*, 86–87.

That conclusion raises yet another question. What does Paul mean when he says that Christ "became life-giving Spirit"? He cannot be confusing or mixing Christ and Spirit as two distinct persons, since elsewhere in his letters he takes care to make personal distinctions between the two (cf. Rom. 8:9–11). In other words, Paul is not erasing the distinction between the person of the Son and the person of the Spirit. He is, however, making an economical or functional identification of Christ and the Spirit (cf. 2 Cor. 3:17). This identification took place at the resurrection, when Christ was raised from the dead by the power of the Holy Spirit (cf. Rom. 8:11; Eph. 1:19–20). Gaffin explains the significance of what transpired at the resurrection:

> At his resurrection the personal mode of Jesus' existence as the last Adam was . . . decisively transformed by the Holy Spirit. The Spirit, who raised him up as the first-fruits, indwells him so completely and in such a fashion that in their functioning he *is* the Spirit who will be instrumental in the resurrection of the full harvest. . . . Only by virtue of the functional identity of the Spirit and Christ, effected redemptive-historically in his resurrection, is Christ the communicator of life.[25]

In light of what Paul has argued earlier in 1 Corinthians 15, and in light of what Paul goes on to say in 15:46–49, we may begin to bring this discussion of 15:45b and of 15:42–49 to a close with two concluding considerations.

First, in 1 Corinthians 15, Paul is underscoring the aeonian significance of the resurrection of Christ.[26] The resurrection of Jesus has inaugurated the age to come, an order whose counterpart is the order standing under Adam (15:46–48). What characterizes and even denominates this age to come is the activity of the Spirit of the risen and exalted Christ. As Paul argues in 15:50, the resources of this present age are categorically insufficient and inadequate to enable one to "inherit the kingdom of God" or to "inherit the imperishable." Such resources are found only in the second Adam, who at his resurrection became life-giving Spirit.[27]

Second, Paul has charted a sweeping representation of human history. The age to come, defined by the second man and last Adam, stands in contrast with the present age, defined by the first man, Adam. That Christ is the "second man" indicates that there is no representative figure or age that stands between Adam and Christ. That Christ is the "last Adam" indicates that there is no representative figure or age that will follow Christ. The "contrast between Adam and Christ" here "is not only pointed but also comprehensive and exclusive."[28]

---

25. Gaffin, *Resurrection and Redemption*, 89; emphasis original.
26. Gaffin, *Resurrection and Redemption*, 89–90.
27. In light of Paul's emphasis in 1 Cor. 15 on Adam in his prelapsarian condition, it is fair to conclude, with both Vos and Gaffin, that Paul is "correlat[ing] protology and eschatology," *not* soteriology and eschatology. Vos, *Pauline Eschatology*, 169n19; Gaffin, *Resurrection and Redemption*, 82n14. See especially the important qualifications and caveat raised in this connection by Gaffin.
28. Gaffin, *Resurrection and Redemption*, 85.

We are now in a position to summarize Paul's statements in 1 Corinthians 15 in relation to the covenant of works. For Paul, Adam and Christ are representative persons. Every ordinary human being claims either Adam or Christ as his representative. Adam and Christ each stand at the head of a distinct eschatological order. Adam stands over the preeschatological order. Had Adam obeyed, he would have brought himself and his posterity into confirmed eschatological life. Adam, however, disobeyed God. In doing so, he plunged himself and his posterity into a state of sin and misery. Death in all its forms, not life, is the just outcome for Adam and all those who are in Adam.

Christ, however, stands over another order. This order was inaugurated in history by his resurrection from the dead in the power of the Holy Spirit. When Christ was raised, he entered into confirmed eschatological life. This life he merited by his obedience, an obedience that led to his accursed death on the cross (Gal. 3:10–14; Phil. 2:8) and that eventuated in his resurrection from the dead (Rom. 4:25). Christ freely and graciously shares this life with all those who are in him. When God graciously transfers a person from being in Adam to being in Christ, God brings that person from the realm of sin, curse, and death into the realm of righteousness, blessing, and life.

Romans 5

In Romans 5:12–21, Paul revisits the two Adams in the context of the exposition of his gospel (1:16–17). He does not, however, merely restate what he said about the two Adams in 1 Corinthians 15. He builds on and advances that teaching in such a way as to help us appreciate the glory of Christ and the sufficiency of his work for our salvation.

There is one important difference between the way Paul portrays Adam in 1 Corinthians 15 and the way he portrays him in Romans 5:12–21.[29] In 1 Corinthians, Paul reflects on Adam before his fall into sin (15:45, citing Gen. 2:7). In Romans, however, Paul reflects on Adam in light of his first sin against God. The burden of Romans's exposition of Adam is to show how his first transgression plunged him and his posterity into ruin and misery.

There is also a difference between the way Paul portrays Christ in 1 Corinthians 15 and the way he portrays him in Romans 5:12–21. In 1 Corinthians 15, Paul emphasizes the epochal resurrection of Christ and the fruit of that work for all who are "in Christ." In Romans 5:12–21, however, Paul's chief concern is the obedience and righteousness of Christ, on the sole basis of which the sinner is justified. In Romans, Paul addresses one dimension of the broader redemptive work of Christ to highlight a particular benefit for the redeemed.[30]

---

29. Richard B. Gaffin Jr., *By Faith, Not by Sight: Paul and the Order of Salvation*, 2nd ed. (Phillipsburg, NJ: P&R, 2013), 53.

30. And yet note how in Rom. 4:25 Paul joins "justification" with the resurrection of Christ, "who was delivered up for our trespasses and raised for our justification." Such statements as these confirm that what Paul is concerned to distinguish—that is, the resurrection of Christ versus the obedience and righteousness of Christ—he is not at all prepared to separate.

With these framing considerations in place, we are in a better position to consider Paul's argument in Romans 5:12–21. Paul's running concern in Romans 5:12–21 is the "one man," that is, Adam (5:12, 15, 16, 17, 19), and more specifically, the "one trespass" of that one man (5:16, 18; cf. 5:14, "the transgression of Adam"). In view is not the whole course of Adam's sinning but a particular sin, the first sin—the sin of eating the fruit that God had said not to eat.

This sin has come into the possession of Adam's ordinary posterity, specifically, "all men" (5:12, 18), or "many" (5:15, 19). There is a relationship between Adam and his posterity such that Adam's sin becomes their sin. That relationship is a covenantal union that God has established between the representative head, Adam, and the represented, all human beings ordinarily descended from Adam. That this relationship is representational and not merely biological is evident from considering the relationship between Adam and Jesus. Jesus is descended from Adam (cf. "son of Adam," Luke 3:38). But while Jesus is "of Adam," he is not "in Adam," because, Paul tells us elsewhere, Jesus is the "second" or "last Adam" (1 Cor. 15:45, 47). Paul testifies to this unique relationship in Romans 5:12–21 when he says that Adam "was a type of the one who was to come" (5:14). When Paul declares Adam a "type" of the coming Christ, he is using the word "type" in the sense of "a person or thing prefiguring (according to God's design) a person or thing pertaining to the time of eschatological fulfillment."[31] Specifically, Paul says that "Adam in his universal effectiveness for ruin is the type which—in God's design—prefigures Christ in his universal effectiveness for salvation."[32] Jesus, then, is "of Adam" but not "in Adam." For this reason, the relationship between Adam and the "all" or "many" whom Adam's sin affects is representational in nature, notwithstanding the biological descent of the "all" or "many" from Adam.[33]

There is, therefore, a representational union between Adam and his posterity. In similar fashion, there is a representational union between Christ and his people. Just as Adam is "one man" (5:12), so Jesus is the "one man Jesus Christ" (5:15, 17), or simply, "one man" (5:19). Paul employs the terms "all" or "many" in this passage in relation to Adam and to Christ. This pattern signals the apostle's conviction that all human beings are federally related to one or the other of two—and only two—representative heads, Adam or Jesus Christ.[34]

---

31. C. E. B. Cranfield, *Romans 1–8*, ICC (Edinburgh: T&T Clark, 1975), 283.

32. Cranfield, *Romans 1–8*, 283. "The universal impact of his one act prefigures the universal impact of Christ's act." Douglas J. Moo, *The Epistle to the Romans*, NICNT (Grand Rapids, MI: Eerdmans, 1996), 334.

33. On which, see Guy Prentiss Waters, "Theistic Evolution Is Incompatible with the Teachings of the New Testament," in *Theistic Evolution: A Scientific, Philosophical, and Theological Critique*, ed. J. P. Moreland, Stephen C. Meyer, Christopher Shaw, Ann K. Gauger, and Wayne Grudem (Wheaton, IL: Crossway, 2017), 879–926.

34. Some commentators have pressed Paul's language in Rom. 5:18 ("so one act of righteousness leads to justification and life for all men") in service of universalism. In other words, Paul is thought to teach the salvation in Christ of every human being, so Arland J. Hultgren, *Paul's Letter to the Romans: A Commentary* (Grand Rapids, MI: Eerdmans, 2011), 229–33. One problem with this view is that Paul elsewhere teaches the final, eternal punishment of all who "do not know God" and who "do not obey the gospel of our Lord Jesus" (2 Thess. 1:8; cf. Rom. 2:8–9, 12).

We have thus far concentrated our attention on the representational character of Adam and Christ, and the nature of their union with those whom each man represents. Paul's primary concern in Romans 5:12–21, however, is the work of each representative head and the implications of that work for the represented. Adam's work is termed "the transgression" (5:14), "one man's trespass" (5:15, 17; cf. 5:18), "one man's sin" (5:16), and "one man's disobedience" (5:19). By way of contrast, Christ's work is termed "one act of righteousness" (5:18) and "one man's obedience" (5:19). In view is the first sin of Adam in eating the forbidden fruit in the garden of Eden, and the perfect obedience of Christ to the Father, an obedience that led to his death on the cross (Phil. 2:8).[35]

To understand adequately these actions, we also need to consider their effects on the represented. Paul's interest in Romans 5:12–21 is in the forensic dimensions both of the sin of Adam and of the righteousness of Christ. If the work of Adam has brought us "condemnation," the work of Christ has brought us "justification" (5:16, 18). If the "one man's disobedience" has constituted the many as "sinners," the "one man's obedience" has constituted the many as "righteous" (5:19).[36]

What is striking is that those who are justified in Christ are those who formerly stood condemned in Adam. But how can sinners be counted righteous or the condemned be justified, that is, declared righteous? Paul is clear—his multiple references to God's "free gift" and "grace" in this passage help us see that it is the work of another, the second Adam, that exhaustively and exclusively grounds the verdict "justified." The sinner is declared righteous solely on the basis of the "free gift of righteousness" (5:17). By this "free gift of righteousness" Paul has in mind Jesus's "one act of righteousness" and his "obedience" as resulting in our justification (5:18, 19). This righteousness is imputed to the sinner and received through faith alone (4:4–5; 5:17). In this way, God justifies the ungodly (4:5).

We may now further probe what Paul has in mind by Jesus's "obedience" and "righteousness." Surely Jesus's propitiatory death is in view (cf. 3:21–26). But Paul has in mind more than the death of Christ. In 5:17, the apostle tells us that those who receive

---

Paul's universal language ("all") is best understood in light of his use of the term "all" throughout this letter to denote the entire scope and range of the human race, Jew and Gentile (cf. Rom. 1:16; 3:9, 22, 23; 4:11, 16). His use of this term in 5:12–21 indicates the fact that the saving work of Christ extends no less farther than the consequences of Adam's first sin extend. No human being, sharing Adam's plight, is ethnically disqualified from sharing in the saving benefits of Christ. Even so, it is only those who put their trust in Christ who may know that they are "in Christ" and therefore justified in him (5:17), so rightly Moo, *Romans*, 343–44. John Murray helpfully summarizes Paul's statement in Rom. 5:18: "What the apostle is interested in showing is not the numerical extent of those who are justified as identical with the numerical extent of those condemned but the parallel that obtains between the way of condemnation and the way of justification. It is the *modus operandi* that is in view." *The Epistle to the Romans*, 2 vols. (Grand Rapids, MI: Eerdmans, 1959, 1965), 1:203.

35. "Undoubtedly it was in the cross of Christ and the shedding of his blood that this obedience came to its climactic expression, but obedience comprehends the totality of the Father's will as fulfilled by Christ." Murray, *Romans*, 1:205.

36. On Paul's language in Rom. 5:19 as forensic in nature, see, representatively, Moo, *Romans*, 344–46. Leading English translations fail to bring out adequately this aspect of Paul's meaning. As Murray notes, Paul speaks here of a double imputation—the imputation of Adam's sin to those whom he represents and the imputation of Christ's righteousness to those whom he represents. *Romans*, 1:205.

the "free gift of righteousness" are they who "reign in life through the one man Jesus Christ." It is for this reason that Paul says in the next verse that "one act of righteousness leads to justification and life for all men" (5:18), that is, the justification that leads to life.[37] The possession of Christ's righteousness for justification does not simply deliver us from a state of condemnation; it equally entitles us to "reign in life." The law requires perfect obedience in order to see life (10:5; Gal. 3:12). For the justified person to be entitled to reign in life, Jesus must not only have paid the penalty due to the sinner for his sin but must also have perfectly obeyed the law of God in that sinner's stead. We are therefore bound to conclude that, for Paul, Jesus's "obedience" and his "righteousness" include not only his full satisfaction for sin but also his perfect obedience to the law. It is this righteousness, imputed to the sinner and received by faith alone, that solely grounds the sinner's justification, his being "constituted righteous" (Rom. 5:19, my trans.).[38]

Christ, then, does not merely reverse or nullify the condemnation and death that are the result of Adam's first sin, transmitted to his posterity. To be sure, Jesus's work does cancel the penalty of sin for his people, freeing sinners from their subjection to the law's curse and their obligation to divine justice. But Christ has done more for them. He has rendered full and perfect obedience to the Father on behalf of his people. In this way, he has fulfilled, in his people's stead, all their obligations to enter into lasting and irreversible possession of eschatological, eternal life. Christ has not only undone what Adam did; he has done what Adam failed to do.

One final observation from Paul's argument in Romans 5:12–21 helps us appreciate the gratuity of what God has done for sinners in Christ. It is, after all, this gratuity that Paul reiterates throughout this passage ("free gift," 5:15 [*bis*]; "free gift," 5:16 [*bis*]; "grace," "free gift," 5:17; "grace," 5:20; "grace," 5:21).[39] God's gratuity in Christ is evident from the fact that Christ's righteousness comes into the possession of his people by imputation. In this respect, Christ's work is parallel to that of Adam. Adam's sin came into the possession of human beings by imputation. Paul says in 5:12 that "death spread to all men because all sinned," that is, they did not sin by imitating Adam (5:13–14), but they sinned when the one sin of their representative head was counted their own. On this basis, they entered into "condemnation" (5:16, 18). When the first sin of Adam was counted to them, they were "constituted" (5:19, my trans.) sinners. In view is not their inward transformation but a change of legal or judicial standing before God. For this reason, the "reign" of death (5:21) is universal, even over "those whose sinning was not

---

37. Taking the genitive ζωῆς as a genitive of result, following Cranfield, *Romans 1–8*, 1:289; Murray, *Romans*, 1:202; Moo, *Romans*, 341n126.

38. Although Paul uses the future tense of the verb "constitute," he is not thinking of "an act that is reserved for the consummation." Rather, "the future tense . . . indicate[s] that this act of God's grace is being continually exercised and will continue to be exercised throughout future generations of mankind." Murray, *Romans*, 1:206.

39. For a recent treatment of "gift" in the writings of Paul, see now John M. G. Barclay, *Paul and the Gift* (Grand Rapids, MI: Eerdmans, 2015). See also my review in *WTJ* 78, no. 1 (2016): 170–74.

like the transgression of Adam" (5:14). Paul views death here as the penalty for sin (cf. Gen. 2:17, "In the day that you eat of it you shall surely die"). That is, he views death in a particularly forensic light—God's just punishment for human sin.

It is by a similar mechanism that God justifies the sinner in Christ. Christ's righteousness is imputed to the sinner, who receives that righteousness by faith alone. It is solely on the basis of the work of "the one who was to come" (Rom. 5:14), Christ, that the sinner is justified or declared righteous before God. This verdict of justification entitles that sinner to eschatological life. At no point does the sinner merit any of these benefits; they have been earned and secured by the sinner's representative, Christ. It is for this reason that the apostle exults in the free and abundant grace of God in Christ. It is not only that the beneficiaries of Christ's work receive what is contrary to their personal desert as sinners. Nor is it simply that what we have received in Christ far exceeds what we forfeited in Adam. It is also that what we have in Christ is entirely the gift of God to us, in no way based on our actions or character in the past, present, or future.

In summary, Paul understood Adam to have been in a covenant of works with God. This covenant predated his fall into sin. God held before him the requirement to continue in obedience to him, not least by obeying the command not to eat of the fruit of the tree of the knowledge of good and evil. God threatened death for disobedience. He promised Adam confirmed eschatological life for obedience. This covenant was made not with Adam alone. God made this covenant with Adam as a representative person. When Adam sinned, therefore, he plunged himself and his posterity into sin, curse, and death. Adam's first sin is our sin because in this covenant God has counted Adam's sin to us. In Adam, then, we are guilty before God, without help or plea.

Paul does not recount this covenant for its own sake, far less to lead his readers into despair. He does so in order to present Jesus Christ as the second man, the last Adam, the one of whom Adam was "type." Like Adam, he is a representative man. He undertook to fulfill the obligations that his people bore before God. Because they were guilty of sin, he willingly died on the cross to pay for all their sins. Because they lacked perfect obedience, he obeyed God perfectly on their behalf, even to the point of laying down his own life at the cross. Because they had no prospect of securing eschatological life, Jesus by his resurrection and the power of the Holy Spirit secured the life of the age to come for them. When God justifies the sinner in Christ, the justified sinner is given title to the eschatological life that Jesus won for his people.

Jesus redresses his people's plight brought about by their breach, in Adam, of the covenant of works. But he also fulfills its unmet demands on their behalf. As a result, in Christ, believers have no further obligations to the covenant of works. Christ has discharged on their behalf all their obligations to the covenant of works. In Christ, God has brought us into a second covenant with himself. This covenant, often called the covenant of grace, is characterized by the superabundance of God's free grace in Christ to sinners. In this covenant, believing sinners' justification is based wholly on Christ's merits in his obedience and death. The life that they enjoy is not one that they have secured through their obedience but one that they have received through faith in the obedient last Adam. It is no exaggeration, then, to say that Paul's gospel finds its setting within God's covenant with sinners in Christ. But we cannot fully understand and appreciate this covenant unless we grasp the covenant that God had first made with Adam. For this reason, we may conclude that the covenant of works lies at the very heart of the New Testament's exposition of the person and work of Jesus Christ.

The Covenant of Works and the Mosaic Covenant?

In the epistles to the Romans and Galatians, the apostle Paul devotes considerable energy to addressing the nature of the Mosaic covenant ("the law") and its role in redemptive history. In the course of that exposition, Paul makes statements about the Mosaic covenant that have suggested to some readers a strong association with the covenant of works. These readers point in particular to Paul's citation of Leviticus 18:5 ("If a person does them, he shall live by them") in Romans 10:5 and Galatians 3:12. In both Romans 10 and Galatians 3, Paul is contrasting two mutually exclusive ways of justification. The first way is that of justification by faith alone. The second is that of justification by works of the law. In the course of demonstrating that one must be justified by faith apart from works of the law, Paul cites testimony from the Old Testament. In both Romans 10:5 and Galatians 3:12, he invokes Leviticus 18:5 to give voice to what Paul calls "the righteousness that is based on the law" (Rom. 10:5). Paul's point is that no sinner can meet the righteous requirements of the law by his personal obedience. Therefore, the sinner cannot see life on the basis of his own works. All that awaits the one who relies on his own works for justification is "curse" (Gal. 3:10).

The principle that life is contingent on one's obedience to the commands of God is familiar to us from Paul's exposition of the covenant of works. But in Romans 10 and Galatians 3, Paul advances this principle in relation to the Mosaic covenant. Is there a connection in Paul's mind between the Mosaic covenant and the covenant of works? Is it the case that Paul understands the Mosaic covenant to be in some sense a republication of the covenant of works? We may offer answers to these questions by giving careful attention to what Paul says about the Mosaic covenant in both Romans 10 and Galatians 3.

Romans 10

Paul's claims about the law in Romans 9:30–10:21 appear in a broader portion of Paul's argument that addresses and explains Israel's rejection of the gospel. In 9:30–10:21, Paul argues that Israel has misused the law that God gave her. She has sought her own "righteousness" from that law, rather than "submit[ting] to God's righteousness" (10:3). She has pursued "righteousness" "as if it were based on works" rather than "by faith"

(9:31–32). It is in 10:5–13 that Paul demonstrates Israel's pursuit to be a misuse of the law. Israel, Paul argues, was not properly attending to her own Scripture.

To that end, Paul compares two "righteousnesses" in Romans 10:5–6.[40] There is the "righteousness that is based on the law" of which "Moses writes" (10:5), and there is "the righteousness based on faith" (10:6). Despite recent efforts to understand these two righteousnesses in complementary fashion, we are bound to take the two righteousnesses in antithesis.[41] Beginning in 9:30, Paul is contrasting two mutually exclusive righteousnesses. The one is associated with "faith" (9:30, 32), and the other is associated with the "law" and "works" (9:31, 32).[42] Strikingly, the contrast between the two righteousnesses in Romans 10:3 along the lines of "their own" and "of God" finds parallel in Philippians 3:9, where Paul there sets these two righteousnesses in undisputed contrast.[43]

One difficulty of this passage is that Paul quotes passages from the Torah in support of each of the two righteousnesses that he sets in antithesis. The "righteousness that is based on the law" is found in the words of Leviticus 18:5, paraphrased in Romans 10:5 as "The person who does the commandments shall live by them." But "the righteousness based on faith" finds support in words that Paul has adapted from Deuteronomy 30:12–14.[44] Paul certainly understands both passages to be Scripture. We would not expect Paul to be setting one portion of Scripture against another, especially given what Paul has said in Romans 3:31 ("We uphold the law"). To see how he understands these two passages in relation to one other, we need first to see what he understands each passage to say.

We can readily understand Paul's point in Romans 10:6–8. He quotes Deuteronomy to say, in the words of John Murray, that "the things revealed for faith and life are accessible: we do not have to ascend to heaven nor go to the utmost parts of the sea to find them."[45] The "righteousness based on faith" is the gift of God to us.[46] We do not strive to merit it by our works. We receive it as the gift of God. Thus, "the grace of God that underlies the Mosaic covenant is operative now in the New Covenant."[47] For this reason, Paul can locate "the word of faith that we proclaim" in the text of Deuteronomy itself (Rom. 10:8).[48]

---

40. What follows summarizes the argument of Guy Prentiss Waters, "Romans 10:5 and the Covenant of Works," in *The Law Is Not of Faith: Essays on Works and Grace in the Mosaic Covenant*, ed. Bryan D. Estelle, J. V. Fesko, and David VanDrunen (Phillipsburg, NJ: P&R, 2009), 210–39.

41. For secondary literature in support of the complementary and antithetical understandings of the two "righteousnesses" in Rom. 10:5–6, see Waters, "Romans 10:5," 213n9, 213n10, respectively.

42. Compare Rom. 4:4–5, where Paul contrasts "working" and "believing" in relation to the righteousness of justification.

43. While Paul uses the particle δέ in Rom. 10:6, he uses the adversative ἀλλά in Phil. 3:9.

44. On the form of which, see Guy Waters, *The End of Deuteronomy in the Epistles of Paul*, WUNT, 2nd ser., no. 221 (Tübingen: Mohr Siebeck, 2006), 162–70.

45. Murray, *Romans*, 2:52.

46. "The best explanation for Paul's use of the Deut. 30 text is to think that he finds in this passage an expression of the grace of God in establishing a relationship with his people." Moo, *Romans*, 653.

47. Moo, *Romans*, 653.

48. C. E. B. Cranfield, *Romans 9–16*, ICC (Edinburgh: T&T Clark, 1979), 526.

But what is Paul doing in setting Leviticus 18:5 not only against Deuteronomy 30:12–14 but also against the gospel? To answer this question, we need to draw a few observations about Paul's argument in Romans 10. Paul's citation of Leviticus 18:5 is, in fact, an abbreviated form of that text. When we read that citation alongside its fuller form, we find that Paul is concerned to say that the "righteousness that is based on the law" is based on a perfect and complete obedience to the totality of the law's requirements.[49] We may fairly conclude that Paul's interest in this passage is not with the Mosaic covenant per se but with the commandments that were given in that covenant.

Furthermore, Paul is concerned with Jews *and* Gentiles in Romans 10:4–13. There is a single, universal solution for all kinds of people, namely, salvation through faith in Jesus Christ alone (10:9). To this universal solution corresponds the universal problem of human sinfulness. It is this problem that Paul underscores in 10:5. Sinners cannot secure through their own obedience the righteousness that they need before God. While Moses gives expression to this problem ("For Moses writes . . . ," Rom. 10:5), this problem is not unique to the recipients of the Torah. It is a problem that Jews share in common with Gentiles. By conscience, Gentiles know and are accountable to the moral core of the Torah (cf. 2:14–15 with 1:18–32). Just like the Jews, Gentiles cannot meet the just requirements of God's law in order to stand righteous before God.

For this reason, "life" is impossible to attain through our own obedience of the law. "Life," rather, is the free gift of God in Jesus Christ. Jesus Christ is the one whose obedience and righteousness secures for the sinner justification and life (5:12–21). What we, in Adam, have failed to secure, the last Adam has accomplished and freely given to the undeserving.

We are now in a position to address how Paul approaches the Mosaic covenant in Romans 10. In light of his citation and interpretation of Deuteronomy 30:12–14 in Romans 10:6–8, Paul understands the Mosaic covenant to be the gracious gift of God to his redeemed people. The way Paul cites and interprets Leviticus 18:5 in Romans 10:5 indicates his understanding that the commandments of the law, independently of their gracious covenantal framework, set forth the standard of righteousness required by the covenant of works.[50] Paul did not understand God to promulgate the Mosaic covenant to Israel as a covenant of works. To those who were inclined to misuse the Mosaic covenant by obeying its commandments to earn eternal life, Paul informed them that the law itself testified to the impossibility of such a task. But to the one who trusts in Christ for salvation, such striving comes to an end (10:4). And to lead men and women to Christ in the way of faith was the goal of the Mosaic covenant all along (10:6–8).

---

49. Waters, "Romans 10:5," 219–20.
50. For articulations of this view in the writings of the Westminster divine Anthony Burgess, the Genevan Reformed scholastic Francis Turretin, and the Free Church divine Patrick Fairbairn, see Waters, "Romans 10:5," 211n2, 237–38.

Galatians 3

Paul also cites Leviticus 18:5 in the course of his argument in Galatians 3:6–14. Galatians 3:1–4:11 constitutes the heart of Paul's argument in this epistle. Paul is writing this letter to persuade the Galatians to turn away from false teachers who have been active in their churches. These false teachers are telling the Galatians that they must observe the Mosaic law to be justified before God (2:16; 5:2–3).[51] Paul insists that this teaching is another gospel (1:6) and that its proponents are accursed of God (1:9).

In Galatians 3:1–4:11, Paul has two primary objectives. The first is to show that God never intended obedience to the Mosaic covenant (what Paul calls the "law") to be the way his people would be justified. God's intention, rather, was that his people in every age would be justified through faith in Christ, solely on the basis of Christ's merits. Before the incarnation of Christ, God revealed Christ to his people in his promises to them, preeminently the promises that he made to Abraham in covenant with him. For this reason, Abraham exemplifies the way people across redemptive history are justified in Christ (3:9). Paul's second objective in Galatians 3:1–4:11 is to show that the Mosaic covenant is an antiquated economy. It is not a timeless covenant. It had a historical beginning, and it has come to its appointed end (3:23). It served God's purposes for when it was in effect. Now that Christ has come into the world, died, and been raised, there is no legitimate reason why someone should place himself under the regimen of the law (4:8–11). For all these reasons, the Galatians should reject the teaching of the Judaizers and commit themselves to the gospel that Paul preached to them.

In the course of these arguments, Paul makes some strong claims about the law. He associates the law with the "flesh" (Gal. 3:3), "slavery" (5:1; cf. 4:1, 21–31), captivity (3:23–24), and "curse" (3:10). It is the Abrahamic, not the Mosaic, covenant that Paul labels "promise" (3:15–29). The law is incapable of supplying either "life" or "righteousness" to its recipients (3:21). Justification, Paul argues, comes through "promise," not "law" (3:6–14).

One such strong claim precedes his citation of Leviticus 18:5 in Galatians 3:12b ("The one who does them shall live by them")—"But the law is not of faith" (3:12a). Does Paul understand the Mosaic covenant to stand in diametric opposition to justification by faith alone? Does he understand the Mosaic covenant to have counseled Israel to pursue eschatological life by obedience to its demands? Is Paul arraying himself, the Abrahamic covenant, and the new covenant against the Mosaic covenant?

Closer inspection of Paul's argument yields negative answers to these questions. To begin, we may make three staging observations. The first is that, for all Paul's negative

---

51. This assumes that the phrase "the works of the law" refers to efforts to observe the law's requirements in order to be declared righteous on that basis. For a defense of this traditional position, in response to the New Perspective on Paul, see Moisés Silva, "Faith versus Works of Law in Galatians," in *Justification and Variegated Nomism*, ed. D. A. Carson, Peter T. O'Brien, and Mark A. Seifrid, vol. 2, *The Paradoxes of Paul*, WUNT, 2nd ser., no. 181 (Grand Rapids, MI: Baker Academic, 2004), 217–48.

statements about the law, he does not draw an absolute antithesis between the law and the promise: "Is the law then contrary to the promises of God? Certainly not!" (3:21a). Paul then observes that God did not give the law as though the law "could give life" (3:21b).[52] The issue in Galatians 3:1–4:11, then, concerns God's intention in giving the law—did God give the law to be "the *source* of righteousness and life," as the Judaizers were teaching?[53]

The second observation is that Paul is responding to false teachers in Galatia who are teaching that obedience to the precepts of the Mosaic law is necessary to achieve justifying righteousness. Paul, then, is not addressing the Mosaic covenant in the abstract but as it had been represented by the Judaizers to the Galatians. He is primarily concerned to refute the Judaizers' contention that one should obey the laws of Moses in order to be justified.[54] In doing so, he probes the competency of the law to justify a sinner who seeks justification by obedience to its demands. In saying that the law could not justify the sinner, Paul insists that he says nothing except what the law has already said.[55] Paul by no means grants that the Judaizers have correctly understood the law. On the contrary, they have profoundly misunderstood it. Paul is helping the Galatians understand, from the law itself, what God intended the law to be and to do in the life of Israel.

The third observation is to recall an important distinction that Paul draws in his letters between the law as covenantal administration and the law as bare commandment (cf. Rom. 9:30–10:21).[56] The former reflects God's purpose to administer Christ to Israel for their salvation (Rom. 10:6–8). The latter—the commandment divorced from the gracious administration in which it had been promulgated—utters the voice of the covenant of works: "Do this and you will live" (Lev. 18:5). The law offers no resources to the sinner who seeks life by the command and does nothing other than pronounce God's curse on the one who fails to meet the command's standard of perfect obedience for eschatological life.

With these observations in place, we may give attention to what Paul says in Galatians 3:12. Paul does, in fact, cite Leviticus 18:5 to articulate the doctrine against which he is arguing, namely, that a person may be justified before God on the basis of his law keeping. This works principle he denominates "law" (Gal. 3:12). But Paul's concern with "law" in Galatians 3:12 is not as a covenantal administration promulgated by God; his

---

52. We may trace Paul's reasoning along the following lines: because the law cannot give life, we sinners cannot achieve righteousness by our law keeping, and because righteousness cannot come by our law keeping, the law is not contrary to God's promises. So Herman N. Ridderbos, *The Epistle of Paul to the Churches of Galatia*, NICNT (Grand Rapids, MI: Eerdmans, 1981), 141.

53. So, rightly, Moisés Silva, *Interpreting Galatians: Explorations in Exegetical Method*, 2nd ed. (Grand Rapids, MI: Baker Academic, 2001), 194. The law "cannot get man to fulfill itself" and is "not a quickening power, as is the promise." Ridderbos, *Galatia*, 141.

54. See here the perceptive comments of Ridderbos, *Paul*, 154–55. Note Venema's extensive discussion of Ridderbos's argument in *Paul*, 154–56, in *Christ and Covenant Theology*, 119–24.

55. Ridderbos, *Paul*, 154.

56. See here Ridderbos, *Paul*, 154–55.

concern is with "law" as commandment.[57] The wider context of 3:10–14 commends this understanding. Paul defines "works of the law" in 3:10 in terms of his citation of Deuteronomy 27:26, "Cursed be everyone who does not abide by all things written in the Book of the Law, and do them."[58] To be "justified before God by the law" in Galatians 3:11 is to be justified by keeping the entirety of what the law requires. When Paul says, "The law is not of faith" (3:12), he envisions the law narrowly, as a body of commandments. Specifically, Paul is addressing individuals who are attempting to be justified on the basis of their law keeping. His point is that this approach to justification stands diametrically opposed to justification by faith alone. These two approaches are mutually exclusive and cannot be reconciled.[59]

In saying what he says in Galatians 3:12, Paul does not deny the original intent of Leviticus 18:5, which is to encourage Israel to observe the law of God in order that they might enjoy the life that God has freely given them in covenant with him.[60] Ridderbos has summarized Paul's understanding of Leviticus 18:5 as follows:

> That there is also a life in the law lived out of the *grace* of God's covenant (Ps. 119) is, of course, not denied by [Paul]. Hence there is no conflict between Hab. 2 and Lev. 18 either, so long as the root of life is sought in the grace of God and thus in faith. If, however, one wants to live out of the works of the law, it is the utterances of the law itself that prove the impossibility of it.[61]

In Galatians 3:12, Paul cites Leviticus 18:5 as the testimony of the law itself to what the Judaizers' teaching about justification requires—the fulfillment of the entirety of the law's commandments for justifying righteousness. In this respect, the Mosaic law gives voice to the covenant of works. God's intention in giving the Mosaic law, however, was not to teach his people to be justified by obedience to his commands. God's intention, as Paul goes on to say, was to prepare his covenant people for Christ (Gal. 3:22–29). It was a regimen appropriate to children (4:1–6) and, from the perspective and vantage point of the freedom and liberty of new covenant believers, a regimen of bondage and slavery. Even so, it was a gracious regimen, pointing Israel to their Messiah, through faith in whom they then had righteousness, justification, and life. Now that Christ has come, that regimen has passed. But Christ places the law as it has come to fulfillment in himself

---

57. Recall our observation above how Paul's text form of Lev. 18:5 in Rom. 10:5 underscores his interest in law *qua* commandment. The same observation applies here in Gal. 3:12. See Douglas J. Moo, *Galatians*, BECNT (Grand Rapids, MI: Baker Academic, 2013), 209; Brandon Crowe, "'By Grace You Have Been Saved through Faith': Justification in the Pauline Epistles," in *The Doctrine on Which the Church Stands or Falls: Justification in Biblical, Theological, Historical, and Pastoral Perspective*, ed. Matthew Barrett (Wheaton, IL: Crossway, 2019), 248.

58. On the text form of Paul's Old Testament citation from Deuteronomy in Gal. 3:10, see Waters, *End of Deuteronomy*, 80–86.

59. See further Ben C. Dunson, "'The Law Evidently Is Not Contrary to Faith': Galatians and the Republication of the Covenant of Works," *WTJ* 79, no. 2 (2017): 243–66.

60. On the context of Lev. 18:5 in relation to Paul's use of this text in Rom. 10, see Murray, *Romans*, 2:249–51.

61. Ridderbos, *Galatia*, 125. Ridderbos helpfully observes in a note to this statement, "Paul is speaking here of the law as a *life-principle*. As such it stands diametrically opposed to faith" (125n7).

into the hands of his people (5:14; cf. Rom. 13:8–10). This fulfillment means that we do not observe the totality of the commands that God gave to Israel through Moses, but we observe its moral core, the Ten Commandments. Furthermore, we observe the law not for justification but for sanctification, the necessary and grateful response of redeemed sinners to our Redeemer. In this respect, we stand alongside Israel who, in covenant with God their Redeemer, took up his law in exactly the same way. We, no less than they, "delight in the law of God" (Rom. 7:22).

Theological Implications

In this brief survey, we have seen that the apostle Paul understood Adam, before his fall, to have been in a special covenant with God. Adam stands parallel with the last Adam, Jesus Christ. As Christ's work to redeem his people is covenantal in character, we must understand Adam's disobedience and its consequences in equally covenantal terms. In this covenant, Adam represented himself and all his ordinary descendants. Had Adam obeyed God, he would have secured for himself and for humanity confirmed eschatological life. But Adam disobeyed God. In so doing, he forfeited life and earned death. As a result, human beings "in Adam" are guilty of Adam's first sin and so liable to God's just judgment. In God's mercy, that was not the end of the story. He sent into history the "last Adam" or "second man," Jesus Christ. By his obedience, death, and resurrection, Jesus paid the penalty for the sins of his people and won for them eschatological life. These are blessings that Jesus merited but that we receive as gifts from his hand. We in no way earn them, but God graciously and freely gives them to us.

In his correspondence with the churches in Galatia and Rome, Paul speaks of the Mosaic covenant in ways that are reminiscent of the covenant of works. His statements have as their background a misunderstanding of the Mosaic covenant represented in first-century Judaism and in the teaching of the Judaizers. This misunderstanding saw obedience to the Mosaic covenant as an instrument of the sinner's justification. In other words, one must obey the laws of the Mosaic covenant in order to be counted righteous before God. For Paul, this is a misreading of the Mosaic covenant. Beginning with the Abrahamic covenant, Paul shows that God has always intended for his people to be justified through faith in the promised Messiah. It is Christ's work that justifies and not our own. To those inclined to misread the Mosaic covenant, Paul points them to the testimony of that covenant. When one removes the Mosaic legislation from the covenant in which it was promulgated, then one is left with the covenant of works. The outcome for the sinner inclined to rely on his obedience to the Mosaic law for justification will always be curse and death. God has built into his gracious Mosaic covenant a testimony or warning against its misuse (Lev. 18:5).

The New Testament's teaching on the covenant of works has profound implications for the way we read the Bible and for the way we live the Christian life. It tells us, in the first place, that the Bible is a grand unity with one goal, the glory of God in the redemption of sinners in Christ. The saving work of the last Adam is tailored precisely to our plight in Adam. From its very beginning, redemptive history advanced toward the appearing of Christ in history in order to save sinners. That advance was marked by fuller and clearer revelation of God's saving purposes for the nations. The whole of the Old Testament, no less than the New Testament, speaks of Christ (Luke 24:25–27, 44–49). No less than believers today, Abraham, Moses, David, and Isaiah looked to Jesus Christ and placed their hope in him for salvation (John 5:45; 8:56; 12:41; Acts 2:29–31). The Old Testament is not a sealed book to believers. It is a book that is full of Christ.

In the second place, the New Testament's teaching on the covenant of works helps us understand and live the Christian life well. Our salvation is entirely based on and rooted in the person and work of Jesus Christ. It is therefore the free gift of God to sinners. In this way, salvation exalts both the justice and mercy of God (see Rom. 3:26). This broad perspective on our salvation in Christ helps us appreciate the various benefits that are ours in him, especially our justification and our sanctification. Our justification is not only the forgiveness of all our sins. It is that and is never less than that, but it is more than that. To be justified in Christ is to be counted righteous before God. In the last Adam, we stand accepted, vindicated, and entitled to eternal life. This justified state will never change (Rom. 8:1). We cannot lose it, and no one will ever take it away from us (Rom. 8:31–39). The whole of the Christian life is lived in light of this fixed and certain reality (cf. Rom. 5:1–11). Our sanctification is not earning a life that we do not have. Jesus has won that life for us already and has freely given it to us (cf. Eph. 2:4–7; Col. 3:3–4). Sanctification is the process by which we experience more and more the life that belongs to us in Christ. We are working out the life that God is working into us in Christ (cf. Phil. 2:12–13). Sanctification is not striving to get into heaven; it is the life of those who have, in Christ, already been seated in heaven (Eph. 2:6; Col. 3:1–4). For these reasons, the true Christian may and ought to have a well-grounded assurance of his or her salvation (2 Pet. 1:5–11). Confident in what Christ has done for us to secure our redemption, we should look to the future with expectation and hope (cf. Titus 2:11–14). We eagerly await God to complete at Christ's return what he has already begun in our lives (Phil. 1:6). This expectation is not abstract or speculative. It has a sanctifying influence in the present (2 Pet. 1:10–11; 1 John 3:1–3).

For the New Testament, covenant theology is the framework within which God gives us his gospel. At the heart and center of God's covenant with sinners is the person and work of Jesus Christ. It is when we understand the New Testament's exposition of this gracious covenant, against the backdrop of the covenant of works with Adam, that we can say with Paul, "For from him and through him and to him are all things. To him be glory forever. Amen" (Rom. 11:36).

4

Adam and the Beginning of the Covenant of Grace

John D. Currid

Mankind's rebellion and disobedience to the covenant of works had devastating consequences. It not only negatively affected Adam and Eve and their posterity, but their defi-
ant behavior also resulted in a curse descending on all creation. John Calvin comments,

> As Adam's spiritual life would have consisted in remaining united and bound to his
> Maker, so estrangement from him was the death of his soul. Nor is it strange that he
> who perverted the whole order of nature in heaven and earth deteriorated his race
> by his revolt. "The whole creation groaneth," saith St. Paul, "being made subject to
> vanity, not willingly" (Rom. Viii 20, 22). If the reason is asked, there cannot be a
> doubt that creation bears part of the punishment deserved by man, for whose use all
> other creatures were made. Therefore, since through man's fault a curse has extended
> above and below, over all the regions of the world, there is nothing unreasonable in
> its extending to all his offspring.[1]

The ubiquitous nature of the results of mankind's revolt can be gleaned directly from
the Scriptures, and therefore, it is to them that we now turn.

Genesis 3:7–24 and the Effects of Sin

The consequences of Adam and Eve breaking the covenant of works through their
sinful behavior were staggering and far reaching, as seen seminally in Genesis 3:7–24

---

1. John Calvin, *Institutes of the Christian Religion*, trans. Henry Beveridge, 2 vols. (1970; repr., Grand Rapids,
MI: Eerdmans, 1983), 2:214.

but also throughout Scripture. First, sin affected and infected all human nature. The Westminster Confession of Faith puts it this way: "By this sin they fell from their original righteousness, and communion with God, and so became dead in sin, and wholly defiled in all the faculties and parts of soul and body" (6.2). This means that each and every aspect of human nature has been adversely affected by sin. As Paul says in Romans 1:21, "For although they knew God, they did not honor him as God or give thanks to him, but they became futile in their thinking, and their foolish hearts were darkened." Sin simply darkened and distorted the hearts and minds of humanity.[2] In addition, sin has resulted in the death of the human body; as Paul comments in Romans 6:23, "The wages of sin is death." God had threatened Adam with that punishment for covenantal disobedience (Gen. 2:16–17), and it came to pass (Gen. 5:5). The upshot is that by their rebellion Adam and Eve lost their lives, both physically and spiritually.

Covenants are communal and generational. So when our first parents revolted against the covenant of works, that rebellion had a debilitating impact on their progeny. The Westminster Confession of Faith defines it well when it says, "They being the root of all mankind, the guilt of this sin was imputed, and the same death in sin and corrupted nature was conveyed to all their prosperity, descending from them by ordinary generation" (6.3). In Eden, Adam was the covenant representative for all mankind. When he broke the covenant, he brought a curse down on all those he represented. Because of Adam's sin, all people are born sinners and are held accountable for Adam's original sin. God simply imputes or credits Adam's sin to all who descend from Adam. As David proclaims in Psalm 51:5,

> Behold, I was brought forth in iniquity,
>   and in sin did my mother conceive me.

Evidence that this curse is in effect for all humanity is clearly seen in the genealogy of Genesis 5, in which all the people (except Enoch) are described by the ringing, insistent refrain ". . . and he died."[3]

The mandate that God had given mankind in their creation to be "fruitful and multiply and fill the earth and subdue it, and have dominion" (1:28) is yet in effect after the fall, but it has been warped by sin. Man and woman at creation were given the task of producing children. Because of their rebellion, however, that duty has become hard, painful, and laborious (3:16). Adam had also been ordered by God to cultivate the ground and to help it produce (2:15). But now the earth is cursed, and it will strive

---

2. For a good study of how sin has twisted mankind's thinking, or what theologians call the noetic effects of sin, see Stephen K. Moroney, *The Noetic Effects of Sin: A Historical and Contemporary Exploration of How Sin Affects Our Thinking* (Lanham, MD: Lexington Books, 2000). Moroney comments that "the most detailed reflection on how sin affects our thinking is found within the Reformed (or Calvinistic) tradition of Christianity" (27).

3. Also in support of the doctrine of imputation is Gen. 5:3, where there appears a reversal of elements from the original creation of mankind to the birth of Seth. In Gen. 1:26, man is created in the image/likeness of God (that is, righteous), but in Gen. 5:3, Seth bears the likeness/image of Adam (that is, unrighteous). This chiasm underscores the twisted nature that Seth inherits directly from Adam, which is a fallen nature and one that ends in death.

against man's efforts to make it productive (3:17). In fact, it will be in "pain" that humans will eat from the ground; that word "pain" is the same one used in 3:16 of woman's labor. Humanity's creational tasks now become difficult, rough, and burdensome.

Mankind's relationship to everything around him and within him has been affected by sin. Man has been *alienated* from God. In Genesis 3:7–24, we see that the man and woman hide themselves in the trees from the presence of the Lord (3:8). They now experience fear and guilt, and so they run from their Creator. Adam's response to God's query "Where are you?" (3:9) highlights his disobedience (3:10) and accentuates the estrangement that exists between God and man.[4]

The man and woman have been *alienated* from one another. Immediately after they sin, Adam and Eve cover their nakedness. Their nakedness had symbolized their innocence, openness, and guiltlessness (see 2:25). The coverings they now manufacture serve as physical symbols of a breakdown of their unity. The distance and estrangement is exacerbated by Adam and Eve's refusal to admit guilt and responsibility for their actions: Adam shifts the blame to God and to his wife (3:12), and Eve blames the serpent (3:13). Because of sin, the creational institution of marriage has been twisted and distorted. Genesis 3:16 likely indicates that the struggles and tensions in the first marriage relationship will prevail in the ongoing marriage institution after the fall.[5]

Adam and Eve are driven from the garden, and thus they are *alienated* from their original, perfect physical environment (3:17–19). They are exiled into a world that has been subjected to vanity, futility, and frustration because of mankind's disobedience. The apostle Paul is clear about the effects of sin on creation: "For the creation was subjected to futility, not willingly, but because of him who subjected it, in hope that the creation itself will be set free from its bondage to corruption and obtain the freedom of the glory of the children of God" (Rom. 8:20–21). Truly, the universe is now in an unending cycle of birth, growth, death, and decay; nature itself is in a state of deterioration and decay.

To be fair, not all biblical commentators agree with this assessment. For example, Arthur Lewis concludes, "Nothing in the narrative suggests that the realm of nature has been altered in a fundamental way."[6] Meredith Kline concurs: "The Bible does not require us, therefore, to think of the character and working of man's natural environment before the Fall as radically different from what is presently the case."[7] I would also point the reader to the work of C. John Collins in this matter.[8] Some theologians, such

---

4. Nahum Sarna points out that the word "heard" in Gen. 3:10 can also be properly translated "obey." Man would thus be claiming that he was obedient to God. This would be ironic, in which the man is deceptive in his reply. See Sarna, *Genesis* בראשית, JPS Torah Commentary (Philadelphia: Jewish Publication Society, 1989), 26.

5. It is customary today to view the woman's "desire" for her husband to be not adversarial but rather one of affection and a longing for intimacy. See Irvin A. Busenitz, "Woman's Desire for Man: Genesis 3:16 Reconsidered," *GTJ* 7, no. 2 (1986): 203–12; Janson C. Condren, "Toward a Purge of the Battle of the Sexes and 'Return' for the Original Meaning of Genesis 3:16b," *JETS* 60, no. 2 (2017): 227–45. This positive reading, in my opinion, misses the contextual thrust of Gen. 3:7–24, which focuses on the dominating effects of sin on all aspects of reality.

6. Arthur H. Lewis, "The Localization of the Garden of Eden," *BETS* 11 (1968): 174.

7. Meredith G. Kline, *The Kingdom Prologue* (South Hamilton, MA: M. G. Kline, 1993), 81.

8. C. John Collins, *Science and Faith: Friends or Foes?* (Wheaton, IL: Crossway, 2003), 135–46.

as Abraham Kuyper and Emil Brunner, exempt certain areas of reality from the effects of sin. They agree that the empirical sciences and mathematics should be excluded. These appear to be mere speculative distinctions, when in fact we should not "exempt any area of study from the potential distorting effects of sin."[9]

These views appear to misunderstand, or at least minimize, the commentary of Paul in Romans 8:20–21. As Charles Cranfield remarks, "There is little doubt that Paul had in mind the judgment related in Gen 3:17–19, which includes (3:17) the words 'cursed is the ground for thy sake.'"[10] The "bondage of corruption" that Paul speaks of "must be taken in the sense of the decay and death apparent even in non-rational creation."[11] Douglas Moo is right when he concludes, "Creation is helplessly enslaved to the decay that rules the world after the Fall."[12]

Finally, mankind is *alienated* from eternal life as God banishes them from the garden (Gen. 3:20–24). God then sets two guardians at the eastern entrance of Eden so that mankind cannot reenter and take from the tree of life. He first places there cherubim, angelic creatures who reflect the very presence of God (see Ex. 36:35). And second, he posts a flaming sword that turns continuously at the gate; it serves as a warning to mankind against attempting to return to the garden.

In summary, Genesis 3:7–24 demonstrates that mankind's violation of and disobedience to the covenant of works produced dire outcomes not only for themselves but for all reality. I state elsewhere,

> And, indeed, it has affected all parts of mankind. All aspects of people's characters have been infected by sin: the physical body, the emotions, the mind, the heart and the will. This understanding of sin properly explains the present condition of the earth and humanity's situation in it. There is simply cosmic and ubiquitous brokenness.[13]

Adam and Eve's sin has had sweeping negative consequences for all creation.

Commencement of the Covenant of Grace (Gen. 3:14–19)

Mankind has thus broken the covenant of works. By their sinister act, the man and the woman have tumbled into sin, and it has had remarkable effects on the entire creation. Sin has simply distorted and twisted how the universe operates. Indeed,

> Cursed is the ground . . . ;
> thorns and thistles it shall bring forth for you. (Gen. 3:17–18 *passim*)

---

9. Moroney, *Noetic Effects of Sin*, 37.

10. C. E. B. Cranfield, *A Critical and Exegetical Commentary on the Epistle to the Romans*, ICC (Edinburgh: T&T Clark, 1975), 413.

11. John Murray, *The Epistle to the Romans*, NICNT (1960; repr., Grand Rapids, MI: Eerdmans, 1968), 304. In this discussion, Murray emphasizes the effects of sin on "the *whole* creation."

12. Douglas J. Moo, *Romans 1–8*, WEC (Chicago: Moody Press, 1991), 553.

13. John D. Currid, *Genesis*, vol. 1, *Genesis 1:1–25:18* (Darlington, UK: Evangelical Press, 2003), 141.

Yet there is good news. God makes a covenantal oath, binding himself to mankind and to his creation. And so we read in the Westminster Confession of Faith 7.3, "Man by his fall having made himself incapable of life by that covenant, the Lord was pleased to make a second, commonly called the Covenant of Grace." O. Palmer Robertson correctly concludes that

> God had absolutely no obligation to man once he had revolted against the Almighty's will and aligned himself with the serpent, who is Satan. . . . But God is gracious—he bound himself by oath. Although man proved to be an ungrateful, self-willed rebel, God chose to obligate himself to the sinner.[14]

God's response to mankind's rebellion is found in Genesis 3:14–19. These verses are prophetic, and they pronounce a new order to the operation of the universe. This prophecy, however, is given not by means of a human prophet or human agent but directly by the Lord himself. In one sense, God is the first prophet. In the opening section of his vision (3:14–15), Yahweh deals with the serpent specifically and then with the forthcoming history of mankind in a general way.

God's Pronouncement on the Serpent (3:14–15)

God now turns to the serpent and pronounces a curse and punishment on that creature because of the part it played in tempting mankind. There is an immediate impact of divine judgment on the serpent in Genesis 3:14. The execration is twofold: first, the serpent is doomed to travel on its belly from now on. It is not clear whether the serpent originally walked erect or not; it may be that the curse subjects the creature to continue in its created posture. Second, the beast is further doomed to eat "dust." Because the transgression involved both speaking and eating, the judgment ironically includes both as well. The two judgments are symbols of defeat and humiliation throughout the Old Testament (see, e.g., Ps. 72:9; Isa. 65:25; Mic. 7:17).[15] As Nahum Sarna concludes, "Having arrogantly aggrandized itself in a challenge to God, it is now permanently doomed to a posture of abject humiliation."[16]

The final line of Genesis 3:14 may indicate that the curse is also eschatological; that is, it is a pointer to the serpent's ultimate defeat and humiliation. Thus, the physical subjugation of the serpent may, in fact, be a symbolic reminder of the final vanquishing of Satan at the hands of the coming Messiah (see the discussion of 3:15 below).

A Hebrew particle called the *min of comparison* (translated "above all" by the ESV) appears twice in this verse. It is there to remind the reader of Genesis 3:1, where the serpent is introduced as "more crafty than" all the animals that God had made. This verse also

---

14. O. Palmer Robertson, *Covenants: God's Way with His People* (Philadelphia: Great Commission, 1987), 24.

15. Observe that in the original Hebrew both the objects "belly" and "dust" precede their verbs; this word order is emphatic, underscoring the depth and certainty of the judgments.

16. Sarna, *Genesis*, 27.

contains a *min of comparison*, and it can rightly be read that the serpent is "crafty above all" (my trans.). In Genesis 3:14 he is "cursed . . . above all." This is biblical irony at work; as the ancient rabbis conclude, "Because he was cunning above all, he is cursed above all."[17]

In 3:15, the theme of God's judgment on the serpent continues and intensifies. That judgment is in the form of conflict in which the serpent will be ultimately defeated. But we should also observe that there is a blessing pronounced in this verse to those who oppose the serpent. That should not be a surprise since both sanctions, blessings and curses, were central to covenant relationships in the Old Testament and throughout the ancient Near East.[18]

The opening of the Lord's pronouncement against the serpent begins with "I will put enmity . . ." (3:15). The first thing to note here is that God is the subject of the verse as the speaker, and he is setting up a new order and direction for history. As Robertson remarks, "The divine initiative in this establishment of animosity must be underscored. God himself shall perpetuate a continuing warfare."[19] His sovereignty and providence are on display, as history will unfold according to his plan. Here God is acting as the king in a suzerain-vassal covenant, in which the king sets down the parameters and substance of the covenant.[20] This new order is defined by the use of the word "enmity" (אֵיבָה). It is emphasized in the sentence because it appears as the first word in the original Hebrew. The noun form appears five times in the Old Testament, and it bears the idea of "hostile disposition"[21] or "personal hostility"[22] (Num. 35:21–22; Ezek. 25:15; 35:5). In each instance of word usage, the animosity displayed by the two parties is a matter of life and death, and it extends to the point of human destruction.

Genesis 3:15 defines three levels or tiers of conflict. The first stage of enmity will be "between you and the woman." The pronoun "you" is second-person masculine singular, and it obviously refers to the serpent to whom God is directly speaking. The "woman," of course, refers to Eve, since Adam had earlier given her that name (2:23). This stage of conflict already was underway in the garden when the serpent dialogued with Eve and tempted her to sin. The Lord is prophesying that this enmity will continue. When Jesus comments on the scene in the garden, he describes the serpent's activity not merely as deception but as an act of murder (which ties back into the meaning of the word "enmity"). He says in his discussion with some of the Jewish

---

17. Quoted in Umberto Cassuto, *A Commentary on the Book of Genesis*, part 1, *From Adam to Noah* (1961; repr., Jerusalem: Magnes, 1989), 159.

18. See, e.g., Kenneth A. Kitchen, *Ancient Orient and Old Testament* (Chicago: InterVarsity Press, 1966), 90–102.

19. O. Palmer Robertson, *The Christ of the Covenants* (Grand Rapids, MI: Baker, 1980), 96.

20. See Meredith G. Kline, *Treaty of the Great King: The Covenant Structure of Deuteronomy; Studies and Commentary* (Grand Rapids, MI: Eerdmans, 1963); Kline, *The Structure of Biblical Authority* (Grand Rapids, MI: Eerdmans, 1972); George E. Mendenhall, "Covenant Forms in Israelite Tradition," *BA* 17, no. 3 (1954): 50–76.

21. *HALOT*, 36.

22. Francis Brown, S. R. Driver, and Charles A. Briggs, *A Hebrew Lexicon of the Old Testament* (Oxford: Clarendon, 1906), 33.

leaders, "You are of your father the devil, and your will is to do your father's desires. He was a murderer from the beginning, and does not stand in the truth, because there is no truth in him. When he lies, he speaks out of his own character, for he is a liar and the father of lies" (John 8:44).

The second stage of the conflict is between "your offspring" and "her offspring" (Gen. 3:15). The Hebrew word זֶרַע ("offspring"/"seed") is a collective, and as Paul Joüon remarks, a "collective noun properly speaking designates a plurality of individuals as forming a group."[23] This Hebrew noun often refers to the lineage/descent/posterity of a human subject. The Septuagint commonly renders the word in Greek as σπερμα, which reflects the idea of issue/descent/family.[24] Interestingly, the first mention of the people of Israel in extrabiblical literature is in the Egyptian *Merneptah Stela*. In it the pharaoh boasts that he has wiped out the people of Israel: "Israel is laid waste, his seed is not."[25] With that collective understanding, then, who is the seed/offspring of the serpent?

The apostle John provides a commentary on the Genesis narrative by defining the very nature of the serpent as "that ancient serpent, who is called the devil and Satan, the deceiver of the whole world" (Rev. 12:9). The offspring of the serpent cannot refer to a physical descent because Satan is a fallen angel and has no reproductive power (cf. Mark 12:25). This must refer to a spiritual posterity in which one can be a child of Satan by will, heart, and intent. As C. John Collins says, "I take his offspring to be those who are seduced into his darkness."[26] Jesus, in fact, when speaking to some of his Jewish opponents, says, "You are of your father the devil, and your will is to do your father's desires. He was a murderer from the beginning" (John 8:44).

The apostle John gives further commentary on this tier of enmity when he defines the seed of the woman in the following way:

> And when the dragon saw that he had been thrown down to the earth, he pursued the woman who had given birth to the male child. But the woman was given the two wings of the great eagle so that she might fly from the serpent into the wilderness, to the place where she is to be nourished for a time, and times, and half a time. The serpent poured water like a river out of his mouth after the woman, to sweep her away with a flood. But the earth came to the help of the woman, and the earth opened its mouth and swallowed the river that the dragon had poured from his mouth. Then the dragon became furious with the woman and went off to make war on the rest of her offspring, on those who keep the commandments of God and hold to the testimony of Jesus. And he stood on the sand of the sea. (Rev. 12:13–17)

---

23. Paul Joüon, *A Grammar of Biblical Hebrew*, part 3, *Syntax* (Rome: Pontifical Biblical Institute, 2005), 497.

24. Henry George Liddell and Robert Scott, *A Greek-English Lexicon* (Oxford: Oxford University Press, 1843), 645.

25. James B. Pritchard, *Ancient Near Eastern Texts* (Princeton, NJ: Princeton University Press, 1955), 376–78.

26. C. John Collins, *Genesis 1–4: A Linguistic, Literary, and Theological Commentary* (Phillipsburg, NJ: P&R, 2006), 156.

Here John describes the "offspring" of the woman as believers who attempt to keep the law of God and are witnesses to the world of the gospel. This seed, then, is also one of a spiritual descent, and it includes those who say, "Our Father in heaven . . ." (Matt. 6:9).

This two-seed theology has immediate consequences in the book of Genesis. In chapter 4, Cain, who was "of the evil one" (1 John 3:12), murders his brother Abel, who was "commended as righteous" (Heb. 11:4). Although they both had the same physical birth mother, they were spiritually of different lines: one was of the seed of the serpent and the other of the seed of the woman. The promised "enmity" of Genesis 3:15 thus begins to play out in the history of mankind.

The third divinely ordained stage of clash and conflict is climactic, and it is a battle between two individuals. The text says that "he" will bruise "your" head, and "you" will bruise "his" heel (all four pronouns are masculine singular). The "you" obviously speaks to the serpent because he is the one to whom God is speaking, but the "he" is unidentified at this point. Some scholars argue, however, that "he" and "his" refer not to an individual but rather to the "offspring"/"seed" of the second tier of the verse. Many of these commentators thus deny that this final line is an expectation of a coming individual but merely a restated proposition that good and evil will clash throughout human history.[27] Collins, to the contrary, has convincingly made the case that if the author had meant to refer to posterity in general, then he would have used plural pronouns.[28] Because the text uses two singular pronouns, Collins concludes that we are justified "in seeing an individual as the referent here."[29] This interpretation fits well into the context of the messianic concept of the entire book of Genesis, and the remainder of the Old Testament for that matter.[30] It also has a long history. Apart from the Old Testament itself, the earliest messianic interpretation of Genesis 3:15 dates to the Septuagint of the third to second centuries BC, and it is confirmed in the New Testament.[31]

It ought to be noted that the sequence of subjects changes in the final tier. Whereas the serpent ("you"/"your") is mentioned first in both previous tiers, the "he" now is placed in the opening position. This alternation of subjects is chiastic, underscoring the primacy and preeminence of the one who is coming to do battle against the serpent. The description of the conflict further emphasizes the supremacy of the "he" over the serpent. The structure of the final tier is in parallel, as follows:

27. See, e.g., Claus Westermann, *Genesis 1–11* (Minneapolis: Augsburg, 1984), 355; Gerhard von Rad, *Genesis: A Commentary* (Philadelphia: Westminster, 1961), 90.
28. C. John Collins, "A Syntactical Note (Genesis 3:15): Is the Woman's Seed Singular or Plural?," *TynBul* 48 (1997): 139–48.
29. Collins, *Genesis 1–4*, 156.
30. See the compelling argument of T. Desmond Alexander, "Messianic Ideology in the Book of Genesis," in *The Lord's Anointed: Interpretation of Old Testament Messianic Texts*, ed. Philip E. Satterthwaite, Richard S. Hess, and Gordon J. Wenham (Carlisle, UK: Paternoster, 1995), 19–39.
31. See Ralph A. Martin, "The Earliest Messianic Interpretation of Genesis 3:15," *JBL* 84 (1965): 425–27.

a	b	c
he	shall bruise you	(on the) head

a'	b'	c'
and you	shall bruise him	(on the) heel

The two combatants will strike one another: the verb used to describe their actions is שׁוּף, which is translated variously in English versions as "bruise" (ESV, NASB) or "strike" (NEB). The NIV oddly translates the two instances differently, the first as "crush" and the second as "strike."[32] The verb שׁוּף is rare in the Hebrew Bible, although when it is used, it highlights the violence of a blow rather than it merely being a glancing stroke (see Job 9:17). Some scholars believe the verb is possibly related to the verb שׁוּף that means "to crush, trample on."[33] The bodily objects of the wounding underscore the primacy of the "he" over the serpent: the blow to the serpent is to the head, which probably reflects a mortal, deadly wound. The serpent will strike the "he" on the heel, a wound that will not be fatal.

At the very heart of the beginnings of the covenant of grace is a divine promise. God takes a prophetic oath that he will send a champion to crush the enemy of his people. And who is this coming hero? Who is the "he" of Genesis 3:15? One major clue is found in the New Testament, where Jesus is portrayed as in the direct lineage of Adam and Eve in Luke 3; Christ is thus being portrayed as a direct male descendant of the woman. It is further significant that immediately after the genealogy, Jesus is led by the Spirit into the wilderness to battle Satan. The champion sallies forth to engage the enemy, as it were, head-on. Thus begins a raging war that reaches its climax at the cross, where the Messiah lands a mortal blow to the head of the serpent. As the apostle Paul says, Jesus "disarmed the rulers and authorities [i.e., serpent, demonic powers] and put them to open shame, by triumphing over them in him [or, 'in it,' ESV mg.; i.e., the cross]" (Col. 2:15).

Theologians have called this covenantal promise the *protevangelium*, that is, the first gospel presentation. The remainder of Scripture is an unfolding of this promise of Genesis 3:15. The beginning of redemption is prophesied in this one verse, and the Bible traces the development of that redemptive theme from Genesis to its end in the book of Revelation. Collins accurately concludes that "Genesis fosters a messianic expectation, of which this verse is the headwaters."[34] In the coming of Christ, we see the fulfillment of the covenantal promise that one would come to defeat the serpent. The writer to Hebrews expresses it well when he says that Christ came that "he might destroy the one who has the power of death, that is, the devil" (Heb. 2:14).

---

32. In fairness, the NIV does provide a footnote on the word "crush" that says, "or *strike*."

33. Brown, Driver, and Briggs, *Hebrew Lexicon*, 983. See the discussion of Cassuto, *Commentary on the Book of Genesis*, 1:161.

34. Collins, *Genesis 1–4*, 157.

Conclusion

Genesis 3 is a watershed chapter in the Bible. Prior to it, we see that everything that God had created was "very good" (1:31). It is worth quoting the Torah scholar Umberto Cassuto at this point:

> On the previous days the words *that it was good* were applied to a specific detail; now *God saw* EVERYTHING *that He had made*, the creation in its totality, and He perceived that not only were the details, taken separately, good, but that each one harmonized with the rest; hence the whole was not just *good*, but *very good*. An analogy might be found in an artist who, having completed his masterpiece, steps back a little and surveys his handiwork with delight, for both in detail and in its entirety it had emerged perfect from his hand.[35]

In that perfect environment, God established a covenant relationship with mankind. It was a covenant of works, in which mankind's obedience led to life and their disobedience to death. The first man failed, and in his sinful failure he was condemned and lost life. Robertson states,

> By his action he forfeited all claim to life for subsequent generations. In the original bond between God and man no provision for blessing had been offered in the event of disobedience. As a result, in Adam all die (1 Cor. 15:22). By the one disobedience of the one man the many were made sinners (Rom. 5:19).[36]

In addition, by mankind's sin the entire order of nature was distorted and twisted; all material reality is now bent. It has simply curdled.

At the core of God's solution to the predicament of sin and its effects is to send one who will set everything right. This is accomplished through the incarnation, death, and resurrection of his Son Jesus Christ. As Paul says, "For God has done what the law, weakened by the flesh, could not do. By sending his own Son in the likeness of sinful flesh and for sin, he condemned sin in the flesh in order that the righteous requirement of the law might be fulfilled in us" (Rom. 8:3–4). Because of Christ's work, Paul can further proclaim, "There is therefore now no condemnation for those who are in Christ Jesus" (Rom. 8:1). God did not leave mankind in the state of sin, misery, and death. The Westminster Shorter Catechism summarizes that truth when it says, "God, having out of his mere good pleasure, from all eternity, elected some to everlasting life, did enter into a covenant of grace to deliver them out of the estate of sin and misery, and to bring them into an estate of salvation by a Redeemer" (q. 20).

The work of the Messiah in the covenant of grace, however, accomplished even more than the defeat of the serpent and the redemption of mankind. As the Westminster Confession of Faith says, the Lord Jesus "purchased, not only reconciliation, but an

---

35. Cassuto, *Commentary on the Book of Genesis*, 1:59.
36. Robertson, *Covenants*, 20–21.

everlasting inheritance in the kingdom of heaven, for all those whom the Father hath given unto him" (7.5). The apostle Peter describes this "purchase" in the following way: "According to his great mercy, he has caused us to be born again to a living hope through the resurrection of Jesus Christ from the dead, to an inheritance that is imperishable, undefiled, and unfading, kept in heaven for you" (1 Pet. 1:3–4).[37] The apostle John describes the eschatological consummation of this aspect of the Messiah's work in the book of Revelation. I have written elsewhere,

> The theological structure of Genesis 1–3 as creation, fall, and redemption is mirrored in the eschatological conclusion of the Bible. The book of Revelation reverses the order of the sequence. The opening sections of John's vision center on the redemptive work of the Messiah (e.g., Rev. 5:5–6; 7:9–10). This is followed by the judgment and defeat of Satan (e.g., Rev. 12:13–17; 20:1–6) and his fall into the lake of fire and sulfur (Rev. 20:7–10). The final chapters of Revelation describe a new heavens and a new earth, a re-created order based upon the garden of Eden in Genesis 1–2. Included in this eschatological picture is a lush garden-like existence with a river of life running through it and the Tree of Life in it (Rev. 22:1–5). In addition, whereas the institution of human marriage was established at the original creation, this re-creation scene contains the marriage feast of the Lamb and his people, they who constitute his bride (Rev. 19:6–9; 21:9).[38]

In the covenant of grace, the work of Jesus Christ, the "he" of Genesis 3:15, defeats the serpent, redeems mankind, *and* restores creation to its originally intended order, state, and purpose. For those who are of the seed of the woman, the promised Redeemer has redeemed them and brought about *reconciliation* for them with God (Eph. 2:16) and with all reality. The solution to mankind's sinful nature and consequential, ubiquitous *alienation* is the cross of Jesus Christ, the promised one "who fills all in all" (Eph. 1:23).

---

37. In the Septuagint, the Greek word for "inheritance" often describes the land of promise that God has prepared for his people Israel (e.g., Num. 32:19; Deut. 25:19; Josh. 11:23; 13:7). This land inheritance in the Old Testament points to a greater and grander heavenly land that awaits the people of God in heaven.

38. John D. Currid, "Genesis," in *A Biblical-Theological Introduction to the Old Testament: The Gospel Promised*, ed. Miles V. Van Pelt (Wheaton, IL: Crossway, 2016), 54. For an in-depth study of this theological echo, see G. K. Beale, *The Temple and the Church's Mission: A Biblical Theology of the Dwelling Place of God*, NSBT 17 (Downers Grove, IL: InterVarsity Press, 2004).

5

THE NOAHIC COVENANT OF
THE COVENANT OF GRACE

Miles V. Van Pelt

The Noahic covenant recorded in Genesis 9 is a universal, unilateral, nonredemptive administration of the covenant of grace restoring and securing the principle of common grace in this world that was suspended during the judgment ordeal of the flood.[1] This covenant of common grace ensures a period of delay from God's final, eschatological judgment until the covenant of grace should be accomplished in its various historical administrations, which include the Abrahamic, Mosaic, Davidic, and new covenants. The current era of common grace established and sustained by the Noahic covenant, where both the elect and nonelect together enjoy the stability of the natural world order, will terminate at the consummation of this age with the advent of the new heavens and new earth (2 Pet. 3:5–7). It is helpful to understand that the name commonly assigned to this covenant, Noahic, derives from the fact that the man Noah was the prophetic mediator with whom God established it.[2] This

---

1. At this point it is helpful to briefly distinguish between the covenant of grace and common grace. The covenant of grace "is a gracious bond between the offended God and the offending sinner in which God promises salvation in the way of faith in Christ and the sinner receives this salvation by believing." Geerhardus Vos, *Reformed Dogmatics*, vol. 2, *Anthropology*, trans. and ed. Richard B. Gaffin Jr. (Bellingham, WA: Lexham, 2012–2014), 92. Bruce K. Waltke explains, "After the fall into original sin, and the loss of Paradise, the covenant of works is no longer a possibility. In his sovereign grace, God establishes his 'covenant of grace' on the basis of the benefits of Christ's active obedience and his atoning death, validated by his resurrection from the dead, his ascension into heaven, and the empowering presence of his Spirit." *An Old Testament Theology: An Exegetical, Canonical, and Thematic Approach*, with Charles Yu (Grand Rapids, MI: Zondervan, 2007), 288. Common grace, on the other hand, represents a period of delay from final judgment at the consummation of history. It is "the antithesis of the Consummation and, as such, epitomizes this world-age viewed under the aspect of a delay during which the Consummation is abeyant." Meredith G. Kline, "The Intrusion and the Decalogue," *WTJ* 16, no. 1 (1953): 3.

2. As a "covenant mediator prophet," Noah is a type of Christ in the tradition of Adam, Abraham, Moses, and David. This identification is significant for understanding Noah as a second Adam figure in the flood narratives.

covenant, however, is universal in scope, applying to all humanity, the animal kingdom, and the earth itself.

The account of the Noahic covenant appears in Genesis 9:8–17, where the nature, parties, and sign of the covenant are set forth. The establishment of this covenant occurs in the context of the worldwide flood recorded in Genesis 7–8, together with the reasons and preparation for that flood in Genesis 6. In order to properly understand the significance of the Noahic covenant in Genesis 9:8–17, we must also consider the larger context in which it appears.

The World That Then Was

Noah's Birth

After the creation prologue of Genesis 1:1–2:3, the book of Genesis is divided into ten sections, each of which begins with the well-known *toledot* (תּוֹלְדֹת) formula, "These are the generations."[3] The Noahic covenant is located in the third *toledot* section (6:9–9:29). The birth of Noah is recorded in 5:28–29: "And Lamech lived 182 years, and he fathered a son, and he called his name 'Noah,' saying, 'This one will bring us relief from our work and from the *pain* of our hands because of the *ground* that Yahweh *cursed*.'"[4] The language of 5:29 recalls 3:17, "*Cursed* is the *ground* because of you. In *pain* you will eat all the days of your life." The words for "cursed," "ground," and "pain" appear in both 5:29 and 3:17. The order in which these three words appear in each instance are reversed. In 3:17, the order is "pain," "ground," "cursed"; in 5:29, the order is "cursed," "ground," "pain." The inversion of word order in 5:29 may express Lamech's hope that his son will serve as the means by which God will reverse the curse of the ground. As such, Lamech's naming of Noah constitutes an expression of faith, much like Adam's naming of Eve in 3:20. With the naming of his son, Lamech expresses his faith that God will not leave his people toiling under the curse of sin forever. He will provide rest for his people and relief from the curse of the ground.[5]

The name Noah (נֹחַ) means "rest," and it constitutes a play on words with the verb translated "bring relief" (נחם).[6] That is, through Noah, God will move his plan of redemption forward, to provide relief from the pain of the curse under which all human-

---

See Jeffrey J. Niehaus, *Biblical Theology*, vol. 1, *The Common Grace Covenants* (Wooster, OH: Weaver, 2014), 178–79.

3. These sections begin at Gen. 2:4; 5:1; 6:9; 10:1; 11:10; 11:27; 25:12; 25:19; 36:1 (cf. 36:9); 37:2. For an excellent study of this structure and its significance for understanding the message of the book of Genesis, see Jason S. DeRouchie, "The Blessing-Commission, the Promised Offspring, and the *Toledot* Structure of Genesis," *JETS* 52, no. 2 (2013): 219–47.

4. All biblical translations in this chapter are my own unless otherwise indicated.

5. Stephen G. Dempster observes, "The linguistic and conceptual associations with Gen. 3:17 are striking, particularly the link between *the birth of a son* and *relief from the curse of the land*. . . . This genealogy—unlike Cain's—moves to a goal that envisions the removal of the fateful curse of Genesis 3. Noah is envisioned as a saviour." *Dominion and Dynasty: A Theology of the Hebrew Bible*, NSBT 15 (Downers Grove, IL: InterVarsity Press, 2003), 71–72.

6. The relationship between נֹחַ and נחם is not etymological. "It is a matter of assonance because the two words sound alike." John D. Currid, *A Study Commentary on Genesis*, vol. 1, *Genesis 1:1–25:18* (Darlington, UK: Evangelical Press, 2003), 168.

ity suffers because of sin. The impending flood will demonstrate the full weight of the curse of sin as it destroys the old (prediluvian) world and all its inhabitants except for Noah and his family. After the flood, the sacrifice of Noah will mitigate the wrath of the curse as its pleasing (restful) smell (נִיחֹחַ, another wordplay on the name of Noah) comes before God (Gen. 8:21).[7]

Finally, in Genesis 5:32, we read that Noah was five hundred years old before he fathered three sons: Shem, Ham, and Japheth. From these three sons, the world would be repopulated after the flood. It is significant to note that Noah was by far the oldest patriarch to father children in the genealogies of Genesis. This fact connects him with Abraham and his old age when he fathered Isaac. The remarkable age at which Noah fathered his three sons may indicate divine intervention in a previously barren or sterile state of marriage.[8] The birth of a son to an infertile couple in the Bible frequently identifies the advent of an important redemptive-historical figure. Examples include Isaac, Jacob, Joseph, Samson, Samuel, and John the Baptist. This important theme or type-scene points to the miraculous nature by which God would preserve the seed of the woman after the judgment ordeal of the flood.

Noah's World

The first eight verses of Genesis 6 bring the second *toledot* section of Genesis to a conclusion. It is commonly recognized, however, that the content of these verses is significant for understanding the flood and the covenant with Noah that follows. There is no doubt that these verses do in fact provide important information for understanding the content of the third *toledot* section (Gen. 6:9–8:22). Equally true, however, is the enigmatic and difficult nature of what we encounter. First, in 6:1–4, we read about the sons of God, the daughters of man, and the Nephilim. Next, in 6:5–7, God evaluates the moral condition of mankind and responds to that condition with the announcement of impending judgment. Finally, in 6:8, we read that "Noah found favor in the eyes of Yahweh," which serves as a contrast to the condition of humanity in 6:5–7 and prepares us for the description of Noah that follows in the third *toledot* section.

The interpretation of Genesis 6:1–4 is filled with challenges. Who are the sons of God and the daughters of man, and how are the Nephilim related to them? With regard to the sons of God and the daughters of man, scholars have provided three different options for interpretation.[9] First, based on the genealogies presented in Genesis 4 and 5, some identify the sons of God as the godly line of Seth and the daughters of man as the

---

7. The relationship between נֹחַ and נִיחֹחַ is etymological. *HALOT*, 2:696; *NIDOTTE*, 3:55.

8. See Meredith G. Kline, *God, Heaven, and Har Magedon: A Covenantal Tale of Cosmos and Telos* (Eugene, OR: Wipf and Stock, 2006), 80.

9. It is important to understand that the larger purpose of this narrative account is not lost to the difficulty of its interpretation. We observe that the flood account and the covenant that follows are bracketed by narratives that record sexual transgression in violation of the marriage covenant instituted by God in Gen. 2. It was the creation of the woman and the institution of the marriage covenant that brought the sixth day of creation from a state of "not good" (2:18) to "very good" (1:31). The events recorded in 6:1–4 and 9:18–28 are clear violations of this

ungodly line of Cain.[10] One difficulty with this interpretation is that the sons of God are presented as immoral and the daughters of man as the victims of their immorality. Additionally, the designation "sons of God" (בְּנֵי־הָאֱלֹהִים) is never applied to humans in the Old Testament but only to beings from the invisible realm (Job 1:6; 2:1; 38:7; see Ps. 29:1 [בְּנֵי אֵלִים]; Dan. 3:25 [בַּר־אֱלָהִין]).

The second interpretation identifies the sons of God as royal tyrants and the daughters of man as common women taken into the harems of these great tyrant kings.[11] This interpretation finds merit in the fact that kings in the ancient world were often considered divine sons (see Ps. 2:7) and polygamy was a common royal way of life, finding its tyrannical roots all the way back in Genesis 4:18, 23 (see 1 Kings 11:3–4; Est. 2). Again, this interpretation does not solve the problem of the use of the designation "sons of God" for beings of the invisible realm. Additionally, it does not account for the mention of the Nephilim in Genesis 6:4 or the nature of God's judgment in Genesis 6:5.

The third interpretation is often considered the most fantastic. It is, however, the oldest known interpretation, and it does find some support from Scripture. With this view, the sons of God are identified as heavenly or angelic beings and the daughters of man refer to human women.[12] This interpretation is supported by the fact that the designation "sons of God" clearly refers to beings of the invisible realm in the rest of Scripture, as identified above. Additionally, 2 Peter 2:4–5 and Jude 6–7 appear to substantiate this interpretation. In 2 Peter 2:4–5, angelic sin is connected with the destruction of the ancient world through the flood. In Jude 6, we read that some angels "did not stay within their own position of authority, but left their proper dwelling" (ESV). We also know that angels could and did appear as human figures in the Old Testament (see Gen. 18:2; 19:1–3). A difficulty with this interpretation, however, is that the judgment of the flood would appear to be the result of angelic corruption and interference in the visible world, but humanity is clearly the object of God's judgment in this account.

How are the mysterious Nephilim connected to the sons of God and the daughters of man? The English designation "Nephilim" is simply a transliteration (not translation) of the Hebrew word נְפִלִים. Though debated, it is likely derived from the verbal root נפל, meaning "to fall," and thus the Nephilim are "the fallen ones." The mention of the Nephilim occurs between the statement in Genesis 6:2 and its reiteration in 6:4 that the sons of God took or came into the daughters of man so that children were born to them. Between these two verses we read that "the Nephilim were in the land in those

---

covenantal institution and help us account for the severity of the corruption of humanity and the corresponding judgment of the flood.

10. See, e.g., Currid, *Genesis*, 1:173–75.

11. See, e.g., Meredith G. Kline, "Divine Kingship and Genesis 6:1–4," *WTJ* 24, no. 2 (1962): 187–204.

12. See, e.g., Willem A. VanGemeren, "The Sons of God in Genesis 6:1–4 (An Example of Evangelical Demythologization?)," *WTJ* 43, no. 2 (1981): 320–48; Peter J. Gentry and Stephen J. Wellum, *Kingdom through Covenant: A Biblical-Theological Understanding of the Covenants*, 2nd ed. (Wheaton, IL: Crossway, 2018), 181–83; Niehaus, *Biblical Theology*, 1:162–73.

days and also afterward."[13] The appearance of these beings is subsequently explained as occurring "when [or because] the sons of God came into the daughters of man."[14] From the context in which the Nephilim are mentioned, it appears that they were the offspring of the illicit unions between the sons of God and the daughters of man. They became the "warriors who were from antiquity, men of the name" (6:4).

Noah's Favor

With the corruption of humanity and the appearance of the Nephilim, God is moved to bring the prediluvian world to an end. In Genesis 6:3, God sets the clock running for the judgment ordeal of the flood. He states, "My Spirit will not remain with mankind forever because they are flesh. Their [remaining] days will be 120 years." The reason provided for judgment appears in Genesis 6:5: "The wickedness of humanity was great," to the degree that "every plan devised in their heart was completely wicked every day." The wicked state of humanity moved God to regret what he had created and so bring every living thing on earth under the curse of judgment.[15] Even in the midst of the decree of total judgment, however, there came the provision of hope. The whole world was about to experience the full wrath of God's judgment on sin, "but Noah found *favor* in the eyes of Yahweh" (Gen. 6:8).[16] This final statement regarding Noah's favor sets the account of the flood and the subsequent covenant with Noah in Genesis 9 squarely in the context of the covenant of grace.

Judgment and the Ark of Salvation

The third *toledot* section of Genesis begins in the same way that the second *toledot* section ends, with reference to Noah, the man of God's favor. Noah was righteous and blameless, and he walked with God. This characterization implies not that Noah was sinless (see Rom. 3:23) but rather that Noah lived in compliance with the will of God

---

13. The inclusion of "and also afterward" may be a reference to Num. 13:33, the only other mention of the Nephilim in the Bible. If correct, this would mean that these illicit unions continued after the flood, producing giants as described in the text of Num. 13:33, "We were in our eyes [small] like grasshoppers, and so we were in their eyes." This accords with the Greek translation of נְפִלִים as γίγαντες, or "giants," in both Genesis and Numbers.

14. In this context, the clause connector אֲשֶׁר can be translated as either "when" (temporal) or "because" (causal). See *HALOT*, 1:98–99. Either option connects the appearance of the Nephilim with the sexual union of the sons of God and the daughters of man.

15. In Gen. 6:6 and 6:7, the biblical text states that God "regretted" and was "sorry" (ESV) that he had created humanity. It is difficult to produce a precise translation of the Hebrew verb נחם in this context whereby the reader is not led to think that God made a mistake or did not know what he was doing when he created humanity in his image. Nothing, however, could be further from the truth (see Num. 23:19). It is important to observe that this is the same verb used by Lamech in the naming of Noah (Gen. 5:29): "This one shall *bring* us *relief* from our work" (ESV) or "*comfort* us in the labor and painful toil of our hands" (NIV). Through Noah, God will bring us relief as he sustains his promise to preserve the seed of the woman who will crush the head of the serpent.

16. The expression of Noah's favor in God's eyes constitutes an idiom meaning "to be pleased with" or "to be favorably inclined toward." Such statements are frequently followed by a request or the granting of permission or favor (see Gen. 6:8; 18:3; 19:19; 30:27; 32:5; 33:8, 10, 15; 34:11; 39:4; 47:25, 29; 50:4; Ex. 33:12–13, 16–17; 34:9; Num. 11:11, 15; 32:5; Deut. 24:1; Judg. 6:17; Ruth 2:2, 10, 13; 1 Sam. 1:18; 16:22; 20:3, 29; 25:8; 27:5; 2 Sam. 14:22; 15:25; 16:4; 1 Kings 11:19; Est. 2:15; 5:2, 8; 7:3).

and in close fellowship with him.[17] Enoch is the only other person in the Bible described as someone who walked with God (Gen. 5:22, 24), and this connection appears to be intentional. Bruce Waltke observes that as Enoch was saved from death, so Noah would be saved from the flood.[18]

The Noahic link between the second and third *toledot* sections of Genesis functions in such a way as to move the narrative of redemption forward. In Genesis 6:7, at the end of the second *toledot* section, God declared that he was planning to exterminate every living creature on the earth: "I will wipe out [or annihilate] mankind whom I have created from the face of the land, from mankind to animals, creeping things, and the birds of heaven." Now, in the third *toledot* section, God announces how he will accomplish his plan: "But as for me, behold, I am bringing the floodwaters upon the earth to destroy all flesh from under the heavens in which there is the breath of life" (Gen. 6:17). The comprehensive nature of this judgment is mitigated only by Noah, his family, and a remnant of the animal kingdom.

In Genesis 6:11–13, God describes the earth and all flesh as "corrupt" and "filled with violence," continuing to build on the themes first presented in the previous *toledot* section in 6:3 and 6:5. In response to this state of affairs, God will bring complete *corruption* on the earth through the *violence* of a great flood. The ironic nature of God's judgment is lost in translation. In Genesis 6:11–12, there are three references to the corruption of the created order employing various forms of the verbal root שחת, meaning "to be(come) corrupted, ruined, spoiled; to ruin, spoil, annihilate, exterminate."[19] This same verb is used in 6:13 and 6:17 to describe what God is going to do to the created order through the flood, though usually translated "to destroy." The point of this connection is to demonstrate that God is simply bringing the corrupt and violent condition of the world to its necessary and logical conclusion, total destruction by way of violence, owing to the pervasive nature of human sin in the day of Noah.

Were it not for the grace of God in his favoring of Noah, the world that then was would never have yielded to the world that now is. But God graciously commands Noah to build an ark with which he and his family, along with that remnant of the animal kingdom, will pass safely through the judgment of the flood.[20] The instruc-

17. See Currid, *Genesis*, 1:182–83. Noah's righteousness, in contrast to the corruption and violence of his day, is all the more impressive. The life of faith lived by Noah is recalled later by the prophet Ezekiel: "Son of man, if a country sins against me by being unfaithful and I stretch out my hand against it to cut off its food supply and send famine on it and kill its men and their animals, even if these three men—Noah, Daniel, and Job—were in it, they could save only themselves by their righteousness, declares the Sovereign LORD" (Ezek. 14:13–14; see 14:19–20; Heb. 11:7).

18. Bruce K. Waltke, *Genesis: A Commentary*, with Cathi J. Fredricks (Grand Rapids, MI: Zondervan, 2001), 133.

19. *HALOT*, 4:1470–71.

20. The word for ark (תֵּבָה) appears twenty-six times in Gen. 6–9, and then only two other times in all Scripture. It is the same term used for the basket in which Moses was placed to escape the judgment of Pharaoh (Ex. 2:3, 5). This is no coincidence. In the administration of the covenant of grace, Moses is also a covenant mediator and prophet who will lead Israel safely through the judgment waters of the Red Sea while Egypt perishes in those same waters.

tions for the building of the ark (Gen. 6:14–16) are strategically located between the decree (6:13) and its reiteration (6:17) that God has determined to destroy "all flesh" on earth. The design of the ark is intended to replicate the cosmos as understood in the ancient world.[21] The ark's three stories represent the heavens above, the earth, and the waters below. The roof represents the dome or expanse of heaven. The window symbolizes the windows of heaven that allow for rain on earth (see 7:11; 8:2). The door below represents the cosmic doors that hold back the waters of the deep (see Job 38:8–11). In the flood, God was about to open the windows of heaven and the doors of the deep to destroy the world. The ark represented a miniature version of the world, a token of the salvation that God was about to provide for Noah and his family. The design of the ark also corresponds in important ways to the wilderness tabernacle (Ex. 25–30; 35–40), the temple built by Solomon (1 Kings 6), and the new Jerusalem (Rev. 21). As such, the ark also constitutes the house of God's saving presence. With the building of the ark, the judgment of the flood, and the emergence of a new humanity, Noah and his family undergo a prophetic act of redemptive judgment that would come to serve as a paradigm for future judgment ordeals.[22] The apostle Peter makes this connection explicit: "By these waters also the world of that time was deluged and destroyed. By the same word the present heavens and earth are reserved for fire, being kept for the day of judgment and destruction of the ungodly" (2 Pet. 3:6–7 NIV).

The Covenant of Genesis 6:18

After the description of the corruption of the world (Gen. 6:11–12), the announcement of coming judgment (6:13, 17), and the command to build the ark (6:14–16), God declares that he will enter into a covenant with Noah. It is recorded in Genesis 6:18, "And I will establish my covenant with you." This is the first time that the word "covenant" (בְּרִית) appears in the Bible, and its occurrence here has occasioned significant discussion. There are two basic issues. First, how does the covenant mentioned in Genesis 6:18 relate to the covenant that God makes with Noah in 9:8–17? Are these two different covenants or one and the same? Second, is God making a new covenant with Noah in 6:18, or is he establishing or confirming with Noah a previous promise, oath, or covenant relationship?

We begin with the first question. Is the covenant recorded in Genesis 6:18 a proleptic reference, or anticipation, of the covenant made in 9:8–17, or are these two different

---

21. Meredith G. Kline, *Kingdom Prologue: Genesis Foundations for a Covenantal Worldview* (Eugene, OR: Wipf and Stock, 2006), 226–27; Kline, *God, Heaven, and Har Magedon*, 87–88; Sandra L. Richter, *The Epic of Eden: A Christian Entry into the Old Testament* (Downers Grove, IL: IVP Academic, 2008), 144–46.

22. In the judgment of the flood, the redemption of God's people advances by means of the covenant of grace. Thus, the flood is an act of *redemptive* judgment. As Jonathan Edwards observes, "God's destroying those enemies of the church by the flood belongs to this affair of redemption: for it was one thing that was done in fulfillment of the covenant of grace." *A History of the Work of Redemption* (1774; repr., Carlisle, PA: Banner of Truth, 2003), 44.

covenants?[23] One way to answer this question is to consider the nature of the covenant described in each instance. First, in 6:18–21, God makes a covenant with the individual Noah, though seven additional members of his family and a remnant of the animal kingdom will share in its benefits. The individual nature of this covenant is identified by the eight occurrences of the second-person masculine *singular* pronoun ("you") in the four verses that describe this covenant arrangement. John Calvin helpfully explains, "Now, the sum of this covenant of which Moses speaks was, that Noah should be safe, although the whole world should perish in the deluge. For there is an understood antithesis, that the whole world being rejected, *the Lord would establish a peculiar covenant with Noah alone*."[24] In the covenant of Genesis 9, the pronouns are second-person masculine *plural*, and there are nine of them ("you"). The covenant of Genesis 9 is made not just with Noah but with his sons, with their future offspring (which would include all humanity), with the animal kingdom, and with the earth itself.

Second, the covenant of Genesis 6 guarantees the survival of Noah and his family in the ark during the destruction of the world. According to 6:19, this is a covenant to preserve life during the flood. The covenant in Genesis 9, on the other hand, guarantees that a worldwide flood will never occur again (see 9:11, 15). Thus, the basic provisions of the covenants suggest that the covenant in Genesis 6 is distinct from the covenant in Genesis 9.

Third, in Genesis 8:1, God remembers (זקר) Noah and the inhabitants of the ark, and this remembering precipitates the receding of the flood waters. The account of God's remembering does not mean that he had forgotten about Noah during the flood. Rather, remembering of this type is covenantal in nature. According to Waltke, "Unlike English 'remembered,' which refers merely to mental recall and entails having forgotten, the Hebrew term, especially with reference to God, signifies to act upon a previous commitment to a covenant partner."[25] Thus, God remembers when he is about to act in light of a previous covenantal commitment. When God remembers in Genesis 8:1, he moves to bring Noah through the flood in light of the covenant identified in 6:18. When God promises to remember in 9:15 (a pledge that he will remember later), he will refrain from destroying the world once again with a flood. These differences suggest that the covenant of 6:18 is a covenant in its own right and one that is distinct from the covenant in Genesis 9.

Table 5.1 provides a brief summary of some of the more distinctive features in each of these two covenants.

---

23. Those who argue that the covenant of Gen. 6 is different from the covenant in Gen. 9 include Dempster, *Dominion and Dynasty*, 73n33; Kline, *Kingdom Prologue*, 230–34; David VanDrunen, *Divine Covenants and Moral Order: A Biblical Theology of Natural Law*, EUSLR (Grand Rapids, MI: Eerdmans, 2014), 107–14. Paul R. Williamson argues that the covenant of Gen. 6 is the same as the covenant in Gen. 9. *Sealed with an Oath: Covenant in God's Unfolding Purpose*, NSBT 23 (Downers Grove, IL: InterVarsity Press, 2007), 59–60.

24. John Calvin, *Commentaries on the First Book of Moses, Called Genesis*, trans. John King (Grand Rapids, MI: Baker, 2003), 258–59; emphasis added.

25. Waltke, *Genesis*, 141. See also Gen. 19:29; Ex. 2:24; 6:5; 32:13; Pss. 105:8; 106:45.

Table 5.1   Covenants in Genesis 6 and 9 Compared

Genesis 6 Covenant	Genesis 9 Covenant
Established with Noah	Established with all humanity, the animal kingdom, and the earth
A covenant of salvation from the judgment of the flood	A covenant of preservation until final judgment
A covenant made with Noah because of his righteousness (Gen. 7:1)	A covenant made with humanity in spite of their wickedness (Gen. 8:21)
A covenant that required Noah's obedience in the building and provisioning of the ark (Gen. 6:22; 7:5)	A covenant without any requirements to experience the blessings of common grace

Having established that the covenant of Genesis 6 is distinct from the covenant of Genesis 9, we move on to consider the second question. Is God making a new covenant with Noah in Genesis 6:18, or is he establishing and confirming a previous promise, oath, or covenantal arrangement? At first glance, this question might seem illogical. Since this is the first mention of a covenant in the Bible, then God must be making or establishing a new covenant with Noah. The question arises, however, because of the verb used in this context for the making of the covenant. By way of reminder, the text of Genesis 6:18 is translated, "And I will *establish* my covenant with you." The verb translated "establish" (קוּם in the Hiphil stem) is one of two primary Hebrew verbs employed in the context of covenant (בְּרִית) formation.[26] When a new covenant is made (e.g., Ex. 24:8), or if a covenant is renewed (e.g., Josh. 24:25), the normal construction includes the Hebrew verb "to cut" (כרת) with the noun "covenant" as its object, normally translated into English as "to make a covenant." The language of "cutting" stems from the sacrificial-oath sign that would customarily accompany the making of a new covenant (see Gen. 15:7–18).[27] When the intention, however, is to confirm a previous or existing covenant relationship, the verb employed is the very same one that appears in Genesis 6:18 (קוּם in the Hiphil stem), frequently translated "to establish," but better "to confirm."[28] A good example of this phenomenon occurs just a few chapters later

---

26. Other verbs include נתן, "to give" (e.g., Gen. 9:12; 17:2; Num. 25:12), and בוא, "to enter" (e.g., 2 Chron. 15:12; Jer. 34:10; Ezek. 16:8).

27. The "cutting" of the animals as the curse-oath sign serves as the background for the "cutting" or "making" of the covenant. To "cut" the animals is to "make" the covenant. This connection is often lost in translation given the historical and sociological distance that exists between the covenant-making world of the ancient Near East and our modern Western world, with its differing set of cultural values and customs related to the making of formal, legal relationships. Geerhardus Vos argues, "All the signs connected with redemption are bloody, sacramentally dividing signs." Vos, *Biblical Theology: Old and New Testaments* (1948; repr., Carlisle, PA: Banner of Truth, 2014), 51. This distinction, however, does not seem to apply to Sabbath observance (Ex. 31:13) or baptism, though baptism is certainly a dividing sign.

28. For a detailed study of the verbs used to describe the making of covenants, see Gentry and Wellum, *Kingdom through Covenant*, 187–95; William J. Dumbrell, *Covenant and Creation: A Theology of the Old Testament Covenants* (1984; repr., Grand Rapids, MI: Baker, 1993), 12–20. For an opposing view, see Williamson, *Sealed with an Oath*, 69–74, who argues that "Genesis 6:18 heralds the formal inauguration of the Noahic covenant that is subsequently set out in Genesis 8:20–9:17" (74).

in the book of Genesis. In Genesis 15, God entered into a new covenant relationship with Abram: "On that day, Yahweh *cut* [כרת] a covenant with Abram" (15:18). Then, in Genesis 17, God confirms his covenant with Abram by extending it to his offspring, "And I will *confirm* [קום] my covenant between me and between you and between your offspring after you throughout their generations as an everlasting covenant" (17:7; see 17:19, 21). Since the text of 6:18 employs the verb "to confirm" and not "to cut," then to what previous covenantal arrangement is it referring?

As stated earlier, the technical term for "covenant" (בְּרִית) appears for the very first time in the Bible at Genesis 6:18. We understand, however, that the word "covenant" is not always required when making a covenant. For example, we know that God made a covenant with David in 2 Samuel 7 (the Davidic covenant), but the word "covenant" does not appear in 2 Samuel 7. We know it is a covenant because of the covenantal features appearing in the narration. Additionally, the covenantal nature of 2 Samuel 7:8–17 is confirmed by the subsequent testimony of Scripture:

> I have *cut [or made] a covenant* with my chosen one,
>> I have sworn to David my servant. (Ps. 89:3[4]; see Isa. 55:3; Jer. 33:21)

And so, then, to what previous covenantal arrangement does the covenant of Genesis 6:18 refer? The best answer locates its antecedent in the redemptive judgment of Genesis 3:14–19, the historical inauguration of the covenant of grace and the institution of common grace.

Recall that the naming of Noah back in Genesis 5:29 connects him to the redemptive curse of 3:17 with the mention of the cursed ground and the subsequent pain caused by working it. The explanation of Noah's name suggests that God intends to move his plan of redemption forward through Noah, who is located genealogically in the line of Seth. Additionally, the covenant of 6:18 guarantees the survival of Noah and his offspring during the flood, when all other human life will be extinguished. This is significant in light of the promise of 3:15, that the offspring of the woman (a human) will in fact crush the serpent. With 6:18, God confirms that the covenantal arrangement of 3:15 still stands and will endure into the postflood world.[29] While common grace is temporarily suspended during the period of the flood, the covenant of grace endures through Noah and then through his offspring (see 9:18–27). As such, the use of the verb "to confirm, establish" (קום in the Hiphil stem) in 6:18 affirms God's covenant faithfulness in the context of the typological, eschatological intrusion of the flood judgment ordeal.

---

29. "There is, therefore, no good reason to deny that God's promise [i.e., in Gen. 3:15] really had the true nature of a covenant." John Owen, *Biblical Theology: The History of Theology from Adam to Christ*, trans. Stephen P. Westcott (first published in Latin in 1661; repr., Orlando, FL: Soli Deo Gloria, 1994), 207. Contra Dumbrell, who argues that "if Genesis 6:18 refers to a previous covenant, this could only have come about by God's actions within Genesis 1 and 2." *Covenant and Creation*, 9. It is vitally important to understand the covenants of Gen. 6 and 9 as administrations of the covenant of grace. Thus, their antecedents are best located in Gen. 3, not in Gen. 1 and 2.

Judgment of the Flood (Gen. 7:1–8:19)

In the building and provisioning of the ark, Noah is faithful to the terms of the covenant (Gen. 6:22; 7:5). Noah's obedience of faith preserves not only his own life but also the life of his family: "By faith Noah, being warned by God concerning events as yet unseen, in reverent fear constructed an ark for the saving of his household. By this he condemned the world and became an heir of the righteousness that comes by faith" (Heb. 11:7 ESV). Noah's evangelical obedience in these matters also marks him as a type of Christ, whose obedience to the terms of the eternal covenant of redemption secured the salvation of his people from judgment.[30] It is to this flood judgment event that we now turn our attention.

The flood event recorded in Genesis 7:1–8:19 is the central event of the third *toledot* section of Genesis, providing the redemptive-historical context for the covenants of Genesis 6 and 9. As previously indicated, the flood is presented as a redemptive judgment ordeal that comes to serve as a paradigm for future judgment events.[31] The flood itself is an act of de-creation, while its abatement is an act of re-creation. After the flood, Noah is presented as a new (second) Adam figure.

Redemptive Judgment Ordeal

The flood is a universal judgment event. This might seem obvious, but it is also unexpected. In Genesis 3:14–19, God delays the final, eschatological judgment required by the sin of Adam and institutes the principle of common grace until the covenant of grace should be fulfilled by the messianic offspring of the woman. Common grace is that principle whereby God allows the offspring of the woman (those in Christ) and the offspring of the serpent (those in Adam) to remain together in this world until final judgment, the consummation of the age, and the advent of the new heavens and new earth. During this period of delay, agriculture, culture, and procreation continue in a fallen world, though now under the curse of sin. And so there will be agriculture but now in pain and frustration, culture but corrupt and perverted, and human reproduction but only with great pain. The apocalyptic announcement of the flood as a world-destroying event prior to the arrival of the messianic offspring appears to place the promise of Genesis 3:15 in crisis.

---

30. With reference to individuals like Noah, Abraham, Phinehas, and David, Kline states, "But it pleased the Lord to invest their exemplary righteousness and outstanding acts of covenantal devotion with special significance so that with reference to a typological manifestation of God's kingdom they prefigured Christ as one who received the kingdom of glory for the faithful performance of the messianic mission stipulated in his eternal covenant with the Father." *God, Heaven, and Har Magedon*, 79. Niehaus correspondingly argues, "In other words, God is telling Noah that he and his family can be saved in the ark because God has found Noah *singularly* to be righteous. By the righteousness of one, many are saved—a salvific arrangement that clearly anticipates the saving work of Christ." *Biblical Theology*, 1:179. It is important, however, to understand that "their ability to do good works is not at all of themselves, but wholly from the Spirit of Christ. And, that they may be enabled thereunto, besides the graces they have already received, there is required an actual influence of the same Holy Spirit to work in them to will and to do of His good pleasure." WCF 16.5.

31. Kline states, "Such redemptive judgments were intrusions of the principle of final judgment into the era of common grace, prototypes of the eschatological judgment." *God, Heaven, and Har Magedon*, 87.

The flood, however, is not simply a judgment event. It is a *redemptive* judgment event. We understand that Noah "built the ark *for the salvation* of his household" (Heb. 11:7). As described above, the covenant recorded in Genesis 6:18 provides for the continuation of the 3:15 offspring in the person and subsequent offspring of Noah. The gospel of 6:18 is that God will establish and confirm the covenant of grace in Noah by causing the ark of salvation to pass safely through the waters of judgment. It is important to understand that Noah and his family are not delivered *from* judgment but *through* judgment.

Future Judgment Paradigm

The flood serves as a type or paradigm for subsequent judgment events. The water judgment ordeal of the flood becomes a pattern repeated in Israel's crossing of the Red Sea (Ex. 14:13–15:21) and the Jordan River (Josh. 3:7–17). The crossing of the Jordan is subsequently rehearsed by Elijah (2 Kings 2:8) and Elisha (2 Kings 2:14), and the water ordeal of Jonah picks up this same theme of water judgment:

> You cast me into the deep,
>   into the heart of the sea,
>   a current surrounded me,
> all of your breakers and waves
>   passed over me. (Jonah 2:3[4])[32]

In the New Testament, Peter compares the final destruction of this world by fire with the destruction of the previous world by water: "The world that then existed was deluged with water and perished. But by the same word the heavens and earth that now exist are stored up for fire, being kept until the day of judgment and destruction of the ungodly" (2 Pet. 3:6–7 ESV).[33]

Additionally, Jesus characterizes the period before the flood as emblematic of the period before the return of the Son of Man and final judgment:

> For as in those days before the flood they were eating and drinking, marrying and giving in marriage, until the day when Noah entered the ark, and they were unaware until the flood came and swept them all away, so will be the coming of the Son of Man. (Matt. 24:38–39 ESV)

Finally, and perhaps most significantly, 1 Peter 3:20–21 connects the redemptive judgment ordeal of the flood to baptism and relates them as type and antitype (ἀντίτυπος).

---

32. It appears that Jonah also understood his judgment ordeal as a redemptive event when he declared from the belly of the great fish, "Salvation belongs to Yahweh" (Jonah 2:9[10]).

33. Both fire and water are employed as agents of divine judgment (see Gen. 19:24–28; 2 Kings 1:10–16; Luke 9:54). Those united to Christ by faith, however, need never fear such judgment:

> When you pass through the waters, I will be with you,
>   and the rivers will not overflow you.
> When you pass through the fire, you will not be burned,
>   and the flame will not burn you. (Isa. 43:2)

The flood's connection with baptism informs our understanding of the baptism of Jesus. He, too, submitted to the waters of judgment, emerged as a new creation with the Spirit hovering over the waters, and received the judgment of the Father's favor. The sacrament of Christian baptism represents this same reality, and those united by faith to Christ receive the same approbation: "This is my beloved son, with him I am well pleased" (Matt. 3:17; Mark 1:11; Luke 3:22; 2 Pet. 1:17). The flood and baptism remind us that, because of sin, salvation comes *through* judgment.

De-Creation and Re-Creation

The judgment of the flood is presented as an act of de-creation and its abatement as an act of re-creation.[34] According to Genesis 7:11, the global deluge comes from two primary sources: "all the springs of the great deep and the windows of heaven." The reunion of the waters above with the waters below reverses what God did on days two and three of creation. First, the expanse (dome) separated the waters above from the waters below (1:6–7), and then the waters below were gathered together in order for dry ground to appear (1:9). The reunion of the waters of chaos destroys all flesh and vegetation, returning the earth to the primordial conditions of Genesis 1:2, when "the earth was uninhabitable and uninhabited, and darkness was over the surface of the deep." But de-creation is not the end. God remembers his covenant with Noah (8:1) and sends a wind over the earth in order to cause the waters to recede. The presence of the wind (רוּחַ) over the waters in 8:1 recalls the presence of the Spirit (רוּחַ) over the deep in 1:2, marking the advent of the (re-)creation process. Once again, dry land appears (8:5), and vegetation returns (8:11) to a postdiluvian world. The process of de-creation and re-creation in Genesis 8 and 9 is artistically portrayed in the presentation of the numbers that appear in the account.[35]

> 7 days of waiting for flood (7:4)
> > 7 days of waiting for flood (7:10)
> > > 40 days of flood (7:17)
> > > > 150 days of water triumphing (7:24)
> > > > 150 days of water waning (8:3)
> > > 40 days of waiting (8:6)
> > 7 days of waiting (8:10)
> 7 days of waiting (8:12)

---

34. Richter's description is helpful: "What we see in the flood is not merely a natural disaster intended to bring about God's judgment on humanity, but a *de-creational* event. What had been done at creation is undone with the flood. The world is brought back to its pre-creation state—'formless and void." *Epic of Eden*, 144. See also Dempster, *Dominion and Dynasty*, 72–73. Additionally, "We observe, then, that one way of reading Genesis 1–9 is along the lines of creation–uncreation–re-creation." Tremper Longman III and John H. Walton, *The Lost World of the Flood: Mythology, Theology, and the Deluge Debate* (Downers Grove, IL: InterVarsity Press, 2018), 103.

35. This presentation of the numbers from Gen. 7 and 8 comes from Gordon J. Wenham, *Genesis 1–15*, WBC 1 (Waco, TX: Word Books, 1987), 157. For a discussion of the structure of the complete third *toledot* section of Genesis, see 155–58.

After the flood, the world that then was gives way to the world that now is, and God moves to reestablish humanity as his image bearers and stewards of the new world. In this final section, God patterns the postdiluvian world after the prediluvian world, with Noah serving as a second Adam figure.[36]

The World That Now Is (Gen. 8:20–9:29)

When the old world emerged from the waters of the chaotic deep, God shaped and governed that world by his word and then through those made in his image. And so, as this new world emerges from the waters of the flood, God again shapes and governs it through his word and those made in his image. As the third *toledot* section of Genesis comes to an end, God restores the principle of common grace (8:20–22), renews the cultural (dominion) mandate (9:1–7), and confirms his covenant with creation (9:8–17). Finally, we discover that the offspring of the serpent is alive and well in this postdiluvian world (9:18–27).

The Restoration of Common Grace

After exiting the ark, Noah builds an altar and offers up whole burnt offerings to God. The scent of these offerings brings to rest the wrath of God's judgment and moves God to restore the principle of common grace suspended in the flood judgment ordeal.[37] The principle of common grace is first established after the fall of Adam in the context of the redemptive judgments of Genesis 3:14–19.[38] Common grace secures a period of delay from final, eschatological judgment where both the elect (offspring of the woman) and nonelect (offspring of the serpent) coexist in the stability of the natural world order, though now groaning under the weight of sin (Rom. 8:19–22), until the arrival of the new heavens and new earth and the permanent theocratic kingdom of God. Waltke helpfully explains,

> God's providential preservation of all life throughout the span of human life until the final eschaton is known as God's "common grace"—the Creator's indiscriminate goodwill by which "He causes his sun to rise on the evil and the good, and sends rain on the righteous and the unrighteous" (Matt. 5:45).[39]

---

36. For a good summary of Noah as a second Adam figure, see J. V. Fesko, *Last Things First: Unlocking Genesis 1–3 with the Christ of Eschatology*, rev. ed. (Fearn, Ross-shire, Scotland: Mentor, 2007), 115–19; Warren Austin Gage, *The Gospel of Genesis: Studies in Protology and Eschatology* (Eugene, OR: Wipf and Stock, 2001), 11, 16 (helpful summary chart); Gentry and Wellum, *Kingdom through Covenant*, 197–98; Waltke, *Old Testament Theology*, 296. For a discussion of Noah as a type of Christ, see Niehaus, *Biblical Theology*, 1:178–79.

37. The word for the scent of the sacrifice is נִיחֹחַ. It is derived from the root נוּחַ, the same root from which Noah's name is derived. Though often translated as "soothing" or "pleasing," the connotation of rest or restfulness should not be neglected. "The odor of the burning sacrifice is not pleasing in a sensuous way, but it is restful. Because a sacrifice is offered in faith, God's anger is put to rest." John N. Oswalt, "נוּחַ," in *NIDOTTE*, 3:58.

38. Michael Horton states, "After the fall, God might have legitimately disowned his creation but for the eternal and unconditional agreement of the Trinity for the redemption of a people. Both to call out this new people he has chosen and to care even for the rest of humanity hostile to his purposes, God has unconditionally pledged his common grace to all of creation." *God of Promise: Introducing Covenant Theology* (Grand Rapids, MI: Baker, 2006), 113.

39. Waltke, *Old Testament Theology*, 291.

The terms for the restoration of common grace appear in Genesis 8:21: (1) God will never again fully curse the ground, and (2) God will never again destroy (strike down) every living thing. This word of promise secures the current world order in spite of the fact that the judgment of the flood did not eradicate sin or the evil nature of humanity, "for the design of the heart of mankind is evil from its youth" (Gen. 8:21). The maintenance of the natural world order is characterized in Genesis 8:22: "While the earth remains, seedtime and harvest, cold and heat, summer and winter, day and night, shall not cease" (ESV).[40] The introductory temporal modifier, "While the earth remains" (ESV) or "As long as the earth endures" (NIV), is better translated "For the duration of all the days of the earth." The explicit rendering of the word for "day" (יוֹם) better captures the temporary nature of this current world order. We are instructed to number our own days (Job 14:5; Pss. 39:4[5]; 90:12), and so too the days of this earth are numbered.

The Renewal of Creation Sanctions

After restoring the principle of common grace in the postdiluvian world, God also renews the sanctions of creation in Genesis 9:1–7, marked off by the repeated command to be fruitful, increase, and fill the earth (9:1, 7). These sanctions are often described as the cultural or dominion mandate, and they find their antecedents in Genesis 1 and 2. The postdiluvian world replicates the prediluvian world in many important ways. Table 5.2 lists those features identified in Scripture as common to the world before and after the flood.[41]

Table 5.2 Similarities of Preflood and Postflood World

Genesis 1–2 Inauguration	Genesis 9 Restoration
God blesses humanity (1:28)	God blesses humanity (9:1)
Command to increase and fill the earth (1:28)	Command to increase and fill the earth (9:1, 7)
Dominion over the animal kingdom (1:26, 28)	Dominion over the animal kingdom (9:2)
Provision for food: vegetation (1:29–30; 2:16)	Provision for food: meat (9:3)
Restriction from food: tree of the knowledge of good and evil (2:17)	Restriction from food: blood (9:4)
Humanity created in the image of God (1:26–27)	Humanity created in the image of God (9:6)

Given the extensive correspondence between the world of Genesis 1–2 and the world of Genesis 9, it becomes important to consider several significant differences that exist

---

40. God's covenantal relationship with nature is picked up in Jer. 33:25–26: "Thus says the LORD: If I have not established my covenant with day and night and the fixed order of heaven and earth, then I will reject the offspring of Jacob and David my servant and will not choose one of his offspring to rule over the offspring of Abraham, Isaac, and Jacob. For I will restore their fortunes and will have mercy on them" (ESV).

41. For a corresponding summary chart, see Gentry and Wellum, *Kingdom through Covenant*, 201.

in the postfall, postflood world. These differences are due to the fact that the Noahic covenant in Genesis 9 "was designed for a fallen world rather than a sinless world."[42] First, humanity's dominion over the animal kingdom is now characterized as a dominion of fear and dread (9:2), unlike the eschatological ideal that will characterize the new heavens and new earth (Isa. 11:6; 65:25). In Genesis 1 and 2, the command to rule over the animal kingdom (1:28) was expressed by the naming of the animals presented by God (2:19–20).

Second, the provision for food in the garden consisted of all seed-bearing fruits and vegetables. Now, however, the provision for food also includes animal flesh without any distinction between clean and unclean animals. The distinction between clean and unclean while on the ark (and in the Mosaic economy) was in force because of its theocratic nature. With the reestablishment of common grace and the absence of theocracy, the distinction between clean and unclean is eliminated. In addition to the provision of food, there is also the corresponding restriction from consuming blood: "However, you may not eat meat with its life, that is, its blood" (Gen. 9:4). The reason for this restriction is difficult to determine from the context. The blood of the animal is characterized as the life (נֶפֶשׁ) of the animal, and this same issue of lifeblood is connected to the subsequent sanction of capital punishment. The full significance of this restriction is perhaps made clear to us in later parts of Scripture. We understand that blood and the spilling of blood can be covenantal in nature (Ex. 24:8), can represent the cost for the forgiveness of sin (Ex. 30:10), and was a central component of the sacrificial legislation in the Mosaic covenant as detailed in the book of Leviticus. Ultimately, however, this restriction finds its true meaning in the antithetical, symbolic requirement to drink the blood of Jesus: "Then Jesus said to them, 'Unless you eat the flesh of the Son of Man *and you drink his blood*, you do not have life in you'" (John 6:53; see also Matt. 26:28; Mark 14:24; Luke 22:20; John 6:54–56; 1 Cor. 11:25; Heb. 12:24; 13:20). Some argue that the prohibition of consuming blood has fallen away in the period of the new covenant with the obsolescence of the Mosaic sacrificial system and the removal of the earthly altar.[43] Given, however, the enduring common-grace context of the inaugurated (not consummated) new covenant order and the postresurrection instructions of the Jerusalem Council (Acts 15:20, 29), it appears that this prohibition remains in force.

The final difference between the world of common grace before and after the flood is the sanction of capital punishment appearing in Genesis 9:5–6. Here God authorizes humanity in the form of the state to restrain evil and protect human life from both animal and human violence: "Whoever pours out the blood of mankind, by mankind

---

42. VanDrunen, *Divine Covenants*, 100.

43. Jeong Koo Kim, *Biblical Theology: Covenants and the Kingdom of God in Redemptive History* (Eugene, OR: Wipf and Stock, 2017), 52–54; Kline, *Kingdom Prologue*, 256–62. Even though, however, the so-called earthly altar no longer exists and the sacrificial system of the Mosaic covenant has been done away with, the reality of those previous shadows remains in the institution of the Lord's Supper: "This cup is the new covenant in my blood. Do this as often as you drink in my remembrance" (1 Cor. 11:25).

his blood will be poured out" (9:6). In the period of common grace prior to the flood, this authority appears to have resided with God alone (4:15), but it was subsequently taken and perverted by the line of Cain in Lamech (4:23–24). This sanction is now to be administered by the state in order to restrain evil during the period of common grace. The postfall preservation of the image of God in humanity provides the reason for the sanction of capital punishment (9:6). Some have understood that the image of God in humanity is what makes murder an offense requiring the penalty of death. In other words, the destruction of the image constitutes an attack on the source of that image. For others, however, the possession of the image of God authorizes humanity to exercise this sanction. This is the royal-judicial aspect of creation in the image of God. In this case, it is perhaps best not to prefer one interpretation over the other but to maintain both without contradiction. The unlawful destruction of human life constitutes an attack on the image of God, *and* that same image invests humanity with the judicial authority to uphold the sanction of capital punishment instituted by God in the current era of common grace.[44]

The Confirmation of the Covenant of Common Grace

With the restoration of common grace (Gen. 8:20–22) and the sanctions that will sustain the created order during this final period of delay (9:1–7), God now confirms his providential preservation of nature and life (9:8–17).[45] This is the second covenantal arrangement identified with Noah. The first one appeared in Genesis 6:11–22 and conferred salvation from the judgment of the flood. That covenant was individual in nature, made with Noah alone, and sustained the covenantal arrangement of 3:15, the promise of the messianic offspring. That covenant also required the obedience of Noah in the building of the ark in order to obtain the salvation offered in that covenant. The covenant of common grace, on the other hand, is universal in nature and does not require obedience to experience its benefits. In fact, the covenant of common grace exists because of human disobedience. It is a covenant of preservation until final judgment.[46] It is not a covenant that provides salvation from that judgment.[47] The exposition of the

---

44. For further study of the capital punishment sanction, see VanDrunen, *Divine Covenants*, 115–32; O. Palmer Robertson, *The Christ of the Covenants* (Phillipsburg, NJ: Presbyterian and Reformed, 1980), 117–21.

45. This passage of Scripture consists of three speeches, each of which begins with "And God said" (Gen. 9:8, 12, 17). The first speech identifies the covenant members and the covenant promise. The second speech describes the covenant sign. The third speech consists of a brief summary statement rehearsing the covenant sign and the covenant members. These ten verses are dense with covenantal language. The word for covenant (בְּרִית) appears seven times. Three times it is stated that the Lord is establishing or confirming (קוּם in the Hiphil stem) his covenant. Three times it explicitly refers to the sign (אוֹת) of the covenant, and twice it mentions the promise to remember (זכר) the covenant.

46. Robertson helpfully employs the language of "preservation": "The covenant with Noah primarily may be characterized as a covenant of preservation. . . . By this decree, God binds himself to preserve the earth in its present world-order until the time of the consummation." *Christ of the Covenants*, 114.

47. VanDrunen states,

The Noahic covenant promises only the preservation of the earth from a flood and the maintenance of the ordinary cycles of nature. It presumes the presence of sin and evil in the human, animal, and cosmic orders

covenant includes the identification of the covenant members (9:9–10), the covenant promises (9:11), and the covenant sign (9:12–17).

Just like Genesis 6:18, the verb used for the making of this covenant is "to establish, confirm" (קוּם in the Hiphil stem; 9:9, 11, 17), not "to make, cut" (כרת). As stated earlier, the verb "to make, cut" is used when making a new covenant, but the verb "to establish, confirm" is used to confirm a previous or existing covenantal relationship. Because the principle of common grace is a postfall reality, the covenant reestablished here must be a postfall covenant. Once again, we find the covenantal antecedent in the redemptive judgment of 3:14–19.[48] With the historical inauguration of the covenant of grace, God instituted a delay before final judgment, during which both the elect and nonelect were sustained by the natural order of the original creation.[49] This principle of common grace was suspended in the judgment of the flood, when both the nonelect and the old world perished in its waters. With the emergence of the new world and the preservation of the promise of the messianic offspring sustained in the Genesis 6 covenant with Noah, God now reinstitutes the principle of common grace and unilaterally binds himself in this covenant to preserve the natural world in the midst of human sin until the final, eschatological judgment, of which the judgment of the flood now serves as a type.

In Genesis 6, the members of the covenant consisted of God and Noah. The individual nature of that covenant was initially substantiated by the eight occurrences of the second-person masculine singular pronoun ("you") in the four verses that described that covenantal arrangement. Here in Genesis 9, however, the members identified in the text include God, all current and future humanity, the entire animal kingdom, and the earth itself. The universal nature of this covenant is vigorously highlighted by the sixfold repetition of the covenant members (9:9–10, 12, 13, 15, 16, 17) and the nine plural pronouns ("you") used with reference to those members.

The promise of the covenant is twofold and appears in Genesis 9:11: "All flesh will not be cut off again by the waters of the flood, and there will not again be a flood to destroy the earth." With this covenant, God promises to not engage in total, global judgment, and so living things and the earth will continue until the consummation of

---

and pledges to manage and constrain evil but not to expunge it. The later biblical covenant promises look forward to a time in which sin and evil are entirely banished from all orders of creation. The promise of preservation *in the midst of* evil is not the same as the promise of salvation *from* evil.
Divine Covenants, 112.

48. Contra Niehaus, who argues that the antecedent to this covenantal arrangement is the "Adamic or Creation covenant." *Biblical Theology*, 1:192; see also 198–99. He further states, "The Noahic covenant, moreover, is actually a renewal of the Adamic covenant, as we have noted, and the two covenants together form one legal package" (211). This argument cannot be sustained given that the Adamic-creation covenant is a covenant of works. The Noahic covenant confirms the covenantal principle of common grace instituted in Gen. 3:14–19. It is a postfall principle that accounts for sin and the breaking of the Adamic-creation covenant.

49. Edwards likewise argues that "the manner of expression, 'I will establish my covenant with you, and with your seed after you,' shows plainly that it was a covenant already in being, that had been made already, and that Noah would understand what the covenant it was [*sic*] by that denomination, namely, the covenant of grace." *History of the Work of Redemption*, 49.

all things.[50] The durative nature of this covenant is marked by the designations "for ever-lasting generations" (לְדֹרֹת עוֹלָם) in 9:12 and "an everlasting covenant" (בְּרִית עוֹלָם) in 9:16.[51] As such, this common-grace covenant remains in force during this current, inau-gurated (not consummated) new covenant era. Only with the advent of the antitypical, eschatological judgment by fire will this arrangement come to its intended conclusion (Gen. 8:22; 2 Pet. 3:5–7). Geerhardus Vos states, "The promise to Noah has its limit in the eschatological crisis, which shall bring the earth to an end."[52]

The vast majority of the exposition of the covenant of common grace in Genesis 9 concerns the sign of the covenant in 9:11–17.[53] It is well known that covenants fre-quently contain corresponding covenant signs. Examples include circumcision with the Abrahamic covenant (17:10–14), Sabbath observance with the Mosaic covenant (Ex. 31:13, 17), and the Lord's Supper with the new covenant (1 Cor. 11:23–26). One of the functions of a covenant sign is to provoke the remembering of the covenant and, there-fore, faithfulness to the promises and regulations of that covenant. This reality is clearly expressed in the words of institution for the Lord's Supper, "Do this *in remembrance of me*" (1 Cor. 11:24). This same reality obtains with the sign of the rainbow designated by God for the covenant of common grace. When God sees the rainbow in the sky, he will remember his covenant and so not break forth in judgment (Gen. 9:15–16). This sign is not reserved for the elect alone but appears in nature as a testimony to God's grace and patience for all creation to observe (see Rom. 1:20).

The significance of the sign of the rainbow is not included in its designation. Usu-ally, a covenant sign has some symbolic relationship to the covenant it signifies. For example, circumcision reminded God's people that they would be cut off if they broke the covenant (Gen. 17:14), and the Lord's Supper symbolizes the death of Jesus and the proclamation of that death until he returns (1 Cor. 11:26). Unfortunately, the emblematic value of the rainbow as the sign for this covenant is not expressly stated here or anywhere else in Scripture. Some have suggested that the rainbow is a symbol of the bow of a warrior.[54] This interpretation stems from the fact that the Hebrew word for rainbow is the same word used for the bow of a warrior (קֶשֶׁת). For this reason, the

---

50. The fact that local floods with corresponding tragic fatalities continue to occur in this current world order is one argument in favor of a global-flood account in Gen. 6–9. If the flood of Genesis was local in nature, then this covenant and the threat of judgment it restrains would be void of any significant meaning. How could something that never took place not take place again?

51. The designation "everlasting covenant" (בְּרִית עוֹלָם) is applied to the Noahic, Abrahamic, Mosaic (Sab-bath), Davidic, and new covenants in the Old Testament (Gen. 9:16; 17:7, 13, 19; Ex. 31:16; Lev. 24:8; 2 Sam. 23:5; 1 Chron. 16:17; Ps. 105:10; Isa. 24:5; 55:3; 61:8; Jer. 32:40; 50:5; Ezek. 16:60; 37:26). For further discus-sion of the meaning of this designation, see Niehaus, *Biblical Theology*, 1:210–13.

52. Vos, *Biblical Theology*, 55.

53. This section is framed by the inclusio "This is the sign of the covenant" (זֹאת אוֹת־הַבְּרִית).

54. Currid, *Genesis*, 1:221; Gage, *Gospel of Genesis*, 135; Gentry and Wellum, *Kingdom through Covenant*, 203–4; Kline, *Kingdom Prologue*, 247–48; Waltke, *Genesis*, 146; Nahum M. Sarna, *Genesis* בראשית, JPS Torah Commentary (Philadelphia: Jewish Publication Society, 1989), 62–63. Some have further suggested that the direction in which the rainbow faces, up toward heaven, indicates a self-maledictory oath taken up by God in the making of this covenant. Though not unprecedented (see Gen. 15:9–18), it is difficult to substantiate in this case.

rainbow may represent the bow (weapon) of God and that it has been placed at rest in the clouds as a symbol of God's rest from judgment (see Deut. 32:23, 42; Pss. 7:12[13]; 18:14[15]; Hab. 3:9). It is also worth noting that the rainbow is a feature associated with the throne of God and the divine presence: "Like the appearance of the [rain]bow in the clouds on the day of rain, so is the appearance of the brightness around him" (Ezek. 1:28). This theme is picked up in the book of Revelation, where the clouds and the rainbow attend the divine presence: "And I saw another strong angel coming down from heaven clothed with a cloud and the rainbow was around his head" (Rev. 10:1; see 4:3). Perhaps the rainbow represents God's royal presence as the one who rules this world and sustains the covenant of common grace.[55] We know that

> Yahweh sits enthroned over the flood,
> Yahweh sits enthroned as king forever. (Ps. 29:10)

The Offspring of the Serpent Survives

Coming to the end of this section of Scripture, we arrive back where we started. The closing of the second *toledot* section in Genesis 6:1–8 closely parallels the closing of the third *toledot* section here in Genesis 9:18–29. First, in 6:1, mankind *begins* to increase in the *land*, and daughters are *born* to them. In 9:18–22, Noah *begins* to farm the *land*, and sons are *born* to him. Second, in 6:2, the sons of God *see* the daughters of man and engage in illicit sexual activity. In 9:22, Ham *sees* the nakedness of his father and also engages in illicit sexual activity. Finally, both events follow with a curse and a blessing that shapes the progression of redemptive history (6:7–8; 9:25–27).

The interpretation of Ham's sin is disputed. The account is cryptic at best. The text only records that "Ham, the father of Canaan, saw the nakedness of his father, and he told his two brothers who were outside" (9:22). The exact nature of Ham's sin has been variously interpreted as voyeurism, castration, paternal incest, and maternal incest. The key to interpretation is the identification of the "nakedness of his father." In Leviticus 18, we find a group of laws related to sexual relationships. Many of those laws describe sinful sexual activity with a relative characterized as the uncovering of nakedness (18:6–18). In Leviticus 18:7 it is recorded, "You shall not uncover the nakedness of your father, which is the nakedness of your mother; she is your mother, you shall not uncover her nakedness" (ESV). From this law we understand that "the nakedness of the father" (which is the nakedness of the mother) is a euphemism for maternal incest.[56] This interpretation

---

55. According to Vos, the appearance of the rainbow against the backdrop of storm clouds is significant because "it is produced against the background of the very clouds that had brought destruction to the earth. But it is produced upon these by rays of the sun which in the symbolism of Scripture represent the divine grace." *Biblical Theology*, 55.

56. For an excellent study of the interpretation of Ham's sin and the curse of Canaan, see John Sietze Bergsma and Scott Walker Hahn, "Noah's Nakedness and the Curse on Canaan (Genesis 9:20–27)," *JBL* 124, no. 1 (2005): 25–40. The interpretation of the sin of Ham is important, but the particular view adopted does not significantly

would also suggest that Canaan was the result of the illicit encounter and explains why Canaan was cursed by Noah.[57]

The sin of Ham (Gen. 9:22) and the cursing of Canaan (9:25) make it clear that the offspring of the serpent also survived the flood judgment ordeal. The enmity of 3:15 will continue with the corresponding blessing of Shem and Japheth (9:26–27). The blessing of Shem consists of Yahweh's identification with him as "the God of Shem." The promise of the offspring of the woman in Genesis 3:15 was preserved in the covenant with Noah identified in 6:18, and it will now continue on through the line of Shem. Japheth will also share in the blessing of Shem as he comes to dwell in the tents of Shem.[58] The threefold reference to the subjugation of Canaan as the "lowest of slaves" anticipates not only Israel's future conquering of the Canaanites as they possess the land of promise but also the ultimate destruction of the serpent and his offspring.

Summary and Conclusions

In our consideration of the Noahic covenant in Genesis 6–9, we discovered that the covenant of 9:8–17 was not the only covenantal arrangement associated with Noah. Before the covenant of common grace in Genesis 9, we encountered a covenant of saving grace in Genesis 6. The covenant identified in 6:18 conferred salvation on Noah through the judgment of the flood. This covenant was individual in nature and sustained the covenantal arrangement of 3:15, the promise of the messianic offspring. This covenant also required the obedience of Noah in the building of the ark in order to obtain the salvation offered.[59] As such, the covenant recorded in Genesis 6 was an individual, bilateral, redemptive administration of the covenant of grace fulfilled in the preservation of Noah, his family, and a remnant of the animal kingdom in the ark.

---

affect the function of Gen. 9:18–27 in its larger narrative context. Both the offspring of the woman and the offspring of the serpent, together with their continuing enmity, have survived the flood.

57. Currid is correct to title this section "The Sin of Ham." *Genesis*, 1:224. Commentators often misrepresent Noah's actions as sinful and reminiscent of the fall of Adam. The text is clear, however, that Ham is the one who sinned and that Noah is the one who was sinned against (see Ezek. 14:14, 20; Heb. 11:7; 2 Pet. 2:5). This tragic event is similar to the account of Lot and his daughters in Gen. 19:30–38 (see 2 Pet. 2:7). From these incestuous relationships came the Canaanites, Moabites, and Ammonites, three of Israel's future enemies. For further study, see Walter E. Brown, "Noah: Saint or Sot? Genesis 9:20–27," in *The Way of Wisdom: Essays in Honor of Bruce K. Waltke*, ed. J. I. Packer and Sven K. Soderlund (Grand Rapids, MI: Zondervan, 2000), 36–60. For a brief, helpful critique of some of Brown's arguments, see Waltke, *Genesis*, 148.

58. The blessing of Japheth is that God would increase (יַפְתְּ) Japheth (יֶפֶת) and that he would dwell in the tents of Shem. The one who dwells in the tents of Shem could be either God or Japheth. The ambiguity of the poetic line allows for both interpretations, and perhaps both are intended. In other words, it is not a case of either-or but rather both-and. Thus, the blessing of Shem is that God would come to dwell in his midst and that a way would be made for Japheth to share in this blessing. Therefore, I am in agreement with Herman Witsius when he states, "But indeed, seeing both these things, the habitation of God by Christ in the tents of Shem, and the habitation of Japheth in the same tents, have been joined not only in time, but also the latter in a consequent and effect of the former, that is no reason that we may not affirm that both are included in the latitude of the words." *The Economy of the Covenants between God and Man: A Complete Body of Divinity*, trans. William Crookshank (1882; repr., den Dulk Christian Foundation, 1990), 2:139–40.

59. Waltke's summary is helpful: "God's *conditional covenant* with Noah at the beginning of the narrative preserves Noah and the earth during the flood, and God's *unconditional covenant* with Noah after the flood guarantees that the earth will endure until the end of the world." *Old Testament Theology*, 284–85; emphasis added.

The Noahic covenant recorded in Genesis 9, however, is a universal, unilateral,[60] nonredemptive administration of the covenant of grace restoring and securing the principle of common grace suspended during the judgment ordeal of the flood. This covenant of common grace ensures a delay of God's final, eschatological judgment until the covenant of grace is fully accomplished. During this current era of common grace, both the elect and nonelect together enjoy the stability of the natural world order. The covenant of common grace does not require obedience to experience its benefits. Rather, it exists because of human disobedience and "provides the foundation for the world-wide proclamation of the gospel in the present age."[61]

---

60. Contra Williamson, who maintains that the sanctions of the covenant in Gen. 9:1–7 constitute "bilateral obligations." *Sealed with an Oath*, 63–64. Covenantal sanctions, however, are not unique to bilateral covenants, as the Abrahamic and Davidic covenants clearly demonstrate. Additionally, the covenant of Gen. 9 includes the animal kingdom and the earth as covenant members. Certainly, these covenant members are not required to uphold the sanctions of 9:1–7. VanDrunen states, "The best way to describe the covenant, then, is a unilateral covenant with regulations." *Divine Covenants*, 115. Dumbrell, on the other hand, argues that all covenants are "unilateral by divine imposition, as they must be since they are, in effect, divine pledges for the course of the human future to fulfill the basic covenant with creation." *Covenant and Creation*, 10.

61. Robertson, *Christ of the Covenants*, 122; see Isa. 54:9–10; Jer. 33:19–26.

6

THE ABRAHAMIC COVENANT

John Scott Redd

Against the backdrop of repeated unmet expectations in Genesis 1–11, the story of Abram/Abraham presents a vivid moment of respite and a glimmer of hope for the plan of redemption. The dream of the original divine intent to rid the world of its chaos and void and to fill it with the order-inducing dominion of divine images seems distant and lost after the accounts of the fall of humanity, Cain and Abel, the violence of Lamech, global exploitation and oppression by the powerful, the flood of judgment, and the recidivist builders of Babel. The story has been one of failed hopes: creation and fall, childbirth and murder, personal deliverance and global rebellion. But in the person of Abram, the Lord initiates a plan for humanity and the world that includes true blessing for an individual, his offspring, and the world.

The reader of Genesis 1–11 is already "in the know" about the Creator-God who has established covenants with humanity. In the curse of Genesis 3, the Lord does not rescind his judgment that creation is "good" (1:10, 12, 18, 21, 25, 31), though he does speak of the conflict that will mark the events of world history, the enmity between the offspring of the woman and the offspring of the serpent (3:15). The narrative that follows traces this conflict through multiple generations of characters; Abel, Enoch, and Noah all show themselves to be faithfully aligned with the woman's offspring, but the work of redemption has been limited to individual instances of protection and deliverance from divine judgment. In the Abrahamic covenant, however, the redemptive program shifts to one of positive benefit—that is, blessing—both for the people of God and for the whole world. In T. Desmond Alexander's view, these key themes show that "the Abraham story forms the heart of the book of

Genesis."[1] Up to this point, salvation has been primarily individual, protective, and occasional, whereas in Abraham, salvation is expanded to become global, beatific, and progressive.

The Unity of the Abrahamic Administration

Redemptive history is structured by a series of covenants initiated by God during progressive epochs, each of which represent a singular phase that includes the covenant's constituent parts, historical foundation, stipulations, blessings and curses, ratification, and so forth. Out of each epoch the covenant emerges to feed the flow of redemption toward fulfillment. Both in its founding and in its application in human history, a covenant is divinely ordained and initiated as part of a larger discourse that includes divine revelation and activity and human beliefs and behaviors. The beliefs and behaviors of the eponymous covenant representative, or "federal head" (Adam, Noah, Abraham [with Isaac and Jacob], Moses, David, Jesus Christ), are of particular importance to the manner in which a covenant is initiated by God.

The Noahic covenant is singular and complete even though it is administered at different points and with different emphases before and after the flood (including a statement of Noah's faithfulness and promises of deliverance and stipulations before the flood, Gen. 6:9–22; covenant promises after the flood, 8:20–22; and formal covenant stipulations and promises after the flood, 9:1–17). Furthermore, the Mosaic covenant is delivered at Sinai (Ex. 19–24) and again renewed and updated on the plains of Moab (Deuteronomy). After the intervening generational experience of the wilderness wandering and the impending conquest of the land, the restatement of the covenant in Deuteronomy seems to be more of a recommitment to the covenant. Moses goes as far as to say that the Sinaitic covenant was not for the previous generation but rather looked forward to the Deuteronomic generation ("Not with our fathers did the Lord make this covenant, but with us, who are all of us here alive today," Deut. 5:3). The latter audience's appropriation of the Sinaitic covenant reminds us that covenants are not for nominal adherents but for the faithful covenant head and his offspring. There are not two covenants with Moses but one, administered during its epochal phase in history and developed, amended, and updated over time.

The administration of each redemptive covenant is based on divine ordination and initiation in light of saving faith. While saving faith alone is instrumental in human salvation throughout redemptive history, however, true faith and the faithfulness that flows organically from it are not always clearly distinguished. Faithfulness is the necessary outflow of true faith (Jer. 17:9–10; James 2:17). Noah is described as blameless (Gen. 6:9). Abraham responds to God's call (Gen. 12:1–4; 15:6). David's heart draws

---

1. T. Desmond Alexander, *From Paradise to Promised Land: An Introduction to the Pentateuch* (Grand Rapids, MI: Baker, 1998), 48.

the Lord's attention (1 Sam. 16:7). Moses is called by God to lead the exodus because of the people's outcry in Egypt (Ex. 3:7), but through an apparent infraction of the circumcision mandate, Moses falls under divine judgment that almost costs him his life (Ex. 4:24–26). Even the promise of the new covenant is predicated on the corporate repentance of the people in exile (e.g., Deut. 30:1–2; Jer. 29:13). An attempt to bring about this repentance can be found in Daniel 9:1–19, and this historical call also appears to be why John's baptism is one of repentance. In some cases, the faith of the human party is foregrounded, and in others, the behaviors that spring from faith, which are the evidence of true faith, are in the foreground, but faith always has the priority. In the well-known biblical agrarian metaphor, the tree planted by streams of water can bear fruit in the drought because of the water around the roots, but the water, not the fruit, gives life (Ps. 1; Jer. 17:7–10; Ezek. 47:12).

The interplay between divine ordination and initiation in redemptive covenants is on display in the Abrahamic covenant, which itself is anticipated, inaugurated, amended, and confirmed over the course of the narrative of Genesis 12:1–25:11. In Genesis 12:1–3, Abram learns the three constituent promises of the Abrahamic covenant: a land, a nation, and, as a result of these, global blessing. In Genesis 15, the covenant is ratified with special focus on the immediate concerns of land and an offspring, as well as timing for the possession of the land. In Genesis 17, God's promise of an offspring is confirmed, as is the timing of the possession of the land and the resultant global blessing. This passage also includes helpful corrective to the previous emphasis on God's unilateral participation in the covenant, indicated by the theophany passing through the viscera alone (15:17).

It should be noted that the covenant-ratification ceremony in Genesis 15 is predicated on Abram's faith in the Lord's promises (15:6), and yet the faithfulness of Abram to the covenant is reiterated and foregrounded in Genesis 17 with the introduction of the covenant sacrament of circumcision (17:1, 9–11). This amendment to the previous covenant arrangement comes after Abraham's failure of faith with Hagar in Genesis 16, and it serves to remind him that the Abrahamic covenant is not universal but contingent on the faith of the human participants, just as it was for Abraham himself.

Finally, Abraham's faith in God is confirmed in the test he undergoes in Genesis 22. In this account, Abraham succeeds where he initially failed with Ishmael and shows that he trusts the Lord with the life of his covenant offspring Isaac. Once Abraham's faithfulness is confirmed, the Lord in turn confirms his promises of a nation and people that will bless the world (22:17–18). While the language of "the mount of the LORD" (22:14) and "possess[ing] the gate of his enemies" (22:17) does remind the reader of the promise of a land for the offspring to inhabit, the primary focus of the passage is the promised offspring Isaac.

In the Abraham narrative, the patriarch covenant is developed over the course of four major beats: covenant introduction (Gen. 12), covenant ratification (Gen. 15), covenant amendment (Gen. 17), and covenant confirmation (Gen. 22). By under-standing these discrete beats and their relationship to each other, we can develop a better understanding of the Abrahamic covenant's individual elements, how the cove-nant is received by its later biblical interpreters, as well as its meaning in the context of the gospel of Jesus Christ.

Covenant Introduction (Gen. 12:1–9)

A series of genealogical accounts (תּוֹלְדֹת, or *toledot*) form the basic backbone of the book of Genesis, and it is in the account of Terah (Gen. 11:27–32) that Abram is introduced to the reader.[2] The account slows slightly to describe the situation of Abram and his wife, Sarai, that she is childless and that together they set out for Canaan from their hometown of Ur. This short introduction is a break from the convention in the previous accounts. The break hints at the unique place of Terah's son, but it does not indicate the grand shift in the redemptive-historical narrative that will unfold in the story of his life.

Bruce Waltke argues that Abram is the culmination of the postdiluvian re-creation in primeval history (6:9–11:32), just as Noah is the culminating figure of the period that begins with antediluvian creation in primeval history (1:1–6:8).[3] Noah is the tenth from Adam, and Abram is the tenth from Noah.[4] Both emerge as faithful representatives of the righteous seed of the woman (3:15).[5] The story now takes a dramatic turn, as the cosmic stability promised to Noah now becomes the theater in which God's redemp-tive purposes are to be worked out through the descendants of the elect Abram and the land they will inhabit. In the divine calling of Genesis 12:1, Abram moves from a brief mention in a genealogy to an individual character.[6] Waltke argues, "The election and call of Abraham begins a new divine initiative, the forming of a new nation to bless the nations. A nation, however, entails the new motif of land. The holy nation needs sanctified space and sustenance."[7] Both of these elements are present in the initial cove-nant promises of chapter 12. The new relationship between God and Abram involved the creation of a new family, marked by the divine call to go out from his father's house (12:1). This new family line will become the nexus of the divine blessing in the world, not only for Abram's descendants but for all who bless them in the world (12:3). The global scope of this blessing echoes the creation mandate to "fill the earth" (1:28; 9:1). It will become more explicit in later covenant reiterations, but here the global implica-

---

2. Bruce K. Waltke states, "The Bible is all about the irrupting kingdom of God, and Genesis all about the elect 'seed,' a metaphor for the people of God who constitute that kingdom. The narrator uses the refrain *tôlĕdôt* . . . to give his book structure and meaning." *An Old Testament Theology: An Exegetical, Canonical, and Thematic Approach*, with Charles Yu (Grand Rapids, MI: Zondervan, 2007), 305.

3. Waltke, *Old Testament Theology*, 307–8.

4. Henri Blocher, *In the Beginning: The Opening Chapters of Genesis* (Downers Grove, IL: InterVarsity Press, 1984), 211; Joseph Blenkinsopp, *Creation, Un-Creation, Re-Creation: A Discursive Commentary on Genesis 1–11* (New York: T&T Clark, 2011), 171–75.

5. Waltke, *Old Testament Theology*, 307–8.

6. Robert Alter, *Genesis: Translation and Commentary* (New York: Norton, 1996), 50.

7. Waltke, *Old Testament Theology*, 306.

tion is clear. God is identifying with Abram and his descendants, so that anyone who blesses them will receive divine blessings, just as anyone who honors God will receive his blessing. By identifying with human community, God establishes the groundwork for his broader redemptive program.

Abram's faith is displayed in his obedient response to the Lord, and the promise that inspired the migration of the family to Shechem is restated upon their arrival. Abram intuits the covenant nature of the promise and demonstrates it by building an altar in the land the Lord had promised to him (12:7). The ensuing events illustrate the faithfulness of the Lord to his promise to bless Abram, first in the case of the Pharaoh's affections for Sarai (12:10–20), then in the choosing of Canaan (13:1–18), the defeat of Chedorlaomer's coalition (14:1–16), and the blessing of Melchizedek (14:17–24).

To the close reader of these stories, the education of Abram about the nature of the deity whom he has fallen in with becomes apparent. This is no family deity or local god. Common belief would have held that a deity's jurisdiction would end at the borders of the land where he is worshiped, and such a misconception is on display in the accounts of Abram's life. Abram seems to fear Pharaoh despite God's promises to protect him, but he learns that God is sovereign even in the land of Egyptian gods. The question is not who will protect Abram from Pharaoh, but who will protect Pharaoh from the Lord. Pharaoh's desperate situation leaves him in a panic. "What is this you have done to me?" he cries, as if he is the one in the weaker position (12:18). The entire episode shows the reader that Abram's God is not a local family deity but a global superpower whose sovereignty extends across geopolitical boundaries.

The account of Abram separating from Lot reveals the Lord's continuing faithfulness even in the details of Abram's life. Given the first choice of pastureland, Lot greedily claims the Jordan Valley, a location that seems more desirable but will ultimately prove to be a hardship for him because of its inhabitants. Abram receives the second option, which is the land of Canaan, where the Lord will prosper his family and their holdings. The Lord restates his promise of a land and a nation after Abram has separated from Lot, indicating again that this covenant is for Abram's descendants, and Abram faithfully responds by building another altar (13:14–18).

The selection of pastureland sets the background for the invasion of Chedorlaomer and his coalition of kings and the abduction of Lot. God's faithfulness is again showcased in Abram's victory in battle, the rescue of Lot, and the blessing of Melchizedek. It should be noted that the blessings in nature (prospering in the land) and in warfare (victory over enemies) are derived from the initial promise of Genesis 12:1–3, but they will also become categories in the subsequent redemptive covenants with Moses and David. These two sorts of blessings, blessings in nature and in warfare, will become common expressions of divine benevolence in redemptive history that will ultimately find their fulfillment in the new heavens and new earth, where the curse of the fall will be lifted from the land and justice and aggressions will be eradicated forever.

The somewhat mysterious and wonderful character of Melchizedek, king of Salem and priest of God, steps into the victory celebrations after Lot's rescue, and he presents Abram with a verbal blessing that both confirms Abram's special relationship with God and clearly states the superiority of God over all other powers (14:19–20). Geerhardus Vos describes Melchizedek as "representative of the earlier, pre-Abrahamic, knowledge of God," whose religion, "though imperfect, was by no means to be identified with the average paganism of the tribes."[8] If Abram was unsure of the extent of God's power, presence, and authority, the epithet "God Most High, Possessor of heaven and earth" (14:19) removes any qualification to God's rule. Abram repeats the epithet verbatim (14:22), revealing that his education in the nature of his Redeemer has been advanced.

Covenant Ratification (Gen. 15)

Ever since the discovery of ancient Near Eastern treaties in the early twentieth century, scholars have intensified their interest in and understanding of biblical passages clearly depicting similar treaty ratification ceremonies.[9] As a result, passages like Genesis 15 can be understood against a considerably expanded background of ancient practice. With that said, biblical interpreters must be careful not to overapply historical backgrounds and cognate texts with any particular biblical text. The biblical covenants were intelligible to the ancient audience in part because they reflected aspects of current practice, but they must be read in their own biblical context and not reduced to the sum of extrabiblical sources. The covenant ceremonies of the Bible traffic in common ancient practices, but they are also uniquely ordained by God for his purposes, and so we must trust the scriptural context to explain their parameters.

The problem of Genesis 15 is one of assurance: How can Abram be sure that the Lord will provide him with an heir? The question is a practical one that engages all the other blessings God has promised to him. Without an heir, there can be no nation. Without a nation, there will be no inhabitants for the land. Will the covenant begin and end with Abram's natural lifespan?

---

8. Geerhardus Vos, *Biblical Theology: Old and New Testaments* (1948; repr., Edinburgh: Banner of Truth, 1975), 77.

9. See George E. Mendenhall, *Law and Covenant in Israel and the Ancient Near East* (Pittsburgh: Biblical Colloquium, 1955); Meredith G. Kline, *The Treaty of the Great King: The Covenant Structure of Deuteronomy; Studies and Commentary* (Grand Rapids, MI: Eerdmans, 1963); Kline, *The Structure of Biblical Authority* (Grand Rapids, MI: Eerdmans, 1972); Dennis J. McCarthy, *Treaty and Covenant: A Study in Form in the Ancient Oriental Documents and in the Old Testament*, AnBib 21 (Rome: Pontifical Biblical Institute, 1963); Delbert R. Hillers, *Covenant: The History of a Biblical Idea* (Baltimore: Johns Hopkins University Press, 1969); Klaus Baltzer, *The Covenant Formulary in Old Testament, Jewish, and Early Christian Writings*, trans. David E. Green (Philadelphia: Fortress, 1971). See also Donald J. Wiseman, ed. and trans., *The Vassal-Treaties of Esarhaddon* (London: British School of Archaeology in Iraq, 1958); Frank Moore Cross, *Canaanite Myth and Hebrew Epic: Essays in the History of the Religion of Israel* (Cambridge, MA: Harvard University Press, 1973), 295–300. Steven L. McKenzie, *Covenant* (Saint Louis, MO: Chalice, 2000), 46–51. Critical scholarship addressed the question of the biblical covenant as promissory oath previous to this period, e.g., Julius Wellhausen, *Prolegomena to the History of Ancient Israel* (New York: World, 1957), 338–42; translation of *Prolegomena zur Geschichte Israels*, 2nd ed. (Berlin: Georg Reimer, 1883).

These concerns underlie the opening promise to Abram: "Fear not, . . . I am your shield; your reward shall be very great" (15:1). This promise comes with the introductory statement "The word of the LORD came to Abram in a vision" (15:1), a common superscript for other prophetic oracles (1 Sam. 15:10; 2 Sam. 7:4; Jer. 1:2; Ezek. 1:3; Jonah 1:1; Hag. 1:1; Zech. 7:1), which corroborates the tradition that Abram was a prophet (Gen. 20:7; Luke 13:28).[10] Abram also uses the title אֲדֹנָי יֱהוִה (Gen. 15:1), a term that is rare in the Pentateuch but more common in the Prophetic Books, linking Abraham's somewhat ambiguous prophetic role to the unambiguous role of the prophet in later Israelite history.[11] In premonarchical times, the office of the prophet is somewhat vague, referring to a person who has a special relationship with God.

At this point in the narrative, the problem of Sarai's barrenness, introduced in Genesis 11:30, has not been solved, and this leads Abram to inquire about some sign of assurance. Perhaps following the logic of his wife's barrenness, Abram suggests an unfortunate solution in the form of his relative Eliezer, but the Lord confirms that it will be his own biological heir who will continue the covenant line. It is interesting to note that Abram will again struggle with the temptation in the next chapter to solve apparent problems by his own contrivance rather than trusting in the Lord.

Nevertheless, Abram trusts in the Lord to fulfill his promises as he has in the preceding chapters, and that faith establishes him as a fitting covenant partner (15:6). The apostle Paul puts much importance in the necessity and singularity of faith for the Abrahamic covenant by noting how Abraham's faith results in his justification even before the covenant sacrament of circumcision is mandated in Genesis 17 (Rom. 4:12–13). Faith in the Lord to fulfill his promises provides the groundwork for the covenant requirements that follow. That Abraham asks for a sign does not discredit him before Lord, but rather, the Lord acknowledges his concern and graciously provides him with a sign in the form of a covenant-ratification ceremony.

Drawing from the findings regarding ancient Near Eastern treaties, we can identify certain elements of the ceremony that begins in Genesis 15:7. The Lord somewhat abruptly recalls the ways in which he has blessed Abraham already, calling him out of Ur to give him the land. This recollection is not a non sequitur in the passage but rather indicates the commencement of the ceremony, beginning with a historical prologue that recounts instances of divine benevolence in the past (cf. the covenants with Moses, Deut. 1:1–4:43, and David, 2 Sam. 7:8). The covenant is founded on God's freely initiated acts of grace toward Abram, not on anything that Abram of Ur has done in the past to merit the promises of God.

The dramatic tension of the passage is heightened in Abram's interruption to again ask for a sign, but the Lord continues by commanding Abram to prepare the sacrificial animals for the ceremony (Gen. 15:8–9). Knowledge of ancient covenant treaties

---

10. The only other place this phrase is used in Genesis is in 15:4.
11. Kenneth A. Mathews, *Genesis 11:27–50:26*, NAC 1B (Nashville: B&H, 2005), 161.

elucidates the purpose of the animal sacrifices. Covenant participants would create sometimes vivid illustrations of the fate that would befall any participant who broke the terms of the covenant. In some cases, effigies of the covenant participants would be burned or melted during a ceremony, while in others, animals would be slaughtered, their viscera scattered on the ground, making a grisly path that the participants would walk down together as the terms of the covenant were read aloud. By protecting the carnage from carrion birds (15:11), Abram shows that he rightly understands the sacred nature of the event that is unfolding.

The coming darkness of night (15:12) creates a dramatic effect as the narrative reaches its climax while also foreshadowing the sobering timetable of a generations-long hiatus before the offspring of Abram will receive their inheritance of the land. The "deep sleep" (15:12) is the same word used to describe the slumber that Adam experiences (2:21) as well as the sleep of spiritual ignorance (Isa. 29:10), and the dreadful darkness evokes images from the exodus and conquest (Ex. 10:21, 22; 14:20; 15:16; 23:27; Deut. 4:11; Josh. 2:9). As the ceremony reaches its crescendo, the weight of entering into a covenant relationship with a deity overwhelms Abram, and he loses consciousness.

The passing of the fire pot and torch through the animal parts poses some problems in terms of what exactly it means in the ceremony,[12] but it is evident that it emphasizes the unconditionality of the covenant. Just as God unilaterally elected Abram and called him from Ur, blessing him along the way, so the Lord alone is bearing the burden of the terms of this covenant. The promises to the offspring of Abram to inherit the land and the length of the period beforehand are the business of a just God who will not give over the land until the act of conquest is warranted by the widespread sin of the inhabitants in the land (Gen. 15:16). The gentilic name Amorite is used to represent all the people currently settled in the land, though a more detailed accounting of the peoples of the region is given later in the narrative (15:19–20). The fact that Abram's offspring will spend the intervening four hundred years in slavery is not fully explained, leading early Jewish interpreters to interpolate verbiage to the effect that Abram must have committed a sin to warrant such a difficult prospect.[13] There is no biblical evidence of such sin, but the reality of future enslavement does complicate the prospective outlook of the covenant.

The use of the suffix form of the verb נָתַתִּי in Genesis 15:18 should be contrasted with the prefix forms used in the rest of the discourse (12:1–3, 7; 13:14–17; 15:4–5) and read as a performative use of the verb form, indicating a solemn vow: "I hereby give . . ." While in previous passages, the Lord is promising the gift of the land, the gift is formally enacted in the covenant ceremony. While the promise of the land to Abram's

---

12. G. Hasel, "The Meaning of the Animal Rite in Genesis 15," *JSOT* 19 (1981): 61–78; supported in the study of R. S. Hess, "The Slaughter of the Animals in Genesis 15: Genesis 15:8–21 in Its Ancient Near Eastern Context," in *He Swore an Oath: Biblical Themes from Genesis 12–50* (Cambridge: Tyndale House, 1993), 55–65.

13. So the Genesis Rabbah (15:13). Gary A. Anderson, *Sin: A History* (New Haven, CT: Yale University Press, 2009), 101–4.

offspring is assured in the hands of the Lord, they will not inherit the land within the borders delineated in this passage until long after the conquest, during the early years of King Solomon's reign (the borders are reiterated in Ex. 23:31; Deut. 1:7; Josh. 1:4; though more restricted boundaries are found in Num. 34:2–12; the fulfillment is found in 1 Kings 4:21), a postponement that is probably due to Israel's failure to drive all the peoples out of the land during the time of Joshua and the judges (Judg. 2:21–22).

Some scholars have pointed out that the format of the covenant in this passage reflects the land-grant type of promissory commitment of one party to another regarding a delineated tract of land,[14] but again, readers should be careful not to overapply such a similarity in an effort to conclude that this covenant is merely unconditional. As will be seen, this covenant emphasizes unconditionality, but like all biblical covenants, certain conditions are required of the receiving party.[15]

Covenant Amendment (Gen. 17)

As already mentioned, readers must understand the development of the covenant with Abram in light of the development of the narrative. The scene that follows the covenant ceremony of Genesis 15 involves Abram's failed attempt to bring about the promised heir through the Egyptian woman Hagar. While Hagar and the child Ishmael receive a unique and particular blessing of the Lord, they are not to be party to the transmission of covenant blessings from Abram to his heir.

In Genesis 17, the Lord revisits Abram and clarifies the terms of the covenant into which they have both entered. Lest the foregrounded unconditionality of the covenant ceremony in chapter 15 be misconstrued as a universalistic arrangement in which Abram has no responsibility, the divine instruction of chapter 17 outlines the expectations of the covenant for Abram. In this covenant arrangement, Abram is called to "walk before me, and be blameless" (17:1), to assume a new covenantal identity represented by the change of his name to Abraham (17:5),[16] and to keep covenant by observing the sacrament of circumcision (17:10–14). Hardly a new covenant, as some have suggested, the covenant in Genesis 17 merely reiterates and amplifies the previous promises that God has made to Abram since his calling out of Ur. Abraham's offspring will be a multitude of nations, drawing attention to the global aspects of the blessing (17:5), and they will inherit the land as their possession (17:8). The promise to make Abraham "exceedingly fruitful" (17:6) ties the redemptive program to the creative one. Where once humanity

14. M. Weinfeld, "The Covenant of Grant in the Old Testament and in the Ancient Near East," *JAOS* 90, no. 2 (1970): 200.

15. Walther Eichrodt is surely correct: "The attempt to understand the *berith* as a solemn assurance which obligates only the giver is seen to be an abstraction, which ignores the sociological aspect of the phenomenon. . . . The *berith*, as part of its very nature, assumes the obligation, also of the receiver." "Covenant and Law: Thoughts on Recent Discussion," *Int* 20 (1966): 306.

16. In his naming, Abraham is being created anew for this redemptive purpose. The close connection between creation and naming is found in both Egyptian and Mesopotamian literature. John D. Currid, *Ancient Egypt and the Old Testament* (Grand Rapids, MI: Baker, 1997), 61–62.

was mandated by God to "be fruitful and multiply" (1:28), now God will ensure Abraham's expansion and provide a new country, which, like the garden of Eden, will be his sanctuary on earth.[17]

An overly atomistic reading of these passages would miss the clear continuity of the covenant development beginning in Genesis 12. The Lord graciously and sovereignly calls Abram from Ur; Abram trusts in the Lord's provision; the Lord articulates the blessings of the covenant and explicitly binds himself to faithful Abram; and Abram, now Abraham, persists in his faithfulness by giving expression to it in the form of covenant obedience. Understood against the backdrop of the fall of humanity and subsequent curse, this redemptive covenant is unquestionably gracious, but it is not universalistic. Waltke explains, "Here we enter into the mystery of divine sovereignty and human accountability. YHWH will fulfill his promises but not apart from the faith of their beneficiaries."[18] The recipient of the blessings must participate in the covenant by his faithfulness, as seen in the prohibition of the uncircumcised male (17:14). This condition of true faithfulness is common to every redemptive covenant following the fall and does not mean that any fallen human can merit covenant blessings. Covenant faithfulness signifies covenant membership.

The sacrament of circumcision amplifies the generational elements of these blessings. As the covenant representative or "head," Abraham will not enjoy the fulfillment of these promises in his lifetime (the only land gains will be Sarah's burial site, 23:19–20), but the conditions of the covenant are nevertheless required of his offspring. To enjoy the promise of a nation and land, the Abrahamic descendants must likewise walk blamelessly before the Lord, assume the Abrahamic identification, and keep covenant by circumcising the males of their households (including servants, some of whom would have likely been Gentiles, a precedent for the "sojourners" of later narratives).[19]

In a more recent debate, some have questioned the conditionality of the covenant with Abraham. John Murray points out the inherent conditionality of the circumcision mandate:

> For does not the possibility of breaking the covenant imply conditional perpetuity? "The uncircumcised male . . . shall be cut off from his people; he hath broken my covenant" (Gn. Xvii. 14, R.V.). Without question the blessing of the covenant and the relation which the covenant entails cannot be enjoyed or maintained apart from the fulfillment of certain conditions on the part of the beneficiaries. . . . Fellowship is always mutual and when mutuality ceases fellowship ceases.[20]

---

17. N. T. Wright, *The New Testament and the People of God* (Minneapolis: Fortress, 1992), 263.

18. Bruce K. Waltke, "The Phenomenon of Conditionality within Unconditional Covenants," in *Israel's Apostasy and Restoration: Essays in Honor of Roland K. Harrison*, ed. Avraham Gileadi (Grand Rapids, MI: Baker, 1988), 129.

19. See also Ex. 12:43–49; Lev. 12:3.

20. John Murray, *The Covenant of Grace: A Biblico-Theological Study* (Phillipsburg, NJ: Presbyterian and Reformed, 1988), 18.

The covenant is not universally applied to all Abraham's descendants, lest Ishmael and Esau be recipients of the covenant line, but only to those who trust in the Lord to provide for the promises he has made to Abraham, Isaac, and Jacob. To make the same point, the apostle Paul will distinguish between children of the flesh and children of the promise (Rom. 9:8). Only the latter, who are marked by faith, are considered the offspring of Abraham. True faith will result in covenant keeping, just as true faith in Christ, the condition for justification, is the sort of faith that results in verbal profession and enjoyment of the means of grace (Mark 16:6; Rom. 10:9; 1 Cor. 12:3).

To be sure, the Mosaic covenant, while in clear continuity with the Abrahamic covenant, includes a heightened focus on faith worked out in covenant obedience. Meredith Kline argues that this focus forms a works principle that operates in "the typological sphere of the provisional earthly kingdom" of Israel in the land.[21] This introduction of multiple strata unique to the Mosaic covenant seems to depend on a reading of the Abrahamic covenant that ignores the clear conditional elements in that covenant, elements that are present in the new covenant as well (Heb. 12:4–11). If one argues, as Vos does, that the interest in obedience to the law is primarily a matter of "appropriateness of expression" of faith and not legal merit,[22] then it follows that the same is true of the Abrahamic covenant requirements of blamelessness and covenant keeping. The reader should recognize the different emphases of both Abraham and Moses while acknowledging that both put the priority on divine grace and the instrumentality of human faithfulness.[23]

Covenant Confirmation (Gen. 22)

Genesis 22 introduces a narratival break with the previous stories of God's preservation of Abraham and his work to sustain the redemptive program begun in Genesis 12. The first line of Genesis 22 offers a proleptic introduction to the events that follow; the clause "After these things God tested Abraham" makes a clean break from the previous series of events and prepares the reader for the jarring command that God is about to give Abraham. It is, after all, a test, not a radical about-face of divine purpose. God tests his people elsewhere in Scripture to give them opportunity to confirm their faithfulness to the covenant (Ex. 15:25; 16:4; Deut. 8:2; Judg. 2:22; 1 Chron. 29:17; Ps. 66:10; cf. Luke 8:13; 1 Cor. 3:13; 2 Cor. 8:2). The testing merely brings into the open what is already true within the heart (Ps. 1:3; Jer. 17:7–8). The display of such outward righteousness does not earn Abraham the promises of the covenant, since these have been secured already through divine promise (Gen. 12) and covenant ceremony (Gen. 15).

---

21. Meredith G. Kline, *Kingdom Prologue: Genesis Foundations for a Covenantal Worldview* (Eugene, OR: Wipf and Stock, 2006), 321.

22. Vos, *Biblical Theology*, 127. See also John M. Frame, *The Doctrine of the Christian Life*, A Theology of Lordship (Phillipsburg, NJ: P&R, 2008), 206–7.

23. For a longer discussion of the similarity of Moses and Abraham in this regard, see John Murray, *Principles of Conduct: Aspects of Biblical Ethics* (Grand Rapids, MI: Eerdmans, 1957), 196–201.

There are several poetic devices that move the story forward. For instance, *naming* plays an important function. The title "God" (אלהים) is used during the first ten verses of the passage while God is behaving in a somewhat estranged, distant manner. As soon as the story shifts in 22:11, and he becomes Savior to the child, the covenantal name "LORD" (יהוה) is used.[24] The phrase "Here I am" also ties the account together (22:1, 7, 11). In each case, Abraham's "Here I am" statement is responding to others (God, Isaac, and the angel of the Lord, respectively), and his response suggests his obedience both in his faithful response to the command and in his trust in the Lord to provide a lamb (22:8). Abraham's faith in the Lord for the boy's protection is also suggested when he instructs the servants to wait until they *both* return (22:5). His past experience with divine benevolence assures him of the Lord's intentions for his offspring. The response "Here I am" further connects Abraham with other prophets who respond in the same way to their own prophetic callings (Gen. 31:11; 46:2; Ex. 3:4; 1 Sam. 3:4; Isa. 6:8; cf. Acts 9:10).

After the resolution of the story, the angel of the Lord communicates a blessing that reiterates and confirms the blessings of the covenant (Gen. 22:15–18), bringing the arc of Abraham's covenant formation to its completion. This leaves nothing but the coda of the story about the transmission to Isaac and Jacob, which plays out through the rest of this section of the book, setting the stage for the Joseph cycles that begin in Genesis 37.

The Abrahamic Covenant in Redemptive History

The covenant with Abraham becomes the theological foundation of the covenant with Israel and one of the earliest formal anticipations of the blessings Israel will enjoy in terms of population, country, and global influence. David Noel Freedman and David Miano show how later covenantal thought and postexilic tradition see the Abrahamic covenant as prior to and influential in later covenantal development.[25] The covenants with Moses and David, and ultimately the new covenant with Christ, take up and amplify the promises of God to Abraham, Isaac, and Jacob.

Abraham and Moses and David

As Israel languishes in Egyptian slavery, the Lord's remembrance of his covenant with Abraham triggers the events that lead to the exodus (Ex. 2:24). Furthermore, in the divine disclosure to Moses, the Lord identifies himself first as the God of Abraham, Isaac, and Jacob (Ex. 3:6). When the Lord threatens to wipe out Israel and begin the people again in the line of Moses, the disaster is avoided when God is reminded of his promises to the patriarchs (Ex. 32:13; cf. Gen. 22:17).[26] The covenant at Sinai and its later reiteration

---

24. Gordon J. Wenham, *Genesis 16–50*, WBC 2 (Dallas: Word Books, 1998), 103; see n14.

25. David Noel Freedman and David Miano, "People of the New Covenant," in *The Concept of the Covenant in the Second Temple Period*, ed. Stanley E. Porter and Jacqueline C. R. de Roo, JSJSup 71 (Leiden: Brill, 2003), 7–26.

26. It should be noted that the threat to begin the line again through Moses, while severe, would not have undermined the promises of the covenant to Abraham, since there is no reason that the offspring from Moses

on the steppes of Moab will expand on the stipulations for the people entering into the land, including how they should behave toward the non-Israelites within the land (Deut. 20:16–20) and without (Deut. 20:10–15). The latter suggests the initial global scope of the conquest program. While the nations within the land were under the חֵרֶם ban, Israel was always meant to engage with nations outside the land and extend its national influence around the world (Gen. 12:3). When such engagements were hostile, Israel was first to sue for peace, while also being prepared to use force.

God identifies with Abraham and his offspring (Gen. 12:1–3; 17:7), as he does with Moses's generation (Ex. 6:7) and the restoration generation (Jer. 30:22; Ezek. 36:28; cf. John 17:20–26). In the covenant with Moses, that close relationship is sharpened by the promise of the Lord to be present with his people in the form of the sanctuary, first the tabernacle and then the temple. Where previously God's presence was notional, now there is a physical, formalized sanctuary that can be experienced personally as a locus of civic life and worship.[27]

The outlines of Mosaic eschatology found in Leviticus 26 and Deuteronomy 28–30 anticipate a period of divine forbearance in the land, followed by a time of dispersal among the nations, which will in turn end with the repentance of the people and the reconstitution of the people and the land to a better situation than they had experienced before (Deut. 30:1–10). These promises of restoration following exile are fully constituent of the Mosaic covenant even though they are adumbrated in the everlasting nature of the Abrahamic covenant and only amplified or expanded in Moses (Gen. 17:7). It is the Abrahamic covenant that is in view in the hopeful restoration oracle found in Isaiah 63:7–64:11, where the covenantal language of "faithfulness" (חֶסֶד, 63:7)[28] and kinship (63:16; 64:8)[29] encourages the people that restoration is sure because God is a faithful covenant partner, even if the patriarchs Abraham and Israel do not know the exiled generation.

While the Mosaic covenant foregrounds the righteous expressions of faithfulness that the Abrahamic covenant assumes (but see Gen. 17:1, 9–10), both covenants require its human parties to participate in the covenant with a faith that finds expression in faithful covenant obedience and humble repentance. Abraham is called to give expression to his faith by pursuing blamelessness and keeping covenant. This same principle is most clearly articulated in the Mosaic doctrine of wholehearted "love" in Deuteronomy 6:4–5, which encompasses all the requirements of the Mosaic law. Such covenantal love remembers the faithful acts of the Lord in the past and trusts him to be true to his

---

could not be enlarged over time to a great covenant people. When added to Moses's other argument based on the reputation of the Lord among the Egyptians (Ex. 32:12), however, it is apparently compelling.

27. J. V. Fesko makes the helpful observation that the altars Abraham built suggest the need for an archetypal temple, but the need is not met as part of divine initiative until God gives the instructions for the sanctuary to Moses (Gen. 12:8; 22:9, 14). *Last Things First: Unlocking Genesis 1–3 with the Christ of Eschatology* (Fearn, Ross-shire, Scotland: Mentor, 2007), 120.

28. Richard J. Bautch, "An Appraisal of Abraham's Role in Postexilic Covenants," *CBQ* 71, no. 1 (2009): 46.

29. Frank Moore Cross, "Kinship and Covenant in Ancient Israel," in *From Epic to Canon: History and Literature in Ancient Israel* (Baltimore: Johns Hopkins University Press, 1998), 3–21.

promises in the future. Furthermore, the character of David is described as "a man after [God's] own heart" (1 Sam. 13:14), a probable allusion to Deuteronomy 6:4–5, and this is the instruction David gives to his son Solomon in 1 Kings 2:4. God's covenantal promises to David are articulated once his faithfulness is confirmed (2 Sam. 7:8–16), and the application of those promises are explicitly contingent on the faithfulness of the Davidic heir (2 Sam. 7:14).[30]

Abraham and Second Temple Literature

The distinction between faith and obedience in the Abrahamic covenant is not always clearly disambiguated in Second Temple literature. For instance, in the wisdom book Ben Sira, Abraham is described as keeping the law and receiving a covenant established by his faithful offering of Isaac (Ben Sira 44.19–23), a chronology that seems to conflict with that of Paul in Romans 4:9–14, which emphasizes the priority of faith before works of righteousness as the grounds for God's covenant with Abraham. In 1 Maccabees 2:52, Abraham is remembered being found faithful in his testing, at which point it was reckoned to him as righteousness (cf. Ps.-Philo 18.5).[31] In the book of Jubilees, Abram is described as a child who rejected the idol worship of his father and recognized that God as Creator was the only god worthy of worship (Jub. 11.16–17; cf. 12.16–21). In each of these cases, the obedience seems to be foregrounded as the foundation for the covenant blessings, though such a reading does not rule out the notion of covenant obedience as an indicator of true reliance on God (cf. Ps. 1; Jer. 17:8).

The problem of ambiguity between Abraham's faith and obedience that we see on display in Second Temple literature sheds light on the discussion of Abraham in the epistle of James in the New Testament. For James, Abraham's righteous works, particularly the offering up of Isaac, reveal the authenticity of his faith, not the other way around (James 2:20–24; cf. Heb. 11:8–9). His aim is polemical, refuting the "foolish" notion that justifying faith can be devoid of faithful activity. Over the years, this issue has been confused by theologians who attach anachronistic connotations to the "justification" word group in biblical passages like this one. A careful reading of James reveals that his understanding of the *ordo salutis* does not differ from that found in Paul or the rest of Scripture.

Abraham and Christ

Henri Blocher is surely correct: "It would require a commentary on the whole New Testament to describe the work of grace, a work which is envisaged by the call of Abraham."[32]

---

30. For a helpful outline of the common themes and structures in the Old Testament covenants, see Roger T. Beckwith, "The Unity and Diversity of God's Covenants," *TynBul* 38 (1987): 93–118; Waltke, "Phenomenon of Conditionality."

31. For more, see Jacqueline C. R. de Roo, "God's Covenant with the Forefathers," in Porter and de Roo, *Concept of the Covenant*, 195–96.

32. Blocher, *In the Beginning*, 211.

The covenant with Abraham points to the global impact of the offspring and land that God has promised to Abraham. Set within the horizon of the Old Testament, the Abrahamic child of the promise must be understood to be believing Israel, meaning all those who persist in faith and repentance, so that even the fire of exile is merely a refining fire leaving them pure and unalloyed, a true remnant (Isa. 1:25; Ezek. 22:20–22; Mal. 3:3). The Gospel writers are quick to identify Jesus with faithful Israel, the one who completes the new exodus, succeeding where the Israel of antiquity had failed. Matthew describes Christ as a new Israel coming out of Egypt (Matt. 2:15; cf. Hos. 11:1), the Israelite who passes through the waters of repentance/baptism on Israel's behalf (Matt. 3:15), the one worthy of the title "Son" of God (Matt. 3:17; cf. Ex. 4:22), the faithful wanderer who resists temptation in the wilderness for a period of time marked by the conspicuous number forty (Matt. 4:1–11; cf. Num. 14:34), and finally, the faithful remnant reentering the land to bring about national restoration (Matt. 4:13–17; cf. Isa. 9:1–2). In each instance, Matthew is closely identifying Jesus with believing Israel of the exodus and restoration; Christ is the remnant, the faithful seed in whom all others can receive the inheritance of Abraham. Jesus himself evokes this tradition when he claims to be the "true vine," a vivid biblical metaphor always used in reference to the people of God (John 15:1–17; cf. Ps. 80:8; Isa. 5:1–7; Jer. 2:21; Hos. 9:10; Matt. 21:33–46).

The apostle Paul contends that Jesus Christ is, in actuality, the singular offspring to whom the covenant with Abraham points (Gal. 3:16). Here Paul is refuting the notion that the covenant with Moses could annul the covenant with Abraham by exchanging the faith principle of Abraham with a works principle of the Mosaic law. For Paul, this distinction creates a false dichotomy between Moses and Abraham that is untenable (Gal. 3:21).[33] Neither the Mosaic law nor the Abrahamic circumcision can give life, but rather both were expressions of faithfulness in the promises of God fulfilled in Jesus Christ, "for in Christ Jesus you are all sons of God, through faith. . . . And if you are Christ's, then you are Abraham's offspring, heirs according to promise" (Gal. 3:26, 29).

In Christ, the promise to Abraham that his offspring would bless the world (Gen. 12:3; 22:17) is also fulfilled in the person of Jesus Christ. He is the righteous seed through whom the nations are brought into the divine program of redemption through saving faith. In Christ, the nations are being gathered into the inheritance of Abraham, a work that is being accomplished even now through the Great Commission (Matt. 28:18–20), and the apostles are empowered by the great solution to Babel at Pentecost (Acts 2). The inclusion of the nations will be completed in the new heavens and new earth (Rev. 21:1–22:5). The global scope of the promises to Abraham mentioned above imply that the divine work of redemption was never meant to stop at the borders of the land of Israel, nor was it ever limited to biological descendants of Abraham. Abraham and his offspring, by faith, were always meant to be "heir[s] of the world" (Rom. 4:13).

---

33. O. Palmer Robertson, *The Christ of the Covenants* (Phillipsburg, NJ: Presbyterian and Reformed, 1980), 59–60.

7

The Mosaic Covenant

J. Nicholas Reid

The Mosaic covenant has been understood in numerous ways within the Reformed tradition.[1] Whether considering Francis Roberts's seventeenth-century taxonomy of views or the recent and further nuanced taxonomy provided by Brenton Ferry,[2] one quickly grasps what John Owen meant when he said that this subject is "wrapped up in much obscurity, and attended with many difficulties," or why Anthony Burgess stated, "I do not find in any point of Divinity, learned men so confused and perplexed (being like Abraham's Ram, hung in a bush of briars and brambles by the head) as here."[3] Unlike some theological diversity that seems to stem primarily from confusion among theologians, the study of the Mosaic covenant is fraught with difficulties that occur primarily from the numerous ways in which the law is considered in the Bible and subsequently how one accounts for such diversity. For example, Paul writes in his epistle to the Romans, "Do we then overthrow the law by this faith? By no means! On the contrary, we uphold the law" (3:31). But three chapters later, he writes, "For sin will have no

---

1. I wish to thank the following for reading and commenting on various drafts of this chapter: Michael Allen, Ben Dunson, J. V. Fesko, Mark Jones, Scott Swain, John Tweeddale, Chad Van Dixhoorn, and Guy Waters. I also want to thank my students, and in particular David Carnes, who assisted me in several ways. Of course, I bear responsibility for any errors that remain.

2. See Francis Roberts, *Mysterium et Medulla Bibliorum: The Mysterie and Marrow of the Bible* (London: George Calvert, 1657), 738–39. While Roberts's taxonomy remains a useful point of reference, more recently Brenton Ferry has provided a nice taxonomy of positions in "Works in the Mosaic Covenant: A Reformed Taxonomy," in *The Law Is Not of Faith: Essays on Works and Grace in the Mosaic Covenant*, ed. Bryan D. Estelle, J. V. Fesko, and David VanDrunen (Phillipsburg, NJ: P&R, 2009), 76–105, though, as Mark Jones has pointed out, Ferry's own taxonomy also makes some mistakes shared by previous attempts. "The 'Old' Covenant," in *Drawn into Controversie: Reformed Theological Diversity and Debates within Seventeenth-Century British Puritanism*, ed. Michael A. G. Haykin and Mark Jones, RHT 17 (Göttingen: Vandenhoeck & Ruprecht, 2011), 18n22.

3. John Owen, *Exposition of Hebrews*, in *The Works of John Owen, D.D.* (London: Johnstone and Hunter, 1850–1855), 23:60; Anthony Burgess, *Vindiciae Legis; or, A Vindication of the Morall Law and the Covenants* (London: Thomas Underhill, 1647), 24 (p. 229).

dominion over you, since you are not under law but under grace" (6:14).[4] How one accounts for these texts shapes one's articulation of covenant theology.

In what must be a highly selective chapter that can attempt to provide only a useful introduction to the topic, I seek to organize this discussion around the place of the Mosaic covenant within the theology of the Westminster Confession of Faith.[5] This is less an attempt to provide a theology of the confession and more an attempt to consider some of the key points about the Mosaic covenant in biblical, historical, and theological perspective by using the seventeenth-century majority position in Reformed theology.

The following chapter discusses initially the nature of the Mosaic covenant from the dichotomist perspective (namely, the view that there are two covenants: the covenant of works and the covenant of grace) set forth in the confession. This is followed by a discussion of the law of God, with particular interest in the divisions and uses of the law. Since one of the larger questions about the law is its applicability for the church, considerable attention must be devoted to this topic. Following Jesus's own summary, the love of God and the love of neighbor are a summary of the law. For this reason, the love of God is also dealt with here. If the Mosaic covenant is considered an administration of the covenant of grace, then it is necessary to explain the exile as an application of the covenantal curses. The exile is one of the key entry points for the discussion of conditionality in the Mosaic covenant. Finally, I consider the republication thesis, the view that the Mosaic covenant republished the covenant of works in some sense.

It is hoped that this chapter fairly represents the doctrine within the Reformed tradition and serves as a useful guide for understanding the many other more important works on the topic. To achieve this goal, numerous decisions had to be made. For example, when discussing the republication thesis below, the focus is on Meredith Kline's view of the Mosaic covenant and the republication of the covenant of works, as he is arguably the most influential figure in the modern discussion.[6] While there is a very

---

4. Numerous attempts have been made to reconcile these diverse statements and others. See the work by Brian S. Rosner, *Paul and the Law: Keeping the Commandments of God*, NSBT 31 (Downers Grove, IL: InterVarsity Press, 2013). See the review by Guy Waters, "Paul and the Law," *Reformation21* (blog), December 2013, http://www.reformation21.org/shelf-life/paul-and-the-law.php.

5. One of the large debates in covenant theology from that period was between the dichotomist and trichotomist views. The dichotomist view said that there were two covenants: the covenant of works and the covenant of grace. The Mosaic covenant was considered part of the covenant of grace. The trichotomist position said that there were three covenants: the covenant of works, the covenant of grace, and a covenant subservient to the covenant of grace (the Mosaic covenant). For an excellent discussion of the historical debate surrounding the dichotomist and trichotomist positions, see Jones, "'Old' Covenant." This article summarizes the trichotomist (subservient covenant) position argued by John Cameron and John Ball. Jones further discusses the debated question about whether John Owen held to a dichotomist or trichotomist position. For this discussion, one should now see John Tweeddale, *John Owen and Hebrews: The Foundation of Biblical Interpretation* (Edinburgh: T&T Clark, 2019). Tweeddale makes a convincing case that Owen was "functionally Cameronian" in his approach.

6. The republication thesis has much deeper historical roots and remains broadly represented today in confessionally Reformed circles. For the historical arguments, see in particular J. V. Fesko, *The Theology of the Westminster Standards: Historical Context and Theological Insights* (Wheaton, IL: Crossway, 2014), 125–67; Estelle, Fesko, and

large debate about how to read Kline and whether his view changed from his early to late writings, I focus mainly on his work in *Kingdom Prologue*, where he offers clear and arguably programmatic statements about the relationship between the Mosaic covenant and the covenant of grace.[7] If one can at least get a handle on Kline's seminal works on the topic, other works building on the thesis will surely be more accessible. It should be noted that dispensational and new covenant theologies, however, are discussed little here, as they are treated more fully elsewhere in this volume.

The Dichotomist Position

In chapter 7 of the confession, the Westminster Assembly sets forth the majority Reformed view, the dichotomist position.[8] Proponents of the dichotomist view maintain that there are two main covenants in redemptive history between God and man: the prefall covenant with Adam and the postfall covenant of grace. From this perspective, the greatest change in redemptive history is not the movement from the old covenant to the new covenant, as significant as that is. The greatest change in redemptive history is the inauguration of the covenant of grace when the *protevangelium* was given to fallen Adam and Eve in Genesis 3:15. Such a perspective recognizes the fundamental unity of both the Old and New Testaments, and yet it seeks to maintain the diversity by which the one covenant of grace was administered. This view can be clarified using the Aristotelian categories of *substance* and *accidents*.

Substance refers to that which belongs to the essence of something. Accidents, however, are those things that belong to something contingently and do not touch directly on the essence of that thing.[9] Applying these categories to the Mosaic covenant, the Westminster Confession of Faith maintains that the Mosaic covenant belongs in substance to the one covenant of grace (WCF 7.5–6). The aspects of the Mosaic covenant that do not touch on its substance, such as the ways in which it was implemented uniquely among the people of Israel prior to the coming of Christ, are the accidents of the covenant. Put differently, the one covenant of grace (substance)

VanDrunen, *The Law Is Not of Faith.* For a critical review, see Cornelis Venema, *Christ and Covenant Theology: Essays on Election, Republication, and the Covenants* (Phillipsburg, NJ: P&R, 2017), 37–144.

7. For a great entry point into the debate about Kline and his views, see the Orthodox Presbyterian Church's "Report of the Committee to Study Republication," 2016, http://www.opc.org/GA/republication.html.

8. The debate surrounding the covenant of redemption is not the concern of this chapter. See in particular Scott R. Swain, "Covenant of Redemption," in *Christian Dogmatics: Reformed Theology for the Church Catholic,* ed. Michael Allen and Scott R. Swain (Grand Rapids, MI: Baker Academic, 2016), 107–25; Joel R. Beeke and Mark Jones, *A Puritan Theology: Doctrine for Life* (Grand Rapids, MI: Reformation Heritage Books, 2012), 237–58. For a brief survey of the covenant of redemption in relation to the Westminster Assembly, see Andrew A. Woolsey, *Unity and Continuity in Covenantal Thought: A Study in the Reformed Tradition to the Westminster Assembly,* RHTS (Grand Rapids, MI: Reformation Heritage Books, 2012), 58–59. See also Guy M. Richard, "The Covenant of Redemption," chap. 1 in this volume.

9. Calvin uses the categories of substance and dispensation in *Institutes* 2.10.2. See the discussion in Venema, *Christ and Covenant Theology,* 44–48. For a discussion of the use of Aristotelian categories by other Reformed theologians, see R. Scott Clark, *Caspar Olevian and the Substance of the Covenant: The Double Benefit of Christ,* RHTS (Grand Rapids, MI: Reformation Heritage Books, 2005), 58–63.

was administered differently (accidents) throughout redemptive history. According to this view, the Mosaic covenant belongs in substance to the covenant of grace, since the forgiveness of sins and salvation promised within this covenant were achieved only through Jesus Christ.

These substantial and administrative distinctions provide helpful categories both to maintain the fundamental unity of Scripture and the arc of the biblical story of creation, fall, redemption, and consummation and to account for the radical shift from shadow to reality with the coming of Christ, who is the substance of the covenant of grace (WCF 7.6).

Continuity and Discontinuity

When holding to this substantial unity, one must still affirm that the new covenant is better (Heb. 8). The Westminster Confession of Faith distinguishes between the administration of the covenant of grace "in the time of the law, and in the time of the gospel" (WCF 7.5). Under the law, the covenant of grace was administered "by promises, prophecies, sacrifices, the paschal lamb, and other types and ordinances delivered to the people of the Jews" (WCF 7.5). The confession goes on to state that these pointed forward to the coming of Christ and were, "for that time, sufficient and efficacious, through the operation of the Spirit, to instruct and build up the elect in faith in the promised Messiah" (WCF 7.5).

In using the language of "the time of the law," the Westminster Confession of Faith sees the Mosaic covenant as being in essential continuity with the other covenantal administrations of the Old Testament, such as the Abrahamic covenant. Put differently, the one covenant of grace was also administered during the time of the law. The administrations of the Old Testament are lumped together without concern to disentangle their accidents in this instance. The main distinctions drawn administratively, as discussed below, relate to the movement from the Old Testament to the New Testament. This broad perspective views "the time of the law" as a time of sacrifices and promises. The sum total of the Mosaic covenant, in other words, was not just a bunch of laws, nor did it entail an anticipation of perfect obedience by Israel. The perfect standard of righteousness was held forth, but the sacrificial system indicates that sin was anticipated and provisions were made for such disobedience. Unlike the giving of the law in the prefall covenant with Adam, which, through the "voluntary condescension" of God is seen as a covenant of works (WCF 7.1–2), the republishing of the moral law at Sinai was in the broader context of a sacrificial system to atone for sins. In fact, the Mosaic covenant was inaugurated because "God remembered his covenant with Abraham, with Isaac, and with Jacob" (Ex. 2:24). Further, the proclamation of the divine name, the tetragrammaton, in Exodus 3:14–17 and later in Exodus 6:1–10 grounds the immeasurable greatness of the divine name in the relatable and understandable: "The LORD, the God of your fathers, the God of Abraham, of Isaac, and of Jacob" (Ex. 3:16; see also 6:2).[10]

At Sinai, the Lord is described not merely as the God of Israel's fathers; he is also described as the God who redeemed them from slavery. The preamble of the giving of the Ten Commandments details God's past benevolence to his people: "I am the LORD your God, who brought you out of the land of Egypt, out of the house of slavery" (Ex. 20:2).[11] This becomes another way that the people of God can know the Lord. Yet the weight of the giving of the law at Sinai must not be missed. When narrowly considered, the law, abstracted from its broader context of redemption, promise, and sacrifice, serves a condemning function. Considered in its broader context, however, the law, by revealing sin, pointed the Old Testament believer to the various promises and sacrifices mentioned above as a means to facilitate communion with God.[12]

When considering the theme of the Pentateuch and the broader context of the Mosaic law, L. Michael Morales asserts the following: "The Pentateuch's main theme [is] *YHWH's opening a way for humanity to dwell in the divine presence*."[13] In relation to this, Morales argues that Leviticus 16, which discusses the Day of Atonement, is the "literary and theological centre" of the Pentateuch.[14] If his thesis is correct, the broader perspective of the law is the context of facilitating worship and dwelling with God, thus facilitating the relationship that already exists between God and his people. The Mosaic covenant, then, as a covenant arrangement, does not use the law to create the relationship between God and Israel. Rather, it provides a way for that relationship to be maintained, especially through ongoing atonement.

Thus considered, the Mosaic covenant, while dipleuric (bilateral) on one level, was fundamentally monopleuric (unilateral). Put differently, the covenant of grace is established and achieved by God; it is unilateral. Yet within the covenant there is an expected response to this fundamental work of God; it is bilateral in its destination. Mark Jones describes it as follows:

> As John Owen (1616–1683) would argue: "if by conditions we intend the duties of obedience which God requireth of us in and by virtue of that covenant; but this I say, the principal promises thereof are not in the first place remunerative of our obedience in the covenant, but efficaciously assumptive of us in the covenant, and establishing

---

10. For an excellent theological interpretation of the tetragrammaton, see Andrea D. Saner, *"Too Much to Grasp": Exodus 3:13–15 and the Reality of God*, JTISup 11 (Winona Lake, IN: Eisenbrauns, 2015).

11. It has long been recognized that such historical prologues feature prominently in the Hittite suzerain-vassal treaties. For further discussion of the ancient Near Eastern background, see J. Nicholas Reid, "Ancient Near Eastern Backgrounds to Covenants," chap. 21 in this volume.

12. See in particular Francis Turretin, *Institutes of Elenctic Theology*, ed. James T. Dennison Jr., trans. George Musgrave Giger (Phillipsburg, NJ: P&R, 1992–1997), 12.8.12–15; Ben C. Dunson, "'The Law Evidently Is Not Contrary to Faith': Galatians and the Republication of the Covenant of Works," *WTJ* 79, no. 2 (2017): 243–66.

13. L. Michael Morales, *Who Shall Ascend the Mountain of the Lord? A Biblical Theology of the Book of Leviticus*, NSBT 37 (Downers Grove, IL: InterVarsity Press, 2015), 30; emphasis original.

14. Morales, *Who Shall Ascend?*, 23–38.

or confirming the covenant." Thus the covenant of grace may be understood as both monopleuric (*foedus monopleuron*) and dipleuric (*foedus dipleuron*).[15]

Likewise for Calvin, the covenant of grace was both monopleuric and dipleuric. On the one hand, all promises are met and fulfilled by God, but God requires "uprightness and sanctity of life" for all those in the covenant; "nonetheless the covenant is at the outset drawn up as a free agreement, and perpetually remains such."[16] In keeping with this understanding, the difference between the covenant of works and the covenant of grace is not the presence of conditions in the former and the absence of conditions in the latter. Rather, the distinction is the relationship of the conditions to the fundamental blessings of the covenant. In the covenant of works, the conditions must be met to receive the blessings of the covenant. In the covenant of grace, the blessings are received, and then the conditions are to flow out of gratefulness for the received blessing.

In traditional Reformed theology, the covenant of works never ended but remains a covenant unfulfilled by any who inherit the fallen nature from original sin, owing to their inherited unrighteousness through Adam and their own sinfulness.[17] Christ, the second Adam (Rom. 5), took on flesh, fulfilled the covenant of works for his people, and paid the penalty for their sins. Thus, through his active and passive obedience, Christ justified a people for God in the covenant of grace. The Mosaic covenant belongs in essence to the covenant of grace, so the conditions in the covenant are to be kept out of gratitude rather than as a means to merit the fuller blessings of the covenant (see, e.g., Deut. 6:10–15).[18]

Despite this fundamental continuity, one must avoid flattening the relationship between the Old and New Testaments. The Westminster Confession continues to describe how the covenant of grace was administered differently under the gospel, concluding, "There are not therefore two covenants of grace, but one and the same, under various dispensations" (WCF 7.6). The differences between the old and new covenants lie at the administrative level rather than the essential level. In sum, the Mosaic covenant is viewed as belonging in substance to the one covenant of grace. Nevertheless, the Mosaic covenant was an inferior and shadowy administration of types and numerous laws.

As an inferior administration, the Mosaic administration of the covenant of grace has a number of distinctive features.[19] Although not exclusively so, the Mosaic covenant is primarily a Jewish administration (Rom. 3:1–2; 9:4–5). It is also a shadowy administra-

---

15. Jones, "'Old' Covenant," 183. On this topic, Richard Muller writes, "The language of monopleuron and dipleuron describes the same covenant from different points of view." *Dictionary of Latin and Greek Terms Drawn Principally from Protestant Scholastic Theology* (Grand Rapids, MI: Baker, 2004), 120. See further Lyle D. Bierma, *The Covenant Theology of Caspar Olevianus* (Grand Rapids, MI: Reformation Heritage Books, 2005).

16. John Calvin, *Institutes of the Christian Religion*, ed. John T. McNeill, trans. Ford Lewis Battles, LCC 20–21 (Philadelphia: Westminster, 1960), 3.17.5. See further the discussion in Jones, "'Old' Covenant," 183–84.

17. Rowland S. Ward, *God and Adam: Reformed Theology and the Creation Covenant* (Wantirna, Australia: New Melbourne, 2003), 140–43.

18. On the gratitude required in response to God's love, see Jon D. Levenson, *Love of God: Divine Gift, Human Gratitude, and Mutual Faithfulness in Judaism* (Princeton, NJ: Princeton University Press, 2016), 48–57.

19. See Randall C. Zachman, *Image and Word in the Theology of John Calvin* (Notre Dame, IN: University of Notre Dame Press, 2007), 107–32. Zachman helpfully lists nine ways Calvin saw the manifestation of Christ in

tion, specifically with respect to its ceremonial aspect (Col. 2:17). The ceremonial law was but a shadow of the realities to come in the new covenant. As the Mosaic covenant was in force until the coming of Christ, it is a temporary administration (Jer. 31:31–36; Gal. 3:24–25; Heb. 8:13). In keeping with being a temporary administration, it is also servile and given to an "underage" church (see Acts 15:10; Gal. 3:21–25; 4:1–3). As the Mosaic covenant is situated prior to the coming of Christ, the condemning function of the law (see the discussion of the second use of the law below) is especially prominent, while the more positive third use is largely but not exclusively spoken of in a prophetic mode (see, e.g., Deut. 30; Jer. 31; cf. Ps. 119). The Mosaic covenant is also a weak administration that results in a curse (e.g., Lev. 26; Deut. 28:15–68; Rom. 8:3). This is particularly seen in the Prophets. Finally, it is a preparatory administration and a means to the fulfillment of God's promised blessing in and through Jesus Christ (Gal. 2:19; 3:10–14; 4:4).[20]

In summary, although the covenant of grace was administered differently throughout redemptive history, there is essential unity to it because Jesus Christ is the true offspring of Abraham. Jesus is the true Israelite, who fulfills the law of Moses in all its dimensions (precept, penalty, promise). Jesus becomes the one in whom all the families of the earth may inherit all God's covenant blessings.

The Law of God[21]

As indicated above, the law of God delivered in the covenant of works continued to be "a perfect rule of righteousness, and, as such, was delivered by God upon Mount Sinai, in ten commandments" (WCF 19.2). In the Westminster Confession of Faith 19.2–4, the assembly lays out the much-disputed threefold division of the law: moral, ceremonial, and judicial.[22] While Israel did not divide their laws in such

---

the law and the gospel. This treatment gets at the heart of the inferior and superior distinction between the old and new covenants.

20. For these distinctive features, I am particularly indebted to Scott R. Swain in personal correspondence.

21. For a recent survey of the law in the Reformed tradition, see Michael Allen, "The Law in the Reformed Tradition," in *God's Two Words: Law and Gospel in the Lutheran and Reformed Traditions*, ed. Jonathan A. Linebaugh (Grand Rapids, MI: Eerdmans, 2018), 45–62.

22. A twofold division of the law as ceremonial and moral goes back at least to Augustine. Augustine, *Answer to Faustus, a Manichean*, in *Works of St. Augustine*, vol. 1/20, ed. Boniface Ramsey, trans. Roland Teske (Hyde Park, NY: New City Press, 2007), 93–94 (6.2). Aquinas argued for a third division. *Summa Theologiae*, 1a2ae.99.4. See further Allen, "Law in the Reformed Tradition," 45–62. See also Tweeddale, *John Owen and Hebrews*, 169–70:

> Owen accepts the classic threefold division of the law into moral, judicial, and ceremonial categories with little qualification. He surmises that "there is no precept but may conveniently be referred unto one or other of these heads." This classification had widespread agreement within reformed theology as evidenced in the writings of Samuel Bolton, James Durham, Obadiah Sedgwick, and Francis Turretin, among others, and in its use in several reformed confessions. Its origin predates the Reformation, as Aquinas utilized it, and Calvin refers simply to "ancient writers" who supported the designation, suggesting that its antiquity was undisputed. While this is not an idea native to the Jewish oral tradition drawn on by Maimonides in his organization of the law, it does have a stronger foundation in the text itself.

For a fuller treatment of the debated history and biblical theological arguments supporting the threefold division, see Philip S. Ross, *From the Finger of God: The Biblical and Theological Basis for the Threefold Division of the Law* (Fearn, Ross-shire, Scotland: Mentor, 2010). For a representative criticism of this division as an imposition on the

manner,[23] the threefold division represents the diverse ways in which the New Testament authors approach portions of the law. This division may be organized around whether the various types of laws are abrogated in the New Testament and whether the principles learned from them directly or indirectly apply to the church. This principle of indirect application is seen rather clearly when Paul writes, "Let the elders who rule well be considered worthy of double honor, especially those who labor in preaching and teaching. For the Scripture says, 'You shall not muzzle an ox when it treads out the grain,' and, 'The laborer deserves his wages'" (1 Tim. 5:17–18; cf. Deut. 25:4).[24] Paul, in this passage, does not view the law about muzzling oxen to be applicable directly to the church; instead, he draws out a principle about a worker deserving wages and applies it specifically to rulers in the church. In what follows, it is seen that the ceremonial and judicial laws do not directly apply to the church, while the moral law, continuing to be "a perfect rule of righteousness," remains in force for the Christian.

Ceremonial

The Westminster Confession of Faith states, "Ceremonial laws, containing several typical ordinances, partly of worship, prefiguring Christ, . . . are now abrogated, under the New Testament" (WCF 19.3). This abrogation is clear in numerous passages (Acts 10; 15; 1 Cor. 8; Heb. 10; etc.). While the church can indirectly learn about holiness or worship from the ceremonial laws, these ceremonial laws do not remain in force. Thus, a Christian may eat pork or worship without bringing blood sacrifices to church, because Christ, the perfect sacrifice once and for all, has fulfilled the ceremonial law. The ceremonial law further teaches the Christian about the fullness of what Christ achieved for them in making them holy and clean.

Judicial

Judicial law relates to Israel as a political body: "He gave sundry judicial laws, which expired together with the State of that people; not obliging any other now, further than the general equity thereof may require" (WCF 19.4). Paul does not seem to envision the church living under political Israel's law when he tells them to submit to the governing authorities (Rom. 13:1). Paul also does not apply judicial law to the church when dealing with incest in the Corinthian church (1 Cor. 5; cf. Lev. 20:11–12). While one can learn

---

text, see Peter J. Gentry and Stephen J. Wellum, *Kingdom through Covenant: A Biblical-Theological Understanding of the Covenants* (Wheaton, IL: Crossway, 2012), 354–56. Such criticisms are not new. Martin Luther calls the division "old and common" but adds that "it is not an intelligent one." *Luther's Works*, ed. Jaroslav Pelikan (Saint Louis, MO: Concordia, 1963), 40:93. See discussion and elaboration on this point in Piotr J. Malysz, "The Law in the Lutheran Tradition," in Linebaugh, *God's Two Words*, 15–44, particularly 30–32. For Luther, the law simply cannot be divided in this manner.

23. For Israel, the laws were not divided. Such divisions only become possible through fulfillment.

24. The Westminster divines use the principle of general equity to discuss the ways in which the civil laws, although abrogated, have some applicability. This would be an example of indirect application (WCF 19.4).

from these laws, they are not directly repeatable, as they are historically conditioned with respect to their application.[25]

Moral

Moral law, by distinction, remains in force: "The moral law doth for ever bind all, as well as justified persons as others, to the obedience thereof; and that, not only in regard of the matter contained in it, but also in respect of the authority of God the Creator, who gave it: neither doth Christ, in the gospel, any way dissolve, but much strengthen this obligation" (WCF 19.5). While many dispute this point, the contention is that unlike the other types of laws, the moral law is directly applicable to the church.[26] For example, the apostle Paul clearly applies the fifth commandment to the church in Ephesians 6:2–3. As the law remains "binding" in the lives of believers, it is useful to turn attention to the "threefold use of the law."

The Threefold Use of the (Moral) Law

The threefold use of the law has been used to articulate the ways in which the moral law functions, as summarized in the Ten Commandments. Echoing the Formula of Concord, article 6, these functions of the law are as follows:

First use: magistrate; external restraint
Second use: pedagogical; reveals sin
Third use: rule for the Christian life[27]

The first use of the law is that it acts as an external restraint. According to Calvin, the threat of punishment contained in the law has the effect of restraining those who do not care for that which is good and right but who for fear of the consequences might be restrained (Rom. 13:1–7; 1 Tim. 1:8–11; 1 Pet. 2:13–14). As they possess poor frames of mind and fail to love what is good, they in no way appear righteous before God.[28]

The second use of the law reveals sin and shows humanity their inability to live up to God's perfect standard of righteousness. Calvin describes the law as a mirror that reveals sin.[29] The revelation of sin induces sinners to seek grace. With respect to the old

---

25. See J. Ligon Duncan III, "Moses' Law for Modern Government: The Intellectual and Sociological Origins of the Christian Reconstructionist Movement" (Greenville, SC: Reformed Academic Press, 1994), a paper originally presented to the Social Science History Association, Atlanta, Georgia, October 1994.

26. For what is, in my view, the most impressive and astute rejection of this point in favor of "natural law" terminology, see David VanDrunen, "Natural Law and the Works Principle under Adam and Moses," in Estelle, Fesko, and VanDrunen, *The Law Is Not of Faith*, 283–314. For the direct application of the moral law, see John Murray, *Principles of Conduct: Aspects of Biblical Ethics* (Grand Rapids, MI: Eerdmans, 1957). For a thorough consideration of the topic, see Oliver O'Donovan, *Resurrection and Moral Order: An Outline for Evangelical Ethics* (Grand Rapids, MI: Eerdmans, 1986).

27. Note that Calvin holds to the same threefold use but discusses one and two in a different order. Calvin, *Institutes*, 2.7.6–13. The WCF also recognizes the threefold use, but it reverses the order in 19.6.

28. Calvin, *Institutes*, 2.7.10–11.

29. Calvin, *Institutes*, 2.7.7.

covenant, the despair one experiences leads one to Christ as typified in the sacrificial system, the promises, and the mediatorial role of the priesthood. The ultimate goal of the second use of the law is to reveal sin in the hopes that by forsaking their own righteousness, sinners might turn to Jesus Christ in the gospel (Rom. 3:20; 4:15; 7:7; Gal. 3:19; etc.). The second use also has the ongoing positive function in the lives of believers. Calvin writes,

> This means that, dismissing the stupid opinion of their own strength, they come to realize that they stand and are upheld by God's hand alone; that naked and empty-handed, they flee to his mercy, repose entirely in it, hide deep within it, and seize upon it alone for all righteousness and merit.[30]

In other words, the second use of the law is not just for the unbeliever. The law induces us to continue seeking Christ and his mercy by revealing our sin.

Finally, in both Testaments, the moral law serves as the guide to the life of the believer. This is the third use of the law. It is worth briefly considering a typical difference between Lutheran and Reformed discussions of the law. It should be noted that the Lutheran and Reformed division on this point is sometimes understood too simplistically. Within the Reformed tradition, there remains significant influence from the Lutheran law-gospel dialectic, and some argue that Luther later in his life articulated a more positive role of the law in the life of the believer.[31] With those caveats in view, the Lutheran position stems from the sharp law-gospel distinction from passages such as Galatians 3:12: "But the law is not of faith, rather 'The one who does them shall live by them.'" With respect to justification, the dialectical relationship between the law and gospel remains at the core of traditional Reformed theology. Lutherans and Reformed agree on this point: with respect to justification, the law can serve only to condemn. The point of departure comes with respect to the relationship of the justified person to the law. In Reformed theology, unlike Lutheran theology, the moral law, as summarized in the Ten Commandments, has a positive function in the life of believers with respect to sanctification.[32] The Westminster Larger Catechism 77 helpfully summarizes the inseparable relationship and differences between justification and sanctification:

---

30. Calvin, *Institutes*, 2.7.8.

31. See the *tertius usus legis* in Philipp Melanchthon, *The Chief Theological Topics (1559)*, trans. J. A. O. Preus, 2nd ed. (Saint Louis, MO: Concordia, 2011), 123–24. On Luther and this proposed theological development, see Carl R. Trueman, *Luther on the Christian Life: Cross and Freedom*, TCL (Wheaton, IL: Crossway, 2015), 159–74. Trueman writes, "Typically, Melanchthon is the one credited with developing the so-called third use of the law, its use as a guide for practical daily life of the Christian. In fact, I would argue that the basic concept, if not the actual terminology, is there in Martin Luther (especially after 1525)" (172). One could also point toward Luther's *Treatise on Good Works*, which applies the Decalogue in a third-use type of way. This text was written in 1520, the same year as his three great Reformational treatises—*To the Christian Nobility of the German Nation, On the Babylonian Captivity of the Church*, and *The Freedom of a Christian*. For a recent discussion of the Lutheran tradition in relation to the law, see Malysz, "Law in the Lutheran Tradition," 38–44.

32. For Calvin, the third use of the law is the most prominent function. See Calvin, *Institutes*, 2.7.12. While the Lutheran view holds to a threefold use of the law yet focuses on the condemning function of the law, "the Reformed," Herman Bavinck explains, "held a very different view. The political use and the pedagogical use of the law

Q. Wherein do justification and sanctification differ?

A. Although sanctification be inseparably joined with justification, yet they differ, in that God in justification imputeth the righteousness of Christ; in sanctification of his Spirit infuseth grace, and enableth to the exercise thereof; in the former, sin is pardoned; in the other, it is subdued: the one doth equally free all believers from the revenging wrath of God, and that perfectly in this life, that they never fall into condemnations; the other is neither equal in all, nor in this life perfect in any, but growing up to perfection.

With these differences in view and with respect to justification, the law is contrary to grace. With respect to sanctification, law has a place in the life of the believer. Thus, Paul can say in Galatians 3:12 that the law is contrary to faith and yet at the same time apply the fifth commandment to believers in Ephesians 6:2–3.

While there are numerous passages that point toward a positive function of the law in the lives of believers (Rom. 8:3–4; 13:8–10; 1 Cor. 7:19; 9:21; etc.), there are other challenging passages (Rom. 7:6). Luther, however, spoke of the law in primarily two uses, the civil and the theological.[33] These two uses correspond to the first and second uses of the law above. The Ten Commandments are an articulation of the natural law that is written on the hearts of humans and so bind all to it. This standard, then, is not primarily Mosaic, and thus it is ongoing. For Luther, the law can only condemn, but it has ongoing implications in the lives of believers who are at the same time justified and sinners (*simul iustus et peccator*).[34] The condemning function of the law continues to point believers back to Christ by revealing their sin. Yet the result is not licentiousness. Rather, the Christian in union with Christ is set free to love God and neighbor. Thus understood, the law can be kept only by faith.[35] Since a fuller treatment of the law in Paul is beyond the scope of this chapter,[36] it is worthwhile to note that this threefold use of the law is commonly held in Reformed theology. The moral law requires perfect love of God, and out of this comes a love for neighbor. Yet it must be remembered that in both the Lutheran and Reformed traditions, pursuit of the love of God and the love of neighbor can occur only by faith and in union with Christ.[37] Abstracted from union

---

have only become 'accidentally' necessary because of sin. Even when these earlier uses cease, the most important one, the didactic or normative use, remains. The law, after all, is an expression of God's being." *Reformed Dogmatics*, vol. 4, *Holy Spirit, Church, and New Creation*, ed. John Bolt, trans. John Vriend (Grand Rapids, MI: Baker Academic, 2006), 55. For the third use of the law in the Puritans, see Beeke and Jones, *Puritan Theology*, 555–71.

33. Malysz, "Law in the Lutheran Tradition," 23–24.

34. Luther, *Luther's Works*, 26:232.

35. For an excellent discussion, see Malysz, "Law in the Lutheran Tradition."

36. See Herman Ridderbos's classic discussion of the third use in *Paul: An Outline of His Theology*, trans. John Richard de Witt (Grand Rapids, MI: Eerdmans, 1975), 278–88.

37. For an excellent discussion of union with Christ and its implications for the transformation from the dominion of sin and weakness of the flesh to the power of the Spirit, see Grant Macaskill, *Union with Christ in the New Testament* (Oxford: Oxford University, 2013), 238–43. John M. G. Barclay writes,

Paul perfects the incongruity of the gift (given to the unworthy) but he does *not* perfect its non-circularity (expecting nothing in return). The divine gift in Christ was *unconditioned* (based on no prior conditions)

with Christ and the power of the Holy Spirit, the third use of the law, which can be applied only to believers, would be merely a form of legalism and works righteousness. In other words, we need God to do a work of transformation.

The Love of God and the Law of God

Martin Luther understood human and divine love differently from one another: "The love of God does not find, but creates, that which is pleasing to it. The love of man comes into being through that which is pleasing to it."[38] Human love is reactive; God's love is creative.[39] Humans react to that which they find lovely, but God creates that which is lovely in his people. If God's love were merely reactive to fallen humanity, there would be no hope. The standard by which a perfect God must judge could serve only to condemn fallen humanity, since the law of God is viewed as an expression of God's own character. Such condemnation is but one use of the law.

Because human love is reactive, the Bible calls humanity to respond to the loveliness of God. Since love of God and love of neighbor are the sum total of the moral law (discussed below), it is fitting that the Ten Commandments begin by inducing Israel to react to God's love by stating what God has done for his people.

Deuteronomy 7 provides what may be viewed as a somewhat programmatic text that expresses the origin of God's love followed by the implications of that love:

> For you are a people holy to the LORD your God. The LORD your God has chosen you to be a people for his treasured possession, out of all the peoples who are on the face of the earth. It was not because you were more in number than any other people that the LORD set his love on you and chose you, for you were the fewest of all peoples, but it is because the LORD loves you and is keeping the oath that he swore to your fathers, that the LORD has brought you out with a mighty hand and redeemed you from the house of slavery, from the hand of Pharaoh king of Egypt. (Deut. 7:6–8)

The origin of the love of God for Israel is not the people. Rather, the source of God's love for his people is God himself (Deut. 7:8). God loves his people because he loves them. Further, the love God has for his people is rooted in keeping his oath that he swore to their fathers (Deut. 7:8). In other words, God delivered Israel out of Egypt and covenanted with them because of his love and in faithfulness to his promises. Of

---

but it is not *unconditional* (carrying no subsequent demands). . . . The incongruous gift that is strongly obliging, and that bears as its "fruit" obedience to God, remains, in fact, *incongruous*. How so? Because the very life that offers this obedience is a miraculous and incongruous phenomenon, the resurrection life of Christ, which is not just the beginning but the continuing reality of the Christian life.

Paul and the Gift (Grand Rapids, MI: Eerdmans, 2015), 500; emphasis original.

38. Luther, *Luther's Works*, 31:41.

39. This is following Trueman's description of Luther's view of God's love. See Trueman, *Luther on the Christian Life*, 66–67.

course, contextually, this is a clear reference to the Abrahamic covenant. In Romans 4, Paul points out that Abraham was justified by faith (Gen. 15) prior to circumcision (Gen. 17). Further, James appeals to Genesis 22 and the (near) sacrifice of Isaac as the fruit of genuine faith. The covenant that God established unilaterally with Abraham in Genesis 15 had a bilateral destination in Abraham. As Jon Levenson points out, the love of God has to be engaged; this love is summarized in action and affection.[40] This characteristic is seen in God's covenant with Israel too:

> Know therefore that the LORD your God is God, the faithful God who keeps covenant and steadfast love with those who love him and keep his commandments, to a thousand generations, and repays to their face those who hate him, by destroying them. He will not be slack with one who hates him. He will repay him to his face. You shall therefore be careful to do the commandment and the statutes and the rules that I command you today.
>
> And because you listen to these rules and keep and do them, the LORD your God will keep with you the covenant and the steadfast love that he swore to your fathers. He will love you, bless you, and multiply you. He will also bless the fruit of your womb and the fruit of your ground, your grain and your wine and your oil, the increase of your herds and the young of your flock, in the land that he swore to your fathers to give you. (Deut. 7:9–13)

The love that is bestowed on Israel comes with commandments for life in the covenant. These commandments contain both threats of curses and promises of blessing.

A key message of the book of Deuteronomy is the Shema ("Hear," the first Hebrew word in this section), found in 6:4–9 but also more succinctly summarized in 10:12–13:

> And now, Israel, what does the LORD your God require of you, but to fear the LORD your God, to walk in all his ways, to love him, to serve the LORD your God with all your heart and with all your soul, and to keep the commandments and statutes of the LORD, which I am commanding you today for your good?

Because God loved his people, his people have to love God with an exclusive love.[41] Levenson writes, "If we put all this together, we come up with an identification of the love of God with the performance of his commandments. Love, so understood, is not an emotion, not a feeling, but a cover term for acts of obedience."[42] This perspective of obedience as an expression of love is in keeping with Jesus's own admonitions in John 14:15 and John 15. The exclusive love that his people owe to God must also result in a love for others. This interpretation is in keeping with Jesus's summary of the law:

---

40. Levenson, *Love of God*, 21–29.
41. See the discussion of מְאֹדְךָ in Levenson, *Love of God*, 72.
42. Levenson, *Love of God*, 4.

"Teacher, which is the great commandment in the Law?" And he said to him, "You shall love the Lord your God with all your heart and with all your soul and with all your mind. This is the great and first commandment. And a second is like it: You shall love your neighbor as yourself. On these two commandments depend all the Law and the Prophets." (Matt. 22:36–40)

All the Law and Prophets depend on the exclusive love owed to God and the resultant love of neighbor. Those who love the Lord keep his commandments (Deut. 7:9–10).

The covenant formalizes the terms of the relationship between God and Israel. God loves his people, and they must respond to that love. But how are they to love God? This love is summarized in the Ten Commandments.[43] As Levenson argues,

> And so, when at Sinai/Horeb God makes his great claim on Israel's service and Israel immediately accepts it, we have a powerful narrative representation of the dynamics of covenantal love—not law as the antithesis of love, or love as a substitute for law, but love made practical, reliable, reciprocal, and socially responsible through law, divine law observed in love.[44]

God's love for his people is so great that it pervades all their lives. Since he is the one true God and is perfect in every way, the best thing that God can do for them out of that love is to produce that which is lovely in them. Since God is the most excellent of all, the greatest good we can experience is being transformed into people who glorify and enjoy him (WSC 1).

Israel was the visible people of God, but not all within it were elect.[45] Since Israel was made up of genuine believers—those who were the spiritual children of Abraham by faith, whether physical descendants (David) or not (Rahab)—and those who were not (Jeroboam),[46] the law functioned in multiple ways in Israel. While the law led to repentance with Josiah, pointing him to the sacrificial system, the law served only to condemn others.

---

43. Stephen A. Kaufman argues that Deut. 12–26 could be divided to correlate with the Ten Commandments. "The Structure of the Deuteronomic Law," *Maarav* 1, no. 2 (1979): 105–58. Some have expanded the correlation to include Deut. 6–11, viewing it not just as a literary framework but as an intent to address the spirit of the law. This approach provides the key to understanding the compositional structure of the book. See John Walton, "Deuteronomy: An Exposition of the Spirit of the Law," *GTJ* 8, no. 2 (1987): 213–25. See further still John D. Currid, *Deuteronomy*, EPSC (Darlington, UK: Evangelical Press, 2006). Contra Daniel I. Block, *Deuteronomy*, NIVAC (Grand Rapids, MI: Zondervan, 2012), 301–2. The argument that the structure follows the Ten Commandments is interesting in the broad strokes but fails to convince in numerous places. Of course, numerous scholars see the structure of Deuteronomy to be covenantal. See, e.g., Meredith G. Kline's helpful little book *Treaty of the Great King: The Covenant Structure of Deuteronomy; Studies and Commentary* (Grand Rapids, MI: Eerdmans, 1963). See also Gentry and Wellum, *Kingdom through Covenant*, 357–63.

44. Levenson, *Love of God*, 57.

45. Meredith G. Kline, *By Oath Consigned: A Reinterpretation of the Covenant Signs of Circumcision and Baptism* (Eugene, OR: Wipf and Stock, 1998).

46. Even the fuller meaning of circumcision as an outward sign of an inward reality must be distinguished from mere outward performance. Geerhardus Vos concludes, "Circumcision teaches that physical descent from Abraham is not sufficient to make true Israelites. The uncleanness and disqualification of nature must be taken away. Dogmatically speaking, therefore, circumcision stands for justification and regeneration, plus sanctification." *Biblical Theology: Old and New Testaments* (1948; repr., Edinburgh: Banner of Truth, 2014), 90.

The multifunctional nature of the law can be seen in Joshua 24. For Joshua and his family, this is the standard rule of life (24:15). This function is in keeping with the third use of the law. When addressing the people, however, Joshua uses the law to expose Israel's inability to keep the law (24:19–20). When they insist that they will serve the Lord, Joshua warns them of the implications of this. Undeterred, the Israelites say they will serve the Lord (24:21). Joshua tells them to put away their idols (24:23). In the first instance, Joshua sees the standard of the law as the rule of life for his family. It would be inconsistent for him to have in view some sort of perfection. Rather, Joshua, despite being a sinner, loves the Lord his God alone, loves his neighbor, and receives forgiveness by faith and through the sacrificial system. With the Israelites, however, Joshua uses the law to reveal their sin (similar to the second use of the law above) in the hopes that they will repent of their idolatry.

The Exile

The Mosaic covenant resulted in the expulsion of Israel from the promised land. In view of the loss of the land, the conditionality within the covenant must be considered further. J. Gordon McConville offers a balanced perspective on the question whether the land is conditional or a gift.[47] Passages like Deuteronomy 4:25–28 point toward a conditionality:

> When you father children and children's children, and have grown old in the land, if you act corruptly by making carved image in the form of anything, and by doing what is evil in the sight of the LORD your God, so as to provoke him to anger, I call heaven and earth to witness against you today, that you will soon utterly perish from the land that you are going over the Jordan to possess. You will not live long in it, but will be utterly destroyed. And the LORD will scatter you among the peoples, and you will be left few in number among the nations where the LORD will drive you. And there you will serve gods of wood and stone, the work of human hands, that neither see, nor hear, nor eat, nor smell.

If the Israelites committed idolatry and forsook the Lord their God, they would be dispersed and removed from the land. This conditionality relates to the continuation of life in the land. There even appears, however, to be some conditionality required prior to entering the land (Deut. 6:18; 8:1; 11:8).

The land is also viewed as a gift. The verb נתן ("to give") occurs 167 times in the book of Deuteronomy; 137 times the Lord is the subject.[48] The object of the verb is usually the land but is also sometimes cities, towns, villages, and the fruit of the ground (26:10). The Lord says that he swore to give the land to Abraham, Isaac, and Jacob (1:8).

---

47. See the discussion in J. Gordon McConville, *Law and Theology in Deuteronomy*, JSOTSup 33 (Sheffield, UK: JSOT Press, 1984), 11–13.
48. See figures in McConville, *Law and Theology*, 13–14.

So reception of the land is based on God's promise. Perhaps it is best to view the land as a gift but one that comes with responsibility. The continuation of the Abrahamic covenant at Sinai had a bilateral destination in the people of God (note, for example, the fifth commandment from Ex. 20:12 in Eph. 6:3, "that it may go well with you and that you may live long in the land"). For some, it resulted only in judgment; for others, it was the means by which they enjoyed life in the covenant of grace.

While the law of God requires perfection as the standard of righteousness, the exile did not occur because of Israel's failure to live to this standard perfectly. Rather, as an administration of the covenant of grace, the Mosaic covenant with its sacrificial system and mediatorial roles of the prophets and priests provided a way for sinful but believing Israelites to enjoy communion with God. When one searches for the actual reasons for the exile, the above summary of the law by Jesus is particularly instructive. The Prophets (both Former and Latter)[49] are also important when answering this question. The Israelites were exiled for their failure to love the one true God and him alone. As an example of this, the exile of the northern kingdom, just like the downfall of Jeroboam, was the result of idolatry (1 Kings 14; 2 Kings 17). Later, Judah went into exile because of the idolatry during the reign of Manasseh (2 Kings 21). Primarily, their failure to love the Lord their God and to worship him according to his commandments resulted in the exile.

As discussed above, the proper love of God must result in a proper love of neighbor. The Prophets also cite instances of injustice in the land as causes for the exile (2 Kings 24:4; Hab. 1). Further, the Prophets use the injustice of both the northern and southern kingdoms to reveal their actual spiritual condition (Isa. 1; Amos 5; Mic. 6). Their failure to love their neighbor exposed the condition of their hearts, which pointed to the manipulative and perfunctory nature of their worship. Even when they worshiped God in the true and stipulated ways, their worship was false if they went on unrepentant of their sinful treatment of others. Their failure to love God alone and, as a result, their failure to love their neighbor caused the exile. Neither physical descent from Abraham nor outward forms of worship were sufficient to make genuine believers. This shows the weakness of the law.

The transition from the weak and shadowy old covenant to the better new covenant goes back to God's love. God overcame and achieved what the law, weakened by the flesh, could not (Rom. 8). Isaiah 54 contrasts God's anger in the exile with his love:

"For a brief moment I deserted you,
    but with great compassion I will gather you.
In overflowing anger for a moment
    I hid my face from you,

---

49. See the discussion of the Hebrew canon and the Former and Latter Prophets in Stephen G. Dempster, *Dominion and Dynasty: A Theology of the Hebrew Bible*, NSBT 15 (Downers Grove, IL: IVP Academic, 2003), 15–51. See more recently Miles V. Van Pelt, "Introduction," in *A Biblical-Theological Introduction to the Old Testament: The Gospel Promised*, ed. Miles V. Van Pelt (Wheaton, IL: Crossway, 2016), 30–41. Earlier, see the work by Meredith G. Kline, *The Structure of Biblical Authority*, 2nd ed. (Eugene, OR: Wipf and Stock, 1997).

but with everlasting love I will have compassion on you,"
    says the LORD, your Redeemer.

"This is like the days of Noah to me:[50]
    as I swore that the waters of Noah
    should no more go over the earth,
so I have sworn that I will not be angry with you,
    and will not rebuke you.
For the mountains may depart
    and the hills be removed,
but my steadfast love shall not depart from you,
    and my covenant of peace shall not be removed,"
    says the LORD, who has compassion on you. (Isa. 54:7–10)

The exile is described as an outpouring of anger that lasted for a moment.[51] Although genuine believers like Daniel and Ezekiel went into exile with the apostate of Israel, God was not finished with his people. His anger with his covenant people was for but a moment, compared to his eternal love for his genuine people. When cast in relation to God's eternal love, the temporary outpouring of wrath is compared to the permanent, unrepeatable event of the flood. This communicates the transition from the wrath that Israel faced in the exile to the security of the eternal new covenant that God was establishing with his people.[52] God achieved the permanent covenant of peace in Isaiah 54 by the sacrifice of the suffering servant in Isaiah 53.[53] So while God requires humans to react to his love, God's love is creating something lovely in his people through their union with Christ and by the power of the Holy Spirit.

Republication Thesis: A Works Principle

Charles Hodge wrote that the Mosaic covenant was in some sense a republication of the covenant of works.[54] Meredith Kline was a champion of republication during the twentieth century. Before attempting to summarize briefly Kline's view of republication,

---

50. The ESV follows here 1QIsaᵃ and the other ancient manuscripts except the Septuagint and Masoretic Text, which read, "For this is like the waters of Noah for me." The difference in readings is not consonantal but a difference in divisions and pointing. See, e.g., Joseph Blenkinsopp, *Isaiah 40–55: A New Translation with Introduction and Commentary*, AB 19A (New Haven, CT: Yale University Press, 2002), 359. For a list of variants, see Moshe H. Goshen-Gottstein, ed., *The Book of Isaiah*, in Hebrew University Bible (Jerusalem: Magnes, 1995), דמו.

51. Mark J. Boda writes, "While he was angry a *little*, the nations exceeded his disciplinary intentions. The anger against his people in view here must refer to that which motivated the destruction of Jerusalem in 586 BC. . . . Yahweh here admits to his angry discipline of his people, something defended by the people in [Zech.] 1:6b." *The Book of Zechariah*, NICOT (Grand Rapids, MI: Eerdmans, 2015), 149; emphasis original.

52. See the description in John Goldingay, *The Message of Isaiah 40–55: A Literary-Theological Commentary* (New York: T&T Clark, 2005), 532.

53. On this progression of a covenant of peace through Isa. 53, see, e.g., Paul R. Williamson, *Sealed with an Oath: Covenant in God's Unfolding Purpose*, NSBT 23 (Downers Grove, IL: InterVarsity Press, 2007), 160–61.

54. Charles Hodge, *An Exposition of the Second Epistle to the Corinthians* (New York: A. C. Armstrong and Son, 1891), 57–58.

it is worthwhile to note the context in which he was writing, as emphases can often be shaped by historical context. Kline wrote in defense of the traditional doctrine of justification by faith alone (contra Norman Shepherd), in defense of the covenant of works (contra John Murray), and in defense of covenant theology (contra Daniel Fuller).[55] Further, Kline defended the doctrine of the active obedience of Christ, the doctrine without which J. Gresham Machen famously said he would be without hope. While there remains much debate about Kline's view of the Mosaic covenant, his programmatic statements will be taken here as primarily informative. So while there is a way to read Kline to make the case that he held to a substantial republication of the covenant of works, in *Kingdom Prologue* Kline says that the Mosaic covenant is an administration of the covenant of grace:[56]

> The Mosaic economy, while an administration of grace on its fundamental level of concern with the eternal salvation of the individual, was at the same time on its temporary, typological kingdom level informed by the principle of works. Thus, for example, the apostle Paul in Romans 10:4ff. and Galatians 3:10ff. (cf. Rom 9:32) contrasts the old order of the law with the gospel order of grace and faith, identifying the old covenant as one of bondage, condemnation, and death (cf. 2 Cor 3:6–9; Gal 4:24–26). The old covenant was law, the opposite of grace-faith, and in the postlapsarian world that meant it would turn out to be an administration of condemnation as a consequence of sinful Israel's failure to maintain the necessary meritorious obedience. Had the old typological kingdom been secured by sovereign grace in Christ, Israel would not have lost her national election. A satisfactory explanation of Israel's fall demands works, not grace, as the controlling administrative principle.[57]

Kline goes on to say that the Mosaic covenant had a typological kingdom overlay (discussed further below) that republished the covenant of works. Kline writes,

> At the same time, Paul affirmed that the Mosaic Covenant did not annul the promise arrangement given earlier to Abraham (Gal 3:17). The explanation for this is that the

---

55. For an overview of the development of Norman Shepherd's theology and the ensuing controversy, see Guy Prentiss Waters, "The Theology of Norman Shepherd: A Study in Development, 1963–2006," in *The Hope Fulfilled: Essays in Honor of O. Palmer Robertson*, ed. Robert L. Penny (Phillipsburg, NJ: P&R, 2008), 207–31; O. Palmer Robertson, *The Current Justification Controversy*, Trinity Paper 63 (Unicoi, TN: Trinity Foundation, 2003); Samuel E. Waldron, *Faith, Obedience, and Justification: Current Evangelical Departures from Sola Fide*, RBDS 1 (Palmdale, CA: Reformed Baptist Academic Press, 2006), 157–86. For interaction with John Murray's covenant theology, see O. Palmer Robertson, "Current Reformed Thinking on the Nature of the Divine Covenants," *WTJ* 40, no. 1 (1977): 63–76; Andrew M. Elam, Robert C. Van Kooten, and Randall A. Bergquist, *Merit and Moses: A Critique of the Klinean Doctrine of Republication* (Eugene, OR: Wipf and Stock, 2014), 12–22. For critiques of Daniel Fuller, see Meredith G. Kline, "Covenant Theology under Attack," *New Horizons* 15, no. 2 (1994); Waldron, *Faith, Obedience, and Justification*, 127–55.

56. See chap. 7 in the Orthodox Presbyterian Church's "Report of the Committee to Study Republication," 2016, http://opc.org/GA/republication.html.

57. Meredith G. Kline, *Kingdom Prologue: Genesis Foundations for a Covenantal Worldview* (Overland Park, KS: Two Age, 2000), 109.

old covenant order was composed of two strata and the works principle enunciated in Leviticus 18:5, and elsewhere in the law, applied only to one of these, a secondary stratum. There was a foundational stratum having to do with the personal attainment of the eternal kingdom of salvation and this underlying stratum, continuous with all preceding and succeeding administrations of the Lord's Covenant of Grace with the church, was informed by the principle of grace (cf., e.g., Rom 4:16). Because the Abrahamic covenant of promise found continuity in the Mosaic order at this under-lying level, it was not abrogated by the latter. The works principle in the Mosaic order was confined to the typological sphere of the provisional earthly kingdom which was superimposed as a secondary overlay on the foundational stratum.[58]

For Kline, at the level of individual salvation, the Abrahamic covenant and its righteousness-by-faith principle remained normative, while at the national level, a king-dom overlay governed by a works principle pointed forward to the merit of Jesus Christ. In other words, covenantal fidelity resulted in the Israelites continuing in the land, while individual salvation remained in fundamental continuity with the Abrahamic covenant.

For Kline, such covenant keeping, however, is not purely meritorious; it is typologi-cally meritorious.[59] Kline does not see the obedience required for continuation of life in the land as perfect in the old covenant. Just as an imperfect mediator like Moses or an imperfect priest like Aaron were types of the perfect mediator and priest, Jesus Christ, so also the imperfect typological obedience pointed forward to the antitypological perfect obedience of Jesus Christ.[60] The Israelites' imperfect obedience for the right to live in the land (a type of heaven) was a type of the perfect and active obedience of Christ, who earned our right to enter heaven. But just as Adam's sin resulted in expulsion from the garden of Eden, so also the sin of Israel resulted in their expulsion from the land. Indeed, when Leviticus 18:5 republishes the principle "Do this and live," it is a republication of the works principle found in the covenant of works, according to this interpretation.[61] To this passage we will return below.

---

58. Kline, *Kingdom Prologue*, 321.

59. This idea of typological merit is challenging. I agree with the Orthodox Presbyterian Church's "Report of the Committee to Study Republication" when it states (4.2),

Given what the confession has to say about types and what it has to say about merit and demerit, real questions are raised which are not easily answered. After all, our imperfection under the moral law is intended to point us to Christ. But does a works principle do the same? This question is especially pointed if the works principle requires a less-than-perfect obedience. What is the typological import of this imperfection with respect to merit and obedience, both ours and Christ's? How is such a principle really analogous—even typologically— to the Adamic covenant of works? It is not particularly controversial to argue for the confessional compatibility of seeing in the Mosaic, indeed, in the whole Old Testament economy, reiterations of Adam's demerit, failure, and rebellion in Ahab and the kings of Israel, or types of Christ's merit in Abraham the patriarch or Aaron the priest. On the other hand, since a type should reflect its symbolized reality, it is quite another step to argue for "typological legibility" and to ask what it might represent about works, faith, and the work of Christ.

60. For a criticism of this typology, see Venema, *Christ and Covenant Theology*, 37–144.

61. For further discussion on Lev. 18:5 and its use in the New Testament, see Bryan D. Estelle, "Leviticus 18:5 and Deuteronomy 30:1–14 in Biblical Theological Development: Entitlement to Heaven Foreclosed and Proffered," in Estelle, Fesko, and VanDrunen, *The Law Is Not of Faith*, 109–46.

The active obedience of Christ merited our right to salvation through our union with Christ.[62] For Kline, this operative works principle is fundamental to understanding the nature of the Old Testament covenants. First of all, if Adam had obeyed God, Adam would have received a covenant of grant that resulted in life in the garden with God:

> In our introductory comments on the Creator's Covenant of Works with Adam we suggested that that covenant was comparable to the proposal of a grant in which a great king offered to give favored treatment to a lesser ruler on the condition of his assuming and performing the obligations of loyal service as a covenant vassal. . . . Noah, unlike Adam, is viewed as a covenant servant who has already demonstrated his fidelity.[63]

Noah, who is introduced as finding favor with God, was righteous (Gen. 6–9). The covenant made with Noah resulted in a grant that Noah's prior typological (not perfect!) obedience secured.[64] Abra(ha)m, in obedience to God's calling, followed God (Gen. 12) and, in refusing to be made rich by the king of Sodom (Gen. 14), was granted a covenant that was (primarily) unconditional. The covenant is established and confirmed after his obedience in Genesis 22.[65] Again, the obedience, albeit imperfect, took on typological significance for Kline. The same may be said of the Davidic covenant. In each instance, the past obedience, imperfect as it was, took on typological significance for God's purposes. The Mosaic covenant, much like the Adamic covenant, held out the conditional blessing of life in the land, which like the garden was a type of heaven. The primary difference is that perfect obedience was required in the original covenant of works, while in the administrative republication of the covenant of works in the Mosaic covenant, an imperfect obedience was acceptable because it pointed forward to the perfect obedience of Christ.

While some have argued that an existential conflict would have existed in Israel if they were living under grace for salvation individually but under a covenant of works at a national level, this does not seem to be a necessary consequence of the republication position.[66] On the level of salvation, the Israelites enjoyed salvation by grace through faith. Yet that grace was costly. That costly grace and the need for it to be achieved was reinforced in the everyday works principle that resulted in life or death for Israel. The deficit of merit continually held forth before Israel highlighted the need for a mediator and sacrifice. By so doing, the active obedience of Christ is prefigured and shown forth as necessary. Nev-

---

62. For recent discussions of the imputation of the active obedience of Christ and the Westminster Assembly, see Alan Strange, "The Imputation of the Active Obedience of Christ at the Westminster Assembly," in Haykin and Jones, *Drawn into Controversie*, 31–51; Jeffrey K. Jue, "The Active Obedience of Christ and the Theology of the Westminster Standards: A Historical Investigation," in *Justified in Christ: God's Plan for Us in Justification*, ed. K. Scott Oliphint (Fearn, Ross-shire, Scotland: Mentor, 2007); Heber Carlos de Campos Jr., *Doctrine in Development: Johannes Piscator and Debates over Christ's Active Obedience*, RHTS (Grand Rapids, MI: Reformation Heritage Books, 2017).

63. Kline, *Kingdom Prologue*, 233.

64. Kline, *Kingdom Prologue*, 234–39.

65. Kline, *Kingdom Prologue*, 323–26.

66. Elam, Van Kooten, and Bergquist, *Merit and Moses*, 125–29.

ertheless, it is incorrect to assume that without a republication of a covenant of works, the active obedience of Christ cannot be foreshadowed in the old covenant. As stated above, the perfect rule of righteousness remains in force since before the fall. While a proper covenant of works was impossible for sinful humanity, the Mosaic administration of the covenant of grace was a covenant of works for Christ, the perfect Son of God.

While much more can be said about the republication thesis, one of the most significant passages that relate to this position is Leviticus 18:5,[67] which Paul quotes in Romans 10:5–6 and Galatians 3:12. While a more extensive discussion of Paul's view belongs elsewhere in this volume, a few observations are warranted here for the sake of completion.

In Romans 10:5, Paul sets forth an antithesis between the righteousness achieved by keeping the law (Lev. 18:5) and the righteousness that comes by faith (Deut. 30:14).[68] This antithesis is also mentioned in Galatians 3:12. For the purposes of this essay, the main question is whether Paul is drawing on a works principle that is inherent in the law or whether he is responding to a misappropriation of the law by his Jewish opponents.

Two main positions on Leviticus 18:5 and Paul's use of it are worth considering in brief. Bryan Estelle offers a thorough exegetical defense of the position that Paul is pointing to an actual works principle contained within the Mosaic administration of the covenant of grace.[69] Estelle argues that this works principle, while not touching on salvation, must be viewed as operable within the old covenant. Estelle writes of Jeremiah 31:33, "The reader is obliged to say that a works principle in the old covenant was operative in some sense because the text clearly states that it was a fracturable covenant, 'not like the one *they broke*.'"[70] In sum, for Estelle and others, Paul is not repurposing Leviticus 18:5 for the sake of argument against legalism; rather, Paul is highlighting an actual antithesis between the righteousness of the law and the righteousness of faith.[71]

The other position worthy of consideration here is articulated by Guy Waters in chapter 11 of this volume. Therefore, it is unnecessary to restate it in full here. Basically, many interpreters within the Reformed tradition argue that Paul is responding to his opponents who would seek to rely on the law.[72] In order to refute their fleshly efforts to

---

67. For an extensive discussion of Lev. 18:5 in the rest of the Old Testament, in Jewish interpretation, and in Paul, see Francis Watson, *Paul and the Hermeneutics of Faith* (London: T&T Clark, 2004).

68. Richard Hays, for example, presents a case against the antithesis view and understands Paul to be saying that Deut. 30:14 explains further what Moses says in Lev. 18:5. See Richard B. Hays, *Echoes of Scripture in the Letters of Paul* (New Haven, CT: Yale University Press, 1989), 75–77. For the antithesis view, consider Watson, *Paul and the Hermeneutics of Faith*, 315–41. See also Barclay, *Paul and the Gift*, 541–44, esp. 542n47; Guy Prentiss Waters, "Romans 10:5 and the Covenant of Works," in Estelle, Fesko, and VanDrunen, *The Law Is Not of Faith*, 210–39; Waters, "Covenant in Paul," chap. 11 in this volume.

69. One should note how careful Estelle is when advancing his arguments. In fact, Estelle situates the argument of his position within the context of Reformed theology; see, e.g., Estelle, "Leviticus 18:5 and Deuteronomy 30:1–14," 132n100, 136.

70. Estelle, "Leviticus 18:5 and Deuteronomy 30:1–14," 130; emphasis original.

71. See, e.g., T. David Gordon, "Abraham and Sinai Contrasted in Galatians 3:6–14," in Estelle, Fesko, and VanDrunen, *The Law Is Not of Faith*, 240–58.

72. Venema writes, "As we have seen in our consideration of the view of the Mosaic Administration in Calvin, Turretin, and Witsius, these formative writers in the history of Reformed theology consistently interpret Paul to be

achieve righteousness, Paul uses the law, abstracted from its gracious context, in order to demonstrate the impossibility of achieving righteousness by law keeping. Crucial to this interpretation is Romans 9:32: "Why? Because they did not pursue it by faith, but as if it were based on works. They have stumbled over the stumbling stone."

Leviticus 18:5 states, "You shall therefore keep my statutes and my rules; if a person does them, he shall live by them: I am the LORD." The preceding verses mention the ways of life and statutes of the Egyptians and the Canaanites (18:3) to distinguish between covenant life in Israel and the ways of the Egyptians and Canaanites. By contrast, God says to Israel, "You shall follow my rules and keep my statutes and walk in them. I am the LORD your God" (18:4). The command to obey and the promise of life is in the immediate context of the partially cited covenant formula: "Speak to the people of Israel and say to them, I am the LORD your God" (18:2). The principle of the offer of life and the threats against various forms of sexual immorality come after the central Day of Atonement and the call to holiness: "You shall be holy, for I the LORD your God am holy" (19:2). In its proper context, then, the expectations for life in the covenant occur in the redemptive context of two key aspects of the Mosaic covenant: deliverance from Egypt and the atonement. Such expectations are not unique to life in the covenant.

In the context of those who want to claim descent from Abraham as evidence of a right relationship with God, Jesus distinguishes between the true descendants of Abraham and those who are not. In this context, he states, "Truly, truly, I say to you, if anyone keeps my word, he will never see death" (John 8:51).[73] Richard Hays further connects John 8 with Paul's discussion in Galatians 3, where Paul argues that those who want to live by the law must do the law perfectly.[74]

As discussed above, the positive use of the law can only ever relate to believers. For this reason, the moment that someone seeks a right relationship with God through law keeping, the law can only condemn, since the law, which is good, is weakened by sinful flesh (Rom. 8). To pursue it in that way would necessarily be to evidence unbelief in Christ as one's way, truth, and life. So whether it is the Judaizers of Galatians 3, the Jews of John 8, or the unfaithful among Israel, the law, which is a blessing within the divinely established covenant relationship, can only reveal and condemn sin in the flesh when abstracted from that covenant context.

Conclusion

In this chapter, I have sought to situate the Mosaic covenant within the covenant of grace. Proponents of this view hold to the fundamental continuity of Scripture, seeing

---

addressing a 'legalistic' abuse or misappropriation of the teaching of Leviticus 18:5." *Christ and Covenant Theology*, 37–144, summary on 109. See also Dunson, "Law Evidently Is Not Contrary to Faith."

73. Gordon J. Wenham connects this passage to Lev. 18:5. *The Book of Leviticus*, NICOT (Grand Rapids, MI: Eerdmans, 1979), 253.

74. Richard B. Hays, *Echoes of Scripture in the Gospels* (Waco, TX: Baylor University Press, 2016), 290–91.

the greatest break in biblical history as occurring with the fall. The arc of biblical history, then, is creation, fall, redemption, and consummation. Although belonging to the covenant of grace, the Mosaic covenant must be considered a weak, shadowy, and inferior administration to the new covenant. While much can be said about the movement from the old to new covenant, perhaps most significant is that believers receive the Spirit of the risen and exalted Christ in the new covenant. Prior to the resurrection and exaltation of Christ, the Spirit was at work in converting and producing fruit in God's people. But in the new covenant, the Spirit is at work more powerfully in the lives of believers who have been united to Christ and have become temples of the living God (1 Cor. 3:16).[75]

Despite administrative inferiority to the new covenant, the Mosaic covenant belongs in essence to the one covenant of grace. The Mosaic covenant, like all the administrations of the one covenant of grace, differs substantially from the covenant of works. Francis Turretin writes about the differences between the covenant of works and the covenant of grace as follows:

> Nor can it be objected here that faith was required also in the first covenant and works are not excluded in the second (as was said before). They stand in a far different relation to each other. For in the first covenant faith was required as a work and a part of the inherent righteousness to which life was promised. But in the second, it is demanded, not as a work on account of which life is given, but as a mere instrument apprehending the righteousness of Christ (on account of which alone salvation is granted to us). In the one, faith was a theological virtue from the strength of nature, terminating on God the Creator; in the other, faith is an evangelical condition after the manner of supernatural grace, terminating on Christ the Redeemer. As to works, they were required in the first as an antecedent condition by way of a cause for acquiring life; but in the second, they are only the subsequent condition as the fruit and effect of the life already acquired. In the first, they ought to precede the act of justification; in the second, they follow it.[76]

In short, the essential difference between the covenant of works and the covenant of grace is not the presence or absence of conditions; it is the function of the conditions. In the covenant of works, the conditions precede the blessing of justification. In the covenant of grace, the blessing of justification precedes the condition of evangelical fruit.

---

75. On the doctrine of union with Christ, see the recent work by Macaskill, *Union with Christ in the New Testament*. See, too, the discussion of the new life and transformation offered in the divine gift of Christ in Barclay, *Paul and the Gift*, 493–519. On the role of the Holy Spirit in the old and new covenants, see Morales, *Who Shall Ascend?*, 279–306. For a balanced dogmatic treatment of the Holy Spirit throughout redemptive history, see Sinclair Ferguson, *The Holy Spirit*, CCT (Downers Grove, IL: InterVarsity Press, 1996). For an alternative view, see James M. Hamilton Jr., *God's Indwelling Presence: The Holy Spirit in the Old and New Testaments*, NACSBT (Nashville: B&H Academic, 2006).

76. Turretin, *Institutes*, 12.4.7.

8

THE DAVIDIC COVENANT

Richard P. Belcher Jr.

God's covenant with David represents the culmination of all the promises of the previ-ous covenants.[1] It not only consolidates those promises but sets the stage for the further outworking of those promises in Old Testament history and for their fulfillment in Jesus Christ. The Davidic covenant is a high point of Old Testament theology because it ad-vances to a new stage prior Old Testament concepts, apart from which the hope of a com-ing king cannot be fully understood.[2] The kingdom of God arrives in a formal manner with indications of how God will rule among his people. God situates his throne in a single locality, and the Davidic line is established as the line through which God will exercise his rule on the earth. This chapter examines the key texts that explain the Davidic covenant in order to understand the promises God makes to David, how those promises are fulfilled in Old Testament history, and also how those promises find their fulfillment in Jesus Christ.

2 Samuel 7: God's Promises to David

Background and Setting

David's life as king reaches a turning point in 2 Samuel 7. The chapter begins with David secure in his kingdom, living in his house, enjoying rest from his enemies, which the Lord had given him. David has time to reflect on the accomplishments of his kingdom and what

---

1. The development of the ideas in this chapter are related to another work on understanding covenant theol-ogy that I have been writing for Christian Focus. I thank Christian Focus for granting me permission to use many of the ideas developed in that work for this chapter.

2. Robert D. Bergen calls the Davidic covenant the flowering of a Torah prophecy, the climax of David's life, and the foundation for a major theme in the writings of the Latter Prophets. *1, 2 Samuel*, NAC (Nashville: Broadman & Holman, 2002), 336. Walter Brueggemann calls it the "dramatic and theological center of the entire Samuel corpus" and "the most crucial theological statement of the OT." *First and Second Samuel*, IBC (Louisville: John Knox, 1990), 253, 259.

this period of rest means for the future. He wants to honor God and proposes that a house of cedar be built for him wherein the ark of God will dwell. This suggestion makes sense in the Old Testament context, where it is the duty of the king to build a temple for the gods who have given him victory. Anything less would be considered ingratitude to God.[3] Other events in 2 Samuel have made this request by David possible. In chapter 5, David is made king over all Israel and moves his capital to Jerusalem after conquering the Jebusites. This location is more centrally located in Israel than Hebron, the prior capital.[4] In chapter 6, David brings to Jerusalem the ark of God, the visible symbol of God's presence, which comes to be identified with God's rule over Israel. God is enthroned and seated as King on the cherubim above the ark. The ark is the footstool of the divine throne.[5] With the ark of God in Jerusalem and with David experiencing rest from his enemies, it is appropriate for the king to contemplate building a more permanent temple for God.

Second Samuel 7:1–3 gives the setting for the chapter. God has granted David victory over his enemies, which has led to a period of rest. This rest does not mean the end of warfare for David, because God also promises him future rest from his enemies in 7:11. David enjoys a period of peace that allows him to reflect on God's blessings and to contemplate that he dwells in a house of cedar, but God dwells in a tent. When David first suggests that he wants to build a house for God, the prophet Nathan gives his blessing to the idea. And yet, his request to build a temple is rejected by God, though not because God is angry with him. There are reasons that David is not the man to build the temple; plus, God has something greater planned for him. Instead of David building a house/temple (בַּיִת) for God, God will build a house/dynasty (בַּיִת) for David. This promise is the main focus in 2 Samuel 7 around which the basic elements of God's other promises to David are given. Although 2 Samuel 7 does not use the term "covenant" (בְּרִית) to describe the relationship established here, other passages identify it as a covenant (2 Sam. 23:5; Pss. 89:3, 28, 34; 132:12). These passages confirm that God gives to David an enduring, unconditional promise, sworn on divine oath.[6]

The Dynastic Oracle

Very quickly the word of the Lord comes to Nathan to communicate to David an oracle concerning the building of the temple and God's plans for his future (2 Sam. 4–17).[7]

---

3. Joyce G. Baldwin, *1 and 2 Samuel: An Introduction and Commentary*, TOTC (Downers Grove, IL: InterVarsity Press, 1988), 213–14.

4. O. Palmer Robertson, *The Christ of the Covenants* (Phillipsburg, NJ: Presbyterian and Reformed, 1980), 230.

5. William J. Dumbrell, *Covenant and Creation: A Theology of the Old Testament Covenants* (Nashville: Thomas Nelson, 1984), 142–43.

6. Baldwin, *1 and 2 Samuel*, 213. For further evidence that the covenant is part of the intention of the author of 2 Sam. 7, see David G. Firth, "Speech Acts and Covenant in 2 Samuel 7:1–17," in *The God of Covenant: Biblical, Theological, and Contemporary Perspectives*, ed. Jamie A. Grant and Alistair I. Wilson (Downers Grove, IL: InterVarsity Press, 2005), 79–99.

7. Bill T. Arnold notes that up to this point in 2 Samuel, speeches are used sparingly but that the content of 2 Sam. 7 is composed almost entirely of speeches. The narrator takes a long pause to consider the magnitude of these developments. *1 and 2 Samuel*, NIVAC (Grand Rapids, MI: Zondervan, 2003), 471.

This oracle first contains a reversal of Nathan's positive response to David's desire to build a temple (7:5–7). God asks David why he wants to build a house for him to dwell in. He has never dwelt in a house from the days he brought Israel out of Egypt, nor has he ever requested that a temple be built for him. In fact, the tent structure of the tabernacle allowed God's presence to travel with his people, a tremendous benefit throughout Israel's history. The section ends with the same question, but this time it is set in the period of the judges (7:7). The fact that this question frames this section (7:4–7) shows how important the question is. The point seems to be that the building of a temple should be at God's initiative.[8] The question of 7:5 puts the pronoun "you" in an emphatic position, indicating a rejection of the person (David) rather than a rejection of the action itself (the building of the temple).[9]

Nathan's oracle also reviews David's rise to power (2 Sam. 7:8–9a).[10] God himself took David from being a shepherd and made him a prince over his people Israel. God has been with him wherever he has gone and has given him victory over all his enemies. God's presence has been the source of his success. Even though David has been elevated to a high position as king, the text emphasizes his subservient role to God. God calls him "my servant," a title of honor but also a reminder that David himself is a servant of God. The use of the word "prince" (נָגִיד) reminds him that he is subservient to the real King of Israel, God himself.[11] But God also reminds David that he will bless him with future blessings (7:9b–11). Scholars debate whether the verbs in these verses should be translated as past or future. The form of the verbs would normally be translated as future.[12] Some argue, however, against a future translation on grammatical grounds but also because the blessings mentioned in these verses have already been provided for David at the beginning of the chapter (a great name, a place for Israel to dwell securely, and rest).[13] H. W. Hertzberg thinks that the statements refer to the past but translates them as present because of the possibility that they have been left intentionally ambivalent. What the Lord has done in the past continues to have relevance.[14] And yet, just because God has granted to David a great

---

8. Dumbrell, *Covenant and Creation*, 148. The fact that Yahweh must initiate the move should have been discernible from David's experience of having to wait for the divine pleasure before moving the ark to Jerusalem, as well as the fact that Jerusalem had been put into David's hands by Yahweh. The marking off of the site and the movement of the ark were divine decisions. The timing of building the temple and the person who would build it must also be divine decisions.

9. A. A. Anderson, *2 Samuel*, WBC (Dallas: Word Books, 1989), 118.

10. The verb forms are imperfect *waw* consecutives recounting what God has done for David in the past.

11. Baldwin, *1 and 2 Samuel*, 215. The subservient role of the king is also emphasized in Deut. 17:14–20 with the restrictions placed on the king.

12. The verbs in 2 Sam. 7:9b–11 change to perfect *waw* consecutives.

13. O. Loretz, "The *Perfectum Copulativum* in 2 Sm 7, 9–11," *CBQ* 23, no. 3 (1961): 294–95; H. W. Hertzberg, *I and II Samuel: A Commentary*, OTL (Philadelphia: Westminster, 1964), 286. The grammatical argument against translating the perfect *waw* consecutives as future is that there is no imperative or imperfect preceding them. In support of translating the perfect *waw* consecutives as future is that 2 Sam. 7:10 includes two imperfect verbs with the negative that have to be translated as future. P. Kyle McCarter Jr., *II Samuel: A New Translation with Introduction, Notes, and Commentary*, AB 9 (Garden City, NY: Doubleday, 1984), 202. These are followed by two other perfect *waw* consecutive verbs after a parenthetical remark about the past days of the judges that uses a perfect verb.

14. Hertzberg, *I and II Samuel*, 286.

name, rest, and a secure dwelling place does not mean that these blessings are permanent. In fact, 7:9b–11 provides the one blessing that God is going to grant to David that will be the linchpin of these other blessings and that will ensure their continuing relevance. The last blessing mentioned in these verses is the key blessing. God will build David a house, a dynasty that will endure forever.[15] Part of the history of Israel shows that without a stable kingship, the other blessings are in jeopardy (Judg. 17:6; 21:25).

David had wanted to build God a house (temple), but God promises that he will build David a house (dynasty). This promise is mentioned at the end of 2 Samuel 7:11 and then is further explained in 7:12–17. This promise will be fulfilled in the future after David has died. The focus is on the one who will immediately follow David and will begin the fulfillment of the promise of an enduring dynasty and will build a house for God. This son will be a descendant of David "from your body" whose kingdom will be established (7:12).[16] The relationship between the kingdom, the temple, and this son born to David is important. David, the man of war, is not allowed to build the temple, which is reserved for his son Solomon, the man of peace.[17] The early reign of Solomon reflects this peace (rest from enemies), which is the proper setting for the building of the temple, because the temple, as the symbolic representation of the kingdom, is to correspond to the nature of that kingdom.[18] God grants this peace by his grace in first establishing David's dynasty and then allowing that dynasty to establish the Lord's temple. This binds David's rule to God's rule, and vice versa.[19] God will maintain his permanent dwelling place as King in Israel through the kingship of the Davidic line.[20]

Other promises that God makes to David are important for understanding the Davidic covenant and its role in the history of Israel (7:14–16). The Davidic covenant establishes a father-son relationship between God and the kings of the Davidic line (7:14). This represents a significant development in redemptive history (discussed below). The king's relationship to God as son, along with his responsibilities to keep the covenant, raises the issue of the discipline of the king and what happens to God's promise of a continuing dynasty if the king breaks the covenant. God specifically states that when the son commits iniquity, God will discipline him with the rod of men, but his steadfast love (חֶסֶד) will not be taken from him as it was taken away from Saul (7:14–15). The covenant has a conditional aspect that relates to each individual king.

15. The promise of an enduring dynasty is introduced with the solemn declaration "The Lord declares to you." McCarter, *II Samuel*, 205.

16. Baldwin comments that the use of the word "seed" implies not only one but many generations, although the immediate reference is to David's heir and successor. *1 and 2 Samuel*, 215. The general reference to the Davidic dynasty is made clear by 2 Sam. 7:16.

17. Anderson points out that the emphatic "he" in 2 Sam. 7:13 is the positive counterpart to the negative emphatic "you" of 7:5, where God rejects David as the person to build God's temple. *2 Samuel*, 118.

18. C. F. Keil and F. Delitzsch, *Joshua, Judges, Ruth, I and II Samuel*, vol. 2 in *Commentary on the Old Testament in Ten Volumes* (Grand Rapids, MI: Eerdmans, 1978), 345.

19. Roland de Vaux comments that because Yahweh was considered the true King of Israel, the royal throne was called the throne of Yahweh (1 Chron. 29:23) and, more explicitly, the throne of the kingship of Yahweh (1 Chron. 28:5) over Israel. *Ancient Israel: Its Life and Institutions* (Grand Rapids, MI: Eerdmans, 1997), 106.

20. Robertson, *Christ of the Covenants*, 233.

Each king must keep the covenant, and if a king does not keep it, then God may use other nations to bring judgment against the king and the people. The covenant also has an unconditional element to it so that the promises of an enduring dynasty and kingdom are not ultimately dependent on the obedience of individual kings. God will not remove his covenant loyalty from the line of David and choose another dynasty in place of it, as he did with Saul.[21] David's dynasty, kingdom, and throne will be established forever (7:14–16). The ultimate realization of the promises made to David are assured because the Davidic covenant fits into God's purpose to redeem a people for himself. God's plan to establish a kingdom among redeemed sinners will come to pass.[22]

The Implications of the Davidic Covenant

The remainder of 2 Samuel 7 consists of David's prayerful, grateful response to the promise of God to build him a dynasty. David appears before the Lord and expresses humility and surprise at the great promises that God has given to him (7:18–21).[23] God's blessing is greater than what he deserves because of the implications for the future of his house and for the rest of mankind (for a discussion of the phrase "This is instruction for mankind," see below). God's blessings to David are no different from his past blessings to his people (7:22–24). He is great and unique among the gods, which makes his people Israel unique, as demonstrated by their redemption out of Egypt through the power of God, who makes a name for himself and establishes his people. Then David asks God to confirm the promises he has made to him concerning his dynasty so that his house will be established and continue forever (7:25–29).[24] Several times throughout this section David uses "Adonai Yahweh" ("Lord GOD") for the name of God. This name does not appear anywhere else in Samuel or in the parallel passage in Chronicles. It is used in Genesis 15:2 and 15:8 by Abraham when God speaks to him about the promise of a seed. David seems to be making a conscious, deliberate response indicating that he is aware that the blessing of Abraham is continued in the blessing that God has promised to him.[25]

The implications of the Davidic covenant for the rest of humanity are expressed in the phrase "This is instruction for mankind" (2 Sam. 7:19). This phrase raises questions: Is it a statement or a question? And what is the meaning of the word תּוֹרָה (*torah*

---

21. The verb used in 2 Sam. 7:15 in a negative way to describe that God's steadfast love will not "depart" from David's descendant (סור) is also key to understanding the turning points in Saul's story. Sara Japhet, *I and II Chronicles: A Commentary*, OTL (Louisville: Westminster John Knox, 1993), 334. The Spirit of the Lord departed from Saul (1 Sam. 16:14); the Lord was with David, but he had departed from Saul (1 Sam. 18:12); and Saul even acknowledges that God has turned away from him (1 Sam. 28:15–16).

22. Robertson, *Christ of the Covenants*, 246.

23. The division of these verses comes from Walter C. Kaiser Jr., "The Blessing of David: The Charter for Humanity," in *The Law and the Prophets: Old Testament Studies Prepared in Honor of Oswald Thompson Allis*, ed. John H. Skilton (Nutley, NJ: Presbyterian and Reformed, 1974), 310.

24. This section begins with "And now," which indicates a transition from praising God for his past actions on behalf of God's people to praying for the future fulfillment of God's promises. Baldwin, *1 and 2 Samuel*, 218–19. This phrase also occurs in 2 Sam. 7:28 and 29, highlighting the truth of God's word (7:28) and supplicating God to bring it to pass (7:29).

25. Kaiser, "Blessing of David," 310.

normally means "law" or "instruction")? One view is that this is the typical way that God deals with humanity. God makes great plans and graciously makes them known.[26] This view is reflected in the NIV (1984) translation: "Is this your usual way of dealing with man, O Sovereign LORD?"[27] There are no contextual or grammatical grounds, however, to translate this as a question, and "instruction" or "law" is a better meaning for תּוֹרָה in this context.[28] Another view is that "the law of man" is the law that regulates the conduct of man as exemplified in the love that God shows to David. This law states that you should love your neighbor as you love yourself.[29] In other words, the way God treats David is the way human beings should treat each other. But the usual meaning for תּוֹרָה is not "manner" or "custom" (meanings usually associated with the Hebrew words חֹק and מִשְׁפָּט).[30] Perhaps the best view of this phrase is that it refers to the Davidic covenant as God's plan for the establishment of his kingdom, which will bless all humanity. The word "this" (זֹאת) refers to the content of God's gracious revelation to David concerning the promises of the covenant. The meaning of תּוֹרָה is "law" or "teaching," and it regularly refers to divine instruction. It refers here to a divinely constituted ordinance that takes its place among the laws that govern human affairs. The word הָאָדָם refers to humanity in general because the promises to David will be the channel of blessing for all the nations, the principle by which all humanity will be blessed. Walter Kaiser calls the phrase in 7:19 the "Charter of Humanity" and translates the phrase, "This is the Charter for mankind, O Lord God."[31]

The parallel phrase to 2 Samuel 7:19 in 1 Chronicles 17:17 seems very different. The context is that David, addressing God, expresses amazement that "you have also spoken of your servant's house for a great while to come," and the next phrase, "and have shown me future generations," is the parallel phrase. This is a general statement that God has shown David important things in the future concerning God's promises to himself and to God's people.[32] There seems to be very little parallel with the statement in 2 Samuel 7:19. Kaiser argues that 1 Chronicles 17:17 supports his understanding of 2 Samuel 7:19. He translates the verse as "And thou are regarding me according to the upbringing torah of mankind." It is not clear that the word כְּתוֹר should be translated "torah" or that the

---

26. Baldwin, *1 and 2 Samuel*, 217.

27. The NIV (2011) translates this phrase, "And this decree, Sovereign LORD, is for a mere human," with a note that says "for the human race." This translation seems to support Kaiser's view.

28. Peter J. Gentry and Stephen J. Wellum, *Kingdom through Covenant: A Biblical-Theological Understanding of the Covenants* (Wheaton, IL: Crossway, 2012), 399.

29. Keil and Delitzsch, *Joshua, Judges, Ruth, I and II Samuel*, 350.

30. Kaiser, "Blessing of David," 313.

31. Kaiser, "Blessing of David," 314. He argues against the view that הָאָדָם refers to "the Man," namely, the man of Pss. 8:5–6 and 80:17—as in A. W. Pink, *The Life of David: Two Volumes in One* (Swengel, PA: Reiner, 1977), 1:337. Although these promises will be fulfilled in the Messiah, this passage is not emphasizing the proper name Adam or a reference to a covenant made with him.

32. There are difficulties with the ESV translation. The phrase "you have shown me" should be translated "you regard me" or "you see me" (reflecting a Qal verb instead of a Hiphil verb). Also, the phrase "future generations" is quite general for the Hebrew phrase כְּתוֹר הָאָדָם הַמַּעֲלָה. Thus, the ESV offers the marginal reading "and you look upon me as a man of high rank."

word "upbringing" should go with "torah." Kaiser discusses the possibility that כְּתוֹר is a shortened form of "torah," but he acknowledges that it is difficult to cite linguistic parallels supporting this view. He sees it as a by-form of כְּתֹאַר, meaning "according to the outline" of mankind, and understands the phrase to be synonymous with the idea expressed in 2 Samuel 7:19 ("the charter for mankind").[33] Yet the word "upbringing" (מַעֲלָה) stands closer to "mankind" (אָדָם), and many translate these two words together instead of taking "upbringing" with כְּתוֹר (understood as "torah"). The third option is to translate 1 Chronicles 17:17 as "And [you] have regarded me according to the rank of a man of high degree" (NKJV; cf. NASB, NIV). This seems to be an interpretation of 2 Samuel 7:19 emphasizing that the Davidic king has the highest rank among human beings because he represents the supreme and universal God. This is equivalent to what David says in 2 Samuel 23:1–7, where he refers to Nathan's oracle as a covenant and calls himself "the man who was raised on high, the anointed of the God of Jacob" (23:1).[34]

Differences between 2 Samuel 7 and 1 Chronicles 17

There are other differences between 2 Samuel 7 and 1 Chronicles 17 that result from the different focus of the author of Chronicles. The books of 1 and 2 Samuel focus on the need for godly leadership in the transition from the period of the judges to the monarchy and show why David is the king chosen by God over Saul to lead God's people. The books of 1 and 2 Chronicles were written to the postexilic community to answer the question "Are God's promises to Israel, David, and Jerusalem still valid for us?" The postexilic community had experienced limited success because many were still in exile, Israel was under the control of other powerful nations, and the promises of the covenant were not evident. The author wrote a history of God's people going all the way back to Adam to demonstrate that God will fulfill his promises. It is, however, a selective history that presents the ideal reigns of David and Solomon as models for the postexilic community.[35]

The different purpose of Chronicles explains some of the different emphases in 1 Chronicles 17 in comparison with 2 Samuel 7.[36] The main differences will be

---

33. Kaiser, "Blessing of David," 315–16.

34. Gentry and Wellum, *Kingdom through Covenant*, 401. They translate 1 Chron. 17:17 as "You see me according to the rank of the man placed high." Second Sam. 23:1–7 is David's prophetic oracle that presents the reign of a righteous king guided by the fear of the Lord. Bergen, *1, 2 Samuel*, 464–67. David was a man "who was raised on high," and his "house" should rule in righteousness and the fear of God so that God's blessings would be poured out on God's people. The blessings that accompany a king who rules in righteousness are also expressed in Ps. 72, which could be a psalm written by David "for Solomon"; for a discussion of this possibility, see Richard P. Belcher Jr., *The Messiah and the Psalms: Preaching Christ from All the Psalms* (Fearn, Ross-shire, Scotland: Mentor, 2006), 268n81.

35. Richard L. Pratt Jr., *He Gave Us Stories: The Bible Student's Guide to Interpreting Old Testament Narratives* (Phillipsburg, NJ: Presbyterian and Reformed, 1990), 297–98. Japhet writes, "The period of David and Solomon is a unified whole" and "is the zenith of Israel's virtues and achievements." *I and II Chronicles*, 48.

36. This is true even though there is almost universal consent that 1 Chron. 17 is dependent on 2 Sam. 7. Roddy Braun, *1 Chronicles*, WBC 14 (Waco, TX: Word Books, 1986), 198. Many of the differences are minor, owing to stylistic variations or problems in transmission, but some variations reveal intentional changes. Richard L. Pratt Jr., *1 and 2 Chronicles*, MC (Fearn, Ross-shire, Scotland: Mentor, 1998), 148.

commented on here.[37] First, 1 Chronicles 17:1 does not mention that God had given rest to David from all his enemies, as in 2 Samuel 7:1, and language to the effect that God will give rest from enemies in 2 Samuel 7:11 is changed to "I will subdue all your enemies" in 1 Chronicles 17:10. Both 2 Samuel 8 and 1 Chronicles 18 recount David's victories over his enemies after the account of the Davidic covenant, so that the main reason for the omission of rest in 1 Chronicles is to avoid confusion concerning the future victories of David. The focus in 1 Chronicles is on Solomon as the man of rest who will build the temple of God. David had only a partial rest, but Solomon will be "a man of rest" who will be given rest from all his enemies (1 Chron. 22:9–10). Solomon is the culmination of the rest that began with David, and when God gives peace and quiet to Israel in his days, he will build a house for God.[38]

Second, the statement in 2 Samuel 7:14 that when the son commits iniquity, he will be disciplined, is omitted in 1 Chronicles 17:13. This omission causes some to think that the unconditional nature of God's promise is not retained in 1 Chronicles 17.[39] The issue is not whether one text is unconditional and the other text is conditional because both elements are present in the overall presentation of both books. Human failure in the Davidic line is well known from 1–2 Kings, and royal obedience is still important for Israel to receive God's blessings.[40] The Chronicler focuses on the role of Solomon in building the temple, emphasizing the positive aspects of the reign of Solomon so that the house of David still provides permanent hope for God's people even after the exile.[41] The reigns of both David and Solomon are presented as in agreement concerning the goal of building a temple for God's people.[42]

Third, an explicit connection is made in 1 Chronicles 17:14 between the human throne of Israel and God's throne. The emphasis in 2 Samuel 7 is on God's promises to David: "Your house and your kingdom shall be made sure forever before me" (7:16). In 1 Chronicles 17:14 God promises, "I will confirm him in my house and in my kingdom forever."[43] The kingdom is God's kingdom, with his rule manifested through the reign of the son of David who sits on the throne. The kingdom of God on earth is established through the Davidic covenant.[44]

---

37. For a chart that compares 2 Sam. 7 and 1 Chron. 17, see Pratt, *1 and 2 Chronicles*, 147.

38. Martin J. Selman, *1 Chronicles: An Introduction and Commentary*, TOTC (Downers Grove, IL: InterVarsity Press, 1994), 177. He calls Solomon the man of peace and rest *par excellence*.

39. Japhet writes, "The Chronicler deviates from the central premise of II Sam. 7 and approaches more closely the Deuteronomistic redaction of 1 Kings, which does see God's promise as conditional." *I and II Chronicles*, 334. Others, interestingly enough, think that the 2 Chronicles text is more unconditionally stated. Arnold, *1 and 2 Samuel*, 488n59.

40. Selman, *1 Chronicles*, 180.

41. Pratt, *1 and 2 Chronicles*, 154.

42. H. G. M. Williamson, *1 and 2 Chronicles*, NCB (Grand Rapids, MI: Eerdmans, 1982), 133.

43. The focus on Solomon in Chronicles is further supported by looking at the clause that follows God's promise to David concerning house and kingdom. In 2 Sam. 7:16, the next sentence is "Your throne shall be established forever," but in 1 Chron. 17:14, the next sentence is "His throne shall be established forever."

44. Pratt, *1 and 2 Chronicles*, 25, 154. Selman calls this a significant contribution to the development of the idea of the kingdom of God. *1 Chronicles*, 180.

Finally, the focus on Solomon and the close association of the Davidic kingdom with God's kingdom in the postexilic context of Chronicles give hope to God's people that David's throne will be established as necessary for the restoration of God's rule on the earth. Such restoration will not be complete until the throne of David is occupied. One of the major elements lacking in the postexilic period is the establishment of a king, which causes this hope to shift to the future.[45] These ideas provide essential background for the teaching of the New Testament that the kingdom of God is established in Jesus, the Son of David (Matt. 12:28; Luke 17:20–21), who sits on David's throne (Acts 2:22–36).[46]

The Davidic Covenant: The Culmination of God's Covenant Promises

The Development of the Idea of Kingship

The promises of the Davidic covenant are the culmination of previous promises that are found in covenants God made with his people. In this way, the Davidic covenant sets the stage for the future of God's people and the ultimate fulfillment of his promises. The idea of kingship does not just appear in Israel's history at the time of the institution of kingship with Saul. The concept of rule goes back to Genesis 1–2, particularly 1:26–28, where every human being is to rule over creation for the glory of God. God's rule on the earth is accomplished through the agency of human dominion, but the fall makes dominion more difficult because in it the earth is cursed. For restoration to take place, an individual will arise who will conquer the serpent so dominion can be established again. The promise in Genesis 3:15 uses the language of warfare to describe the conflict between the seed of the serpent and the seed of the woman. The covenant with Abraham includes the promise of kings (15:12–16; 17:6) and the prospect of Abraham's descendants establishing dominion over the land of Canaan (17:8). One will come with royal power from the tribe of Judah whose dominion is demonstrated in the unleashing of abundant blessings in creation (49:8–12).

Deuteronomy 17 sets forth how this king shall rule "when [Israel] come[s] to the land" and desires a king "like all the nations" (17:14). God will grant them their desire for a king, but it must be a king "whom the LORD [their] God will choose" (17:15). Deuteronomy sets out the parameters of kingship in a theocracy in which Yahweh is the true King; the king must be kept aware of his relationship to Yahweh and to his fellow Israelites. Limits on the law of the king in Deuteronomy are antithetical to the usual assumptions of royal power. Deuteronomy 16:18–18:22 places all authority in the nation under the authority of Yahweh and within the covenant character of the law for

---

45. Pratt comments that the lack of attention to royal matters in the ministries of Ezra and Nehemiah shows that the hopes for the immanent restoration of the line of David had faded, causing messianic hopes to be cast into the indefinite future. *1 and 2 Chronicles*, 25.

46. Pratt, *1 and 2 Chronicles*, 154; Selman, *1 Chronicles*, 180–81. A focus on Solomon in Chronicles does not preclude a messianic emphasis, because Chronicles clearly points both to the special significance of Solomon and to another son of David who will establish God's house and kingdom *forever*. Selman, *1 Chronicles*, 176.

the nation.[47] The law is a higher power than the word of the king (17:18–20), keeping the king from the temptations of royal power and the abuses of it. The law will be the standard by which the nation and the king will be judged, such that obedience will bring covenant blessings, and disobedience will bring covenant curse (Deut. 27–28). A balance of power among the leaders limits the power of all the offices, particularly the king, so that the laws work together as a constitution for the nation. The typical marks of success among kings are limited by Yahweh. The limit on horses (17:16) signifies a cap on a professional standing army and has implications concerning Yahweh's leadership in "holy war." Israel is to trust in Yahweh, not military strength, for victory. The limit on wives (17:17) curtails foreign entanglements and temptations to apostasy. Wives would come as a part of treaties and would bring foreign influence and the temptation to worship false gods. The limit on wealth signifies constraints on commerce with foreign nations and a check on the king's accumulation of power and status above other Israelites.[48]

As the ministry of Samuel comes to a close, the elders of Israel ask God, "Now appoint for us a king to judge us like all the nations" (1 Sam. 8:5). When Samuel warns the people of the dangers of kingship, the people respond, "But there shall be a king over us, that we also may be like all the nations, and that our king may judge us and go out before us and fight our battles" (8:19–20). God tells Samuel to give them a king because they have rejected God as their King (8:7, 22). Although Deuteronomy 17 had mentioned the future appointment of a king, the people request a king out of wrong motivations. Israel wants to be like the nations, and a king will give her power and political influence with the nations. Deuteronomy 17 did not mention that the king would be responsible for fighting the battles of Israel, probably because it was clear that Yahweh is the one who fights for his people and wins their battles (see the descriptions of the battles in Joshua and in the victory over the Philistines in 1 Sam. 7:5–11). The request for a king to lead them in battle betrays Israel's lack of trust in Yahweh to defend the nation. Samuel makes it clear in his farewell address that both the people and the king are subject to the word of God and that if either one disobeys the law of God, then the hand of God will be against both of them (1 Sam. 12:13–16). The prophets will be raised up by God to speak the word of God to the king. Many times throughout the history of Israel the kings reject the word from God. Saul is a good example. Israel requests a king like the nations, and God grants them a king like they request. Saul looks like a good choice, but he is rejected by God because he rejects the word of God (1 Sam. 15).[49] David is God's choice, and through the promises of the Davidic covenant, the kingdom of God reaches its zenith in the early reign of Solomon.[50]

---

47. Patricia Dutcher-Walls, "The Circumscription of the King: Deuteronomy 17:16–17 in Its Ancient Social Context," *JBL* 121, no. 4 (2002): 603–4.

48. Dutcher-Walls, "Circumscription of the King," 603–4.

49. Bergen has an excellent discussion of the character of Saul in *1, 2 Samuel*, 118–19.

50. The statement that Yahweh "has sought out a man after his own heart" (1 Sam. 13:14) has been understood to refer to David as God's choice (Jason DeRouchie, "The Heart of YHWH and His Chosen One in 1 Samuel

Fulfillment of Earlier Covenant Promises

The culmination of the promises of God in the Davidic covenant is evident in how the Davidic covenant and the early reign of Solomon fulfill prior covenant promises. The Davidic covenant stands in an organic relationship with the other covenants so that the Davidic covenant builds on and assumes the promises of the other covenants but does not replace them.[51] God promised Abraham many descendants who would one day inherit the land that Abraham experienced only as a sojourner. God promised to make Abraham's name great (Gen. 12:2) and to give him many descendants, as numerous as the stars of heaven (Gen. 15:5) and the dust of the earth (Gen. 13:16). These promises are restated to David (2 Sam. 7:9–10) and fulfilled in the early reign of Solomon. The people are as numerous as the sand by the sea (1 Kings 4:20), and the kingdom experiences peace and safety throughout the whole region (1 Kings 4:24–25). Also, the promise that all families of the earth will be blessed (Gen. 12:3) is fulfilled in Solomon's reign: "People of all nations came to hear the wisdom of Solomon, and from all the kings of the earth, who had heard of his wisdom" (1 Kings 4:34).[52] Several promises in the Mosaic covenant are also fulfilled in the Davidic covenant, including the rest God granted David, the experience of covenant blessings by God's people in the land (Deut. 28:1–14; 1 Kings 4:25), and the nations witnessing God's blessings on Israel (Deut. 28:10; 1 Kings 4:30). The promise that God will be with the people, expressed in some form of the phrase "I will take you to be my people, and I will be your God" (Ex. 6:7), is fulfilled in David (2 Sam. 7:9) and God's people (Ezek. 34:24).[53] This principle is also fulfilled when God dwells among his people through the temple that Solomon built (1 Kings 8:54–61). The Davidic dynasty is fully integrated into the religious and social dimensions of the Mosaic covenant so that the covenant is administered by the Davidic king who takes on a prominent role in the leadership of the nation.[54]

The King as Mediator of God's People

Not only is the Davidic covenant the culmination of the covenant promises of God, but also the king's position is advanced as the nation stands on the threshold of a new political era.[55] Up to this point, Israel was God's firstborn son (Ex. 4:23), but now the king of Israel is the son with God as his Father.[56] This special relationship of sonship

---

13:14," *BBR* 24, no. 4 [2014]: 467–89) or to refer to David as a man who will be like-minded with the Lord and surrender to his word (Bergen argues that both views are possible meanings of 1 Sam. 13:14; *1, 2 Samuel*, 151).

51. Robertson, *Christ of the Covenants*, 27–52.

52. The early reign of Solomon is a partial fulfillment of the mission of Israel to the nations. Richard P. Belcher Jr., *Prophet, Priest, and King: The Roles of Christ in the Bible and Our Roles Today* (Phillipsburg, NJ: P&R, 2016), 13–16.

53. Robertson summarizes this phrase as "I shall be their God and they shall be my people" and discusses it as the thematic unity of the covenants. *Christ of the Covenants*, 46–48.

54. Bergen, *1, 2 Samuel*, 334n52.

55. Dumbrell, *Covenant and Creation*, 136.

56. Adoption does not mean deification of the king. The character of Yahweh as transcendent and unique made deification of the king impossible. Plus, the kings do *not* claim deity, and if they did, the prophets certainly would condemn them for doing so. De Vaux, *Ancient Israel*, 112–13.

means that the king serves as a covenant mediator. As son, he shares the throne with God his Father and has access to the Father. He represents God to the people, but he also represents the people to God.[57] The special status of the king as son of God has implications for his role within the nation of Israel.

First of all, the king is empowered to perform certain religious functions in relationship to worship. David sets up the first altar for Yahweh in Jerusalem (2 Sam. 24:25), conceives the idea of building the temple, and then makes plans for it. The kings are able to perform certain priestly acts. Solomon offers sacrifices at the dedication of the temple (1 Kings 8) and then at the three great feasts of the year (1 Kings 9:25). Both David and Solomon bless the people in the sanctuary (2 Sam. 6:18; 1 Kings 8:14), and David wears the loincloth, which was the vestment of officiating priests (2 Sam. 6:14).[58] This special role of the king, however, does not mean that he is a priest or can perform all the priestly functions (2 Chron. 26:16–21).[59] The king's role in worship occurs in special or exceptional circumstances, such as the transference of the ark to Jerusalem, the dedication of an altar, or the great annual festivals. Ordinarily, the conduct of worship is left to the priests (2 Kings 16:15). The king is the religious head of the people, but he is not a priest in the strict sense.[60]

Second, the special status of the king as son has implications for the role of the king in keeping the covenant. The king represents the people so that his actions of obedience or disobedience become part of the basis for whether God's people experience God's judgment or God's blessings. The people are still indicted for their sin, and they are held responsible for the judgment of exile (Jer. 2–6), but special responsibility falls on the king to follow God and obey the law; otherwise, he is held responsible for God's judgment (Jer. 22; Ezek. 34).

There are also implications for Jerusalem as the center of God's plan for the nations. The throne of God is identified with the throne of the Davidic king so that Jerusalem becomes the center from which God will exercise his sovereignty over the nations through the king.[61] When Solomon builds the temple, Jerusalem becomes the place of God's presence and the focal point of the religious life of God's people in worship and in looking to Jerusalem for God's help in times of need (1 Kings 8). It also becomes the geographical location for the fulfillment of Israel's mission to the nations to become a kingdom of priests and a holy nation. As king and people live in obedience to God, the nations will see the abundant blessings that God will pour out on his people, and they

---

57. Robertson, *Christ of the Covenants*, 235–36.

58. De Vaux, *Ancient Israel*, 113–14.

59. For a discussion of the view that a royal priesthood was established in Israel in relationship to David and his descendants, see Belcher, *Prophet, Priest, and King*, 131–38.

60. De Vaux, *Ancient Israel*, 114.

61. The correlation of God's rule in Jerusalem through the Davidic king with the temple as his dwelling place factors into the development of "Zion theology." Mount Zion, a high mountain, is the place of God's rule with a river flowing out of Zion to bring fertility to the land. The Lord as the divine King rules over heaven and earth, providing security for Jerusalem as the place where the nations will come to acknowledge God's sovereignty. John T. Strong, "Zion: Theology of," in *NIDOTTE*, 4:1314–21.

will come to learn about the great God that Israel worships and the wonderful law that he has given to his people (Deut. 4:5–8). The early reign of Solomon is a partial fulfillment of this mission (1 Kings 4:29–34; 10:1–13). The promises of the Davidic covenant are fulfilled in David's son Solomon, and the early reign of Solomon brings Israel as a nation to the height of its power and influence.[62]

The Davidic Covenant in Redemptive History

The early reign of Solomon represents the high point of Israel's history. Solomon is the immediate fulfillment of the covenant promises to David, and Israel fulfills her mission to the nations. This period of blessing, however, does not last, because of disobedience. It starts with Solomon turning away from the Lord because of his foreign wives (1 Kings 11:1–8). God responds by raising up adversaries against Solomon and taking ten tribes away from David's line with the division of the kingdom under Rehoboam. But God keeps his promise to David by not taking the whole kingdom away from his descendants (11:34–36), represented in the dynasty that continues in the southern kingdom of Judah. God even tells Jeroboam that he is leaving one tribe to Solomon's son "that David my servant may always have a lamp before me in Jerusalem, the city where I have chosen to put my name" (11:36).[63]

The division of the kingdom does not terminate the covenant commitment on behalf of David and Jerusalem. God's faithfulness to his covenant promise to David is expressed in the phrase "for the sake of my servant David" (11:32, 34). This phrase, or the shortened "for David's sake," occurs at several points of the history of the southern kingdom.[64] Two times it is used in a positive sense as a promise to Hezekiah that God will defend the city of Jerusalem from Sennacherib (2 Kings 19:34; 20:6). The other uses are in response to the disobedience of the kings of the southern kingdom. It is used with Abijam, the first king to rule after Rehoboam. Abijam walks in the sins of his father before him, and his heart is not wholly true to the Lord (1 Kings 15:3). The phrase is used when the northern kingdom influences the southern kingdom to do evil during the reign of Jehoram, son of Jehoshaphat, "yet the Lord [is] not willing to destroy Judah, for the sake of David his servant" (2 Kings 8:19). The apostasy of the kings of Judah culminate in the reign of Manasseh (see 2 Kings 21 for a list of his idolatrous practices, even setting up idols in the temple of Jerusalem). His evil is characterized as

62. Even after the division of the kingdom, the mission of Israel is kept alive in various prophetic passages, such as Isa. 2:2–5; Zech. 8:20–23; 14:16–21.

63. It is striking that Jeroboam is promised by God the same promises that God had given to David. If Jeroboam would keep God's commandments, as David did, God promised to be with him and to build him a sure house as God built for David (1 Kings 11:38). The opportunity for Jeroboam was a lasting dynasty over the northern kingdom of Israel. This did not remove God's promises to David, for God told Jeroboam, "I will afflict the offspring of David because of this, but not forever" (11:39). Jeroboam disobeyed God by setting up opposing places of worship in the northern kingdom in Dan and Bethel to keep his people from worshiping in Jerusalem. This nullified God's promises to him.

64. For a brief review of the history of Israel from the perspective of God's faithfulness to David, see Robertson, *Christ of the Covenants*, 236–43.

more despicable than the practices of the nations that inhabited the land before Israel (21:2, 11). Such idolatry, including child sacrifice (21:6), leads to a pronouncement of God's judgment against the city of Jerusalem. The same disaster that overtook Samaria of the northern kingdom will also overtake Jerusalem (21:13–16).[65]

The destruction of the city of Jerusalem in 586 BC is a momentous event. Not only is the city destroyed, but so is the beloved temple. The king is exiled to Babylon, and the line of David ruling over the Davidic kingdom comes to an end. Such events are hardly believable to the people (see the sentiment in Jer. 7:4), even though Jeremiah and Ezekiel prophesied these very events. One major question is, What do these events have to do with the promises that God made to David that he would build him an eternal dynasty? Does the removal of the Davidic king from Jerusalem and the lack of a king to rule over God's people in the postexilic period mean that God's promises to David have come to an end?

Psalm 89 wrestles with these questions. It has three sections: a hymn to Yahweh for his faithfulness (89:1–18), a review of the promises of the Davidic covenant (89:19–37), and a lament over the apparent failure of the promises to David in light of the condition of the monarchy (89:38–51).[66] The psalm closes with a doxology (89:52) that marks the end of book 3 of the Psalter (Pss. 73–89). The key words of the psalm are "steadfast love" (חֶסֶד) and "faithfulness" (אֱמוּנָה).

The hymn praises God's faithfulness by showing how the heavens and the heavenly hosts praise the power of God, whose rule exemplifies God's steadfast love and faithfulness (89:5, 14). The promises of God to David display the same enduring stability as the creation because the God who rules creation made an oath to his servant David (89:3) to establish his throne (89:29). The close relationship between Yahweh and the Davidic king that was expressed in Psalm 2:7 is also expressed in David's cry "You are my Father" (89:26) and in the close relationship between Yahweh and David.[67] Just as Yahweh is head of the heavenly assembly (89:6–8), so he will make David the firstborn, the highest of the kings of the earth (89:27).[68] Just as Yahweh rules the raging sea and scatters his enemies by the strength of his hand (89:9–10, 13), so Yahweh will place David's hand on the sea and his right hand on the rivers (89:25). David, as Yahweh's representative, rules the sea. The heavenly rule of Yahweh is manifested on earth through the reign of David. The blessings to David (89:20–28) are also extended to his descendants (89:29–37), in line with the promise of 89:36 that David's throne will last as long as the sun.

The strong statements of God's "steadfast love" and "faithfulness" to establish David's throne and his affirmations that he will not lie to David or violate the covenant make the lament that questions God's faithfulness all the more jarring to the reader (89:38–45).

---

65. August H. Konkel, *1 and 2 Kings*, NIVAC (Grand Rapids, MI: Zondervan, 2006), 622–23.

66. For a discussion of the setting and date of the psalm, see Belcher, *Messiah and the Psalms*, 270n101.

67. Marvin E. Tate, *Psalms 51–100*, WBC 20 (Dallas: Word Books, 1990), 423.

68. The firstborn as the highest of the kings of the earth refers not to the one born first but to the one who has the privileges and blessings that come with having the highest place. Belcher, *Messiah and the Psalms*, 140.

Instead of David being the highest of the kings of the earth, his throne and crown are cast down to the dust (89:39, 44). Instead of David's right hand ruling the sea, the right hand of the enemy is exalted (89:42), and the kingdom has experienced the humility of defeat (89:43–44). The current humiliation of the king has an explanation that goes back to the Davidic covenant itself (2 Sam. 7:14–15). The Davidic kings have not obeyed God, and God's wrath has been poured out against his anointed (Ps. 89:31–33, 38). The problem is not the faithfulness of God but the unfaithfulness of the king. The questions in 89:46–51 are a cry for God to fulfill his covenant promises to David by moving beyond discipline and wrath to show his faithfulness again to the Davidic line. Even though the disobedience of the king has led to the destruction of the kingship and temple, the question of God's steadfast love is raised in the question in 89:49: "Lord, where is your steadfast love of old, which by your faithfulness you swore to David?" God has been faithful to the covenant to bring the discipline of judgment; will he also be faithful to show his steadfast love as promised?

The conditional nature of the Davidic covenant is demonstrated in the removal of the king in Judah, but the unconditional nature of the covenant is seen in the continued hope that God will establish the Davidic line again at some point in the future. The loss of kingship in the Babylonian exile puts a strain on the promises of God to David that one of his descendants will sit on the throne forever. This hope, however, is kept alive during the postexilic period. The royal psalms keep alive the hope that the Davidic dynasty will rise again. Two groups of Davidic psalms in book 5 of the Psalter (Pss. 108–110; 138–145) remind God's people of the need for a Davidic king to complete the restoration.[69]

Psalm 132 is a royal psalm that focuses on God's promise to David that one of his descendants will sit on the throne "forever" (132:12). The psalm also emphasizes Jerusalem as God's dwelling place. The basic structure of the psalm highlights the parallels between David's concern to establish a dwelling place for Yahweh (132:1–10) and Yahweh's covenant promises regarding David's descendants (132:11–18), with reference to the "anointed one" (מָשִׁיחַ) in 132:10 and 132:17. The first section asks God to remember all the hardships that David endured in finding a proper place for the ark, Yahweh's dwelling place, to rest (2 Sam. 6). The significance of the ark cannot be overlooked since it represents the rule of God on the earth.[70] God is to remember the efforts of David for the ark so that he will take action on behalf of the Davidic king to establish his throne (Ps. 132:11–12). God promises that the strength ("horn") of David will be restored and that his dynasty will not be extinguished but rather will shine like a lamp.[71]

---

69. For how kingship and the Davidic covenant relate to the theme and structure of the Psalter, see Belcher, *Messiah and the Psalms*, 17–18.

70. Belcher, *Messiah and the Psalms*, 150.

71. Both horn and lamp may refer to the permanence of the Davidic dynasty. Willem A. VanGemeren, *Psalms*, vol. 5 of *The Expositor's Bible Commentary*, rev. ed., ed. Tremper Longman III and David E. Garland (Grand Rapids, MI: Zondervan, 2008), 930.

Psalm 132 is part of the songs of ascent, and it gives a rationale for making the pilgrimage to Jerusalem: Zion is God's dwelling place and the site of the Davidic throne.[72] It is also a call for the restoration of the Davidic dynasty in the postexilic period.[73] It demonstrates that the rejection of the king in Psalm 89 is not final. Psalm 89:39 laments the defilement of the crown of the "anointed one," but 132:18 affirms that the crown of the "anointed one" will shine.[74] In 89:42 the enemies have triumphed over the king, but in 132:18 the enemies are defeated and humiliated. Psalm 132 gives hope that the promises related to the Davidic covenant will be fulfilled. A king will come; a horn will sprout for David.

Psalms 89 and 132 are fulfilled in Christ, who is the descendant of David, the son who will sit on the throne forever. He is the horn who sprouted for David (see also Ezek. 29:21; Luke 1:69) and the highest of the kings of the earth as the firstborn of creation (Ps. 89:27; Col. 1:15), both Son of David and Son of God (Rom. 1:3–4). Jesus is the fulfillment of the prayer in Psalm 132:1–10 for God to remember his covenant promises "for the sake of your servant David." This psalm also speaks of the triumph of the king with associations of resurrection (132:8) and ascension (132:8, 14). It describes the fulfillment of the Davidic promises related to kingship, temple, and Zion through the ministry of Christ as he sits at the right hand of the Father, occupying the very throne of David.[75] Jesus fulfilled the conditions of the covenant by keeping the law perfectly and bearing in himself the chastening judgments deserved by David's seed through their covenant violations (89:38–45).[76] God was faithful to his covenant promises to David, and those who believe in Jesus Christ are the beneficiaries of the rest, salvation, and security that result from his person and work.

Conclusion

The Davidic covenant established God's rule in Israel through the line of David. The king of David was established as the son of God who was to lead God's people in faithfulness to God. Israel had the opportunity to fulfill its mission as a light to the nations. The disobedience of Solomon and the kings following him led to the judgment of exile and the loss of kingship. But the promises of the Davidic covenant kept the hope alive that one from the throne of David would come to rule over God's people. Christ established a kingdom that will never end, and even today he rules over this world at

---

72. For an analysis of the songs of ascent that treats them as a unity with the theme of Yahweh's restoration of Zion, see Philip E. Satterthwaite, "Zion in the Songs of Ascents," in *Zion, City of Our God*, ed. Richard S. Hess and Gordon J. Wenham (Grand Rapids, MI: Eerdmans, 1999), 105–28.

73. For a discussion of the possible setting of Ps. 132, see Belcher, *Messiah and the Psalms*, 274n168.

74. For connections between the sprouting of the horn in Ps. 132 and the passages in the Prophets that speak of the Branch (Isa. 4:2; Jer. 23:5; Zech. 3:8; 6:12), see F. Delitzsch, *Psalms*, vol. 5 in *Commentary on the Old Testament in Ten Volumes*, by C. F. Keil and F. Delitzsch (Grand Rapids, MI: Eerdmans, 1978), 316.

75. Robertson, *Christ of the Covenants*, 251–52.

76. Belcher, *Messiah and the Psalms*, 142–43. Robertson comments that the role of Jesus as the seed of David speaks to the question of the conditionality of the covenant. *Christ of the Covenants*, 248.

the right hand of the Father for the sake of his people (Eph. 1:22–23). The promises of the Davidic covenant should bring great comfort to God's people, for we live in a world that does not recognize the rule of our King. We can be assured that one day he will return as the King of kings to defeat all his enemies. God made a promise to David that he has already begun to fulfill, and there is no doubt that he will bring it to completion for our good and his glory.

9

The New Covenant as Promised in the Major Prophets

Michael G. McKelvey

The topic of the new covenant within the Old Testament Scriptures is difficult to confine to a brief chapter such as this one. To begin with, there is much to consider about the relationship between the prior covenants in Scripture and the new covenant, especially how they prepare for and anticipate the new covenant and how they build on one another as redemptive history unfolds. But space prohibits an extended discussion on the covenantal progression of the Bible since the purpose of this chapter is to look at specific texts that reveal the coming new covenant and to address how these texts shape our understanding of covenant theology. So while we endeavor to consider these texts in light of the covenantal development in Scripture, we need to keep in mind a wider discussion regarding the relationship of the covenants to each other, and the other chapters in this book provide the collective portrait of this relationship.

Since the Prophetic Literature of the Old Testament contains the primary passages concerning the new covenant, in this chapter we spend our time examining those prominent passages in the Prophets on this subject. The Major Prophets in particular contain most of the content on the new covenant, and they take center stage in this section. But this does not imply that the Minor Prophets are silent on this topic. We also consider some overarching biblical-theological themes that elucidate the topic of the new covenant throughout both the Old and New Testaments. Starting with the book of Jeremiah and ending with the book of Isaiah, we highlight the theme of the new covenant and show just how central it is in Prophetic Literature. The rationale for starting with Jeremiah is that it contains the only occurrence of the phrase "new covenant" (31:31) in the

Old Testament, and this phrase occurs at the center of a large section of Jeremiah that focuses on the coming new covenant administration. In addition, after looking at the book of Ezekiel, we end with the book of Isaiah because it contains the only occurrences of the "new heavens" and "new earth" (65:17; 66:22) in the Old Testament. Since the new heavens and the new earth are the restorative consummation of the new covenant (and all God's covenantal purposes), it seems fitting to conclude our study with the book of Isaiah.

Ultimately, the goal of this chapter is to show that the new covenant is a central concern of Prophetic Literature, as well as of the whole Old Testament. But before moving on to the Prophets, an additional word needs to be said about the unity of God's covenants. Within the Old Testament Scriptures, there are five main covenants, and each one moves God's grand redemptive plan forward. The covenants with Adam, Noah, Abraham, Moses, and David lay the foundation for the new covenant, and they provide the context for understanding it. Comprehending the progressive nature of these covenantal administrations is key to grasping the new covenant and its purposes. All these covenants are working toward the same *telos*, or goal, namely, the restoration of humanity and creation after the fall of Adam and Eve. This continuity provides the basis for seeing the new covenant as inherent (at least in its goal) in the previous covenants of the Bible. Without appreciating this covenantal unity, we fail to see the harmony of God's overarching redemptive scheme for the world. With that said, let us begin to see how the new covenant obtains a prominent place in the prophetic corpus and how it echoes, extends, and fulfills the previous Old Testament covenants.

Jeremiah 30–33 (The Book of Consolation)

In a book that largely deals with the judgment of Judah and Jerusalem, Jeremiah 30–33 contains the central message of hope. This section of Jeremiah is often called "the Book of Consolation" because of its hopeful tenor regarding the coming restoration and salvation of God's people.[1] Within this segment, Jeremiah 31:31–34 distinctly summarizes the new covenant, and the author of Hebrews cites this passage in 8:8–12 and 10:16–17. When discussing the new covenant in the book of Jeremiah, many interpreters examine 31:31–34 without discussing the entire context of Jeremiah 30–33.[2] But such an ap-

---

1. Some scholars limit the Book of Consolation to Jer. 30–31, such as Peter J. Gentry and Stephen J. Wellum, *Kingdom through Covenant: A Biblical-Theological Understanding of the Covenants*, 2nd ed. (Wheaton, IL: Crossway, 2018), 492, 536. In Gentry's outline of Jeremiah, however, the Book of Consolation is listed as Jer. 30–33 (528; this is an emendation from the first edition of the book [Crossway, 2012], found on page 484). For reasons that follow in this present chapter, Jer. 30–33 must be understood as a unit in light of its structure and symmetry. See also the structure and outline of Jeremiah in Peter J. Lee, "Jeremiah," *A Biblical-Theological Introduction to the Old Testament: The Gospel Promised*, ed. Miles V. Van Pelt (Wheaton, IL: Crossway, 2016), 280–83. See also J. A. Thompson, *The Book of Jeremiah*, NICOT (Grand Rapids, MI: Eerdmans, 1980), 551–53; John L. Mackay, *Jeremiah: An Introduction and Commentary*, vol. 2, *Chapters 21–52*, MC (Fearn, Ross-shire, Scotland: Mentor, 2004), 180–83.

2. While examining how Jer. 31:26–40 forms a smaller unit in the chapter, Gentry also notes the tendency in scholarly discussions to limit examinations to Jer. 31:31–34. Gentry and Wellum, *Kingdom through Covenant*, 538.

proach to interpreting this passage is inadequate since the entirety of Jeremiah 30–33 addresses the coming salvation of the new covenant and provides the immediate interpretive context for 31:31–34. When Hebrews cites Jeremiah 31:31–34, it does so as a summary of the entire Book of Consolation in Jeremiah. In other words, 31:31–34 represents all that is contained in Jeremiah 30–33. In what follows, we consider what this section of Jeremiah reveals about the new covenant and see how it corresponds to the previous covenants while pointing to its inauguration and fulfillment in Jesus Christ.

Days Are Coming

First, Jeremiah provides a repetitive expression that ties Jeremiah 30–33 together: "days are coming" (יָמִים בָּאִים). While this phrase occurs fifteen times throughout the book of Jeremiah, the five times it occurs in Jeremiah 30–33 refer to the positive message of the coming salvation. Additionally, the distribution of the five occurrences is quite revealing. The phrase bookends this section of Jeremiah (30:3; 33:14), and the other three occurrences are concentrated within eleven verses in chapter 31 (31:27, 31, 38),[3] suggesting that this is the central, climatic section of the Book of Consolation—one that represents the whole of Jeremiah 30–33. In other words, this expression indicates the parameters and the center of this section of Jeremiah.[4] This means that the entire Book of Consolation addresses the central subject of the Book of Consolation—the new covenant.

David

Second, David also occurs as an *inclusio*, or as bookends, to this section. The name "David" (דָּוִד), referring to the messianic king, occurs once in Jeremiah 30:9 ("But they shall serve the Lord their God and David their king, whom I will raise up for them") and five times in 33:14–26, showing that the coming Davidic king "surrounds" this Book of Consolation.[5] In other words, the coming covenant is centered on the coming Messiah. The figure of David is inextricably linked to the coming salvation, which implies that the new covenant extends and fulfills the Davidic covenant. This becomes especially clear when examining 33:14–26 because it emphasizes that the covenant with David will never be broken and is a permanent fixture in God's redemptive purposes.[6] As the new

---

3. See the *Qere* reading in the Masoretic Text for Jer. 31:38.

4. As noted above, Gentry also sees Jer. 31:29–40 as a unit. Gentry and Wellum, *Kingdom through Covenant*, 538.

5. It is interesting to note that prior to Jer. 30–33, the name "David" (דָּוִד) also occurs eight times in Jer. 1–29 (13:13; 17:25; 21:12; 22:2, 4, 30; 23:5; 29:16), and the name occurs only once after the Book of Consolation (36:30). Of all these occurrences, only one time outside Jer. 30–33 does "David" clearly refer to the coming Messiah: "Behold, the days are coming, declares the Lord, when I will raise up for David a righteous Branch, and he shall reign as king and deal wisely, and shall execute justice and righteousness in the land" (23:5).

6. For discussion of the covenant with the Levitical priests mentioned in this passage, see Paul R. Williamson, *Sealed with an Oath: Covenant in God's Unfolding Purpose*, NSBT 23 (Downers Grove, IL: InterVarsity Press, 2007), 105; Gentry and Wellum, *Kingdom through Covenant*, 576–78; John A. Davies, *A Royal Priesthood: Literary and Intertextual Perspectives on an Image of Israel in Exodus 19.6*, JSOTSup 395 (London: T&T Clark, 2004), 170–88.

covenant also has a permanent nature, these two covenants are shown to be integrally connected. In fact, this passage also notes the permanent character of the covenant with creation (Noahic covenant) in 33:25 (see also 31:35–37)[7] and the permanent nature of the covenant with Abraham ("Abraham, Isaac, and Jacob") in 33:26.[8] In addition, the final sentence in this passage is the *telos*, or goal, of all God's covenants—restoration and salvation: "For I will restore their fortunes and will have mercy on them" (33:26).

With this in mind, the only nonpermanent covenant in Jeremiah 30–33 is the Mosaic administration. As 31:32 indicates, the new covenant is "not like the covenant that I made with their fathers on the day when I took them by the hand to bring them out of the land of Egypt, my covenant that they broke, though I was their husband, declares the LORD." So the only covenant fulfilled and replaced by the new covenant is the Mosaic covenant. The Noahic, Abrahamic, and Davidic covenants are all shown to be permanent, as they are fulfilled and extended by the new covenant.[9] We see here the unity and diversity of the covenant of grace. The unity is that each administration finds fulfillment in the new, while the diversity is that the fulfillment looks different for the Mosaic administration than for the other administrations.

Restoration and Peace

Reference to God restoring "the fortunes" (שְׁבוּת, שְׁבִית) of specific people groups occurs eleven times in the book of Jeremiah. Eight of those references refer to Judah and Israel, and the other three refer to Gentile nations.[10] Most significant is that almost every reference of God restoring the fortunes of his people occurs in the Book of Consolation (Jer. 30:3, 18; 31:23; 32:44; 33:7, 11, 26). The single exception to

---

7. There is much debate regarding whether the covenant with creation existed prior to Gen. 6–9 and the Noahic covenant. For various views on the relation of the covenant with creation to the Noahic covenant, see, e.g., Miles V. Van Pelt, "The Noahic Covenant of the Covenant of Grace," chap. 5 in this volume; Williamson, *Sealed with an Oath*, 59–76; Gentry and Wellum, *Kingdom through Covenant*, 187–95, 211–58; William J. Dumbrell, *Covenant and Creation: A Theology of the Old Testament Covenants* (Nashville: Thomas Nelson, 1984), 11–46; Charles Lee Irons, "*Hēqîm Bĕrît* in Gen 6:18: Make or Confirm a Covenant?," Academia, accessed October 3, 2019, https://www.academia.edu/35833018/Hēqîm_Bĕrît_in_Gen_6_18_Make_or_Confirm_a_Covenant; Peter J. Gentry and Jason T. Parry, "*hēqîm bĕrît* in Gen 6:18—Make or Confirm a Covenant?—A Response to Charles Lee Irons," Academia, accessed October 3, 2019, https://www.academia.edu/36844287/hēqîm_bĕrît_in _Gen_6_18_Make_or_Confirm_a_Covenant_A_Response_to_Charles_Lee_Irons; O. Palmer Robertson, *The Christ of the Covenants* (Phillipsburg, NJ: Presbyterian and Reformed, 1980), 67–86, 109–25; Meredith G. Kline, *Kingdom Prologue: Genesis Foundations for a Covenantal Worldview* (Eugene, OR: Wipf and Stock, 2006), 230–34.

8. With the permanence of the Abrahamic covenant, why is the sign of circumcision no longer applicable in the New Testament? The simple answer is that the New Testament reveals that baptism replaces circumcision in the new covenant era (e.g., Col. 2:8–12). Both circumcision and baptism point to the same realities: circumcision looks forward to what Christ does at the cross, and baptism looks backward to what Christ did on the cross. For more on the relationship between circumcision and baptism, see Robertson, *Christ of the Covenants*, 157–66; J. V. Fesko, *Word, Water, and Spirit: A Reformed Perspective on Baptism* (Grand Rapids, MI: Reformed Heritage Books, 2010), 228–48; Mark E. Ross, "Baptism and Circumcision as Signs and Seals," in *The Case for Covenantal Infant Baptism*, ed. Gregg Strawbridge (Phillipsburg, NJ: P&R, 2003), 85–111; Cornelis P. Venema, *Christ and Covenant Theology: Essays on Election, Republication, and the Covenants* (Phillipsburg, NJ: P&R, 2017), 274–76.

9. The fact that only the Mosaic covenant is in view in Jer. 31:31–34, and *not* the Abrahamic covenant, is missed by some theologians or not clearly distinguished in some discussions on this passage. Fesko also notes this trend. *Word, Water, and Spirit*, 355nn50–51.

10. Moab (Jer. 48:47), Ammon (49:6), and Elam (49:39). Note God's mercy to the Gentiles in these texts.

this pattern is found in the chapter just prior to Jeremiah 30–33. Jeremiah 29:14 prepares the reader for the heavy emphasis on the coming restoration of God's people in Jeremiah 30–33: "I will be found by you, declares the LORD, and I will *restore your fortunes* and gather you from all the nations and all the places where I have driven you, declares the LORD, and I will bring you back to the place from which I sent you into exile."

In light of the judgment and misery that Israel and Judah experience through exile, Yahweh will save them and their offspring

> from the land of their captivity.
> Jacob shall return and have quiet and ease,
>   and none shall make him afraid. (30:10)

Yahweh will restore his people and defeat all their enemies (30:11–20). Instead of a foreign ruler, one "from their midst" will be king over them (30:21). Then God says, "And you shall be my people, . . . and I will be your God" (30:22; see 31:1, 33; 32:38).[11] This sentiment notably occurs in 31:33 and 32:38 regarding the outcome of the new covenant. God will establish peace so that there might be uninterrupted communion between God and his people. Furthermore, the coming restoration is pictured as God bringing his people back in joyful repentance to a land of abundance (31:1–26) because he has remembered Ephraim (31:20).

As a sign that this restoration will truly come, God commands Jeremiah to buy a field while the Babylonians have Jerusalem under siege (32:1–25). The reason for having Jeremiah purchase land in the face of certain destruction and exile is because Yahweh "will bring them back to this place" and "make them dwell in safety" (32:37). The Lord then says, "And they shall be my people, and I will be their God" (32:38). God will plant them in this land (a repeated idea in the book of Jeremiah), with all his heart and soul (32:41). Yahweh then further explains,

> Just as I have brought all this great disaster upon this people, so I will bring upon them all the good that I promise them. Fields shall be bought in this land of which you are saying, "It is a desolation, without man or beast; it is given into the hand of the Chaldeans." Fields shall be bought for money, and deeds shall be signed and sealed and witnessed, in the land of Benjamin, in the places about Jerusalem, and in the cities of Judah, in the cities of the hill country, in the cities of the Shephelah, and in the cities of the Negeb; for I will restore their fortunes, declares the LORD. (32:42–44)

---

11. Mark J. Boda refers to this expression as the "core relational formula," which occurs throughout the Old Testament. *The Heartbeat of Old Testament Theology: Three Creedal Expressions*, ASBT (Grand Rapids, MI: Baker Academic, 2017), 71. See also Robertson's discussion on how this phrase shows the thematic unity of the divine covenants. *Christ of the Covenants*, 45–52. For an in-depth investigation of this "formula," see Rolf Rendtorff, *The Covenant Formula: An Exegetical and Theological Investigation*, trans. Margaret Kohl, OTS (Edinburgh: T&T Clark, 1998).

Following this declaration, in Jeremiah 33:1–13, the Lord promises health and heal-ing, prosperity and security (33:6). He says,

> I will cleanse them from all the guilt of their sin against me, and I will forgive all the guilt of their sin and rebellion against me. And this city shall be to me a name of joy, a praise and a glory before all the nations of the earth who shall hear of all the good that I do for them. They shall fear and tremble because of all the good and all the prosperity I provide for it. (33:8–9)

This language is repeated from the passages that directly mention the new covenant in 31:31–34 and 32:37–41. Forgiveness of sin (see 31:34) will lead to the fear of God (see 32:40), and thus, God's redeeming restoration of his people will lead to their faithful obedience and worship. Voices will be heard singing,

> Give thanks to the Lord of hosts,
> for the Lord is good,
> for his steadfast love endures forever! (33:11)

The Lord explains, "For I will restore the fortunes of the land as at first" (33:11). This restoration and peace is then tied to David in 33:14–26, the final passage of the Book of Consolation.

The portrait of renewal described in Jeremiah 30–33 is presented in both tem-poral and eschatological terms.[12] This means that the text exhibits an anticipation of this restoration happening in the not-so-distant future but also an anticipation of con-summation or eschatological finality, which has clearly not yet happened. And the "near and far" imagery is intermingled in Jeremiah, which is often the case in the Old Testament Prophets. So the initial restoration of Israel to the land after exile was a partial fulfillment of this portrait. Christ coming to take away the sins of his people and to inaugurate the new covenant also fulfills this portrait. And the final, ultimate expression of this restoration and peace will be realized in the new heavens and new earth (Rev. 21–22). One must grasp the "already and not yet" nature of God's redemp-tive purposes in order to see how Christ fulfills the message of Jeremiah 30–33 and how these things have been partially fulfilled now (regarding our experience in the New Testament era) even as we await the fullness of what is prophesied in the Book of Consolation.

Jeremiah 31:31–34

With the book of Hebrews citing this passage twice, Jeremiah 31:31–34 provides a syn-opsis of the Book of Consolation, and it presents a picture of the new covenant's *telos*, or goal. In 31:31, God declares that he will make a "new covenant with the house of

---

12. See Dumbrell, *Covenant and Creation*, 184–85.

Israel and the house of Judah." The phrase "new covenant" (בְּרִית חֲדָשָׁה) occurs only in this verse in the Old Testament, but the new covenant arrangement is addressed many times. The term חָדָשׁ means "new" or "fresh,"[13] and it should not be interpreted as if this "new" covenant were "brand new," that is, that it has no relation to the previous covenants. In fact, as the context of Jeremiah 30–33 shows, this covenant is necessarily connected to those previous covenants.[14]

First, the new covenant is not like the Mosaic covenant (31:32), but it is related to it in that it achieves that to which the Mosaic administration typologically pointed—life and restoration (cf. Heb. 8:1–13; 10:1–18). Notably, Yahweh will put his law "within" his people (lit., "in their midst," בְּקִרְבָּם) and will write it on "their heart" (לִבָּם) (Jer. 31:33). The law written on the heart is (at least in some way) the moral law[15] that was not codified until the Mosaic covenant (see Gal. 3:17). So Jeremiah 31:33 shows that through the new covenant administration, the moral law (summarized in the Ten Commandments) is internalized, indicating that God will conform his people to his law (i.e., God's moral image and likeness). In doing this, God says, "And I will be their God, and they shall be my people" (31:33), which constitutes the goal of the Mosaic administration (Ex. 29:45; Lev. 26:12). In this way, the new covenant replaces the Mosaic covenant, and it fulfills and extends its objective. Second, the new covenant is also connected to the Noahic covenant in that it will never end (Jer. 31:35–37; 33:25), and it brings about complete restoration. Third, as has already been established, the new covenant is intimately tied to the Davidic covenant (30:9; 33:14–26), and it fulfills the promises of the Abrahamic covenant (33:26). These facts entail that the new covenant cannot be isolated from the previous covenants, and it must be understood as extending God's redemptive purposes that he has been progressively working out through those covenants.

It is also important to note that as the central summarization of the new covenant in Jeremiah 30–33, this passage presents the eschatological outcome of this covenant. Jeremiah 31:34 portrays this finalized realization of redemption: "And no longer shall each one teach his neighbor and each his brother, saying, 'Know the LORD,' for they shall all know me, from the least of them to the greatest, declares the LORD. For I will forgive their iniquity, and I will remember their sin no more." This verse must not be interpreted in an overrealized manner in the present day in light of Christ's inauguration of this covenant. Believers do indeed have the law written on their hearts, they know the Lord, and their sins are forgiven. But there is still the need within the

13. *HALOT*, 294; Pieter A. Verhoef, "חדש," in *NIDOTTE*, #2542, #2543.
14. Mackay also notes that the passage in Jeremiah indicates continuity between the covenants. *Jeremiah*, 233–34.
15. Gentry states that תּוֹרָה in this passage is "inappropriately" translated "law" because it refers to God's overall "instruction" for his people. Gentry and Wellum, *Kingdom through Covenant*, 551. While I would grant that the concept of God's overall instruction is in view, the moral law is at the heart of God's word/instruction and affects all that he desires for and requires of his people. Thus "law" is a perfectly valid and appropriate translation in the context of Jer. 31:33.

covenant community today (and outside it) to teach one's neighbor and to exhort one's brother to "know the Lord." This need will continue until Christ returns to make all things new. So while we see this verse fulfilled in new covenant believers today, the verse ultimately presents an idyllic, eschatological portrait of the redeemed community (i.e., the new heavens and new earth, Rev. 21–22), when all will know God perfectly because sin is removed and the creation is restored. In other words, while the realities of this wonderful new covenant have already begun, history is progressing toward an eschatological completion of the pure covenant community anticipated in this passage.[16] As Dumbrell notes (after observing the inaugurated nature of the new covenant today), "In Jeremiah [31:31–34], we are looking beyond the New Testament age to the community of the end-time, to a situation when the kingdom of God has finally come and is all in all."[17]

Jeremiah 32:36–41

One final passage to consider in Jeremiah 30–33 also addresses the new covenant but from another angle. Jeremiah 32:36–41 explains that after Babylon conquers Jerusalem, God will gather his people from "all the countries" to which he drove them in judgment: "I will bring them back to this place, and I will make them dwell in safety" (32:37). Then the Lord echoes the previous promise of 31:33 by saying, "And they shall be my people, and I will be their God" (32:38). This clearly indicates that the covenant being addressed in Jeremiah 32:36–41 is the same covenant as found in 31:31–34.

While 31:31–34, however, presents an eschatological picture of the consummation of the new covenant (see discussion above), 32:36–41 speaks of the new covenant in a manner that highlights the enduring nature of this administration:

> I will give them one heart and one way, that they may fear me forever, for their own good and the good of their children after them. I will make with them an everlasting covenant [בְּרִית עוֹלָם], that I will not turn away from doing good to them. And I will put the fear of me in their hearts, that they may not turn from me. I will rejoice in doing them good, and I will plant them in this land in faithfulness, with all my heart and all my soul. (32:39–41)

---

16. An example of an overrealized interpretation of Jer. 31:34 (and Isa. 54:13) for the covenant community today can be seen in Gentry and Wellum, *Kingdom through Covenant*, 555–56. Gentry writes, "Only believers are members of the new covenant community: all *members* are *believers*, and *only* believers are members. Therefore in the new covenant community there will no longer be a situation where some members urge other members to know the Lord. There will be no such thing as an unregenerate member of the new covenant community" (555; emphasis original). What Gentry fails to distinguish between is membership in the covenant by *true faith* and membership in the covenant *community* (and he repeatedly uses the word "community" in the above quote). The visible expression of the covenant community (i.e., the church) in this present life reveals that there are those who do not believe (e.g., Matt. 7:22–23; John 6:60–65; 15:6; 2 Tim. 4:3–4; Heb. 6:4–6; 10:28–29; 1 John 2:18–19; Rev. 2:14–16, 20–23; 3:1–4). The rigor with which Gentry argues his point simply will not hold up when examining what the Old Testament and New Testament reveal about the *visible* and *invisible* dimensions of the church prior to the final judgment and re-creation of all things.

17. Dumbrell, *Covenant and Creation*, 183; see also 182–85.

The language of these verses draws attention to the ongoing nature of the "fear" of Yahweh from one generation to the next. God's people will never turn away from God because he will put the fear of him within their hearts.

Like the previous covenants of the Old Testament, there is also a familial aspect to the new covenant as subsequent generations will receive and benefit from this administration.[18] God will do this "for their own good and the good of their children [lit., 'their sons'] after them" (32:39). This does not necessarily entail that all the children of God's people will automatically receive personal salvation, just as not every child of the believers in the previous covenants were saved (Rom. 9:6–8). The promises of God's covenant must always be received by faith in order for salvation to be realized (Gen. 15:6; Rom. 3:27–31; 4:1–8; 9:30–33; Gal. 3:7).

Peter Gentry notably says very little about Jeremiah 32:39, and he dismisses covenant theologians' use of it to support the teaching that the children of believers are part of the covenant community.[19] He simply notes that New Testament believers could pass on the gospel to their children throughout the following generations. His discussion of this text is unfortunately brief and does little to substantiate his claim that covenant theologians misinterpret this verse. In addition, his statement that 32:39 does not guarantee "that the children of believers will automatically become believers,"[20] while true, seems to miss the point of the text regarding the familial benefit of the new covenant (i.e., that the children of believers in some way benefit from being a part of the covenant community). Such a statement also seems to imply that *all* covenant theologians interpret this verse as a guarantee "that the children of believers will automatically become believers," which is simply not true and is a distraction from the real issues in the text. Actually, the familial aspect of the new covenant highlighted in this text shows that the covenant community will consist of those who fear the Lord and their children. As with previous covenants in the Old Testament, this covenant is the heritage of the subsequent generations of God's people, but the promises of life and salvation through this covenant will either be received by faith or rejected in unbelief.[21]

This familial aspect of the new covenant has direct implications regarding the covenant sign of entrance into the covenant community, namely, baptism (i.e., the baptism of believers and their children). While other chapters in this book examine the relationship between circumcision and baptism,[22] it is worth noting that these new covenant

---

18. Mackay states, "Not only does it [i.e., the new covenant] bring good (covenant blessing) on them, it also rebounds to the good of subsequent generations, which is a notable feature of the LORD's covenant dealings with his people." *Jeremiah*, 263.

19. Gentry and Wellum, *Kingdom through Covenant*, 571.

20. Gentry and Wellum, *Kingdom through Covenant*, 571.

21. At this point, it is worth noting that the New Testament demonstrates this familial facet of the covenant being worked out in passages such as Acts 2:39; 16:15, 33; 1 Cor. 7:14; Eph. 6:1–4; Col. 3:20–21.

22. See John Scott Redd, "The Abrahamic Covenant"; O. Palmer Robertson, "Israel and the Nations in God's Covenants"; and Derek W. H. Thomas, "Covenant, Assurance, and the Sacraments," chaps. 6, 24, and 27, respectively, in this volume. See also Fesko, *Word, Water, and Spirit*, 337–67.

texts in Jeremiah 31 and 32 must be evaluated and interpreted in light of each other and the whole of Jeremiah 30–33. And when this is done, these texts do not undermine the familial nature of God's covenant. One should not prioritize one text and diminish another, and if an interpreter employs an overrealized eschatology in interpreting one passage, he or she will face significant difficulty in interpreting other passages or will end up elevating one text above another.

Conclusion on Jeremiah 30–33

The Book of Consolation in Jeremiah reveals the richness of God's coming salvation. Jeremiah 30–33 is foundational for understanding the new covenant and its relationship to the previous Old Testament covenants. Its message encourages God's people that the days are coming in which the Lord will establish a better covenant that will achieve the goal of life and restoration promised by God in times past. As New Testament believers, we have seen this covenant inaugurated by Christ through his death and resurrection. Now, living under this administration, God preserves us and keeps us from turning away from him, and we look forward to the consummation of the covenant when all things are restored in the new heavens and new earth and all God's people will "know the Lord."

Ezekiel

Two passages occupy much of the following discussion on the new covenant in the book of Ezekiel. It is worth noting, however, that the structure of the whole book not only provides the key to its interpretation but also points to the restoration promised in the new covenant. In Ezekiel, the otherworldly description of "the glory of Yahweh" signifies the presence of God. In the Old Testament, God's presence dwells among his people in the temple, and the connection between God's presence and the temple highlights his relationship to Israel in the book of Ezekiel.[23] For instance, the visions of Yahweh's glory occur in Ezekiel 1:1–3:27; 8:1–10:22; and 40:1–48:35. First, "the glory of Yahweh" appears in a vision to Ezekiel by the Chebar Canal in the province of Babylon as he is summoned to prophetic ministry. Then, Ezekiel 8–10 contains the vision of "the glory of Yahweh" leaving the temple in Jerusalem as a sign of the coming judgment of destruction and exile at the hands of the Babylonians. Finally, Ezekiel 40–48 shows a future temple to which "the glory of Yahweh" returns. God's eschatological presence in this new temple will bring complete restoration to God's people and the land. Jerusalem itself will be restored and will have the name "Yahweh is there" (48:35, my trans.).[24]

---

23. David Noel Freedman writes, "The theme of the Temple runs through the entire book, and is the key to its unity. In a sentence, it is the story of the departure of the glory of God from the Temple, and its return." "The Book of Ezekiel," *Int* 18 (1962): 456.

24. For further discussion on the "the glory of Yahweh" in the book of Ezekiel, see Michael G. McKelvey, "Ezekiel," in Van Pelt, *Biblical-Theological Introduction to the Old Testament*, 310–13.

This promise of future restoration for the people of Israel and their environment is essentially the same message that was seen above in Jeremiah 30–33, the Book of Consolation. The entire book of Ezekiel moves the reader forward to anticipate a coming time in which God will return to dwell among his people in a fuller manner than Israel knew under the Mosaic administration before the exile. In this future time, God's presence will bring life to a dead land (Ezek. 47:1–12), and his people will be built up and substantially established from then on (47:13–48:35). In this manner, the promises of the new covenant are inherent in the message of the whole book of Ezekiel. With this in view, we turn to give attention to two particular passages.

Ezekiel 34:20–31

Ezekiel 34 begins with the condemnation of "the shepherds of Israel" (34:1), which is a metaphor for the leadership of the nation. The Lord denounces their corrupt rule and selfish ambition (34:1–10). He says, "Behold, I am against the shepherds, and I will require my sheep at their hand and put a stop to their feeding the sheep. No longer shall the shepherds feed themselves. I will rescue my sheep from their mouths, that they may not be food for them" (34:10). Instead of false shepherds, Yahweh himself will seek out his sheep and rescue them from the lands into which they have been scattered (34:11–13); he will bring them into their land and provide them with lush pastures (34:13–14). God promises, "I myself will be the shepherd of my sheep, and I myself will make them lie down" (34:15). He will also judge between the bad sheep and the good sheep and will rescue his flock from further predation (34:16–22).

God clearly states that he himself will be the shepherd of his people (34:15). But the passage further highlights that this future restoration is tied to the Davidic covenant: "And I will set up over them one shepherd, my servant David, and he shall feed them: he shall feed them and be their shepherd. And I, the LORD, will be their God, and my servant David shall be prince among them. I am the LORD; I have spoken" (34:23–24). The text highlights the unification of God's kingship and Davidic kingship in this time of restoration. Both God himself and David himself will shepherd Israel in unified manner.[25] Much like Jeremiah 30–33, this passage in Ezekiel shows that the Davidic covenant is integral to the new covenant and is a means of bringing about this coming salvation.

In the next verse, God states that he will make with his people a "covenant of peace" (בְּרִית שָׁלוֹם, Ezek. 34:25; see also Isa. 54:10; Ezek. 37:26).[26] The Hebrew term

---

25. Jesus fulfills this promise by being both the Son of God and the Son of David, the one person in whom we see both divine kingship and Davidic kingship. See the emphasis in Jesus's words on how he and the Father are *one*, in view of his being the good shepherd in John 10:22–30.

26. The phrase בְּרִית שָׁלוֹם occurs four times in the Old Testament. The only occurrence outside the Prophets is God's "covenant of peace" with Phinehas (Num. 25:12).

"peace" (שָׁלוֹם) is rich with meaning and conveys a restitution of well-being.[27] As Philip Nel states, "The *berît šālôm* is, therefore, the promissory covenant of God given to his restored people as an eternal blessing and salvation."[28] The description of restoration follows in 34:26–31, with the people's knowledge of Yahweh's presence among them being central to this eschatological peace: "And they shall know that I am the LORD their God with them, and that they, the house of Israel, are my people, declares the Lord GOD" (34:30). This knowledge of God echoes Jeremiah 31:34, showing that the new covenant administration achieves the eschatological restoration of God's people to God himself. It is the restoration of life to which the previous covenants pointed.

Ezekiel 36:22–37:38

Yahweh's concern for his holy name is a central matter in Ezekiel 36, and he will vindicate his holiness before the eyes of the nations. The manner in which he will do this is the restoration of Israel from the nations (36:22–24) and the cleansing of them from their sin and idolatry (36:25). God will transform them inwardly: "And I will give you a new heart, and a new spirit I will put within you. And I will remove the heart of stone from your flesh and give you a heart of flesh. And I will put my Spirit within you, and cause you to walk in my statutes and be careful to obey my rules" (36:26–27). Like Jeremiah 31:33 and 32:40, this change of heart in the new covenant leads to obedience to God's law ("my statues" and "my rules," Ezek. 36:27).[29] Note that God's presence in them brings about this transformation ("I will put my Spirit within you," 36:27). God will also restore their land (to be become "like the garden of Eden," 36:35) and their cities that have been desolated (36:28–36). He will multiply his people like a flock (36:37), and "then they will know that I am the LORD" (36:38). Restoration (in re-creational terms), forgiveness, God's presence, obedience from the heart, and the knowledge of God are all motifs central to the new covenant (see discussion on Jer. 30–33 above).

Ezekiel 37 continues the description of God's salvation through the new covenant, first with the great vision of the valley of dry bones (37:1–14). This highlights the deadness of God's people. The utter impossibility of these "very dry" (37:2) bones coming back to life is evidenced in Ezekiel's response that only "the Lord GOD" knows if they can live (37:3). As Ezekiel prophesies over the bones, they regrow flesh but do not yet have "breath" in them. The word for "breath" is the Hebrew term רוּחַ, which is often translated "spirit" when it refers to the Spirit of God, as in 36:27; 37:1, 14; or to the spirit of human beings, as in 36:26. It is also the same word translated "winds" in 37:9.

---

27. See *HALOT*, 1509–1510; Philip J. Nel, "שָׁלֵם," in *NIDOTTE*, 4:130–32.

28. Nel, "שָׁלֵם," in *NIDOTTE*, 4:132.

29. The occurrences of "statute" (מִשְׁפָּט) and "rule" (חֹק/חֻקָּה) in the plural have a notable connection to Lev. 18:5 throughout the book of Ezekiel, especially in 36:27 and 37:24. See Preston Sprinkle, "Law and Life: Leviticus 18:5 in the Literary Framework of Ezekiel," *JSOT* 31, no. 3 (2007): 275–93.

The use of רוּחַ ten times in 37:1–14 emphasizes the spiritual restoration that God will bring to Israel. This text, however, implies not only spiritual restoration but total renewal, including bodily resurrection:[30]

> Behold, I will open your graves and raise you from your graves, O my people. And I will bring you into the land of Israel. And you shall know that I am the LORD, when I open your graves, and raise you from your graves, O my people. And I will put my Spirit within you, and you shall live, and I will place you in your own land. Then you shall know that I am the LORD; I have spoken, and I will do it, declares the LORD. (37:12–14)

The promise of future restoration continues in the remainder of Ezekiel 37:15–28. God's people will become one as Israel and Judah are reunited (37:15–23), and they will never defile themselves again (37:23). For Yahweh says, "I will save them from all the backslidings in which they have sinned, and will cleanse them; and *they shall be my people, and I will be their God*" (37:23; see Jer. 31:33; 32:38). The next verses once again reference David's connection to this new covenant era. Note several things in Ezekiel 37:24–27 regarding this coming time of restoration.

First, "David" will be the king, the one shepherd (37:24), and the forever prince (37:25) over God's people. The promise to David is realized in the inauguration and consummation of the new covenant (see Jer. 30–33).

Second, Israel will dwell in the land promised to Jacob (Ezek. 37:25); the generational/familial nature of God's covenant is also highlighted ("They and their children and their children's children shall dwell there forever," 37:25); and the Lord will multiply their number (37:26). These are all elements inherent in the Abrahamic covenant (Gen. 12:1–4; 15:1–20; 17:1–14).

Third, this covenant that God will make with them is called "a covenant of peace" (בְּרִית שָׁלוֹם) and "an everlasting covenant" (בְּרִית עוֹלָם), and both expressions refer to the new covenant in Ezekiel 34:25 and Jeremiah 32:40 respectively.[31]

Finally, God's presence among them will be permanent with his "sanctuary in their midst forevermore" (Ezek. 37:26, 28). The mention of the Lord's sanctuary (2x) and "my dwelling place" (37:27) highlights the temple motif that is prominent in the book of Ezekiel.[32] The Lord may have symbolically left his sanctuary in Jerusalem as a sign of judgment in the exile (Ezek. 8–10), but in the future, he will return to them and renew them completely (Ezek. 40–48). His permanent presence among his people signifies his possession of them, for he says, "*I will be their God, and they shall be my people*" (37:27; see Jer. 31:33; 32:38; Ezek. 37:23). And this will affect the whole world: "Then *the*

30. See G. K. Beale, *A New Testament Biblical Theology: The Unfolding of the Old Testament in the New* (Grand Rapids, MI: Baker Academic, 2011), 229–30.

31. See earlier discussions on these texts.

32. See the above discussion on "the glory of Yahweh" and the temple in the book of Ezekiel.

nations will know that I am the LORD *who sanctifies Israel, when my sanctuary is in their midst forevermore*" (37:28). In this way, God's everlasting presence with humanity is the goal of both redemption and the new covenant.

Conclusion on Ezekiel

The message of Ezekiel shows that God's ultimate purpose in redemption is that "the glory of Yahweh" (i.e., God's presence) will dwell permanently in the midst of his people. As the reality of judgment for sin in the form of exile sets in, God's people must look forward to the time in which the Lord will restore his people and dwell with them forever. As New Testament believers, we have seen this new covenant inaugurated by Christ through his incarnation, death, and resurrection. Jesus is the presence of God in its fullness (Col. 1:19; Heb. 1:1–3). He is the new temple of God (John 1:14; 2:19–22) from which living water flows (John 4:10, 13–15; 7:37–38). He has poured out the Spirit of God into the hearts of believers, who are now the temple of the Holy Spirit (1 Cor. 3:16; 6:19), and because his people love him, they seek to keep his commandments (John 14:15, 21). He is the firstfruits of the resurrection of the dead (1 Cor. 15:20, 23), and through him, his people are resurrected spiritually (John 3:3–8; Eph. 2:5) and will be resurrected bodily in the last day (Rom. 8:23; 1 Cor. 15). He is the good shepherd who reigns over his people (John 10:1–30). And when he returns, he will establish the fullness of his presence in the restoration of the new heavens and new earth (Rev. 21–22). His presence will be centered on the new Jerusalem, and there will be no temple, "for its temple is the Lord God the Almighty and the Lamb" (Rev. 21:22). And in that place, there will be

> the river of the water of life, bright as crystal, flowing from the throne of God and of the Lamb through the middle of the street of the city; also, on either side of the river, the tree of life with its twelve kinds of fruit, yielding its fruit each month. The leaves of the tree were for the healing of the nations [see Ezek. 47:12]. No longer will there be anything accursed, but the throne of God and of the Lamb will be in it, and his servants will worship him. They will see his face, and his name will be on their foreheads. (Rev. 22:1–4)

In these ways, the promises of the new covenant in the book of Ezekiel point us to the reality of redemption and restoration found in Jesus Christ, both now and in the age to come![33]

Isaiah

The book of Isaiah contains many references to the Messiah and the coming salvation of God's people—so many that it would be difficult to examine all the pas-

---

33. For further discussion on the message of Ezekiel and the New Testament, see McKelvey, "Ezekiel," 316–18.

sages that touch on the promises of the new covenant. Therefore, in this section, we briefly summarize the central messianic themes in Isaiah, which can be clearly divided into at least two major sections: Isaiah 1–39 and 40–66. These sections address Israel's situation both before the exile and during and after the exile, respectively. Within each section the future hope of the people is tied to a coming figure that will bring God's salvation and restoration. In Isaiah 1–39, that figure is the Davidic Messiah, and in Isaiah 40–66, it is "the servant of the LORD."[34] As I show here, both of these figures refer to the same person—the coming Savior-King of Israel—as he establishes justice, righteousness, and equity for his people and restores creation to a harmonized order.

The Davidic Messiah

The man Isaiah prophesies of a coming Davidic king in 9:1–7; 11:1–12:6; and 16:5. The first two passages occur in Isaiah 7–12, which reflect the time of the Syro-Ephraimite conflict.[35] In both passages, after a time of judgment, God will raise up a Davidic king who will rule righteously forever (9:6–7; 11:3–9) and will bring restoration to Israel from among the nations (11:6–16), with even the nations themselves seeking this king (11:10). Similarly, 16:5 speaks of the future Messiah reigning righteously:

> Then a throne will be established in steadfast love,
>> and on it will sit in faithfulness
>> in the tent of David
> one who judges and seeks justice
>> and is swift to do righteousness.

The book of Isaiah shows that the righteous and just nature of the Messiah's reign entails a renewal of order within creation. As sin has caused disorder within creation, God will redeem his people and their environment, and the Davidic king will faithfully rule over the restored creation, allowing for peace and harmony within this renewed world.

The Servant of the Lord

Remarkably, "the servant of the LORD" found in Isaiah 40–66 engages in the same activity as the Davidic king of Isaiah 1–39. Isaiah 42:1–9; 49:1–12; 50:4–11; and

---

34. For an extended treatment of these figures in the book of Isaiah, see Andrew T. Abernethy, *The Book of Isaiah and God's Kingdom: A Thematic-Theological Approach*, NSBT 40 (Downers Grove, IL: InterVarsity Press, 2016), 119–70. See also Willem A. VanGemeren, "Isaiah," in Van Pelt, *Biblical-Theological Introduction to the Old Testament*, 267–68.

35. The prophecy of Isa. 7:14 regarding the "virgin" bearing a son named "Immanuel" is linked to the Davidic Messiah of 9:1–7 and 11:1–12:6 in the context of Isa. 7–12. See O. Palmer Robertson, *The Christ of the Prophets* (Phillipsburg, NJ: P&R, 2004), 213–15; J. Alec Motyer, *The Prophecy of Isaiah: An Introduction and Commentary* (Downers Grove, IL: InterVarsity Press, 1993), 86; John L. Mackay, *A Study Commentary on Isaiah*, vol. 1, *Chapters 1–39*, EPSC (Darlington, UK: Evangelical Press, 2008), 198. For a different perspective on the "Immanuel" of 7:14, with "Immanuel" having a more immediate referent in Isaiah's time, see Abernethy, *Book of Isaiah*, 119–24.

52:13–53:12 portray a servant who rules righteously, achieves the salvation of God's people, and brings restoration to the world. In two of these passages, God states that he gives the servant himself as a "covenant" (בְּרִית, 42:6; 49:8). This means that the servant is the embodiment of all that the new covenant reveals. All God's saving, life-giving, restorative, covenantal purposes are found in him and brought about through him. Notably, the portrayal of the servant's suffering in behalf of his people in Isaiah 52:13–53:12 provides one of the most remarkable prophecies of the Messiah's saving work. While he will be exalted as king (52:13–14; 53:12), the servant will first endure humiliation by being rejected by men (53:1–3) and by suffering for the sins of his people (53:4–9, 11), yet he will rise from the dead to see the salvific outcome of his work (53:10–12).[36] His justification of the many (53:11) entails his restoration of people to a right standing with God, mankind, and creation.

Following the suffering servant of Isaiah 53, the phrase "a covenant of peace" (בְּרִית שָׁלוֹם) occurs in Isaiah 54:10. We noted above while discussing the book of Ezekiel (34:25; 37:26) that there this phrase refers to the new covenant, and it appears to do so in the context of Isaiah as well. In view of the servant's saving work in Isaiah 53, Isaiah 54 begins with God promising to permanently restore Israel (54:1–3), though he has briefly "deserted" Israel like the deserting of a wife (54:4–8). This everlasting restoration is called "a covenant of peace" in 54:10. In fact, this covenant is compared to the Noahic covenant:

> "This is like the days of Noah to me:
>   as I swore that the waters of Noah
>   should no more go over the earth,
> so I have sworn that I will not be angry with you,
>   and will not rebuke you.
> For the mountains may depart
>   and the hills be removed,
> but my steadfast love shall not depart from you,
>   and my covenant of peace shall not be removed,"
>   says the LORD, who has compassion on you. (54:9–10)

As God's covenant with creation/Noah is everlasting, in that he will never destroy the earth again with water, so this new covenant of peace, brought about by the servant of the Lord, will restore God's people forever.[37]

In the next chapter, Isaiah refers to the new covenant again, but this time he calls it "an everlasting covenant" (בְּרִית עוֹלָם, Isa. 55:3; see also 61:8). As noted above, this same expression also occurs in both Jeremiah 32:40 and Ezekiel 37:26 in reference to the new

---

36. See Beale, *Biblical Theology*, 494–95.

37. Note the discussion earlier on the relationships between the previous Old Testament covenants and the new covenant. See especially the discussion on the Book of Consolation in Jeremiah.

covenant. In the context of Isaiah 55, God is calling for the people to come to him that they may freely receive salvation. He declares,

> Incline your ear, and come to me;
>> hear, that your soul may live;
> and I will make with you an everlasting covenant,
>> my steadfast, sure love for David.
> Behold, I made him a witness to the peoples,
>> a leader and commander for the peoples. (55:3–4)

The connection of this covenant with "David" is significant since it is the only occurrence of David's name in Isaiah 40–66. The servant of Yahweh has been the prominent figure in the second part of Isaiah, but now in the context of God's coming salvation through his "servant" in Isaiah 52–55, David's name reappears for the first time since Isaiah 1–39. This connection follows the pattern that we have seen in Jeremiah and Ezekiel in that the new covenant is intimately linked to the Davidic covenant. The messianic Davidic king will usher in this new covenant era (55:3), he will bring God's salvation to his people (55:1–3), and he will rule over the nations (55:4, "peoples" [2x]).

In view of the redeeming work of the servant of the Lord, a Redeemer is later promised in Isaiah 59 who is connected to the covenant that God makes with his people:

> "And a Redeemer will come to Zion,
>> to those in Jacob who turn from transgression," declares the LORD.

> "And as for me, this is my covenant with them," says the LORD: "My Spirit that is upon you, and my words that I have put in your mouth, shall not depart out of your mouth, or out of the mouth of your offspring, or out of the mouth of your children's offspring," says the LORD, "from this time forth and forevermore." (59:20–21)

While the Redeemer is not named, nor is he called "servant," his connection to the Davidic Messiah / servant in Isaiah is apparent because he redeems God's people, just as the messianic servant of the Lord in the previous passages. Also, the text reveals that the new covenant entails God's Spirit (see Ezek. 36:37; 37:14) and word (see Jer. 31:33) being perpetually in his people, and this covenant will continue from one generation to the next (Isa. 59:21).[38]

Furthermore, the figure in 61:1–3 clearly matches up with the Davidic king and the servant of the Lord.[39] While the term "servant" does not occur in this text, the one in view has the Spirit of God (see 11:2) and is "anointed" (מָשַׁח) by Yahweh. He brings the

---

38. See the discussion above on Jer. 32:36–41 regarding the familial aspect of the new covenant. Interestingly, Gentry does not comment on the familial language of this verse. Gentry and Wellum, *Kingdom through Covenant*, 509.

39. John N. Oswalt, *The Book of Isaiah*, vol. 2, *Chapters 40–66*, NICOT (Grand Rapids, MI: Eerdmans, 1998), 563.

good news of restoration to the poor, deliverance to the captives, the year of the Lord's favor, and the day of God's vengeance (61:1–2). He will bring permanent joy to those who mourn and establish them in righteousness forever (61:3). Then, after promising abundant restoration (61:4–7), God says,

> For I the LORD love justice;
>> I hate robbery and wrong;
> I will faithfully give them their recompense,
>> and I will make *an everlasting covenant* [בְּרִית עוֹלָם] with them.
> Their offspring shall be known among the nations,
>> and their descendants in the midst of the peoples;
> all who see them shall acknowledge them,
>> that they are an offspring the LORD has blessed. (61:8–9)

Conclusion on Isaiah

The restoration that God will bring about through his Davidic king / servant of the Lord by means of the new covenant culminates in the "new heavens and new earth" at the end of Isaiah. In Isaiah 65:17–66:24, God reveals a universal picture of the restored creation.[40] God's people will be at peace, God's enemies will be judged, and "all flesh shall come to worship" before Yahweh (66:23). This is the *telos*, or goal, of the covenantal purposes of God—life in a restored creation. The author of Revelation shows us more fully what Isaiah revealed in part:

> Then I saw a new heaven and a new earth, for the first heaven and the first earth had passed away, and the sea was no more. And I saw the holy city, new Jerusalem, coming down out of heaven from God, prepared as a bride adorned for her husband. And I heard a loud voice from the throne saying, "Behold, the dwelling place of God is with man. He will dwell with them, and they will be his people, and God himself will be with them as their God. He will wipe away every tear from their eyes, and death shall be no more, neither shall there be mourning, nor crying, nor pain anymore, for the former things have passed away."
> And he who was seated on the throne said, "Behold, I am making all things new." (Rev. 21:1–5)

Summary and Conclusion

The book of Isaiah functions together with Jeremiah and Ezekiel to reveal God's saving purposes through the coming new covenant administration. These purposes have been revealed through the previous Old Testament covenants, but now the Major Prophets show how the new covenant will achieve God's great redemption of humanity and

---

40. See Abernethy, *Book of Isaiah*, 171–98; VanGemeren, "Isaiah," 270–73.

creation through the messianic Davidic king. The above prophetic books, however, are not the only texts that portray the coming new covenant. The so-called Minor Prophets (i.e., the Twelve) and Daniel also say much about the coming redemption through the Messiah. Space prohibits us from looking at the coming Davidic king who will reign over his people in Hosea 3, Amos 9, and Micah 5; the "son of man" who will reign over the eternal kingdom of God in Daniel 7; the shepherd-king who will be rejected in Zechariah 9–11 and 13; the descendant of Zerubbabel who will reign in Haggai 2; the promise of God's Spirit being poured out on "all flesh" in Joel 2; and the expectations of a restored cosmos for the benefit of Israel and the nations found throughout the book of the Twelve. From this portrait we understand that all the covenants in all redemptive history are working toward the ultimate goal of redeeming the fallen creation. There are continuities and discontinuities between the covenants, but what was foreshadowed in the old is realized in the new, and God's salvation is essentially the same in both eras (i.e., eternal life by grace alone through faith alone, e.g., Rom. 4:1–25).

With the coming of Jesus Christ, however, the new covenant has been inaugurated, redemption has been procured, and restoration has begun—first, spiritually, and in the last day, materially. We who live on this side of the cross are blessed to live in the time of the new covenant because we have received its benefits now and await its consummation when Christ returns. We have seen the messianic King come in his Father's glory and inaugurate God's kingdom. We now see the Spirit of God extending that kingdom as the church of Christ is built up throughout the generations. We also know the restoring, resurrecting power of God in the new birth. And we look forward to the fullness of God's everlasting presence in the new creation. We who know the grace of God in Christ by means of the new covenant are eternally blessed. And we can rejoice in all God's covenantal workings because they are the means by which God is our God and we are his people.

10

COVENANT IN THE GOSPELS

Michael J. Kruger

When it comes to tracing the covenant theme throughout the books of the New Testament, the Gospels have received comparably little attention.[1] Instead, covenantal discussions have tended to focus on either Pauline texts or the book of Hebrews. This neglect is no doubt due (in part, at least) to the fact that the word "covenant" (διαθήκη) is used only sparsely in the canonical Gospels—four times, to be exact (Matt. 26:28; Mark 14:24; Luke 1:72; 22:20). And three of these instances occur in the Synoptic accounts of the Last Supper, while John never uses the word at all. As I argue below, however, the word "covenant" may be absent, but the *concept* is not.[2] Indeed, it is woven throughout the very fabric of the Gospel narratives.

The Genre of the Gospels: Gospels as Covenant Documents

As we explore the theme of covenant in the Gospels, it is appropriate that we begin by considering the kinds of documents that are before us. Of course, the last few generations of scholarship have produced a considerable amount of material pertaining to

---

1. There are some exceptions; e.g., Alistair I. Wilson, "Luke and the New Covenant: Zechariah's Prophecy as a Test Case," in *The God of Covenant: Biblical, Theological, and Contemporary Perspectives*, ed. Jamie A. Grant and Alistair I. Wilson (Leicester, UK: Apollos, 2005), 156–77; Theophilus John Herter, *The Abrahamic Covenant in the Gospels* (Houston: Classical Anglican, 1992); Cleon L. Rogers, "The Davidic Covenant in the Gospels," *BibSac* 150 (1993): 458–78; Sherri Brown, *Gift upon Gift: Covenant through Word in the Gospel of John*, PrTMS 144 (Eugene, OR: Pickwick, 2010).

2. Some scholars have made the same mistake in regard to Second Temple Judaism, assuming that the lack of the term "covenant" during this time must mean there was little interest in the subject. But this has been challenged by E. P. Sanders, *Paul and Palestinian Judaism: A Comparison of Patterns of Religion* (Philadelphia: Fortress, 1977), 420–21. For more on this subject, see Stanley E. Porter and Jacqueline C. R. de Roo, eds., *The Concept of the Covenant in the Second Temple Period*, JSJSup 71 (Leiden: Brill, 2003).

the genre of these writings.[3] Suggestions have ranged all over the map, including the Gospels as oral folk literature,[4] as a summary of the early Christian *kerygma*,[5] as accounts of a "divine man" (or aretalogy),[6] and beyond. But most popular today is the view that our Gospels are a form of Greco-Roman biography, or "lives" (Gk. *bioi*), similar to the accounts of Plutarch, Suetonius, or Xenophon.[7] To be sure, there is much to commend this view. On the surface, our Gospels share a certain family resemblance with the *bioi* genre, including a similar length; a focus on a single protagonist; extra attention to the protagonist's final days; and various types of content, such as sayings, stories, and great deeds.

If we look at the Gospels merely as *bioi*, however, we miss one of their most salient features, namely, the manner in which their story connects to, and even continues, the story of the Hebrew Scriptures. If we are searching for a literary model readily available for our Gospel authors—three of whom were Jews—then we might ask why we would look to the broader Greco-Roman context when "much closer to hand is the Hebrew Bible."[8] Or as Loveday Alexander has argued,

> It is to the biblical tradition, surely, that we should look for the origins of the "religious intensity" of the gospel narratives and their rich ideological intertextuality with the biblical themes of covenant, kingdom, prophecy, and promise—all features hard to parallel in Greek biography.[9]

So while our Gospels may be similar to Greco-Roman biography in terms of *structure*, they are indebted to the Old Testament in terms of their *narrative*. And when we consider the narrative features of the four Gospels, it quickly becomes clear that they are stories of God's eschatological, redemptive, covenant-fulfilling activity through the person of Jesus of Nazareth. Or, put differently, they are not merely history—which would be implied by the *bioi* genre—but are, in fact, *redemptive history*.[10] As Jonathan Pennington has observed, "This is good news, not just a biography!"[11]

---

3. For an up-to-date survey of the various options, see Michael F. Bird, *The Gospel of the Lord: How the Early Church Wrote the Story of Jesus* (Grand Rapids, MI: Eerdmans, 2014), 221–98; Loveday Alexander, "What Is a Gospel?," in *The Cambridge Companion to the Gospels*, ed. Stephen C. Barton (Cambridge: Cambridge University Press, 2006), 13–33.

4. Martin Dibelius, *From Tradition to Gospel* (Cambridge: J. Clarke, 1971).

5. C. H. Dodd, *The Apostolic Preaching and Its Developments* (New York: Harper, 1949).

6. H. Koester, "One Jesus and Four Primitive Gospels," *HTR* 61, no. 2 (1968): 203–47.

7. Richard A. Burridge, *What Are the Gospels? A Comparison with Graeco-Roman Biography*, 2nd ed. (Grand Rapids, MI: Eerdmans, 2004).

8. Jonathan T. Pennington, *Reading the Gospels Wisely: A Narrative and Theological Introduction* (Grand Rapids, MI: Baker Academic, 2012), 26.

9. Alexander, "What Is a Gospel?," 27–28.

10. G. K. Beale defines "redemptive history" as "God's salvific dealings with his people throughout the entire history, from the fall of Adam until the final consummation." *A New Testament Biblical Theology: The Unfolding of the Old Testament in the New* (Grand Rapids, MI: Baker Academic, 2011), 174. Thus, redemptive history, in contrast to mere (or secular) history, explores how God has acted in the various stages of history to save his people through Christ. In short, it looks at the (unfolding) historical timeline of our redemption.

11. Pennington, *Reading the Gospels Wisely*, 31.

Indeed, the openings of the Gospels exhibit this redemptive-historical focus. Mark plainly tells us, in his very first line, that he is writing "the *gospel* [εὐαγγελίου] of Jesus Christ, the Son of God" (Mark 1:1).[12] And thus, as Robert Stein has observed, "the entire work is to be understood as the good news about Jesus Christ."[13] Likewise, Luke's opening line reminds us that he is not merely writing a historical narrative but rather is writing about "the things that *have been accomplished* [πεπληροφορημένων] among us" (Luke 1:1).[14] In other words, "they are not mere events, but form part of a series planned and carried into effect by God."[15] Matthew begins his Gospel by describing it as a Βίβλος γενέσεως—a vivid echo of the title of the book of Genesis—which has prompted scholars to suggest that Matthew should be understood as the "Book of the New Genesis wrought by Jesus Christ."[16] Similarly, John's opening phrase, "in the beginning," is a clear nod to the opening line of Genesis but now with the λόγος standing in the place of *Elohim*.[17] Thus, John presents his Gospel as a "new Genesis" with Jesus as the Creator and the author of life.

This intertextual indebtedness to the Old Testament narrative raises questions about how to best characterize what the Gospels are as documents. Meredith Kline, recognizing the unequivocal Old Testament backdrop, has argued that the Gospels are best understood as *covenant documents*.[18] In particular, Kline suggests that the book of Exodus is the closest counterpart to the Gospels: "The Book of Exodus appears to have the same thematic focus and to exhibit comprehensively the same literary structure as the gospels. . . . The book of Exodus is an Old Testament gospel—the Gospel of Moses."[19] Both documents have a clear covenantal purpose: they focus on the life of the covenant mediator, the deliverance of God's covenant people, the inauguration of the covenant, and a new law delivered by the covenant mediator.

These structural connections between the Gospels and Exodus are confirmed in two ways. First, extensive Moses-Exodus typology is found throughout all four Gospels. Jesus is portrayed as the new Moses (Matt. 5:1; John 5:46; 7:40), leading a new exodus (Matt. 2:15; 4:1–17; Mark 1:1–13; Luke 3:4–6), giving a new law (Matt. 5–7), supplying new bread from heaven (John 6:32–34), and offering a new/final Passover sacrifice (Matt. 26:26; Mark 14:22; Luke 22:19).[20] We revisit this subject in more depth below. Second, much of the teaching of Jesus fits into standard treaty language

---

12. Gerd Theissen argues that Mark's opening line is similar in structure to that of Old Testament prophetic books (e.g., Hos. 1:1–2). *The New Testament: A Literary History* (Minneapolis: Fortress, 2012), 54.

13. Robert H. Stein, *Mark*, BECNT (Grand Rapids, MI: Baker Academic, 2008), 39.

14. See the discussion in Darrell L. Bock, *Luke*, vol. 1, *1:9–9:50*, BECNT (Grand Rapids, MI: Baker, 1994), 56–57.

15. I. Howard Marshall, *Luke: Historian and Theologian* (Grand Rapids, MI: Zondervan, 1970), 41.

16. W. D. Davies and Dale C. Allison Jr., *The Gospel according to Saint Matthew*, vol. 1, *Matthew 1–7*, ICC (Edinburgh: T&T Clark, 1997), 153.

17. D. A. Carson, *The Gospel according to John*, PNTC (Grand Rapids, MI: Eerdmans, 1991), 113–14.

18. Meredith G. Kline, "The Old Testament Origins of the Gospel Genre," *WTJ* 38 (1975): 1–27. See also Jacob J. Enz, "The Book of Exodus as a Literary Type for the Gospel of John," *JBL* 76, no. 3 (1957): 208–15.

19. Kline, "Gospel Genre," 3–4.

20. Kline, "Gospel Genre," 9–20.

of covenantal texts: Jesus's self-declarations as the God of the covenant (John 6:35; 8:12, 51), condemnation of Israel's covenant breaking (Matt. 21:40–41; Mark 12:9), teachings on how to live within the covenant community (Matt. 5–7), blessings and curses of the covenant (Matt. 23; Luke 6:20–26), and even covenant discipline (Matt. 16:18–19; 18:15–20).

We might also observe that the church fathers seemed to recognize the covenantal nature of the earliest Christian writings—of which the Gospels were a part—by the fact that they often used the term διαθήκη to refer to these writings.[21] Indeed, the collection of Christian Scripture was often called the "new testament" or "new covenant."[22] By the time of Clement of Alexandria, this covenantal language had become standard nomenclature for the church's canon.[23] Everett Ferguson observes that for Clement, "'Covenant' meant or referred to written documents."[24] One particularly illuminating instance is that of the anonymous anti-Montanist writer who referred to the church's canonical books as "the word of the new covenant of the Gospel."[25] While the author may have been referring to the entire corpus, the use of the word "Gospel" suggests the possibility that he may have had our canonical Gospels in mind.

If indeed our Gospels should be construed as covenant documents, two important implications follow. First, the covenantal nature of these books means they are not so much human testimony about God as they are God's testimony to humans about the terms of his covenant through Jesus. God is the maker of divine covenants and therefore rightly understood to be the author of covenant documents (e.g., Ex. 24:12; 31:18; 32:16). Thus, the Gospels are authoritative not by virtue of some later ecclesiastical court, nor by virtue of the fact that the human authors are reliable eyewitnesses (though they are), but because the Gospels are, from their very inception, a legal and divine witness for covenant keepers and against covenant breakers.[26]

Second, the covenantal nature of these books allows us to see, perhaps more clearly than before, the remarkable *unity* between the old covenant and the new covenant, and the place of the Gospels in that unified structure.[27] Although the Bible is made up of diverse types of writings—law, history, wisdom books, prophecy, letters, and so forth—Kline argues that each of these different writings serves a singular covenantal

21. W. C. van Unnik, "Η καινὴ διαθήκη—A Problem in the Early History of the Canon," *StPatr* 4 (1961): 212–27; W. Kinzig, "Καινὴ διαθήκη: The Title of the New Testament in the Second and Third Centuries," *JTS* 45, no. 2 (1994): 519–44; Everett Ferguson, "The Covenant Idea in the Second Century," in *Texts and Testaments: Critical Essays on the Bible and the Early Church Fathers*, ed. W. Eugene March (San Antonio, TX: Trinity University Press, 1980), 135–62; J. Ligon Duncan, "The Covenant Idea in Melito of Sardis: An Introduction and Survey," *Presb* 28 (2002): 12–33.

22. Tertullian preferred the Latin *instrumentum* or *testamentum*: *Pud.* 1; 10; *Marc.* 4.2; *Prax.* 15.

23. Clement of Alexandria, *Strom.* 1.44.3; 3.71.3; 5.85.1.

24. Ferguson, "Covenant Idea," 151.

25. Eusebius, *Hist. eccl.* 5.16.3.

26. Kline, "Gospel Genre," 22. For more on the eyewitness nature of the Gospels, see Richard Bauckham, *Jesus and the Eyewitnesses: The Gospels as Eyewitness Testimony* (Grand Rapids, MI: Eerdmans, 2006).

27. Michael Horton, *God of Promise: Introducing Covenant Theology* (Grand Rapids, MI: Baker, 2006), 15–21.

purpose.[28] History (which includes the Gospels) recounts God's great covenantal acts, law provides God's covenantal stipulations (usually with blessings and curses), wisdom literature provides guidance on how to live as a member of the covenant, and prophecy and letters function as covenant "lawsuits" to those who break the terms of God's covenant. For this reason, Michael Horton has observed that the covenant idea is the "architectonic structure, a matrix of beams and pillars that hold together the structure of biblical faith and practice."[29]

The Story of the Gospels: Gospels as the Fulfillment of God's Covenantal Promises

Leaving aside the genre of the Gospels, we now turn our attention to the story of the Gospels. As shown below, the story of Jesus of Nazareth is presented by the Gospel authors not merely as history but as the fulfillment of God's covenantal promises in the Old Testament. The new covenant inaugurated by Jesus is the realization and completion of the prior covenantal administrations—both the covenant of works and the covenant of grace.[30]

The Covenant of Works

Reformed theologians have long described the original administration with Adam in the garden as a covenant—in particular a *covenant of works*.[31] Although the early chapters of Genesis do not employ the word "covenant," all the features are there of a formal arrangement between God and Adam as the federal head of the human race.[32] This is echoed in places like Hosea 6:7, "But like Adam, they transgressed the covenant,"[33] as well as in the headship of Adam expressed in Romans 5:18, "As one trespass led to condemnation for all men . . ."[34] The Westminster Confession affirms the covenant of works and, in particular, the requirement of perfect obedience from Adam: "The first covenant made with man was a covenant of works, wherein life was

28. Meredith G. Kline, *The Structure of Biblical Authority*, 2nd ed. (Eugene, OR: Wipf and Stock, 1997), 45–75.

29. Horton, *God of Promise*, 13.

30. If space allowed, we could also explore the "covenant of redemption" (*pactum salutis*) theme in the Gospels. For a helpful overview of that important doctrine, see David VanDrunen and R. Scott Clark, "The Covenant before the Covenants," in *Covenant, Justification, and Pastoral Ministry*, ed. R. Scott Clark (Phillipsburg, NJ: P&R, 2007), 167–96.

31. Other names have been used; e.g., "covenant of life" and "covenant of creation." For discussion, see Horton, *God of Promise*, 83–104.

32. Josh Bolt, "Why the Covenant of Works Is a Necessary Doctrine: Revisiting the Objections to a Venerable Reformed Doctrine," in *Faith Alone: Answering the Challenges to the Doctrine of Justification*, ed. Gary L. W. Johnson and Guy P. Waters (Wheaton, IL: Crossway, 2006), 171–90; Oswald T. Allis, "The Covenant of Works," in *Basic Christian Doctrines*, ed. Carl F. Henry (New York: Holt, Rinehart and Winston, 1962), 96–102; Meredith Kline, "Of Works and Grace," *Presb* 1 (1983): 88–89.

33. See Byron G. Curtis, "Hosea 6:7 and Covenant-Breaking like/at Adam," in *The Law Is Not of Faith: Essays on Works and Grace in the Mosaic Covenant*, ed. Bryan D. Estelle, J. V. Fesko, and David VanDrunen (Phillipsburg, NJ: P&R, 2009), 170–209.

34. See John Murray, *The Imputation of Adam's Sin* (Grand Rapids, MI: Eerdmans, 1959).

promised to Adam, and in him his posterity, upon condition of perfect and personal obedience" (7.2).

Upon the fall of Adam, God enacted the *covenant of grace*, by which God would save humanity and forgive their sins through the sacrifice of the coming Savior, Jesus Christ, the offspring of the woman who would crush the head of the serpent (Gen. 3:15). Even so, the requirements of the covenant of works were still in effect—God still demanded perfect obedience. And this requirement was met by the active obedience of Christ. His perfect law keeping achieved a righteousness that is imputed to us by faith.[35]

It is in the Gospel accounts that we see this representative and meritorious obedience of Christ highlighted most plainly. Indeed, it is this aspect of Jesus's salvific work that explains why the Gospels include more than simply his birth and his death.[36] For generations, scholars have struggled to explain the rationale for this material in the "middle" of the Gospel accounts.[37] Is it offered merely to show Jesus as a moral example? Is it just a "warm-up" for the passion narratives? We have an explanation for why Jesus died, but do we have an explanation for why he *lived*? The Gospels answer these questions (at least in part) by presenting Jesus as the second Adam who lived as the obedient son, thus fulfilling the obligations of the covenant of works on behalf of his people.[38]

Numerous passages in the Gospels highlight Jesus's active obedience, but we draw our attention to a select few here. Most noteworthy, of course, is his temptation in the wilderness, where Jesus, like the first Adam, is tempted directly by Satan (Matt. 4:1–11; Mark 1:12–13; Luke 4:1–13).[39] While the first Adam was in paradise and yet failed, the second Adam is in a desert and succeeds. Luke's Gospel makes the link to Adam even more explicit by the fact that his temptation account is directly preceded with the acknowledgment that Jesus ultimately descends from "Adam, the son of God" (Luke 3:38). Although Matthew's genealogy does not go back to Adam, it does begin with the curious phrase Βίβλος γενέσεως ("book of generation," Matt. 1:1, my trans.), taking the reader back to the book of Genesis and particularly Genesis 5:1: "This is the book of the generations of Adam [man]."[40] Thus, "Jesus is being painted with the genealogical brush of Adam."[41] Matthew completes this echo of Genesis by presenting the second

35. John Calvin, *Institutes of the Christian Religion*, ed. John T. McNeill, trans. Ford Lewis Battles, LCC 20–21 (Philadelphia: Westminster, 1960), 2.12.3.

36. For full discussion of this theme, see Brandon D. Crowe, *The Last Adam: A Theology of the Obedient Life of Jesus in the Gospels* (Grand Rapids, MI: Baker Academic, 2017).

37. E.g., N. T. Wright, *How God Became King: The Forgotten Story of the Gospels* (New York: HarperOne, 2012).

38. Crowe, *Last Adam*, 16–17. This is not to deny, of course, that there are additional reasons for including this Gospel material, including the fact that Jesus is a moral example for us to follow (e.g., John 13:15).

39. Beale, *Biblical Theology*, 381–437; Joel Marcus, *Mark 1–8: A New Translation with Introduction and Commentary*, AB 27 (New York: Doubleday, 1999), 170–71. See the further discussion in Richard Bauckham, "Jesus and the Wild Animals (Mark 1:13): A Christological Image for an Ecological Age," in *Jesus of Nazareth: Lord and Christ; Essays on the Historical Jesus and New Testament Christology*, ed. Joel B. Green and Max Turner (Grand Rapids, MI: Eerdmans, 1994), 3–21.

40. See Davies and Allison, *Matthew*, 1:151.

41. Beale, *Biblical Theology*, 389.

Adam's birth as the product of the work of the Spirit (Matt. 1:20), which mirrors the first Adam's "birth" (see Gen. 2:7).

In addition, when the Gospels present Jesus as the Son of God, they often highlight the obedient and faithful nature of his sonship. In particular, it is at his baptism by John that the obedience of the Son is expressed in the heavenly voice: "This is my beloved Son, with whom I am well pleased" (Matt. 3:17; cf. Mark 1:1; Luke 3:22). And in this act of baptism, Jesus is (again) acting as a representative of his people—his baptism is "vicarious," as he takes on the role of the sinner in place of disobedient Israel.[42] Thus, Jesus's baptism is done "to fulfill all righteousness" (Matt. 3:15).[43] Similarly, the voice of the centurion also affirms the obedient sonship of Jesus when, after beholding the manner in which Jesus died, he declares, "Truly this man was the Son of God!" (Mark 15:39). And again, this affirmation of Jesus's obedience is heard at his transfiguration: "This is my beloved Son, with whom I am well pleased; listen to him" (Matt. 17:5). Even the bright, shining clothing of Jesus is, in some sense, a picture of the glory that could have belonged to the first Adam if he had only obeyed.[44]

The righteous status of Jesus is also affirmed by other characters in the Gospels. Demons are quick to note that Jesus is the "Holy One of God" (Mark 1:24; Luke 4:34), a status that stands in obvious contrast to the "unclean" nature of these spirits. Peter, reflecting the collective conviction of the disciples, also affirms that Jesus is the "Holy One of God" (John 6:69). Even Jesus's enemies affirm his righteous nature. Pilate's wife, for example, calls Jesus a "righteous man" (Matt. 27:19), and Pilate himself realizes that Jesus is pure and innocent (Luke 23:22). And the centurion in Luke's account reaches the same conclusion: "Certainly this man was innocent!" (Luke 23:47).[45] Whereas the first Adam was guilty and rightly punished, the second Adam is innocent and wrongly convicted.

We should also consider the implications of the title "Son of Man"—used exclusively by Jesus throughout the four Gospels as a way to refer to himself.[46] Without exploring all the complexities of the phrase here, there are good reasons to think that it alludes to the mysterious figure of Daniel 7:13–14.[47] And the human figure in that passage not only is given authority to rule but has a rule that is representative of the corporate people of God. As such, the Daniel 7 figure "builds upon the royal imagery for humanity originally given to Adam; the son of man in Daniel is the fulfiller of the Adamic task of

---

42. Geerhardus Vos, *Biblical Theology: Old and New Testaments* (1948; repr., Edinburgh: Banner of Truth, 1975), 318–20.
43. See Beale, *Biblical Theology*, 416.
44. Crowe, *Last Adam*, 49–50.
45. It should be noted that the English word "innocent" (ESV) is a translation of the Greek δίκαιος, which means "righteous."
46. For a helpful overview of the debate regarding "Son of Man," see Larry W. Hurtado and Paul L. Owen, eds., *Who Is This Son of Man? The Latest Scholarship on a Puzzling Expression of the Historical Jesus*, LNTS 390 (London: T&T Clark, 2012).
47. See especially how the phrase is used by Jesus at his trial: Matt. 26:64 // Mark 14:62 // Luke 22:69.

ruling in God's image."[48] Thus, Jesus's invocation of the "Son of Man" language positions himself as the representative second Adam who exhibits the long-awaited kingly rule on behalf of his people.[49]

In sum, we see in the canonical Gospels a presentation of Jesus as the second Adam, the obedient son who succeeds where the first Adam failed. Thus, we can say that the Gospels present Jesus as the one who meets the righteous requirements of the covenant of works on behalf of those he represents. As Jesus declared about himself, "I have kept my Father's commandments" (John 15:10).

The Covenant of Grace

While Jesus's obedience as the second Adam is technically part of the covenant of grace—because Jesus graciously obeys on our behalf—we have treated it under the "covenant of works" above in light of how Jesus's obedience echoes the Adamic arrangement in the garden. We now turn our attention to the covenant of grace proper and its various administrations, particularly the way the Gospels present Jesus as fulfilling the Abrahamic, Mosaic, and Davidic covenants. Jesus fulfills these prior covenants by inaugurating a "new covenant," the final stage of the covenant of grace. Needless to say, our treatment here can be only cursory, owing to the vast amount of material in the Gospels.

Abrahamic Covenant

When it comes to the Abrahamic covenant, the Gospels regularly affirm (1) that the ministry of Jesus fulfills the promises given to Abraham by which God will bless the nations through his offspring (Gen. 12:2; 15:5–6)—that is, Jesus is the ultimate "seed" of Abraham; and (2) one must trust in Jesus to be a "son of Abraham"—that is, true Abrahamic sonship is not physical but spiritual. Thus, the Gentile "nations" can now be included in the people of God.

Matthew traces the genealogy of Jesus back to Abraham (Matt. 1:1–2), portraying Jesus as the ultimate "seed" of Abraham (cf. Gal. 3:15–18), by which salvation will come to the nations—thereby indicating that salvation is not by ethnic descent but by being connected to Jesus.[50] This reality is confirmed by John the Baptist, who makes it clear that Jesus is ushering in a new era, one in which the children of Abraham are no longer the result of physical lineage: "Do not presume to say to yourselves, 'We have Abraham as our father,' for I tell you, God is able from these stones to raise up children for Abraham" (Matt. 3:9).[51] This same message is repeated at the end of Matthew as Jesus offers the Great Commission with a decidedly Abrahamic echo: "Go therefore and make

---

48. Crowe, *Last Adam*, 39.

49. Beale, *Biblical Theology*, 393–400.

50. Herter, *Abrahamic Covenant*, 24–35.

51. Of course, it should be acknowledged that being a true child of Abraham had *always* required belief in the coming Savior. Nevertheless, John the Baptist is clearly battling against those who misunderstand this reality and insist that their physical lineage is sufficient.

disciples of *all nations* [πάντα τὰ ἔθνη]" (Matt. 28:19; cf. Gen. 18:18 LXX), indicating again that through faith in Christ, all people can become part of Abraham's children.

Luke is even more direct in drawing connections to Abraham.[52] Mary's song acknowledges that the coming of Jesus is God remembering his promise "to Abraham and to his offspring forever" (Luke 1:55).[53] Likewise, Zechariah acknowledges that the coming of Jesus is

> to show the mercy promised to our fathers
>   and to remember his holy covenant,
> the oath that he swore to our father Abraham. (Luke 1:72–73)

For Luke, the coming ministry of Jesus is God fulfilling his promises to Abraham in Genesis 12; 15; and 17.[54] Jesus also affirms that true sons of Abraham are not according to bloodline when he says of Zacchaeus, "Today salvation has come to this house, since he also is a son of Abraham" (Luke 19:9). It is Zacchaeus's repentance and faith, not his ethnicity, that identifies him as a "son of Abraham."[55] Since covenantal membership is not based on bloodline, Luke plainly indicates that the gospel message is for all nations. He not only mentions that God's people will experience "the times of the Gentiles" (Luke 21:24), but he even ends his Gospel with another Abrahamic echo: "Forgiveness of sins should be proclaimed . . . to *all nations*" (Luke 24:47).

In John's Gospel Jesus continues to affirm that ethnic descent is not enough to qualify as true sons of Abraham when he describes children of God as those "born, not of blood nor of the will of the flesh nor of the will of man, but of God" (John 1:13). Later, Jesus affirms this same theme when he says that unbelieving Jews are decidedly not Abraham's children: "If you were Abraham's children, you would be doing the works Abraham did" (John 8:39).[56] The promises given to Abraham were realized not through natural descent but ultimately through Christ's own coming: "Abraham rejoiced that he would see my day. He saw it and was glad" (John 8:56).

Mosaic Covenant

The Mosaic covenant, also known as the "old" covenant, refers to that legal arrangement that God made with the nation of Israel on Mount Sinai upon her deliverance from Egypt.[57] Central to the Mosaic covenant was, of course, the law of God—not only the moral law in the Ten Commandments but also the ceremonial law, which

---

52. Darrell L. Bock, *A Theology of Luke and Acts: God's Promised Program, Realized for All Nations*, BTNT (Grand Rapids, MI: Zondervan, 2012), 292–97.

53. Herter, *Abrahamic Covenant*, 45–48.

54. Wilson, "Luke and the New Covenant," 170–71.

55. Joel B. Green affirms that the Abrahamic sonship here is "not a reference to his bloodline." *The Gospel of Luke*, NICNT (Grand Rapids, MI: Eerdmans, 1997), 672.

56. See Craig S. Keener, *The Gospel of John: A Commentary* (Peabody, MA: Hendrickson, 2003), 756.

57. The degree to which the Mosaic economy has "works" elements is debated among Reformed theologians. For more on that issue, see essays in Estelle, Fesko, and VanDrunen, *The Law Is Not of Faith*.

would govern the cultic life of Israel and the manner in which they would worship Yahweh. In order to be ritually "clean," Israelites were required (among other things) to engage in various washings, abstain from certain foods, and offer the appropriate animal sacrifices. The Gospels present the ministry of Jesus as completing or fulfilling various aspects of the Mosaic covenant, but we will focus our attention here on just three: temple, sacrifice, and law.

Temple. We begin with that feature of the Mosaic economy that was perhaps most central to the life of Israel: the temple.[58] Jesus tells us plainly, "Something greater than the temple is here" (Matt. 12:6), implying that his ministry fulfilled and surpassed all that the temple represented. Jesus is the presence of God with his people—the true "Immanuel," God with us (Matt. 1:23). Thus, in the midst of cleansing the earthly temple, Jesus can refer to his own body as the temple of God, "Destroy this temple, and in three days I will raise it up" (John 2:19; cf. Matt. 26:61).[59] Herman Ridderbos comments on this passage, "[Jesus] is also the temple that will replace the existing temple and in whom the indwelling of God among people will be truly and fully realized."[60] This same image is picked up earlier in John's prologue when he declares that the Word became flesh and "dwelt" (ἐσκήνωσεν) among us (John 1:14).[61] The term ἐσκήνωσεν has connotations of pitching one's tent, an indicator that Jesus has come to "tabernacle" with his people so that they "have seen his glory" (John 1:14)—an allusion to the glory cloud around the tent of meeting (Ex. 40:34–35).[62]

And if Jesus is the new temple, then we can see why the physical location of worship will no longer matter under the new covenant: "The hour is coming when neither on this mountain nor in Jerusalem will you worship the Father. . . . True worshipers will worship the Father in spirit and truth" (John 4:21, 23). Indeed, the now obsolete status of the physical temple is confirmed by the great ripping of the temple veil upon the death of Jesus (Matt. 27:51; Mark 15:38; Luke 23:45) and by Jesus's prediction of its future destruction (Matt. 24:1–2; Mark 13:1–2; Luke 21:5–6). In the new covenant, Jesus has paved the way into God's presence—an earthly temple is no longer needed.

Sacrifice. Closely related to Jesus fulfilling the temple is Jesus fulfilling the Mosaic sacrificial system. Just as animals were sacrificed under the Mosaic economy as an atonement for sin, so Jesus is presented as the "Lamb of God, who takes away the sin of the world"

---

58. Of course, in the early period of Israel's history, God's presence centered on the mobile sanctuary called the tabernacle. But inasmuch as the tabernacle anticipated the temple, we will focus on the latter here.

59. Andreas J. Köstenberger, *A Theology of John's Gospel and Letters*, BTNT (Grand Rapids, MI: Zondervan, 2009), 427–29.

60. Herman Ridderbos, *The Gospel of John: A Theological Commentary*, trans. John Vriend (Grand Rapids, MI: Eerdmans, 1997), 120.

61. For more on how John's prologue presents Jesus as fulfilling (and surpassing) the Mosaic covenant, see Alexander Tsutserov, *Glory, Grace, and Truth: Ratification of the Sinaitic Covenant according to the Gospel of John* (Eugene, OR: Pickwick, 2009).

62. Raymond F. Collins, *These Things Have Been Written: Studies on the Fourth Gospel*, LTPM 2 (Grand Rapids, MI: Eerdmans, 1990), 198–209; Keener, *John*, 410.

(John 1:29).[63] Indeed, Jesus affirms the same purpose for his death: "The Son of Man came not to be served but to serve, and to give his life as a ransom for many" (Mark 10:45; cf. Matt. 20:28). Even Jesus's enemies, perhaps inadvertently, acknowledge his substitutionary sacrifice: "Better for you that one man should die for the people" (John 11:50). The crucifixion accounts themselves are shaped in such a way that Jesus takes on the role of the innocent Passover Lamb offered as a sacrifice for sins. John describes the crucifixion by directly quoting from Exodus 12:46, "Not one of his bones will be broken" (John 19:36), a reference to how the Passover lamb must be pure and spotless.[64] Jesus drinks from a sponge on a "hyssop branch" (John 19:29), an item that was used to sprinkle the blood on the doorposts during the original Passover (Ex. 12:22).[65] Likewise, the crucifixion accounts present Jesus as largely silent (Matt. 27:11–14; Mark 15:1–5), not only evidence of his innocence but a vivid echo of Isaiah's suffering servant:

> Like a lamb that is led to the slaughter,
>   and like a sheep that before its shearers is silent,
>   so he opened not his mouth. (Isa. 53:7)[66]

That Jesus's death fulfills the Mosaic covenant's cultic requirements is most aptly seen in the accounts of the Last Supper.[67] Jesus's words of institution indicate that his death functions as the Passover Lamb given in the place of sinners: his body is "given *for you*" (Luke 22:19), and his blood will be shed "for the forgiveness of sins" (Matt. 26:28).[68] As a result, the sacrificial death of Jesus marks the inauguration of a "new covenant in [his] blood" (Luke 22:20), which supersedes the covenant given to Moses. Indeed, Jesus's words in Matthew 26:28—"my blood of the covenant" (τὸ αἷμά μου τῆς διαθήκης)— are nearly identical with the words used by Moses in Exodus 24:8, where an atoning sacrifice was used to inaugurate the Mosaic covenant.[69] Moreover, Jesus's "forgiveness of sins" language (Matt. 26:28) echoes the promise of Jeremiah 31:31–34 (cf. Isa. 53:12), where God says he will make a new covenant, in which he "will forgive their iniquity" and "will remember their sins no more."[70] Thus, the theme of the forgiveness of sins throughout the Gospels can be seen as a reference to the promise of the new covenant.[71]

---

63. Keener, *John*, 452–54; Köstenberger, *Theology of John's Gospel*, 414–15.

64. Leon Morris, *The Gospel according to John* (Grand Rapids, MI: Eerdmans, 1971), 727.

65. Keener, *John*, 1147.

66. For more on this theme, see Michael J. Wilkins, "Isaiah 53 and the Message of Salvation in the Four Gospels," in *The Gospel according to Isaiah 53: Encountering the Suffering Servant in Jewish and Christian Theology*, ed. Darrell L. Bock and Mitch Glaser (Grand Rapids, MI: Kregel Academic, 2012), 109–32.

67. For more details on these accounts, see I. Howard Marshall, *Last Supper and Lord's Supper* (Grand Rapids, MI: Eerdmans, 1980); Joachim Jeremias, *The Eucharistic Words of Jesus*, trans. Arnold Ehrhardt (Oxford: Blackwell, 1955). In terms of the historicity of the event, see I. Howard Marshall, "The Last Supper," in *Key Events in the Life of the Historical Jesus: A Collaborative Exploration of Context and Coherence*, ed. Darrell L. Bock and Robert L. Webb, WUNT 247 (Tübingen: Mohr Siebeck, 2009), 481–588.

68. See John Kimbell, "Jesus' Death in Luke–Acts: The New Covenant Sacrifice," *SBJT* 16, no. 3 (2012): 28–48.

69. Marshall, *Last Supper*, 43.

70. Jeremias, *Eucharistic Words*, 113.

71. Wilson, "Luke and the New Covenant," 172–75.

Matthew refers to this new covenant promise in his opening chapter: "He will save his people from their sins" (Matt. 1:21)—a likely allusion to the promises of forgiveness made in Ezekiel 36–37.[72] Similarly, Luke tells us that in Christ God "remember[ed] his holy covenant" with Abraham (Luke 1:72), which resulted in "the forgiveness of [the] sins" of the people (Luke 1:77). Even more, Luke ends his Gospel with Jesus declaring that "the forgiveness of sins should be proclaimed in his name to all nations" (Luke 24:47). This is yet another echo of Jeremiah 31:34, where God says that in the new covenant, "I will remember their sin no more."

Law. Just as Moses was given the law on the mountaintop (Ex. 19:20), so Jesus "went up on the mountain" (Matt. 5:1) and delivered the law in the Sermon on the Mount (Matt. 5–7).[73] Scholars have observed that Matthew's Gospel can be divided into five sections, which may be a structural echo of the five books of the Pentateuch,[74] thus presenting Jesus as the new Moses.[75] Indeed, Matthew presents Jesus as a new Moses from the very start—both are in danger as infants (Ex. 1:22; Matt. 2:16–18), are rescued miraculously (Ex. 2:1–10; Matt. 2:13–14), and flee out of Egypt (Ex. 13–14; Matt. 2:14–15).[76] And the "law" Jesus presents in the Sermon on the Mount is the fulfillment of the law of Moses: "Do not think I have come to abolish the Law or the Prophets; I have not come to abolish them but to fulfill them" (Matt. 5:17; cf. Luke 24:44).[77] Other Gospels share the same theme. In John, Jesus can say, "For if you believed Moses, you would believe me; for he wrote about me" (John 5:46). In fact, in John's Gospel Jesus even delivers "bread from heaven" like Moses (John 6:32)[78] and also performs "signs" like Moses (e.g., John 2:11, 23; 3:2; 4:54).[79] Luke observes at the transfiguration that Jesus is talking to Moses about his upcoming "exodus" (ἔξοδον, Luke 9:31).[80] And the heavenly voice in Luke even says, "Listen to him" (Luke 9:35), an unmistakable echo of the Old Testament prophecy about a new prophet like Moses: "The LORD your God will raise up for

72. Charles L. Quarles, *A Theology of Matthew: Jesus Revealed as Deliverer, King, and Incarnate Creator*, EBT (Phillipsburg, NJ: P&R, 2013), 56.

73. Quarles, *Theology of Matthew*, 37–39.

74. B. W. Bacon, "The Five Books of Matthew against the Jews," *Exp* 15 (1918): 56–66; R. T. France, *Matthew: Evangelist and Teacher* (Grand Rapids, MI: Zondervan, 1989), 142–45.

75. For works on Jesus as a new Moses, see Dale C. Allison Jr., *The New Moses: A Matthean Typology* (Edinburgh: T&T Clark, 1993); John Lierman, *The New Testament Moses: Christian Perceptions of Moses and Israel in the Setting of Jewish Religion*, WUNT 173 (Tubingen: Mohr Siebeck, 2004); Vern Poythress, *The Shadow of Christ in the Law of Moses* (Phillipsburg, NJ: Presbyterian and Reformed, 1991).

76. Of course, there is overlap in the typological imagery of Jesus as the new Moses and Jesus as the new Israel; these two motifs should not be too sharply divided. See France, *Matthew*, 186–91.

77. In the Sermon on the Mount, Jesus is not contrasting himself with the Mosaic law, but with Pharisaical distortions of the Mosaic law. For more on this issue, see John Murray, *Principles of Conduct: Aspects of Biblical Ethics* (Grand Rapids, MI: Eerdmans, 1994), 149–80.

78. Carson, *Gospel according to John*, 268–69.

79. Keener, *John*, 277–79; Raymond E. Brown, *The Gospel according to John*, AB 29–29A (New York: Doubleday, 1966), 528–29; Robert H. Smith, "Exodus Typology in the Fourth Gospel," *JBL* 81, no. 4 (1962): 329–42.

80. For more on the exodus motif in the Gospels (Mark and Luke–Acts), see Rikki Watts, *Isaiah's New Exodus in Mark* (Grand Rapids, MI: Baker Academic, 2001); David W. Pao, *Acts and the Isaianic New Exodus* (Tübingen: Mohr Siebeck, 2000).

you a prophet like me from among you, from your brothers—it is to him you shall listen" (Deut. 18:15; cf. Acts 3:22).[81]

Davidic Covenant

In many ways, the Davidic covenant could be construed as a more mature and developed version of the Mosaic.[82] When God made his original covenant with Moses, Israel was wandering in the desert with no king, no land, and no permanent temple. Thus, David's reign marked significant progress in God's redemptive plan. Now, finally, God's duly appointed king—"a man after his own heart" (1 Sam. 13:14)—sat on the throne in God's city, Jerusalem, in God's promised land, Canaan. Through David, God had finally given Israel its long-awaited "rest" (2 Sam. 7:1). In a sense, the kingdom of God had arrived.

Son of David. Even though David's reign marks a key stage in the covenant of grace, God's redemptive purposes were by no means complete in it. Within the Davidic covenant itself, God promised to raise up a son from David's line and to "establish the throne of his kingdom forever" (2 Sam. 7:13; see also Isa. 11:10; Jer. 23:5; 33:15). The Gospel accounts clearly set forth Jesus as this long-awaited Davidic King, the Messiah who would deliver Israel.[83] Most definitive is Luke 1:32–33: "The Lord God will give to him the throne of his father David, and he will reign over the house of Jacob forever, and of his kingdom there will be no end" (cf. Luke 1:69). Although Matthew's genealogy is traced back to Abraham (as noted above), it is actually David who is at its center. The purpose of the genealogy is to confirm Christ's messianic pedigree as the "son of David" (Matt. 1:1), making it likely that the symbolic fourteen generations are a play on the numerical value for the name David.[84] Of all the Gospels, Matthew uses the title "Son of David" most frequently,[85] often on the lips of the crowds wondering if this Jesus is the Messiah (Matt. 9:27; 12:23; 15:22; 20:30–31; 21:9).[86]

And, of course, throughout the Gospels Jesus is given the title "King," a clear allusion to his status as David's long-awaited son (Matt. 21:5; 27:42; Mark 15:2; Luke 19:38; John 1:49; 6:15; 12:13–15). His role as the new King of Israel is perhaps best exemplified in the act of cleansing the temple. Such an act would not only foreshadow a new era in which a physical temple would no longer be needed (as mentioned above under the Mosaic covenant), it would also constitute a claim of *royal status.*[87] It was the

---

81. David M. Miller, "Seeing the Glory, Hearing the Son: The Function of the Wilderness Theophany Narratives in Luke 9:28–36," *CBQ* 72 (2010): 502.

82. For discussion, see O. Palmer Robertson, *The Christ of the Covenants* (Phillipsburg, NJ: Presbyterian and Reformed, 1980), 229–69.

83. Sherman E. Johnson, "The Davidic-Royal Motifs in the Gospels," *JBL* 87, no. 2 (1968): 136–50.

84. Davies and Allison, *Matthew*, 1:161–65.

85. Jack Dean Kingsbury, "The Title 'Son of David' in Matthew's Gospel," *JBL* 95, no. 4 (1995): 591–602.

86. The title occurs less frequently in other Gospels: Mark 10:47–48; 12:35; Luke 18:38–39; 20:41–44 (none in John).

87. N. T. Wright, *Jesus and the Victory of God*, vol. 2 of *Christian Origins and the Question of God* (Minneapolis: Fortress, 1996), 490–93.

king of Israel's place to build, protect, cleanse, and restore God's holy temple, as seen in the legacies of Solomon, Hezekiah, Josiah, Zerubbabel, and even Judas Maccabaeus. As N. T. Wright has observed, "Temple and kingship went hand in hand."[88] Thus, Jesus's act of temple cleansing was an expression of kingly authority over the temple—which is why the Jewish authorities felt so threatened by it.

Son of God. Within the Davidic covenant, the prophecies about the Messiah went even further. Not only was he to be the Son of David, he was also to be the Son of God.[89] Indeed, God makes such a promise about David's future son: "I will be to him a father, and he shall be to me a son" (2 Sam. 7:14). Again, we see Jesus fulfilling this promise as the title "Son of God" is explicitly used of him throughout the Gospels.[90] While the genealogy of Matthew clearly positions Jesus as the Son of David, it is followed immediately by the affirmation that Mary's child is "from the Holy Spirit" (Matt. 1:20)—that is, Jesus is also the divine Son of God. In addition, we have the various instances of the divine voice from heaven, at both Jesus's baptism and transfiguration, affirming that Jesus is the special Son of God (Matt. 3:17; cf. 17:5; Mark 1:1; 9:7; Luke 3:22; 9:35). Key confessions plainly affirm the same title for Jesus—the confession of Peter, "You are the Christ, the Son of the living God" (Matt. 16:16); the confession of Nathanael, "You are the Son of God! You are the King of Israel!" (John 1:49); and the confession of Martha, "I believe that you are the Christ, the Son of God" (John 11:27). Even Jesus's enemies (Matt. 26:63; Mark 14:61; Luke 22:70) and demons (Mark 3:11; 5:7; Luke 4:3, 41) refer to him as the Son of God. And most pointedly, Jesus expressly debates with the Pharisees over the status of David's Son: "If then David calls him Lord, how is he his son?" (Matt. 22:45). The implications here are obvious: the Messiah must not only be David's Son, he must also be God's Son; that is, he must be the divine "Lord."

Kingdom of God. The Davidic covenant promised not only a new king but a new *kingdom*, which would last forever (2 Sam. 7:13). David's theocratic rule was only temporary; it was merely a type of the future messianic kingdom that would be inaugurated by Jesus. The dominant theme of the "kingdom of God" in the Gospels confirms that Jesus is the promised Davidic King.[91] The inaugural sermon of Jesus has this theme as its centerpiece: "The time is fulfilled, and the kingdom of God is at hand; repent and believe" (Mark 1:15; cf. Matt. 4:17, 23). Jesus talks about kingdom ethics (Matt. 5–7;

---

88. Wright, *Jesus and the Victory of God*, 483.

89. For further discussion of how the phrase "Son of God" has implications for Jesus's divinity, see Michael F. Bird, *Jesus the Eternal Son: Answering Adoptionist Christology* (Grand Rapids, MI: Eerdmans, 2017), 64–106.

90. For more on this theme, see Martin Hengel, *The Son of God: The Origin of Christology and the History of Jewish-Hellenistic Religion* (Philadelphia: Fortress, 1976).

91. The classic work on the kingdom of God is George Eldon Ladd, *The Gospel of the Kingdom: Scriptural Studies in the Kingdom of God* (Grand Rapids, MI: Eerdmans, 1971). See also Herman Ridderbos, *The Coming of the Kingdom*, trans. H. de Jongste, ed. Raymond O. Zorn (Philadelphia: Presbyterian and Reformed, 1962); Wright, *How God Became King*; Christopher W. Morgan and Robert A. Peterson, eds., *The Kingdom of God*, TiC (Wheaton, IL: Crossway, 2012).

Mark 12:33–34), kingdom entrance (John 3:3–5), kingdom parables (Matt. 13), the mystery/secret of the kingdom (Mark 4:11; Luke 8:10), and also the future of the kingdom (Mark 14:25). In addition, the link between Jesus's kingdom and the promised Davidic kingdom is made explicit at Jesus's triumphal entry: "Blessed is the coming kingdom of our father David!" (Mark 11:10).

It should also be noted that this new messianic kingdom has a new type of kingdom membership.[92] Jesus the Son of David will constitute and regather a new Israel—a renewed people of God. And as we noted with the fulfillment of the Abrahamic covenant, membership in the new kingdom is not predicated on ethnic descent: "I tell you, many will come from east and west and recline at table with Abraham, Isaac, and Jacob in the kingdom of heaven, while the sons of the kingdom will be thrown into the outer darkness" (Matt. 8:11–12). One of the definitive marks of eschatological Israel, therefore, will be the inclusion of the Gentiles. This is captured in the parable of the vineyard (Matt. 21:33–41; Mark 12:1–12; Luke 20:9–19), in which the rebelliousness of Israel leads to its judgment and reconstitution: "The kingdom of God will be taken away from [Israel] and given to a people producing its fruit" (Matt. 21:43). As a result, we should not be surprised to find that the partakers of Christ's new kingdom include, among others, a Samaritan (Luke 10:25–37; John 4:1–42), a Roman centurion (Matt. 8:5–13), a Syrian (Luke 4:27), and a Canaanite (Matt. 15:22). The idea that Gentiles would be included in the renewed eschatological Israel was anticipated by numerous Old Testament passages: Psalm 87:1–6; Isaiah 19:18–25; 56:1–7; 66:18–21; Ezekiel 47:21–23; Zechariah 2:11.[93] Thus, we can say that this ethnically mixed church is "not merely like Israel but actually is Israel."[94]

In sum, we have seen that the Gospels are very much focused on how the ministry of Jesus is a completion/fulfillment of the prior administrations of the one covenant of grace. God's promises to bless the offspring of Abraham (Gen. 12; 15) are realized in Abraham's "seed"—namely, Jesus—and all who trust in him. Thus, the heirs of Abraham's promise are rightly recognized to be his spiritual descendants in Christ. Jesus also fulfills the Mosaic covenant, by taking on the role of a new Moses, the prophet of Deuteronomy 18, who speaks for God and delivers a new law. In addition, Jesus offers himself as the Passover Lamb, sacrificed in the place of sinners. And in regard to the Davidic covenant, Jesus is the long-awaited messianic King, the Son of David and the Son of God, who ushers in a new kingdom that will never end.

Conclusion

Since the term "covenant" occurs very infrequently in the Gospels, it has long been assumed that the Gospels can teach us very little about this important concept. As

92. Kim Huat Tan, "Community, Kingdom and Cross: Jesus' View of Covenant," in Grant and Wilson, *God of Covenant*, 122–55.
93. For discussion of these texts, see Beale, *Biblical Theology*, 657–65.
94. Beale, *Biblical Theology*, 653.

a result, theologians have often turned elsewhere (Paul, Hebrews, etc.) to build their understanding of covenant theology. As we have seen, however, the word "covenant" may be largely absent from the Gospels, but the underlying concept is not. Indeed, the covenant concept provides the theological architecture of the Gospel accounts—it is the invisible foundation of the house, holding everything in its place.

Within the Gospel accounts, the bicovenantal nature of God's dealings with mankind—a covenant of works and a covenant of grace—is clearly visible. As the second Adam, Christ takes on the role of the obedient Son, obeying where the first Adam failed. As a result, he fulfills the requirement of the covenant of works on our behalf; he achieves a perfect obedience that is imputed to us by faith. Additionally, we see echoes of the various administrations of the covenant of grace. Christ's work is the fulfillment of God's promises to Abraham to bless the nations and bring the Gentiles into the covenant community. Likewise, Christ takes on the role of a new prophet in the likeness of Moses, leading a second exodus, delivering a new law, and offering himself as the perfect Passover Lamb. Thus, the physical temple is made obsolete through Christ's fulfillment of the Mosaic economy. And as David's Son, Christ is presented as the long-awaited King—both Son of God and Son of David—who will establish a new kingdom that will never end.

Thus, we can affirm that the Gospels are, in every way, covenant documents. Not only is this evident in the very genre of the Gospels, it is evident in their content. They express, as well as any book in the New Testament, that God's work in Jesus Christ is the fulfillment and completion of all God's covenantal promises that have come before.

11

COVENANT IN PAUL

Guy Prentiss Waters

At first glance, it may seem that "covenant" is of little importance to Paul.[1] The Greek word (διαθήκη) appears only nine times in his correspondence (Rom. 9:4, 11:27; 1 Cor. 11:25; 2 Cor. 3:6, 14; Gal. 3:15, 17; 4:24; Eph. 2:12), half as many times as in the epistle to the Hebrews.[2] Of these nine instances, one is a quotation of Jesus (1 Cor. 11:25), and not fewer than four refer to the covenants that God made with Israel (Rom. 9:4; 2 Cor. 3:14; Gal. 3:15; Eph. 2:12). Over half these nine references, furthermore, are concentrated in just three chapters (2 Cor. 3; Gal. 3–4). These statistics may suggest to some that "covenant" is either peripheral or incidental to Paul's thought.

But such a conclusion would be mistaken.[3] These few verbal references are, in fact, reflective of a deeper and guiding current in Paul's thought. Paul understands not only

---

1. The role and significance of "covenant" in Paul's theology is an ongoing and unresolved debate in the secondary literature. Such scholars as E. P. Sanders, James D. G. Dunn, and J. Louis Martyn have argued, in different ways, that covenant occupies a muted or negligible place in Paul's thought. E. P. Sanders, *Paul and Palestinian Judaism: A Comparison of Patterns of Religion* (Philadelphia: Fortress, 1977), 236–37, 420–22, 550–52; Sanders, *Paul: The Apostle's Life, Letters, and Thought* (Minneapolis: Fortress, 2015), 605–11; James D. G. Dunn, "Did Paul Have a Covenant Theology? Reflections on Romans 9.4 and 11.27," in *The Concept of the Covenant in the Second Temple Period*, ed. Stanley. E. Porter and Jacqueline C. R. de Roo, JSJSup 71 (Leiden: Brill, 2003), 287–307; J. Louis Martyn, *Theological Issues in the Letters of Paul*, SNTW (Edinburgh: T&T Clark, 2005), 161–75. Others such as Stanley E. Porter, Scott W. Hahn, and N. T. Wright have argued that covenant plays a considerable role in the apostle's writings. Stanley E. Porter, "The Concept of Covenant in Paul," in Porter and de Roo, *Concept of the Covenant*, 269–86; Scott W. Hahn, *Kinship by Covenant: A Canonical Approach to the Fulfillment of God's Saving Promises*, ABRL (New Haven, CT: Yale University Press, 2009), 19–21; N. T. Wright, *Paul and the Faithfulness of God*, vol. 4 of *Christian Origins and the Question of God* (Minneapolis: Fortress, 2013), 780–82. For recent analyses of the debate, see David A. Shaw, "Apocalyptic and Covenant: Perspectives on Paul or Antinomies at War?," *JSNT* 36, no. 2 (2013): 155–71; E. C. van Driel, "Climax of the Covenant vs Apocalyptic Invasion: A Theological Analysis of a Contemporary Debate in Pauline Exegesis," *IJST* 17, no. 1 (2015): 6–25.

2. For these references, see W. S. Campbell, "Covenant and New Covenant," in *Dictionary of Paul and His Letters*, ed. Gerald F. Hawthorne, Ralph P. Martin, and Daniel G. Reid (Downers Grove, IL: InterVarsity Press, 1993), 179.

3. On the problems with reducing the concept of "covenant" in Paul to the lexical instances of the underlying Greek word, see now Porter, "Concept of Covenant in Paul."

the whole of the Christian's salvation but also the whole of human history in terms of the covenants that God has made with people. "Covenant," for Paul, demonstrates the unity of God's purposes for human beings in creation and redemption. It is, therefore, an architectonic principle of Paul's thought.[4]

For Paul, there are two primary covenants governing God's relationship with all people throughout human history—the covenant that God made with Adam in the garden and the covenant that God made with Christ. It is this former covenant that explains the universal human predicament of sin, shame, and death. It is the latter covenant that offers humanity both rescue from this predicament and entrance into righteousness, glory, and life. Although these blessings were not historically accomplished until Jesus Christ lived, died, and rose again two thousand years ago, God has made them available to human beings since the fall. In fact, for Paul, these blessings have never been available to human beings apart from Christ and the covenant that God made with him.

We first survey the evidence in Paul for these two covenants that structure both human history and God's dealings with people across space and time. We then give particular attention to the way that Paul understands God to have unfolded this second covenant across redemptive history. We conclude by offering some reflections on the implications of Paul's covenantal theology for our understanding of Scripture and the central concern of Scripture, the person and work of Jesus Christ.

Two Adams, Two Covenants

In two passages, 1 Corinthians 15:20–23, 42–49, and Romans 5:12–21, Paul compares and contrasts the first human being, Adam, and the God-man, Jesus Christ. Another chapter in this book advances the case for understanding Adam and Christ as representative heads of two distinct covenants. I simply summarize those findings here.[5]

In 1 Corinthians 15, Paul contrasts Adam and Christ along the lines of death and life, "for as by a man came death, by a man has come also the resurrection of the dead" (15:21). The sin of Adam resulted in death for human beings, while the resurrection of Christ has secured life for his people (15:22). Adam and Christ are therefore representative men. The eternal destiny of every human being is suspended on the action of one or the other of these two representatives. Those who are "in Adam" will die; those who are "in Christ shall all be made alive" (15:22).

Paul's interest in Adam in this chapter extends to before Adam's first transgression. In 1 Corinthians 15:42–49, Paul returns to his running contrast between Adam and Christ. Now, however, the contrast is not between fallen Adam and Christ. It is between prefallen Adam and Christ. That Paul has prefallen Adam in mind is evi-

---

4. For this reason, the infrequency of the term "covenant" in Paul's letters is an unreliable measure of its importance to Paul's thinking.

5. See Guy Prentiss Waters, "The Covenant of Works in the New Testament," chap. 3 in this volume.

dent from the fact that he quotes Genesis 2:7 ("The first man Adam became a living being," 1 Cor. 15:45). Paul's point in his running comparison between Adam and Christ in 1 Corinthians 15:42–49 is twofold. First, Adam failed to bring the creation to its intended goal. Had Adam obeyed God, he would have won confirmed life for himself and for his posterity. But Adam disobeyed God, and the result was death. Second, Christ did what Adam failed to do. By his obedience and death, he secured eschatological life for his people, a life that Paul understands in terms of the ministry of the Holy Spirit (15:45).

In this chapter, Paul calls Adam "the first man" (15:45, 47) and Christ "the last Adam" and "the second man" (15:45, 47). In putting matters this way, Paul stresses that there is no representative person or age that stands between Adam and Christ. Neither is there any representative person or age that will follow Christ. The "contrast between Adam and Christ" here "is not only pointed but also comprehensive and exclusive."[6] The Adam-Christ parallel embraces not only all humanity but also all history, extending back to the garden of Eden.

In Romans 5:12–21, Paul once again takes up the contrast between Adam and Christ as representative persons. Adam is "a type of the one who was to come," that is, Jesus (5:14). For this reason, Paul stresses an important similarity between Adam and Christ—each is a representative person whose action is imputed, or counted, to those whom he represents. But the actions of Adam and Jesus radically differ, as do the consequences of those actions. Adam's one sin has resulted in condemnation and death for his ordinary descendants. Christ's obedience has resulted in justification and life for his people. Christ's work does not merely undo the damage wrought by Adam's one sin. It accomplishes what Adam has failed to do, namely, to usher the people of God into eschatological life. For this reason, Paul stresses in this passage that Christ's work exceeds Adam's work in sheer scope ("much more," 5:17; "all the more," 5:20).[7]

Paul, then, tells us in 1 Corinthians 15 and Romans 5 that Adam and Jesus are the representative heads of two distinct covenants. God made the first covenant with Adam in the garden.[8] Confirmed eschatological life was stipulated on Adam's ongoing and unblemished obedience to God. For this reason, many have referred to this covenant as the "covenant of works." But God also threatened death for his disobedience. When Adam first sinned against God, he broke this covenant. The result of Adam's one sin was death for himself and his ordinary posterity.

---

6. Richard B. Gaffin Jr., *Resurrection and Redemption: A Study in Paul's Soteriology*, 2nd ed. (Phillipsburg, NJ: Presbyterian and Reformed, 1987), 85. The material in this paragraph has been drawn from Guy Prentiss Waters, "1–2 Corinthians," in *A Biblical-Theological Introduction to the New Testament*, ed. Michael J. Kruger (Wheaton, IL: Crossway, 2016), 214.

7. Much of the material in this paragraph has been drawn from Guy Prentiss Waters, "Romans," in Kruger, *Biblical-Theological Introduction*, 186–87.

8. For a recent treatment and defense of this covenant in the Gospels, see now Brandon D. Crowe, *The Last Adam: A Theology of the Obedient Life of Jesus in the Gospels* (Grand Rapids, MI: Baker Academic, 2017).

There is, however, a second covenant. This covenant God made with his people in Jesus Christ. By his obedience and death, Christ conquered death and secured eschatological life for himself and for his people. The benefits that Christ won for his people are not something that they merit. Christ has merited these benefits. They are Christ's gracious provision to the undeserving. For this reason, many have referred to this covenant as the "covenant of grace." What Christ secured by his obedience he freely and graciously bestows on his people.[9] We are not in the position of Adam, who was commanded to obey God in order to secure life. Christ has rendered that obedience to God for us. The life we receive by grace is the life that he earned by his works.

Paul understands all human beings to stand in covenantal relation to one of the two Adams. Every person is either "in Adam" or "in Christ." This is true of all human beings who are alive today, and it is true of humanity across history. As Adam's one sin resulted in "condemnation for all men," so Christ's righteous obedience resulted in "justification and life for all men," that is, all men who are united with Jesus Christ (Rom. 5:18). The tragedy of Adam's trespass is that every human being after Adam (Jesus excepted) has been conceived and born in sin. The glory of Christ's work is that even before his incarnation, people like Abraham and David received him and his benefits through faith for salvation (Rom. 4:1–25).

There is, therefore, since the fall one gracious covenant across history. Since Adam's fall into sin, God has been saving sinners by the work of his Son, Jesus Christ. For Paul, human history finds its culmination and climax in the life, death, and resurrection of Christ (Gal. 4:4; Eph. 1:10). The apostle sees the period of history before Christ as one of anticipation and preparation for the Son of God. But he does not view this period of history in undifferentiated fashion. Paul sees a succession of covenants that God made with human beings. These covenants served God's purpose of preparing the world for the person and work of Christ. These covenants are not independent of the one gracious covenant that God has made with his people in Christ. They are, rather, successive administrations of that one covenant of grace. Each administration, for Paul, has its own characteristics, and each prepares for Christ in distinct fashion. We may now turn to what the apostle Paul has to say about these covenantal administrations, in the order in which they appear in redemptive history.

One Gracious Covenant, Many Administrations
The Beginning of the Covenant of Grace
For Paul, God's one gracious covenant in Christ was inaugurated in the garden of Eden, immediately after the fall: "The God of peace will soon crush Satan under your feet.

---

9. On which, see Brandon D. Crowe, "The Passive *and* Active Obedience of Christ: Retrieving a Biblical Distinction," in *The Doctrine on Which the Church Stands or Falls: Justification in Biblical, Theological, Historical, and Pastoral Perspective*, ed. Matthew Barrett (Wheaton, IL: Crossway, 2019), 444–47.

The grace of our Lord Jesus Christ be with you" (Rom. 16:20).[10] The background of this statement is God's words to Satan shortly after Adam's first sin:

> I will put enmity between you and the woman,
>   and between your offspring and her offspring;
> he shall bruise your head,
>   and you shall bruise his heel. (Gen. 3:15)

In Genesis 3:15, God declares his intention to distinguish within the human race two offsprings.[11] These offsprings will be at "enmity" with one another. One line stems from Satan ("your offspring") and the other from Eve ("her offspring"). Since Satan is physically incapable of spawning human offspring, the relation in view is spiritual, not biological. In other words, God will set apart for himself a line of human beings who are spiritually opposed to Satan and spiritually aligned with himself. This promise finds its focus in a single descendant ("he"). This single descendant, a descendant of Eve, will deliver Satan a mortal blow ("bruise your head") even as he shall suffer from Satan in the process ("you shall bruise his heel").

This descendant, the New Testament writers tell us, is Jesus Christ. The battle between Satan and Christ was joined at the cross. The cross, Paul tells us, was the place where God "disarmed the rulers and authorities and put them to open shame, by triumphing over them in him" (Col. 2:15). When Jesus died on the cross for the sins of his people, that death nullified both the authority of the usurper, Satan, and Satan's bondage over those for whom Jesus died.[12]

With this background in mind, we may better understand what Paul is saying to the Roman Christians in Romans 16:20. In the preceding verse, Paul charges the church to be "wise as to what is good and innocent as to what is evil" (16:19). This command certainly echoes Jesus's exhortation to be "wise as serpents and innocent as doves" (Matt. 10:16).[13] But it may well have suggested to Paul's mind the failure of Adam and Eve to obey God by not eating of the fruit of "the tree of the knowledge of good and evil" (Gen. 2:17).[14] It is in Romans 16:20, then, that we have a statement of the promise that "the

---

10. For a defense of the textual integrity of Rom. 16:17–20a, 25–27, see now Richard N. Longenecker, *The Epistle to the Romans*, NIGTC (Grand Rapids, MI: Eerdmans, 2016), 1073–76.

11. For a more detailed exegetical argument supporting the observations that follow, see John D. Currid, "Adam and the Beginning of the Covenant of Grace," chap. 4 in this volume.

12. It is on the basis of this death that God "has provided for the full cancellation of the debt of obedience that we had incurred." Douglas J. Moo, *The Letters to the Colossians and to Philemon*, PNTC (Grands Rapids, MI: Eerdmans, 2008), 212. Paul understands Christ's death on the cross to be penal and to have offered satisfaction to divine justice (Col. 2:14). It is precisely in this light that Paul understands the cross to be the triumph over Satan that it is (2:15). As Moo observes, "The connection between these is the power that Satan and his minions hold over human beings because of their sin." *Colossians*, 216.

13. So Douglas Moo, *The Letter to the Romans*, NICNT (Grand Rapids, MI: Eerdmans, 1996), 932.

14. Compare here Gen. 3:5, "You will be like God, knowing good and evil," and Gen. 3:22, "Behold, the man has become like one of us in knowing good and evil." For the connection between Gen. 3:5 and Rom. 16:20, see Mark A. Seifrid, "Romans," in *Commentary on the New Testament Use of the Old Testament*, ed. G. K. Beale and D. A. Carson (Grand Rapids, MI: Baker Academic, 2007), 692.

God of peace will soon crush Satan under your feet." Here Paul echoes the promise of Genesis 3:15. Strikingly, the promise comes in the future tense. Paul has in mind the "eschatological consummation," when the already-defeated and nullified Satan will cease altogether to be a threat to the church.[15]

Paul says that God will crush Satan not under Jesus's feet but "under your feet." Because of the union between Jesus and his people (cf. Rom. 5:12–21), the people of God share in Jesus's triumph over Satan. Just as surely as they benefit from Christ's victory over Satan at the cross, so also shall they stand with Jesus on the last day, "when Satan is thrown into the 'lake of fire.'"[16] Importantly, the one who will deliver the final blow to Satan is the "God of peace" (cf. 1:7, 15:33). The peace that God grants to his people is the peace that results from the atoning death of Christ, by which they have been reconciled to God (5:1, 10, 11).[17] God's people may be assured of this final victory over Satan because of the victory that he has already accomplished in Christ over Satan on their behalf.

These words of Paul shed light on his understanding of covenant in the era of history before Christ. The apostle sees the promise of Genesis 3:15 as finding its intended fulfillment in Christ and the church. Since the work of Christ lies at the very heart of the gracious covenant that God made with his people in Christ, we should see the promise of Genesis 3:15 in light of that covenant. When we recall Paul's claim in Romans 5:12–21 that since the fall God has saved sinners only through the last Adam, we may fairly conclude that God inaugurated this one gracious covenant in Genesis 3:15.

This covenant began with God's word of promise in Genesis 3:15 and culminates in the life, death, and resurrection of Christ.

Abraham

The earliest covenant in redemptive history that Paul acknowledges with the word "covenant" (διαθήκη) is the covenant that God made with Abraham (cf. Gal. 3:15). The importance of this covenant to Paul emerges from the fact that he devotes no fewer than three chapters in two letters (Rom. 4; Gal. 3–4) to explaining its significance for the church. Galatians 3–4, in fact, is widely regarded as the argumentative heart of the epistle to the Galatians.

In Galatians 3–4, Paul's preferred word for the Abrahamic covenant is "promise" (ἐπαγγελία). The promises that God made to Abraham, Paul believes, constitute the heart of this covenant. Throughout these chapters, Paul describes the content of these promises in various ways. The promises include righteousness (3:6), blessing (3:9), the Holy Spirit (3:14), and inheritance (3:18). The same promises that God extended to Abraham are, Paul insists, the very promises that believers now

---

15. C. E. B. Cranfield, *Romans 9–16*, ICC (London: T&T Clark, 1979), 803.

16. Moo, *Romans*, 933.

17. C. E. B. Cranfield, *Romans 1–8*, ICC (London: T&T Clark, 1975), 72.

receive.[18] It is for this reason that Paul can preface his citation of Genesis 12:3 with the statement "The Scripture . . . preached the gospel beforehand to Abraham" (Gal. 3:8). God offered the same gospel to Abraham that he now offers to new covenant believers.

Not only does God extend to Abraham and to Christian believers the same promises, but we receive those promises in the same way, through faith. For this reason, Paul says that the "sons of Abraham" are "those of faith" (3:7). Jews *and* Gentiles may therefore claim covenantal descent from Abraham (3:8).

Paul notes that the promises that God made to Abraham were made "to Abraham and to his offspring [σπέρμα]" (3:16). The word "offspring" (σπέρμα) is a collective singular. That is, it is "singular in form" and "plural in meaning."[19] In Galatians 3:16, Paul accents the singularity of this word. The offspring, he insists, is Christ. Later in his argument, however, Paul accents the plurality of this word: "And if you are Christ's, then you are Abraham's offspring [σπέρμα], heirs according to promise" (3:29). There is no contradiction between these two claims. Christ is the intended recipient of the Abrahamic promises, and all those who are "Christ's" are, in and with him, recipients of those same promises.[20] That is, it is through faith in Jesus Christ that people in every age have received what God promised to Abraham.

In Romans 4, Paul elaborates one of the chief promises that God gave to Abraham and to his offspring, namely, the gift of justifying righteousness that Abraham received through faith alone, apart from works (4:1–5).[21] Circumcision was in no way a qualifying condition for receiving this righteousness. After all, Abraham received the promise of righteousness *before* he received circumcision (4:10). In fact, circumcision is both "sign" and "seal" of "the righteousness that [Abraham] had by faith" (4:11). Paul tells us, then, that the covenant ordinance of circumcision signified and confirmed to Abraham an evangelical reality, namely, justification by faith alone. Just as the Abrahamic covenant was and remains an evangelical covenant, administering gospel promises to the undeserving through faith (4:5), so its appointed sign, circumcision, is no less evangelical in character.

Paul also shows us how the Abrahamic covenant relates to the covenantal administrations that precede and follow it. The word "offspring" (σπέρμα), which Paul highlights from the Abrahamic narratives, is a word that features prominently in the promise that God makes in Genesis 3:15.[22] In both Romans 16:20 and Galatians 3:16, Paul understands this offspring to be Christ. There is, then, covenantal continuity between the

---

18. See here the helpful reflections of Thomas R. Schreiner, *Galatians*, ZECNT (Grand Rapids, MI: Zondervan, 2010), 196–97.

19. Douglas J. Moo, *Galatians*, BECNT (Grand Rapids, MI: Baker Academic, 2013), 229.

20. As Schreiner puts it, "Jesus is *the representative* offspring of Abraham and David," the intended and "final fulfillment" of the "typological . . . offspring promises in the OT." *Galatians*, 230.

21. Note the reappearance of the word "offspring" (σπέρμα) in Rom. 4:13, 16, 18.

22. In the Septuagint, Gen. 3:15 reads, καὶ ἔχθραν θήσω ἀνὰ μέσον σου καὶ ἀνὰ μέσον τῆς γυναικὸς καὶ ἀνὰ μέσον τοῦ *σπέρματός* σου καὶ ἀνὰ μέσον τοῦ *σπέρματος* αὐτῆς· αὐτός σου τηρήσει κεφαλήν, καὶ σὺ τηρήσεις

inaugural administration of God's one gracious covenant in the garden of Eden (Gen. 3:15) and the subsequent administration of that covenant to Abraham and his family (Gen. 12; 15; 17). The Abrahamic administration serves to reveal more of the person and work of Christ and, in this way, continue to administer Christ to human beings through faith.

Paul, moreover, understands the new covenant not to terminate or replace the Abrahamic covenant but to bring that covenant to its intended fulfillment. Christ, Paul argues, places the blessings of the Abrahamic covenant into the hands of his people, who are "Abraham's offspring, heirs according to promise" (Gal. 3:29). It is "in Christ Jesus," Paul tells us, that "the blessing of Abraham" has "come to the Gentiles," namely, "the promised Spirit," whom we "receive . . . through faith" (Gal. 3:14). As Christians, we possess the same blessings that were promised to Abraham and to his believing descendants. But we are in an incomparably better position. Abraham knew Christ and received his benefits, but from afar, in the shadows. We now know Christ, crucified and raised, and we receive these blessings as they have been secured by Christ in his death and resurrection (Rom. 4:24–25; Gal. 3:13–14).

Moses

The Mosaic covenant—or what Paul calls both the "old covenant" (2 Cor. 3:14) and, in places, "the law" (see Gal. 3:19)—loomed large in the ministry of the apostle.[23] In both Galatia and Corinth, opponents appealed to this covenant in their attacks on Paul and his ministry. It is important to bear this situation in mind as we turn to the passages in which Paul speaks at greatest length of the Mosaic covenant. The majority of his reflections on this covenant are stated not in the abstract but in the throes of specific controversies. He is addressing individuals whom he regards as having fundamentally corrupted the gospel of grace (2 Cor. 11:4; Gal. 1:6–8). Paul is, then, both correcting his opponents' misreading of the Mosaic covenant and advancing the way this covenant should be properly understood. Part of the complexity of reading Paul, however, is that commentators are not always agreed on how to take some of his statements about the Mosaic covenant. With this background in mind, we may attempt to sketch the way that Paul understood this covenant to work within the broader scope of God's redemptive purposes in history.

It is in Galatians 3–4 and 2 Corinthians 3:1–4:6 that Paul devotes his most concentrated attention to the Mosaic covenant. In Galatians 3:19, Paul asks the question "Why then the law?" This is an understandable question. If Christ is the substance of the Abrahamic promise, if he has secured those blessings for his people, and if his people

---

αὐτοῦ πτέρναν. The same Hebrew word (זֶרַע) underlies the Greek word σπέρμα in both Gen. 3:15 and several of the Abrahamic promise passages (Gen. 12:7; 13:15, 16; 15:5, 13, 18; 17:7, 8, 9, 10, 12, 19).

23. It is widely recognized that the word "law" (νόμος) admits of several denotations in Paul's writings. While "Mosaic covenant" is among them, it is by no means the exclusive or exhaustive meaning of this term for Paul.

across redemptive history receive him and those blessings through faith, what need is there for the Mosaic covenant? Paul knows that God gave the law and that it therefore served good and constructive purposes in God's unfolding redemptive plan.[24] Which are these purposes?

Paul insists, before he identifies those purposes, that the law and the promise, that is, the Mosaic covenant and the Abrahamic covenant, are fundamentally complementary: "Is the law then contrary to the promises of God? Certainly not!" (Gal. 3:21). Although each covenant plays a different role on the stage of redemptive history, the law did not cancel out the promise. The Mosaic covenant does not replace what preceded it.

Having posited that complementarity, Paul identifies in these chapters at least two distinct but intertwined purposes of the Mosaic covenant. The first is that God intended this covenant to show his people their need for a Savior: "For if a law had been given that could give life, then righteousness would indeed be by the law. But the Scripture imprisoned everything under sin, so that the promise by faith in Jesus Christ might be given to those who believe" (Gal. 3:21–22). Paul says here that the law is incapable of "giv[ing] life" or "righteousness." It requires perfect obedience and holds out blessing and life to the one who fulfills its requirements. But it "cannot arouse [a person] from his impotence and grant him the ability to do what it demands."[25] But because the law is given to sinners, sinners will invariably transgress God's law to greater and greater degrees (cf. Rom. 5:20). The fault lies not in the law. As Paul stresses elsewhere, the law is "holy and righteous and good" (Rom. 7:12).[26] The fault lies squarely with those who transgress the law.

As a result of this state of affairs, those to whom the law came found themselves "imprisoned . . . under sin" (Gal. 3:22). As Herman Ridderbos has explained this statement, "Scripture has left open no avenue of escape within the pale of the law, but has brought together as in a prison-house all human life and all efforts to fight itself free."[27] Paul explains the purpose of this mass incarceration in the remainder of 3:22: "so that the promise by faith in Jesus Christ might be given to those who believe." God wanted his people to see their need for a Savior. He wanted them to see that they had no hope of righteousness, life, or blessing in themselves. They were to look outside themselves for that help and relief.

Elsewhere in his correspondence, Paul tells us that the law pointed Israel to the Savior they needed. In Colossians 2:16–17, Paul tells the Colossians that "a festival," "a new moon," and "a Sabbath" are all "a shadow of the things to come, but the substance

---

24. As Moo states, "Paul is no Marcionite." *Galatians*, 232.

25. Herman N. Ridderbos, *The Epistle of Paul to the Churches of Galatia*, NICNT (Grand Rapids, MI: Eerdmans, 1953), 141.

26. Paul makes this statement in the context of a larger set of reflections on what happens when the law enters into the life of a sinner (Rom. 7:7–13). Here Paul stresses that this entrance not only serves to define sin but also results in the sinner sinning more. This result is not the fault of the law but of sin.

27. Ridderbos, *Galatia*, 141–42.

belongs to Christ." In Ezekiel 45:17 (LXX), these three nouns ("festivals," "new moons," "Sabbaths") appear together and in the same order. Preceding this list are "burnt offerings, grain offerings, and drink offerings," and following this list are "all the appointed feasts of the house of Israel" (Ezek. 45:17). Paul has in mind, then, the entirety of the system of worship that God appointed for Israel under the Mosaic covenant. He tells us that this system, inclusive of its offerings and feast days, was "a shadow of the things to come" (Col. 2:17). This system was eschatological. It was not self-referential but pointed beyond itself for its ultimate meaning and significance. That ultimate meaning ("substance") is "Christ." Christ, Paul tells us, was casting his "shadow" back into redemptive history through the ceremonial system of the Mosaic covenant. By this means, Israel had sight of the Savior they needed. The law was intended to bring them to an end of themselves so that they might flee for refuge to the Savior whom the law revealed to them.

The fact that the law, good in itself, served as the instrument of aggravating the situation in which its sinful recipients found themselves helps explain one feature of Paul's teaching about the law. In 2 Corinthians 3:1–4:6, Paul speaks of the law in fairly severe terms.[28] It "kills" (3:6), results in "death" (3:7), and brings "condemnation" (3:9). Paul, however, is not describing the law in the abstract. He is describing what happens when the law enters into the life of a sinner without the intervention of divine grace. As Ridderbos aptly summarizes, "The consequence of this monstrous alliance of sin and the law is that all kinds of qualifications that describe the corruption and curse of sin now also apply to the law."[29] Furthermore, the law, as a written code, is unable to convey to those under its administration the power to keep its demands. The law cannot give life (Gal. 3:21). It "can only condemn those who fail to meet its demands."[30] As such, the law brings its recipients into captivity and imprisonment (3:23).

There is a second and related purpose to the Mosaic covenant. The law functioned as a "guardian" (παιδαγωγὸς) to lead its recipients to Christ (Gal. 3:24). The "guardian" in the ancient world was typically a slave whom a father appointed to oversee his son.[31] The "guardian" did not primarily serve as a tutor, who taught or instructed his young charge. His role was more of a disciplinarian. He ensured that the boy went to school, did his lessons, and stayed out of trouble. He was authorized to administer punishment for infraction of the father's rules.

When Paul compares the Mosaic covenant to a guardian for Israel, he is making a number of important points about this covenant and those who were subject to its administration. First, this covenant's recipients were in a state of relative youth and im-

---

28. For more extensive discussion of this passage, see Waters, "1–2 Corinthians," 223–27.

29. Herman N. Ridderbos, *Paul: An Outline of His Theology*, trans. John Richard de Witt (Grand Rapids, MI: Eerdmans, 1975), 147.

30. Colin G. Kruse, *2 Corinthians*, 2nd ed. (Downers Grove, IL: InterVarsity Press, 2015), 95.

31. On the guardian (παιδαγωγὸς) in Paul's day, see the still-valuable surveys of Richard N. Longenecker, *Galatians*, WBC 41 (Dallas: Word Books, 1990), 146–48; Ben Witherington III, *Grace in Galatia: A Commentary on Paul's Letter to the Galatians* (Grand Rapids, MI: Eerdmans, 1998), 262–67.

maturity. This is a point that Paul develops at some length in Galatians 4:1–7. Israel, he insists, had the status of son and heir (4:1). But they were minors. Therefore, their circumstances were "no different from a slave, though [they were] the owner of everything" (4:1). They required the regimen and discipline of the "guardians and managers" whom their father set over them (4:2).

It is in this analogy that Paul makes an important point about the Mosaic covenant's role in the economy of salvation. It was, by design, temporary in duration. It had a point of origination: "It was added, . . . and it was put in place" (3:19). And it had a built-in terminus: "until the coming faith would be revealed" (3:23); "but now that faith has come, we are no longer under a guardian" (3:25); "but when the fullness of time had come" (4:4). Thus, when Christ (cf. "faith," 3:23) appeared, God's people entered into the fullness of their status as sons and of their inheritance (4:7).

The built-in, temporary character of the law is something that Paul addresses in 2 Corinthians 3. The Mosaic covenant was transitory, "being brought to an end" (3:7). But what has followed it (the new covenant) is "permanent" (3:11). For this reason, the Mosaic covenant had "glory," but the new covenant has "even more glory" (3:7, 8; cf. 3:9–11). The fact that each administration has glory means that each administration functioned in just the way that God intended—to reflect the perfection of his character. In performing its own assigned office, each covenant brought glory to its divine author.

How, then, does Paul answer the question "Why then the law?" (Gal. 3:19)? His answer is, "It was added because of transgressions, until the offspring should come to whom the promise had been made." Here we see some of the main lines of Paul's teaching about the Mosaic covenant. The Mosaic covenant was temporary in nature ("until the offspring should come"). It was designed to be subservient to the Abrahamic "promise" that would find its realization in the incarnation and ministry of the "offspring" to whom that promise was made. As such, the law provided a divine regimen to prepare the immature people of God for that offspring. It was given to a sinful people ("because of transgressions") and therefore showed them their sin and helplessness apart from Christ as well as the Savior whom they needed for righteousness, life, and blessing.

Given these purposes of the Mosaic covenant, and given their fundamental complementarity with the Abrahamic covenant that precedes ("promise") and the new covenant that follows ("faith"), we may ask a further question. Did Paul regard the Mosaic covenant to be an evangelical administration of the one gracious covenant that God inaugurated in Genesis 3:15? Did this covenant, no less than the Abrahamic covenant, administer gospel promises to Israel?

In light of Paul's writings about the law, we may offer an affirmative answer to these questions. The Mosaic covenant not only pointed to evangelical realities but also administered those promises to Israel. We have seen indication of this from Colossians 2:16–17. The ceremonial system of the law was a "shadow" that Christ cast back into redemptive history. As such, the feasts and sacrifices were instruments by which Christ was administered to the souls of believing Israelite worshipers.

Paul makes two statements in his letter to the Ephesians that suggest he understood the Mosaic covenant as an evangelical administration of God's one gracious covenant. In Ephesians 2:12, Paul tells the Gentile members of the church in Ephesus that they were formerly "alienated from the commonwealth of Israel and strangers to the covenants of promise." These persons were separated from a plurality of covenants that were characterized by promise.[32] Which covenants does Paul have in mind?[33] Commentators differ, but it is likely that Paul is referring to all the administrations of the one gracious covenant that God has made with sinners in Christ.[34] These administrations include at least the Abrahamic, Mosaic, and Davidic covenants. The broad generality of the expression "covenants of promise" commends the inclusion of all covenantal administrations in redemptive history. Furthermore, because Paul's argument in Ephesians 2:11–22 addresses what had formerly distinguished and set apart Jew from Gentile, we are bound "to include the covenant of Israel" in this grouping of covenants.[35] This covenant, after all, was characterized by the way it had distinguished Jew from Gentile. For Paul, then, the Mosaic covenant stands with the other administrations of the one gracious covenant as a covenant that administered promises to Israel. The Mosaic covenant is an essentially evangelical covenant.

A second passage in Ephesians that reinforces this point is Ephesians 6:2–3: "'Honor your father and mother' (this is the first commandment with a promise), 'that it may go well with you and that you may live long in the land.'" Paul here quotes the fifth commandment, likely from Exodus 20:12 (LXX). This command, of course, constitutes part of the Decalogue, the foundational legislation of the Mosaic covenant. Paul inserts a parenthetical observation in the midst of his quotation, "This is the first commandment with a promise." This observation serves to introduce the promise that follows ("that it may go well with you and that you may live long in the land"). Paul is concerned, then, not only to quote the command but also to call attention to the fact that it was promulgated with an accompanying promise.[36] It is in this same form (command with promise) that the fifth commandment is set before the children of the church in Ephesus. These observations tell us at least two things about Paul's understanding of the Mosaic covenant. The first is that he understood the Mosaic covenant to be an administration of "promise." As such, it stands alongside and in continuity

32. The genitive "of promise" is likely an attributive genitive, so Clinton E. Arnold, *Ephesians*, ZECNT (Grand Rapids, MI: Zondervan, 2010), 155.

33. For a survey of opinion, see Harold W. Hoehner, *Ephesians: An Exegetical Commentary* (Grand Rapids, MI: Baker Academic, 2002), 358–59. More recently, see Arnold, *Ephesians*, 155.

34. So, rightly, Arnold, who sees specifically the Abrahamic, Mosaic, Davidic, and new covenants in view. *Ephesians*, 155. *Pace* Hoehner, who sees only "unconditional covenants" in view, that is, the Abrahamic, Davidic, and new covenants but not the Mosaic covenant. *Ephesians*, 358–59.

35. Peter T. O'Brien, *The Letter to the Ephesians*, PNTC (Grand Rapids, MI: Eerdmans, 1999), 189.

36. Significantly, the word translated "promise" (ἐπαγγελία) is the same Greek word that Paul used in Eph. 2:12 in describing the "covenants" from which the Gentiles were formerly alienated.

with other covenants that administered promises to the people of God. The second is that Paul expects new covenant members to obey God's law on the same terms that old covenant members were to obey God's law. This parity indicates that the Mosaic covenant, no less than the new covenant, is an evangelical administration. Under both administrations, believing obedience is the way that the redeemed respond to their gracious, promise-making God.

Paul, then, understood the Mosaic covenant to be an administration of the one gracious covenant that God has made with sinners in Christ. The purpose of this covenant was twofold. First, it served to define sin clearly and to impress on God's people their helplessness through sin and their need for a Savior. Second, this covenant served as a guardian to prepare Israel for and lead them to Jesus Christ. This covenant was never intended to be a permanent fixture of the life of God's people. It served to complement the Abrahamic covenant, and it terminated when Christ died and rose from the dead. Even so, this covenant was not only part of God's good purpose toward his people, it was also good in itself (Rom. 7:12).

We are now in a position to assess in brief why Paul reacted so strongly to his opponents' teaching about the Mosaic covenant. We may take as an example Paul's opponents in Galatia. According to Paul, his opponents mistook the law on two fundamental grounds. First, they were treating the Mosaic covenant as though it were an active or perpetual administration (cf. Gal. 4:21). But, Paul argues, the Mosaic covenant was brought to an end by the new covenant (3:25). Good for its time, the Mosaic covenant has been abrogated and succeeded by an even better administration. Why, Paul asks the Galatians, would they want to exchange what is better for what is comparatively inferior (cf. 4:9).

Second, Paul's opponents misunderstood how the Mosaic covenant operated in its own time. They were counseling the Galatians to obey the commands of the law in order to be justified, or declared righteous, before God (2:16). But, Paul stresses, God never gave the law to his people so that they could be justified by their obedience to its commands (3:11–12, 21). Those who seek justification by the law must perfectly obey all its commands, something no sinner can do (3:10; 5:3). All that the law is empowered to do for the sinner is to pronounce him accursed for his disobedience. God's intention in this covenant, rather, was to drive his people to Christ, in whom alone they could find justification.

David

One further covenant to which Paul gives attention is the covenant that God made with David (2 Sam. 7; 1 Chron. 17). This covenant does not appear to have independent significance in the Old Testament. In many ways it is an extension and specification of the Abrahamic covenant. From David, the descendant of Abraham, God will raise up one who will be his own Son and who will reign forever. The New Testament writers with one voice declare Jesus to be that Son of David, the one in whom the covenant that God made with David found its intended fulfillment.

Although Paul does not make frequent reference to this covenant, two occasions when he does address it are significant:

Remember Jesus Christ, risen from the dead, the offspring of David, as preached in my gospel. (2 Tim. 2:8)

[. . . the gospel of God] concerning his Son, who was descended from David according to the flesh and was declared to be the Son of God in power according to the Spirit of holiness by his resurrection from the dead. (Rom. 1:3–4)

Both passages serve as summaries of Paul's teaching. In Romans 1:3–4, Paul gives to the church in Rome an initial overview of the gospel that he will devote the remainder of the letter to explaining. In 2 Timothy 2:8, Paul is calling Timothy to remember the substance of the gospel that Paul preached and that Timothy was to preach as well. In both summaries, Paul highlights the Davidic descent of Jesus. Significantly, Paul identifies Jesus to Timothy as "the offspring of David" (ἐκ σπέρματος Δαυίδ). The Greek word translated "offspring" (σπέρμα) is the same word that Paul uses to describe Jesus as the "offspring" of Abraham (Gal. 3:16; cf. 3:29). This verbal link suggests that Paul understands the Davidic covenant as related to and advancing the Abrahamic covenant—the promised offspring in whom the nations will be blessed is a descendant of David, namely, Jesus.

We may also notice how, in Romans 1:3–4, Paul links Jesus's Davidic sonship with Jesus's resurrection from the dead. At the resurrection, Jesus was "appointed" (NIV; "declared," ESV) the messianic Son of God.[37] That is, Jesus then entered into a "new and more powerful" phase of his messianic sonship.[38] This phase is characterized by the presence, power, and life of the Holy Spirit.

This advance in Jesus's Davidic sonship helps us understand his present reign. Jesus's never-ending and universal reign over his people is characterized by the ministry of the Holy Spirit, the "Spirit of Christ" (Rom. 8:9). It is the Holy Spirit who prompts a person gladly to acknowledge and submit to the lordship of Christ (1 Cor. 12:3). The Christian is one who has "set [his] mind on the things of the Spirit" and who lives his life "according to the Spirit" (Rom. 8:5). The risen, reigning Jesus has so given his Spirit to his people as to bring them under his saving reign. And what characterizes this reign is the blessedness and life that Jesus won for them and shares with them by the Holy Spirit.

Paul's references to the Davidic covenant are few, but attending to those references yields rich returns. Christ is the fulfillment of the Davidic covenant. Paul understands

---

37. So Herman N. Ridderbos, *Aan de Romeinen* (Kampen: J. H. Kok, 1959), 26; C. E. B. Cranfield, *Romans 1–8*, 61–62.

38. Moo, *Romans*, 49. I am taking, with Moo, the prepositional phrase "in power" to modify the noun clause "the Son of God." *Romans*, 48.

Jesus's messianic sonship and saving reign in light of this covenantal fulfillment. When we take into account both the weight and scope of Christ's sonship and saving reign within and across Paul's writings, we not only realize the importance of this covenantal administration to Paul's understanding of Christ but also find confirmation of the importance of the covenants of the Old Testament to Paul's thinking generally.

New

For Paul, the climactic administration of God's one gracious covenant with his people is the "new covenant" (1 Cor. 11:25; 2 Cor. 3:6). The term "new covenant" is not unique to Paul. It first appears in the prophet Jeremiah (Jer. 31:31) and resurfaces in the teaching of Jesus (Luke 22:20). With Jesus, Paul understands the new covenant to come to expression in the life and ministry of Jesus Christ. How specifically does Paul see this covenantal administration realized in Christ? In Romans 11:27, Paul indicates that he understands the whole of Jesus's life, ministry, death, and exaltation in light of this new covenant. Quoting Isaiah 59:20–21 and Isaiah 27:9 from the Septuagint, Paul tells the Roman Christians,

> "The Deliverer will come from Zion,
>   he will banish ungodliness from Jacob";
> "and this will be my covenant with them
>   when I take away their sins." (Rom. 11:26–27)[39]

There is at least one significant difference between Isaiah 59:20 as Paul cites it and Isaiah 59:20 as it appears in the Masoretic Text and Septuagint. The Masoretic Text says that the Redeemer comes "to" Zion; the Septuagint, "on account of" Zion; and Paul, "from" Zion.[40] To appreciate this difference, one must first discern what Paul understands "Zion" to be. "Zion," for Paul, refers here to "heaven or the heavenly sanctuary" (cf. Gal. 4:26).[41] Paul is likely thinking of the return of Christ, at which point "ungodliness" will have been "banish[ed]" from elect Israel.[42] Here Paul identifies the work of Christ in terms of the complete and comprehensive removal of sin from his people, which in this context means his Jewish people.[43] Paul denominates this work of Christ a "covenant": "And this is my covenant with them" (Isa. 59:21 LXX). In the following clause ("when I take away their sins"), which serves to "interpret this covenant," Paul intentionally stops

---

39. On the text form, see Cranfield, *Romans 9–16*, 577–78.

40. Seifrid, "Romans," 674. On the faithfulness to the Hebrew original of Paul's rendering, see John Murray, *The Epistle to the Romans*, 2 vols., NICNT (Grand Rapids, MI: Eerdmans, 1959, 1965), 2:99n54.

41. Cranfield, *Romans 9–16*, 578; cf. Moo, *Romans*, 728, 728n73.

42. Notice that Paul does not necessarily say that Christ's return in glory will be the moment at which these realities will take place but that his return in glory will accompany these realities' consummate expression in the life of "all Israel" (Rom. 11:26).

43. This work, of course, is not unique to Jewish individuals. It is the work of Christ for all his people, Jew and Gentile. Paul is stressing in this passage the application of that work to the Jewish elect.

referencing Isaiah 59 (LXX) and draws wording from Isaiah 27:9 (LXX).[44] Paul may also have had in mind here Jeremiah 31:31, 34, in which the prophet announces the "new covenant," one blessing of which is said to be the forgiveness of sins.[45]

This passage describes the work of Christ comprehensively in at least two respects. First, Paul addresses Christ's work from the vantage point of consummation, namely, his return in glory. Second, Paul addresses the totality of what Christ has come to do, namely, to remove sin comprehensively from his people. Although Paul's concern in these verses is the Jew, his argument throughout the epistle to the Romans has been that Jews and Gentiles share a common plight and can be saved in only one and the same way, namely, the work of Christ. What Paul says of the Jew here applies, *mutatis mutandis*, to the Gentile.

This comprehensive work of Christ Paul labels "covenantal." Although he does not here use the term "new covenant," it is probable that Paul intends us to understand Christ's work of redemption in terms of the new covenant, which served as the climax of all preceding redemptive covenantal administrations. Paul's statements in Romans 11:26–27, therefore, invite his readers to reflect on the whole of Christ's ministry in terms of the one gracious covenant that God has made with sinners in Christ, specifically, the administration of the "new covenant."

For Paul, the heart of this covenant and the heart of this covenantal work of Christ is the death of Christ, which has secured forgiveness for the sins of sinners. Paul expresses this conviction in the way he explains the Lord's Supper to the church in Corinth (1 Cor. 11:23–26). In this passage, Paul stresses that what he has "delivered" to the Corinthians and now reiterates to them is what he has "received from the Lord," that is, the Lord Jesus Christ. It is in 11:25 that he invokes the covenantal character of the Supper: "In the same way also he took the cup, after supper, saying, 'This cup is the new covenant in my blood.'" The term "new covenant" is, of course, drawn from Jeremiah 31:31. Both Jesus and Paul link the cup, which represents the redemptive death of Jesus Christ, to the new covenant of which Jeremiah spoke centuries earlier. Further, the association of "covenant" and "blood" recalls Exodus 24:8, "Behold the blood of the covenant that the LORD has made with you in accordance with all these words."[46] As the Mosaic covenant had been founded on God's work of redemption in the exodus, so the new covenant will be founded on God's work of redemption in Christ, in the "second exodus."[47]

---

44. Moo, *Romans*, 729. Isa. 27:9 (LXX) reads, ὅταν ἀφέλωμαι αὐτοῦ τὴν ἁμαρτίαν.

45. So Murray, *Romans*, 99; Cranfield, *Romans 9–16*, 578–79. Jer. 38:34 (LXX) [=Jer. 31:34 MT] reads, ὅτι ἵλεως ἔσομαι ταῖς ἀδικίαις αὐτῶν καὶ τῶν ἁμαρτιῶν αὐτῶν οὐ μὴ μνησθῶ ἔτι. What commends this verse as lying in the background of Rom. 11:26 is the fact that it falls in a paragraph (Jer. 38:31–34 LXX [=Jer. 31:31–34 MT]) that conjoins "covenant" with the forgiveness of sins. So Cranfield, *Romans 9–16*, 579.

46. See Roy E. Ciampa and Brian S. Rosner, "1 Corinthians," in Beale and Carson, *New Testament Use of the Old Testament*, 736; David E. Garland, *1 Corinthians*, BECNT (Grand Rapids, MI: Baker Academic, 2003), 547; cf. Gordon D. Fee, *The First Epistle to the Corinthians*, NICNT, rev. ed. (Grand Rapids, MI: Eerdmans, 2014), 614.

47. Roy E. Ciampa and Brian S. Rosner, *The First Letter to the Corinthians*, PNTC (Grand Rapids, MI: Baker, 2010), 552.

Paul's statements in 1 Corinthians 11:23–26 carry significant implications for the way he would have us understand the nature of the biblical covenants and their relationship with one another. The substance of both the Mosaic and the new covenant is Christ and his redemptive work. The Mosaic covenant represents Christ prospectively and through types and shadows. The new covenant represents Christ in light of his finished work in history. As such, these two covenants stand in complementary, even organic, relationship with one another. Although they present Christ from different vantage points, their common concern is Christ and his saving work for sinners.

It is in 2 Corinthians 3 and Galatians 3–4 that Paul helps us see some of the ways in which the new covenant differs from the old covenant. That is, with the framework of essential continuity between these two covenantal administrations, Paul highlights certain areas of discontinuity. These lines of discontinuity help us appreciate what, for Paul, the distinguishing character of the new covenant is and the privilege that it is for believers in Christ to be under that covenant.

In both passages, Paul sees the distinguishing character of the new covenant along two lines. The first is the finished, or accomplished, work of Christ. As Paul puts it in Galatians 3:25, "Now . . . faith has come." Paul does not mean that people did not believe in Christ before Christ's death and resurrection.[48] He is saying, rather, that the object of faith, Christ, has now come and accomplished what God's people had been expecting him to do, to save them from their sins. Consequently, Paul declares "a new mode of existence that has been given with Christ's advent, . . . with the manifestation of the grace of God in the death and resurrection of Christ."[49]

It is in light of this reality that Paul can stress "adoption as sons" as a hallmark privilege of the new covenant (Gal. 4:5; cf. 3:25–26). To be sure, God's people who lived before Christ were sons (4:1–3). But new covenant believers understand adoption with more clarity and fullness (cf. 2 Cor. 3:12–18) and experience its benefits to a degree that old covenant believers did not. Christ's accomplishment in history of the work of redemption furnishes adoption with "new, deepened significance."[50]

Paul's teaching on adoption highlights the second distinguishing character of Paul's exposition of the new covenant, the ministry of the Holy Spirit. Paul tells new covenant believers, "Because you are sons, God has sent the Spirit of his Son into our hearts, crying, 'Abba! Father!'" (Gal. 4:6). One of the privileges of our adoption in Christ is the abiding presence and ministry of the one whom Paul calls "the Spirit of his Son."[51] The Spirit whom the exalted Christ has poured out in fullness has taken up residence in our beings and lives.

---

48. So, rightly, Ridderbos, *Paul*, 154.
49. Ridderbos, *Paul*, 174.
50. Ridderbos, *Paul*, 198.
51. On the way that this sending of the Spirit of Christ constitutes fulfillment of such new covenant prophecies as Jer. 31:31–34 and Ezek. 36:26–27, see Moo, *Galatians*, 269.

In 2 Corinthians 3–4, Paul reflects at length on the new covenant privilege of the plenary ministry of the Spirit. Paul associates the new covenant with the "Spirit" and the old covenant with the "letter" (3:6). He terms the new covenant the "ministry of the Spirit" and the old covenant the "ministry of death" (3:7–8). The law has no power either to effect what it demands or to overcome the sin of those to whom it comes. It is simply capable of confirming and aggravating sinners' "condemnation" (3:9).[52] But the Spirit has the power to bring inward transformation (3:18), even the "life" of the new creation, to those who are dead and helpless in their sins (3:6; 4:6). He conveys the "righteousness" of Christ to sinners, who are brought out of the state of "condemnation" (3:9).

What accounts for this work of the Spirit? Paul tells us that the "Lord is the Spirit" (3:17). That is, there is a functional identity between the Lord Jesus Christ and the Holy Spirit. It is for this reason that Paul calls the Spirit the "Spirit of [God's] Son" (Gal. 4:6) and the "Spirit of Christ" (Rom. 8:9). As Paul teaches elsewhere, this functional identity was forged at the resurrection of Christ (1 Cor. 15:42–49). At his resurrection, Christ so possessed and was so possessed by the Spirit that, upon his ascension and session, he poured out the Spirit in fullness on his people. What Christ secured for sinners in his obedience, death, and resurrection, the Spirit applies to them in time.

Paul is not saying that either Christ's benefits or the Spirit's ministry was unknown before the resurrection.[53] Neither is he saying that since the resurrection, the Spirit works in a saving manner on every human being (cf. 2 Cor. 2:15, 16). Rather, Paul emphasizes the privilege of living in the era inaugurated by the accomplished redemptive work of Christ in history. The scope and power of the Spirit's ministry under the new covenant far exceed the scope and power of the Spirit's ministry under the old covenant.[54]

Conclusions

Although Paul uses the word "covenant" (διαθήκη) only a handful of times in his correspondence, it is nevertheless fair to characterize Paul as a covenant theologian.[55] The framework of human history, from creation to consummation, is, for Paul, covenantal. In particular, the progress of redemptive history and the culmination of that progress, the person and work of Christ, are covenantal. The way that redemption in Christ is applied to and experienced by human beings is covenantal.

---

52. On this dimension of Paul's teaching about the Mosaic covenant in 2 Cor. 3:1–4:6, see Waters, "1–2 Corinthians," 224–25.

53. In Rom. 4, Paul stresses that both Abraham and David possessed the "righteousness" of Christ not by observing God's commandments but through faith in the promised Messiah. In 1 Cor. 10:1–13, he shows that the Spirit had a distinct ministry in the lives of God's redeemed old covenant people, Israel.

54. See further Richard B. Gaffin Jr., "The Holy Spirit," *WTJ* 43, no. 1 (1980): 58–78, esp. 72–73; Gaffin, *The Work of the Holy Spirit* (Willow Grove, PA: Committee on Christian Education of the Orthodox Presbyterian Church, 2012), esp. 9–13.

55. *Pace* Dunn, who sees Paul as having a "covenant theology" but nevertheless concludes that "the theme of 'covenant' was not a central or major category within his own theologizing." "Did Paul Have a Covenant Theology?," 306.

Paul's understanding of covenant helps us see how the whole of Scripture points to Christ. The last Adam not only remediates the damage of the first Adam's sin but also carries the purpose of God for humanity forward to its consummation. Beginning with the first promise of redemption announced to human beings in Genesis 3:15, "all the promises of God find their Yes in [Christ]" (2 Cor. 1:20). Similarly, the covenants that administered those promises to God's people were all designed to point and lead God's people to Jesus Christ.

Paul's understanding of the covenant also helps us better understand the Christian life. All the blessings and benefits of the Christian life come to us in Christ, our faithful covenant keeper. They are in no way rewards that we have merited. On the contrary, Christ has merited them for the undeserving. We receive them in union with Jesus Christ and through faith in him (Gal. 2:16–21). This reality does not render us passive or permit us to be indifferent to the commands of God. On the contrary, the ministry of the Spirit under the new covenant is transforming us after the glorious image of the Lord Jesus (2 Cor. 3:18). It is our duty and delight to strive to be conformed to the image of our covenant head, Christ, who "though he was rich, yet for [our] sake . . . became poor, so that [we] by his poverty might become rich" (2 Cor. 8:9).

Covenant in Paul helps us see more clearly the one who sat at the heart of Paul's teaching and ministry, Jesus Christ. Covenant shows us how the mercies of God in Christ run the whole length of Scripture. And covenant shows us how all God's mercies for sinners are bound up in Christ. For Paul, then, covenant is ancillary neither to his teaching nor to that teaching's center, his gospel. And in line with the other authors of the Old and New Testaments, Paul understands the covenants of Scripture as the means by which God is advancing history to its purposed goal, the glory of God in Christ.

12

Covenant in Hebrews

Robert J. Cara

Covenants are significant in Hebrews.[1] This book's treatment of them must be an important part of any presentation of the Bible's overall understanding of covenants. Below are a few preliminary comments about covenants in Hebrews that show aspects of their importance, which are fleshed out later in this chapter.

The author of Hebrews uses the word διαθήκη ("covenant"[2]) more than all the other New Testament writers combined—seventeen times in Hebrews and sixteen times elsewhere.[3] To put a finer point on the author of Hebrews's usage, διαθήκη is used explicitly

---

1. Unfortunately, many tend to downplay the overall significance of "covenant" in Hebrews, e.g., Michael D. Morrison, *Who Needs a New Covenant? Rhetorical Function of Covenant Motif in the Argument of Hebrews* (Eugene, OR: Pickwick, 2008); Barnabas Lindars, *The Theology of the Letter to the Hebrews*, NTT (Cambridge: Cambridge University Press, 1991), 94–98, 124–27. Others see it as one of the main categories, e.g., Geerhardus Vos, "Hebrews, the Epistle of the *Diatheke*" (part 1), *PTR* 13, no. 4 (1915): 587–632, esp. 592; Vos, "Hebrews, the Epistle of the *Diatheke*" (part 2), *PTR* 14, no. 1 (1916): 1–61, esp. 52; Susanne Lehne, *The New Covenant in Hebrews*, JSNTSup 44 (Sheffield, UK: Sheffield Academic Press, 1990), 94–95.

2. As is well known, many argue that διαθήκη should be translated as "testament"/"will" in Heb. 9:16–17, e.g., Philip Edgcumbe Hughes, *A Commentary on the Epistle to the Hebrews* (Grand Rapids, MI: Eerdmans, 1977), 368–73; Vos, "Hebrews, the Epistle of the *Diatheke*" (part 1), 613–18; Craig R. Koester, *Hebrews: A New Translation with Introduction and Commentary*, AB 36 (New York: Doubleday, 2001), 417–18; WCF 7.4. Arguing for "covenant" as the proper translation are, e.g., John J. Hughes, "Hebrews IX 15ff. and Galatians III 15ff.: A Study in Covenant Practice and Procedure," *NovT* 21, no. 1 (1979): 27–96; Scott W. Hahn, "A Broken Covenant and the Curse of Death: A Study of Hebrews 9:15–22," *CBQ* 66, no. 3 (2004): 416–36.

3. Similarly, the cognate verb διατίθημι ("to make a covenant or arrangement," "to establish or confer") is used four times in Hebrews (8:10; 9:16, 17; 10:16) and only three times elsewhere in the New Testament, all by Luke (Luke 22:29 [*bis*]; Acts 3:25). All uses in Hebrews of διατίθημι are in the same verses where διαθήκη is also used. In the "Protestant" Septuagint (the Septuagint proper includes more books than the Protestant/Jewish Old Testament canonical books), διατίθημι occurs eighty-one times. Among other uses in the Septuagint, the term primarily translates כרת ("to cut") as part of the common idiomatic phrase "to cut a covenant" (e.g., Gen. 15:18; Ex. 24:8; Pss. 89:3; 105:9). Other Greek verbs are used for כרת when it is not used in the phrase "to cut a covenant" (e.g., Ex. 4:25; Prov. 2:22). (All references in this chapter, including the Septuagint, are based on English Bible chapter and versification, unless specifically noted.)

seventeen times and is idiomatically implied (e.g., the "first" and the "second" [Heb. 8:7]) an additional eight times for a total of twenty-five references.[4]

Of the twenty-five uses of διαθήκη in Hebrews, twenty-two of them are included in one major section, Hebrews 7:1–10:18 (the remaining three are 10:29; 12:24; 13:20). This section especially emphasizes the priesthood of Christ and his sacrificial labors on our behalf. Although Christ is conceptually assumed to be our priest in many New Testament texts, only in Hebrews is Christ explicitly called "priest" (ἱερεύς, e.g., 7:11; 8:4; 10:21) and "high priest" (ἀρχιερεύς, e.g., 2:17; 3:1; 4:14; 6:20; 8:1; 9:11). Hence, in Hebrews 7:1–10:18 there is the unusual concentration of *both* "covenant" and "priest"/"high priest."

In Hebrews, the term διαθήκη is used to refer to both the first/old covenant and the second/new/better/eternal covenant (e.g., 7:22; 8:7, 13; 13:20), that is, the Mosaic covenant and the new covenant. In addition to these two covenants, Hebrews also includes arguments from the Abrahamic covenant (e.g., 6:15; 11:9, 17–18) and the Davidic covenant (e.g., 1:5, 13; 5:5–6), though without using the term διαθήκη. Therefore, the author of Hebrews makes significant reference to four covenants: Abrahamic, Mosaic, Davidic, and new.

Although implied in all books of the Bible, the grand sweep of redemptive history with its emphasis on Christ is very explicit in the book of Hebrews (e.g., 1:1–2; 9:15; 10:9–10; 11:39–40). Within this grand sweep, the book displays both continuities and discontinuities within God's plan. The author of Hebrews uses his understanding of biblical covenants and other realities to explicate these.

The Old Testament has many terms and expressions that describe the triune God's multifaceted promises. Often multiple terms describe the same reality. Jeremiah's promise of a "new covenant" (Jer. 31:31) is the only use of this expression in the Old Testament. In the New Testament, outside of Hebrews, this exact expression occurs only three times (Luke 22:20; 1 Cor. 11:25; 2 Cor. 3:6). The author of Hebrews, however, quotes twice from the Jeremiah 31:31–34 passage (Heb. 8:8–12; 10:16–17) and has by far the longest sustained discussion of the "new covenant" and its relationship to the old covenant in the New Testament (7:1–10:18).

Within this chapter, my primary aim is to present an exposition of the details of the Abrahamic, Mosaic, Davidic, and new covenants as found in Hebrews. To do this adequately, I also note the broad redemptive-historical movement within Hebrews, which I term *contrast within continuity*. Not surprisingly, I conclude that Hebrews conforms to the traditional Reformed view of one covenant of grace administered differently during various dispensations. Because of space, I do not discuss the covenant of redemption, the covenant of works, or the Noahic covenant.[5]

---

4. Explicit use of διαθήκη: Heb. 7:22; 8:6, 8, 9 (*bis*), 10; 9:4 (*bis*), 15 (*bis*), 16, 17, 20; 10:16, 29; 12:24; 13:20. Idiomatically implied: Heb. 8:7 (*bis*), 13 (*bis*); 9:1, 18; 10:9 (*bis*).

5. Texts that may apply to the covenant of redemption include Heb. 3:2; 6:18–20; 7:20–22; 9:15; 10:5–9; 13:20. The primary texts that relate at some level to the covenant of works are Heb. 3:16–19; 8:8–9. As to my

Contrast within Continuity

Hebrews presents discontinuities or contrasts between the Old Testament and the current ("now") New Testament age and also between the "now" New Testament age (partial eschaton) and the final "not yet" New Testament age (full eschaton). This final "not yet" New Testament age is the full eschatological new heavens and new earth. Hebrews also presents aspects of continuity between the Old Testament, the "now" New Testament, and the new heavens and new earth. I prefer to designate this relationship of discontinuities and continuities as *contrast within continuity*. There are two basic types of *contrasts* throughout redemptive history: (1) antithetical, for example, oath versus no oath (Heb. 7:20) or stand versus sit (10:11–12); and (2) graded (better, superior, escalating), for example, shadow versus reality (10:1). Both of these types of contrasts are set within a more fundamental *continuity*. That is, the continuity of *God* and his redemptive plan is more basic than the contrasts taking place as this plan unfolds.

Included in Hebrews are both God's redemptive actions (e.g., 1:3; 4:1; 6:15; 10:17; 11:40; 13:20) and God's speaking his word in a variety of ways (e.g., 1:1–2; 3:7; 4:12; 8:8; 10:15; 13:7).[6] These actions and words are presented as occurring throughout redemptive history. This is not simply a "flat" line of equal blessings throughout redemptive history; rather, God's unfolding plan includes *progressive* escalation of God's presence and benefits.[7] This general-progressive aspect matches well to the covenant idea that clearly includes it. As Vos persuasively argues, the author of Hebrews uses and assumes the "covenant-idea" because it well matches the "historic progress of the movement of redemption and special revelation."[8] This covenantal movement inherently includes, to

view, the Mosaic covenant is part of the covenant of grace (WCF 7.5), but there is a secondary sense that a works principle is included in it. I do not believe, however, in the "republication" view, although my view has continuity with it. See Robert J. Cara, *Cracking the Foundation of the New Perspective on Paul: Covenantal Nomism versus Reformed Covenantal Theology*, REDS (Fearn, Ross-shire, Scotland: Mentor, 2017), 43–50, esp. 46, 46n24. John Owen strongly ties the covenant of works to the Mosaic covenant and at points denies that the Mosaic covenant is a covenant of grace, but he also makes distinctions between a testament, a covenant, and an absolute covenant that complicate the issue. See Owen, *An Exposition of the Epistle to the Hebrews*, vols. 17–23 of *The Works of John Owen*, ed. William H. Goold (Carlisle, PA: Banner of Truth, 1991), 21:391–92; 22:58–113. For an excellent discussion of Owen's view, see Joel R. Beeke and Mark Jones, *A Puritan Theology: Doctrine for Life* (Grand Rapids, MI: Reformation Heritage Books, 2012), 293–303. The Noahic covenant could be included based on Heb. 11:7.

6. Concerning God's speaking in Hebrews, see Jonathan I. Griffiths, *Hebrews and Divine Speech*, LNTS 507 (London: T&T Clark, 2014).

7. The superiority or escalation of the New Testament relative to the Old Testament is important in Hebrews. Andrew T. Lincoln comments, "The exposition sections are all variations on the theme of the comparison between the previous stage of God's revelation to Israel and the final and superior stage of that revelation in Christ." *Hebrews: A Guide* (London: T&T Clark, 2006), 52. Lehne opts for the "hermeneutical scheme of 'correspondence, contrast, superiority.'" *New Covenant in Hebrews*, 97–104, esp. 97. Richard B. Hays presents eight exegetical arguments that the author of Hebrews used to show that the new covenant comes from the Old Testament. "'Here We Have No Lasting City': New Covenantalism in Hebrews," in *The Epistle to the Hebrews and Christian Theology*, ed. Richard Bauckham, Daniel R. Driver, Trevor A. Hart, and Nathan MacDonald (Grand Rapids, MI: Eerdmans, 2009), 151–73, esp. 156–64.

8. Vos, "Hebrews, the Epistle of the *Diatheke*" (part 2), 1–19, esp. 1. For connecting Old Testament covenants to God's words, see Dennis J. McCarthy, *Treaty and Covenant: A Study in the Ancient Oriental Documents and in the Old Testament*, rev. ed., AnBib 21A (Rome: Biblical Institute Press, 1981), 157, 277. For connecting covenants to redemptive history, God's words, and canon, see Michael J. Kruger, *Canon Revisited: Establishing the Origins and Authority of the New Testament Books* (Wheaton, IL: Crossway, 2012), 108–11.

use my language, a contrast-within-continuity character. That is, some of the movement includes escalating (progressive) contrasts, as Vos emphasized, but some also includes antithetical contrasts. Hence, I view all aspects of this contrast within continuity as broadly related to the covenant idea.

The majestic opening of Hebrews presents contrast within continuity: "Long ago, at many times and in many ways, God spoke to our fathers by the prophets, but in these last days he has spoken to us by his Son" (Heb. 1:1–2). The contrast is obvious between the two redemptive periods, with the "last days" being superior because of the Son. The continuity is shown by God's speaking in both the Old Testament and the New Testament. The importance of God's speaking even in the Old Testament is further emphasized in context as Hebrews 1:5–13 has seven Old Testament quotes (in order of quotation: Ps. 2:7; 2 Sam. 7:14 // 1 Chron. 17:13; Deut. 32:43; Pss. 104:4; 45:6–7; 102:25–27; 110:1).

Another aspect of continuity is the people of God, and this is especially related to their "faith."[9] Hebrews 3:7–4:13 narrates the Old Testament and New Testament "people of God" and their search for "rest." Hebrews 4:2–3 reads, "For good news came [εὐαγγελίζω] to us [New Testament people] just as to them [Old Testament people], but the message they heard did not benefit them, because they were not united by *faith* [πίστις] with those who listened. For we who have *believed* [πιστεύω] enter that rest."[10] Hebrews 10:36–11:40 famously uses the faith of the "people of old" (πρεσβύτερος, 11:2) as an encouragement for New Testament saints to persevere.[11] The author of Hebrews simply assumes continuity between the Old Testament and New Testament relative to faith. The "house" metaphor is also used to connect the Old Testament and New Testament people of God (3:5–6; 10:21).[12] A final example of continuity between the Old Testament and New Testament relative to the people of God is Hebrews 13:5–6. The readers are being exhorted, "Be content with what you have." In this context, the author of Hebrews quotes Joshua 1:5 and Psalm 118:6 and applies these verses directly to the readers (similarly, Heb. 12:5–6 // Prov. 3:11–12).[13] That is, these two Old Testament words of assurance apply to both Old Testament and New Testament believers, which in turn emphasizes the continuity between them. On the other hand, the author of Hebrews introduces some contrast between the Old

---

9. "The relationship between the old and new systems is not simply one of contrast. There is also a strong element of continuity. This is provided by the concept of faith." I. Howard Marshall, *New Testament Theology: Many Witnesses, One Gospel* (Downers Grove, IL: InterVarsity Press, 2004), 613.

10. See the discussion by Hughes, who concludes that there is a "real equivalence between the *promise* of the Old Testament and the *evangel* of the New Testament." He also notes the connections of Heb. 4:2 with Gal. 3:8 and Rom. 10:14. *Hebrews*, 156–57; emphasis original.

11. Also, Abraham (Heb. 6:13–14) is used as an example of "those who through *faith* and patience inherit the promises" (6:12).

12. Similarly, the comment that Christ "helps the offspring [seed] of Abraham" refers to Old Testament and New Testament believers (Heb. 2:16).

13. Not all agree that "I will never leave you nor forsake you" comes from Josh. 1:5. Other options include Gen. 28:15; Deut. 31:6, 8; 1 Chron. 28:20.

Testament and New Testament believers based on Jeremiah's new covenant prophecy (Heb. 8:10–11).

A significant example of contrast within continuity is the relationship between the Old Testament tabernacle, the heavenly tabernacle, and Christ's atoning work. The Old Testament tabernacle is associated with the Mosaic covenant. The tabernacle clearly looks forward to the reality of Christ's atoning work. Moses's faithful actions, including his speaking, writings, and the tabernacle itself, did "testify to the things that were to be spoken later" (3:5). "The law has but a shadow of the good things to come" (10:1). Christ was "the greater and more perfect tent" (9:11). The Old Testament blood sacrifices foreshadowed Christ's blood atonement (e.g., 9:12–22; 10:19; 12:24; 13:20).

In addition to the Old Testament tabernacle's looking forward, it also looks "up" to the heavenly temple. That is, the Old Testament tabernacle is not simply a shadow of the future reality of Christ, it is also a shadow of the heavenly reality about the preincarnate Christ, who existed when Moses wrote the Pentateuch.[14] The Old Testament priests "serve a copy and shadow of the heavenly things. For when Moses was about to erect the tent, he was instructed by God, saying, 'See that you make everything according to the pattern that was shown you on the mountain'" (8:5, quoting Ex. 25:40; cf. Heb. 9:23–24). To say it another way, in the new covenant, the old covenant and its heavenly reality of the preincarnate Christ became the full substance of that reality in Christ's New Testament work. The Old Testament tabernacle was a shadow of the new covenant both as it relates to the heavenly, preincarnate Christ and the future, full New Testament reality of Christ.[15] This heavenly reality that always existed explains well (1) the use of "eternal" (αἰώνιος) with "salvation" (5:9), "redemption" (9:12), "inheritance" (9:15), and "covenant" (13:20), and (2) the fact that Christ is "the same yesterday and today and forever" (13:8). Hence, this heavenly reality provides a fundamental grounding of the continuity between the old and new covenants.

Exposition of Four Covenants in Hebrews
Abrahamic Covenant

Although not using the term "covenant," the Old Testament Abrahamic and Davidic covenants are a significant part of the author of Hebrews's theology and understanding of biblical covenants.

---

14. By "preincarnate Christ," I am referring to Christ as the eternal, divine Son of God before he took on flesh at conception. The word "incarnate" means to have taken on flesh (cf. WCF 8.6).

15. Vos puts it wonderfully, "The bond that links the Old and New Covenant together is not a purely evolutionary one, inasmuch as the one has grown out of the other; it is, if we may so call it, a transcendental bond; the New Covenant in its preëxistent, heavenly state reaches back and stretches its eternal wings over the Old." "Hebrews, the Epistle of the *Diatheke*" (part 2), 12. Also see Geerhardus Vos's often-used triangle to represent this idea. *The Teaching of the Epistle to the Hebrews*, ed. Johannes G. Vos (Phillipsburg, NJ: Presbyterian and Reformed, 1956), 57.

To state the obvious, the Abrahamic covenant is prominent in the Old Testament.[16] Key events are the calling of Abram to go to Canaan and his being a blessing to many (Gen. 12:1–4); the explicit making of a covenant (a smoking fire pot) and the promise of giving the land to Abram's seed (15:12–21); an everlasting covenant between God and Abraham and his seed, a covenant of circumcision, and a promise that he will be a father of many nations (17:1–14); and Abraham's offering up of Isaac and God's oath to bless Abraham and his seed (22:1–19).

In Hebrews, Abraham is mentioned in four contexts and implied in one.[17] First, Christ "helps the offspring [seed] of Abraham" (Heb. 2:16). This has a clear connection to Genesis 17:9 and the Abrahamic covenant. It implies the continuity of Old Testament and New Testament believers.

Second, Hebrews 6:12 encourages the reader to imitate those who have inherited the promises. Hebrews 6:13–14 assumes and quickly summarizes Genesis 22:1–19. God's promise (oath) to Abraham after Isaac's rescue is "I will surely bless you, and I will surely multiply your offspring" (Gen. 22:16–17). Hebrews 6:15 concludes that Abraham is an example of one who inherited an aspect of the promise (i.e., Isaac and the seed continue). In context, both the inviolability of God's promises/oath/blessing and the resulting example of Abraham are encouragements to the reader.[18] The promise mentioned from Genesis 22:17 probably evokes all the promises to Abraham (Gen. 12:2, 3, 7; 13:14–17; 15:5–7; 17:4–8, 19),[19] which promises are intimately connected to the Abrahamic covenant.

Third, Abraham is mentioned several times in reference to the Melchizedek discussion (Heb. 7:1–10; cf. Gen. 14:17–24; Ps. 110:4). In context, the author of Hebrews is demonstrating the superiority of the Melchizedekian priesthood (Christ's) to the Levitical. Abraham represents the Levitical, and the superiority of Melchizedek is shown by Abraham giving a tithe to him. Abraham is given the epithets "the patriarch" (Heb. 7:4) and "him who had the promises" (7:6). Note that (1) through Levi, Abraham is associated with the Mosaic covenant and its deficiencies (7:7, 18, 22, 28), and (2) Abraham is again positively associated with promises.

Fourth, Abraham is included in the great heroes-of-the-faith chapter (Heb. 11:8–12, 17–19). Hebrews 11 refers to Abraham's initial call to receive his inheritance, land promise, and being a fellow heir of promise with Isaac and Jacob (Gen. 12:1–4; 15:7; Ex.

16. Prominent New Testament discussions include Acts 7; Rom. 4; Gal. 3. For other texts from noncanonical Second Temple Judaism literature, see Harold W. Attridge, *A Commentary on the Epistle to the Hebrews*, Hermeneia (Philadelphia: Fortress, 1989), 322n11.

17. For discussions of Abraham in Hebrews, see J. Swetnam, *Jesus and Isaac: A Study of the Epistle to the Hebrews in the Light of the Aqedah* (Rome: Biblical Institute Press, 1981); Lehne, *New Covenant in Hebrews*, 19–22; N. Calvert-Koyzis, "Abraham," in *Dictionary of the Later New Testament and Its Developments*, ed. Ralph P. Martin and Peter H. Davids (Downers Grove, IL: InterVarsity Press, 1997), 1–6, esp. 2–4.

18. For a similar exegesis, see Thomas R. Schreiner, *Commentary on Hebrews*, BTCP (Nashville: Holman Reference, 2015), 197–200.

19. So also Paul Ellingworth, *The Epistle to the Hebrews: A Commentary on the Greek Text*, NIGTC (Grand Rapids, MI: Eerdmans, 1993), 335.

2:24); Abraham's understanding that he was ultimately looking for a city built by God; Sarah and Abraham's having a child past age (Gen. 21:1–7); Abraham's seed being like the "stars of heaven" and "the sand that is on the seashore" (22:17; cf. 15:5; 32:12); and the offering up and rescue of Isaac (22:1–19), with the fulfillment that "through Isaac shall [Abraham's] offspring [seed] be named" (21:12; cf. Rom. 9:7). Here, as one of the heroes of faith, Abraham is presented as a positive example. Again, God's promises are associated with Abraham. These promises include the land (Heb. 11:9), the multitude of seed (11:12, 18), and the understanding that the promise includes the new heavens and new earth, with a "better" and "heavenly" country (11:10, 13–16; cf. 13:14). Note (1) that the term "promise" is clearly associated with the Abrahamic covenant in this context and (2) that the terms "better" (κρείττων) and "heavenly" (ἐπουράνιος) from Hebrews 11:16 are also associated with the new covenant (e.g., 7:7, 22; 8:6; 11:35; 12:24), which shows that the Abrahamic covenant itself included an unfolding and escalating component that is being fulfilled in the new covenant.

Fifth, the author of Hebrews says, "Do not neglect to show hospitality to strangers, for thereby some have entertained angels unawares" (Heb. 13:2). As to entertaining angels without realizing it, the author of Hebrews implicitly reminds the reader of Abraham, Lot, Gideon, and the parents of Samson (Gen. 18:1–15; 19:1–22; Judg. 6:11–23; 13:3–21).[20] The Old Testament people of God are again used as an example for the New Testament people of God. Abraham is the most prominent of the examples. This exemplary exegesis shows continuity between the Old Testament and the New Testament.

Allow me to expand the discussion based on the above. In Hebrews God's "promises" (ἐπαγγελία, noun; ἐπαγγέλλομαι, verb) are prominent in the texts featuring Abraham. These promises are clearly related to the Abrahamic-covenantal contexts in the Old Testament, even though the author of Hebrews does not use the term "covenant."[21] Promises in Hebrews have been partially realized in the Old Testament (Heb. 6:15; 11:9, 33) and have significant continuity with (and escalation into) the current New Testament age and the coming new heavens and new earth (e.g., 4:1; 10:18, 36; 11:39). In fact, the word "promise" itself implies a starting point when the promise was given but also has a forward, progressive aspect. Hence, the word "promise" itself shows escalating contrast within an overarching continuity between the Abrahamic and new covenants. In addition, these Old Testament promises are contrasted, or better yet, the Christological work to obtain these promises is contrasted, with the new covenant—"better promises" (8:6) and "promised eternal inheritance" (9:15).

---

20. List from Simon J. Kistemaker, *Exposition of the Epistle to the Hebrews*, NTC (Grand Rapids, MI: Baker, 1984), 408.

21. The terms ἐπαγγελία and ἐπαγγέλλομαι are rare in the "Protestant" Septuagint. Lehne believes that the distinction in Hebrews between ἐπαγγελία and διαθήκη "shows the hand of a careful theologian" in order to maintain the distinction between the new covenant (ἐπαγγελία) and the Mosaic covenant (διαθήκη). *New Covenant in Hebrews*, 19. Morrison comments, "To avoid confusing the contrast [between the Mosaic and new covenants, Hebrews] does not use the word 'covenant' for Abraham—probably due to rhetorical strategy." *Who Needs a Covenant?*, 141.

Two of the primary benefits/promises of the Old Testament Abrahamic covenant are land and the people of God. The author of Hebrews discusses both. The "land of promise" (11:9) (also alluded to by the terms "rest" and "city") is seen as escalating from the physical land of Canaan to the complete fulfillment in the new heavens and new earth (e.g., 3:7–4:13; 11:13–15; 13:14). The people of God attached to the Abrahamic covenant are seen as a straight-line continuity from Abraham to the New Testament age and to the new heavens and new earth (e.g., 6:14; 11:18; 12:22–24).[22]

Within Hebrews 7:1–10, Abraham is associated with the Levitical priesthood and its connection to the Mosaic law, which is contrasted with Melchizedek and his connection to the new covenant. Hence, this shows some level of antithetical contrast. This is a minority use of Abraham in Hebrews, but it does fit the Old Testament biblical data and does dovetail with the author of Hebrews's nuanced understanding that some aspects of Old Testament covenants have an antithetical contrast to the new covenant.

In sum, the author of Hebrews has a clear understanding and use of the Abrahamic covenant. It is associated with promise, land, and the people of God. This understanding is presented primarily as a progressive and escalating contrast within a significant continuity that spans from Abraham to the new heavens and new earth. The author of Hebrews includes a minor antithetical contrast by comparing the Levitical and Melchizedekian priesthoods.

Davidic Covenant

Similar to its treatment of the Abrahamic covenant, Hebrews highlights the Davidic covenant, though without using the term "covenant."[23]

In the Old Testament, the inauguration of the Davidic covenant is narrated by the influential 2 Samuel 7 // 1 Chronicles 17 passage (cf. 2 Sam. 23:5; 1 Chron. 22:10; 28:6; 2 Chron. 1:8; Pss. 89:3–4; 132:11–12; Isa. 7:14; 9:6–7; 11:1; Jer. 23:5; 33:14–22; Ezek. 34:23–24; Mic. 5:2; Luke 1:32; Acts 2:30; Rom. 1:3–4).[24] David is concerned that the ark of God needs a "house" (temple) (2 Sam. 7:1–3). God tells Nathan to tell David that his son (Solomon) will build the "house" (both temple and dynasty) and that David's throne and kingdom will be established forever (2 Sam. 7:4–17). In fact, God declares that he will be a father to David's line and that the line will be a son to God (2 Sam. 7:14 // 1 Chron. 17:13). After hearing Nathan's words, David thanks God for these covenantal promises (2 Sam. 7:18–24) and asks for the fulfillment of these promises (2 Sam. 7:25–29).

---

22. In association with the new covenant and the Jeremiah prophecy, the author of Hebrews introduces aspects of contrast between the Old Testament and New Testament people of God (Heb. 8:10–11).

23. See Lehne's discussion of the "Royal-Priestly (Davidic) Traditions" in Hebrews, in *New Covenant in Hebrews*, 27–30, 32.

24. For an extended discussion of the Davidic covenant, see O. Palmer Robertson, *The Christ of the Covenants* (Phillipsburg, NJ: Presbyterian and Reformed, 1980), 229–69.

In Hebrews 1, the author of Hebrews especially connects Christ the (divine) Son to the Davidic covenant. Preeminently, he shows this relationship by quoting from the 2 Samuel 7 passage, "I will be to him a father, and he shall be to me a son" (2 Sam. 7:14 // 1 Chron. 17:13 // Heb. 1:5). The author of Hebrews asserts that ultimately this promise to (or covenant with) David was really the promise to (or covenant with) Christ. With this understanding of Christ as the true Davidic King, three royal psalms are quoted and applied to Christ in Hebrews 1. Psalm 2:7 emphasizes Christ's sonship (Heb. 1:5); Psalm 45:6–7, Christ's throne, anointing, and divinity (Heb. 1:8–9); and the often-quoted Psalm 110:1, Christ's ascension and coming judgment (Heb. 1:13; cf. 1:3).[25] Also, Psalm 102:25–27 (Heb. 1:10–12), concerning God's actions in creation and providence, is also applied to Christ the Son. Finally, the royal/Davidic imagery in Hebrews 1 includes "heir of all things" (1:2), "right hand" (1:3), "firstborn" (1:6), and divine/kingly power in creation and providence (1:2–3). Within Hebrews 1, the Davidic covenant is simply assumed to be the covenant with Christ. It emphasizes Christ's royal office: his sonship, kingship, divinity, power over all things, ascension, and coming in judgment.[26] Foreshadowing what will become explicit later in Hebrews, Christ's royal office is also connected to his priestly office in Hebrews 1:3: "After making purification of sins, he sat down at the right hand of the Majesty on high."

In addition to Hebrews 1, Hebrews 5:4–6 also clearly assumes the Davidic covenant. Here Aaron's action of not taking honor to himself but obeying God's call to be a high priest (Ex. 28:1; Lev. 8; Num. 3:10; 18:1) is paralleled by Christ. To prove this about Christ, the author of Hebrews quotes from Psalm 2:7 ("You are my Son, today I have begotten you," Heb. 5:5) and Psalm 110:4 ("You are a priest forever, after the order of Melchizedek," Heb. 5:6). In addition to showing that Christ did not wrongly take the priestly honor but was appointed[27] by God, the author of Hebrews uses these two quotes to connect the kingship of Christ ("Son") with his priesthood. He connects the two *not* through the Mosaic covenant but through the kingly/priestly connections to Melchizedek.[28]

After Psalm 110:4 is quoted in Hebrews 5:6, it is quoted again in Hebrews 7:17 and 7:21. Within Hebrews 7:13–17, Psalm 110:4 is quoted to confirm that Christ is in the "likeness of Melchizedek" because he (1) is not bodily from Aaron based on law and (2) does have an indestructible life ("You are a priest forever").[29] The royal/Davidic office is assumed by the use of Psalm 110 and the previous connection between Psalms 2

25. The standard critical studies of Ps. 110 in the New Testament are David M. Hay, *Glory at the Right Hand: Psalm 110 in Early Christianity*, SBLMS 18 (Atlanta: Society of Biblical Literature, 1989); Martin Hengel, *Studies in Early Christology* (Edinburgh: T&T Clark, 1995), 119–226, concerning Hebrews, 145–48, 221–22.

26. Cf. WSC 26 and WLC 45.

27. William L. Lane comments, "[The author of Hebrews] correctly interprets Ps. 2:7 ['begotten'] as a declaration of appointment, not of parentage." *Hebrews 1–8*, WBC 47A (Dallas: Word Books, 1991), 118.

28. For a discussion of Ps. 110:4 in Hebrews, see Simon Kistemaker, *The Psalm Citations in the Epistle of Hebrews* (1961; repr., Eugene, OR: Wipf and Stock, 2010), 37, 116–24.

29. F. F. Bruce clarifies, "The Aaronic priesthood itself is described as 'an everlasting priesthood' (Ex. 40:15; cf. Jer. 33:18), but no individual member of the priesthood is described as an everlasting priest." *The Epistle of Hebrews*, rev. ed., NICNT (Grand Rapids, MI: Eerdmans, 1990), 169n58.

and 110 in Hebrews 5:5–6, and it is explicitly confirmed by the comment "Our Lord was descended from Judah" (Heb. 7:14).[30]

Within Hebrews 7:20–22, the author of Hebrews includes the first half of Psalm 110:4, which refers to an oath. Christ is antithetically contrasted with the Aaronic priests. Although the Aaronic priestly line was appointed by God, it was not done with a direct oath from God. God the Father, however, did make an oath with Christ the priest.[31] Psalm 110:4 is quoted to prove this point. Following the quote, the author of Hebrews concludes with the first explicit reference to the term "covenant" in Hebrews: "This makes Jesus the guarantor [ἔγγυος] of a better covenant [διαθήκη]" (Heb. 7:22). The oath appears to confirm that a covenant was made.[32] The covenant with Jesus is "better" because (1) it is founded on an oath from God and (2) it is guaranteed forever since Jesus will live forever.[33] This "better covenant" (Heb. 7:22) refers to the new covenant, but it has close associations to the Davidic through Psalm 110:4. In sum, in Hebrews 7:20–22 the priests of the Mosaic covenant are antithetically contrasted with Christ the priest in relation to God's oath. This contrast makes Christ the guarantor of the new and better covenant. Psalm 110:4 as part of a royal psalm brings in Davidic covenant assumptions with the focus on the priestly office to show that the new covenant is better than the Mosaic covenant.

Hebrews 10:12–13 includes a partial quote of Psalm 110:1. This again connects the royal office of Christ to his priestly office as he performed his priestly duties and then sat on a throne (cf. Heb. 1:3; 8:1).[34] In context, the author of Hebrews is comparing the Aaronic priests, who must *stand* and offer *many* sacrifices, with Christ, who *sat* and offered *one* sacrifice: "But when Christ had offered for all time a single sacrifice for sins, he sat down at the right hand of God, waiting from that time until his enemies should be made a footstool for his feet" (Heb. 10:12–13). The sitting of Christ in context implies that he does not have to stand and offer continual (hence ineffectual) sacrifices.[35] The sitting at the right hand of God also evokes a royal aspect of the Davidic covenant. Christ is certainly a priest but a priest on his throne.[36]

---

30. Contra Attridge, who sees no "christological reflections on the basis of a Davidic relationship." *Hebrews*, 201.

31. This recalls Heb. 6:13–20 and the inviolability of God's promises related to oaths.

32. J. V. Fesko well connects oaths to covenants and then to the covenant of redemption. *The Trinity and the Covenant of Redemption* (Fearn, Ross-shire, Scotland: Mentor, 2016), 96–105. McCarthy emphasizes that Old Testament covenants, paralleling ancient Near Eastern treaties, include oaths. He lists Gen. 21:22–24, 27, 31; 26:26–30; Josh. 9:15; Neh. 6:18 with Gen. 14:13. *Treaty and Covenant*, 185, 253, 253n18.

33. John Calvin states, "This principle is to be continually kept in mind, that a priest is made to be the guarantor of a covenant." *The Epistle of Paul the Apostle to the Hebrews and the First and Second Epistles of St. Peter*, trans. William B. Johnson, vol. 12 of *Calvin's New Testament Commentaries*, ed. David W. Torrance and Thomas F. Torrance (Grand Rapids, MI: Eerdmans, 1963), 100.

34. Some see royal imagery mixed with priestly also in Heb. 13:20–21 by combining the "great shepherd" with the "blood of the eternal covenant." E.g., Hurtado, "Christology," in Martin and Davids, *Dictionary of the Later New Testament*, 170–84, esp. 172.

35. So also William L. Lane, *Hebrews 9–13*, WBC 47B (Dallas: Word Books, 1991), 267; Luke Timothy Johnson, *Hebrews: A Commentary*, NTL (Louisville: Westminster John Knox, 2006), 253–54.

36. So emphasized by John Brown, *An Exposition of Hebrews*, GSC (1862; repr., Carlisle, PA: Banner of Truth, 1961), 446.

For completeness, it is noted that Hebrews refers to the historical person David only twice. In Hebrews 4:7, God speaks "through David" in a quote of Psalm 95:7–8. In Hebrews 11:32, the author of Hebrews states that he does not have time to discuss David and several others.

To summarize so far, the Davidic covenant is prominent in the Old Testament and in Hebrews. In Hebrews 1:5, this covenant is clearly referenced by the quote of 2 Samuel 7:14 // 1 Chronicles 17:13. By use of this quote, the covenant is also explicitly connected to Psalm 2:7 (Heb. 1:5) and Psalm 110:1 (Heb. 1:13). These verses in Hebrews 1 emphasize the Son and the royal aspects of the Davidic covenant. Later, the author of Hebrews also explicitly connects Psalm 2:7 to 110:4 (Heb. 5:5–6). This then connects the royal aspects of Christ's work to its priestly aspects for the first time in Hebrews. Psalm 110:4 is later quoted in Hebrews 7:17 and 7:21, again with the emphasis on Christ's priesthood and a close verbal connection to the new covenant. Finally, Hebrews 10:12–13 references Psalm 110:1 again, and here Christ as priest sits on his royal throne.

In terms of contrast within continuity, there is a straight-line continuity between the Davidic covenant and Christ because the Davidic covenant is ultimately assumed to have been made with Christ. In Hebrews 7:20–22, there is a very close verbal connection between the new covenant and the Davidic covenant. This is another aspect of continuity. The connection between Melchizedek and Christ is typological, which is an escalating contrast. There are several examples of antithetical contrast between Christ and the Aaronic priesthood. Interestingly, there is one example of continuity with the Aaronic priesthood (Heb. 5:4).

To conclude concerning the Davidic covenant in Hebrews, the key Old Testament texts are 2 Samuel 7:14 // 1 Chronicles 17:13; Psalms 2:7; 110:1; and 110:4.[37] These texts all assert that the Davidic covenant was in reality made with Jesus Christ. The importance of the Davidic covenant in Hebrews is that it (1) emphasizes and confirms the divine sonship of Christ and (2) connects Christ's kingly office to his priestly office.[38]

Mosaic Covenant

The Mosaic covenant is prominent in Hebrews and is contrasted primarily with the new covenant in Hebrews 7:1–10:18.[39] As opposed to the Abrahamic and Davidic covenants, the Mosaic and new covenants are both identified using the term "covenant" (διαθήκη).

To state the obvious, Moses and the Mosaic covenant are significant in the Old Testament. The first use of the word "covenant" (ברית) in clear reference to the Mosaic

---

37. Other possible texts that may relate to the Davidic covenant are Heb. 2:5–10; 4:16; 8:10; 9:28; 10:5–7; 13:20.

38. Hurtado comments, "Throughout the book the author is primarily concerned to emphasize two christological themes: [1] Jesus' salvific death in imagery and language drawn from OT cultic traditions and [2] Jesus' exalted status in imagery drawn from OT royal tradition." "Christology," 172.

39. See Lehne's discussion of the "Mosaic Traditions, Sinai, and the Law" in Hebrews, in *New Covenant in Hebrews*, 22–27.

covenant is Exodus 19:5 (cf. Ex. 2:24; 6:4–5). Here God recounts how he saved Israel from the Egyptians. He will make them a "treasured possession," "a kingdom of priests," and "a holy nation" if they will keep his covenant (Ex. 19:5–6). The Mosaic covenant includes a significant amount of legislation. The Christian tradition has often summarized this legislation with three categories: moral (e.g., the Ten Commandments, Ex. 20:2–17; Deut. 5:6–21), ceremonial (e.g., sacrificial offering, priestly regulations, Lev. 1–8), and civil/judicial (e.g., divorce, roof regulations, Deut. 22:8; 24:1–4).[40]

Before getting directly to the Mosaic covenant in Hebrews, a few comments about Moses himself in Hebrews are enlightening.[41] Moses is emphasized in two passages.[42] First, in Hebrews 3:1–6, he is called God's "servant" and is "faithful in all God's house" (cf. Num. 12:7). Moses testified about the "things that were to be spoken later" (cf. Heb. 1:2; 8:5; 9:9, 23; 10:1). In context, Moses is used as a positive foil to Christ. Christ was also faithful (continuity) but exceeded Moses in that he is a "Son" and is a "builder" who is "over" the "house" (contrast).

The second major passage about Moses is Hebrews 11:23–28. Here he is included with the heroes of faith and is part of the "people of God" (11:25). While in Egypt, Moses was not entrapped by the "treasures of Egypt" (11:26) nor "afraid of the anger of the king" (11:27; cf. Ex. 2:14–15; Deut. 9:19; Heb. 12:21). He was aware of the "reproach of Christ" (11:26; cf. 2:9) and was aware of God, who is "invisible" (11:27). It was "by faith" that Moses "kept the Passover and sprinkled the blood, so that the Destroyer of the firstborn might not touch them" (11:28; cf. Ex. 12:1–27; Heb. 2:14). Interestingly, Moses is commended for keeping a ceremony (i.e., the Passover) in a book that contrasts sacrificial ceremonies with the reality of Christ.

The two passages above concerning Moses himself are very positive. This background about Moses predisposes the reader to see the Mosaic covenant and its legislation as part of God's plan and not, in principle, as *un*godly. That is, this "softens" the emphasis on contrast between the Mosaic and new covenants.

Now let us consider the presentation of the Mosaic covenant itself. The discussion of this covenant occurs only within Hebrews 7:1–10:18, where the primary concern is to compare the Aaronic priesthood and sacrifices with Christ's priesthood and sacrifice of himself.

The terms "covenant" and "law" are especially pertinent. The term "covenant" and "first" are used to refer to the Mosaic covenant eight times in Hebrews (8:7, 9 [*bis*], 13; 9:1, 15, 18; 10:9). "Covenant" is also used three additional times in the expressions "ark," "tablets," and "blood" of the covenant (9:4 [*bis*], 20).

In these uses of "covenant," what adjectives are used to describe the Mosaic covenant? It is most consistently called "first" (πρῶτος) (8:7, 13; 9:1, 15, 18; 10:9).[43] In

---

40. WCF 19.3–4.
41. For an in-depth discussion of Moses in Hebrews, see Mary Rose D'Angelo, *Moses in the Letter of Hebrews*, SBLDS 42 (Missoula, MT: Scholars Press, 1979).
42. Also see Heb. 3:16 (cf. 8:9); 8:5; 12:21.
43. Only in Heb. 9:15 is the full expression "first covenant."

these immediate contexts, the "first" covenant is explicitly contrasted with the "second" (δεύτερος, 8:7; 10:9), "new" (καινός, 8:13), and "better" (κρείττων, 8:6–7; cf. 7:22). Technically, the adjective "old" is never used to describe the Mosaic covenant; in Hebrews 8:13, however, the Mosaic covenant, while being called "first" and contrasted with the "new covenant," is described with two different verbs that both mean "becoming old" (παλαιόω, γηράσκω). Finally, in the quote of Jeremiah 31, the Mosaic covenant is called "my [the Lord's] covenant" (Heb. 8:9). Why the emphasis on the term "first"? I assume it relates to the first *priesthood* (Aaronic) and the second *priesthood* (Christ's) (cf. Heb. 7:11–19; 9:8; Lev. 26:45).[44]

Another important term related to the Mosaic covenant is "law" (νόμος).[45] "Law(s)" is used fourteen times in Hebrews, and, excepting one (10:28), all are within 7:1–10:18. Twelve times "law" is singular, and it always refers to the Mosaic legislation (7:5, 12, 16, 19, 28 (*bis*); 8:4; 9:19, 22; 10:1, 8, 28). Eleven of the twelve singular occurrences are within Hebrews 7:1–10:18, and all eleven refer to the *ceremonial* aspects of the law. The remaining singular occurrence refers to the *civil* use (10:28; cf. Num. 35:30). The two plural uses of "law" are both from the quote of Jeremiah 31:33 and clearly refer to the new covenant ("I will put my *laws*" into/on their minds/ hearts, Heb. 8:10; 10:16).[46] This data concerning "law" confirms that the author of Hebrews is primarily interested in the Mosaic covenant as it relates to the ceremonial aspects of the Mosaic legislation because he is interested in priesthood and sacrifices: "For when there is a change in the priesthood, there is necessarily a change in the law as well" (7:12). The further logic is that when there is a change in the law, a change in covenant is also required.

Broadening our discussion beyond the terms "covenant" and "law," many other aspects of the Mosaic covenant are presented in Hebrews 7:1–10:18. Interestingly, many times the same concept is presented using a variety of words and phrases. This covenant had a beginning by blood (8:9; 9:18–19) and was coming to an end (8:9, 13; 9:10; 10:9). The Mosaic covenant had an earthly character (7:16; 8:4; 9:1, 13) but was (and is) also a copy of the heavenly reality (8:5; 9:9, 23, 24; 10:1). Negatively, the Mosaic covenant did not achieve "perfection" for the believer (7:11, 19; 9:9; 10:1),[47] could not ultimately forgive sins (9:15; 10:4, 18), was weak and useless (7:18, 28), and had faults (8:7). These negative aspects all relate to the variety of so-called deficiencies

44. WCF 7.2–3 refers to the "first covenant" and the "second covenant." These, however, are explicitly referring to the "covenant of works" and "covenant of grace," respectively. Hence, the WCF is not taking its "first" and "second" language from Hebrews. There are no scriptural footnotes to Hebrews in WCF 7.2–3, although there are for WCF 7.4.

45. The cognate verb νομοθετέω ("to enact law") is used twice, once in reference to the Mosaic legislation (Heb. 7:11) and once, to the new covenant (Heb. 8:6).

46. The Masoretic Text has "law" as singular, and the Septuagint has plural. I discern no special importance to whether "law" is singular or plural. The plural use is simply due to the Septuagint quote.

47. "Perfection" in Hebrews relates to reaching the intended goal or being made fit for service. See David Peterson, *Hebrews and Perfection: An Examination of the Concept of Perfection in the "Epistle to the Hebrews,"* SNTSMS 47 (Cambridge: Cambridge University Press, 1982).

of the Aaronic priesthood and sacrifices, that is, the ceremonial aspects of the Mosaic legislation.[48] Of course, these deficiencies are an intended part of God's Old Testament revelation, and they point ultimately to Christ.

In addition to these deficiencies, the author of Hebrews adds the sin of Israel, "for he [God] finds fault with them . . . for they did not continue in my covenant" (Heb. 8:8–9; cf. 3:19).[49] Here, within the Jeremiah 31 quote, the Mosaic covenant is clearly referred to, but technically it is not restricted to the ceremonial aspects as elsewhere in Hebrews 7:1–10:18.[50] As the context of the whole book of Jeremiah shows, Israel sinned against all aspects of the Mosaic legislation (moral, ceremonial, and civil).

As to the contrast-within-continuity theme, I will use "blood" as one example of many within Hebrews 7:1–10:18.[51] Continuities include that both the high priest and Christ took blood into the Most Holy Place (9:7, 12), blood was required to inaugurate the two covenants (9:18–19), and shedding of blood is required for forgiveness (9:22). There is an escalating contrast in that since the blood of animals purified the flesh, how much more will Christ's blood purify believers (9:13–14; cf. 10:29; 12:24). The contrasts include the following: the high priest must appear every year with blood, as opposed to Christ's one appearance (9:25–26); Christ brought his own blood, not that of animals, into the Most Holy Place (9:25); and only Christ's blood, not animals' blood, can take away sins (10:4).

Hebrews 13:10–16 makes several applications to believers from the ceremonial aspects of the Mosaic covenant. The applications include "bear[ing] reproach" like Christ did while suffering "outside the camp" (Heb. 13:13; cf. Lev. 16) and "offer[ing] up a sacrifice of praise" (Heb. 13:15; cf. Lev. 7:11–18; Ps. 50:7–15). These applications show another use of the Mosaic covenant; the ceremonial law applies not in a one-to-one way to moral obligations and motivations of believers.[52]

To summarize, the person Moses is presented very positively. The Mosaic covenant is termed the "first," "becoming old," and "my (Lord's) covenant." It is primarily connected to the ceremonial aspects (priesthood, sacrifices) of the "law" in contrast to Christ's priesthood and sacrifice.[53] This covenant is a copy of the heavenly realities, but as a copy,

---

48. For an in-depth list of seventeen differences between the Mosaic and the new covenant, with discussion for each one, see Owen, *Hebrews*, 22:87–97.

49. So all major English translations. In support of the traditional translation, see Koester, *Hebrews*, 385. Some translate "finding fault with *it* [Mosaic covenant], he [God] says *to them*." This view is based partially on a variant textual reading (αὐτοῖς instead of αὐτούς). It assigns fault to the Mosaic covenant and not Israel's sin; so Hughes, *Hebrews*, 298–99.

50. So also Calvin, *Hebrews*, 109–11.

51. For a discussion of "blood" in Hebrews, see John Dunnill, *Covenant and Sacrifice in the Letter to the Hebrews*, SNTSMS 75 (Cambridge: Cambridge University Press, 1992), 227–38.

52. The Westminster divines perceptively noticed that ceremonial laws may also have moral implications for the believer: "Ceremonial laws, containing several typical ordinances; partly of worship, prefiguring Christ, His graces, actions, sufferings, and benefits; and *partly of divers instructions of moral duties.*" WCF 19.3; emphasis added.

53. There are only three exceptions to an explicit ceremonial-only use: (1) entire moral, ceremonial, civil laws as opposed to just ceremonial (Heb. 8:10); (2) civil law as opposed to ceremonial (10:28); and (3) ceremonial aspects being applied to believers as opposed to being applied to Christ (13:10–16). One citation worth mention-

it has intentional God-ordained deficiencies. Israel sins and does not keep this covenant. It ends when the heavenly reality, Christ, comes as the God-man to accomplish his work. There are numerous contrasts and continuities between the Mosaic and new covenants that occur in almost every sentence of Hebrews 7:1–10:18. To conclude, the author of Hebrews uses the Mosaic covenant primarily to understand Christ's priesthood and sacrifice within a context of the "vertical" earthly-heavenly realities and within the context of the "horizontal" redemptive-historical movement ("first" to "second").

New Covenant

Much has already been said about the new covenant as part of the previous Abrahamic, Davidic, and Mosaic covenant discussions, especially by way of contrasts and continuities. Also, in a significant sense, everything said about Christ in Hebrews—for example, his sonship, his priesthood, his being Creator, his interactions with the Father and Holy Spirit—could be subsumed under the new covenant. Therefore, for purposes of this section, I will limit the discussion from Hebrews to direct references to new covenant terminology and to the two Jeremiah 31 quotes (Heb. 8:8–12; 10:16–17).

Concerning terminology, within Hebrews the new covenant is referred to using five Greek adjectives, two of which are synonymous: "better" (7:22; 8:6), "second" (8:7; 10:9), "eternal" (13:20), "new"/καινός (8:8, 13; 9:15), and "new"/νέος (12:24).[54] Clearly, "better," "second," and "new" are primarily contrasted with the Mosaic covenant's priesthood and sacrifices. The expression "eternal covenant" brings broader nuances to the new covenant. As discussed above in the "Contrast within Continuity" section, "eternal" connects Christ's eternal, heavenly realities to believers' eternal benefits of "salvation" (5:9), "redemption" (9:12), and "inheritance" (9:15). In Reformed theology's categories, the new covenant is both an aspect of the unfolding of the covenant of grace ("better," "second," "new,") and the reality of the covenant of grace ("eternal").

In Hebrews "mediator" (μεσίτης) is a key term related to covenant and is only used explicitly of Christ and the new covenant (8:6; 9:15; 12:24; cf. 7:22, 25). Conceptually, it is contrasted to Old Testament high priests (5:1) and implicitly to Moses himself (3:2–5; 9:19–20). Andrew Lincoln argues that *mediator* is "the key [Christological] concept" in Hebrews because it (1) bridges the immense gap between a holy God and sinful man and (2) explains the dual emphasis in Hebrews of Christ being both God and sinless man.[55] Importantly, Christ's death as the one mediator is explicitly said to redeem those who have sinned in the Old Testament (9:15; cf. 1 Tim. 2:5). That Christ's death applies to Old Testament believers is a significant aspect of the heavenly reality that confirms the continuity of God's covenant structure. Similar to "covenant,"

---

ing, though it is not from the Mosaic legislation per se, is Deut. 32:35–36, which is used to describe God the Judge (Heb. 10:30).

54. With the notable exception of C. Spicq, virtually all commentators agree that καινός and νέος are synonymous in Hebrews. *L'Épître aux Hébreaux*, 2 vols., EBib (Paris: Gabalda, 1952–1953), 2:409.

55. Lincoln, *Hebrews*, 85–89, esp. 85.

"mediator" is an important term in Hebrews but is used sparingly in the remainder of the New Testament. Conceptually, however, both terms are assumed everywhere in the New Testament.[56]

Now I turn to the Jeremiah quotes. Jeremiah 31:31–34 is quoted in Hebrews 8:8–12 and a truncated Jeremiah 31:33–34 in Hebrews 10:16–17. But first, a brief discussion of the book of Jeremiah.

In the Old Testament, the term "new covenant" is used only once, in Jeremiah 31:31.[57] What is the context of Jeremiah 31? Although much of Jeremiah includes condemnation as God is sending Judah off to exile, Jeremiah 31 is part of the "Book of Consolation" (Jer. 30–33), which gives comfort to the exiles and looks forward to restoration.[58]

Within Jeremiah as a whole, explicit covenantal statements abound. Judah and Israel are condemned for not following the Mosaic covenant (7:21–26; 11:1–8; 22:8–9; 31:32; cf. 16:14–15; 23:7–8). Positively, the Mosaic covenant includes the promise "I will be your God, and you shall be my people" (7:23; cf. 30:22) and an everlasting "covenant with the Levitical priests" (33:18, 21). The Davidic covenant is very prominent and includes "righteous Branch" language (23:5–6; 30:9; 33:15–17, 21–22; cf. 30:22). The new covenant will include a renewed "heart" (24:7; 31:33; 32:39–40), the promise "you shall be my people, and I will be your God" (30:22; cf. 24:7; 31:33), and the assurance of being brought back to the land (16:14–15; 23:7–8; 25:11–12; 29:10),[59] and it is called an "everlasting covenant" (32:40; 50:5). Finally, the permanence of the day-and-night aspect of the Noahic covenant is used to confirm the permanence of God's covenantal promises (33:20–21; cf. Gen. 8:22; Jer. 31:35). As is mentioned in virtually every scholarly discussion of Jeremiah's new covenant compared to the previous covenants, there are both discontinuities and continuities.[60]

Hebrews 8:8–12 is a quote of Jeremiah 31:31–34.[61] On initial glance, it is not completely clear how this quote relates to the Hebrews 8:1–7 argument about the ceremonial law.[62] The introductory comment before the quote states that Israel sinned by not

---

56. Properly so, WCF titles chapter 8, the chapter about Christ, "Of Christ the Mediator."

57. Cf. the use of "new" in Ezek. 11:19–20; 36:26–28.

58. Peter Y. Lee comments on the book of Jeremiah, "Although the curse sections dominate the book quantitatively, the qualitative worth of the blessings is a bright beacon of hope in what would otherwise be dismal prophecies of doom." "Jeremiah," in *A Biblical-Theological Introduction to the Old Testament: The Gospel Promised*, ed. Miles V. Van Pelt (Wheaton, IL: Crossway, 2016), 277.

59. These land promises implicitly refer also to the Abrahamic covenant (cf. Jer. 33:26).

60. For a standard discussion, see Willem A. VanGemeren, *Interpreting the Prophetic Word: An Introduction to the Prophetic Literature of the Old Testament* (Grand Rapids, MI: Academie, 1990), 313–17.

61. There are no major differences between the Masoretic Text, Septuagint, and Hebrews; there are, however, several minor differences, of which two at best relate tangentially to our topic. (1) "Law" and the related pronoun "it" are singular in the Masoretic Text (Jer. 31:33), and both are plural in the Septuagint (Jer. 38:33) and Hebrews (8:10). (2) The Masoretic Text uses the idiomatic verb כרת ("to cut, establish") three times in Jer. 31:31–33. It is consistently translated three times by διατίθημι in the Septuagint (Jer. 38:31–33). In Heb. 8:8–10, however, three different functionally synonymous verbs are used: συντελέω, ποιέω, and διατίθημι.

62. Calvin rhetorically comments, "The apostle seems to do violence to this prophecy in order to suit his purpose." *Hebrews*, 109. Similarly, see David Peterson, "The Prophecy of the New Covenant in the Argument

keeping the Mosaic covenant (8:8). This obviously relates to the clause "they did not continue in my covenant" (8:9), a portion of the quote. But how does this sin of Israel explain the weakness of the Mosaic covenant itself, which has been the primary point from Hebrews 7:1 up to 8:7? Also, as some scholars suggest, is not the author of Hebrews using "laws" wrongly and assuming it is simply the ceremonial law?[63]

I present several arguments to justify the author of Hebrews's use of the Jeremiah quote:

1. A weakness of the Mosaic covenant itself is that its laws were not adequately written on hearts (Heb. 8:10).[64]
2. The fact that Jeremiah uses the expression "*new* covenant" implies that aspects of the old covenant were not adequate. This matches the author of Hebrews's concluding comments (Heb. 8:13) following the Jeremiah quote (Heb. 8:8–12).[65]
3. "Laws" as used by Jeremiah, although not exclusively referring to the ceremonial law, certainly includes them (Heb. 8:10).
4. The book of Jeremiah condemns many ceremonial, in addition to civil and moral, sins (e.g., Jer. 7:8–10; 8:19; 17:21–23); hence, it is proper in prophetic language to indicate that ceremonial laws, among others, would be written on hearts.
5. The author of Hebrews, although not agreeing that the ceremonial laws continue in a straight one-to-one manner, does apply ceremonial-law language to his audience (e.g., Heb. 10:22; 13:10–16). Hence, at some level ceremonial laws are written on New Testament believers' hearts.
6. "I will remember their sins no more" (Heb. 8:12) is taken absolutely by the author of Hebrews, based on the work of Christ (cf. Heb. 10:18). Therefore, this shows the inadequacies of the ceremonial laws to forgive sins.

The following discussion moves beyond the above broader argument to exposition. The author of Hebrews understands "behold, the days are coming" and "after those days" as referring to the new covenant being inaugurated by Christ (Heb. 8:8, 10).[66] He uses the expressions "house of Israel," "house of Judah," and "my people" to refer especially to New Testament believers (8:8, 10).

---

of Hebrews," *RTR* 38 (1979): 74–81. Both Calvin and Peterson do believe that the author of Hebrews used Jeremiah legitimately.

63. Lehne complains that the author of Hebrews "infuses the new covenant metaphor, which bears no relationship whatsoever to the cult in Jeremiah's prophecy on the new covenant, with cultic content that is rooted elsewhere in the OT." *New Covenant in Hebrews*, 120.

64. So also Calvin, *Hebrews*, 109.

65. So John Chrysostom, who notes that after showing priestly reasons, the author of Hebrews "shows more clearly by express words" that the Mosaic covenant has ended. "Homily 14 on Hebrews," in *Homilies on the Gospel of St. John and the Epistle to the Hebrews*, trans. Frederic Gardiner, vol. 14 of *Nicene and Post-Nicene Fathers*, 1st ser., ed. Philip Schaff (Peabody, MA: Hendrickson, 1995), 433–38, esp. 434.

66. From the book of Jeremiah, one might get the impression that the new covenant begins at the end of exile and their return to Canaan. But this is not the author of Hebrews's view. Therefore, the return from exile must be another aspect of typology pointing toward Christ's inauguration of the new covenant at his first coming.

That God will "write them [his laws] on their hearts" emphasizes the grace and divine initiative of the new covenant (8:10). This grace is strengthened further when one considers Christ's priesthood. Within Hebrews the reading audience is exhorted not to have an "unbelieving heart" (3:12; cf. 3:8) but to draw near to God with a "true heart" (10:22). Also, the author of Hebrews refers to "heart" in a similar way for Old Testament believers (3:8, 14). Hence, the heart aspect of the new covenant cannot imply that no one in the Old Testament had the law in their hearts. When we join the new covenant emphasis on grace and divine initiative as it relates to "heart" with the fact that at some level the Old Testament people of God had a "heart" for God, we end up with a proportional understanding of the heart. The new covenant emphasis on heart is not *absolutely* different from that of the Old Testament—God's initiative versus no initiative. It is, rather, *proportionally* different—more emphasis on God's initiative in the new covenant as compared with the old.[67]

The Jeremiah quote includes the grand covenantal language of "I will be their God, and they shall be my people." This language is part of the new covenant (Heb. 8:10; Rev. 21:3) and has connections to all covenants (e.g., Gen. 17:7; Ex. 6:7; 29:45; 2 Kings 11:17; Jer. 7:23; 24:7; 30:22).[68] Within Hebrews, similar language is used in a Davidic covenant context, "I will be to him a father, and he shall be to me a son" (Heb. 1:5), and in an Abrahamic context, "God is not ashamed to be called their God" (11:16). This all points to significant continuity across the covenants. In addition, this covenantal language dovetails well with the emphases in Hebrews to "draw near to God" (4:16; 7:25; 10:22; 11:6) and "not [neglect] to meet together" (10:25).[69]

The Jeremiah quote includes the notion that in the new covenant there will be no need for teaching each other. Why is no teaching required? "They shall all know me" (8:11). I take the emphasis of this verse as parallel to the preceding "mind"/"heart" language. God will sovereignly put his laws in our "minds," and equally so, he will make all true believers to "know" him (cf. John 6:45). As John Owen rightly states, "In the new covenant, there being an express promise of an *internal, effectual, teaching by the Spirit of God* . . ."[70] Again, similar to the heart language, I take this new covenant reality as proportional to the old covenant—God did make believers know him in the Old Testament, but relative to that, he will do so with greater emphasis in the New Testament. Also, this internal knowledge does not negate the New Testament teaching ministry, since the whole book of Hebrews is itself a teaching ministry (Heb. 13:22) and the author of Hebrews refers to teachers (5:11–12; 13:7).

---

67. See WCF 7.6 and 20.1, where new covenant realities offer "more."

68. See the classic discussion by Robertson, *Christ of the Covenants*, 45–52.

69. Though in my view he overstates his case, Morrison sees the covenant motif as primarily used in Hebrews for exhortations related to the community. *Who Needs a New Covenant?*, 158–60.

70. Owen, *Hebrews*, 17:160; emphasis original. Schreiner goes a step beyond me and further infers that the old covenant was a "mixed community" (regenerate and unregenerate) and that the new covenant community is not mixed. *Hebrews*, 252–53, 476.

Portions of Jeremiah 31:33–34 are quoted again in Hebrews 10:16–17.[71] In context this is at the end of the major Hebrews 7:1–10:18 section, which argues that Christ's priesthood is better than the Aaronic priesthood. The quote includes two basic points: (1) God's putting his laws in their hearts and (2) God's not remembering their sins.[72] Then Hebrews 10:18, the next verse, summarizes by picking up on the forgiveness-of-sins aspect of the quote: "Where there is forgiveness of these [sins and lawless deeds], there is no longer any offering for sin." It concludes that since there truly was absolute forgiveness in the new covenant, then this proves that Christ as priest has offered one eternal sacrifice and does not need to offer multiple offerings like the Aaronic priesthood (10:11–14). As opposed to the longer quote of Jeremiah 31 in Hebrews 8:8–12, which has many angles, this quote focuses on the forgiveness of sins and its implication for Christ's priesthood.[73]

Summary and Conclusion

Hebrews emphasizes both an eternal, heavenly reality and a redemptive-historical movement from Old Testament to New Testament. From this contrast-within-continuity structure, four covenants are significantly discussed: Abrahamic, Mosaic, Davidic, and new. All of them match Old Testament expectations.

The Abrahamic covenant is used to highlight "promise," the arrival in the "land" of the new heavens and new earth, and the unified people of God. The Davidic covenant emphasizes Christ as the kingly Son and is also used to connect his kingship to his priesthood. The ceremonial aspects of the Mosaic covenant are primary as opposed to the moral and civil. Although being a shadow of the heavenly reality, these ceremonial aspects are contrasted with Christ's priesthood and his sacrifice. The new covenant is both eternal and inaugurated at Christ's first coming. In addition to the multifaceted work of Christ, it emphasizes God's initiative in our salvation, which is at some level greater than it was under the Mosaic covenant.

The above discussion matches the traditional Reformed view that the covenant of grace is "not two covenants of grace differing in substance, but one and the same under various dispensations" (WCF 7.6). The one "substance" is Christ. The eternal, heavenly realities ensure that there is one substance. The contrasts, although within continuity, explain the "various dispensations."

For some, the problem with the Reformed view is usually the Mosaic covenant and the antithetical contrasts between it and the new covenant in Hebrews. The problem, however, should be mitigated upon realizing that (1) the contrast is primarily between the *ceremonial* aspects of the Mosaic covenant's priesthood and sacrifices as compared

---

71. In addition to the portions skipped, the Greek of Heb. 10:16–17 has several minor differences from the Greek of Heb. 8:10, 12. The most notable is the reversal of "mind" and "hearts."

72. One might say this summarizes justification and sanctification. Calvin's Catechism 17 (1537) makes this exact point and references Jer. 31:33; Heb. 8:10; 10:16.

73. So also Johnson, *Hebrews*, 254.

to the reality of Christ's priesthood and sacrifice, and (2) the heavenly reality did exist during the Old Testament, and the Mosaic covenant is a shadow of this reality.

"I will be their God, and they shall be my people" (Heb. 8:10). This core promise of the covenant of grace reflects the character of our gracious God and his covenantal love toward believers. May the book of Hebrews with its significant discussion of various covenants be used to remind us anew of our covenantal relationship with the triune God.

13

COVENANT IN THE JOHANNINE
EPISTLES AND REVELATION

Gregory R. Lanier

The epistles and the Apocalypse written by the apostle John conclude the Scriptures of the new covenant era. These writings are often overlooked within covenant theology,[1] and at first glance this may seem reasonable. Many covenant-related terms rarely appear in the corpus: "covenant" and "promise" (once each); "law" (never); Moses (once); Adam, Noah, Abraham, Isaac, and Jacob (never); David (3x). On closer inspection, however, this corpus offers a complex and glorious picture of the covenant-making God, his covenant people, the consummation of the covenant in history, and the author's work as self-consciously covenant documentation. In what follows, I trace each of these points thematically (rather than chapter by chapter) to allow the reader to see the full picture.

---

1. In the Reformation era, the debates about Revelation's canonicity among Erasmus, Luther, Zwingli, and Bullinger influenced how Melanchthon, Bucer, and Calvin largely ignored it. Irena Backus, *Reformation Readings of the Apocalypse: Geneva, Zurich, and Wittenberg*, OSHT (Oxford: Oxford University Press, 2000), 7–35. Many major works on covenant theology rarely mention these writings: e.g., a handful of references to Revelation and 1 John in the nearly 900-page volume by Peter J. Gentry and Stephen J. Wellum, *Kingdom through Covenant: A Biblical-Theological Understanding of the Covenants* (Wheaton, IL: Crossway, 2012); roughly three Revelation references in Michael Horton, *God of Promise: Introducing Covenant Theology* (Grand Rapids, MI: Baker, 2006); only a few scattered sentences in O. Palmer Robertson, *The Christ of the Covenants* (Phillipsburg, NJ: Presbyterian and Reformed, 1987); no references in the covenant discussions in Louis Berkhof, *Systematic Theology*, combined ed. (1938; repr., Grand Rapids, MI: Eerdmans, 1996); no references in Calvin's *Institutes*, 2.10–11. Herman Witsius would be an exception in appealing to Revelation numerous times, though typically only in passing. *The Economy of the Covenants between God and Man: Comprehending a Complete Body of Divinity*, 2 vols. (London: T. Tegg and Son, 1837). Within scholarship on Revelation, some authors are conversant with covenant theology—e.g., G. K. Beale, *The Book of Revelation*, NIGTC (Grand Rapids, MI: Eerdmans, 1999)—while others are less so—e.g., Richard Bauckham, *The Theology of the Book of Revelation*, NTT (Cambridge: Cambridge University Press, 1993).

The Covenanting God

Covenant theology is grounded in the gracious condescension of God to engage his people in covenant. Thus, we begin with how the Father, Son, and Holy Spirit are described in covenantal terms in 1–3 John and Revelation.

God the Trinity

The mutual relations of the persons of the Godhead are prominent in John's writings. It is from this fountainhead that all covenantal dealings flow.

The equality in essence of Father and Son stands out the clearest. In Revelation we find interpretive glosses on the divine name (Ex. 3:14)[2] and monotheistic declarations of God as "first" and "last" (Isa. 41:4; 44:6; 48:12) applied to both persons (see table 13.1):[3]

Table 13.1   Essential Equality of Father and Son in Revelation (divine name glosses in italics; monotheistic declarations in bold)

Father	Rev. 1:4	[He] *who is and who was and who is to come*
Father	1:8	I am **the Alpha and the Omega** . . . *who is and who was and who is to come*
Son	1:17	I am **the first and the last**
Son	2:8	The words of **the first and the last**
Father	4:8	*Who was and is and is to come*
Father	11:17	*Who is and who was*
Father	16:5	*Who is and who was*
Both?*	21:6	I am **the Alpha and the Omega, the beginning and the end**
Son	22:13	I am **the Alpha and the Omega, the first and the last, the beginning and the end**

* The speaker is the "voice from the throne" (21:3); as discussed below, in Revelation the Lamb takes the throne with the Father, so John holds out the possibility that they speak these words *jointly*.

Key assertions of the old covenant era are now understood more fully in light of Christ. What the Father speaks, the Son speaks—culminating in the fullest statement on the lips of the Son in Revelation 22:13. The fact that the phrase "is to come" as spoken by the *Father* (1:4, 8; 4:8) drops out in 11:17 and 16:5 implicitly identifies the *Son* as the one who fulfills that "coming."

Moreover, the Son uniquely shares the singular throne of the Father (Rev. 3:21; 5:13; 7:17; 22:1–3), the kingdom of the Father (11:15), and worship due to the Father

---

2. Particularly the Greek rendering of the divine name (ἐγώ εἰμι ὁ ὤν, "I am the one who is"); see further in Bauckham, *Theology*, 28–29. Targum Ps.-Jon. to Ex. 3:14 glosses the divine name similarly—"I am the one who is and who is to come." Moreover, "the one who is to come" also may reflect other Old Testament passages anticipating the future coming of God (Pss. 96:13; 98:9; Isa. 40:10; 66:15; Zech. 14:5) *and* a human deliverer-figure (Ps. 118:26).

3. Similarly, the Father is described as the one "who is from the beginning" in 1 John 2:14.

(5:13).[4] Yet further, the Apocalypse ends with the picture that the final temple "is the Lord God the Almighty and the Lamb" and that "the glory of God gives it light, and its lamp is the Lamb" (21:22–23). One could scarcely bring Father and Son closer together in invoking the Old Testament temple and "glory" (כבוד/δόξα) as the presence of God. While John affirms the humanity of the Son (1 John 4:2), he doubtless places him "on the divine side of distinction between God and creation,"[5] such that we have fellowship with and abide in both Father and Son (1 John 1:3; 2:24; 2 John 9). In this way we realize fully what John means in saying that Jesus is specifically *his Father's* Son (2 John 3; Rev. 1:6) and that the Father has "sent his Son" (1 John 4:10) and given him "authority" (Rev. 2:27).[6] This Son was "first" and in his preexistence shared eternal glory with the Father; he was sent to save his covenant people; and he will reign as "last" with the Father.

Yet John's understanding of the Godhead is far from binitarian. The Spirit is the one sent from the Father (1 John 3:24; 4:1) to testify to the Son (4:1; 5:6–8; Rev. 22:17), showing the mutuality of their triune relations. Revelation begins precisely here, with blessings from the Father (the one "who was," etc.), the Spirit ("seven spirits who are before the throne"),[7] and the Son (Rev. 1:4–5).

John holds the covenant-making God to be a plural unity, which is entirely consistent with his Gospel. Yet his Trinitarianism, of course, does not obliterate Father-Son-Spirit distinctions, and covenantal thinking permeates his description of each divine person.

God the Father

Fatherhood

While θεός ("God") is used around 160 times in this corpus, John also specifically uses "Father" around 20 times. That is, the foundational relation between God and the people of the covenant is one of *fatherhood*. The *Father-son* relation can be traced at least as early as the Mosaic administration, when God declares the exodus to be a redemption of his "firstborn son," Israel (Ex. 4:22–23; Hos. 11:1). It becomes further concretized in the kingly representative, denoted God's "son," in the Davidic administration (2 Sam. 7:14; Ps. 2:7).

This idea is extended further by John's famous statement "God is love" (1 John 4:8). Far from a fuzzy feeling of sentimentality, this predication taps into something essential about God: not only is the Godhead constituted by a plural expression of love, but so also is God's loving relation to his covenant people. In fact, both the Abrahamic and Mosaic administrations are grounded not in the worthiness of Israel but rather in the

---

4. See Richard Bauckham, "The Worship of Jesus in Apocalyptic Christianity," *NTS* 27, no. 3 (1981): 322–41; Bauckham, *The Climax of Prophecy: Studies on the Book of Revelation* (Edinburgh: T&T Clark, 1993), 118–40. The angels' refusal of worship (Rev. 19:10; 22:9) accentuates this theme.

5. Bauckham, *Climax*, 140.

6. As opposed to adoptionistic Christology or limiting "son" to royal kingship.

7. Douglas F. Kelly, *Revelation*, MEC (Fearn, Ross-shire, Scotland: Mentor, 2012), 24; Beale, *Revelation*, 189.

assertion "The LORD loves you" (Deut. 7:7–8). John, in short, articulates God's covenantal identity as the *Father* who *loves*.

Presence

In addition to the core ways in which John articulates the identity of the Father in Revelation, he also uses several images drawn from the Mosaic administration to portray his tan-
gible presence. For example, God's terrifying theophanies (Rev. 4:6; 6:12; 8:5; 16:17–21)
draw directly on the Sinai theophany, the prototype for all cosmic manifestations of God.[8]

Moreover, John's visions of God's presence in his heavenly dwelling are saturated
with tabernacle/temple imagery.[9] We encounter seven golden lampstands in 1:12, an
intensification of the seven-pronged *single* lampstand of the tabernacle (Ex. 25:31–35)
and temple (2 Chron. 13:11). Heavenly worship of God is depicted as taking place in
a temple (Rev. 7:15), with an altar attended by angels (14:18). Before God's presence is
the incense burning on the golden incense altar (traditionally housed within the Most
Holy Place, Ex. 30)—only the incense is now transfigured into the prayers of the saints
(Rev. 8:3).

When John is asked to measure God's temple in the heavenlies (11:1), he testifies,
"God's temple in heaven was opened, and the ark of his covenant was seen within his
temple. There were flashes of lightning, rumblings, peals of thunder, an earthquake, and
heavy hail" (11:19). Much like the author of Hebrews (Heb. 9:24), Moses (Ex. 25:40),
and the psalmist (Pss. 11:4; 78:69), John sees heaven as a temple of God's presence,
for which the earthly tabernacle/temple were mere temporary copies. Fascinatingly,
we see the reappearance of the ark of the covenant, which had disappeared during the
monarchy.[10] The ark was the most sacred temple furnishing: the repository of covenant
documents, the centerpiece of Israel's priestly worship, the place of atonement via the
splattering of blood, and the physical locus of God's כבוד as he quite literally "guarded
the covenant."[11] Put differently, the ark in some sense *incarnated* God's old covenant with
Israel—and its heavenly type now appears at the climax of history. But notice how the
temple "was opened" and the ark "was seen." This was decidedly untrue for the earthly
ark, which was separated from the people by layers of curtains and rituals. The Son,
however, has given access to God himself; the temple stands open; and the ark bears
witness to the intimacy by which we now draw near to God.[12] This combination of

---

8. Bauckham, *Climax*, 199–200; on the influence of the Sinai theophany, see Jeffrey J. Niehaus, *God at Sinai:
Covenant and Theophany in the Bible and Ancient Near East* (Carlisle, UK: Paternoster, 1995).

9. See Robert Briggs, *Jewish Temple Imagery in the Book of Revelation*, StBibLit 10 (New York: Peter Lang, 1999).

10. Though the ark was set in the inner sanctuary by Solomon (1 Kings 8:3–7), it is not part of the temple
furnishings removed by Nebuchadnezzar (nor is it mentioned in the Maccabean literature). Jeremiah asserts that
the postexilic community would forget it entirely (Jer. 3:16); see Briggs, *Jewish Temple Imagery*, 89–96. It is mentioned elsewhere in the New Testament only once (Heb. 9:4–5), though Paul's use of ἱλαστήριον (Rom. 3:25)
evokes the old Greek translation of the lid of the Hebrew "ark."

11. Laszlo Gallusz, *The Throne Motif in the Book of Revelation*, LNTS 487 (London: T&T Clark, 2014), 238.

12. William Hendriksen, *More Than Conquerors: An Interpretation of the Book of Revelation* (1940; repr., Grand
Rapids, MI: Baker, 1998), 133.

temple imagery is a beautiful picture of the new access Christians have to the presence of God the Father.

Yet the Sinai-like theophany in Revelation 11:19 also reminds us of the terrifying holiness of this God of presence. When John subsequently describes how the "sanctuary of the tent of witness in heaven was opened," this opening enables God to send out his judgment (15:5–8).

Rule

Finally, we see throughout Revelation that God is the ruler on the heavenly throne. The nearly fifty occurrences of "throne" in Revelation are too numerous to cover in detail.[13] The structure of heaven in John's vision is something like a court of angels (bearing attributes of the cherubim in Ezek. 1; 10) and saints radiating out from the central throne of God. The throne is imbued with characteristics from Old Testament throne-room visions (chiefly Isaiah and Ezekiel). It is also surrounded by a rainbow (Rev. 4:3) that evokes the Noahic covenant (Gen. 9:13) and anticipates the start of a new creation.[14] The throne structure of heaven reminds us that God alone reigns on the true throne surrounded by his heavenly court (1 Kings 22:9); the monarchs of the Davidic dynasty sit on a throne that ultimately belongs to God (1 Chron. 29:23), such that even when the dynasty fails, "the LORD sits enthroned forever" (Ps. 9:7).

To summarize, the Johannine epistles and Revelation use covenantal concepts and language to construe the first person of the Godhead in terms of his fatherhood, presence (Sinai/temple), and rule (throne).

God the Son

The two primary aspects of the Son's identity in this corpus are priest/sacrifice (Mosaic covenant) and King (Davidic covenant). We will take them in turn and then see how John takes us back to the Adamic administration in a key scene in Revelation 12.

Priest and Sacrifice

While none of the Johannine epistles nor Revelation directly refers to Jesus as "priest," he clearly fills that office. In the first scene of Revelation, Jesus appears clothed in a priestly robe ministering "in the midst of the lampstands" of the heavenly temple (1:13; 2:1), now revealed to be the "seven churches" (1:20).[15] He later appears in a priestly

---

13. See the extensive discussion in Gallusz, *Throne Motif*.

14. Robertson, *Christ of the Covenants*, 124. Bauckham observes about the rainbow, "Revelation portrays God as faithful to the Noahic covenant and indeed surpassing it in faithfulness to his creation: first by destroying the destroyers of the earth, finally by taking creation beyond the threat of evil." *Theology*, 53.

15. Briggs, *Jewish Temple Imagery*, 55–54. In the heavenly temple of Rev. 11, we have another interesting vision of "two witnesses," "two lampstands," and "two olive trees" (11:1–4). Most likely, these cryptic symbols evoke Zech. 3–4 and, specifically, the priestly function of Joshua and kingly function of Zerubbabel. Charles E. Hill, "Revelation," in *A Biblical-Theological Introduction to the New Testament: The Gospel Realized*, ed. Michael J. Kruger (Wheaton, IL: Crossway, 2016): 537.

garment consecrated with blood (19:13, 16), much like the Aaronic high priest (Lev. 8:30). Rightly John can say that the Son is the consummate priestly "intercessor/helper" (παράκλητος, my trans.) before the Father (1 John 2:1).[16]

These Johannine writings further present the Son as the consummate atoning sacrifice of the Mosaic administration. As with burnt/guilt offerings of the temple cultus, the blood of Jesus is understood to cleanse sin and ransom the sinner (1 John 1:7–9; Rev. 1:5; 5:9). Jesus is, moreover, the "propitiation" (ἱλασμός) provided by God to deal with the wrath incurred by sin (1 John 2:2; 4:10).[17] And his atonement is specifically of a substitutionary nature, whereby his life is exchanged for another ("laid down his life for [ὑπέρ] us," 3:16). John explains *how* all this is possible by describing the Son as the "Lamb" (about 30x in Revelation) who has been "slain" and who bled for sin (Rev. 5:6, 12; 7:14; 12:11; 13:8).[18] Jesus is the summation of the entire sacrificial system; he is that to which the blood of all the substitutionary animals was pointing in a provisional way.

This sacrificial function of the lamb is essential to biblical thought, and its *personal* embodiment is anticipated in Isaiah 52–53. But John unveils the beautiful fullness of Christ when he fuses the Lamb—typically a picture not of victory but of weakness—with the conquering King: "The Lamb will conquer them, for he is Lord of lords and King of kings" (Rev. 17:14), which is reiterated after the Lamb executes wrath (19:15).[19] Let us turn, then, to the Son's kingly identity.

King

Inasmuch as the Mosaic covenant frames the sacrificial work of the Son, so also the Davidic covenant frames his resulting reign, particularly in Revelation.[20] Jesus holds the "key of David" (3:7). He is "the Root of David" (5:5; cf. Isa. 11:1–10) and "the descendant of David" (Rev. 22:16; cf. 2 Sam. 7:12).[21] Within this Davidic identity, Jesus is the "ruler of kings on earth" (Rev. 1:5). He is the "Lion of the tribe of Judah" (5:5), tracing his Davidic/kingly origins yet deeper into Israel's history (Gen. 49:9).[22] He, like the first (1 Sam. 16–17) and eschatological David (Ezek. 34:23), is royal "shepherd" (Rev. 7:17) but in a fuller way: whereas David describes YHWH as the shepherd leading his people beside still waters (Ps. 23), in Revelation it is *Jesus* who will "guide them to springs of

---

16. This is striking since the Holy Spirit is designated παράκλητος in John 14–16.

17. Henry George Liddell and Robert Scott, *A Greek Lexicon*, rev. Henry Stewart Jones (Oxford: Oxford University Press, 1996), 828; BDAG 474; Friedrich Büchsel, "ἵλεως, κτλ.," *TDNT*, 3:300–323. Ἱλασμός is used in Greek Leviticus for the "Day of Atonement," and various forms of the ἱλασ- lexeme are used throughout the Greek Old Testament for propitiation/atonement.

18. See Loren L. Johns, *The Lamb Christology of the Apocalypse of John: An Investigation into Its Origins and Rhetorical Force*, WUNT, 2nd ser., no. 167 (Tübingen: Mohr Siebeck, 2003); though imposing a nonviolence grid on Revelation, this work includes helpful research on the "lamb" motif in Old Testament and Jewish sources.

19. In Second Temple Judaism, the *messianic* use of "Lamb" was nearly nonexistent. Bauckham, *Climax*, 183.

20. See Cleon L. Rogers Jr., "The Davidic Covenant in Acts–Revelation," *BSac* 151 (1994): 71–84.

21. For more on the Davidic covenant, see Gregory R. Lanier, "Davidic Covenant," in *Lexham Bible Dictionary*, ed. John D. Barry (Bellingham, WA: Lexham, 2016).

22. "Lion" is occasionally a messianic metaphor, as in, e.g., 1Q28b 5.20–29. Bauckham, *Theology*, 74; Rogers, "Davidic Covenant," 83.

living water" (Rev. 7:17). By conquering sin, the Son assumes the heavenly throne with his Father (3:21; see above) to reign over an eternal kingdom (1:9; 11:15–18). And so, in a climactic throne vision, praise is rendered to the "Lord" and to "his Christ" (χριστός), the classic epithet for the anointed Son of David (11:15).[23] This confession that "Jesus is [ἔστιν] the Christ"—which renders more emphatically what is encoded in the shorthand "Jesus Christ"—is, indeed, the sine qua non of Christianity in 1 John 2:22 and 5:1 (cf. John 20:31).

Seed of the Woman

The dual designation of Jesus as Lamb and King leads us to a key scene where they coincide once more: Revelation 12. In this complex cosmic vision, the "male child, one who is to rule all the nations with a rod of iron" (12:5)—evoking nearly word for word Psalm 2:6–9 about the "Anointed" (2:2)—is also God's "Christ" *and* "Lamb" (Rev. 12:10–11). A radiant woman suffering tremendous birth pains is attacked by a "great red dragon . . . that ancient serpent, who is called the devil and Satan, the deceiver" (12:3, 9). Though the serpent attempts to devour her son, she successfully gives birth to him and is protected by God. After a heavenly battle, the serpent/dragon turns instead to attack the "offspring" (σπέρμα) of the woman, that is, those who "hold to the testimony of Jesus" (12:17).

One immediately recognizes allusions to the Adamic administration, as John's combination of images takes us directly back to Genesis 3.[24] Out of the wreckage brought by the serpent's temptation and man's sin (3:1–13), God promises the first woman that her "offspring" (זֶרַע/σπέρμα) will conflict with that of the serpent (3:15) and that she will suffer greatly in childbirth (3:16). By expanding apocalyptically on every element of this Genesis scene, Revelation discloses how Jesus is that promised "offspring," the eschatological Adam.[25]

In sum, John has painted the Son of God in colors pigmented by the gracious covenants with Adam (as the one who conquers the serpent on behalf of his people), Moses (as both priest and sacrificial lamb), and David (as King, shepherd, and "anointed"/χριστός).

God the Holy Spirit

We can discuss briefly the covenant identity of the Holy Spirit in this corpus. In 1 John 5:6 the Spirit is "the one who testifies" to Christ, which may evoke the role of covenant witness/testifier.[26] In a more pronounced way, the Spirit is the one who "[speaks] to

---

23. "The Lord's Anointed" (or "Messiah"/"Christ") is also prominent in Pss. Sol. 17:32 and 18:7, which refer to an eschatological Davidic king.

24. Hendriksen, *More Than Conquerors*, 136–40; Hill, "Revelation," 538. Some argue that the "woman" is the church or Mary or both.

25. Compare with Paul's similar treatment of Christ and Adam in Rom. 5 and 1 Cor. 15. Furthermore, in Rev. 12:17, the "offspring" of the woman is understood plurally, as the church of believers in Christ. This is consistent with the federal principle within covenant theology, wherein Christ as offspring represents and is united to believers as offspring (cf. the allusion to Gen. 3:15 in Rom. 16:20).

26. One thinks also of the "ark of the testimony [or witness]" (Ex. 25:22) and the "tent of witness" (Acts 7:44; cf. Ex. 27:21). "Witnessing" is essential to covenant making (Gen. 31:44).

the churches" in each of the seven letters of Revelation (2:7, 11, 17, 29; 3:6, 13, 22). While these phrases corroborate the personhood of the Spirit and the Spirit inspiration of Scripture, the weight of emphasis falls on how the Spirit is the one who mediates covenant warnings to the covenant people on behalf of Christ (2:1). The Spirit also pronounces blessing on (future) martyrs to encourage them (14:13). Indeed, John's inscripturation of Revelation itself is attributed to the work of the Spirit (1:10; 4:2; 17:3; 21:10).

In other words, the Holy Spirit is witness to and communicator of covenantal warnings, blessings, and scriptural documentation—consistent with the rest of Scripture (e.g., Zech. 7:12, numerous others).

The Covenant People

While the redemptive covenants in the Bible are unilaterally established by God, they are administered bilaterally with a second party, namely, the covenant people. We turn, then, to examine how John grounds the identity and formation of the people of God extensively in covenantal language/ideas.

Identity

We begin with two patterns by which this corpus employs covenant concepts to configure the identity of the people redeemed by the Lamb.

(New) Israel

For John, the life of ancient Israel is the raw material from which the church of Christ is carved. Those redeemed by Christ are thus not something entirely *new* but rather *new Israel*: organically connected to the historical covenant people but a group that has reached greater fullness upon the inbreaking of the eschatological age.

Just as the first person of the Godhead is manifestly the Father and the second person the Son (recall above), so also the people in covenant with God are identified as *sons*. The great promise held out is this: "The one who conquers will have this heritage, and I will be his God and he will be my son" (Rev. 21:7).[27] Yet this is not entirely future, for John also speaks of Christians *now* as those who are "called children of God" (1 John 3:1) and—almost inverting Revelation 21:7—asserts that "whoever is born of God conquers the world" (1 John 5:4, my trans.; cf. 4:7).[28] This notion of the corporate people as *sons* of God for whom he gives victory runs very deep into Israel's history (Ex. 4:22).

These children of God are determined as such by God alone from eternity past. John speaks of the covenant people as "elect" (ἐκλεκτός) in 2 John 1 and 13, where he figu-

---

27. The second phrase evokes the Immanuel principle, to which we will return. "Inheritance," likewise, is common old covenant language.
28. See the discussion in Rudolf Schnackenburg, *The Johannine Epistles: Introduction and Commentary*, trans. Reginald and Ilse Fuller (New York: Crossroad, 1992), 228–30. Cf. John 1:12–13; 3:8.

ratively refers to the church as, respectively, an "elect lady" and "elect sister."[29] Likewise, the church consists of "those [who] are called and chosen" (Rev. 17:14). Such "choosing" or "electing" is, of course, profoundly covenantal, tracing back to God's choice of Abraham's offspring to be the objects of redemption (e.g., Ezek. 20:5; Mal. 1:2–3).[30] In addition, Revelation speaks regularly of the saints or Christians as those, and only those, whose names are written in the "book of life" (3:5; 13:8; 17:8; 20:12, 15; 21:27) and who are numbered precisely by God (7:4; 14:1, 3), though the specific numbers used in Revelation are symbolic.[31]

Over twenty times the Johannine epistles and Revelation describe the people of God as ἐκκλησία ("assembly," "church"). As in Paul and other New Testament writings, this particular use of an otherwise common Greek word is rooted in the Second Temple Jewish language used for the Israelite assembly or congregation (קהל or עדה).[32] A more specific form of this pattern is the denotation of the redeemed as "sons of Israel" (Rev. 7:4; 21:12).

Probing a bit further in Revelation in particular, John envisions "twenty-four" elders who lead the assembly in worship in the heavenly temple (4:4, 10; 5:8; 11:16; 19:4). Their number likely connotes the twelve tribal leaders of the old covenant and the twelve apostles of the new covenant, thus conveying in compact fashion a theology of one covenant people across time (a similar double use of "twelve" connecting the tribes and apostles is found in 21:12–14).[33] These elders bring the incense of the "prayers of the saints" before the Lamb and are seated on thrones around *the* throne (5:8). Thus, they combine elements of the covenant administrations with Abraham (twelve tribes), Moses (priestly role in the heavenly temple), and David (thrones).

This Abraham-Moses-David pattern, however, does not stop with these "elders." It applies to the saints as a whole. They are the "tribe of Judah" from and for whom Jesus comes as Lion (5:5), and their full number is "sealed from every tribe of the sons of Israel" (7:4–8).[34] They are redeemed in order to be "priests to . . . God" (1:6), wearing robes "washed" in the "blood of the Lamb" (7:14)—evoking the Aaronic consecration by blood. Yet even this priestly role is fused with that of king, drawing on Exodus 29:6: the saints are "a kingdom and priests to our God, and they shall reign on the earth" (Rev. 5:10), and "they will be priests of God and of Christ, and they will reign with him" (20:6).

---

29. "Church" in Greek is grammatically feminine, allowing John to make this figuration.

30. See Dan Lioy, *The Book of Revelation in Christological Focus*, StBibLit 58 (New York: Peter Lang, 2003), 123.

31. Beale, *Revelation*, 58–64.

32. K. L. Schmidt, "ἐκκλησία," in *TDNT*, 3:501–36.

33. Hendriksen, *More Than Conquerors*, 85; Hill, "Revelation," 531. While the significance of the number twenty-four is well settled, the nature of these "elders" is debated; some argue that they are angelic beings. Bauckham, *Theology*, 34; Briggs, *Jewish Temple Imagery*, 48.

34. The listing of the tribes in this verse varies from other Old Testament lists; John may be doing so to signal how the original twelve tribes have been shaped by exile, restoration, and the coming of Christ. George Eldon Ladd, *A Theology of the New Testament*, rev. ed. (Grand Rapids, MI: Eerdmans, 1993), 678.

Other details round out the picture. The covenant people are promised "hidden manna" (Rev. 2:17), evoking the manna that nourished the Israelites in the wilderness (Ex. 16; Num. 11). They will be a "pillar in the temple," abiding in the presence of God forever (Rev. 3:12). And, borrowing language from the Mosaic covenant pertaining to the offering of firstfruits (e.g., Ex. 23:19; Deut. 18:4), the saints are "redeemed from mankind as firstfruits for God and the Lamb" (Rev. 14:4). In the Mosaic economy, the "firstfruits" are always given *to God alone*, but now they are given to God and the Lamb.

We are left with a richly covenantal picture: those who are saved by the Lamb consummate what Israel was consecrated to be, namely, a tribe of priests and kings to God. Interestingly, then, John envisions those gathered in Zion before the Lamb and states that "in their mouth no lie was found" (14:5). John is alluding to Zephaniah 3:12–13, where the postexilic prophet describes how those who find refuge in the Lord, "who are left in Israel" during its future restoration, shall

> speak no lies,
> nor shall there be found in their mouth
>   a deceitful tongue.[35]

By appealing to Zephaniah in this subtle way, John is conveying that the redeemed church is eschatological Israel.

Ingathered Nations

While John weaves Israelite concepts into the identity of the new covenant people, he also expands it by incorporating the nations—which, in fact, fulfills God's original promise to Abraham (Gen. 12; 15). In Revelation, though judgment is poured out on the nations who oppose God, the promise is that "all nations will come and worship" the Lamb, who is "King of the nations" (Rev. 15:3–4; cf. 1:5). We can fill in the details by examining John's varied use of "tribes," "languages," "peoples," and "nations"— traditional Old Testament language associated with the Abrahamic promise. There is a clear pattern of opposition and restoration among these groups about whom John is commanded to prophesy (10:11), displayed in table 13.2.

It is a testament to John's literary skill that the order of these descriptors varies in every instance, yet amid this complex picture a profound sense of God's patient grace emerges. Among the nations are those who were set against Christ and his people but hear the gospel, are ransomed by Christ's blood, and worship the Lamb. The covenant people will be extended to the ends of the earth.

Stepping back to view the whole, we see how John proves himself to be a skilled covenant theologian in how he portrays the identity of the people of God as what they always were promised to be: Israel and the nations united in Christ.

---

35. Bauckham, *Theology*, 78. See a similar use of this passage in John 1:47.

Covenant in the Johannine Epistles and Revelation 277

Table 13.2 Opposition and Restoration in "Nations" Language in Revelation ("nations" language in italics)

Opposed to Christ	Rev. 11:18*	The *nations* raged.
Ruled by evil	13:7–8	[The beast of the sea] was allowed to make war on the saints and to conquer them. And authority was given it over every *tribe* and *people* and *language* and *nation*.
Ruled by evil	17:15	The waters that you saw, where the prostitute is seated, are *peoples* and *multitudes* and *nations* and *languages*.
Fearful of Christ	1:7	All *tribes* of the earth will wail on account of him.
Under judgment	11:9	For three and a half days some from the *peoples* and *tribes* and *languages* and *nations* will gaze at their dead bodies.
Recipients of the gospel	14:6	Then I saw another angel flying directly overhead, with an eternal gospel to proclaim to those who dwell on earth, to every *nation* and *tribe* and *language* and *people*.
Ransomed by Christ	5:9	You ransomed people . . . from every *tribe* and *language* and *people* and *nation*.
Worshiping Christ	7:9	A great multitude that no one could number, from every *nation*, from all *tribes* and *peoples* and *languages*, standing before the throne and before the Lamb, clothed in white robes . . .

* Due to the iterative structure of Revelation, I am listing these verses in thematic rather than chapter order.

Moreover, for John there is a pronounced sense of being *inside* this covenant body. In his visions, the redeemed are clearly demarcated: they are visible, clothed in renewed garments, precisely numbered, and gathered corporately to sing. Likewise, there is also a strong sense of others being *outside* this body. Chiefly, "antichrists" (plural) are, somewhat shockingly, those who "went out from us, but they were not of us; for if they had been of us, they would have continued with us" (1 John 2:18–19; see also 2:22; 4:3; 2 John 7).[36] They seemed to be part of the covenant community but proved otherwise. For our purposes the point is this: firmly distinguishing those inside from those outside is inherently a covenantal way of thinking rooted in Jacob/Esau, Isaac/Ishmael, Shem/Ham, and even Cain/Abel.

Formation

Essential to covenant relationships is the establishment of promises, obligations, and warnings that shape life in the covenant. We see several ways in which John, having defined the identity of those who are redeemed, indicates how they are to be formed.

36. See Charles E. Hill, "1–3 John," in Kruger, *Biblical-Theological Introduction*, 483.

Belief and Worship

The primary index of true Christianity, as fleshed out in this corpus, is responding to God with faith in his Son (e.g., "believes that Jesus is the Son of God," 1 John 5:5, and similar phrases in 3:23; 4:16; 5:1–13) and worship (Rev. 4:10; 11:1–16; 15:4; 19:1–8). These formative elements of God's people can be traced back to Abraham's seminal response of faith (Gen. 15:6) and God's redeeming the Israelites from Egypt specifically to worship him (e.g., Ex. 3:12).

Keeping the Commandments

Obedience to God is also the proper response of his people. Though John does not use "law" (νόμος) in this corpus (versus around 15x in his Gospel), he does use "commandment" (ἐντολή) and related language frequently, reflecting how the moral law plays a formative role in the life of the church.[37] Some of his language is frank. Those who know God are the ones who "keep his commandments" (1 John 2:3); we receive whatever we ask of God because "we keep his commandments and do what pleases him" (3:22); the "love of God" *is* "that we keep his commandments" (5:3); and the eternally blessed are those "who [keep] my works" (Rev. 2:26). This commandment keeping is not crass externalism/legalism; rather, it is annexed to faith (1 John 3:22; Rev. 2:19; 14:12) and stimulated by the Spirit (1 John 3:24).[38] It is a normal way of framing how those redeemed by God are to strive to please him. The specifics of these "commandments" are not spelled out by John,[39] but they bear a clear imprint of the law of Moses. John asserts that he is not writing a "new commandment" but reinforcing the "old commandment," which "you had from the beginning" (1 John 2:7; cf. 2 John 5–6).[40] Sin is defined as "lawlessness" (ἀνομία) (1 John 3:4). And the essence of the commandments is this: "Whoever loves God must also love his brother" (1 John 4:21). This twofold summary of the law—combining the Shema (Deut. 6:5) and love for neighbor (Lev. 19:18)—is squarely aligned with Jesus (Matt. 22:36–38), Paul (Rom. 13:9; Gal. 5:14), and James (James 2:8).

Warnings

Running parallel to the generally positive sense of commandment keeping in this corpus is the prominent place of warnings imposed *on the church*. First John regularly exhorts Christians toward self-examination as to whether they are deceiving themselves (1:10; 2:4–15; 3:4). The seven letters in Revelation 2–3 feature how Christ "know[s] [their] works" (typically negative, 2:19; 3:1, 8, 15), has something "against" them (2:4, 14, 20), and warns them sternly to repent (e.g., 2:5, 16; 3:2–3).

---

37. Schnackenburg, *Johannine Epistles*, 95–98.
38. Hill, "1–3 John," 501.
39. Andreas Köstenberger describes this as "sanctified reductionism." *A Theology of John's Gospel and Letters: The Word, the Christ, the Son of God*, BTNT (Grand Rapids, MI: Zondervan, 2009), 524.
40. "Old" (παλαιός) here may parallel Paul's description of "Moses" as the "old" (παλαιᾶς) covenant in 2 Cor. 3:14.

In short, John indicates his covenantal understanding of the people of God by showing how belief, worship, commandments, and warnings function in the life of the community to form it into Christ, the mediator, so that "when he appears we shall be like him" (1 John 3:2).

The Covenant's Consummation in History

John's Apocalypse famously depicts God's final judgment on human rebellion and the future restoration of all things. It is the latter that typically receives the most attention in terms of covenant themes (and rightfully so), though judgment is also depicted using old covenant language.

Judgment

From the earliest days of Christianity, much ink has been spilled in coming to grips with Revelation's complex visions of judgment involving beasts, fiery sulfur, the millennium, bowls, trumpets, and much more. Competing theories abound as to the timing and sequence of the various events portrayed. For our purposes, we can find stable common ground in sketching how John uses numerous covenantal themes to depict the present period in which the church advances amid opposition.

The Current Exile

John describes the great enemy of God's people as "Babylon the great," the "great prostitute" who is drunk with the blood of the saints/martyrs (e.g., Rev. 14:8; 16:19; 17:1–16; 18:1–21). In the apostolic era, "Babylon" is often a code word for the Roman Empire (i.e., 1 Pet. 5:13), but John extends it to all nations who oppose God and oppress his people (Rev. 17:18).[41] The symbolic label recalls the historical Babylon that subjugated the southern kingdom (605–539 BC), destroying Jerusalem and its temple. Though there was a partial restoration under Zerubbabel (not to mention the Hasmonean era in the second century BC), Second Temple Jews as well as early Christians still *theologically* understood themselves to be dispersed in exile.[42] Therefore, John's use of "Babylon" expresses how Christians, though redeemed, "are still in a continuing exile under Babylonian oppression."[43] When we read, then, of how the second beast makes an image of the first beast, we are reminded of Nebuchadnezzar's image worship in Babylon (Dan. 3).[44] John takes us even further back to other foreign cities and nations who have opposed Israel in the past, namely, "Sodom and Egypt" (Rev. 11:8). When, therefore, the nations and beast turn on the prostitute Babylon and destroy her—and "God has put it into their hearts to

---

41. Bauckham, *Theology*, 128. Hendriksen rightly notes, "Babylon thus viewed is past, present, and future. Its form changes; its essence remains." *More Than Conquerors*, 168.

42. See John 7:35; James 1:1; 1 Pet. 1:1. Also, the Jewish writings of Baruch, Psalms of Solomon, and several scrolls from Qumran (among others) convey a strong sense of ongoing exile.

43. G. K. Beale, *A New Testament Biblical Theology: The Unfolding of the Old Testament in the New* (Grand Rapids, MI: Baker Academic, 2011), 550.

44. Steve Moyise, *The Old Testament in the Book of Revelation*, JSNTSup 115 (Sheffield, UK: Sheffield Academic Press, 1995), 48.

carry out his purpose" (17:17)—history is repeating itself, for God used foreign powers to destroy original Babylon.[45] In other words, in the consummation of times portrayed in John's visions, the covenant curse of exile is being decisively unwound.

Judgment Outpoured

Israel's history also shapes John's depiction of eschatological judgment and wrath. Two judgment scenes in Revelation intentionally echo the plagues of the original exodus.[46] We can summarize them as shown in table 13.3.

Table 13.3   Echoes of the Exodus in Two Judgment Scenes in Revelation

Exodus 7–12	Trumpets (Rev. 8:6–9:19)	Bowls (Rev. 16)
1. Water into blood	"third of the sea became blood," 8:8	"rivers . . . became blood," 16:4
2. Frogs	—	"unclean spirits like frogs," 16:13
3. Gnats	—	—
4. Swarm of flies	—	—
5. Plague on livestock	—	—
6. Boils caused by furnace soot	"plagues . . . by the fire and smoke and sulfur," 9:18	"harmful and painful sores," 16:2
7. Hail and fire	"hail and fire, mixed with blood," 8:7	"great hailstones," 16:20
8. Locusts	"locusts on the earth," 9:3	—
9. Darkness	"third of their light . . . darkened," 8:12 "the sun and the air were darkened," 9:2	"kingdom was plunged into darkness," 16:10
10. Death of firstborn	—	—

Within Revelation's various cycles of judgment are battle scenes—culminating in the battle at "Armageddon" (Rev. 16:16)[47]—that blend topography, imagery, and prophecies from Israel's history, along with cosmic upheaval and destruction modeled on Old Testament prophecies of the day of the Lord.[48] John is appealing to past biblical events to describe the present and future.

---

45. As observed by Marko Jauhiainen, "The OT Background to 'Armageddon' (Rev. 16:16) Revisited," *NovT* 47, no. 4 (2005): 388.

46. Laszlo Gallusz, "The Exodus Motif in Revelation 15–16: Its Background and Nature," *AUSS* 46, no. 1 (2008): 21–43; Bauckham, *Climax*, 204.

47. The debate on what John means by "the place that in Hebrew is called Armageddon" is unresolved; see Jauhiainen, "OT Background." It may combine Megiddo (Zech. 12:11) with other eschatological/Zion imagery (such as Ezek. 38–39).

48. Ranging from Ezek. 38:19–22 to Hos. 10:8 (and numerous others). For instance, the four horsemen of Rev. 6 are patterned after those of Zech. 6:2–3.

A high point in Revelation is reached when, after the passing of the "seven plagues" (15:1), those who were delivered by God gather alongside a "sea of glass mingled with fire" to sing praises to God (15:2). What is the song they sing? John describes it as "the song of Moses, the servant of God, and the song of the Lamb" (15:3). This title recalls Moses's famous ode to God for judging their oppressor, Egypt, as Israel stood on the opposite side of the sea (Ex. 15)—only now, the sea has become in some sense eschatological. The song has been fused with that "of the Lamb," and the lyrics are modified, though they still share the same theme of the power of God over the nations. The point is quite clear: the salvation achieved by the Lamb through the plagues of judgment is a recapitulated and, now, consummated new exodus. It is only appropriate, then, that God's people celebrate by dusting off an old song, by which they express covenantal solidarity with the Israel of God.[49]

Consummation

We arrive at the culmination of John's writing and, indeed, at the consummation of redemptive history: Revelation 21–22. In saving this section for last—rather than jumping directly to it for its rich covenant themes—we can better sense how these chapters are not outliers but rather tie together the covenantal threads found elsewhere in John's writings. Full verse-by-verse analysis is not feasible here.[50] Instead, we summarize along covenant themes.

New Creation

In John's vision, the final state is that of "a new heaven and a new earth," for the original heaven and earth had "passed away" (Rev. 21:1). The voice from the throne declares, "I am making all things new" (21:5), and subsequently John sees a "spring of the water of life" (21:6), "the river of the water of life" (22:1), and the "tree of life with its twelve kinds of fruit" (22:2). By combining these elements, John has taken us simultaneously to the original creation and Adamic Eden (Gen. 1–2) as well as to Isaiah's prophecy of "new heavens and a new earth" (Isa. 65:17). Moreover, John describes the reversal of days one and four of the first creation: the sun and other luminaries created on day four are no more (Rev. 21:23; 22:5), for God himself—the Father and Son on the throne— "will be their light" (22:5; cf. 1 John 1:5), as on the very first day. Finally, John observes that "the sea was no more" (Rev. 21:1). This detail evokes how the originally created sea (Gen. 1:2, 9) is often a symbol for the domain of evil or tumult in the Old Testament (e.g., Job 7:12) and Revelation (e.g., 13:1), as well as the barrier overcome in the original (Ex. 14) and new (Isa. 11:15–16; 51:9–11) exodus events. Thereby, this sea, as a symbol

---

49. See further in Steve Moyise, "Singing the Song of Moses and the Lamb: John's Dialogical Use of Scripture," *AUSS* 42, no. 2 (2004): 347–60; Gallusz, "Exodus Motif," 30.

50. For a detailed treatment, see David Mathewson, *A New Heaven and a New Earth: The Meaning and Function of the Old Testament in Revelation 21.1–22.5*, JSNTSup 238 (Sheffield, UK: Sheffield Academic Press, 2006).

of the separation of God from his people, is completely eradicated.[51] The future state is, through and through, a transformed Edenic creation.

Removal of the Curse

Consequently, we also see how the curse pronounced on Adam in the old Eden is unwound in the final state. John writes that death, mourning, crying, and pain will "be no more" (Rev. 21:4). Death was the chief curse of the prefall Adamic covenant (Gen. 2:17; also Rom. 5:12–14), and the curse on creation (Gen. 3:17; also Rom. 8:20–22) brings with it mourning, crying, and pain. All this, however, is entirely undone: John writes, "No longer will there be anything accursed" (Rev. 22:3). Things are reset to Eden *before* the fall and curse.[52]

Jerusalem, the Bride

The essence of this Eden-like new creation is "the holy city, new Jerusalem, coming down out of heaven from God" (Rev. 21:2; cf. 21:10). Jerusalem was the city at the heart of the land promised in the Abrahamic covenant, the nucleus of the sacrificial system of the Mosaic covenant, and the city of David's dynastic throne—but also the place of covenant curse via its Babylonian destruction. In Revelation's earlier chapters, *earthly* Jerusalem is not yet what it was designed to be; rather, it is "where their Lord was crucified" (11:8). But God has not given up on his promises, and John's description of the new creation *as* the holy city, a heavenly Jerusalem, is pregnant with all the covenantal memory of God's people: they will finally enter their eschatological dwelling place.[53] This, too, fulfills Isaiah's prophecy of the new heavens and new earth, wherein God declares, "I create Jerusalem to be a joy. . . . I will rejoice in Jerusalem" (Isa. 65:18–19).

Yet John goes further and personifies Jerusalem as "a bride adorned for her husband" (Rev. 21:2) and the "wife of the Lamb" (21:9), expanding on his previous description of the "marriage supper of the Lamb" (19:9).[54] Jerusalem is not, on the final accounting, a concrete *city* but a *people* betrothed to Christ.[55] This eschatological wedding banquet

---

51. Jonathan Moo, "The Sea That Is No More: Rev 21:1 and the Function of Sea Imagery in the Apocalypse of John," *NovT* 51, no. 2 (2009): 148–67; Bauckham, *Theology*, 53; David Mathewson, "New Exodus as a Background for 'The Sea Was No More' in Revelation 21:1c," *TJ* 24, no. 2 (2003): 243–58. There remains debate about whether this "sea" refers instead to the laver/basin positioned outside the Holy Place in the old temple (as, perhaps, in Rev. 4:6; see Briggs, *Jewish Temple Imagery*, 52); if that were the case, it still remains that its disappearance conveys how the people can now directly approach God, with the external barriers of the temple court now abolished.

52. Beale, *Biblical Theology*, 465; Mathewson, *New Heaven*, 220.

53. See further in Celia Deutsch, "Transformation of Symbols: The New Jerusalem in Rv 21:1–22:5," *ZNW* 78, no. 1 (1987): 106–26. This scene is all the more potent if Revelation was written *after* AD 70.

54. For detailed treatment of the "bride" motif, see Sebastian Smolarz, *Covenant and the Metaphor of Divine Marriage in Biblical Thought: A Study with Special Reference to the Book of Revelation* (Eugene, OR: Wipf and Stock, 2010).

55. Berkhof, *Systematic Theology*, 557. This is consistent with how "Jerusalem" is often treated as a metonym for the Israelites/Jews in so-called "Apostrophes to Zion" (e.g., Isa. 52:1–12; Qumran's 11Q5/Ps^a 22.1–11; Luke 13:34–35).

is profoundly connected to three significant prophecies of Isaiah (connections to Revelation are italicized below):

Isaiah 61:8–10
> [God] will make an everlasting *covenant* with them . . .
> They are an offspring the LORD has blessed . . .

> He has clothed me with the garments of salvation . . .
>   as a *bride* adorns herself with her jewels.

Isaiah 62:1–6
> For *Jerusalem's* sake I will not be quiet,
> until her righteousness goes forth as brightness . . .
> The LORD delights in you,
>   and your land shall be married.
> For as a young man marries a young woman,
>   so shall your sons marry you,
> and as the bridegroom rejoices over the bride,
>   so shall your God rejoice over you.

> On your walls, O *Jerusalem*,
>   I have set watchmen.

Isaiah 25:6–8
> On this *mountain* the LORD of hosts will make for all peoples
>   a *feast* of rich food, a feast of well-aged wine. . . .
> He will swallow up death forever;
> and the Lord GOD will *wipe away tears* from all faces,
>   and the reproach of his people he will take away from all the earth.

John combines Isaiah's ancient expectations into one breathtaking depiction of the finale, the wedding of God (revealed in the Lamb) to his "Jerusalem," the people of God.

Eschatological Temple

Just as the centerpiece of old Jerusalem was the temple of Solomon, so also temple language reappears here—but with a twist. When an angel shows John the new Jerusalem from afar, *the city itself* resembles the old temple. It has gates on each side and is an enormous cube with equal sides (Rev. 21:12–16), just like the Most Holy Place (1 Kings 6:20). Its walls and their twelve foundations are made of various precious stones (jasper, onyx, etc., Rev. 21:18–21) that correlate closely to the stones of the priestly ephod, which, in turn, represented the twelve original tribes (Ex. 28:6–14). The entire city is made of "pure gold" (Rev. 21:18), just as the apparatus of the Most Holy Place (Ex. 25). The "throne of God and of the Lamb will be in it" (Rev. 22:3), which combines both Mosaic (ark as throne of God) and Davidic (Messiah/Lamb reigning on David's throne) elements. In short, the archetypal temple is no longer manifested in a man-made temple in Jerusalem nor confined to heaven. Rather, as the new-creational "Jerusalem" comes down from heaven, the entire cosmos becomes the temple of God's presence. This vision is a fulfillment of Ezekiel's idealized temple (Ezek. 40–48)[56] as well as, possibly, another instance of the notion of an eschatological return to Eden, which many scholars argue is subtly described in Genesis as a kind of temple, with Adam as priest.[57]

John has even more in store: "I saw no temple in the city, for its temple is the Lord God the Almighty and the Lamb" (Rev. 21:22). At this point, the reader may well be completely overwhelmed! From one perspective, as described beforehand, the heavenly Jerusalem—a symbol for the people of God—does not need a separate temple because *it is a temple* where God dwells. But from the perspective introduced here, the *Lamb himself* is also the temple (cf. John 2:21). Only a robust covenantal theology can make sense of this: the Son/Lamb is the true temple of God, but because he federally incorporates in himself all God's covenant people (i.e., heavenly "Jerusalem," his "bride"), so they, too, are the temple (cf. 1 Cor. 3:16).

Immanuel Promise, for All Nations

In this light, we read perhaps the most glorious words of Revelation: "Behold, the tent [σκηνή] of God is with man. He will dwell [σκηνώσει] with them, and they will be his people, and God himself will be with them as their God" (Rev. 21:3, my trans.). The first part draws twice on the "tent"/"tabernacle" language of the old covenant to reiterate how God himself is dwelling, or "tenting," with his people. The second part is, famously, the final scriptural occurrence of what is called the "Immanuel promise." Within covenant theology it is generally recognized that the essence of God's covenant relationship is "I will be your God, and you will be my people" (see especially Deut. 29:12–15).[58] Variations on this promise appear throughout the Old Testament (e.g., Ex. 6:7; Lev. 26:12; 2 Sam. 7:24; Ezek. 36:26), and it is applied to Christ himself in Matthew 1:23 ("Immanuel . . . God with us") and 28:19–20 ("I am with you always"). Revelation climaxes in this very truth: the triune God is—finally, eternally—dwelling with his people, and they with him.

But the Immanuel promise is not just for ancient Israel, nor has it ever been. Just as Zechariah 2:11 declares that "many nations . . . shall be my people. And I will dwell in your midst" (cf. Ezek. 37:26–28), so also John specifies that God's dwelling is "with man" (ἀνθρώπων) (Rev. 21:3). As anticipated in prior chapters of Revelation, the "na-

---

56. Many of John's descriptions evoke those of Ezekiel, though with modifications.
57. See, e.g., Beale, *Biblical Theology*, 617; detailed further in Beale, *The Temple and the Church's Mission: A Biblical Theology of the Dwelling Place of God*, NSBT 17 (Downers Grove, IL: InterVarsity Press, 2004).
58. Robertson, *Christ of the Covenants*, 49–51; Berkhof, *Systematic Theology*, 278–79.

tions" will walk by the light of God, and the "kings of the earth" will bring their "glory" (21:24) and "the honor of the nations" (21:26) into the new Jerusalem. The Edenic tree of life will bring the "healing of the nations" (22:2). And thus will come to pass how the redeemed of every tribe, tongue, and nation will praise God forever.

To summarize the nearly unsummarizable, embedded throughout John's Apocalypse are numerous covenantal ideas (Adamic, Abrahamic, Mosaic, Davidic, along with prophetic anticipation of a new covenant) that he uses to depict judgment and, in a final symphony, the restoration of all things. Indeed, not only do covenant themes shape John's literary product, but the *telos*, indeed the very meaning, of history itself is the consummation of God's covenant.

The Conclusion to Covenant Documentation

On the evidence of these writings, one obtains the distinct impression that John is a covenant theologian on par with any other. In a variety of ways, he invokes every covenant administration in portraying the Godhead, the identity and formation of the covenant people, and the culmination of redemptive history.

But his incorporation of robust covenant themes is not the only means by which we observe this. His authorial method, too, provides insight that John sees himself to be a writer—likely the last one—of covenant documentation.[59]

Engagement with Scripture

As is well known, John does not explicitly cite or quote any passage of the Old Testament in 1–3 John or Revelation.[60] Yet as we have seen, the imprint of the Scriptures is found on every page. John is particularly indebted to Daniel, Ezekiel, Zechariah, and Isaiah in Revelation—without which the reader would be at a severe disadvantage in understanding the book.[61] What explains this puzzling procedure of relying exclusively on Old Testament allusions? It reflects how deeply John has digested the old covenant, such that in nearly every breath he is giving it a new configuration in the new. Additionally, he is also following best practices within the genre of apocalypse. Though often lost in modern debates that pit "apocalyptic" against "covenantal" or "redemptive-historical,"[62] any cursory examination of actual apocalyptic writings reveals that they are saturated with covenantal ideas. To take 1 Enoch as a premier example, the pseudepigraphal author shows indebtedness to the Old Testament by using "election" over fifty times; describing eternal reward as "covenant" (1 En. 60.6); recasting Ezekiel's throne vision in his own

---

59. For more on the notion of Scripture as covenant documentation, see Gregory R. Lanier, *A Christian's Pocket Guide to How We Got the Bible: Old and New Testament Canon and Text* (Fearn, Ross-shire, Scotland: Christian Focus, 2018).

60. The NA28 and UBS5 Greek New Testaments indicate no direct Old Testament quotations.

61. See G. K. Beale, *John's Use of the Old Testament in Revelation*, LNTS 166 (Sheffield, UK: Sheffield Academic Press, 1999); Moyise, *Old Testament*, 15–16.

62. For a survey of this tension, see David A. Shaw, "Apocalyptic and Covenant: Perspectives on Paul or Antinomies at War?," *JSNT* 36, no. 2 (2013): 155–71.

(1 En. 14; 18); portraying God as King on a temple-throne (1 En. 25); promising that a deliverer ("Elect One"/"Son of Man") will sit on a throne (1 En. 45–47); describing the final state as dwelling under the wings of God (1 En. 39); and envisioning a remade Jerusalem (1 En. 90). In other words, John reflects the typical apocalyptic mode that is deeply influenced by covenantal reflection.

Macro- and Microstructures[63]

Furthermore, the macroshape of Revelation may, at least at a high level, mimic a covenant arrangement. It opens with a declaration of the parties (Rev. 1:1–4); rehearses (several times) the historical basis of the covenant relationship (e.g., 1:5–7; 4:11); holds out promises of blessing (e.g., 1:3; 14:13); stipulates obligations and warnings (e.g., 2:3–3:22); and at both beginning and end includes documentation provisions (1:11; 21:5). In fact, the angelic intermediary himself states that "the words of this book"—the very βίβλος John is composing—are something to be "kept" or "obeyed" (22:9), which is quite a covenantal way of thinking about a written document. In addition, at a microlevel each of the seven letters in Revelation 2–3—and one might extend this to 2 John and 3 John—are miniature covenant documents. Each of these letters identifies the parties, recounts the historical situation, and features a mix of promises, obligations, and warnings.

The End of Scripture

If these hypotheses are correct—if, in other words, John is self-consciously engaged in writing covenant documentation—then the closing words of Revelation take on immense significance. He writes,

> I warn everyone who hears the words of the prophecy of this book: if anyone adds to them, God will add to him the plagues described in this book, and if anyone takes away from the words of the book of this prophecy, God will take away his share in the tree of life and in the holy city, which are described in this book. (Rev. 22:18–19)

John here takes up the instruction in Deuteronomy not to "add to" or "take from" the word given by God (Deut. 4:2; 12:32) and applies it to his own writing.[64] While at one level he is directly referring to his specific book, the fact that the consummation of God's covenantal dealings is the content of what he has "described in this book" suggests more might be going on. If Revelation is chronologically the final New Testament writing,[65] John may see himself—the last living apostle—as the one who writes the last inspired covenant document of the new covenant era.

---

63. Key studies on this topic include William H. Shea, "The Covenantal Form of the Letters to the Seven Churches," *AUSS* 21, no. 1 (1983): 71–84; Kenneth A. Strand, "A Further Note on the Covenantal Form in the Book of Revelation," *AUSS* 21, no. 3 (1983): 251–64; Lioy, *Revelation*, 84–85.

64. Beale argues that this reappropriation of Deuteronomy is a key reason why a "covenantal scheme forms at least part of the general background" of Revelation. *Biblical Theology*, 305–6.

65. For the cumulative case for a late date (ca. AD 95), see Beale, *Revelation*, 4–27; David E. Aune, *Revelation 1–5*, WBC 52 (Dallas: Word Books, 1997).

He may be, in other words, intentionally bringing all Scripture to a close. The era of the Spirit-filled church has begun in the death, resurrection, and ascension of Christ. In this era there are no anticipated special acts of verbal revelation of God—no more covenant documents to be written. None are needed, for the next and final act on the horizon is the return of Christ. And so Christians as the "bride" join with the Spirit in saying, "Come," Lord Jesus (Rev. 22:17).

PART 2

HISTORICAL THEOLOGY

14

Covenant in the Early Church

Ligon Duncan

The early church's theology of the covenants informed the covenant theology of the Reformers and their successors, but the covenants were important in early Christianity on their own grounds and were deployed for their own hermeneutical, catechetical, apologetic, and polemic purposes.[1] The very earliest postbiblical writings of the church show a full appreciation for the importance of the biblical covenants and expound a covenantal view of redemptive history.

Early Christian writers employed the Bible's teaching on the covenants (1) to stress moral obligations incumbent on Christians; (2) to show God's grace in including the Gentiles in the Abrahamic blessings; (3) to deny the reception of these promises to the Israel of the flesh, that is, unbelieving Israel considered merely as an ethnic entity; (4) to demonstrate continuity in the divine economy; and (5) to explain discontinuity in the divine economy. In the first two hundred or so years of postapostolic Christianity, pre-Nicene theologians (1) freely applied Old Testament covenant passages as the starting point of their paraenesis; (2) understood the covenant between God and his people to be both unilateral and bilateral, both promissory and obligatory, to bring divine blessings and entail human obedience; (3) employed the covenants as a key structural idea in their presentations of redemptive history; and (4) explicitly linked the covenant idea to the early Christian self-understanding as the people of God.

When reading the New Testament, the apostolic fathers, and Justin with an eye to the presence, usage, and significance of a theology of the covenants, one can see that this emphasis is more important to them than is often appreciated. Furthermore, when

---

1. This chapter is a distillation of J. Ligon Duncan, "The Covenant Idea in Ante-Nicene Theology" (PhD diss., University of Edinburgh, 1995).

one turns to Melito, Irenaeus, Tertullian, Cyprian, Origen, Clement of Alexandria, Hippolytus, Novatian, and others, one can detect a definite "covenant tradition" of interpretation. That is, there are genetic connections of exegesis and theologizing relating to covenants that we find passed down from one generation of Christian theologians to the next in the earliest years of Christianity.

Is There a Theology of the Covenants in Early Christianity?

Ever since Delbert Hillers (1969) denied the importance of the covenants in the theology of the New Testament and early Christianity, scholars have been proving him wrong. He infamously asserted,

> The Essenes had a covenant, but it was not new; the Christians had something new, but it was not a covenant. That is to say, to call what Jesus brought a covenant is like calling conversion circumcision, or like saying that one keeps the Passover with the unleavened bread of sincerity and truth. For Christians, the coming of the substance made shadows out of a rich array of Old Testament events, persons, and ideas, among them covenant. *Figuram res exterminat*; the reality brings the image to an end.[2]

The literary deposit of early Christianity, however, tells a very different story, and researchers in two very different fields of historical study have contributed to reviving our awareness of and appreciation for the theological importance of the covenants in the early church. First, scholars studying the origins of the covenant theology of the sixteenth-century Reformation have established a link between the early Reformers' covenant thought and patristic sources.[3] They have shown, for instance, that Heinrich Bullinger appealed to a number of early church fathers for confirmation of his teaching on the covenant idea in his *De testamento seu foedere Dei unico et aeterno* (1534).[4] Charles S. McCoy and J. Wayne Baker assert,

---

2. Delbert R. Hillers, *Covenant: The History of a Biblical Idea* (Baltimore: Johns Hopkins University Press, 1969), 188.

3. See, for instance, J. Wayne Baker's *Heinrich Bullinger and the Covenant: The Other Reformed Tradition* (Athens: Ohio University Press, 1980), 1–25; Joachim Staedke, *Die Theologie des jungen Bullinger*, SDST 16 (Zurich: Zwingli Verlag, 1962), 43; D. A. Stoute, "The Origins and Early Development of the Reformed Idea of the Covenant" (PhD diss., University of Cambridge, 1979), 23; cf. W. N. Todd, "The Function of the Patristic Writings in the Thought of John Calvin" (ThD diss., Union Theological Seminary, 1964), 169–227; Charles S. McCoy and J. Wayne Baker, *Fountainhead of Federalism: Heinrich Bullinger and the Covenantal Tradition; With a Translation of "De testamento seu foedere Dei unico et aeterno" (1534)* (Louisville: Westminster John Knox, 1991), 14–15; Andrew A. Woolsey, *Unity and Continuity in Covenantal Thought: A Study in the Reformed Tradition to the Westminster Assembly* (Grand Rapids, MI: Reformation Heritage Books, 2012), 161–83; Peter Y. De Jong, *The Covenant Idea in New England Theology, 1620–1847* (Grand Rapids, MI: Eerdmans, 1945), 15–17; Peter A. Lillback, *The Binding of God: Calvin's Role in the Development of Covenant Theology* (Grand Rapids, MI: Baker Academic, 2001), 67–74; Mark Walter Karlberg, "The Mosaic Covenant and the Concept of Works in Reformed Hermeneutics: A Historical-Critical Analysis with Particular Attention to Early Covenant Eschatology" (ThD diss., Westminster Theological Seminary, 1980), 37–45.

4. The McCoy and Baker annotated translation of *De testamento* (or *A Brief Exposition of the One and Eternal Testament or Covenant of God*) may be found in their *Fountainhead of Federalism*, 99–138; for Bullinger's appeals to the fathers, see 119–30. Bullinger had earlier appealed to Irenaeus, Tertullian, Lactantius, Eusebius, and Augustine

Bullinger drew heavily on the Bible and used several church fathers to give his idea of covenant a past, in order to demonstrate that it was not an innovation but the very fabric from which the history of salvation was woven through the centuries, from Adam to his own day. He cited Augustine, Irenaeus, Tertullian, Lactantius, and Eusebius for patristic support.[5]

This discovery has led a number of Reformation specialists to conduct preliminary surveys of the covenant idea in the fathers in order to set the stage for analysis of the Reformers' covenant theology.[6] Andrew Woolsey, for instance, offers these concluding remarks in his brief overview of the use of the covenant concept in the epistle of Barnabas, Justin Martyr, Irenaeus, Clement of Alexandria, and Augustine:

> First, they all used the idea of covenant to stress the unity, and explain the differences, between the Old and New Testaments. Secondly, they saw the covenant soteriologically as one eternal covenant in Christ manifest throughout all ages from the time of Adam. Thirdly, there was a dual emphasis in their presentation of the covenant. It was a unilateral promise of grace given sovereignly by God, but it also required a response of faith and obedience from man, though this response was only by divine enabling and not by any natural inherent power resident in fallen man. Fourthly, in the case of Augustine, there was a definite use of the idea of covenant in a legal sense, though still in a context of "grace," with respect to Adam in his fallen state. Finally, again in Augustine especially, there was a close association of the covenant with baptism, so that it is erroneous to locate the origin of the idea of covenant in this connection in the Zurich reformation.[7]

Hence, a new interest in the role of the covenant idea in the early church has been created through research into the sources of Reformation-era covenant theology.

Second, specialists in early Christian studies have recently given attention to the place of the covenant idea in the theology of the early church.[8] Chief among them is

---

in support of his covenant teaching in *De originis erroris, in divorum ac simulachrorum cultu* (Basel, 1529), sig. Bii(v); see McCoy and Baker, *Fountainhead of Federalism*, 127n20.

5. McCoy and Baker, *Fountainhead of Federalism*, 14–15.

6. The best of these is in Woolsey, *Unity and Continuity*, 161–83; but see also Baker, *Bullinger and the Covenant*, 19–25; Karlberg, "Mosaic Covenant," 37–45.

7. Woolsey, *Unity and Continuity*, 183.

8. See Everett Ferguson, "The Covenant Idea in the Second Century," in *Texts and Testaments: Critical Essays on the Bible and the Early Church Fathers*, ed. W. Eugene March (San Antonio, TX: Trinity University Press, 1980), 134–35; Ferguson, "Covenant," in *Encyclopedia of Early Christianity*, ed. Angelo di Berardino, trans. Adrian Walford (New York: Oxford University Press, 1992), 239–40. W. C. van Unnik discusses the significance of the application of the phrase καινὴ διαθήκη to the collection of writings that became the New Testament, and in passing he highlights the import of the covenant idea in Irenaeus's theology in "'Η καινὴ διαθήκη—A Problem in the Early History of the Canon," *StPatr* 4 (1961): 212–27. Robert Verelle Moss concentrates primarily on the covenant as a theological category in Old Testament and New Testament canonical writings but briefly considers its role in the periodization of redemptive history in Barnabas, Justin Martyr, Irenaeus, and Clement of Alexandria in "The Covenant Conception in Early Christian Thought" (PhD diss., University of Chicago, 1964). W. H. C. Frend notes Irenaeus's employment of the covenant idea in "The Old Testament in the Age of the Greek Apologists, A.D. 130–180," *SJT* 26, no. 2 (1973): 129–50, esp. 148–49. David Sterling Kolb discusses how the idea of

Everett Ferguson, whose essay "The Covenant Idea in the Second Century" is an important, brief review of the covenant concept in the theology of the early church. He surveys 1 Clement, Barnabas, Justin Martyr, Gnostic and Ebionite literature, Irenaeus, Tertullian, Clement of Alexandria, Melito of Sardis, the Pseudo-Cyprian *Adversus Judaeos*, and Origen and draws the following conclusions:

1. Covenant was part of the Old Testament–Jewish heritage of the church.
2. The covenant idea had its significance in structuring holy history against Jewish claims for and Gnostic repudiation of the law, and a covenantal "history of salvation" view was one of the fundamental hermeneutical tools employed by many early Christian writers in doing so.
3. This covenantal structure may fairly be claimed to be rooted in the early kerygma and to be based on the first developments of it by Paul and Luke.
4. The covenant concept is closely related to the theme of "God's people."
5. Both Hebraic (i.e., relationship) and Hellenistic (i.e., testament) components persisted in early Christian texts about διαθήκη.
6. The association with "law" and "gospel" prepared for the adoption of the term "covenant" as the title for the Scriptures.[9]

So in the work of Ferguson and others, there are signs that patristic scholars are showing more attention to covenant thought and are acknowledging its theological importance in early Christianity. Even a cursory reading of studies on patristic literature reveals the significance of the theology of the covenants for early Christianity. This can be seen most manifestly in the ways in which the early church employed covenants in controversial writings against the Jews; their use of covenants in the second- and early third-century polemics against Gnostics; and, more positively, the ways in which they employed the covenant idea to teach both the continuity and discontinuity between the Old Testament and the New.

A Theological Summary of Explicit New Testament Usage of "Covenant"[10]

The doctrine of the covenants in the New Testament has been addressed at length elsewhere in this volume, which leaves it to us to summarize the main lines of the theological

---

the incarnation modified the church's inherited covenant concept through a survey of Justin Martyr, Tatian, Athenagoras, Irenaeus, Theophilus of Antioch, Melito of Sardis, Minucius Felix, Tertullian, Hippolytus, and Clement of Alexandria, but he assumes (rather than demonstrates) the concept's presence and content in the fathers' writings in "The Impact of the Incarnational Motif on the Churches' Understanding of Covenant Faith in the Period AD 150 to AD 230" (PhD diss., Southern Baptist Theological Seminary, 1988). E. G. Hinson suggests that the "three pillars of the covenant concept" are monotheism, high moral standards, and mission and that the covenant was an important theological concept in the early church in *The Evangelization of the Roman Empire* (Macon, GA: Mercer University Press, 1981), 151. We may note in passing that, over a century ago, Adolf von Harnack (characteristically) did not allow the significance of the covenant idea in the fathers to escape his notice, see *History of Dogma*, trans. Neil Buchanan, 3rd ed. (ca. 1900; repr., New York: Dover, 1961), 2:230–318, esp. 244–45.

9. Ferguson, "Covenant Idea in the Second Century," 155–56.

10. For extensive evidence of the following summary points, see Duncan, "Covenant Idea in Ante-Nicene Theology", 21–75.

usage of the covenants in the New Testament, in order to indicate in what areas to expect its deployment within the postapostolic writings of the early church.

1. In the Synoptic Gospels, Acts, Paul, and Hebrews, Christ's incarnation and saving work are seen as the fulfillment of the Abrahamic promise. Hence, each book evidences belief that the blessings of God's covenant with Abraham are now coming to rest on the followers of Christ. Additionally, and this is particularly clear in the "son of David" and "kingdom" sayings of Matthew, the Davidic covenant is strongly applied to Jesus as recipient of God's promises to David, both as King and bringer of the kingdom.

2. In the Synoptics, Paul, and Hebrews, the new covenant established in the blood of Christ is identified as the fulfillment of the new covenant prophecy in Jeremiah 31.

3. The Synoptics and Hebrews interpret the death of Christ in light of the covenant-inauguration ceremony of Exodus 24. The Synoptics relate Christ's death to the Passover lambs of the exodus in the eucharistic narratives, and explicit paschal imagery is also found in 1 Corinthians 5:7; 1 Peter 1:19; and the Johannine writings.

4. In the Synoptics, Acts, Paul, and Hebrews, the covenant idea is explicitly linked with the forgiveness of sins. This forgiveness of sins is seen as a fulfillment of both the Abrahamic promise and Jeremiah's new covenant prophecy, and it is a hallmark of the new covenant established by Christ.

5. Throughout the New Testament writings, διαθήκη is best rendered "covenant." There are only two passages in the New Testament, Galatians 3:15 and Hebrews 9:16–17, where it is even possible that διαθήκη means "testament," and even these are best read as "covenant."

6. Both Paul (in 2 Cor. 3 and Gal. 3) and Hebrews interpret the history of redemption in covenant terms. For each of them, the new covenant is vastly superior to the old. When they are contrasting the new redemptive economy with the old, they represent the era before Christ in the form of the Mosaic economy.

7. Paul tends to stress discontinuity between the Mosaic economy and the new (letter and Spirit), while emphasizing continuity between the Abrahamic covenant and the new (promise and fulfillment). At the same time, Hebrews, while also acknowledging continuity between the Abrahamic covenant and the new, displays *both* continuity and discontinuity between the Mosaic and new covenants. For the author of Hebrews, the new covenant not only sets aside the old order, it fulfills it.

8. Contrary to the view of Hillers already quoted, in none of these strands of the New Testament's total witness is the covenant idea itself seen as one of the shadows that passes away with the coming of a new era in redemptive history.[11] The covenant idea is appealed

---

11. Howard C. Kee has observed, "As Christianity reached out ever wider into the Gentile world, the nature of its links with its Jewish heritage became more ambiguous and controversial. Yet all the evidence before and after 70 points to the insistence of the early Christians that they were the heirs, and had the proper keys to interpretation, of the covenant tradition of Israel embodied in the Jewish Scriptures." "After the Crucifixion: Christianity through

to in the Synoptics, Acts, Paul, Hebrews, and Revelation as an adequate expression of the relationship between God and his people established by the work of Christ. In both Hebrews and Paul, the covenant relationship transcends the temporal characteristics of the Mosaic administration and finds its ultimate realization in the face-to-face communion with God of the new covenant.

For the New Testament theologians, then, the covenant idea is inextricably tied to the death of Christ. His blood inaugurated a new covenant, and without that bloodshed, there would have been no new covenant. His death is the ground of forgiveness of sins in the new covenant, and his covenantal mediation ensures everlasting communion with God.

With these categories and usages in mind, we turn now to the extrabiblical evidence for a theology of the covenants in early Christianity. We concentrate on pre-Nicene material because it is the most overlooked in terms of covenant thought and because it is foundational for later influences on the church (Augustine et al.).

Apostolic Fathers and Apologists[12]

Everett Ferguson has pointed out that the word διαθήκη occurs in three principal contexts in the New Testament (in the Supper narratives; in Paul's discussions of the covenant in 2 Cor. 3 and Gal. 4; and in Heb. 7–13). In these passages the authors appeal to the covenants

1. to explain the significance of Jesus's death;
2. to show the relationship between the Mosaic and Christian eras, and carnal and spiritual Israel; and
3. to demonstrate the superiority of the Christian economy.[13]

It is not surprising, then, to find that the covenant concept fulfills similar roles in early post–New Testament writings. The theology of the covenants can be shown to be present in the writings of the early church via the explicit use of covenant terminology; the treatment of key biblical "covenant passages"; the usage of covenant-related concepts (e.g., election, the people of God); the authors' approach to the continuity of redemptive history; and the employment of inherited patterns of interpretation and views on the covenants. A survey of the writings of the apostolic fathers and apologists reveals the following observations relating to the theology of the covenants.

1. Clement and Barnabas employ the covenant in the context of moral exhortation (see, e.g., 1 Clem. 15.4, 35.7; Barn. 4.6–8). Clement in particular stresses

---

Paul," in *Christianity and Rabbinic Judaism: A Parallel History of Their Origins and Early Development*, ed. Hershel Shanks (Washington, DC: Biblical Archaeology Society, 1992), 124.

12. For extensive evidence of the following summary points, see Duncan, "Covenant Idea in Ante-Nicene Theology," 76–100.

13. Ferguson, "Covenant Idea in the Second Century," 136.

the consequences of Christian disobedience and the attendant responsibilities in the covenant relationship. Barnabas also uses the story of Israel's loss of the covenant as a warning to Christians (Barn. 4.9, 14). While Justin's accent on mutuality is less pronounced than Barnabas's or Clement's, he nevertheless recognizes the bilateral aspects of the covenant.

2. According to Barnabas, Israel lost the covenant at the start through disobedience (Barn. 4.6, 8) and never understood it rightly (i.e., allegorically, see Barn. 7–12), whereas Justin affirms the historical reality, reception, and function of the old covenant. He simply teaches that it has now been superseded in Christ.

3. Both Barnabas and Justin connect law and covenant closely and view Jesus as the covenant, via Isaiah 42:6–7 (Barn. 14.7; *Dial.* 26). For Barnabas, however, Jesus is the covenant; for Justin he is the *new* covenant.

4. Following on the previous point, for Barnabas there is only one covenant (he never speaks of a new covenant), and Christians are the only recipients of it (Barn. 13.1, 6). For Justin there is an old and a new covenant, and Christians are the recipients of the new, as Israel was of the old (*Dial.* 11–12).

5. Both Barnabas and Justin relate the covenant idea to inheritance (Barn. 13.6, 14.5; *Dial.* 122). This does not necessarily mean that they view the διαθήκη to be testamentary. It may well simply reflect themes they have lifted from Isaiah (e.g., Isa. 49:8) in their Christological exegesis.

6. In Barnabas, Israel is "the people," though he sometimes qualifies this appellation (e.g., "the first people" or "those people," Barn. 13.1). For Justin the church is the fulfillment of Old Testament prophecy concerning the salvation of the Gentiles and is the true spiritual Israel (*Dial.* 11).

7. Barnabas links the covenant idea with God's redemptive plan, forgiveness, the person of Christ, Jesus's suffering, and our receipt of the inheritance (Barn. 14.4–7). Clement employs the covenant as an example for Christians to follow, or rather, not to follow (1 Clem. 15, 35). Justin links the covenant with Christ (virtually equating the new covenant with Christ), the law, the people of God, God's promises, and the Gentiles (*Dial.* 11, 24, 122).

8. Without denying the influence of New Testament interpretive patterns, we may note that the covenantal thought of Barnabas, Justin, and Clement appeals to Old Testament, rather than New Testament, covenant passages for support of their respective discussions. This is a hallmark of second-century *demonstratio evangelica* (in which Old Testament passages are used to establish the gospel message and appealed to for apologetic and evangelistic purposes).

9. The Abrahamic, Mosaic, Davidic, and new covenants are mentioned or alluded to in writings of the apostolic fathers and apologists (Barn. 4.6–8; *Dial.* 11, 12, 24). Neither an Adamic nor a Noahic covenant, however, is explicitly cited.

10. Variations in covenant thought are evident in the second-century theologians. Indeed, Ferguson identifies seven contemporary competing views of the covenant in the second century.[14]

It is apparent in examination of the occurrences of covenant thought in the fathers and apologists (at least in Clement, Barnabas, and Justin) that covenant is often used in the context of exhorting Christians to moral responsibility and, hence, clearly retains its Hebraic sense of mutuality, without in any way denying the priority and necessity of the grace of God. Furthermore, early Christian writers claimed "to have the correct insights [into the Jewish Scriptures] and to be the true heirs of the covenant promises,"[15]

---

14. Everett Ferguson, "Justin Martyr: On Jews, Christians, and the Covenant," in *Early Christianity in Context: Monuments and Documents*, ed. F. Manns and E. Alliata (Jerusalem: Franciscan Printing, 1993), 398–402. In this article, Ferguson surveys seven varieties of covenant thought in the second century, identifying Justin's as the version (as taken up and modified by Irenaeus) that later came to be predominant. The following is a synopsis of his review of competing solutions to the question of the Christian attitude toward the Jewish Scriptures and the Jewish heritage of the church:

(1) Justin Martyr: (a) taught that *covenant* means "disposition" (not "testament"); (b) was primarily concerned with the question "Who are God's people?"; (c) commonly associated "law" and "new" with "covenant"; (d) taught, in his history-of-salvation view, that "the covenant with Israel at Sinai was replaced with another covenant inaugurated by Jesus" (Ferguson, "Justin Martyr," 396); (e) affirmed one and the same God of Israel and Christians; (f) taught that Christians are not led to God through Moses or the law; (g) viewed the final law and covenant as ethnically universal; (h) asserted that Christ *is* the new law and new covenant; (i) deemed Christians to be the true spiritual Israel; (j) maintained that the new covenant accomplished the purpose of the old; (k) identified a number of Septuagint passages as significant for Christian covenant thought (e.g., Isa. 51:4; 55:3; Jer. 38:31; cf. Isa. 43:6); (l) argued for the identification of the new covenant with Christ via Isa. 42:6 (LXX); (m) taught that the new covenant replaced the Mosaic covenant; (n) viewed the new covenant to be everlasting; (o) held that the church fulfills the Old Testament Gentile passages.

(2) Barnabas: (a) distinguished between covenant and law; (b) saw the covenant as still binding, but for Christians, not Jews; (c) taught that the Jews misunderstood the law and lost the covenant by disobedience; (d) did not speak of a new covenant, only a new people; (e) associated covenant with the idea of inheritance, and hence probably had a testamentary understanding of διαθήκη; (f) argued that Christians had superseded the Jews as God's people.

(3) Marcion: (a) rejected the Jewish heritage of the church; (b) viewed the Old Testament as a Jewish book; (c) attempted a radical separation of law and gospel; (d) argued for two dispensations (fundamentally distinct); (e) taught that Christians and Israel worshiped different gods. [Ferguson calls Barnabas's and Marcion's resolutions "all or nothing approaches." "Justin Martyr," 399.]

(4) Ptolemy: (a) suggested that the New Testament attributes part of the Pentateuch to God, part to Moses, and part to elders; (b) believed that God wrote the Ten Commandments and that they were perfected by Jesus; (c) said that Old Testament civil legislation had been abolished by Jesus, being foreign to his nature; (d) taught that Old Testament ceremonial laws were transformed from material to spiritual in the new covenant.

(5) Ebionites: (a) attempted to be both Jews and Christians; (b) saw (some) Old Testament ritual law as binding on Gentile converts; (c) posited a distinction in the Old Testament Scriptures (false pericopes) and hence could maintain loyalty to Moses while rejecting certain portions of the law (sacrifices, monarchy, false prophecy); (d) maintained that Moses and Jesus taught the same things.

(6) *Didascalia*: (a) viewed moral law (Ten Commandments) as eternal; (b) taught that ceremonial law (second law) was temporary; (c) considered Sabbath as part of the deuterosis.

(7) Irenaeus: (a) taught that one and the same God administered his saving plan through successive covenants; (b) did not have the same anti-Jewish concerns as Justin; (c) built on Justin's distinction between dispensations of God, to explain differences between old and new covenant; (d) acknowledged each covenant to be historical and valid in its own time; (e) taught that the covenants find their consummation in Christ; (f) explained the similarities in covenants by noting that the same God arranged them all; (g) identified several covenants but most commonly two; (h) made the (later) common connection between Moses and law, Jesus and gospel; (i) developed his principal discussion of covenants in *Haer.* 4.32–34; (j) said that there were two covenants for two peoples but only one God; (k) explained, with the illustration of the returning king, that Jesus is the new thing about the new covenant; (l) taught two successive covenants, one for Jews, the other for all; (m) maintained that both covenants were adapted by God to the level of human maturity.

15. Kee, *Christianity and Rabbinic Judaism*, 124.

and their exposition of the theology of the covenants was influenced as much by the Old Testament as by the New. W. H. C. Frend has expressed this continuity strongly:

> In [Celsus's, ca. 175] day the thought-world of Christianity still belonged largely to Judaism. It was the Jewish concept of God, of creation, of history and morality that the Christian accepted on Baptism, and the Jewish arguments against paganism that he adopted in his defence of his new faith.[16]

What is clear is that the theology of the covenants was as important to Clement, Barnabas, and Justin as to the New Testament writers, and both groups saw the theology of the covenants as a key Old Testament inheritance for the New Testament church, which also enabled the church to distinguish itself from Judaism.

Melito of Sardis, Preaching the Covenant[17]

Melito of Sardis's extant writings contain only one use of the term "covenant," but his theology bears ample evidence of the theology of the covenants of his predecessors and contemporaries. His sermon Περὶ Πάσχα [*Peri Pascha*, or *PP*] explains the church's receipt of the blessing of Israel, the Jewish people's loss of the inheritance, and the newness and oldness of the divine economy—all in light of the standard early Christian theology of the covenants.

The only surviving passage from Melito's writings in which the word διαθήκη occurs is found in a fragment preserved by Eusebius of Caesarea: "So, going back to the east and reaching the place where it was proclaimed and done, I got precise information about the books of the Old Covenant" (cf. *Hist. eccl.* 4.26).[18] Here, Melito designates the Old Testament Scriptures the "books of the Old Covenant," an appellation that would soon after become commonplace in Christian writings but that (as far as we know) had not heretofore been employed outside the New Testament in written reference to the church's Old Testament Scriptures.[19] There is little internal evidence to assist in determining Melito's exact understanding of διαθήκη in the phrase "the books of the Old Covenant."[20] What is clear is that in Melito's time (ca. 170), the διαθήκη

16. Frend, "Age of Greek Apologists," 130.

17. For extensive evidence of the following summary points, see Duncan, "Covenant Idea in Ante-Nicene Theology," 118–31.

18. Translation from Stuart George Hall, ed., *On Pascha and Fragments: Texts and Translations* (Oxford: Clarendon, 1979). A. D. Nock and others have disputed the historicity of this claim, but see Hall, *On Pascha*, 53n55, 66n10, 67n12. For further argument defending the genuineness of the event, see Roger T. Beckwith, *The Old Testament Canon of the New Testament Church and Its Background in Early Judaism* (London: SPCK, 1985), 184–85.

19. Of course, Paul had referred to the writings of Moses as the "old covenant" (2 Cor. 3:14). J. N. D. Kelly believes that Christian designation of the Scriptures as Old and New Testaments/covenants can be traced to this usage in Paul. *Early Christian Doctrines*, 5th ed. (San Francisco: Harper, 1978), 56. Van Unnik rejects Kelly's view, see, "Ἡ καινὴ διαθήκη," 220.

20. That is, does the phrase involve a covenantal (relational), dispositional (administrative), historical (epochal), or testamentary (legal documentary) understanding of διαθήκη? Hall translates it "books of the Old Covenant." G. A. Williamson, "The Old Testament Books," in *History of the Church* (Harmondsworth, UK: Penguin, 1965), 189; A. C. McGiffert, "books of the Old Testament," *ANCL* 1:206 (2nd ser.).

idea was deemed important enough in the church's understanding of redemptive history to serve as a standard designation for its sacred writings. In fact, not long after this time (ca. 192–193), an anonymous Christian writer applied καινος διαθήκης ("new covenant") to the New Testament Scriptures.[21] In light of the instinctive usage of this terminology in the last quarter of the second century, it is safe to assume that the connection between covenant and Scripture was a conventional one for Christians at least as early as the mid-second century. Even Wolfram Kinzig, who finds the covenant references in Melito and the anonymous anti-Montanist to be inconclusive as evidence of the use of διαθήκη as a title for Scripture, concedes that "it is no doubt correct to assume that there is a close relation between 'New Testament' as a book title and the theology of the time." He furthermore admits that "the development of 'the theological concept of God's covenant with his people' is one of the necessary preconditions for the emergence of the title under discussion."[22] Whatever the case may be, Melito's *Peri Pascha* provides us with testimony to another representative use of covenant thought in this era.

Ferguson and Kinzig both have concluded that a covenantal history-of-salvation approach was typical of the second-century Christian theologians.[23] This is confirmed in Melito's *Peri Pascha*, which was produced sometime in the third quarter of the second century (ca. 160–170).[24] It is an ancient homily, bearing the distinctive marks of Greek rhetoric[25] and commemorating "the whole saving work of Christ as the fulfillment of the ancient Pascha."[26]

In *Peri Pascha* we find Melito employing a covenant approach to redemptive history not dissimilar to that of Justin Martyr but without using the term διαθήκη. This is evidenced in three ways: (1) Melito's treatment of continuity and discontinuity in redemptive history, (2) his anti-Jewish polemic, and (3) the possible sacramental significance of *Peri Pascha*.

---

21. The full phrase is τί τάς τόυ εὐαγγελίου καίνος διαθήκης λόγῳ, which seems to allude to Rev. 22:18–19 (*Hist. eccl.* 5.16.3). The presence of ἐπιδιατάσσεσθαι in the context confirms that διαθήκη is here employed in a documentary (perhaps even a testamentary) sense; see the comments of van Unnik in "'Η καινὴ διαθήκη," 217–18. Note, however, that Ferguson believes this is a reference to "the total message" or "an era," not only a collection of books. "Covenant Idea in the Second Century," 150. In contrast, Kelly argues that Irenaeus is the first to apply καινὴ διαθήκη to the New Testament Scriptures. *Early Christian Doctrines*, 56. Wolfram Kinzig has put forward yet another view, asserting that "the first unequivocal testimonies" to καινὴ διαθήκη being used to designate the New Testament "are found around the year 200 in the writings of Clement of Alexandria." "Καινὴ διαθήκη: The Title of the New Testament in the Second and Third Centuries," *JTS* 45, no. 2 (1994): 529.

22. Kinzig, "Καινὴ διαθήκη," 522.

23. Ferguson, "Covenant Idea in the Second Century," 155. Kinzig corroborates Ferguson's claim when he says that Justin, Irenaeus, Tertullian, and Clement "championed the theology of the covenants." "Καινὴ διαθήκη," 522. See also Kinzig, *Novitas Christiana: Die Idee des Fortschritts in der Alten Kirche bis Eusebius*, FKD 58 (Göttingen: Vandenhoeck und Ruprecht, 1994).

24. Exact dating is perilously dependent on Eusebius's identification of the work Περὶ του Πάσχα with Melito's Περὶ Πάσχα (*Hist. eccl.* 4.26.3–4) and the resolution of the difficulties connected with the attendant chronological note. See Hall's comments in *On Pascha*, xix–xxii. Robert J. Daly suggests AD 165–170 in Origen, *Treatise on the Passover and Dialogue with Heraclides*, trans. and ed. Robert J. Daly, ACW 54 (New York: Paulist, 1992), 7.

25. See A. Wifstrand, "The Homily of Melito on the Passion," *VC* 2, no. 4 (1948): 201–23.

26. Hall, *On Pascha*, xxv.

Melito's stress on redemptive-historical continuity may be seen in a variety of ways. In the first lines of *Peri Pascha*, Melito takes as the starting point of his sermon the exodus as Scripture: "The Scripture about the Hebrew Exodus has been read" (*PP* 1). Here we have a parallel with Clement of Rome's exhortation to Christians based on Old Testament covenant texts (see 1 Clem. 15.4, 35.7).[27] Hence, Old Testament historical events are seen to relate directly to God's dealings with the church (*PP* 40). The relatively meager evidence of covenantal thought in the writings of Melito currently accessible to us allows us neither to assess the total shape of his opinions nor to estimate the significance of the covenant idea in his theology. Nevertheless, there is more than enough material for comparison with the covenantal thought of his predecessors and contemporaries.

1. As "Israel" served as an Old Testament sacral term for the people of God, and as New Testament writers saw themselves to be essentially related to "the people" (Rom. 9–11), so also Melito sees Israel as "the people" and "the church" as its new covenant fulfillment (*PP* 40, 41), indeed, "an eternal people personal to him" (*PP* 68).

2. Whereas Melito repeats the New Testament identification of Jesus as the Paschal Lamb (*PP* 4), he does not duplicate the New Testament connection of the incarnation and work of Christ and the Abrahamic covenant, nor does he link the death of Christ with the Mosaic covenant and Jeremiah's new covenant. Barnabas's and Justin's expressions of covenant thought are much more explicit in this area than is Melito's in *Peri Pascha*.

3. Melito shares with the New Testament and Justin an emphasis on both continuity and discontinuity when relating the old and new covenants (*PP* 3, 40–45), but neither explicitly employs the covenant motif as an instrument to structure redemptive history, nor expressly links the covenant idea and forgiveness of sins (though Melito treats the latter in *PP* 103).

4. Melito's extant writings do not offer enough evidence to determine the denotation and connotation of διαθήκη in his theology. It is clear, however, that the διαθήκη idea is significant enough for Melito that the term διαθήκη can serve as part of his appellation for the church's Hebrew Scriptures.

5. Whereas Clement and Barnabas employ covenant thought in the service of moral exhortation, Melito's covenant thought primarily serves the didactic cause of gospel explanation (e.g., *PP* 6–10).

6. Melito stands with Justin and over against Barnabas in his view of Israel's reception of the old covenant (*PP* 83–85).

7. Like Barnabas, Justin, and Clement of Rome, Melito appeals to Old Testament rather than New Testament passages as the basis of his teaching (in the standard manner of second-century *demonstratio evangelica*) and manifests the influence of the Old Testament and Judaism (*PP* 1, 66, 68, 86, 93).[28]

---

27. Incidentally, if Melito is doing in *Peri Pascha* what Clement was doing in his epistle, then it is possible to read even the strongly anti-Jewish polemic in the sermon as admonitory exhortation for Christians.

28. See Hall, *On Pascha*, xxvi–xxvii.

8. Whereas the Abrahamic, Mosaic, Davidic, and new covenants are mentioned or alluded to in writings of the New Testament, apostolic fathers, and apologists, Melito never explicitly does so in *PP*. He does speak of Adam (*PP* 83), Noah (*PP* 83), Abraham (Frag. 15), Isaac (as a type of Christ, Frag. 9), Moses (*PP* 59, 61), David (*PP* 59, 62), and Jeremiah (*PP* 63), but he never links them to a covenant. Melito does, interestingly, articulate the giving of the law to Adam (an important theme in Tertullian) in the garden as a major part of his discussion of the need for human redemption (*PP* 47–48). There he explicitly equates the command with the prohibition and designates Adam's sin as disobedience.

9. As with the apostolic fathers and apologists, we note slight variations in the cove-nant thought of Melito and his predecessors and contemporaries.

One of the interesting examples of "genetic connections" in the theology of the covenants in early Christianity is the set of threads that can be detected from Justin to Melito to Irenaeus to Tertullian. We turn next to Irenaeus.

Irenaeus, Covenant Theologian[29]

In his seminal article "The Covenant Idea in the Second Century," Ferguson suggests that "Irenaeus was a 'covenant' theologian." He makes clear what he intends by that designation when he says, "The covenant scheme of the interpretation of holy history became the foundation of Irenaeus' theological method."[30] Nevertheless, the Irenaean contribution to second-century covenant theology remains a generally unrecognized and relatively neglected subject, in spite of the work of Philippe Bacq,[31] Ferguson, Kinzig[32] and others;[33] in spite of Irenaeus's significance as a second-century Christian theologian;[34] and in spite of the ongoing interest in Irenaean theology.[35] Indeed, W. C. van Unnik

---

29. For extensive evidence of the following summary points, see Duncan, "Covenant Idea in Ante-Nicene Theology," 132–57.
30. Ferguson, "Covenant Idea in the Second Century," 144.
31. Philippe Bacq has made a splendid contribution to the discussion of Irenaeus's theology with his *De l'ancienne à la nouvelle Alliance selon S. Irénée*. His work counters the opinions of earlier source critics of Irenaeus (in particular Harnack) and argues for the literary and theological unity of *Adversus haereses*. The theological unity of the work, according to Bacq, is built on the concept of the unity of God and the consequent unity of the cove-nants in salvation history; see Bacq, *De l'ancienne à la nouvelle Alliance selon S. Irénée* (Paris: Le thielleux, 1978), 41–46, 153–61, 235–40, and esp. 290–93. While Bacq's work concentrates on book 4 of *Adversus haereses* and is not intended to oppose the importance of the idea of "recapitulation" (or any other theme for that matter) in Irenaeus's thought, it does serve to make clear the significance of "covenant" in Irenaeus's argument for the unity of God and salvation history. This aspect of Irenaean thought has been virtually overlooked in most of the work on his writings before Bacq.
32. See Kinzig, *Novitas Christiana*; Kinzig, *Erbin Kirche: Die Auslegung von Psalm 5,1 in den Psalmenhomilien des Asterius und in der Alten Kirche* (Heidelberg: Universitätsverlag, 1990), 78–96.
33. Among them, van Unnik, see "Ἡ καινὴ διαθήκη," 225.
34. Irenaeus has been described as the "most considerable Christian theologian" of his time. F. L. Cross, *The Early Christian Fathers* (London: Gerald Duckworth, 1960), 110. See also Johannes Quasten, *Patrology*, vol. 1, *The Beginnings of Patristic Literature* (Utrecht: Spectrum, 1950), 287. Berthold Altaner says, "Irenaeus is the most important of the second century theologians and in a certain sense the Father of Catholic dogmatics." *Patrology*, trans. Hilda C. Graef (Edinburgh: Nelson, 1960), 150.
35. Irenaeus's theology has been the subject of a number of major works in the past century. In 1930 (English trans., 1931), Gustaf Aulén, in his famous *Christus Victor*, put Irenaeus in the theological spotlight by suggesting

complains that it is "remarkable that so little attention is given to this theme [covenant] in the descriptions of Irenaeus' theology."[36] In this section, I offer a brief summary of Irenaeus's theology of the covenants, including his use of covenant terminology and the title he uses for the New Testament canon.

J. N. D. Kelly has argued that "the first writer to speak unequivocally of a 'New' Testament parallel to the Old was Irenaeus" and that "after Irenaeus's time . . . the fully scriptural character of the specifically Christian writings was universally acknowledged, and the description of them as the 'New Testament' (a title harking back to St. Paul's designation of the Jewish Scriptures as 'the old covenant') came into vogue."[37] Van Unnik questions the conclusiveness of Kelly's claim that Irenaeus was the first writer to speak unequivocally of a "New" Testament, yet he generally confirms Kelly's assessment of Irenaeus's importance in the development of this terminology.[38] Significantly, however, he expands on and modifies Kelly's view of the origin of the use of the term καινὴ διαθήκη for the Christian Scriptures, linking this terminology to Irenaeus's covenant theology and insisting that the New Testament idea of διαθήκη is not Hellenistic ("testament") but rather Hebraic ("covenant").[39] The background of καινὴ διαθήκη for Irenaeus, according to van Unnik, is the Old Testament prophetic promise of a "New Covenant."[40] With Irenaeus, says van Unnik, "it is remarkable that διαθήκη has here always the biblical notion of 'covenant' and never any relation to 'testament.'"[41] He concludes,

> In this climate were the Gospels and Apostolic writings first styled "books of the καινὴ διαθήκη." . . . This rich title was generally accepted. But soon afterwards it lost its dynamic weight and became nothing more than just a title. . . . In the West the translation *testamentum* and not *foedus* for διαθήκη had, as far as I can see, very

---

that Irenaeus's presentation of the central ideas of the Christian faith provided the basis for a *via media* (between "objective" and "subjective" views) in the construction of a theology of the atonement. Aulén saw Irenaeus's theology of the atonement as revolving around the idea of Christ's triumph over the forces of sin, death, and Satan, which in turn was part of the larger idea of "recapitulation." Aulén's work assured that *recapitulatio* would be considered by subsequent students to be Irenaeus's "most comprehensive theological idea." See Aulén, *Christus Victor: An Historical Study of the Three Main Types of the Idea of the Atonement*, trans. A. G. Hebert (1931; repr., New York: Macmillan, 1969), 37. Consequently, Irenaeus's covenant thought has been ignored. John Lawson reviewed Irenaean theology, all but ignoring Irenaeus's contribution to second-century covenant theology, in his *Biblical Theology of St. Irenaeus* (London: Epworth, 1948), esp. 140ff. Gustaf Wingren continued the focus on recapitulation, discussing Irenaeus's relation to the Old Testament, but neglected the covenant idea, in *Man and the Incarnation: A Study in the Biblical Theology of Irenaeus*, trans. Ross Mackenzie (Edinburgh: Oliver and Boyd, 1959). André Benoît, in *Saint Irénée: Introduction à l'étude de sa théologie* (Paris: Presses universitaires de France, 1960). The only scholars who pay much attention at all to the significant role of the covenants in Irenaeus's history of salvation are F. R. Montgomery Hitchcock, *Irenaeus of Lugdunum: A Study of His Teaching* (Cambridge: Cambridge University Press, 1914); and Auguste Luneau, *L'Histoire de salut chez les Pères de l'Eglise: La doctrine des ages du monde* (Paris: Beauchesne, 1964).

36. Van Unnik, "Ή καινὴ διαθήκη," 225.

37. Kelly, *Early Christian Doctrines*, 56.

38. Van Unnik, "Ή καινὴ διαθήκη," 217; see also Hans von Campenhausen, *The Formation of the Christian Bible*, trans. John Austin Baker (London: A&C Black, 1972), 264–65.

39. Van Unnik, "Ή καινὴ διαθήκη," 225.

40. Van Unnik, "Ή καινὴ διαθήκη," 222–25.

41. Van Unnik, "Ή καινὴ διαθήκη," 225.

serious consequences. In the Greek speaking world διαθήκη was soon misunderstood as "testament" and a change in outlook robbed it of its influence.[42]

This view has since been challenged by Kinzig, who gives some evidence of a testamentary usage of διαθήκη by Irenaeus (cf. *Haer.* 5.9.4).[43] Whatever are the precise origins of διαθήκη becoming employed as a scriptural title, even Kinzig (as we have already seen) does not deny that the development and prevalence of covenant thought in the second century were necessary preconditions for its eventual service as a designation for the Scriptures. In this foundational work, Irenaeus played an undoubted role.

Furthermore, it has been argued that Irenaeus's stress on the essential unity of salvation history paved the way for the consolidation of the Hebrew Scriptures and the Christian writings into the Christian Bible. Rowan A. Greer says that by speaking of the differing economies of the same God, "Irenaeus offers a Christian transformation of the Hebrew Scriptures that makes them wholly integral to a Christian Bible."[44] Irenaeus argued against Marcion's rejection of the Hebrew Scriptures, as seen later, by stressing the unity of the old and new covenants. Hence, it can be argued that the church's bipartite Bible is, at least in part, a legacy of Irenaeus's covenant theology.[45]

Irenaeus's teaching on the covenants has received very little attention from those who have studied his theology.[46] But we have seen, even in this brief survey, that it is a theme of no small significance in the writings of this great theologian of the second century. Woolsey suggests that "Irenaeus was one of the clearest expositors of the covenant amongst the fathers."[47] It seems, then, that Irenaeus's fellow Christians in Lyons spoke precisely and appropriately (and perhaps with a little prescience) when they described him as "zealous for the covenant of Christ" (Eusebius, *Hist. eccl.*, 5.4.2). Van Unnik comments on this lacuna in Irenaean studies:

---

42. Van Unnik, "Ἡ καινὴ διαθήκη," 226–27.

43. Kinzig, "Καινὴ διαθήκη," 519–44, esp. 524–25; see also Dirk van Damme, *Pseudo Cyprian: Adversus Iudaeos; Gegen die Judenchristen; Die älteste lateinische Predigt* (Freiburg: Universitätsverlag, 1969), 46–50.

44. Rowan A. Greer, "The Christian Bible and Its Interpretation," in *Early Biblical Interpretation*, by James L. Kugel and Rowan A. Greer, ed. Wayne A. Meeks (Philadelphia: Westminster, 1986), 154.

45. Campenhausen, *Formation of the Christian Bible*, 209.

46. Only Ferguson (in "Covenant Idea in the Second Century"), Woolsey (in *Unity and Continuity*), and I ("Covenant Idea in Ante-Nicene Theology") have deliberately concentrated on the subject of Irenaean covenant theology. Woolsey's survey, though brief (three pages), accurately concludes,

> Here, then, in outline is the "covenant theology" of one of the early church fathers. Several points are worth underlining. Irenaeus regarded the covenant relationship between God and man as a divine arrangement, involving a condescension by God to man's capacity and condition. He saw the covenant as the central factor in the unfolding of salvation history. While there were different expressions of covenant, the covenant in Christ was requisite for the saints of all ages, with one way of salvation for the church going back to the time of Adam. Irenaeus distinguished between the mere letter of the law and its spirit. He identified both the natural law, the moral law and the love of God with the righteousness of God. Ceremonial laws were abrogated with the coming of Christ, but the moral law continued in force and has a continuing function in the lives of those who have been liberated by the gospel as a means of testing the reality and strength of their faith. The covenant of grace, therefore, while unilateral in its initiation and accomplishment, had for Irenaeus a strong bilateral and ethical emphasis in its outworking in Christian experience.

Unity and Continuity, 165–66.

47. Woolsey, *Unity and Continuity*, 164.

In reading the passages where Irenaeus deals with the New Covenant one notices that he is using general notions with a typically polemical application viz. to show to the Gnostics who rejected the O.T. that it is the same God in both. It is a fundamental part of his theology as may be seen from the *Epideixis* where he gives the positive exposition. This combined with the fact that he is called "zealous for the covenant of Christ" makes it the more remarkable that so little attention is given to this theme in the descriptions of Irenaeus' theology. It is too important to be dealt with in a chapter on the relation between the two parts of the bible by way of introduction as is generally done.[48]

This expression ("zealous for the covenant of Christ"), according to van Unnik, is unique in patristic literature.[49] In any case, it is certainly a most apposite moniker for Irenaeus. We may summarize some of the emphases of his covenant theology as follows.

1. Irenaeus understands διαθήκη primarily as a relationship between God and his people (what van Unnik calls the "Hebraic" sense) (*Haer.* 4.9.3). This relationship is so essential to the purposes of the divine economy that διαθήκη often serves Irenaeus to delineate the main eras of redemptive history (*Haer.* 4.11.3). He is also fond of speaking of covenants in the plural (*Haer.* 4.32.2). Hence, "covenant" (rather than "testament" or "disposition") is the primary sense of διαθήκη in Irenaeus.

2. With the New Testament writers and Justin, Irenaeus sees the incarnation and work of Christ as a fulfillment of the Abrahamic covenant, the Mosaic covenant, and the new covenant prophesied by Jeremiah (*Haer.* 4.13.1; *Epid.* 24, 90). In contrast, Melito nowhere makes this connection explicitly in his extant writings.

3. The covenant concept is of major significance in Irenaeus's presentation of redemptive history (*Haer.* 1.10.1, 3). He perhaps makes more of the covenants than any of his contemporaries. He emphasizes both continuity and discontinuity when relating the old (Mosaic and Abrahamic) and new covenants (*Haer.* 4.11.3).

4. The linkage of the covenant idea with forgiveness of sins is not as prominent in Irenaeus as it is in the New Testament and Justin. Irenaeus does, however, affirm the graciousness of the divine economy, especially in stressing the divine adaptation of the various covenants for the education and glorification of humanity (*Haer.* 3.11.8; 3.12.11–12).

5. Irenaeus (like Clement and Barnabas) employs covenant thought in the service of moral exhortation, and his emphasis on obedience is unmistakable (*Haer.* 4.15–16).[50]

6. Irenaeus stands with the New Testament, Melito, and Justin over against Barnabas and the Gnostics in his view of Israel's reception of the old covenant (*Haer.* 4.15.2).

---

48. Van Unnik, "Ἡ καινὴ διαθήκη," 225.
49. Van Unnik, "Ἡ καινὴ διαθήκη," 212–13.
50. See also Woolsey, *Unity and Continuity*, 164–66. Even Baker sees this. *Bullinger and the Covenant*, 23. Consequently, D. A. Stoute is quite obviously wrong when he claims that there is no discussion of mutual obligations in the patristic teaching on the covenant. "Origins and Early Development," 23.

7. Like Barnabas, Clement of Rome, Justin, and Melito, Irenaeus makes a strong appeal to the Old Testament in establishing covenant thought (in the standard manner of second-century *demonstratio evangelica*).

8. The Abrahamic, Mosaic, Davidic, and new covenants are mentioned or alluded to in writings of the New Testament, Barnabas, and Justin (though not in Melito's *PP*). Irenaeus refers to these frequently and, additionally, to the covenants with Adam and Noah (*Haer.* 3.11.8; *Epid.* 22).

9. Irenaeus links natural law and moral law (epitomized in the Ten Words) and sees this law both as extant prior to Moses (indeed, like Melito, Irenaeus speaks of God's giving of the law to Adam) and binding in the new covenant as well as in the old (*Haer.* 4.15.1; 4.16.3).

Tertullian, Law, and Covenant[51]

In Tertullian, whatever his idiosyncrasies, we find a reaffirmation of the Irenaean solution to the Gnostic challenge. Indeed, Irenaeus and Tertullian bequeathed to the church a legacy regarding Old Testament interpretation and the unity of old and new covenants, Harnack reckons, that has remained with us to the present day.[52] This observation alone warrants an investigation of Tertullian's theology of the covenants.

It has already been suggested that the covenant idea was deployed in three contexts in the early church. Covenant was important in the discussion between the Jews and Christians. It remained conspicuous during the Gnostic controversies when the Jewish heritage of the church was called into question. And as church leaders recognized a two-part canon, they naturally discussed the role of the old covenant in the Christian religion.[53] This certainly holds true for Tertullian. His theology of the Testaments and redemptive history is most clearly expressed in his controversial writings against the Jews and Gnostics. It is surely no accident that Tertullian's covenant terminology (e.g., *testamentum, instrumentum, dispositio*) is more pronounced and appears more frequently in his polemical works: *Adversus Judaeos, De anima, De carne Christi, De praescriptione haereticorum, Adversus Praxean, De resurrectione carnis, Adversus Hermogenem*, and, most importantly, *Adversus Marcionem*.

Furthermore, Tertullian's theological formulations concerning Old and New Testament relations and salvation history bear striking resemblances to those of the great anti-Gnostic polemicist and bishop of Lyons, Irenaeus. Indeed, Tertullian acknowledged this debt to Irenaeus and occasionally reproduced his arguments without modification.[54]

---

51. For extensive evidence of the following summary points, see Duncan, "Covenant Idea in Ante-Nicene Theology," 159–226.

52. Harnack, *History of Dogma*, 2:305.

53. Ferguson, "Covenant Idea in the Second Century," 135–36; D. L. Baker, *Two Testaments, One Bible: A Study of Some Modern Solutions to the Theological Problem of the Relationship between the Old and New Testaments* (Leicester, UK: Inter-Varsity Press, 1976), 43–48.

54. See, e.g., *Val.* 5. Though the context refers explicitly to the refutation of Gnosticism, it effectively illustrates the theological debt that Tertullian self-consciously owed to Irenaeus (among others). Furthermore, *De*

Hence, in Tertullian, as in Irenaeus, there is an emphasis on the continuity of salvation history, the movement from old covenant to new covenant, the unity of the two Testaments, and God's maturing of humanity by bringing mankind along in successive stages of revelation. In fact, Harnack says that, regarding the theology of the Old and New Testaments, Tertullian "only differs from Irenaeus in the additions he invented as a Montanist."[55] This is an interesting and provocative verdict, but it could blind us to the differences between Irenaeus's and Tertullian's respective presentations of salvation history. A comparison of the two yields variations and emphases that are subtle but momentous. We want to appreciate the distinctions without losing sight of the similarities, as well as to characterize the main emphases of Tertullian's covenant thought. Tertullian's theology of redemptive history may be summarized as follows.

1. Tertullian teaches that the Jews have been rejected, because of disobedience and idolatry, from the covenant (which sounds like Barnabas). The Gentiles, to the contrary, have turned from idolatry to God, and so Christians are now "the people" (*Adv. Jud.* 1.52–54; *Praescr.* 8.17–20).

2. Tertullian argues that the Testaments have always been (that is, from apostolic times) together. The Marcionites had only recently tried to separate them (*Praescr.* 30.28–30).

3. Marcion contended that the differences in the covenants prove the discontinuity of the Testaments (and hence of the "Gods" of the Testaments). Tertullian replied by arguing that, in fact, the unity of the Testaments is proved by the diversity of the covenants (*Marc.* 4.1, 6, 12, 34). This is an argument he learned from Irenaeus, which he deploys with his typical rhetorical panache.

4. The movement from old to new is not an afterthought in God's economy but was planned by God and predicted from the beginning in such passages as Genesis 25:23 (*Marc.* 4.9). The one God has one plan, but the Old Testament itself, in its earliest chapters (e.g., the account of Cain and Abel), foretells diversity in the "economy" (*Adv. Jud.* 5.1–7). God's "eternal dispensation" is a unified plan that deliberately contains diversity. In the second and third centuries, theological terms like *economy* and *dispensation* function like the terms *covenant of redemption* and *covenant of grace* in Reformed covenant theology.

5. The law originated not with Moses or Abraham but with Adam in paradise (*Adv. Jud.* 2.11–12, 22–23). The law in Eden contained all the principles of the Decalogue in seed form (*Adv. Jud.* 2.15–17). Law existed among all nations between the time of

praescriptione haereticorum provides evidence of Tertullian's borrowing from Irenaeus's *Adversus haereses*. See Tertullian, *The Prescriptions against the Heretics*, in *Early Latin Theology*, trans. and ed. S. L. Greenslade (Philadelphia: Westminster, 1956); Greenslade, "Appendix I: Irenaeus," in *Early Latin Theology*, where Greenslade gives examples of Tertullian's use of Irenaeus's *Adversus haereses*.

55. Harnack, *History of Dogma*, 2:311. Harnack writes these words as justification for not reviewing Tertullian's presentation of old and new covenant relations (having already surveyed Irenaeus's). This seems to intimate that Harnack thought the differences between the two to be relatively insignificant. If so, then surely the great historian underestimated the matter.

Adam and Moses (*Adv. Jud.* 2.46–47). Tertullian calls this "natural law" (*Adv. Iud.* 2.9) and argues for progressive stages of its development in the law of the old dispensation. In this way the law is adapted to the times (*Adv. Jud.* 2.66–67).

6. Circumcision foreshadowed spiritual circumcision (*Adv. Jud.* 4.24–28). Tertullian does not link it to baptism here.

7. The Jewish Sabbath foreshadowed the eternal Sabbath (*Adv. Jud.* 4.24–28). Tertullian is typical of early Christian writers in not relating the fourth commandment to the Lord's Day.

8. Sacrifices foreshadowed spiritual sacrifices—a contrite heart and praise (*Adv. Jud.* 5.1–7, 21–30, 39–45). It is interesting that Tertullian makes the link here not to Christ's sacrifice but, not unlike Romans 12:1–2, to our godliness.

9. The old law foreshadowed the new law. Tertullian's idea of a "new law" is unique to him and is all the more interesting given his insistence on the original, natural, and universal character of the law.

10. Mankind's knowledge of God precedes Moses's writings and originates with God's revealing of himself to Adam, a corollary of the fifth point (*Marc.* 1.10). Thus, Tertullian's salvation history is not just one movement from old to new but a succession of stages or administrations that advance mankind in knowledge of God and his law, and hence, the law is truly preparatory to the gospel.

11. Though Marcion's doctrine of God seems to be at the bottom of his rejection of catholic teaching, his view of old and new covenant relations is near the heart of the issue. So also, Tertullian's theology of redemptive history is intimately related to the rest of his theology.

Conclusion

This brief chapter has been necessarily selective and has focused on the pre-Nicene era of early Christianity especially because of its foundational importance and the ongoing historical-theological nescience about its extensive use of the covenants and the importance it assigned to them. A study of later patristic writers, especially Augustine, serves students well in helping them appreciate the earliest Christians' theology of the covenants and how it was received by and transmitted to the Middle Ages and how it was recovered in the Reformation. The following things are apparent even from our short survey.

The terms on the very title pages of the two parts of our Bible are an important theological artifact of the early Christian theology of the covenants. The covenants were appreciated as so important in explaining the unity, continuity, and progress of redemptive history and the content of Christian verbal revelation that they supplied the name for the book of God's people.

From the earliest days of the composition of the New Testament documents, every part of that written revelation has testified to a detailed and commonly received theology of the covenants.

1. The work of Christ is explicitly recognized as the fulfillment of God's covenant promises to Abraham and David. This is so central to the New Testament understanding of the person and work of Christ that one cannot understand its teaching about the message and ministry of Jesus without it.

2. The Gospels, Paul, and Hebrews explicitly link Jesus's death, and our remembrance and understanding of it, to the fulfillment of the new covenant prophecy in Jeremiah 31:31–34.

3. Every part of the New Testament links Jesus's death to the Mosaic covenant in Exodus. Luke tells us that Jesus accomplished an exodus in Jerusalem (Luke 9:31). The Gospels and Hebrews quote or reference the covenant inauguration ceremony of Exodus 24 and interpret the death of Christ in light of it. The Passover of Exodus 12 is connected to Christ's death in Paul, Peter, and John.

4. In the Gospels, Acts, Paul, and Hebrews, Jesus's fulfillment of the reality signified in the Mosaic sacrifice of Exodus 24 and especially of Jeremiah's new covenant prophecy is explicitly linked with the forgiveness of sins. This forgiveness of sins is seen as a fulfillment of the Abrahamic promise, the Mosaic sacrificial system, and Jeremiah's new covenant prophecy, and it is a hallmark of the new covenant established by Christ.

5. Throughout the New Testament writings, διαθήκη retains its profound Hebrew sense of "covenant." The only two passages in the New Testament where it can possibly be translated "testament" make better and richer sense when rendered "covenant."

6. The New Testament writers from the Gospels to Paul to Hebrews interpret the history of redemption in covenant terms and categories. This is the theology of the covenants that early postapostolic Christianity inherited, expounded, preserved, and passed on to the later church.

7. While relating the Mosaic economy to the new is the most complicated biblical-theological challenge for the New Testament writers and their interpreters, all the strands of the New Testament witness to a fundamental, underlying unity to God's saving plan in history and to both continuity and discontinuity when relating the Old Testament covenants to the new. It is from this picture that the theological idea of an overarching gracious plan of salvation with both unity and progress emerges. Early Christians talk about this with terms like "economy," "administration," and "dispensation," while the Reformers speak of a covenant of redemption and a covenant of grace.

8. Far from supporting Hillers's claim that the covenant idea is obsolescent in New Testament thought, the total witness of the New Testament writers is to a common and robust theology of the covenants that has hermeneutical implications for everything they say, that is essential to their exposition of the meaning and significance of the death of Christ, that is vital to their doctrine of assurance, that is necessary for their self-understanding as the people of God, and that is critical for their doctrine and practice of baptism and the Lord's Supper.

9. When we turn to the postbiblical writings of early Christianity, we see that they explicitly received, understood, and expanded on the main outline of the New Testament theology of the covenants.

10. The early church generally understood διαθήκη ("covenant") as a special, gracious, secured relationship between God and his people, with attendant promises and obligations, rather than as merely a legal document ("testament") or commercial disposition or arrangement.

11. The early church generally understood and explained the work of Christ as the fulfillment of the Abrahamic covenant, the Mosaic covenant, and the new covenant prophesied by Jeremiah (e.g., *Haer.* 4.13.1; *Epid.* 24, 90).

12. Various theologians of the early church wrote about covenants with Adam, Noah, Abraham, Moses, David, Jeremiah's new covenant, and Christ's fulfillment of the covenants, and used them in the recounting of redemptive history in catechesis. This didactic use of the covenants in discipleship shows that the early church considered the covenants' significant place in redemptive history to be important for the believer's life.

13. The early church appealed to the Bible's teaching on the covenants in the service of moral exhortation, sometimes warning Christians with the reminder of Israel's disobedience to the covenant and its consequences, sometimes positively appealing to Christians' covenantal obligations, even from Old Testament texts.

14. The early church viewed the moral law as summarized in the Decalogue as obligatory for Christians. They spoke of the natural law and moral law (epitomized in the Ten Words) as being given to Adam and as binding in the new covenant as well as the old.

15. The early church regarded the promises of God to Abraham to belong by faith to the people of God, the church, made up of both believing Jews and Gentiles, and they denied that these promises were in the proper possession of unbelieving Israel.

16. The early church learned from the Scriptures and taught in their writings both the overarching continuity (and eternal origins) of God's plan of salvation and its unfolding in history *and* the discontinuities and progress in redemptive history articulated especially in the New Testament, though forecast also in the Old.

17. The early church fully appreciated the link between Jesus's fulfillment of the new covenant in his death and the forgiveness of sins.

When the Reformers appealed to the early church's theology of the covenants as corroborating their own interpretation of Scripture's articulation of redemptive history, they were correct, and they recovered an essential part of the theological legacy of early Christianity that had been largely forgotten, overlooked, underappreciated, neglected, misunderstood, and unapplied.

15

COVENANT IN MEDIEVAL THEOLOGY

Douglas F. Kelly

The Middle Ages saw the longest period of theological development of any time frame within the Western Christian tradition. Though competent historians date it in somewhat different ways, I shall consider that it lasted roughly from sometime in the sixth century to somewhere near the close of the fifteenth century—that is, about eight or nine hundred years, all told.

As for its beginning, E. Clausier said that "Gregory [the Great] and the Middle Ages were born on the same day" (AD 540).[1] This was after the Roman Empire had finally broken down, and within two or three centuries, smaller territorial states (generally with some kind of Christian basis) arose throughout Europe.[2] The ending is less clear but was hastened by the problems of the fourteenth century: the Great Western Schism (1378–1417), the spread of black death, the beginning of the Little Ice Age, and—even more so in the next century—the rise of nominalism. The nominalist movement was, at the end of the day, skeptical about the reality (or "realism") of the traditional categories of theology, and along with that went a skepticism about Christian morality in the church, all of which lowered the public's respect for the clergy and others.

We must look first at the sources of medieval Christian theology and then at some of the major theologians of the period. That should prepare us for a serious consideration of what the leading Western Christian thinkers made of the biblical doctrine of the covenant.

---

1. Quoted in Etienne Gilson, *History of Christian Philosophy in the Middle Ages* (New York: Random House, 1955), 606.
2. William Carroll Bark gives a good overview of this development of early medieval Europe in *Origins of the Medieval World* (Stanford, CA: Stanford University Press, 1968).

Sources of (Western) Medieval Christian Theology

In summary fashion, we may note that there are three major sources of the Christian theology that developed in the medieval West. First are the Scriptures of the Old and New Testaments; second, the Christian patristic heritage; and third, what we now call the Greek and Roman classics. Edouard Jeauneau, in his *La Philosophie Medievale*, held that there were two sources for medieval thought—the book of Scripture and the book of nature—and that Scripture was of preponderant importance.[3]

Without my delving into the details, we should note that Teutonic and Celtic ways of life and thought,[4] and somewhat later, Jewish[5] and Muslim[6] writings, also entered into this theological mix. But my emphasis for this chapter is largely devoted to the first three sources.

I later point out that the medieval theologians did not develop a separate subheading on the covenant, in contrast to the sixteenth-century Protestant Reformers. The Swiss Reformer Heinrich Bullinger (1504–1575), however, who extensively reemphasized the *biblical* doctrine of the covenant, sought to show that he was not a theological innovator in doing so. Thus, he referred to early Christian writers, as having already to some degree made use of the covenant concept. He referred to such as Irenaeus, Tertullian, Lactantius, Eusebius, and Augustine.[7] These, of course, lived before the Middle Ages, unless one counts the extremely influential Augustine as having been at the headwaters of the medieval period.

Even Bullinger, who wished to demonstrate his long theological heritage in the Western Christian tradition, functionally had to go back earlier than the medieval period. Much of his teaching on this matter is found in his fifty sermons *The Decades*. These were translated into English in 1577, and in 1588 the archbishop of Canterbury required candidates for the ministry to read them.

There was good reason for this lacuna in his list of historical-theological predecessors on the covenant: the remarkably rich theology that developed between the sixth and fifteenth centuries made massive contributions to Christian doctrine and life but did relatively little with covenant, at least overtly. As Jaroslav Pelikan observes, "The distinctive

---

3. Edouard Jeauneau writes,

That the Bible played a role in the eyes of the medieval thinkers—even those who are called in some early writings "rationalists"—that it played a prestigious role absolutely without equal, will be clearly seen by anyone who frequents their writings. That the book of Nature was also consulted, is proven among a thousand other testimonies, as much in the pages of *Le Roman de la Rose* or the works of Albertus Magnus, not to mention the fauna and flora which adorn the stone of medieval cathedrals.

La Philosophie Medievale (Paris: Presses Universitaires de France, 1963), 7–8. Unless otherwise noted, all English translations in this chapter are mine.

4. See Christopher Dawson, "The Barbarians," chap. 4 in *The Making of Europe: An Introduction to the History of European Unity* (New York: World, 1970).

5. E.g., Moses Maimonides (1135–1204).

6. E.g., Avicenna, or Abu Ibn-Sina (980–1037).

7. See Heinrich Bullinger, *De origine erroris in divorum ac simulachrorum cultu* (Basel, 1529); Bullinger, *De testamento seu foedere Dei unico et aeterno* (Basel, 1534).

achievement of Western theology in the Middle Ages [was] . . . a further development of the doctrine of the work of Christ rather than of the doctrine of the person of Christ."[8]

No one knows exactly why a particular age turns its greatest minds to thinking through certain doctrines, while relatively neglecting others. James Orr in his *Development of Dogma* offers some interesting suggestions for the precise development of Christian thought from the apologists to the nineteenth century.[9] Orr argues that across the centuries, the teachers of the Christian church could be seen as having followed something like the order of theological topics in a traditional textbook of systematic theology: beginning with the oneness of God (as in the apologists) and then moving to the person of Christ, the Trinity, man's fallen state, then grace, and so forth.

From a very different perspective, Cardinal John Henry Newman proposes a sort of gradual (evolutionary) growth of Christian thought and practice, winding up with the doctrines of the Roman Catholic Church.[10] Newman argues that the development of theology is to be compared to the natural (or supernatural) growth of a living object of nature, so that many things came out of this growth that were in some sense included in the original stock but could not have been foreseen in it, such as the sacramental life of the church, the growing authority of the ecclesiastical hierarchy, and other realities of what became Roman Catholicism. This means that some issues were extensively developed, while other matters were given less official attention in the church's teaching.[11]

I am not certain why the Christian tradition, especially after the ante-Nicene fathers, offered very little discussion of the biblically important concept of covenant, insofar as granting to it theological headings (or "distinctions"). The ante-Nicene covenant heritage has been carefully surveyed by J. Ligon Duncan,[12] and more recently, a small section in Petrus J. Gräbe's *New Covenant, New Community* has added some details to Duncan's study (without reference to it, as far as I could see) and has certainly confirmed Duncan's original thesis.[13]

Any careful reading of the Western Christian tradition, after about the sixth century and down through the fourteenth, does not reveal any serious development of the covenant, though I am suggesting that it was very much present without being emphasized. For instance, in Peter Lombard's (ca. 1100–1160) *The Sentences*, there is

---

8. Jaroslav Pelikan, *The Growth of Medieval Theology (600–1300)* (Chicago: University of Chicago Press, 1978), 22.

9. James Orr, *The Progress of Dogma* (London: Hodder and Stoughton, 1902).

10. John Henry Newman, *An Essay on the Development of Christian Doctrine* (New York: Longmans, Green, 1903).

11. For further assessment of why the church historically emphasized some theological topics, while largely leaving others to the side, see Peter Toon, *The Development of Doctrine in the Church* (Grand Rapids, MI: Eerdmans, 1979).

12. J. Ligon Duncan III, "The Covenant Idea in the Ante-Nicene Fathers" (PhD diss., University of Edinburgh, 1995).

13. Petrus J. Gräbe, *New Covenant, New Community: The Significance of Biblical and Patristic Covenant Theology for Contemporary Understanding* (London: Paternoster, 2006). In chap. 7, "The New Covenant in the Second Century," Gräbe discusses the Epistle of Barnabas, Justin Martyr, Irenaeus, and Clement of Alexandria. He explores other streams of development in chap. 8, "The New Covenant in the Syrian Tradition: Aphrahat."

no separate "distinction" on the covenant. His *Sentences* are published in four volumes, with forty (or usually more) "distinctions" in each volume. Volume 1 contains forty-eight "distinctions."[14] Lombard's four volumes cover God, creatures and sin, the incarnation and redemption, and the sacraments and last things. But nowhere is the covenant specifically discussed.

In a real sense, Lombard set the tone for some three or so centuries in the "High Middle Ages," for his *Sentences* were long used as the standard textbook in the medieval universities. Those who commented on this standard text were known as *sententarii*. They included the luminaries of the Western theological tradition, such as Alexander of Hales, Albertus Magnus, Bonaventure, Thomas Aquinas, Duns Scotus, and William of Ockham. Indeed, Roger Bacon complained in the thirteenth century that Lombard's *Sentences* had usurped the place of the Bible.[15]

The most distinguished and influential *sententarius* by far was Thomas Aquinas (ca. 1225–1274), whose theological teaching centuries later became known as "the perennial philosophy." His *Summa Theologiae* would eventually surpass even Lombard. Aquinas, with great success, thus overcame the crisis that had arisen in the early thirteenth century in the Western intellectual realm by the rediscovery (and Latin translations)[16] of the nondialectical writings of Aristotle, which were profoundly secular and antithetical to Christian doctrine (e.g., the eternal existence of the world rather than creation; the mortality—or actual nonexistence—of the individual soul). Medievals relied almost universally on Aristotle for logic and dialectic, which had long been worked into Christian teaching (with a Platonic tinge). But with the spread of the influence of such thinkers as Averroes (1126–1198), who (as a Muslim) followed in the naturalistic line of the original Aristotle, renewed theories of eternal creation, the mortality of the soul, and one universal intellect for all people began to affect the Christian intellectual elite. To say the least, this growing movement constituted a serious intellectual problem for orthodox Christian theology.

Aquinas answered them by appropriating significant elements of Aristotelian thought (e.g., his distinctions between general and specific, substance and accidents, form and matter, potentiality and actuality), and probably above all else, he followed the *a posteriori* account of human knowledge, based on sense perception.[17] He fit these ideas into orthodox Christian theology, while rejecting—with carefully articulated reasons—Aristotle's secular assumptions. This was especially important for the Christian doctrine of

---

14. See, e.g., Peter Lombard, *The Sentences*, book 1, *The Mystery of the Trinity*, trans. Giulio Silano, Mediaeval Sources in Translation 42 (Toronto: Pontifical Institute of Mediaeval Studies, 2007).

15. Cited in F. C. Copleston, *A History of Medieval Philosophy* (London: Methuen, 1972), 100, 101.

16. E.g., by William of Moerbeke, a contemporary and friend of Thomas Aquinas.

17. "The first thing which is known by us in the state of our present life is the nature of the material thing, which is the object of the intellect, as has been said above many times." Aquinas, *Summa Theologiae*, 1a.88.3. All references to the *Summa* are translated from *Sancti Thomae Aquinatis doctoris angelici Opera omnia*, vols. 4–12, *Summa Theologiae*, ed. Thomas de Vio Cajetan, edition issued by Leo XIII (Rome: Typographia Polyglotta S. C. de Propaganda Fide, 1882).

creation as opposed to the ancient Greek assumption of an eternally existing world, with which God was codependent and thus from which he was not free.

Far from seeing God as codependent on an eternal world, the Christian belief of creation by God was an item of joyful reflection for them in the Middle Ages. The sheer wonder of creation out of nothing by the triune God was praised by Peter Lombard, with special reference to Christ, the agent of creation. He quoted "Augustine" (actually Fulgentius of Ruspe): "That child created the stars."[18]

Etienne Gilson observes concerning God's creation and providence: "All the Fathers and mediaeval theologians agree in referring the idea of providence to creation. Thus it is the metaphysic of Being that makes it possible to hold a contingence and a liberty, the indetermination of which is nevertheless, an object of the divine forethought."[19] Gilson draws three conclusions:

1. There is first the solution for which Thomas has provided the formula: God is Being, therefore the cause of all being. The divine causality, which nothing escapes, must consequently produce the necessity, but also the accidental, and even the free. . . .

2. Like Aristotle's, his God is necessary; but, unlike Aristotle's, His infinite actuality makes Him a free creative will. . . .

3. The very concept of omnipotence, which is essentially Christian, implies that of liberty and suffices of itself to separate any philosophy in which it is recognized from the Aristotelian necessitarianism.[20]

We can see how Aquinas did this kind of thing when he refuted the teaching of "the Philosopher" that God is the member of a genus in Aristotle's *Metaphysics*. Aquinas denied this claim and replied, "We think of a genus as prior to what it contains. But there is nothing prior to God, whether in reality or in the understanding. Therefore God does not belong to any genus."[21] Aquinas then gave three proofs why this has to be the case.

I would say that basically this is a way of applying the Hebraic truth of creation out of nothing by God, though in a very logical fashion. He carried through this procedure with all the doctrines. That is, at a deep and generally unspoken level, he assumed the truth of Scripture and then demonstrated why it makes the most logical sense, when precisely worked through. That does not mean that he was insincerely smuggling Scripture into his argument, but rather, knowing the truth (e.g., that God is the Creator of

---

18. Peter Lombard, *The Sentences*, book 3, *On The Incarnation of the Word*, trans. Giulio Silano, Mediaeval Sources in Translation 45 (Toronto: Pontifical Institute of Mediaeval Studies, 2010), 47 (drawing from Fulgentius of Ruspe, *Sermo* 4n6, 4n8).

19. Etienne Gilson, *The Spirit of Mediaeval Philosophy* (1936; repr., Notre Dame, IN: University of Notre Dame Press, 1991), 479.

20. Gilson, *Spirit of Mediaeval Philosophy*, 479–80.

21. Aquinas, *Summa Theologiae*, 1a.3.5.

all things out of nothing), he used clear reasoning, in accord with the dialectic of "the Philosopher," to show how to avoid logical pitfalls and to wind up at the divinely given truth about the matter. Although he employed *a posteriori* reasoning—which starts with the givens of sense experience and then works forward to truth that makes more sense than anything else—he was somehow coordinating much biblical truth with major aspects of the Aristotelian dialectic.

Etienne Gilson remarks,

> Thomism was not the upshot of a better understanding of Aristotle. It did not come out of Aristotelianism by way of evolution, but of revolution. . . . As a philosophy, Thomism is essentially a metaphysics. It is a revolution in the history of the metaphysical interpretation of the first principle, which is "being."[22]

Aquinas's achievement was massive for the continuing Christian theological tradition, and few across the ages have ever exercised such powerful influence. Yet in Aquinas's largest and greatest work, *Summa Theologiae*, there is no single discussion of covenant. It is divided into four major parts: *Prima Pars, Prima Secundae Partis, Secunda Secundae Partis, Tertia Pars*. Each of the four treatises is divided into various "questions," and each "question" is divided into numbered "articles" (like essays, discussing the question that was first raised).

Each "article" has five sections. The question is formulated in a "yes or no" formula, beginning with the word "whether" (*utrum*). Then Aquinas provides several objections (usually three) to the answer he will give. The objections are apparent proofs of the opposite answer, and he deals with them seriously and fairly. Next, Aquinas gives what he believes is the right position, usually beginning with "on the contrary" (*sed contra*). He uses Scripture and the fathers of the church to do this. After that, he gives the body of the article: "I answer that . . ." (*Respondeo dicens . . .*). Finally, he deals carefully with each objection and does so by patiently explaining why each one is wrong.

In all ninety-seven of these questions, we do not find a single article, nor even an objection and its answer, given to covenant. Covenant is no more explicitly discussed in Aquinas than it is in Lombard. And for that matter, neither John Henry Newman nor James Orr in their fairly comprehensive surveys of the development of dogma over the previous nineteen centuries indicates any discussion of covenant, including in the Middle Ages part of these long centuries.

This question arises: Why was there scarcely any discussion of covenant between the ante-Nicene fathers and the Protestant Reformers? After much thought and reading in the medieval period, I would suggest two pale illustrations to show that even in the absence of explicit use of the word *covenant*, it was always quietly assumed and gave structure to the rest of the theological enterprise.

---

22. Gilson, *Christian Philosophy in the Middle Ages*, 365.

First, we can make mention of the air we breathe. We take it for granted and usually say very little about this factor that makes our lives possible. Or second, a more apt illustration may be the usually hidden steel girders that provide lasting structure for tall brick and concrete buildings. We look at the facades but do not see their undergirding structures deep inside.

It is like that with the church's assumption of covenant: it was little discussed, but it provided a sound structure for her life and teaching. Let us look at this hidden substructure in terms of two major issues that constituted the basis of medieval theology: (1) medievals' use of Holy Scripture and (2) their doctrine of God. Both these pillars of medieval Christianity rested on the constant assumption of one true covenant, running through all the Holy Scriptures. Medieval thinkers worked out their most essential teaching very thoroughly, as it was supported by these two pillars, which were based on the constant assumption of a lasting covenant.

The Medieval Use of Holy Scripture

It is clear that the theologians of the medieval era were as committed to the full authority of the Holy Scriptures as were the church fathers. They understood the Bible to be the fully true word of God to his people, first in Israel, then in the New Testament church. Augustine called the Scriptures "the countenance of God,"[23] and much later, Peter Lombard quoted Augustine on the necessity of "seeking God's face" (as we are instructed in Ps. 105:4):

> Augustine says concerning himself in *On the Trinity*, book 1: "In case of doubt, I will not be loath to ask; in case of error, I will not be ashamed to learn. And so let whoever hears or reads these things, if he shares my certainty, continue on with me; if he shares my hesitations, continue to search with me; if he acknowledges his error, return to me; if he notes an error of mine, call me back. In this way, we can enter together upon the path of love, moving towards him of whom it is said: *Seek ye my face always.*"[24]

I will not go into a discussion of the development of the canon among the church fathers, but from Augustine and Jerome, who stood on the edge of the late patristic and very early medieval periods, we can see that they were in line with the high estimate of the Holy Scriptures held by the early church.[25] Thomas Aquinas, for example, is an

---

23. Augustine, "Sermo XXII: Sermo Sancti Augustini de Psalmo LXVII," in *Corpus Christianorum*, vol. 41, *Sancti Aurelii Augustini Sermones de Vetere Testamento* (Turnhout, Belgium: Brepols, 1961), 297.

24. Lombard, *Sentences*, book 1, *Mystery of the Trinity*, 12, quoting Ps. 105:4.

25. See, e.g., Augustine, *On Christian Teaching*, 8.13, where he lists the canon of Scripture and then adds,

These are all the books in which those who fear God and are made docile by their holiness seek God's will. The first rule in this laborious task is, as I have said, to know these books; not necessarily to understand them but to read them so as to commit them to memory or at least make them not totally unfamiliar.

Augustine, *On Christian Teaching*, trans. R. P. H. Green (Oxford: Oxford University Press, 1997), 37. Similarly, of Jerome it is said,

image of many when, in his inaugural lecture at the University of Paris (*Commendatio Sacra Scriptura*), he stated,

> The doctors of Holy Scripture must excel by their excellent conduct in life, to be apt to preach with good success; they must be illuminated, to be able to instruct well; they must be well instructed and able to refute errors in their disputations, in accordance with the words of the Apostle, who says that the ecclesiastical authority must be able to diminish with sane doctrine and to refute adversaries.

That follows because Aquinas believed that "the author of Holy Scripture is God."[26] He quoted 2 Timothy 3:16 ("All Scripture is given by inspiration of God," KJV) as showing that the Bible is "divinely inspired Scripture."[27] Aquinas taught that "in prophetic revelation the prophet's mind is moved by the Holy Spirit as an effective instrument to its principal cause."[28] Concerning all the books of Scripture, he believed that "none of their authors have erred in composing them."[29] Therefore, Aquinas held that whoever rejects the Scriptures should be anathema: "The reason for this is that only the canonical Scriptures are normative for faith."[30]

In the fifth article of *Prima Pars*, Aquinas showed the value of various human sciences and stated that at first they may look superior ("nobler") than the Scriptures. But he responded,

> *On the contrary*, Other sciences are called the handmaidens of this one: *Wisdom sent her maids to invite to the tower* (Prov. 9:3).
>
> *I answer that*, Since this science is partly speculative and partly practical, it transcends all others speculative and practical.
>
> Now one speculative science is said to be nobler than another, either by reason of its greater certitude, or by reason of the higher worth of the subject matter. In both these respects this science surpasses other speculative sciences. . . . [T]his science surpasses other speculative sciences, in point of greater certitude from the natural light of human reason, which can err, whereas this derives its certitude from the light of divine knowledge which cannot be misled.[31]

After enumerating the "twenty-two" (or perhaps twenty-four) books recognized by the Jews, he decrees that any books outside this list must be recognized as "apocryphal": they are not in the canon. Elsewhere, while admitting that the Church reads books like Wisdom and Ecclesiasticus which are strictly uncanonical, he insists on their being used solely "for edifying the people, not for the corroboration of ecclesiastical doctrine."

Quoted in J. N. D. Kelly, *Jerome: His Life, Writings, and Controversies* (New York: Harper and Row, 1975), 160–61. Both Augustine and Jerome are so thoroughly quoted throughout the Middle Ages, that they may be considered a fountainhead of it.

26. Aquinas, *Summa Theologiae*, 1a.1.10.

27. Aquinas, *Summa Theologiae*, 1a.1.1.

28. Aquinas, *Summa Theologiae*, 2a2ae.172.4 *ad* 1.

29. Aquinas, *Summa Theologiae*, 1a.1.8.

30. Thomas Aquinas, *Commentary on the Gospel according to St. John*, lecture 6, on John 21, in *Commentary on the Four Gospels Collected Out of the Works of the Fathers* (London: Rivington, 1845).

31. Aquinas, *Summa Theologiae*, 1a.1.5.

Peter Kreeft comments with keen psychological insight on this distinction:

> We have the *objective right* to be more certain of theology's principles (data) than of any products of human reason, which can err, for theology's data have been revealed by God, who can neither deceive nor be deceived; but the data God revealed can be (and are) doubted with more *subjective, psychological* ease than the data of the human sciences. Perhaps we should use two different words for these two different dimensions of certainty, the objective ("certain-*ness*," or certainty) and the subjective (*certitude*, or intellectual confidence).[32]

Florent Gaboriau, a traditional Roman Catholic, has extensively argued that in a certain sense, with some careful distinctions, the famous phrase taken up by the sixteenth-century Protestant Reformers "by Scripture alone" (*sola scriptura*) could and should be applied to Aquinas! In his *L'Ecriture Seule?*, Gaboriau—with massive citations from Aquinas and with frequently critical references to traditional and modern "neo-Thomists"—holds that Aquinas does not put tradition and Scripture on the same level; *Scripture alone* is supreme. Gaboriau writes,

> Looking back, our authors always have the word "Tradition" on their lips, and they speak out of the abundance of their hearts. There can be no doubt historically that the most common conception of theology—which is not that of the Common Doctor—places Scripture in the background (Tradition is first, even if they often make excellent usage of it—Thank the Lord—thereby rectifying in many ways their deficient epistemology).[33]

Later, Gaboriau goes on to quote a lecture of Aquinas on John: "Whoever wishes to instruct the people, misses the door who does not enter by the Holy Scriptures."[34] Gaboriau comments on this statement, "We have made the effort of verifying this to have been the meaning of the initial question introducing *Summa Theologiae*."[35] Gaboriau summarizes what he believes to be the correct relationship between Scripture and tradition, in contradistinction to much of Roman Catholicism, which holds "the two-source theory," or even to the idea that Scripture is included under the broader concept of tradition:

> Far from going back on this promise (i.e. Deut. 7:7–8), God carried it out. Such is the *fact* of which Tradition records the *fulfillment* and which one must keep in mind in order to understand what the Scriptures mean. This is of highest importance

---

32. Thomas Aquinas, *A Summa of the "Summa": The Essential Philosophical Passages of St. Thomas Aquinas' "Summa Theologica,"* ed. Peter Kreeft (San Francisco: Ignatius, 1990), 41.

33. Florent Gaboriau, *L'Ecriture Seule?* (Paris: FAC-éditions, 1997), 174.

34. Thomas Aquinas, *Commentary on the Gospel of St. John*, no. 1366 (treating John 10:1–5), cited in Gaboriau, *L'Ecriture Seule?*, 177n17. The original Latin reads, *Ille ergo non intrat per ostium qui ad docendum populum non ingreditur per sacram Scripturam.*

35. Gaboriau, *L'Ecriture Seule?*, 178.

indeed, outside of which one risks misunderstanding that Scripture alone is the norm of faith, for this good reason, that even guided from above, "Tradition" is a human activity which responsibility weighs upon us, while it provides our guidance. But Scripture is on the contrary the work of God, the doing of God.[36]

Although few of the medieval writers spoke specifically of "covenant," all the orthodox ones always assumed one of the mainstays of the covenant: that the same God inspired both Old and New Testaments in his great plan of redemption of his people, for Israel first in the Old Testament and then for the Gentiles in the New. It had been one of the great tasks of Irenaeus (who lived about four centuries before the Middle Ages) to confound the Gnostics, who held that the God who gave the Old Testament was different from the God who gave the New Testament.[37] Irenaeus did speak of "four catholic covenants"—that is, the Noahic, Abrahamic, Davidic, and new covenants. He also spoke of "two testaments."[38] In the third century, Tertullian spoke of *testamentum*, *instrumentum*, and *dispositio*. He included Old and New Testaments in these covenant synonyms and was careful never to separate Old and New Testaments, or law and gospel. Another early Christian writer, Clement of Alexandria, spoke of one overarching covenant, which included both Old and New Testaments.[39]

Origen, though condemned for some heretical teachings, nonetheless bore a heavy influence on the medieval theologians, and he wrote the following against the aggressively anti-Christian Platonist Celsus:

> It is true that for Christians the introduction to the faith is based on the religion of Moses and the prophetic writings. And after the introduction the next stage of progress for beginners consists in the interpretation and exegesis of these. They seek the mystery "according to revelation," which has been kept in silence through times eternal, but now is manifested by the prophetic utterances and by the appearing of our Lord Jesus Christ.[40]

Augustine's deep commitment to the one authority of both Testaments caused him to uphold the importance of knowing both Greek and Hebrew.[41] So high was Jerome's estimate of the Old Testament that he termed Isaiah "an apostle and an evangelist."[42] Leo the Great (b. ca. AD 390–400) extensively held together Old and New Testaments as the one way of salvation, from Old Testament sacrifices to the death of the Lamb of God on Calvary. A passage from his "Sermon LXXI" is typical:

---

36. Gaboriau, *L'Ecriture Seule?*, 193.
37. See Irenaeus, *Haer.* 4.9.3.
38. Irenaeus, *Haer.* 4.9.1.
39. Clement of Alexandria, *Strom.* 6.13, 106.
40. Origen, *Contra Celsum*, trans. Henry Chadwick (Cambridge: Cambridge University Press, 1985), 69.
41. Augustine, *On Christian Teaching*, 2.38.
42. From Jerome, *Commentary on Isaiah*, in Corpus Christianorum Series Latina, 73:1, cited in Pelikan, *Growth of Medieval Theology*, 122.

For a peerless victim was being offered to God for the world's salvation, and the slaying of Christ the true Lamb, predicted through many ages, was transferring the sons of promise into the liberty of the Faith. The New Testament also was being ratified, and in the blood of Christ the heirs of the eternal Kingdom were being enrolled; the High Pontiff was entering the Holy of Holies, and to intercede with God the spotless Priest was passing in through the veil of his flesh. In fine, so evident a transition was being effected from the Law to the Gospel, from the synagogue to the Church.[43]

It is similar with Gregory the Great (ca. 540–604), with whom (as we previously noted) the Middle Ages were born. A very typical illustration of how he binds both Old and New Testaments together is found in "Epistle LXIV":

> For as in the old Testament outward acts were attended to, so in the New Testament it is not so much what is done outwardly that is regarded with close attention, that it may be punished with searching judgment. For while the law forbids the eating of many things as being unclean, the Lord nevertheless says in the Gospel, *Not that which goeth into the mouth defileth a man, but the things which come forth from the heart, these are they which defile a man* (Matth. xv.11).[44]

As we have seen, the great teacher of the medieval universities was Peter Lombard. He constantly thought together Old and New Testaments, law and gospel—all from the same God. He is in line with the rest of the church teachers in showing the immense advance of the New over the Old Testament:

> ON THE DIFFERENCE BETWEEN THE LAW AND THE GOSPEL.—AUGUSTINE. But the letter of the Gospel differs from the letter of the Law because different things are promised: earthly ones by the latter, heavenly ones by the former. The sacraments differ too, because the ones of the Law only signified grace, those of the Gospel confer it. The commandments also differ, insofar as the ceremonial ones are concerned; the moral ones are the same, but they are contained more fully in the Gospel.[45]

And we have already surveyed the teaching of Peter Lombard's greatest successor, Thomas Aquinas, who with equal firmness honored Old and New Testaments as the same Word of God, though seeing a tremendous advancement from one to the other, as the foreshadowings of the gospel are made explicit after the incarnation of Christ.

What could have held together over the ages such a mighty structure between Hebrew Old Testament and Greek New Testament, between law and gospel, except for the

---

43. Leo the Great, "Sermon LXXI," in *Nicene and Post-Nicene Fathers of the Christian Church*, 2nd ser., ed. Philip Schaff and Henry Wace (Grand Rapids, MI: Eerdmans, 1969), 12:181.

44. Gregory the Great, "Epistle LXIV," in Schaff and Wace, *Nicene and Post-Nicene Fathers of the Christian Church*, 13:79.

45. Lombard, *Sentences*, book 3, *On the Incarnation of the Word*, 170. Lombard is referring to Augustine, *Enarrationes in Psalmos*, on Ps. 73.

ever-abiding assumption of the one covenant from the one and triune Creator-Redeemer God, traced from the apostolic fathers and apologists down to Thomas Aquinas over a thousand years later? A deep structure tends to be hidden from immediate view, and that is the case with the steel girders of a modern skyscraper, just as it is with the underlying theological foundations of faith in the triune God, who has always worked redemptively with his creation, from Old to New Testament. The Creator is the Redeemer, and his word in various ages comes from the same mouth that utters nothing but saving truth, whether in warning or in promise, whether through patriarchs, prophets, sages, or apostles.

Unlike some of the sixteenth-century Reformers, the medieval theologians did not speak very explicitly concerning covenant, but it gave their doctrine structure, and they assumed it and built their edifice of teaching on its solid foundations. Another structural undergirding of the doctrine of the covenant is the most crucial issue in all Christian theology: their grasp of who God is.

The Medieval Doctrine of God

God is the mighty Creator and Redeemer whom we meet in both Old and New Testaments. Well before the Middle Ages, Epiphanius, bishop of Salamis (ca. 315–403), wrote, "If I reject the Old Testament, I am not a Catholic."[46] In line with this high estimate of the Old Testament, Thomas Aquinas expounded one of the crucial names for God in the Old Testament as the basis of his doctrine of who God is. Like so many earlier church fathers, Aquinas went back to the burning bush, where God told Moses who he most essentially was:

> Then Moses said to God, "If I come to the people of Israel and say to them, 'The God of your fathers has sent me to you,' and they ask me, 'What is his name?' what shall I say to them?" God said to Moses, "I AM WHO I AM." And he said, "Say this to the people of Israel: 'I AM has sent me to you.'" (Ex. 3:13–14)

In the immediate context, it is clear that God is saying to Moses, "I will be present with you in this humanly impossible task." "I AM WHO I AM" means that God depends on nothing, while everything else depends on him. God needs no explanation and no origin. Pharaoh and his harsh captivity of the Hebrew slaves can well be handled.

The fathers of the church understood that they were in line with Old Testament Israel and thus that the name "I AM" means that God is the ultimate, transcendent triune Being yet is sovereignly present with his people. Athanasius commented on this reality in *De Synodis* 34. Hilary of Poitiers made use of Exodus 3:14 in *De Trinitate* 1.5, as did Gregory of Nazianzus (also in the fourth century) in *The Fourth Theological Oration* xviii.

---

46. Epiphanius, *The Panarion*, trans. Frank Williams, NHMS 63 (Leiden: Brill, 1997), 2.408.

A century later, Augustine took the name of God as "Being" to indicate that because the supreme reality is Being and is good, therefore, even lesser (created) realities are also good:

> Magnificently and divinely, therefore, our God said to his servant: "I am that I am," and "Thou shalt say to the children of Israel, He who is sent me to you." For He truly is because He is unchangeable. For every change makes what was not, to be: therefore He truly is, who is unchangeable; but all other things that were made by Him have received being from Him each in its own measure. To Him who is highest, therefore nothing can be contrary, save what is not; and consequently as from Him everything that is good has its being, so from Him is everything that by nature exists; since everything that exists by nature is good. Thus every nature is good, and everything good is from God; therefore every nature is from God.[47]

Some six centuries later, in the first half of the twelfth century, Peter Lombard quoted Augustine on Exodus 3:14:

> Augustine says in *On the Trinity*, book 5: "And God is without doubt a substance, or, if it is better said, an essence, which the Greeks call *usia*. For just as wisdom is called from being wise, and just as knowledge is called from knowing, so essence is so called from being (*esse*). And who is more than he who said to his servant Moses: *I am that I am*, and *You shall be the children of Israel. He who has sent me to you?*[48]

Lombard immediately went on to comment on Augustine, by way of Jerome,

> He is truly and properly called essence whose essence does not know past or future. Hence Jerome, writing to Marcella says: "God alone, who has no beginning, truly preserved the name of essence; by comparison to him who truly is, because he is unchangeable, things which are changeable are almost as if they are not. For whatever we can say 'will be' about, is not yet. God alone, on the other hand, is, who does not know 'used to be' or 'will be.' Thus, God alone truly is, by comparison with whose essence, or being is as if it is not."[49]

Aquinas also followed these fathers as he sought to state (in a philosophical-theological way, in accordance with the needs of his time) the foundational distinction between Creator (or uncreated Being) and creature (or created being). In *Summa contra Gentiles* he said,

> Everything, furthermore, exists because it has being. A thing whose essence is not its being, consequently, is not through its essence, but by participation in something,

---

47. Augustine, *De Natura Boni*, 19, in *A Select Library of Nicene and Post-Nicene Fathers of the Christian Church*, 1st ser., ed. Philip Schaff (Edinburgh: T&T Clark, 1994), 4:354–55.

48. Lombard, *Sentences*, book 1, *Mystery of the Trinity*, 44 (dist. 8).

49. Lombard, *Sentences*, book 1, *Mystery of the Trinity*, 44 (dist. 8), quoting Jerome, *Epistola*, 15n4 (to Damasus).

namely, being itself. But that which is through participation in something cannot be the first being, because prior to it is the being in which it participates in order to be. But God is the first being, with nothing prior to Him. His essence is, therefore, his being.

This sublime truth Moses was taught by our Lord, When Moses asked our Lord: If the children of Israel say to me: what is his name? What shall I say to them? The Lord replied: I AM WHO I AM. . . . Thou shalt say to the children of Israel: HE WHO IS hath sent me to you (Exod. 3:13, 14). By this our Lord showed that his own proper name is HE WHO IS. Now, names have been derived to signify the natures or essences of things. It remains, then, that the divine being is God's essence or nature.

Catholic teachers have likewise professed this truth. For Hilary writes in his book *De Trinitate*: "Being is not an accident in God but subsisting truth, the abiding cause and the natural property of his nature" (Hilary, *De Trinitate*, Bk. VII, 11). Boethius also says in his own work *De Trinitate*: "The divine subsistence is being itself, and from it comes being" (Boethius, *De Trinitate*, II).[50]

Aquinas wrote in *On Being and Essence,*

Whatever is not of the understood content of an essence or quiddity [i.e., "what it is" or its "whatness"] is something which comes from without and makes a composition with the essence, because no essence can be understood without the things which are parts of it. Now, every essence or quiddity can be understood without anything being understood about its existence. For I can understand, what a man is, or what a phoenix is, and yet not know whether they have existence in the real world. It is clear, therefore, that existence is other than essence or quiddity, unless perhaps there exists a thing whose quiddity is its existence.[51]

Ralph McInerny comments,

The upshot of this teaching is quite clear. God alone is a being for whom to be is *what* he is; God alone is such that he cannot not be. He is, in short, a necessary being. Whatever other than God exists does so, not because it is its nature to exist, a definitional necessity, as it were, but because it has received existence.[52]

Etienne Gilson explains in like fashion:

In order to know what God is, Moses turns to God. He asks his name, and straight-way comes the answer: *Ego sum qui sum, Ait sic dices filius Israel; qui est misi mi ad vos* (Exod. 3:14). No hint of metaphysics, but God speaks, *causa finita est*, and Exodus

50. Thomas Aquinas, *Summa contra Gentiles*, book 1, *God*, trans. Anton C. Pegis (Notre Dame, IN: University of Notre Dame Press, 1975), 1.22.9–11 (120–21).
51. Thomas Aquinas, *On Being and Essence*, in Joseph Bobik, *Aquinas on Being and Essence: A Translation and Interpretation* (Notre Dame, IN: University of Notre Dame Press, 1965), 159–60 (par. 77).
52. Ralph McInerny, *St. Thomas Aquinas* (Notre Dame, IN: University of Notre Dame Press, 1977), 97.

lays down the principle from which henceforth the whole of Christian philosophy will be suspended. From this moment it is understood once and for all that the proper name of God is Being and that, according to the word of St. Ephrem, taken up again later by St. Bonaventure, this name denotes his very essence. Now to say that the word *being* designates the essence of God, and the essence of no other being but God, is to say that in God alone essence and existence are identical. That is why St. Thomas Aquinas, referring expressly to this text of Exodus, will declare that among all the divine names there is one that is eminently proper to God, namely, *Qui est*, precisely because this *Qui est* signifies nothing other than being itself: *non significat formam aliquam sed ipsum esse*.[53] In this principle lies an inexhaustible metaphysical fecundity; all the studies that follow here will be merely studies of its results. There is but one God, and this God is Being, that is the corner-stone of all Christian philosophy; and it was not Plato, it was not Aristotle. It was Moses who put it in position.[54]

The great medieval theologians, of necessity, had to speak in terms of the intellectual concerns of their own day. Aquinas, for example, had to come to terms with the increasingly popular "integral Aristotelianism" of the thirteenth century, by using what he properly could of it and showing why the rest was unacceptable, as we have seen above. For all his usage of crucial elements of Aristotle's methodology as concerns the place of sense experience, his final doctrine of God came from Moses (and the New Testament) and definitely not from Aristotle.

To have relied so directly on Moses demonstrates that Aquinas knew well of the lasting covenant established by God, which undergirded both Old and New Testaments. I would suggest that, for the most part, this assumption of the covenant that was always upheld by the triune God, at a deep level constituted the warp and woof of medieval theology, although it did not give color to the threads of the beautiful pattern. The colors came from the doctrines that were discussed. Without the constitutive warp and woof, the final results of the colorful weaving could not have taken place, though it was not addressed as part of the doctrinal synthesis of either Lombard or Aquinas. But it was nonetheless powerful for all that, giving solid substance to what we now call medieval theology.

53. Gilson draws this Latin quotation from Aquinas, *Summa Theologiae*, 1.13.11.
54. Gilson, *Spirit of Mediaeval Philosophy*, 51.

16

COVENANT IN REFORMATION THEOLOGY

Howard Griffith

The Protestant Reformation moved the church forward on an uneven road. Its doctrinal development had ups and downs as it progressed over time. We should expect, then, that the Reformers developed different views of the theology of the covenant and even had disagreements about it. In Wittenberg, Martin Luther (1483–1546), the most important and influential Reformer, rediscovered and taught the Reformation's most important doctrine: justification by faith alone. Luther was perhaps the least interested in the covenant as a way of interpreting Scripture and understanding the Christian life. In Zurich, Huldrych Zwingli (1484–1531) was writing about the relationship between the Old and New Testaments before the Anabaptists challenged the practice of infant baptism in 1525. But then, responding to their claims, he brought the covenant of grace prominently into his theology. Zwingli's successor in Zurich, Heinrich Bullinger (1504–1575), built on Zwingli to write the first theological treatise devoted to the covenant in Scripture. It lay with John Calvin (1509–1564), however, to develop the ideas of his Swiss brethren and make the covenant of grace a comprehensive way of understanding redemptive history, Christ, and the Christian life.[1]

As we begin, let us think a bit about the theological context. In Scripture, God relates to his people through the covenant. The Reformers shared two broad and important commitments in relation to the covenant: opposition to the medieval theology of grace and opposition to the radical Anabaptist movement. The issues were interwoven, but we may unwind them in terms of personal salvation (how God saves the individual sinner,

---

1. Other Reformers, such as Martin Bucer, Philipp Melanchthon, Peter Martyr Vermigli, and Johannes Oecolampadius, made contributions. I have limited this chapter to the most important figures.

called the *ordo salutis*[2]) and redemptive history (the relationship of the Old and New Testaments, called the *historia salutis*[3]). Let us take these up in turn.

What was the basic approach to salvation as the Reformation emerged? In the late medieval theological movement called nominalism, Gabriel Biel (1420–1495), whom Luther studied, and Robert Holcot proposed a "covenant of acceptance" in which human and divine activity were blended for the individual to appropriate salvation. The term "covenant" in this phrase is not an exposition of Scripture but a construction expressing a doctrine. Their slogan was "To the one who does his very best, God does not deny his grace." Fallen man has innate dignity to the degree that he can love God above all things. This was "doing his very best." Heiko Oberman describes this as an "outer structure" of justification by grace alone, with an "inner structure" of justification by works alone.[4] What does this mean? It means that a fallen person, by an act of will, could prepare himself, with an act of love for God, to receive grace in the sacraments. Grace would then enable him to do good works formed by supernatural love for God, which God would finally reward with eternal life. At the first moment of this process of justification, it was the fallen, sinful person who moved toward God's grace, not God who moved toward the sinner.[5] This was called the "covenant of acceptance," by which God agreed to accept one's doing "his very best" and which set him on the road to meriting eternal life. They called this "gracious" because God was not obliged to provide this opportunity for sinful humans.[6]

This theology of grace contrasts with the Reformers' idea of grace like night with day. The chief article of Reformation belief was justification by faith alone. Justification is not the recognition of virtue or merit. Justification is a free forensic gift, a declaration of the status of righteous, not a virtue "in" a person, and it is received by faith alone. That faith is itself a gift of grace, not a virtue. It comes only to those whom God, in his love, has freely and eternally predestined to save. Christ, the mediator of this grace, was himself a gift to the lost. Grace in Christ comes not to the one who does well but to the hopelessly guilty and resistant. God initiates it based purely on his own loving will, not on account of any inward or outward act the sinner prepares for, does, or will do.

In his combat with Pelagius, Augustine championed saving grace as a matter of sovereign, divine monergism (God alone working grace, without any human contribu-

---

2. I am using the term to indicate that there is, distinct from Christ's accomplishment of redemption, a further, necessary application of that redemption by the Holy Spirit to the elect individual.

3. This term refers to the once-for-all accomplishment of salvation for the whole of God's elect people, that is, the incarnation of the Son, his death and resurrection, and so forth, as well as, broadly speaking, the relationship of Old and New Testaments.

4. Heiko A. Oberman, *The Harvest of Medieval Theology: Gabriel Biel and Late Medieval Nominalism* (Cambridge, MA: Harvard University Press, 1963), 176.

5. Biel taught that even fallen human beings, by the free will that remained theirs after the fall, could "do their very best." Simply as fallen (not yet in a "state of grace"), human beings could be sorry for sin and could recognize that God is supremely worthy of their love. The soul thus infused with grace could now do acts of condign merit and so receive God's acceptance and the beatific vision. Thus, in its inner structure, the human being's justification was by works alone, but only because God limited his power in such a way as to accept this.

6. Oberman, *Harvest*, 176.

tion) and eternal predestination. Those who followed Augustine in the Middle Ages opposed the possibility of fallen man meriting anything. How did the biblical theme of covenant—which included the relationship of the sovereign God and responsible, yet fallen, man—cohere with predestination? Neo-Augustinian theologians like Thomas Bradwardine of Canterbury found the synergism of the nominalists contrary to the sovereignty of divine grace. Each of the Protestant Reformers was also deeply influenced by Augustine. They shared his strong view of original sin[7] and stressed fallen man's complete inability to do spiritual good apart from predestined saving grace. Each objected to Pelagian and semi-Pelagian notions of free will.[8] Fallen man is unable to will any good in his own power. God must raise the spiritually dead, and his saving grace is irresistible.

Yet the idea of covenant in Scripture not only expresses God's sovereign, monergistic grace, it also speaks of God's relation to humanity in terms of the necessary human response of faith and obedience.[9] Can a covenant doctrine be stated that does justice to both? Can it teach sovereign grace and human responsibility without also teaching human merit? Is the covenant of grace one-sided (or unilateral), God alone promising salvation unconditionally (Calvin's supposed view), or is it two-sided (or "bilateral"), both God and sinful-but-regenerate man acting in relationship (Zwingli and Bullinger's view)?

Much debate on the Reformed development of the covenant hangs on this question. One scholarly school asserts a divergence between the covenant doctrines of the Swiss and that of Calvin.[10] Lyle Bierma and Peter Lillback have challenged this "two traditions" approach. They provide clear evidence of continuity between the Swiss and Calvin. They also question the notion that the bilateral idea of covenant necessarily undermines God's absolute sovereignty both in the initiation of the covenant relationship and throughout its development in the believer's life.[11] Lillback writes, "Foundationally, all three [Zwingli, Bullinger, and Calvin] affirm a conditional, mutual covenant of grace that is worked out in the context of a sovereign predestination that includes reprobation."[12] I follow their lead in this chapter, in which I show how Luther, Zwingli, Bullinger, and Calvin answered this question.

The Anabaptist movement criticized the Reformation, sometimes radically, for not establishing an order and discipline that admitted only true believers to the church. All Anabaptists opposed infant baptism, seeing the standard of an entirely pure church

---

7. They understood this as an inborn depravity or the disinclination to love God. I comment on the covenant aspect of it below.

8. This was especially clear in Luther's *Bondage of the Will* (1525).

9. See Anthony A. Hoekema, "The Centrality of the Covenant of Grace," *RJ* 5, no. 11 (1955): 3–5.

10. Leonard J. Trinterud, "The Origins of Puritanism," *CH* 20, no. 1 (1951): 37–57; J. Wayne Baker, *Heinrich Bullinger and the Covenant: The Other Reformed Tradition* (Athens: Ohio University Press, 1981).

11. Lyle D. Bierma, "Federal Theology in the Sixteenth Century: Two Traditions?," *WTJ* 45, no. 2 (1983): 304–21; Peter A. Lillback, *The Binding of God: Calvin's Role in the Development of Covenant Theology* (Grand Rapids, MI: Baker Academic, 2001), 13–28; Lillback, "The Continuing Conundrum: Calvin and the Conditionality of the Covenant," *CTJ* 29 (1994): 42–74.

12. Lillback, "Continuing Conundrum," 74.

as a major difference between Israel in the Old Testament and the church in the New Testament. As the Reformers returned to Scripture to answer Anabaptist claims, the biblical theme of covenant became important to the Swiss and to Calvin, prompting them to stress the importance of the Old Testament and the unity of the Old and New Testaments.

Martin Luther's Views of Covenant

In his first *Lectures on the Psalms* (1513–1515), Luther views "covenant" as equivalent to "law" or "testament." In the relation of Old to New, both the Old Testament, in which Christ's death is promised, and the New Testament, in which his death is exhibited, are one "testament of Christ."[13] All Scripture either promises or testifies to the death of Christ. The Old Testament is incomplete without the New. In these lectures, Luther understands the old covenant as a covenant of merit, one that, in fact, was voided by Israel's wickedness. By contrast, the new covenant is of faith and grace by God's promise.[14] The notions of Biel and his "covenant of acceptance" are clearly present in Luther's comments on the Psalms. On Psalm 115:1, "Not to us, O LORD, not to us, but to your name give glory, for the sake of your steadfast love and your faithfulness!" Luther says,

> The coming of Christ into the flesh was given out of the pure mercy of the promising God, and was neither bestowed by the merits of human nature nor denied by demerits. . . . He required nothing but preparation, that we might be capable of this gift. . . . Hence the teachers correctly say that to a man who does what is in him God gives grace without fail, and though he could not prepare himself for grace on the basis of worth (*de condigno*), because the grace is beyond compare, yet he may well prepare himself on the basis of fitness (*de congruo*), because of this promise of God and the covenant of his mercy. . . . As the Law was the figure and preparation of the people for receiving Christ, so our doing as much as is in us disposes us toward grace. And the whole time of grace is the preparation for the future glory and the second advent. Therefore He orders us to watch, and be prepared and wait for him.[15]

Luther sees both Old and New Testaments requiring preparation for grace. Believers in the old era prepared for Christ's advent; in the new they prepare anticipating Christ's second coming. The individual in both eras must merit grace by her own fitness (*de congruo*). Luther grasps the pure grace that moved God to send his Son (grace that motivated the redemption Christ accomplished). But despite some hints to the contrary,[16] preparation is necessary for the individual to appropriate grace received in

---

13. Kenneth Hagen, "The Problem of Testament in Luther's *Lectures on Hebrews*," *HTR* 63, no. 1 (1970): 87.

14. Lillback, *Binding*, 63.

15. Martin Luther, *LW*, 11:396.

16. Bernhard Lohse notices hints in the Psalms lectures that Luther was also beginning to think of grace in a new way, including a Pauline use of the ideas of "impute" and "reckon." *Martin Luther's Theology: Its Historical and Systematic Development*, trans. and ed. Roy A. Harrisville (Minneapolis: Fortress, 1999), 60.

the *ordo salutis*. There are two actors in the covenant of acceptance, but grace depends on meritorious human action.

Luther's commitment to a "meriting" *ordo salutis* would not last much longer. By the time of his *Disputation against Scholastic Theology* in 1517, Luther had explicitly rejected Biel's "covenant of acceptance." In theses 29 and 30, Luther writes, "The best and infallible preparation for grace and the sole disposition toward grace is the eternal election and predestination of God. On the part of man, however, nothing precedes grace except indisposition and even rebellion against grace."[17] Lillback comments that by 1517 Luther "advocated a vigorous statement of the Augustinian concepts of sin, grace and election."[18] His vigor would only grow stronger.

Between the *Lectures on the Psalms* and Heidelberg, Luther had been lecturing on Romans. From 1516 on, Luther had a new understanding of law and gospel. No longer did he understand law as Old Testament, the first stage of God's revelation of his way of saving sinners, and gospel was no longer the historical fulfillment of Old Testament prophecy and figures. Law was the word of God in either Testament that requires human action and condemns human sin. It reaches to the heart and includes all that God requires. Sinners cannot fulfill it, and so it is a word of wrath, leading one to despair of her own ability to please God. By contrast, gospel, in either Testament, is the word of grace, life, and salvation. It offers only blessing and remission of sins.[19]

As he renounced the medieval merit scheme of covenant and worked out the law-and-gospel principle of interpreting Scripture, Luther came also to proclaim a more clearly testamentary, or unilateral, idea of covenant. In his *Lectures on Galatians* in 1517, Luther expounds Galatians 3:18, "God gave it to Abraham by a promise":

> The apostle calls the promises of God a testament. The same term is used in other passages of Scripture. In this way it was indicated darkly that God would die, and that thus, in God's promise, as in a formally announced testament, God's incarnation and suffering were to be understood. . . . Hence one can at the same time harmonize with this what Jerome mentions, that in the Hebrew one finds "covenant" rather than "testament." He who stays alive makes a covenant; he who is about to die makes a testament. Thus Jesus Christ the immortal God made a covenant. At the same time, He made a testament, because he was going to become mortal. Just as He is both God and man, so He made both a covenant and a testament.[20]

Abraham received the inheritance by faith, resting on the publicly announced testament. Testament and covenant amount to the same thing: a unilateral gift on God's

17. Martin Luther, *Martin Luther's Basic Theological Writings*, ed. Timothy F. Lull and William R. Russell, 2nd ed. (Minneapolis: Fortress, 2005), 36.

18. Lillback develops the Heidelberg material more fully in *Binding*, 65.

19. Robert Kolb, *Martin Luther: Confessor of the Faith* (New York: Oxford University Press, 2014), 52.

20. Luther, *LW*, 27:268. At this early stage, "testament" is also Luther's concept of the sign in the Lord's Supper.

part. Luther's preferred word is "testament." Apparently, after this, Luther used the word "covenant" only in describing Christian baptism. Through baptism understood as a divine word, God promises to put sin to death throughout a Christian's life and, finally, at his death. Again, this is a unilateral, even an effective, promise.[21]

The hermeneutic of law and gospel became Luther's essential tool for exegesis and for preaching. In his 1535 *Lectures on Galatians*, he says that only as it is understood and applied can the right doctrine of justification by faith alone be maintained. Since the law requires activity, he calls this "active righteousness." But faith rests in the gospel word of God and receives Christ's righteousness freely, by a forensic gift. This Luther calls "passive righteousness." Justification is passive righteousness:

> As the earth itself does not produce rain, and is unable to acquire it by its own strength, worship and power, but receives it only by a heavenly gift from above, so this heavenly righteousness is given to us by God without our work or merit. . . . [W]e can obtain it only through the free imputation and indescribable gift of God. . . . For if you do not ignore the Law and thus direct your thoughts to grace as though there were no Law but as though there were nothing but grace, you cannot be saved.[22]

Justified believers need the law because they are still sinners. As far as they are "old man," the law still functions to convict of sin, require righteousness, and condemn. But this is all. The "new man" in the believer does not need or use the law.[23] This dominant law-gospel dialectic means that Luther always views the Christian in the context of temptation (*Anfechtung*): the Christian is always challenged by suffering, the devil, and the law. In other words, she is always struggling and always *simul justus et peccator*, sinful and righteous at the same time.[24] The law, then, always functions to accuse and condemn, and the gospel always relieves this condemnation. We might suppose, then, that any notion of the *necessity* of the believer's obedience to the law will be difficult to place within this framework.

Nevertheless, it would be a serious mistake to infer from this that Luther completely rejected obedience and good works. He struggled and wrote against preachers, some in the Lutheran movement, who wished to do away with the law and the commandments altogether. Given the strength of his polemic against medieval works righteousness, we should not be surprised that some Lutherans misunderstood him or went too far. In response, Luther called for the preaching of the Ten Commandments in the churches and expounded them in his catechisms. The Commandments are God's will for the Christian as he lives in the various callings of life, especially in

---

21. Kolb, *Martin Luther*, 135–41.
22. Luther, *LW*, 26:6.
23. Paul Althaus, *The Theology of Martin Luther*, trans. Robert C. Schultz (Philadelphia: Fortress, 1966), 268–69.
24. Kolb, *Martin Luther*, 130.

horizontal relationships in society.[25] Luther's stress on good works in society answered Rome's claim that the Lutherans were licentious. Still, the believer's good works, even as evidence of real faith,[26] and as necessary to society, do not have a natural place in Luther's wider doctrine of salvation. Their place in his social ethic is more obvious. For Luther, human activity and good works always at least present the danger of being associated with merit. They represent the soteriology he rejected as contrary to grace and justification. This contributed to Luther's unilateral view of covenant as testament.[27] As seen below, the Reformed differed keenly with Luther on the value of the believer's good works. This is because the Swiss, and Calvin, understood the covenant of grace to include human response, while at the same time denying human merit.

What about Luther's debate with the Anabaptists? Luther argued for infant baptism but along a different path from his Reformed peers. Luther replied in different ways to the anti–infant baptism arguments of the Anabaptists.[28] One scholar counts seventeen arguments for infant baptism in Luther's writings. He pursues these from biblical texts, from theological considerations, and from the history of the church.[29] A striking difference appears, however, between Luther and the Reformed theologians: among these arguments, the claim that infants were circumcised as a sign of the covenant is quite rare, and nowhere does he suggest that circumcision was a sacrament. In 1528 he does say, "Baptism has the same import as circumcision," but he does not develop this idea any further, except to say that God accepted the biological children of Abraham.[30] Nor does Luther call circumcision and baptism signs of the same covenant. Why was this so? The Reformer viewed circumcision as the sign of a covenant that was unique to Israel, "a covenant of law." Abraham had received two covenants, one of promise, in Genesis 15, the other of law, in Genesis 17. The promise belongs to Isaac alone, but the law, also to Ishmael:

> The covenant of circumcision . . . is solely a covenant of the law and is temporal
> . . . but the other covenant, which excludes Ishmael, and is made with Isaac alone,
> is spiritual and eternal. The covenant of circumcision is given for our performance
> before the Law of Moses, and is established for a definite people, in a definite land,
> and for a definite time, namely, while the generations of Abraham are in existence.
> The covenant of Isaac, however, is not given for our performance; it is entirely free,

---

25. Kolb, *Martin Luther*, 172–96.

26. Stephen J. Chester shows Luther's clear statement that living faith always does good works in "Faith Working through Love (Galatians 5:6): The Role of Human Deeds in Salvation in Luther and Calvin's Exegesis," *CovQ* 72, no. 3 (2014): 41–54.

27. Kolb states, "Luther's Ockhamist instructors had spoken of God's pledge to sinners with the term 'covenant,' interpreting it to mean that human performance upholding the human side of the covenant played a role in salvation. So Luther largely avoided the term." *Martin Luther*, 140.

28. See Nathan A. Finn, "Curb Your Enthusiasm: Martin Luther's Critique of Anabaptism," *SwJT* 56, no. 2 (2014): 163–81.

29. Paul H. Zietlow, "Martin Luther's Arguments for Infant Baptism," *ConcJ* 20, no. 2 (1994): 147–71.

30. Martin Luther, "Instruction for the Visitation of Parish Pastors in Electoral Saxony," in *LW*, 40:288.

without a name, without a time, and yet, from the seed of Isaac, lest one look for the blessing from another source.[31]

Circumcision is the sign of a different, time-limited, and now-expired covenant. As Luther considers the Anabaptist insistence on receiving baptism after professing faith, he comes to see this as a work, just the kind of work that circumcision had become for the Jews. This is how he understands Paul's arguments in Galatians against the Judaizers. They required the Gentiles to receive circumcision, just as the Anabaptists require baptism. Luther is deeply concerned that Christians not be diverted from faith to good works to receive justification ("lest one look," as he comments above, "for the blessing from another source"). He roots this thinking in his understanding of God's intention in the covenant of circumcision, which has ceased. Luther's most important criticism of the Anabaptist position, then, is that it indicates dependence on baptism as an act of works righteousness. This, no doubt, explains his reticence to appeal to infant circumcision with more force.

In any event, in his matured thought, Luther understood covenant in a testamentary form, as a unilateral promise. To introduce human responsibility in its exposition seems to be to reintroduce the merit scheme, which denies the passive righteousness imputed in justification. Everything stands or falls with maintaining the distinction between law and gospel—and thus with justification by faith alone. This distinction is the key to Christian living in both Testaments.

Covenant Theology in Zurich

If Martin Luther separated the "covenant of circumcision" as law from the "covenant of Isaac" as promise, Huldrych Zwingli came to identify them as one covenant of grace. This was largely through his encounters with leading Anabaptist Balthasar Hubmaier (ca. 1480–1528). Hubmaier understood baptism as a public witness to the crisis experience of conversion. Preaching was to convict of sin, then to bring to repentance and faith. The third step in his *ordo salutis* was water baptism. As Hughes Oliphant Old describes Hubmaier's view, "Baptism is the outward witness on the part of the believer to his or her own inward belief in the forgiveness of sins through Christ."[32] No infant could do this, so no infant ought to be baptized.

Though he never opposed infant baptism, Zwingli, in his earliest writing, was not far from Hubmaier's understanding of the sacraments. He opposed the traditional Roman view that baptism removed original sin.[33] Only grace, given by the Spirit,

---

31. Luther on Gen. 17:19–21, *LW*, 3:162–63; also cited in Lillback, *Binding*, 118.

32. Hughes Oliphant Old, *The Shaping of the Reformed Baptismal Rite in the Sixteenth Century* (Grand Rapids, MI: Eerdmans, 1992), 99.

33. Zwingli denied that infants have guilt from Adam's sin but argued that they have sin as a disease, a complete inability to do any good. Sin as transgression flows out of sin as disease. See W. P. Stephens, *The Theology of Huldrych Zwingli* (New York: Oxford University Press, 1986), 149.

and no outward ceremony, can cleanse the soul. Rather, baptism and the Supper are a "pledge" or "oath" of allegiance, even a testimony to the church.[34] In 1525 Zwingli wrote, "The man who receives the mark of baptism is the one who is resolved to hear what God says to him, to learn the divine precepts and to live his life in accordance with them."[35] This pledge is made by adults, and by parents, who intend to instruct their children in the faith.[36]

What was his view of the covenant relationship? At first, Zwingli seems to view covenant as the believer's commitment. But as he delves into Scripture in response to Hubmaier, his doctrine of the sacraments shifts. W. P. Stephens explains:

> Zwingli's understanding of the sacraments moves from the earlier writings, where they are signs of the covenant, with which God assures us, through a period where the emphasis is on them as signs with which we assure others that we are one with them in the church, to the later writings, where something of both these emphases is present.[37]

Without dismissing the believer's responsibility, Zwingli ultimately holds that the priority belongs to God, who graciously includes believers and their children in his covenant.

In a 1525 response to Hubmaier, Zwingli reads the Old Testament as promise and the New Testament as fulfillment. By this time, Lillback says, Zwingli has come to a mature expression of the continuity of the one covenant from the Old Testament to the New Testament.[38] The Züricher develops this continuity according to the pattern of God's covenant in Genesis 17. Kenneth Hagen summarizes: "The Christian covenant or testament is the old covenant of Abraham. . . . We do not have a new faith or covenant, but the faith and covenant of Abraham."[39]

By 1526 "*foedus, pactum, testamentum* are synonyms that apply to Abraham and his seed and to Christ and Christians."[40] Both the *ordo* and the *historia* are included in the covenant: both the promise to be Abraham's God, or to save him, and the promise to send Christ.[41] God promised Christ and has now fulfilled the promise. He is Almighty Savior of Abraham and of Christians. The requirement is that both must "walk before [God], and be blameless" (Gen. 17:1). The signs are circumcision and baptism: "Our baptism looks altogether to the same thing as circumcision did formerly. It is the sign of the covenant God struck with us through his Son."[42] He is the God of

---

34. See Stephens, *Theology*, 184–85.

35. Huldrych Zwingli, "Of Baptism," in *Zwingli and Bullinger: Selected Translations with Introduction and Notes*, ed. and trans. G. W. Bromiley, LCC (Philadelphia: Westminster, 1953), 131.

36. Stephens, *Theology*, 205.

37. Stephens, *Theology*, 192.

38. Lillback, *Binding*, 95.

39. Kenneth Hagen, "From Testament to Covenant in the Early Sixteenth Century," *SCJ* 3, no. 1 (1972): 19.

40. Hagen, "From Testament to Covenant," 19.

41. Stephens, *Theology*, 207n32.

42. From Zwingli, *The Eucharist* (1525), quoted in Stephens, *Theology*, 206.

Abraham's offspring and of the Christian's offspring. As Lillback notices, the implications of covenant continuity between the Testaments are far wider than the defense of infant baptism.[43] Zwingli has set a trajectory for interpreting the relation of Old and New Testaments. He has also described the Christian's relation to God as one of gracious promise and believing responsibility.

Zwingli presents his position on the covenant in his 1527 *Refutation of the Tricks of the Catabaptists*. He describes the covenant in terms of its unity, its graciousness, and its inclusive, corporate character.

God first made the covenant with sinful Adam. Promising to crush the "old serpent's" head and so to provide a body for his Son, who would die, God then renewed the same covenant with Noah, Abraham, Israel, David, and finally us. He disclosed more light to his people as the incarnation drew closer. Also to Abraham he promised the seed who would save mankind, as well as "innumerable posterity," "not only after the flesh, but also according to the Spirit," and the land of Palestine.[44] To Israel God promised, in the same covenant, to bear them up on his wings and required that they walk before him (Ex. 19:4–5). Should the Anabaptists suggest that Christians and Israel are under different covenants because Paul says there were two covenants (Gal. 4:22, 24), Zwingli answers that Paul speaks of "two testaments by a misuse of language,"[45] referring to the Jews who rejected Christ, and claimed to be, but were not, truly God's people. Two distinct covenants and peoples would be possible only if there were two gods! The same mercy of God promised to the world that saved Adam and Noah also saved Peter, Paul, Ananias, Gamaliel, and Stephen.[46] Zwingli supports this unity by appealing to the parable of the laborers in the vineyard, as also to Romans 11; Ephesians 2:11–20; Hebrews 12:22–24; and 1 Peter 2:9–10. The peripheral differences between Israel and the church are "figures," ceremonies and sacrifices, and types. For the church, now that Christ has come, believers enter heaven at death, the testament is now preached to all nations, and we have the model of Christ's life. But in the "chief thing," more than one covenant and covenant people would require more than one God. Zwingli summarizes: "Since therefore there is one immutable God and one testament only, we who trust in Christ are under the same testament, consequently God is as much our God as he was Abraham's, and we are as much his people as was Israel."[47]

God established this one saving covenant in pure grace. First, he predestined the covenant before the race fell in Adam, setting apart one family through which Christ would come. Through it, he would save mankind. The family of Abraham and David participate in the covenant as a matter of pure grace. Faith in the promise, like Abraham's

43. Lillback, *Binding*, 96.

44. Huldrych Zwingli, *Refutation of the Tricks of the Catabaptists*, in *Selected Works of Huldreich Zwingli (1484–1531)*, ed. Samuel Macauley Jackson (Philadelphia: University of Pennsylvania, 1972), 221.

45. Zwingli, *Refutation*, 223.

46. Zwingli, *Refutation*, 229.

47. Zwingli, *Refutation*, 235.

faith, brings justification. But faith, too, is the gift of God, by the Spirit, coming only to those whom God has eternally predestined to receive it. Zwingli argues this from Romans 8:29–30:

> For those whom he foreknew he also predestined to be conformed to the image of his Son, in order that he might be the firstborn among many brothers. And those whom he predestined he also called, and those whom he called he also justified, and those whom he justified he also glorified.

We know this by synecdoche, or one part standing for the whole. When we read that anyone has "believed," we know that this is so only because God elected, predestined, and called him. Though Scripture may in places speak only of believing, all the rest is implied, based in God's free election. Election makes faith certain. Since this series of acts in the application of grace is unbreakable, faith itself is not the criterion of identifying God's grace, nor the only way of judging someone to be God's son. In effect, the elect are sons before they believe. Thus Zwingli answers the Anabaptist claim that only believers may rightly be considered the church. And this means that children, too, may be in the church before they believe.

The Anabaptists claimed that only the elect—and thus not those rejected, like Esau (Rom. 9:11–13)—could be counted as God's people. But Esau was circumcised. They asked how he could have been considered God's son. Zwingli's answer was that if the elect are sons even before they believe, like Jacob, then faith is not the only mark distinguishing the sons from the rejected. In fact, those like Esau who in maturity do not show faith, the fruit of election, may be judged to have been rejected by God. Only those who have heard and disbelieved may be judged rejected.

This means that eternal election and rejection are distinct from and "above" the covenant relationship. Both are the result of grace, but election and rejection are determinative. There are those properly in the covenant, like Esau, who will be rejected. But this cannot be discerned regarding the infants of believers.[48] Eternal election and rejection are not the rule for the church's judgment or action, because (except in the singular case of Esau) they are secret. God's law or covenant must be the rule of judgment. "So I regard," Zwingli states, "the whole Catabaptist argument as now overturned, and it is demonstrated that election is above baptism, circumcision, faith and preaching."[49]

Zwingli has another use for synecdoche: to show that the covenant is correctly understood as made with a *body* of people. The covenant has a corporate character. This corporate character, however, does not diminish the individual responsibility of the members. Zwingli's discussion of Esau's unbelief underscores this point. Yet in the covenant, God spoke to the whole people:

---

48. Zwingli states, "For the statement that they are in the covenant, testament and people of God assures us of their election until the Lord announces something different of someone." *Refutation*, 244.

49. Zwingli, *Refutation*, 247.

When, in giving command or prohibition, he addresses that whole people, the infants are not excluded because they understand nothing of what is said or commanded, but he speaks synecdochically, so that so far from excluding that part which could receive nothing that came because of the times or its age he even includes it. . . . So that he often addresses the whole people as one man: Hear, O Israel, and: Say to the house of Jacob.[50]

The Anabaptists assumed an individualistic character to the covenant, based on the experience of the Christian. But this is not how God dealt with the family of Israel, nor how he now deals with us.

Zwingli's doctrine of the covenant maintains the absolute sovereignty of God in saving grace,[51] the expression of that grace administered in one covenant of grace throughout redemptive history, and the responsibility of the believer in relation to it.[52] The Old and New Testaments are unified by one covenant that provided one Savior. The Spirit enables the elect in the covenant to walk in believing fellowship with God.

Heinrich Bullinger succeeded Zwingli in Zurich as a theologian and pastor of remarkable ability. Bullinger did not follow Zwingli at every point, but he did build on Zwingli's exposition of Genesis 17 in his important 1534 work *A Brief Exposition of the One and Eternal Testament or Covenant of God.*[53] This document shares Zwingli's fundamental positions, though it does not mention eternal election as the basis of the covenant, nor does it include explicit answers to Anabaptist arguments against infant baptism. Bullinger clearly held the same views as Zwingli on these important matters,[54] so perhaps his treatise had a more popular, less polemical aim.[55]

Clear from its title, the unity of the covenant from old to new is central. God, the all-sufficient, to provide fellowship with himself, entered into this "pact" with "miserable, sinful man," again out of grace, not merit. Like human covenants, God solemnized it with ceremonies in Genesis 15 and 17. Holy Scripture documents the covenant so it may

---

50. Zwingli, *Refutation*, 227.

51. Zwingli states, "The election of God is free and gratuitous. For he elected us before the foundation of the world, before ever we were born. Consequently, God did not elect us because of works, for he executed our election before the foundation of the world. Hence works are not meritorious." "An Exposition of the Faith," in Bromiley, *Zwingli and Bullinger*, 271.

52. Lyle Bierma challenges Richard Greaves's thesis of "two-traditions of covenant theology" in relation to Zwingli's comment on Gen. 17:1:

The correct translation of the Latin is not, "The covenant of God with man is that he will be our God *only if* we walk wholly according to his will," but "The covenant of God with man is that he is our God; *let us* walk wholly according to his will" (or "*that* we walk wholly according to his will"). Nowhere here is there any indication that God's promised blessing is contingent upon human fulfillment of certain conditions.

"Federal Theology," 311.

53. *A Brief Exposition of the One and Eternal Testament or Covenant of God*, in Charles S. McCoy and J. Wayne Baker, *Fountainhead of Federalism: Heinrich Bullinger and the Covenantal Tradition; With a Translation of "De testamento seu foedere Dei unico et aeterno" (1534)* (Louisville: Westminster John Knox, 1991), 101–38.

54. Cf. Bierma, "Federal Theology," 312–13; Peter Stephens, "Bullinger's Defence of Infant Baptism in Debate with the Anabaptists," *RRR* 4, no. 2 (2002): 168–89.

55. Cf. Lillback, "Continuing Conundrum," 49.

be transmitted to posterity. Genesis 17:1–14 is the simplest summary of the covenant, especially Genesis 17:1: "The LORD appeared to Abram and said to him, 'I am God Almighty; walk before me, and be blameless.'" Its parties are God, the "all-sufficient," and Abraham and his children (cf. Gen. 17:7). These children are both his physical offspring, including infants,[56] and those whom the Spirit brings to faith throughout the world.

The terms of the pact are that God—or El Shaddai, the sole source of all good—promises to supply everything for needy humans, especially and finally Christ himself. Included are the land of Canaan and its true referent, the "heavenly" country of Hebrews 11:16. God offers himself "that he will be their protector, confederate, and savior, who is going to strengthen the otherwise weak human race in spirit and flesh, and who through Christ the Lord is going to liberate the human race from sin and eternal death, and going to give eternal life."[57]

Humanity is required to keep its side of the covenant as well. God said in effect, "'Arrange your life in every respect according to my will.' . . . For firmness and sincerity of faith, along with innocence and purity of life, is that integrity and strait way by which the saints walk before God."[58] This integrated faith and living are the requirement of the covenant throughout Scripture, what Bullinger calls the "conditions of the covenant."[59] The law of Moses and the exhortations of the prophets, apostles, and evangelists all express this "target," or sum, of piety. When Christ came, he was the fulfillment of God Almighty's promise, pouring out himself for us "and receiving us who have been cleansed by him into partnership and into the eternal kingdom."[60] Jesus's life instructs us how to walk before God.

What about the differences between the old and new covenants, and the difference between Israel and the church? Jeremiah 31, which speaks of "old" and "new" covenants, simply addresses the "carnalities" of the disobedient among the people, while "new" reveals the richness of what Christ brings. "Even the Spirit is the same in both testaments," Zwingli notes.[61] Mosaic ceremonies and sacrifices were types, predicting what Christ would accomplish in his death. Though the church of Christ is one with Israel, it surpasses it, insofar as the ceremonies and types have now been fulfilled and Christ has now come and spread his gospel around the world.

Circumcision was the sign of the covenant with Abraham. The blood shedding committed Abraham and his children to keep the covenant. The corresponding blood shedding in Genesis 15 taught that God, as a testator, would one day take on a human nature and die for his people.[62] This is the meaning of baptism and

---

56. Lillback states, "The seed of Abraham includes infants, even though they cannot yet keep the condition of walking blamelessly before the Lord." *Binding*, 111.

57. Zwingli, *One and Eternal Testament*, 110.

58. Zwingli, *One and Eternal Testament*, 111.

59. Zwingli, *One and Eternal Testament*, 113.

60. Zwingli, *One and Eternal Testament*, 116.

61. Zwingli, *One and Eternal Testament*, 124.

62. Note that his wording is very close to Luther's comment above on Gal. 3:18.

the Eucharist. As the whole covenant was contained in the old signs, so the entire "renewed covenant" is contained in the new signs.[63] These signs indicate both God's promise and our responsibility. But even before circumcision was instituted, the covenant was in place. Noah, Enoch, Seth, Abel, and Adam "pleased God through faith without circumcision."[64]

Bullinger does not present the covenant as unilateral. Both God and man mutually have responsibilities. Those who serve other gods or who ignore the promises receive God's curse. The covenant is bilateral in its functioning. Bullinger presents human responsibility more vividly in the covenant than either Luther or Zwingli. As we noted, he calls it a "condition." We can easily imagine that Luther would abhor such a title for human responsibility.

In this treatise, Bullinger does not found the covenant in election. It does not follow, however, that he minimizes grace or that he has returned to a medieval soteriology. Bierma points to Bullinger's authorship of the Second Helvetic Confession (1566). There, election to salvation is based on unconditional grace, not on works (10.1–2); also, faith and love, patterned after God's law, are solely the gift of God's gracious Holy Spirit (16.2, 5). Bierma concludes, "For Bullinger, therefore, as for Zwingli, the benefits of God's covenant grace do not ultimately depend on faith and obedience; they include faith and obedience."[65]

Calvin's Covenant Theology

Like his Swiss peers, John Calvin sought to establish the Christian life in the one covenant of grace. And like them, his presentation of the unity of Old and New Testaments responded to Anabaptist teaching. Richard Muller rightly states that Calvin does not make covenant a distinct topic in his *Institutes*. Neither does he organize his theology around it. Instead, he develops the ideas in his exegetical work—in commentaries and sermons.[66]

Covenant in the Historia Salutis

We will first take up his presentation of the history of salvation. Then we will be in a better position to understand how he relates the covenant to matters of individual salvation and the Christian life. Stephen Edmondson argues that integral to understanding Calvin's presentation of Christ as mediator is his understanding of "the covenant history."[67] Calvin understands redemptive history itself as a coherent whole, God's one covenant with the church, enacted by Christ in both Old and New Testaments and brought to

---

63. Zwingli, *One and Eternal Testament*, 132.
64. Zwingli, *One and Eternal Testament*, 135.
65. Bierma, "Federal Theology," 313.
66. Richard A. Muller, *The Unaccommodated Calvin: Studies in the Foundation of a Theological Tradition,* OSHT (New York: Oxford University Press, 2000), 155.
67. Stephen Edmondson, *Calvin's Christology* (Cambridge: Cambridge University Press, 2004), 46–69. I am indebted to his nuanced articulation of redemptive history as "covenant history." The term is his.

consummation in Christ in the fullness of time. Calvin shows his admiration of God's plan in lyrical words:

> In the beginning, when the first promise of salvation was given to Adam, it glowed like a feeble spark. Then, as it was added to, the light grew in fullness, breaking forth increasingly and shedding its radiance more widely. At last—when all the clouds were dispersed—Christ, the Sun of Righteousness, fully illumined the whole earth.[68]

Each of the biblical covenants is part of this one work of salvation. Yet Calvin describes them not as separate or new covenants but as the renewal of the singular eternal covenant: "What was promised to Abraham was enacted under types through Moses and the law and David and his kingdom before it was fulfilled in Christ."[69] In fact, the whole of Scripture, unfolding in its various parts, is a unified, God-given account of this saving work of God in Christ. As Edmondson comments, "Even the work of Christ is seen by Calvin as the renewal of the covenant with Abraham."[70]

This means, for Calvin, that the Old Testament is far from inferior to the New, as the Anabaptists claimed. It is vital to the whole message of the gospel. This conviction of the Reformer is evident in his literary labors. Though Calvin's theology of the covenant was very similar to Zwingli and Bullinger (contrary to the "two traditions" theory), his task in expounding it took on a much wider scope than that of the Swiss. He did not focus strictly on a polemic, as Zwingli, nor offer his exposition in an important treatise, as Bullinger.[71]

God's response to the sin of the human race in Adam was the establishment of his covenant. "Wherever the word 'covenant' appears in Scripture, we ought, at the same time, to call to remembrance the word 'grace.'"[72] By the divine word, God graciously promised eternal life to the patriarchs. All the fathers, Adam, Abel, Noah, and Abraham were joined to God by this promise.[73] But God formally founded the covenant with Abraham in Genesis 12, elaborating on it in Genesis 15 and adding the covenant sign of circumcision in Genesis 17. Here God promised him a family, the land of Canaan, and Christ the mediator. In Genesis 12:2, "I will make of you a great nation," God

---

68. John Calvin, *Institutes of the Christian Religion*, ed. John T. McNeill, trans. Ford Lewis Battles, LCC 20–21 (Philadelphia: Westminster, 1960), 1:464 (2.10.20).

69. Edmondson, *Calvin's Christology*, 49.

70. Edmondson, *Calvin's Christology*, 50.

71. According to Muller, Calvin's theology of covenant was very much like Zwingli's and Bullinger's, in terms of the unity of Old and New and of the covenant's bilateral character. *Unaccommodated Calvin*, 124–25, 155.

72. John Calvin, *Commentary on Isaiah*, on 55:3, quoted in Edmondson, *Calvin's Christology*, 50. Edmondson follows the "Calvin versus the Calvinists" school, rejecting a prefall covenant. *Calvin's Christology*, 50n19. Lillback argues for a "non-meritorious, proto-covenant of works" in Calvin. *Binding*, 278–304. Aaron Denlinger, however, challenges Lillback's presentation of Adam's representative relationship to humankind in "Calvin's Understanding of Adam's Relationship to His Posterity: Recent Assertions of the Reformer's 'Federalism' Evaluated," *CTJ* 44, no. 2 (2009): 226–49. This does not by itself distance Calvin from later Calvinism, but it points to both continuity and development, a matter that D. Blair Smith addresses in "Post-Reformation Developments," chap. 17 in this volume.

73. Calvin, *Institutes*, 1:434 (2.10.7).

promised him the church. Calvin refers to Israel as Abraham's descendants, along with the Gentiles whom God would add, as "Church."[74] The heart of both was the promise of Christ, who by his death would reconcile the covenant people to God. Calvin comments on Genesis 12:3 as follows:

> God . . . pronounces that all nations should be blessed in his servant Abram, because Christ was included in his loins. In this manner, he not only intimates that Abram would be an *example* but a *cause* of blessing; so that there should be an understood antithesis between Adam and Christ.[75]

Abram would be an example of faith to the church forever, as well as the genealogical source of Christ's redemption. That redemption would save Adam's fallen race. Calvin takes the land of Canaan as a type that was confirmed as such when Christ came. It pointed forward to Christ's task "to renovate the world." He reads this in light of Paul's allusion in Romans 4:13 to "the promise to Abraham and his offspring that he would be heir of the world." Calvin comments, "Since under the type of the land of Canaan not only was a heavenly life displayed to Abraham, but also the full and perfect blessing of God, the apostle rightly teaches us that the dominion of the world was promised to him."[76] His encounter with the typical figure Melchizedek in Genesis 14 intimated to Abraham Christ's priestly intercession and his messianic kingship.[77] The covenant provides both for Christ's redeeming and royal work. The first was then revealed more fully in the covenant mediated by Moses, the second in the covenant with David.

Interpreting the relationship between the old (Mosaic) covenant and the new covenant has challenged the best of theologians.[78] Calvin framed his *Institutes*, from the 1539 edition on, to resolve matters of doctrinal debate, so that ministerial candidates could attend properly to the reading of the divine word.[79] In 1539 he added a chapter to the *Institutes* on the similarity and difference between the Old and New Testaments. He expanded it to three chapters (2.9–11) in the final edition of 1559.[80] This answered the Anabaptist slighting of the value of the Old Testament; the unity of the covenant plays a major role in his defense of the value of the Old Testament.[81]

---

74. Edmondson notes that Calvin finds here, not at Pentecost, the birth of the church. *Calvin's Christology*, 54.

75. John Calvin, *Commentary on the First Book of Moses, Called Genesis*, trans. John King, in *Calvin's Commentaries* (hereafter *Comm.*), 22 vols. (Grand Rapids, MI: Baker, 1989), 1:348–49; emphasis original.

76. John Calvin, *The Epistles of Paul to the Romans and to the Thessalonians*, trans. Ross Mackenzie, in *Calvin's New Testament Commentaries* (hereafter, *CNTC*), ed. David W. Torrance and Thomas F. Torrance, 12 vols. (Grand Rapids, MI: Eerdmans, 1979), 8:91.

77. Calvin, *Comm.*, 1:389 (Gen. 14:18).

78. Lillback provides a thorough analysis of Calvin's interpretation of the Mosaic covenant. For his presentation the reader may consult *Binding*, 142–61.

79. Muller, *Unaccommodated Calvin*, 120. "Covenant" was not a disputed topic in the medieval theological books.

80. Willem Balke, *Calvin and the Anabaptist Radicals*, trans. William Heynen (Grand Rapids, MI: Eerdmans, 1981), 99.

81. Calvin, like Zwingli, defended infant baptism on the basis of the unity of the covenant of grace from Old Testament to New. Cf. Calvin, *Institutes*, 2:1324–58 (4.16).

Calvin's understanding of the unity of the covenant of grace is both simple and complex. The simplicity lies in Christ as the single and unique mediator of salvation in the Old and the New Testaments. The complexity is also found in the mediator, because the history of salvation unfolded, "by an orderly plan," in several administrations of the covenant.[82]

On one side, the Old and New Testaments are simply continuous, revealed more and more clearly in history.[83] What God promised to Abraham—a family, a mediator who would accomplish salvation, and a land of blessing—he initially fulfilled in the Mosaic administration of the covenant. In fact, there is ultimately only one covenant. From the beginning of the world, all who were adopted into the covenant had the same law and the same doctrine as Christians have: "The covenant made with the patriarchs is so much like ours in substance and reality that the two are actually one and the same. Yet they differ in the mode of dispensation."[84]

Moses did not abolish the Abrahamic covenant, evidenced by the fact that God saved Israel in the exodus as the fulfillment of the specific promises to Abraham. The Jews had the same hope of immortality that Christians have. They were "adopted" into this hope not by merit but by God's mercy. They had union with God through their knowledge of the mediator, in order to share his promises. Paul teaches that this was revealed in the Law and the Prophets (Rom. 1:2–3).[85] They were justified by God's fatherly mercy, in the "covenant of the gospel," as we are. They can no more be separated from Christ than we.[86] If they had the same gracious covenant, then their sacraments must have meant the same. This is Paul's assumption in 1 Corinthians 10. Their baptism "in the sea" and "spiritual food" and "spiritual drink" referred to Christ (1 Cor. 10:2–4).[87] The "formula of the covenant" belongs to both: "I . . . will be your God, and you shall be my people" (Lev. 26:12). This means that his presence brought them salvation, union with him in righteousness, and thus eternal life.[88] This continuity of substance belies the Anabaptist claim that the old covenant promises were merely carnal and earthly. Through the mediator whom they trusted as "pledge of the covenant," old covenant believers looked forward to future blessedness.[89]

Yet this is not to diminish the discontinuity between Old and New. These are the differences in "administration" of the one covenant of grace. Scripture reveals these also, and Calvin is quick to account for the differences, lest the Anabaptist critics seem to win the day. First, the old covenant used material blessings to teach Israel, as an underage

82. Calvin, *Institutes*, 1:464 (2.10.20).
83. Cf. Peter A. Lillback, "Calvin's Interpretation of the History of Salvation: The Continuity and Discontinuity of the Covenant (2.10–11)," in *A Theological Guide to Calvin's "Institutes": Essays and Analysis*, ed. David W. Hall and Peter A. Lillback (Phillipsburg, NJ: P&R, 2008), 168–204.
84. Calvin, *Institutes*, 1:429 (2.10.2).
85. Calvin, *Institutes*, 1:429 (2.10.2). We return to this union below when we consider Calvin's *ordo salutis*.
86. Calvin, *Institutes*, 1:431 (2.10.4).
87. Calvin, *Institutes*, 1:432 (2.10.5).
88. Calvin, *Institutes*, 1:435 (2.10.8).
89. Calvin, *Institutes*, 1:449 (2.10.23).

people, of their future, heavenly inheritance.[90] The people of the new covenant now meditate on the future life directly. Before the coming of Christ, the Lord taught the church as though it were a child. Now he teaches as though it is an adult. Old Testament physical punishments were signs of the spiritual death of eternity now revealed.[91]

Second, the Old Testament revealed a substance in a certain sense as "absent," under ceremonies, but the New reveals the substance as present. The book of Hebrews teaches this reality regarding the sacrifices of the old covenant, which could never actually take away sins. In the New Testament, we have the true priest, Christ, whose sacrifice on the cross has provided eternal redemption (Ps. 110:4; Heb. 7:19). The ceremonies of the Mosaic covenant were signs of what Christ would do. The new covenant is final in that now Christ's blood has actually been shed for us (Luke 22:20).[92] Everything depended on the accomplished work of Christ. With his death and resurrection and the sending of the Spirit at Pentecost, the old covenant actually *became* the new covenant: "The children of the promise [Rom. 9:8], reborn of God, who have obeyed the commands by faith working through love [Gal. 5:6], have belonged to the new covenant since the world began."[93] That was God's intention all along.[94]

We should not infer that Calvin believed there was no gracious eternal benefit for the believing Israelite. In fact, though the sacrifices were in themselves only typical, they were also sacramental, in that they actually presented the grace they represented, even before Christ's coming and cross. Calvin comments on Exodus 29:38, regarding the sacrifice of "two lambs a year old day by day regularly":

> [It was] not as though these brute animals availed in themselves unto expiation, except insofar as they were testimonies of the grace to be manifested by Christ. Thus the ancients were reconciled to God in a sacramental manner by the victims just as we are now cleansed through baptism. Hence it follows that these symbols were useful only as they were exercises to faith and repentance, so that the sinner might learn to fear God and seek pardon in Christ.[95]

Under the shadow form of typical sacrifices and ceremonies, the old covenant was made "new and eternal only after it was consecrated and established by the blood of Christ."[96]

In this discontinuity, Calvin must account for biblical passages that state the difference between the old and new covenants in absolute terms (Jer. 31:32; 2 Cor. 3:6–9;

---

90. Calvin, *Institutes*, 1:450 (2.11.1).

91. Calvin, *Institutes*, 1:452 (2.11.2–3).

92. Calvin, *Institutes*, 1:454 (2.11.5).

93. Calvin, *Institutes*, 1:459 (2.11.10).

94. The Old Testament "was temporary because it remained, as it were, in suspense until it might rest upon a firm and substantial confirmation. It became new and eternal only after it was consecrated and established by the blood of Christ." Calvin, *Institutes*, 1:454 (2.11.4).

95. Quoted in Edmondson, *Calvin's Christology*, 62.

96. Calvin, *Institutes*, 1:454 (2.11.5). This point underscores that matters of the *historia salutis*, like the inadequacy of the sacrificial system, are distinct from, though not separable from, the saving acts of God toward the individual.

Heb. 8:8–13). Perhaps the sharpest antithesis is found in 2 Corinthians 3:6–9, where Paul contrasts old and new covenants as, respectively, ministries of "death" and "life." Does the apostle sponsor the Anabaptist denigration of the Old Testament? Calvin's answer is twofold. Moses as lawgiver had a narrower ministry of condemnation, in which he exposed the pride of the self-righteous, because the commandment did not provide the ability to keep its precept. Its outcome is condemnation.[97] On the other hand, Moses had a wider ministry, as did the old covenant as a whole. It borrowed from the gospel the promises of grace and redemption. The Holy Spirit was active in the old covenant period, working faith in believers like Abraham and David. But he is more active in the new covenant period, when Christ's redemption has now, finally, been accomplished.

Calvin considers the law as functioning in both the narrow sense (to condemn) and the broad sense (the old covenant as a whole) at the same time under the Old Testament. In other words, under the Mosaic economy, people were saved by faith in Christ (under the covenant of grace in the Old Testament), while at the same time, the law in the narrow sense functioned to show them that the righteousness they needed was not available to them apart from Christ.[98] Though the distinction between old and new covenants is absolute, it is so only in terms of two realities: (1) the progress of the history of redemption and (2) the abuse of the old covenant by those who sought to be justified by their works. The antithesis is relative when related to persons but absolute in terms of administration. Thus, the old covenant was characterized by bondage and fear, while the new is a matter of freedom and trust. The final difference he treats is that the new covenant will include all the nations.[99]

Covenant in the Ordo Salutis

With such an expansive treatment of the covenant of grace as God revealed it in the history of salvation, it might be supposed that Calvin was blasé about the use of the covenant in the salvation of individuals, whether Israelites or Gentile believers. Not so.

From Adam onward, God established the covenant, his "sacred bond," uniting the pious to himself for eternal life.[100] God's monergistic grace was its foundation from beginning to end. Thus no human act or contribution of virtue was involved in establishing the bond.[101] Commenting on Genesis 17:7, Calvin stresses that the covenant was made with all

---

97. So far, Calvin agrees with Luther on this *ordo salutis* use of the law.

98. Commenting on Rom. 8:15, Calvin writes, "We are not to infer from this either that no one was endowed with the Spirit of adoption before the coming of Christ, or that all who received the law were slaves, and not sons. Paul compares the ministry of the law with the dispensation of the Gospel, rather than persons with persons." That is, it is not "persons" but covenant administrations that are contrasted. Calvin, *CNTC*, Rom. 8:15.

99. For more on the issues of law and gospel in Calvin, see I. John Hesselink, *Calvin's Concept of the Law*, PrTMS 30 (Allison Park, PA: Pickwick, 1992), 155–216.

100. Calvin, *Institutes*, 1:434 (2.10.7).

101. This section adapts material from Howard Griffith, "'The First Title of the Spirit': Adoption in Calvin's Soteriology," *EvQ* 73, no. 2 (2001): 135–53. Used by permission of *Evangelical Quarterly*.

the natural children of Israel: "God made his covenant with those sons of Abraham who were naturally born of him."[102] This distinguished the children of Israel from all the nations of the earth, who still wander, exiled from Eden. It came by promise and grace, not by nature. The promise "by which God adopted them all as children" was common to all, and salvation was *offered* to all in it. There are not two offers but one. But not all respond in faith:

> Since the whole body of the people is gathered together into the fold of God, by one and the same voice, all without exception, are, in this respect, accounted children, . . . but in the innermost sanctuary of God, none others are reckoned sons of God, but they in whom the promise is ratified by faith.[103]

The covenant relationship is gracious, but there is more to it than this, as respects eternal election and salvation. Calvin sorts out the relationship of covenant and particular election in his comment on Romans 9:11:

> Paul's first proposition, therefore, is as follows: "As the blessing of the covenant separates Israel from all other nations, so also the election of God makes a distinction between men in that nation, while he predestines some to salvation and others to eternal condemnation." The second proposition is, "There is no basis for this election other than the goodness of God alone, and also his mercy since the fall of Adam, which embraces those whom he pleases, without any regard whatever to their works."[104]

In other words, within the covenanted people, God distinguishes his eternally elect from those whom he has rejected. Election and covenant are not identical, but the covenant is the means by which God works out his eternal election. He does this by working faith in the covenant promises by the inward work of the Holy Spirit. Anthony A. Hoekema comments, "We see how balanced Calvin's theology was. His conception of the covenant of grace as a 'middle way,' as a circle wider than particular election, enables him to do full justice to God's sovereign grace and to man's crucial responsibility within the covenant relationship."[105]

The relationship is purely gracious, but this does not imply that the covenant member is without meaningful responsibility as it is worked out. The interplay between the Israelite's responsibility in the covenant and God's sovereignty has been described as "duality,"[106] "conditionality," and "mutuality."[107] The description does not refer to the ob-

---

102. Calvin expresses the personal nature of the covenant relation by calling it "adoption." Covenant and adoption are twin concepts. His biblical foundation is Rom. 9:4, "to them belong the adoption," which he understands as referring to Ex. 4:22–23.

103. Calvin, *Comm.*, Gen. 17:7.

104. Calvin, *CNTC*, Rom. 9:11. Calvin uses the words "adoption" and "election" interchangeably. Both are subject to "degrees." That is, covenantal adoption and covenantal election must both be ratified by faith. Cf. his discussion of adoption in *Comm.*, Gen. 17:7, and of election in *Institutes*, 2:929–32 (3.21.6–7).

105. Anthony A. Hoekema, "The Covenant of Grace in Calvin's Teaching," *CTJ* 2 (1967): 151.

106. J. Mark Beach, "Calvin and the Dual Aspect of Covenant Membership: Galatians 3:15–22—The Meaning of '"the Seed" Is Christ'—and Other Key Texts," *MJT* 20 (2009): 49–73.

107. Hoekema, "Calvin's Teaching," 133–61; Lillback, *Binding*, 210–41.

ligation on Christ the mediator to meet the terms of life, death, and resurrection for his people. That is a given and is absolutely certain.[108] The work of Christ is not set on a level with the obedience of the believer. The two are distinct, necessarily so. The question is, What is the relation of faith, repentance, obedience, and perseverance to the covenant? Are there necessary stipulations that man must fulfill? The Reformer's answer is clear and oft repeated: yes. References to human responsibility in the covenant are abundant.[109]

God's sovereign grace, worked by the Holy Spirit, does not cancel human responsibility but enables proper, faithful use of it. Calvin uses the offers of grace and the "threatenings" in God's word to engage the human response:

> Let us also note that the threatenings of God are very necessary for us. For we see how great pride and rebelliousness is in all of us, so much so that though we be not rebellious of set purpose to set our God at naught, and to cast off his yoke, yet we are so bleary-eyed that we think not on him, and the enticements of the world seduce us in such wise that we do not receive any warning that God gives us. If he calls us by gentleness he can get nothing at our hands; therefore he is compelled to use threatenings. . . . God, perceiving that that [gentle language] is not enough to move us, uses threatenings, and says, Take heed, if you think to cast away my word, and yet to remain unpunished, you deceive yourselves. . . . I must double your punishment and my vengeance must fall more horribly upon you. . . . Therefore being stirred up by the goodness and gentleness of God, . . . let us also spur ourselves on by his threatenings. . . . We may well dedicate ourselves unto God, and be held in his fear, if on the one side his promises be in force with us, and again on the other side we give ear to his threatenings.[110]

Calvin delivered the sermon from which this quotation is drawn to his congregation in 1555. Clearly, he believed that the conditionality or mutuality of the relationship was not restricted to the Mosaic administration of the covenant of grace! For confirmation of this point, he comments on Romans 11:22 that in the church of the new covenant, as in Israel of the old, covenant breaking is real, and thus so is the possibility of apostasy.[111] Calvin is not asserting that any regenerate or justified person can lose his regeneration or justification. When apostasy really happens, it happens only to the hypocrite. When the covenant achieves its saving purpose, however, the relationship is unilateral in its initiation, continuance, and consummation, as well as bilateral in its outworking in the lives of God's people. There is profound mystery involved in the covenant relation

---

108. See Calvin, *Comm.*, Ps. 132:12.

109. Cf. Calvin, *Institutes*, 1:807 (3.17.5); *The Sermons of M. Iohn Calvin Upon the Fifth Book of Moses called Deuteronomie*, trans. Arthur Golding (1583; repr., Edinburgh: Banner of Truth, 1987), 46a (Deut. 1:34–40), 323–24 (Deut. 7:11–15); Calvin, *Comm.*, Ps. 78:37.

110. Calvin, *Fifth Book of Moses called Deuteronomie*, 925 (Deut. 27:11–15), cited in Hoekema, "Calvin's Teaching," 154–55.

111. Cf. Calvin, *CNTC*, Rom. 11:22. The biblical passage reads, "Note then the kindness and the severity of God: severity toward those who have fallen, but God's kindness to you, provided you continue in his kindness. Otherwise you too will be cut off."

between God and man. Calvin does not tone down the mystery or resolve the tensions but teaches both aspects of the covenant in beautiful profundity.

The covenant promise comes to the entire church, and the Spirit works to unite the elect with the covenant mediator, the risen Christ. In the justly famous beginning of book 3 of the *Institutes*, Calvin writes,

> We must now examine this question. How do we receive those benefits which the Father bestowed on his only-begotten Son—not for Christ's own private use, but that he might enrich poor and needy men? First, we must understand that as long as Christ remains outside of us, and we are separated from him, all that he has suffered and done for the salvation of the human race remains useless and of no value for us. Therefore, to share with us what he has received from the Father, he had to become ours and to dwell within us. . . . Yet since we see that not all indiscriminately embrace that communion with Christ which is offered through the gospel, reason itself teaches us to climb higher and to examine into the secret energy of the Spirit, by which we come to enjoy Christ and all his benefits.[112]

What are these benefits? They are the "double benefit of the covenant," justification and sanctification (which Calvin sometimes identifies as "repentance").[113] Justification answers to the guilt of sin, and sanctification answers to the slavery or corruption of sin. The two benefits must be distinguished but cannot be separated from each other. To separate justification and sanctification from each other is "to tear apart the covenant" and "to tear apart Christ."[114]

We observed above the contrast between Luther and the Swiss theologians regarding the good works of the believer. This contrast is even sharper between Luther and Calvin. Luther opposed antinomians and stressed the necessity of keeping the Ten Commandments. But he was uncomfortable with the function of the Commandments as a guide to pleasing God. Self-righteousness was a too-real danger, and "passive righteousness" (free justification) too precious to throw into doubt. Calvin read the Scriptures much differently at this point. The great value of the law of God for the believer is that it shows him how to please God as a Christian. Referring to the Commandments, Calvin writes, "Here is the best instrument for them to learn more thoroughly each day the nature of the Lord's will to which they aspire, and to confirm them in the understanding of it."[115] In the new covenant, God has written the law on the believer's heart, by the Spirit. This corresponds to God's written commands.

This estimate of the sanctifying work of the Spirit brought Calvin to teach that God is truly pleased with the good works of the believer. Those works are never meritorious,

---

112. Calvin, *Institutes*, 1:537 (3.1.1).
113. Lillback, *Binding*, 180–83.
114. Calvin, *CNTC*, 1 Cor. 1:30; cf. Calvin, *Institutes*, 1:798 (3.16.1).
115. Calvin, *Institutes*, 1:360. See Calvin's explanation of the three "uses" of the law in *Institutes*, 2.7.6–12. His treatment has much overlap with Luther, but the tone and expectation of the Spirit's work in the believer is much more positive in Calvin.

nor even inherently good. But because the believer's person has been justified, God also accepts and even "justifies" his good works. These are the good works that are inspired by the Spirit and by faith yet are not worthy of reward. But in his covenant, God imputes righteousness to them, and so rewards them as good. This is a grand vision of the Christian life and of believers' living fellowship with God, one sadly lost sight of by too many of the heirs of the Reformation. It is possible for Calvin because he grounds both justification and sanctification in union with Christ in the covenant of grace.

Conclusion

In our analyzing the nuance of Calvin's covenant theology, we must not miss the deeply personal character of the covenant fellowship between God and his people that the Reformer presents. Calvin has followed the Scriptures in holding together the great mystery of God's sovereign saving grace and its outworking in the believing lives of unworthy sinners. He accounts for the distinction of covenant and saving election, laying the foundation for his doctrine of the church as both visible and invisible. Like Luther, Calvin's doctrine of justification is entirely forensic and gracious; human merit has no place in the way of salvation. Like Zwingli, Calvin stresses the corporate character of the covenant. He accounts for both the unity and diversity of Old and New Testaments. Like Bullinger, Calvin stresses the Spirit-wrought responsibility of man in the covenant.

But there is more. God draws near to his covenant people to bless them; he humbles himself to give them life. In July 1555 Calvin preached these words in his sermon on Deuteronomy 4:44–5:3:

> For if God only demanded his due, we should still be required to cling to him and to confine ourselves to his commandments. Moreover, when it pleases him by his infinite goodness to enter into a common treaty, and when he mutually binds himself to us without having to do so, when he enumerates that treaty article by article, when he chooses to be our father and savior, when he receives us as his flock and his inheritance, let us abide under his protection, filled with its eternal life for us. When all of those things are done, is it proper that our hearts become mollified even if they were at one time stone? When creatures see that the living God humbles himself to that extent, that he wills to enter into covenant that he might say, "let us consider our situation. It is true that there is an infinite distance between you and me, and that I should be able to command of you whatever seems good to me without having anything in common with you, for you are not worthy to approach me. . . . *But behold, I set aside my right. I come here to present myself to you as your guide and savior. I want to govern you. You are like my little family. And if you are satisfied with my Word, I will be your King.* Furthermore, do not think that the covenant which I made with your fathers was intended to take anything from you. For I have no need, nor am I indigent in anything. . . . But I procure *your* well-being and *your* salvation.

Therefore, on my part, I am prepared to enter into covenant, article by article, and pledge myself to you."[116]

If Luther cleared the church's road by renouncing human merit and finding free justification, and Zwingli showed that the path was wide enough for the whole church to walk on as God increased the light from the Old Testament to the New, Bullinger taught the redeemed how to walk on that road. It lay with Calvin to formulate the covenant of grace as God's life-comprehending and sacred bond with his church. Sovereign grace, tender love, absolute divine authority and power, saving condescension, perfect redemption by Christ, applied by the Spirit in union with Christ—all are found in the Reformer's preaching of the covenant of grace. Such is the legacy of the Reformation's developing doctrine of the covenant to the church.

---

116. *John Calvin's Sermons on the Ten Commandments*, ed. and trans. Benjamin W. Farley (Grand Rapids, MI: Baker, 1980), 45; emphasis added. The Reformer's use of the concept of "adoption" and of family metaphors for covenant fellowship ensures the very personal character of God's dealings with his people.

17

Post-Reformation Developments

D. Blair Smith

The torrent of grace that flowed down from the teaching of the first generation of Reformers made its way into the seventeenth century through channels of increasing theological reflection.[1] These channels flowed into an eventual vast sea bounded by the organizing principles of covenant theology. It is not an exaggeration to say that in this century classical covenant theology took on its distinct federal shape, reflected in its most significant consensus document, the Westminster Confession of Faith, and articulated by some of its leading theologians.

Recent scholars have helpfully schematized the history of Reformed theology during this period in a way that recognizes development and continuity. From roughly 1565 to 1640 was the time of "Early Orthodoxy," with "the initial framing and formulation of orthodoxy," and from 1640 to 1685 was the first phase of "High Orthodoxy," which contains the "large-scale elaboration of the theology" of Early Orthodoxy.[2] The late 1550s to the 1570s saw the making of many national confessions[3] as well as the death

---

1. My former student and now the assistant pastor at Grace Presbyterian Church in Winnetka, IL, Nicholas Swan, has been of immense help in the writing of this chapter, both in tracking down resources and thinking through pertinent theological issues. In addition, my teaching assistant, Nathan Groelsema, has helped find sources in a timely manner and proofed various drafts of this chapter. I'm very grateful for both.

2. Richard A. Muller, *After Calvin: Studies in the Development of a Theological Tradition*, OSHT (Oxford: Oxford University Press, 2003), 4–5. Muller also covers this schema in *Post-Reformation Reformed Dogmatics: The Rise and Development of Reformed Orthodoxy, ca. 1520 to ca. 1725*, 2nd ed., vol. 1, *Prolegomena to Theology* (Grand Rapids, MI: Baker Academic, 2003), 3–32. Willem J. van Asselt follows a slightly modified schema: Early Orthodoxy (ca. 1560–1620), High Orthodoxy (ca. 1620–1700), and Late Orthodoxy (ca. 1700–1790). *Introduction to Reformed Scholasticism*, RHTS (Grand Rapids, MI: Reformation Heritage Books, 2011), 130–93. Still another set of dates, connecting more consciously with the Reformation, is provided by Carl R. Trueman: Early Orthodoxy (from the Reformation until 1640), High Orthodoxy (1640–1690), and Late Orthodoxy (1690 onward). "Introduction," in *Reformed Orthodoxy in Scotland: Essays on Scottish Theology 1569–1775*, ed. Aaron Clay Denlinger (London: Bloomsbury, 2015), 3.

3. Namely, the Gallican Confession (1559), the Scots Confession (1560), the Belgic Confession (1561), the Thirty-Nine Articles of the Church of England (1563), the Heidelberg Catechism (1563), and the Second Helvetic

of significant second-generation theologians of the Reformation.[4] These deaths and the making of confessions did not mark a

> major shift in ethos or direction but as the transition from one generation to another and, specifically, as the transition from the work of a group of thinkers who produced the fundamental Reformed confessional and theological perspective to the work of another group of thinkers whose theology tended to develop within confessional boundaries and along trajectories of argument set by the writers of the second generation.[5]

The dawn of the Early Orthodox era is where we find the initial uses of "covenant of works" language and thus the emergence of federal theology. Significantly, this era is marked not by departure but by theological development along existing trajectories.[6]

The purpose of this chapter is to explore the covenant theology of the post-Reformation era, focusing especially on key documents and figures from the seventeenth century.[7] I argue, in contrast to significant voices in twentieth-century scholarship, that the consensus theology of this era is largely in continuity with the covenantal thought of the Reformers of the sixteenth century. That is not to say that there was no development. Indeed, we set this study in context by first looking to the shaping influence of federalism, which has roots in the Reformers' writings yet is presented with more distinction as Reformed theology flows into the seventeenth century. Because federal theology provides the contours for the covenantal thought of this period, this chapter devotes significant discussion to the bicovenantal theology of the Westminster Standards—the Westminster Confession of Faith (WCF), the Westminster Larger Catechism (WLC), and the Westminster Shorter Catechism (WSC)—and to further refinements evident in the development of the covenant of redemption. Throughout, I demonstrate that while federalism is consequential for covenant theology, it also has profound ramifications for Christology and soteriology.

Confession (1566). Muller notes that the Heidelberg Catechism and its primary author, Zacharias Ursinus, really belong to the beginning of the Early Orthodox era. *After Calvin*, 5. For a study of Ursinus's bicovenantalism, see Todd Smedley, "The Covenant Theology of Zacharias Ursinus" (PhD diss., University of Aberdeen, 2011).

4. Namely, Philipp Melanchthon (1560), Jan à Lasco (1560), Peter Martyr Vermigli (1562), Wolfgang Musculus (1563), John Calvin (1564), Guillaume Farel (1565), Pierre Viret (1571), and Heinrich Bullinger (1575).

5. Muller, *After Calvin*, 5.

6. In supporting Muller's periodization and trajectories of theological continuity, I am not saying that Reformed orthodoxy can be found only by tracing a straight line from Calvin to, say, Turretin. Protestant orthodoxy is not to be found in a single "school" (a Genevan one, for example) or theologian. The Reformation was a multinational theological movement, and the orthodoxy of the Reformed tradition embraces a variety of theologians, confessions, and schools of this era. See Muller, *Post-Reformation Reformed Dogmatics*, 1:78–80. For more on Reformed orthodoxy, in addition to Muller's *Post-Reformation Reformed Dogmatics* volumes, see essays in Carl R. Trueman and R. Scott Clark, eds., *Protestant Scholasticism: Essays in Reassessment*, SCHT (Carlisle, PA: Paternoster, 1998); Willem J. van Asselt and Eef Dekker, eds., *Reformation and Scholasticism: An Ecumenical Enterprise*, TSRPRT (Grand Rapids, MI: Baker Academic, 2001).

7. Dutch covenantal thought, which is significant in its own right, is treated in Bruce P. Baugus, "Covenant Theology in the Dutch Reformed Tradition," chap. 18 in this volume.

Federal Theology

With the Reformation came a greater attentiveness to the text and scope of Scripture, reflecting a desire to tell the story of redemption from Genesis to Revelation. This greater attentiveness gave birth to a federal theology characterized by its twofold nature, that is, a covenant of works and a covenant of grace.[8] In the covenant of works, all humanity was united to Adam as head in his fall into sin. The covenant of grace, which is centered on Jesus Christ the mediator, started with the promise of Genesis 3:15 and continued to draw up the covenantal promises of God throughout Scripture to demonstrate how they are all "Yes" and "Amen" (2 Cor. 1:20) through the person and work of Jesus Christ. As mediator, Christ joins all his elect people to himself as their new federal head, obediently following the path where Adam failed, fulfilling the precepts of the covenant of works for his people even as on the cross he takes on the penalty for their failure in Adam. Christ our mediator then gives of his righteousness to elect sinners, and through his death and resurrection, the elect inherit all the rich blessings of the covenant.

While the covenant of grace highlights the unilateral grace given by God through his Son, it also provided a way for Reformed theologians to address what God requires of his people. We explore the dynamics of this covenant below, including questions around its unilateral and bilateral aspects. For now it serves as a backdrop to the development of federalism and the covenant of works. We trace this development by looking first at the origins of the language and doctrine of the covenant of works. This brings us into a variety of debates over whether the bicovenantalism that the covenant of works introduces is in continuity or discontinuity with John Calvin. Before turning to the WCF as a consensus confessional document, this section concludes with some observations on the theological integrity of bicovenantalism in light of those who consider it a departure from the spirit of the early Reformers.

Origins

Geerhardus Vos notes that within the earliest writings on Reformed theology there was a "representation principle" that took into account Adam in his original state and his relationship with the rest of humanity. As theologians examined parallels between the two Adams found in texts such as Romans 5:12–21 and 1 Corinthians 15:22, there developed a covenant of works, which, along with the covenant of grace, resulted in a bicovenantal structure that is at the heart of federalism. Joel Beeke and Mark Jones put it simply: "Federalism (from Latin, *foedus*, 'covenant') is the idea that by virtue of the covenant of works, sin and death entered the world through Adam and passed on to all

---

8. In many ways, "federal theology" is synonymous with the "covenant theology" of this era. This chapter uses the term *federal theology* to refer to bicovenantalism within covenant theology. In a more general sense, however, federal theology used the "covenant concept as an architectonic principle" in order to systematize Christian truth. That is, it became a way of presenting the whole "body of divinity." Donald Macleod, "Covenant Theology," in *Dictionary of Scottish Church History and Theology*, ed. Nigel M. de S. Cameron (Downers Grove, IL: InterVarsity Press, 1993), 214.

men. . . . What is imputed to all of humanity is specifically the guilt of Adam's sin."[9] The "representation principle" resulted from discerning this "seed" of the doctrine of the covenant of works, and where this principle was applied, a federalism emerged.[10] Thus, to find the origins of federal theology, we must locate the development of the covenant of works.

Scholars remain uncertain as to the explicit origins of the covenant of works.[11] Part of the issue, as Jones has noted, is the diversity of ways Reformed theologians have described the Creator-creature relationship in the garden.[12] Peter Lillback has made a strong argument for finding a seed of the covenant of works in Calvin, even if Calvin did not build his theology using the overarching framework of the covenants, nor use the language of later theologians.[13] More explicitly, the works of Huldrych Zwingli and, especially, Heinrich Bullinger provided seeds for federal theologians. The first- and second-generation Reformers planted these seeds throughout Europe,[14] which naturally developed as Reformed theologians continued to study Scripture. Rowland Ward's judgment on development from the sixteenth to the seventeenth century is correct when he considers the move to "covenant of works" language as "from implicit to explicit, as God's relationship to humanity was further reflected upon."[15]

It is in the second half of the 1580s that *foedus operum* (Lat. "covenant of works") is first used, most likely by the English theologian Dudley Fenner (ca. 1558–1587) in his *Sacra theologia*, where he writes, "The covenant of works is the covenant where the condition of perfect obedience is annexed. . . . The covenant of the promise of grace is the covenant, (a) concerning Christ and blessings prominent in him, freely promised, and (b) where the condition is: if Christ is received [by faith]."[16] Fenner studied with

---

9. Joel R. Beeke and Mark Jones, "The Puritans on the Covenant of Works," in *A Puritan Theology: Doctrine for Life* (Grand Rapids, MI: Reformation Heritage Books, 2012), 235.

10. Geerhardus Vos, "The Doctrine of the Covenant in Reformed Theology," in *Redemptive History and Biblical Interpretation: The Shorter Writings of Geerhardus Vos*, ed. Richard B. Gaffin Jr., trans. S. Voorwinde and W. VanGemeren, rev. trans. Richard B. Gaffin Jr. (Phillipsburg, NJ: Presbyterian and Reformed, 1980), 234–67.

11. See, e.g., Mark Jones, "The 'Old' Covenant," in *Drawn into Controversie: Reformed Theological Diversity and Debates within Seventeenth-Century British Puritanism*, ed. Michael A. G. Haykin and Mark Jones, RHT 17 (Göttingen: Vandenhoeck & Ruprecht, 2011), 183–203; Robert Letham, "The *Foedus Operum*: Some Factors Accounting for Its Development," *SCJ* 14, no. 4 (1983): 457–67; D. A. Weir, *The Origins of the Federal Theology in Sixteenth-Century Reformation Thought* (Oxford: Clarendon, 1990).

12. Jones, "'Old' Covenant," 184. Jones cites Willem J. van Asselt, who lists the following terms: *foedus naturae* ("covenant of nature"), *foedus naturale* ("natural covenant"), *foedus creationis* ("covenant of creation"), *foedus legale* ("covenant of law"), *amicitia cum Deo* ("friendship with God"), and *foedus operum* ("covenant of works"). *The Federal Theology of Johannes Cocceius (1603–1669)*, SHCT 100 (Leiden: Brill, 2001), 254–57.

13. Peter A. Lillback, *The Binding of God: Calvin's Role in the Development of Covenant Theology* (Grand Rapids, MI: Baker Academic, 2001), 276–304.

14. These seeds spread in two significant ways: through works being translated and published, including into English, and through exiles during Mary's reign in England. Michael McGiffert, "Grace and Works: The Rise and Division of Covenant Divinity in Elizabethan Puritanism," *HTR* 75, no. 4 (1982): 468–75.

15. Rowland S. Ward, "Covenant Theology and the Westminster Confession," *VR* 69 (2004): 9.

16. Dudley Fenner, *Sacra theologia, sive, Veritas quae est secundum pietatem* (1585), 88. The Latin reads, *Operum foedus, est foedus ubi conditio annexa est perfecta obedientia. . . . Foedus gratuitae promissionis, est foedus (a) de Christo & eulogia in ipso extante, gratuito promissionis, (b) ubi conditio est, si recipiatur Christus.* For more on Fenner's involvement in the development of this doctrine, see Michael McGiffert, "From Moses to Adam: The Making of the Covenant of Works," *SCJ* 19, no. 2 (1988): 131–55.

Thomas Cartwright at Cambridge, who probably taught the doctrine to him. To avoid confusion, though, it should be noted that Cartwright's works postdate Fenner's because they were published posthumously. Cartwright's *A Methodicall Shorte Catechism* follows the theological outline of Fenner's *Sacra theologia* and had a role in bringing federalism into the English language.[17] Neither writer simply used "covenant of works" language, but both developed it within a federal scheme, "set[ting] off the prelapsarian covenant against the postlapsarian covenant [of grace]."[18] What is more, both men were intimately acquainted with the writings and thought of Reformers on the Continent, especially in Zurich and Geneva, and saw themselves as carrying forward themes that were finding increasing dominance in Reformed thought.[19]

The fact that Fenner was expressing something already in the theological atmosphere is apparent by how quickly the twofold covenant scheme appeared in theologians as spread out as Robert Rollock (1555–1599) of Edinburgh, William Perkins (1558–1602) of Cambridge, and Amandus Polanus (1561–1610) of Basel. With the turn into the seventeenth century, the teaching is found everywhere.[20] The first confessional document where a clear bicovenantalism is found is the Irish Articles of 1615, largely compiled by James Ussher (1581–1656) and affirmed by church leaders in Dublin.[21] The Irish Articles' importance for this present study is magnified by the fact that they were a main source of the WCF.[22]

---

17. Weir, *Origins of the Federal Theology*, 137–47.

18. Weir, *Origins of the Federal Theology*, 147. Continental theologians of this time who were also developing a second, parallel covenant to the covenant of grace were Wolfgang Musculus, Zacharias Ursinus, and Caspar Olevianus.

19. For details connecting Fenner and Cartwright to the Continent, see Andrew A. Woolsey, *Unity and Continuity in Covenantal Thought: A Study in the Reformed Tradition to the Westminster Assembly*, RHTS (Grand Rapids, MI: Reformation Heritage Books, 2012), 442–48. It is argued that Cartwright, in particular, learned the concept of the covenant of works in Heidelberg under Ursinus. Weir, *Origins of the Federal Theology*, 118–19.

20. Jones, "'Old' Covenant," 185. Ward has given a sampling of writings in which "covenant of works" language, or its equivalents, can be found: William Bucan of Lausanne; John Ball's catechism with notes first issued in 1615; George Walker's *The Manifold Wisdom of God* (written in 1616); William Ames's *Marrow of Theology* (1623); *A Body of Divinity*, which was from various authors but compiled by James Ussher in the early 1620s; Johannes Wollebius of Basel's *Compendium* (1626); John Preston's *The New Covenant* (1629). "Covenant Theology and the Westminster Confession," 8–9. As explored in Bruce P. Baugus, "Covenant Theology in the Dutch Reformed Tradition," chap. 18 in this volume, the scheme of two covenants, a covenant of works and another of grace, is found in Dutch theology from the 1620s on.

21. Article 21 of the Irish Articles states,

> Man being at the beginning created according to the image of God (which consisted especially in the wisdom of his mind and the true holiness of his free will), had the covenant of the law ingrafted in his heart, whereby God did promise unto him everlasting life upon condition that he performed entire and perfect obedience unto his commandments, according to that measure of strength wherewith he was endued in his creation, and threatened unto him if he did not perform the same.

Quoted in Jaroslav Pelikan and Valerie Hotchkiss, eds., *Creeds and Confessions of Faith in the Christian Tradition*, 4 vols. (New Haven, CT: Yale University Press, 2003), 2:615.

22. Woolsey, *Unity and Continuity*, 38–44. For a discussion of the influence of James Ussher and the Irish Articles on the Westminster Assembly, see Robert Letham, *The Westminster Assembly: Reading Its Theology in Historical Context* (Phillipsburg, NJ: P&R, 2009), 63–69. B. B. Warfield comments on the scope of influence:

> From [the Irish Articles the divines] derived the general arrangement of their Confession, the consecution of topics through at least its first half, and a large part of the detailed treatment of such capital Articles as those on the Holy Scripture, God's Eternal Decree, Christ the Mediator, the Covenant of Grace, and

The Question of Continuity

The portrayal thus far of federal theology has been one of natural doctrinal *development* yet in significant *continuity* with the early theology of the Reformation. This has not been the view of many twentieth-century scholars, who have attempted to make the case that the federalism of the Early and High Orthodox eras of Reformed theology is a departure from what came before, especially from Calvin. In this section we address two narratives of discontinuity: the first attempts to drive a wedge between seventeenth-century covenantal thought and Calvin; the second creates a division within sixteenth-century covenantal thought itself, with federalism as representative of merely one tradition.

Historical-theological scholarship in the twentieth century is famous for its "fall narratives," which isolate in the history of Christianity an era of supposed theological or ethical purity followed by one of corruption. Early in the century, you had the strong influence of Adolf von Harnack's accusations against the church fathers of putting a Hellenistic husk around the pure kernel of the simple gospel.[23] Later in the century, the Reformation era was given the same treatment, where the purity of Reformed thought as expressed by Calvin (the kernel) was corrupted by the Protestant scholastics of the seventeenth century (the husk). One author holding this view expressed it personally: "It was Calvin who rescued me from the Calvinists."[24]

A figure as consequential as Karl Barth provided the framework through which these critiques are made.[25] By placing a law covenant prior to the fall, Barth feared that federalism jeopardized the priority of God's grace in all his dealings with humanity. Opposed to a differentiation in God's economy with his creation as a result of the fall, Barth taught God's covenant of grace as internal to his creation.[26] Holmes Rolston III picked up this theme and judged that federalism, with its covenant of works, leads to legalism, reintroducing the specter of merit into the pure grace of Calvin's teaching.[27] Perhaps most dogged in this approach has been J. B. Torrance, who accused the bicovenantalism of federal theology with shaping divine-human relations in terms of a conditional contract (with responsibility ultimately resting with humanity); distorting one's

---

the Lord's Supper. These chapters might almost be spoken of as only greatly enriched revisions of the corresponding sections of the Irish Articles.

The Westminster Assembly and Its Work (Grand Rapids, MI: Baker, 1991), 59.

23. Adolf von Harnack, *The History of Dogma*, trans. Neil Buchanan (London: Williams and Norgate, 1894). A more recent variation on this thesis is the fascination with the "purity" of the supposed diversity of early Christianity before the corrupting orthodoxy of the fourth-century councils.

24. Holmes Rolston III, *John Calvin versus the Westminster Confession* (Richmond, VA: John Knox, 1972), 6.

25. For more on Barth and his legacy of antifederalism, see Mark I. McDowell, "Covenant Theology in Barth and the Torrances," chap. 19 in this volume.

26. Barth, *Church Dogmatics*, 3.1, *The Doctrine of Creation*, ed. G. W. Bromiley and T. F. Torrance (Edinburgh: T&T Clark, 1958), 97. For Barth's concern that covenant theology distorts Calvin, see also Barth, *Church Dogmatics*, 4.2, *The Doctrine of Reconciliation*, 54–66.

27. Rolston, *John Calvin versus the Westminster Confession*; Rolston, "Responsible Man in Reformed Theology: Calvin versus the Westminster Confession," *SJT* 23, no. 2 (1970): 129–56.

view of God (from a merciful to a justice-obsessed deity); prioritizing nature over grace (thus subordinating grace to law); skewing human nature (in favor of a legal rather than a filial relation with God); and subverting the status of Scripture (turning it from a revelation of grace into a code of duty).[28]

Space precludes a full engagement with these proposals. Needless to say, ever since R. T. Kendall's trenchant apologia for "Calvin against the Calvinists,"[29] the wedge between Calvin and his successors has been dutifully removed through careful scholarship.[30] Scholars who have pushed this agenda have been rightfully excoriated for their lack of historical methodology.[31] In the process, it has been revealed that the likes of Rolston and Torrance "have typically been interested in proving dogmatic claims rather than trying to understand the doctrine of the covenants [in the WCF] in its own right."[32] In the exposition of the WCF below, I seek to push back against the mischaracterization that bicovenantalism prioritizes law over grace in the garden. Here it is enough to question these theologians' own presuppositions. As David McWilliams has noted, they have not adequately grappled with the unique economy of the garden because of an *a priori* denial of the historicity of Adam. Consequently, they possess a shallow appreciation for the radically new situation brought about by human sin:

> A rejection of the historicity of Adam must inevitably result in the rejection of federalism. Torrance, Rolston, and other existentialist theologians homogenize the prefall and postfall situations, collapsing them into a sort of *Ever Present*. The "before" and "after" of creation and fall are transmuted into a timeless "above" and "below" of creation and the fall.[33]

McWilliams goes on to note that once sin has been reconceptualized, altering the nature of redemption follows. In contrast, federal theology seeks to uphold the structure of redemptive history and to account for the reality of demerit that sin has brought into the God-human relation.

The second view of federal theology that majors on discontinuities puts the wedge not between Calvin and the orthodox of the seventeenth century but within the early

---

28. J. B. Torrance, "The Concept of Federal Theology—Was Calvin a Federal Theologian?," in *Calvinus Sacrae Scripturae Professor*, ed. Wilhelm H. Neuser (Grand Rapids, MI: Eerdmans, 1994), 15–40. See also Torrance, "Covenant or Contract? A Study of the Theological Background of Worship in Seventeenth Century Scotland," *SJT* 23, no. 1 (1970): 51–76; Torrance, "The Covenant Concept in Scottish Theology and Politics and Its Legacy," *SJT* 34, no. 3 (1981): 225–43. For a trenchant and probing analysis of both Rolston's and Torrance's approach to the question of a prelapsarian covenant, see David Gibson, "Prelapsarian Federalism and the Shape of Reformed Theology: A Response to James B. Torrance and Holmes Rolston III" (master's thesis, King's College London, 2004).

29. R. T. Kendall, *Calvin and English Calvinism to 1649*, SCHT (Oxford: Oxford University Press, 1979).

30. Preeminent among scholars seeking to dismantle this false divide has been Richard Muller. See especially his *After Calvin*, chaps. 4–5.

31. Weir, *Origins of the Federal Theology*, 28.

32. J. V. Fesko, *The Theology of the Westminster Standards: Historical Context and Theological Insights* (Wheaton, IL: Crossway, 2014), 125.

33. David B. McWilliams, "The Covenant Theology of the *Westminster Confession of Faith* and Recent Criticism," *WTJ* 53, no. 1 (1991): 113.

Reformers themselves, thus creating "two traditions" of covenant theology within the Reformation. Scholars like Leonard Trinterud, Jens Møller, Richard Greaves, Kenneth Hagen, and J. Wayne Baker[34] pit a Calvin/Genevan tradition of covenant theology against a Zurich/Rhineland one.[35] According to this scheme, the former holds the covenant as unilateral, based on God's unconditional promise, with the burden of fulfillment resting with God and fulfilled in Christ. The latter sees the covenant as bilateral, with the burden of fulfillment resting with the human partner, who is rewarded for obedience.[36] Interestingly, this dichotomous presentation has served writers who would like to take it in very different directions. On the one hand, there are those who paint the German-speaking theologians as developing a richly relational theology of the covenant and the Genevans as coldly fastidious about double predestination; on the other hand, there are those who hold up Calvin as the champion of grace and judge incipient federalism (and the Puritans who adopted it) as proponents of conditioned obedience.[37] Whatever is the case, in this scheme a legacy remains that suggests a synergistic account of human salvation in contrast to a predestinarian one—a strange claim to make regarding Reformed thought![38]

Like the "Calvin versus Calvinists" position, the "two traditions" approach to covenant theology in the sixteenth and seventeenth centuries has been met with a forceful scholarly backlash. Lyle Bierma puts it quite devastatingly: "For all its popularity . . . this 'two traditions' thesis has never been very well documented, and [does] not hold up under a closer scrutiny of the primary texts."[39] Examination of those texts reveals differences in emphasis, for sure. Bullinger wrote extensively on the covenant within doctrinal treatises, whereas Calvin's covenantal thought comes out more in his com-

---

34. Leonard J. Trinterud, "The Origins of Puritanism," *CH* 20, no. 1 (1951): 37–57; Jens Møller, "The Beginnings of Puritan Covenant Theology," *JEH* 14, no. 1 (1963): 46–67; Richard L. Greaves, "The Origins and Development of English Covenant Thought," *Historian* 31, no. 1 (1968): 21–35; Kenneth Hagen, "From Testament to Covenant in Early Sixteenth Century," *SCJ* 3, no. 1 (1972): 1–24; J. Wayne Baker, *Heinrich Bullinger and the Covenant: The Other Reformed Tradition* (Athens: Ohio University Press, 1980). These English scholars are dependent on a narrative that goes back to the dominant voice of Heinrich Heppe and his *Dogmatik des Deutschen Protestantismus im sechzehnten Jahrhundert*, 3 vols. (Gotha: Perthes, 1857).

35. In this scheme, Calvin and Theodore Beza represent those concerned with unilateral grace and absolute predestination, and Zwingli and Bullinger, those concerned with bilateral agreement and the responsibilities of the human partner in the covenant.

36. Lyle D. Bierma, "Federal Theology in the Sixteenth Century: Two Traditions?," *WTJ* 45, no. 2 (1983): 305.

37. Another twist on this narrative is Perry Miller's scholarship. See his *The New England Mind: The Seventeenth Century* (Boston: Beacon, 1939). Miller sought to present the Puritans as a positive alternative to Calvinism. In his opinion, the Puritans' development of federal theology created room for human responsibility by softening the hard predestinarianism of Calvinism. In a helpful précis of Miller's work, Ligon Duncan concludes, "Miller's work has exerted a tremendous influence on subsequent writing on the idea of covenant in the Reformed tradition." "Recent Objections to Covenant Theology: A Description, Evaluation, and Response," in *The Westminster Confession into the 21st Century*, ed. Ligon Duncan (Fearn, Ross-shire, Scotland: Mentor, 2009), 3:468. Duncan references George M. Marsden's classic analysis of Miller's work on the Puritans, "Perry Miller's Rehabilitation of the Puritans: A Critique," *CH* 39, no. 1 (1970): 91–105.

38. Vos notes, "If it were true, the covenant concept would have to be regarded with suspicion as a strange intrusion into Reformed territory." "Doctrine of the Covenant," 235.

39. Bierma, "Federal Theology," 309. See also Bierma, "The Role of Covenant Theology in Early Reformed Orthodoxy," *SCJ* 21, no. 3 (1990): 453–62.

mentaries and sermons (and not his *Institutes*). The differences are more of presentation and precision than of content. The same goes for subsequent Reformed writers. Richard Muller states it well:

> Although there are some minor differences in formulation, both Calvin and Bullinger proposed a thoroughly gracious covenant given unilaterally by God as the basis of salvation and both used bilateral language in describing human responsibility in covenant with God. The Reformed doctrine of covenant is, therefore, neither opposed to nor in tension with the Reformed doctrine of predestination, which also declares grace unilaterally bestowed by God and assumes human responsibility and obedience under and enabled by grace.[40]

The attempt, then, to create divergent trajectories in covenantal thought—one following unilateral grace, the other bilateral cooperation—falls apart on hard evidence. Indeed, as seen in the Westminster Confession of Faith, consensus covenantal thought in the seventeenth century did not choose one trajectory over another but held together a strong monergistic soteriology with a covenantal theology that has both unilateral and bilateral dimensions.[41]

The Integrity of Federal Theology

As we move toward an exposition of the Westminster Confession of Faith that highlights how the various elements of federal theology fit together, a remaining question is whether federalism itself is the result of a "foreign" intrusion into Christian theology. That is, has the federal structure of covenant theology been unduly shaped by a methodology born out of the philosophical movements of its day, namely, Peter Ramus's logic? According to Robert Letham, "The great feature of Ramist methodology was that by usual dichotomous subdivision the entire field of knowledge could be mapped out for virtually instant comprehension."[42] Some have charged that the bifurcation at the center of this methodology influenced bicovenantalism with its covenant of works on one side and covenant of grace on the other.[43] In other words, rather than the covenant-of-works doctrine developing naturally within covenant theology from further reflection on Scripture, it was grafted in with roots outside divine revelation. Our investigation thus far has supported federalism's substantial continuity with the theology of the Reformation, but

---

40. Muller, *After Calvin*, 12.

41. John von Rohr expresses it well: "For the mainstream of Puritanism, therefore, it would appear that basically the bilateral and unilateral were conjoined, human responsibility and divine sovereignty were unitedly maintained, and the covenant of grace was seen as both conditional and absolute." *The Covenant of Grace in Puritan Thought* (Atlanta: Scholars Press, 1986), 33.

42. Letham, *"Foedus Operum,"* 465. More simply, Ramus engaged in "the art of classification by dichotomy." John Coffey, *Politics, Religion and the British Revolutions: The Mind of Samuel Rutherford*, CSEMBH (Cambridge: Cambridge University Press, 1997), 68.

43. Prominent in this assertion is Jürgen Moltmann, "Zur Bedeutung des Petrus Ramus für Philosophie und Theologie im Calvinismus," *ZKG* 68 (1957): 295–318.

the question remains whether covenant theology has, on the whole, been malformed as a result of the influence of Ramism.

Letham has demonstrated that as federal theology was being shaped in the sixteenth century, it developed in places significantly influenced by Ramism: Heidelberg, Oxford, Cambridge, Glasgow, Aberdeen, and Saint Andrews. This correlation is hardly questionable. What is questionable is whether a historical connection between Ramism and bicovenantalism means that the covenant of works and federalism were *caused* by Ramism. Here I agree with the judgment of David McWilliams:

> [A] pre- and postlapsarian distinction is not Ramist. It is dualistic, but rather than being Ramist dualism it is a given resident in the structure of biblical revelation. Now, Letham does not claim that federalism could not have developed apart from Ramism. If what he means is that the dualism of Ramism merely helped to facilitate the development of sixteenth-century covenant theology, then we are prepared to agree. Nonetheless, it cannot be assumed . . . that Ramism was indispensable to covenant theology so that federalism would not have developed apart from it.[44]

In the end, it is safest to conclude that Ramism's greatest effect on covenant theology was methodological and structural. That is, its bifurcations helped refine the structure and cohesiveness of federal theology in the seventeenth century, but bicovenantal thought was not beholden to it.[45] This picture is more nuanced, scriptural, and theological. As Carl Trueman notes, the method of Reformed orthodoxy in accounting for God's relations with humanity

> indicates that [covenant] is no naïve intrusion of commercial categories into the interpretation of Scripture, but conceptual vocabulary developed in careful relation both to exegesis, linguistics, conceptual reflection, and trinitarianism. At one level, covenant is a typical 17th-century way of expressing relationships of various kinds between two or more parties: it is thus useful in explaining the relationship between God and humanity in the garden of Eden, both as it helps explain the federal headship of Adam and the nature of human merit in relation to an infinite God who, in himself, is no one's debtor.[46]

Thus the integrity of federal theology, as it matures into the orthodox periods of the seventeenth century, holds in an enduring substance; it holds even in the midst of meth-

---

44. McWilliams, "Covenant Theology," 118. For a similar judgment, see Christoph Strohm, "Methodology in Discussion of 'Calvin and Calvinism,'" in *Calvinus Praeceptor Ecclesiae: Papers of the International Congress on Calvin Research, Princeton, August 20–24, 2002*, ed. Herman J. Selderhuis, THR 388 (Genève: Librairie Droz, 2004), 97–99.

45. Smedley notes the incongruity of suggesting that key bicovenantal theologians were overly influenced by Ramism in their methodology when, in the case of Ursinus, he was vehemently opposed to Ramist thought—even writing two works against it! "Covenant Theology of Zacharias Ursinus," 55–56.

46. Carl R. Trueman, *John Owen: Reformed Catholic, Renaissance Man* (2007; repr., New York: Routledge, 2016), 98–99.

odological tools that facilitated its presentation.[47] Furthermore, as covenant theologians continued to study texts like Romans 5 and 1 Corinthians 15, they developed integral connections with entailments for soteriology and Christology. The "representation principle" mentioned by Vos above was drawn out as theological reasoning engaged, for example, Romans 5:19 (cited in article 22 of the Irish Articles) and connected imputation with the Thirty-Nine Articles' (1563) affirmation of a corruption naturally engendered in Adam's offspring. Article 9 of the draft revision of the Thirty-Nine Articles by the Westminster Assembly (1643) says that Adam's corruption is "together with his first sin imputed." As Ward notes,

> Thus a more Scriptural presentation of the relationship of Adam and Christ (Romans 5) is possible in terms of the principle of representation or federal headship—and this of course counters the Arminian view of the extent of the atonement, and also assures the final salvation of those for whom Christ died.[48]

As we move now to an examination of the WCF, we see the importance of these Christological and soteriological threads within the rich tapestry of the confession's dual account of the covenant centering on Christ the mediator.

The Westminster Standards

The Westminster Confession of Faith is a confessional document summarizing the Christian faith in twelve thousand words. It stands on the far end of the long Reformation, or, as it is sometimes referred to, the "post-Reformation" era. Because of its place on the Reformational timeline, the more than 120 eminent theologians involved, and, most important, the quality of the enduring text as a whole, the WCF and its catechisms serve as representative examples of the high Protestant covenant theology of this era. Covenant theology is the warp and woof of the theology of the WCF, and its "architectonic principle" was bequeathed to it by federal theology.[49]

---

47. Because federal theology is not considered "innovative" or beholden to the movements of its day, we have left unexplored here the unquestionable appropriation of the traditional language and methods of medieval scholasticism within Reformed orthodoxy. In the end, our judgment of its effect would be more or less the same as that of Ramism's. Trueman is correct:

> Scholasticism is a specific pedagogical method and should not, therefore, be confused with metaphysical content or philosophical commitments, as the practice of disputation, and the technical vocabulary associated with it, did not represent a single, unified system of thought, nor even a consensus position on the scope and competence of logic and human reason. Rather, they represented simply the pedagogical procedures of higher learning during a particular period of time, broadly speaking from the twelfth century to the end of the seventeenth.

John Owen, 14. Richard A. Muller also highlights the limited use of scholasticism within this era yet notes that, though it was prevalent in academic settings, it had little impact on catechesis, and its methods were not used in ecclesial settings. *Calvin and the Reformed Tradition: On the Work of Christ and the Order of Salvation* (Grand Rapids, MI: Baker Academic, 2012), 33.

48. Ward, "Covenant Theology and the Westminster Confession," 11.

49. Warfield, *Westminster Assembly and Its Work*, 56.

Our study thus far has served the purpose of providing the origins and contours of this principle in order to illuminate the bicovenantalism at the heart of the WCF. As enlightening as this backdrop can be, this chapter has also sought to make the case that the reality of theological development and added nuance should not overshadow the more general judgment that the "fundamental source of the Westminster doctrines must be regarded as Reformed theology in general."[50] Accordingly, the confession and catechisms gleaned from "the best biblical exegesis of the Reformers" but also, because the Reformers themselves were indebted to what came before, harvested "the most useful doctrinal structures of the medieval theologians, and the most enduring insights of the church fathers."[51] The Westminster divines had no interest in theological innovation or ecclesiastical provinciality. They saw themselves squarely in the stream of the Reformation, which they saw squarely in the stream of the historic Christian faith.

In this section we (1) briefly look at the immediate background behind the WCF before breaking down the covenant theology in the confession and catechisms, addressing (2) the nature of the covenant of works and (3) the nature of the covenant of grace. The latter introduces questions such as unilateral versus bilateral dimensions of the covenant, covenantal conditions and grace, and the status of the Mosaic covenant as an administration of the covenant of grace. We close this section (4) by examining why the covenant of redemption is not explicitly included in the WCF yet is a doctrine developed within this period and articulated by many of its finest theologians.

Background

The Reformation of the English church and the state of English politics were closely intertwined in the sixteenth and seventeenth centuries. King Henry VIII (r. 1509–1547) broke the church from Rome but did not allow Reformers in the church to fully align it with the reforms in worship and doctrine that were taking place on the Continent. For those wishing for a more thorough reformation of the church, Henry VIII's son, the evangelical and Reformed boy-king Edward VI, provided great hope, but his reign lasted only from 1547 to 1553. After the tumultuous reign of Queen Mary I (r. 1553–1558) and her attempt to return England to Roman Catholicism, the church eventually settled into an enforced moderation under Queen Elizabeth I (r. 1558–1603) and King James I (r. 1603–1625). One unintended consequence of the upheaval of this period was the number of exiled English Puritans whose time on the Continent placed them under the influence of Reformed churches in Switzerland, Germany, and Holland. As a result, their return to England over the course of the seventeenth century brought with it an instinct for thoroughgoing

---

50. Woolsey, *Unity and Continuity*, 38.

51. Chad Van Dixhoorn, *Confessing the Faith: A Reader's Guide to the Westminster Confession of Faith* (Carlisle, PA: Banner of Truth, 2014), xix.

reformation and a depth of theological reflection that heavily influenced their covenantal thought.[52]

The accession of King Charles I (r. 1625–1649) brought with it an abandonment
of the religious *via media* established and maintained by Elizabeth I and James I. This
termination of religious moderation, along with Charles I's unyielding assertion of
the divine right of kings, precipitated England's descent into a bloody civil war. The
political instability that ensued prompted the English Parliament, under the influence
of English Puritans and Scottish Covenanters, to summon an assembly to meet at
Westminster Abbey (from whence the Standards derive their name). In the spirit of the
more thoroughgoing reforms found in churches on the Continent and in Scotland, the
Westminster Assembly was charged to propose to Parliament "any corrections which
might need to be made to the existing structures, worship, and teaching of the church."[53]
The Westminster Confession of Faith was written between 1644 and 1647, and the
Larger and Shorter Catechisms were finished in 1647. The assembly rewrote texts for the
churches of England and Wales, Scotland, and Ireland.[54] And though power was given
back to the monarchy in 1660, and with it the reestablishment of Anglicanism and the
Book of Common Prayer, the Standards have continued to bind the faith of millions of
Reformed Christians all the way up to today.

This brief overview of the historical setting of the Standards suggests that they, like
all creeds and confessions, were not created in a vacuum. There were theological pressures that helped shape, in particular, its covenant theology. While the nuances of the
seventeenth-century debates captured by the WCF are beyond the scope of this chapter,
it is worth noting that its covenant theology was formulated in the face of significant
theological crosswinds that were raging in the middle of the century—winds that swept
from the Continent to the British Isles and back again.

The polemical crosswinds included continued pushback from Roman Catholics,
Arminians, and Socinians.[55] These winds swirl in the background of the WCF's pointed

---

52. The aforementioned Thomas Cartwright is an example of this cross-fertilization. Under Elizabeth he
was deprived of his chair at Cambridge University because he advocated for further reformation along biblical
lines. He eventually proceeded to Geneva, Heidelberg, Basel, and the Netherlands before returning to England
in 1585–1586. His movements among the Reformed on the Continent and the impression they left on him
are important for the cause of reformation in England, not least in the area of covenant theology. According to
Woolsey, Cartwright's "work remained strong enough for him to serve as a link between Elizabethan Puritanism
and the Westminster theologians." It is even considered that his two catechetical works served as models for the
WSC and WLC. *Unity and Continuity*, 16–17. Other consequential theologians for the WCF were Robert Rollock
(1555–1599), John Preston (1587–1628), William Perkins (1558–1602), William Ames (1576–1633), John Ball
(1585–1640), Edward Fisher (fl. 1627–1655), and David Dickson (1583–1663).

53. Van Dixhoorn, *Confessing the Faith*, xvii. For detailed background on the summoning of the assembly, see
Chad Van Dixhoorn, ed., *The Minutes and Papers of the Westminster Assembly 1643–1652*, vol. 1, *Introduction*
(Oxford: Oxford University Press, 2012), 1–19.

54. In addition to the confession and catechisms, the texts that the assembly drafted included directions
for church government, a guide for public worship, statements on doctrine, and correspondence with foreign
churches.

55. Trueman, *John Owen*, 17–33; see also Jeffrey K. Jue, "The Active Obedience of Christ and the Theology
of the Westminster Standards: A Historical Investigation," in *Justified in Christ: God's Plan for Us in Justification*,
ed. K. Scott Oliphint (Fearn, Ross-shire, Scotland: Mentor, 2007), 99–130.

discussions of the extent of sin, the covenant, and the person and work of Christ the mediator. What is more, as we see in the latter part of this section, the WCF is a consensus document, meaning that there were disagreements among the divines themselves. Those disagreements show up in what is left out of the Standards and what is alluded to but not explicitly stated.[56]

Discussions of the covenant in the Standards naturally begins with chapter 7 of the WCF (along with WLC 30–36 and WSC 20). Our examination focuses on this chapter but also ventures into other relevant sections, including the chapters on Christ the mediator (WCF 8) and on the law of God (WCF 19). What is clear from the outset is that the Westminster divines understood all God's ways with humanity as covenantal. This side of the fall, God's covenantal dealings are mediated through Christ, and so the covenant theology of the WCF has a Christological and soteriological focus—emphasized clearly enough through the WCF's placement of chapter 8 immediately after chapter 7. But to understand the postfall covenantal situation, the WCF deals with the covenantal situation in the garden before the stain of sin ever entered the world and altered the economy of God's ways with us.

Covenant of Works

A common complaint against bicovenantalism, as we have seen, is the assertion of a prefall covenant containing a works principle, often called simply the "covenant of works" (WCF 7.2) or, as in WSC 12 and WLC 20, the "covenant of life." The strongest complaints come from those who take issue with the implications of the word "works" and those who do not see explicit biblical footing for this covenant.[57] In its own way, the WCF addresses both of these complaints through foundational teachings that have relevance reaching beyond just this covenant. We address these complaints in turn before turning to a more positive exposition of the first covenant.

In Genesis 1–3 are two radically shaping events for God's economy of relations with humanity. Before Scripture ever introduces the fall in Genesis 3, the Creator-creature distinction is made manifest in the creation account. The WCF reflects this reality through these lines:

> The distance between God and the creature is so great, that although reasonable
> creatures do owe obedience unto Him as their Creator, yet they could never have

---

56. For a helpful discussion of how the WCF is inclusive of a "principled diversity of views," which is often seen in what the confession does *not* say on a particular issue, see Fesko, *Theology of the Westminster Standards*, 167. Similarly, Letham notes that in some cases the assembly purposefully used ambiguous terminology in the confession in light of diverse views held by assembly members. *Westminster Assembly*, 261–62.

57. Influential in this complaint has been John Murray, who saw the development of the covenant of works as a departure from Calvin and the earliest Reformers. He demurred to using either "covenant" or "works" to describe Adam's prelapsarian relationship with God in the garden. Murray preferred the term "Adamic Administration," which in his description ended up serving a similar theological function as the covenant of works. In his evaluation of the confession and catechisms of the Westminster Assembly, he preferred the catechisms' use of "covenant of life" as "much more in according with the grace which conditions the administration than is the term 'covenant of works.'" "Covenant Theology," in *Collected Writings of John Murray* (Carlisle, PA: Banner of Truth, 1982), 4:222.

any fruition of Him as their blessedness and reward, but by some voluntary condescension on God's part, which He has been pleased to express by way of a covenant.
(WCF 7.1)

The distinction between Creator and creature shapes God's ways with humanity from
the start, such that we always stand in need of God's initiation—in need of grace.[58] Thus,
from the very beginning, "some voluntary condescension on God's part" is needed for
human beings to know, to love, and to glorify their Lord.[59] To judge the WCF as first and
foremost concerned with cold "legal relations" is to misread the gracious and personal
context in which God establishes all his relations with mankind. Indeed, prior to the word
"works" ever being mentioned in the WCF, the divines set the context for its theological
understanding. What is more, if we go back to chapter 4, rather than Adam and Eve's
legal relationship with God being one mediated through an external and impersonal
code, the law was "written on their hearts" (WCF 4.2) by virtue of being created in his
image. The result: Adam is God's "son" (Luke 3:38), and he and Eve were "happy in their
communion with God" (WCF 4.2). This all serves as backdrop to WCF 7.2, which says,
"The first covenant made with man was a covenant of works, wherein life was promised
to Adam, and in him to his posterity, upon condition of perfect and personal obedience."
With the whole picture taken together, McWilliams is surely correct when he considers
the first covenant as "simultaneously gracious and legal, personal and federal."[60]

This rich theological context constrains our interpretation of the "works" language
of the covenant in the WCF. The importance of broader theological context informing

---

58. The notion of "grace" prior to the entry of sin into the world has troubled some contemporary Reformed
theologians. But this did not seem to be an issue for seventeenth-century Reformed theologians, who, as Rowland
Ward has noted, understood grace in a more general sense than simply redemptive favor. *God and Adam: Reformed
Theology and the Creation Covenant* (Wantirna, Australia: New Melbourne, 2003), 116. Similarly, Letham argues,
in contrast to the position of Meredith Kline, that the "Westminster documents clearly affirm that grace was
present before the fall." *Westminster Assembly*, 232. Beeke and Jones put it succinctly: "Primarily, grace refers to
God's free favor to His creatures and the blessings He gives to them. In the covenant of works, Adam received
the grace of benevolence; in the covenant of grace, he received the grace of mercy. The covenant of works was
gracious; the covenant of grace is doubly gracious." *Puritan Theology*, 230. One grace clearly not evident in the
garden was the grace of perseverance.

59. This wording is not to suggest that Adam entered into covenant with God only *after* he was created. This
was the position of some seventeenth-century divines. But WLC 93 seems to tie the promise of life in the covenant
of works to the law written on the heart, which would connect the covenant to creational realities. This leads Ward
to maintain that, according to the Standards, God and Adam were already "in covenant in some sense from the
moment of creation, and that God's goodness and favour was richly evidenced from the beginning." "Covenant
Theology and the Westminster Confession," 14. This understanding is confirmed below where we note the language of WCF 4.2. Still, as Cornelis Venema observes, "The prefall covenant must not be identified with creation
simpliciter, since WSC 12 and WLC 20 do place the 'covenant of life,' as a work of God's providence, subsequent
to creation." *Christ and Covenant Theology: Essays on Election, Republication, and the Covenants* (Phillipsburg, NJ:
P&R, 2017), 28n37. For the seventeenth-century background on the debate over whether Adam was created *in*
or *for* a covenant, see Beeke and Jones, *Puritan Theology*, 223–24; and for a more recent argument demonstrating
Adam as being originally *in* covenant through creation, see Mark Vander Hart, "Creation and Covenant, Part
One: A Survey of the Dominion Mandate in the Noahic and Abrahamic Covenants," *MJT* 6, no. 1 (1990): 3–18.

60. McWilliams, "Covenant Theology," 110. The English Puritan Francis Roberts represented many Westminster divines when he wrote, "The Covenant of Works even in innocency was merely Gratuitous." *The Mysterie and
Marrow of the Bible: viz. God's Covenants with Man* (London, 1657), 1099. The assembly saw no incompatibility
between grace and law. See Letham, *Westminster Assembly*, 225–26.

use and interpretation of words also comes into play in answering the complaint that the covenant of works is biblically unfounded. There have been, of course, a number of attempts to explicitly root the covenant of works in a specific biblical text, such as Hosea 6:7 or the covenantal elements found in Genesis 2 (parties, promise, stipulation, penalty).[61] The problem has been that no singular text indisputably uses "covenant" to describe God's relationship with Adam before the fall. This did not concern the Westminster divines, however, who, along with the Reformed orthodox theologians of the day, understood that doctrine "is either expressly set down in Scripture, or by good and necessary consequence may be deduced from Scripture" (WCF 1.6). The divine Anthony Burgess expressed the same notion similarly: "[The covenant of works] must only be gathered by deductions and consequence."[62] Accordingly, this doctrine was not based on any one scriptural text "but drawn as a conclusion from the examination and comparison of a series of biblical *loci* or *sedes doctrinae*. The concept of the covenant of works belongs . . . to a secondary or derivative albeit still fundamental category of doctrine."[63] As suggested above, the most significant biblical inference in support of the development of the covenant of works is the work of Christ as the second Adam, which is found especially in the writings of the apostle Paul (Rom. 5; 1 Cor. 15).[64]

Adam as representative head of the human race is the starting point for a positive articulation of the covenant of works. The promise at the heart of this covenant was "life"—life for Adam and all humanity joined to him—if Adam met the condition of the covenant through "personal, perfect, and perpetual obedience" (WLC 20).[65] This promise is the focus of the "covenant of life" language of WSC 12 and WLC 20.

61. In addition to the elements of a covenant being found in Gen. 2, one of the more interesting arguments for a case of explicit covenantal language is that God's *covenantal name* is used in this chapter.

62. Anthony Burgess, *Vindiciae Legis: or, A Vindication of the Morall Law and the Covenants, From the Errours of Papists, Arminians, Socinians, and More Especially, Antinomians* (London, 1646), 120.

63. Muller, *After Calvin*, 175. Trueman puts it simply: "Underlying the seventeenth-century articulation of the concept [of the covenant of works] is a world of linguistic and theological reflection." *John Owen*, 71. For more on the exegetical sophistication of seventeenth-century theologians who were behind the covenant of works, see Richard A. Muller, "'Either Expressly Set Down . . . or by Good and Necessary Consequence': Exegesis and Formulation in the Annotations and the Confession," in Richard A. Muller and Rowland S. Ward, eds., *Scripture and Worship: Biblical Interpretation and the Directory of Public Worship* (Phillipsburg, NJ: P&R, 2007): 59–82.

64. For more on the exegetical and biblical-theological work of locating a "covenant" in the prefall situation despite the absence of the language of "covenant" in Gen. 1–2, see Richard P. Belcher Jr., "The Covenant of Works in the Old Testament"; Guy Prentiss Waters, "The Covenant of Works in the New Testament"; John D. Currid, "Adam and the Beginning of the Covenant of Grace"; and Guy Prentiss Waters, "Covenant in Paul," chaps. 2, 3, 4, and 11, respectively, in this volume.

65. See also WCF 19.1: "God gave to Adam a law, as a covenant of works, by which He bound him and all his posterity, to personal, entire, exact, and perpetual obedience, promised life upon the fulfilling, and threatened death upon the breach of it, and endued him with power and ability to keep it." This is not to say that Adam was not already beginning to experience the blessings of "life." While there was a probationary period within the garden where the mutability of Adam's commitment to the covenant was real, equally real was Adam and Eve's covenantal communion with God before the disastrous rupture brought on by their fall. Seventeenth-century theologians debated what that "life" would be like if Adam's probationary period ended with his obedience. Some thought Adam would be carried away to heaven. Others thought God's promise only entailed continued life in the garden of Eden upon completion of his probationary period. Many, such as John Ball, remained agnostic: "To say that God would have translated [Adam] to the state of glory in Heaven, is more than any just ground will warrant." *A Treatise of the Covenant of Grace: Wherein the graduall breakings out of Gospel-grace from Adam to Christ are clearly discovered* (London, 1645), 10.

WCF 7.2's "works" language, rather, draws attention to the means by which Adam could attain the promise. Conversely, failure to obtain the promise through disobedience to the command not to eat from the tree of the knowledge of good and evil results in the penalty of death. Obedience leads to life; disobedience leads to death.[66] The confession and catechisms, then, speak in complementary ways about the prefall covenant made with Adam. When we turn to the covenant of grace, we will see the relevance of this complementary language for the work of Christ as mediator.

Because this covenant was made prior to man's fall into disfavor with God, however, Adam had no need for a mediator in this covenant. He received God's favor in the covenant, bore God's image, and in obedience maintained blessed fellowship with his loving God. A sacramental sign of this obedience was divinely given by means of a tree. That is, obedience would be enjoying every tree in the garden save one: "This prohibition was a kind of seal to God's natural covenant with Adam, whereby Adam would be able to assess his performance and strengthen his obedience and that of his posterity in covenant."[67] It bears repeating, given the implications of the first covenant for the second, that not only does Adam's communion with God hang in the balance; as representative of the human race, the penalty for disobedience will be experienced not only by him but by all those who come after him.

A significant question that follows from Adam's federal obedience is whether it should be considered *meritorious*. This is where the gracious context of the first covenant shapes understanding of the "works" demanded within it: WCF 7.1 makes clear that God owes man nothing and promises a reward disproportionate both to his status as a creature and his work to be performed. Just as in redemption, in creation the gifts God gives—including the gift of communion with the loving Father—are wholly undeserved and flow from his goodness and kindness, not from "strict justice," where Adam merits life through work accomplished. Be that as it may, how does the confession understand Adam's obedience and its function within God's economy of relations before the fall? Cornelis Venema gives a careful and balanced answer to this question:

> The fact is that God, by entering into covenant with man, has bound himself by the promises as well as the demands of that covenant. This means that Adam's obedience to the stipulated obedience, though it were an outworking and development within the covenant communion in which he was placed by God's prevenient favor, would nonetheless "merit" or "deserve" the reward of righteousness God himself

---

66. In the words of the highly influential James Ussher, the first covenant with Adam was "a conditionall covenant . . . whereby on the one side God commandeth perfection of godlinesse and righteousnesse, and promiseth that he will be our God, if we keepe all his commandments; and on the other side Man bindeth himself to perform intire and perfect obedience to God's Law by that strength wherewith God hath endued him by the nature of his first creation." *A Body of Divinitie, or the Summe and Substance of Christian Religion catechistically propounded, and explained, by way of Question and Answer: Methodically and familiarly handled* (London, 1647), 125.

67. Woolsey, *Unity and Continuity*, 51. The tree of life was also sacramental, holding forth the immortality offered if Adam would persevere in the conditions of the first covenant.

had promised. In the covenant itself God bound himself to grant, as in some sense a reward well-deserved, the fullness of covenant fellowship into which Adam was called. The terms of the stipulation of obedience—the explicit threat of death in the case of disobedience, the implicit promise of life in the case of obedience—warrant a qualified use of the language of "merit" or "reward."[68]

Merit thus understood is according to the favorable conditions of the covenant and not according to notions of "strict justice." In the history of Reformed theology, this has been understood as merit *ex pacto*, that is, merit according to the covenant. The economy of God's relations in the first covenant is, therefore, God sovereignly granting favor according to his promise conditioned on an obedience that gains covenantal merit.[69] As we turn now to the covenant of grace, this arrangement is significant when we consider the work of Christ our mediator, the second Adam.

Covenant of Grace

The covenant of grace is not a separate covenant per se, insofar as its aim, like the first covenant, is to establish loving communion between God and man. But it is distinct in that its unique economy deals with the new situation brought about by Adam's failure to fulfill the conditions of the first covenant. God does not abandon his creation as a result of the fall in Genesis 3. Instead, on the heels of the fall, he establishes a second covenant, the covenant of grace, and thereby introduces a new economy of relations that takes into account human demerit. The basis for this covenant is Christ fulfilling the conditions of the covenant of works, and on account of his work, he offers life, forgiveness, and salvation. If God enters into the covenant of works as Creator, he enters into the covenant of grace as Creator *and* Savior. All one must do to receive the blessings of this covenant is have faith in Jesus Christ. The covenant of grace, as articulated in the WCF, "forms the heart and soul of Reformed soteriology and declares that salvation, whether in the Old or New Testament, is by grace alone, through faith in Jesus Christ."[70]

As noted above, the WCF's discussion of covenantal relations begins with the need for God to condescend to humanity in light of the vast difference between God and man. The covenant of works was designed to overcome this Creator-creature difference. With the entry of sin into the situation, humanity does not lose its status as creatures made in God's image. Nonetheless, man, now fallen in Adam, is unable to do what is good. Outside God's initiating grace, man is "dead in sin, and wholly defiled in all parts and faculties of soul and body" (WCF 6.2). Furthermore, Adam's federal headship means that because he is "the root of all mankind, the guilt of this sin is imputed; and

68. Venema, *Christ and Covenant Theology*, 33.
69. See Richard A. Muller, *Dictionary of Latin and Greek Theological Terms Drawn Principally from Protestant Scholastic Theology* (Grand Rapids, MI: Baker, 1985), s.v. *ex pacto*, 108–9.
70. Beeke and Jones, *Puritan Theology*, 260.

the same death in sin, and corrupted nature, conveyed to all their posterity descending from them by ordinary generation" (WCF 6.3). Adam and all those sharing in his humanity are incapable of meriting any favor from God. The barrier to communion with God is not man's creatureliness but his sin: "Sinful man now stands in need of God's grace which is defined differently after the fall in terms of new needs. Sinful man stands in need of the grace of mercy and reconciliation. The grace that God now displays is peculiarly redemptive grace."[71] It is into this situation that the WCF not only speaks of the second covenant but does so with a considerable focus on Christology:

> The Lord was pleased to make a second, commonly called the covenant of grace; wherein He freely offereth unto sinners life and salvation by Jesus Christ; requiring of them faith in Him, that they may be saved, and promising to give unto all those that are ordained unto eternal life His Holy Spirit, to make them willing, and able to believe. (WCF 7.3)

WLC 36 likewise zeroes in on Christ:

> Q. Who is the Mediator of the covenant of grace?
>
> A. The only Mediator of the covenant of grace is the Lord Jesus Christ, who being the eternal Son of God, of one substance and equal with the Father, in the fullness of time became man, and so was, and continues to be, God and man, in two entire distinct natures, and one person forever.

The "representation principle" of federalism established in the covenant of works creates the matrix for the Standards' Christology. The Standards' bicovenantalism flows naturally from the two-Adam representative structure found in Romans 5 and 1 Corinthians 15, the first covenant with Adam establishing the conditions of the second covenant made with the second Adam, Jesus Christ. That is, the salvific work that Christ performs in the second covenant is understood insofar as it relates to the terms of the first covenant. Indeed, WLC 31 says, "The covenant of grace was made with Christ as the second Adam, and in him with all the elect as his seed."[72] The Adam-Christ parallel is necessary for seeing clearly the continuities between the first and second covenant, for "the graciousness of the covenant of grace is rooted in God's willingness to accept the work of Christ on our behalf."[73] But there are clear discontinuities: "Because Christ is the surety, the covenant of grace has an enduring stability and certainty of fulfillment never possible in the covenant of works."[74]

WCF 8.4 brings together the "two Adams" and, therefore, the two covenants: "This office [of mediator] the Lord Jesus did most willingly undertake; which that he might

---

71. McWilliams, "Covenant Theology," 110.
72. WCF 7 and WSC 20 do not state the parties to the covenant of grace.
73. Beeke and Jones, *Puritan Theology*, 261.
74. Beeke and Jones, *Puritan Theology*, 261.

discharge, he was made under the law, and did perfectly fulfill it." The nexus between the two covenants is the obedience of the second Adam:

> The Lord Jesus, by his perfect obedience and sacrifice of himself, which through the eternal Spirit he offered up unto God, hath satisfied the justice of his Father; and purchased not only reconciliation, but an everlasting inheritance in the kingdom of heaven, for all those whom the Father hath given unto him. (WCF 8.5)[75]

Where Adam failed both personally and representatively, Christ succeeded personally and representatively. For those in Christ to know redemption, though, the obedience and satisfaction of Christ must be imputed to them:

> Justification is an act of God's free grace unto sinners, in which he pardoneth all their sins, accepteth and accounteth their persons righteous in his sight; not for anything wrought in them, or done by them, but only for the perfect obedience and full satisfaction of Christ, by God imputed to them, and received by faith alone. (WLC 70; cf. WCF 11.1)

In this answer from the WLC, soteriology, Christology, and covenant come together: our salvation depends on *imputation* according to the terms of God's covenant. First, our sins are imputed to Christ on the cross, where they are judged in his humanity and atoned for; thus, God's justice is satisfied, and death is defeated (hence, "pardoneth all their sins"). Second, the perfect righteousness of the second Adam is imputed to the elect (hence, "accepteth and accounteth their persons righteous in his sight"). The blessed result of this double imputation is "an everlasting inheritance."

The "inheritance" aspect of the covenantal blessings flows from, in the words of WCF 7.4, "the death of Jesus Christ the testator." A vital biblical text standing behind this idea is Hebrews 9:15–17, which states that, like a will that releases only when a death occurs, the blessings of the covenant are released to heirs only through the death of the mediator (cf. Luke 22:20; 1 Cor. 11:25). The testamentary character of the covenant of grace shapes the dynamics of the covenant in significant ways. Through it we are able to see that while a covenant always has two parties, and is thus genuinely bilateral, its bilateral dimension is still cast in light of God's "initiating" grace and, further, God's "completing" grace in and through the mediator, Jesus Christ. Holding together both the unilateral and bilateral dimensions of the covenant is essential to understanding the covenant theology of the post-Reformation era.[76]

---

75. According to the Standards, there is a unity in Christ's full obedience imputed to believers, an obedience that has both "active" and "passive" aspects: "Active obedience refers to Jesus's full realization of all that God requires of humanity, whereas passive obedience refers to his suffering the penalty due to humanity as a result of sin." Brandon D. Crowe, *The Last Adam: A Theology of the Obedient Life of Jesus in the Gospels* (Grand Rapids, MI: Baker Academic, 2017), 205.

76. While this aspect of covenantal theology took on greater precision in the seventeenth-century Reformed writers, it should be noted that the first generation of Reformers also held these dimensions together in their

Thus far, this chapter's discussion has examined elements of the covenant of grace in the Standards that are "unilateral," that is, what God establishes out of his unilateral grace offered in the promises of the covenant found in both the Old and New Testaments. Apart from any human initiative, these are freely given to God's people in and through the person and work of Jesus Christ, the mediator of the covenant. The covenant of grace is in this sense accurately described as unilateral, or "one-sided." But a covenant contemplates *two* parties, and there are bilateral, or "two-sided," dimensions to the covenant. John Ball (1585–1640), one of the most significant covenant theologians behind the theology of the Standards, not only noted the blessings flowing from one side—the divine side—but also observed that in the administration of the covenant of grace, conditions were attached to the human side.[77] "Faith" is a condition of entry into the covenant.[78] Though nonmeritorious, faith is a *necessary* instrument by which the elect receive the grace of the covenant.[79] Another condition is "evangelical obedience" (see Gen. 17:1). Ball and the Westminster divines understood obedience to naturally follow entrance into the covenant of grace. It was not a ground for obtaining salvation but a consequent reality of the grace granted in the covenant.[80] WLC 32 provides a helpful summary of these conditions:

Q. How is the grace of God manifested in the second covenant [i.e., the covenant of grace]?

A. The grace of God is manifested in the second covenant, in that he freely provideth and offereth to sinners a Mediator, and life and salvation by him; and requireth faith as the condition to interest them in him, promiseth and giveth his Holy Spirit to all his elect, to work in them that faith, with all other saving graces; and to enable them unto all holy obedience, as the evidence of the truth of their faith and thankfulness to God, and as the way which he has appointed them to salvation.

Following Ball, the Standards were keen to emphasize that the conditions of the covenant were promised in the covenant itself.[81] That is, the conditions of the covenant are granted unilaterally on the basis of the death of Jesus Christ.[82] The testamentary

---

writings. For more on how Zwingli, Bullinger, and Calvin held together divine initiative and human response in their covenantal thought, see Bierma, "Federal Theology," 310–16.

77. See Ball, *Covenant of Grace*, 3–4.

78. WCF 7.3 speaks of "requiring of them faith in him, that they may be saved." Cf. WLC 73; WCF 11.2.

79. Ball called it "the instrument of the soule, wrought there by the Holy Ghost," and said that it "is the free gift of God." *Covenant of Grace*, 19.

80. See Ball, *Covenant of Grace*, 19–21. For the ways seventeenth-century Reformed theologians wrestled with "antecedent" and "consequent" conditional language in covenant theology, see Beeke and Jones, *Puritan Theology*, 305–18.

81. See WCF 8.8; 9.4; 10.1, 2; 11.1, 2; 14.1; 15.2; 16.3; 17.2; 19.7.

82. Woolsey puts it succinctly: "Man is responsible for exercising the repentance, faith, obedience, and love required of him, but unlike a human covenant, what is required was also given in the covenant of grace." *Unity and Continuity*, 78.

character of the covenant of grace demonstrates that it was the death of the mediator that ensured delivery of the grace of faith and obedience to the elect. *Both* the blessings promised by God *and* the duties required of us (i.e., faith and obedience) are ultimately guaranteed, according to the Standards, by God's sovereign initiative, almighty power, and covenantal self-commitment. Consequently, the second covenant is truly a covenant of *grace*. One question that was swirling at the time, though, was whether every postfall covenant in Scripture was an administration of the covenant of grace or whether the Mosaic covenant, in particular, had a different character.

WCF's seventh chapter does make a distinction between the Old (time of the law) and New (time of the gospel) Testaments, yet it also says, "There are not . . . two covenants of grace differing in substance, but one and the same under various dispensations" (WCF 7.6). While the law given at Sinai did have heightened legal demands that led the people of God to look for a Redeemer to come, in substance it was not distinct from the covenant of grace. If there is a contrast, it is to be found between provisional prefiguring (Mosaic administration) and the reality revealed in the coming of Jesus Christ (new covenant), not between the economy of the Mosaic covenant (a "law covenant") and other administrations of the covenant of grace. Such a contrast would establish a third covenant along with the covenants of works and grace. As it is, according to the Standards, there is one pattern of salvation from Abraham throughout the rest of history—justification by faith by virtue of the work of Christ.[83] Thus, there is a fundamental unity to the covenant of grace across its various administrations. This is the position of the Standards and the majority position of seventeenth-century theologians. But it was not the only position.[84] The WCF's language of "differently administered in the time of the law" provided "a gateway into a debate among Reformed theologians that caused Anthony Burgess (d. 1664) to remark that on the relation between Sinai and the covenant of grace he did 'not finde in any point of Divinity, learned men so confused and perplexed . . . as here.'"[85] There was a minority position among seventeenth-century Reformed theologians that disagreed with the Standards' way of relating the Mosaic covenant to the covenant of grace.[86]

---

83. WLC 34: "The covenant of grace was administered under the Old Testament, by promises, prophecies, sacrifices, circumcision, the passover, and other types and ordinances, which did all fore-signify Christ then to come, and were for that time sufficient to build up the elect *in faith in the promised Messiah, by whom they then had full remission of sin, and eternal salvation*" (emphasis added).

84. Scholars have attempted to understand the various views of the covenants by putting together taxonomies. In the seventeenth century, Edmund Calamy provided a brief taxonomy of views among the Westminster divines in his *Two solemne covenants made between God and man: viz. [brace] the covenant of works, and the covenant of grace* (London, 1647), 1–2. More recently, Brenton C. Ferry put together a taxonomy to reflect the variety of views in "Works in the Mosaic Covenant: A Reformed Taxonomy," in *The Law Is Not of Faith: Essays on Works and Grace in the Mosaic Covenant*, ed. Bryan D. Estelle, J. V. Fesko, and David VanDrunen (Phillipsburg, NJ: P&R, 2009), 76–105. For evaluations of these taxonomies, see Jones, "'Old' Covenant," 187–89; Fesko, *Theology of the Westminster Standards*, 147–53; Venema, *Christ and Covenant Theology*, 48–51.

85. Jones, "'Old' Covenant," 187–88, quoting Burgess, *Vindiciae Legis*, 219.

86. Richard Muller has argued for the essential continuity of the minority position with the Reformed orthodox view in the seventeenth century. See his "Divine Covenants, Absolute and Conditional: John Cameron and the Early Orthodox Development of Reformed Covenant Theology," *MJT* 17 (2006): 11–56. For further

For those in the seventeenth century who dissented, there were many nuances to the debate.[87] By and large, though, they were concerned with the law-gospel distinction and how it was applied. If the law, as it was given in the Mosaic economy, mostly had a negative function, and is to be sharply contrasted with the gospel of the new covenant, then the redemptive-historical shift from the old to the new covenant served to heighten this contrast. The position of the Westminster divines was, certainly, to contrast law and gospel in justification. Nonetheless,

> they also applied this distinction less strictly to the time of the law and the time of the gospel where not only justification, but sanctification was also in view. In the time of the law there was gospel, and in the time of the gospel there is law. In justification the law and the gospel are opposed, but in sanctification they are friends.[88]

For those who saw the Mosaic covenant as a third covenant, subservient in some way to the covenant of grace, they emphasized the law's function of leading us *to* faith in Christ; they emphasized *less* the role of the law in the life *of* faith. Diversity of views among the divines shaped everything from how things were said in the Standards to what was said and not said. As mentioned above, while the WCF, WSC, and WLC are confessional statements containing clear boundaries, they are also, in the end, consensus documents with a background in compromise.

Covenant of Redemption?

Perhaps the consensus nature of the WCF is most clearly seen in how it handles an important doctrinal development of the sixteenth and seventeenth centuries, the covenant of redemption (or *pactum salutis*). This covenant holds together God's eternal decree and his Trinitarian nature by articulating an agreement between God the Father and God the Son in eternity in which the Son agreed to be head of his people and accomplish on their behalf the work of salvation.[89] Despite many divines holding to this doctrine, it is not explicitly stated in the confession or catechisms. Rather, it is alluded to, specifically in WCF 8.1, which states,

---

understanding of the debate, see Sebastian Rehnman, "Is the Narrative of Redemptive History Trichotomous or Dichotomous? A Problem for Federal Theology," *NAK* 80, no. 3 (2000): 296–308.

87. Advocating the confessional integrity of the minority position, Fesko gives extensive space to its views in his chapter on the covenant in *Theology of the Westminster Standards*, 147–58.

88. Jones, "'Old' Covenant," 199.

89. Fesko notes, "From the earliest days of the reception and interpretation of the Confession, the covenant of redemption was viewed as compatible with it." *Theology of the Westminster Standards*, 165–66. Evidence for this claim is seen in *The Summe of Saving Knowledge*, written by David Dickson (ca. 1583–1662) and appended to the Westminster Standards by the Scottish Church, which explicitly articulates the covenant of redemption. See David Dickson, *The Summe of Saving Knowledge with Practical Use Thereof* (Glasgow: Robert Sanders, 1669), head 2, in *The Confession of Faith and the Larger and Shorter Catechisms. First Agreed upon by the Assembly of Divines at Westminster. And now Appointed by the General Assembly of the Kirk of Scotland* (Glasgow: Robert Sanders, 1669). Space does not allow an examination of the Holy Spirit's role in the covenant of redemption. For insight on this critical issue, see J. V. Fesko, *The Covenant of Redemption: Origins, Development, and Reception*, RHT 35 (Göttingen: Vandenhoeck & Ruprecht, 2016), 61–68.

It pleased God, *in His eternal purpose*, to choose and ordain the Lord Jesus, His only begotten Son, to be the Mediator between God and man, the Prophet, Priest, and King, the Head and Savior of His Church, the Heir of all things, and Judge of the world: unto whom He did from all eternity give a people, to be His seed, and to be by Him in time redeemed, called, justified, sanctified, and glorified.[90]

It appears that the divines saw the origins of the covenant of grace as reaching back into eternity. Since, however, they disagreed over how exactly to articulate this, the divines held to a strict two-covenant presentation, and the language of covenant was not used in reference to the Trinity.

While the Standards reflected a theological consensus on this point, individual Reformed theologians of the seventeenth century reflected their unique perspectives and the growing theological trends. The High Orthodox era of the century contained further refinements in Reformed covenant theology, especially in the development of a theologically integrated covenant of redemption. Traces of this covenant can be found in the earliest Reformers, such as Luther and Calvin,[91] yet it was not until the middle of the seventeenth century that it was articulated with clarity as a third covenant.[92] This happened as Reformed theologians deepened their exegesis of specific biblical texts (e.g., 2 Chron. 7:18; Pss. 2:7; 110; Isa. 42; 49; Zech. 6:13; Luke 22:29; John 10:18; 17; Heb. 10; 1 Pet. 1:10), honed their "conceptual vocabulary out of prior doctrinal discussion,"[93] and faced theological aberrations such as Arminianism, Antinomianism, and Socinianism.

In his opposition to Remonstrant theology in a 1638 address to the General Assembly of the Church of Scotland, theologian David Dickson (1583–1663) focused on the Remonstrants' denial of the covenant of redemption as their chief offense. In Dickson's mind a covenant between God the Father and God the Son in eternity secured the inviolability of the covenant of grace among the elect, thus providing a bulwark against additional Arminian errors, such as conditional election and a denial of the perseverance of the saints.[94] Antinomian errors were growing in the seventeenth century as well. Reformed theologians perceived a root of their errors in not distinguishing the covenant of grace from that of redemption. Rather, Antinomian theologians held to a justification from eternity and "collaps[ed] the covenant of grace into the covenant of redemption . . . [and had an] inclination to see as much as possible in the divine act and to keep

---

90. Emphasis added. Other sixteenth- and seventeenth-century Reformed confessions and catechisms hint at the covenant of redemption: Belgic Confession 26; Heidelberg Catechism 31; Canons of Dort 1.7. Most explicit, perhaps, is the Savoy Declaration 8.1, which added to WCF 8.1 the phrase "according to a covenant made between them both."

91. Muller locates its origins in the Reformers' "meditation on the trinitarian nature of the divine decrees." *After Calvin*, 187.

92. For thorough investigations into the origins of the *pactum salutis*, see Richard A. Muller, "Toward the *Pactum Salutis*: Locating the Origins of a Concept," *MJT* 18 (2007): 11–65; Fesko, *Covenant of Redemption*, 29–108.

93. Trueman, *John Owen*, 80.

94. David Dickson, "Arminianism Discussed," in *Records of the Kirk of Scotland, containing the Acts and Proceedings of the General Assemblies, from the year 1638 Downwards*, ed. Alexander Peterkin (Edinburgh: Peter Brown, 1845), 156–58.

the covenant as far away as possible from human contracting."[95] The great Puritan theologian John Owen (1616–1683) opposed these errors, as well as Socinianism, and in the *pactum salutis*, he saw the connection needed between the divine plan and the incarnate Christ's work of mediation. In bringing the covenant of redemption to bear on the Socinian rejection of the incarnation of the Son of God, Owen taught that God the Father meted out proportional justice on the cross in punishing the incarnate Son. This was in accord with their eternal arrangement, in which Christ was designated mediator of a sinful people.[96] Thus, the punishment he received on the cross at the hands of the Father was commensurate with the sins of elect.[97] What is more, in Owen the "covenant of redemption serves to make explicit Christ's role as the Second Adam, as the one who acts on behalf of those given to him in the covenant of grace to remedy the disastrous results of the breaking of the original covenant."[98] The Trinitarian dimensions of the cross articulated by Owen cut at the root of the Socinian rejection of the eternal Son of God. Eternity and history kiss when accounts of salvation are integrated with an orthodox Trinitarian and Christological theology.

In addition to Owen, another theological giant of this century to give full-throated affirmation to the *pactum salutis* was Francis Turretin (1623–1687), an articulate and representative defender of High Orthodoxy.[99] He considers the covenant of redemption in "three periods,"[100] rooting it in the economy of redemption itself: "The relationship between the Father and the Son in the way of *historia salutis* points back and testifies to the eternal agreement within the Godhead to be implemented in the fullness of time."[101] In Turretin's own words,

> The pact between the Father and the Son contains the will of the Father giving his Son as *lytrōtēn* (Redeemer and head of his mystical body) and the will of the Son offering himself as sponsor for his members to work out redemption (*apolytrōsin*). For thus the Scriptures represent to us the Father in the economy of salvation as stipulating the obedience of the Son even unto death, and for it promising in return a name above every name that he might be the head of the elect in glory; the Son as offering himself to do the Father's will, promising a faithful and constant performance of the duty required of him.[102]

---

95. Von Rohr, *Covenant of Grace*, 44.

96. John Owen, *The Works of John Owen*, ed. William H. Goold (Edinburgh: Banner of Truth, 1967), 10:441; cf. 10:458; 19:89.

97. Owen, *Works*, 10:269: "It [Christ's satisfaction] was full, valuable compensation, made to the justice of God, for all the sins of all those for whom he made satisfaction, by undergoing the same punishment which, by reason of the obligation that was upon them, they themselves were bound to undergo."

98. Trueman, *John Owen*, 88.

99. Van Asselt provides a crisp overview of what makes Turretin a representative example in *Introduction to Reformed Scholasticism*, 157–63.

100. Francis Turretin, *Institutes of Elenctic Theology*, trans. George Musgrave Giger, ed. James T. Dennison Jr. (Phillipsburg, NJ: P&R, 1994), 2:178.

101. J. Mark Beach, *Christ and the Covenant: Francis Turrretin's Federal Theology as a Defense of the Doctrine of Grace*, RHT 1 (Göttingen: Vandenhoeck & Ruprecht, 2007), 168.

102. Turretin, *Institutes*, 2:177.

Turretin's three periods of the covenant of redemption thus include (1) the Trinity's eternal decision, (2) the gospel promise given right after the fall, and (3) "the execution of that promise in Christ's incarnation."[103] The perspective of "execution" guides theological reflection *from* the earthly work of Christ the mediator in fulfillment of the Father's will *to* its eternal purpose. That is, it vividly depicts

> the official character of Christ's mediatorial work and the "sentness" or apostolic nature of his operations, for he is one appointed and sent to fulfill a task, being assigned a mission, and in fact willingly offered himself for this sacrificial and substitutionary role. More specifically, it defines Christ's mediatorial role as that of Surety—the Guarantor of all the blessings of this covenant, inclusive of its conditions and stipulations.[104]

In his emphasis on the mediatorship of Jesus Christ, Turretin echoes WCF 8 while expanding on the theme by further integrating it into covenant theology. Like Owen above, Turretin's teaching on Christ the mediator ties together the covenants of works and grace, for Christ as man acts on behalf of man, fulfilling the stipulations of the covenant of works, and Christ as God fulfills God's promises to the elect based on his mercy in the covenant of grace. Turretin, and along with him the best of seventeenth-century covenant theology, therefore centers the covenant and salvation wholly on the person of Christ. Because all is offered and accomplished in him, including the very conditions required of human beings as parties to the covenant, it is of sheer grace:

> [Through the mediator] a twofold obstacle to a covenant had to be removed. On the part of God, his enmity on account of man's sin and on the part of man, his enmity on account of the righteousness of God; God was to be reconciled to man and man to God. Christ effected the former by the merit of his blood, by which he satisfied for us and reconciled us to God; the latter by the efficacy of the Spirit, by which he sanctifies and converts us and by converting, reconciles us to God. And thus he perfectly fulfilled what had to be done either on God's part with us or on man's part with God, unto a full consummation of the covenant of grace.[105]

Conclusion

In Turretin's covenant of redemption, the variety of elements introduced through the bicovenantalism of seventeenth-century federal theology find their coherence. Reformed orthodoxy's highly intricate covenant of redemption not only draws in the covenants of works and grace and centers them on Christ the mediator but also considers the historical scope of his work and rivets it to the Trinitarian shape of God's election. The basic structure of the biblical story of creation, fall, and redemption is given theological

103. Beach, *Christ and the Covenant*, 169.
104. Beach, *Christ and the Covenant*, 171.
105. Turretin, *Institutes*, 2:179.

expression through the covenants of works, grace, and redemption. At the same time, these are put into eloquent conversation with the ancient doctrines of the Trinity and Christology. The result, according to Trueman,

> is neither crass proof-texting nor a situation where dogmatics overrides exegesis; it is, rather, a classic example of the Reformed Orthodox move from exegesis to doctrinal synthesis within the context of the analogy of faith and the need to coordinate a Trinitarian understanding of God with the historical action of Jesus Christ in salvation.[106]

The harvest of Reformed teaching in seventeenth-century covenantal thought is thus a systematic theology that is mindful of biblical theology and a biblical theology that reaches beyond itself, even into the deep things of God.

---

106. Trueman, *John Owen*, 85.

18

Covenant Theology in the Dutch Reformed Tradition

Bruce P. Baugus

Given how central covenant, or federal, theology is to Reformed theology, and the significant contributions Dutch theologians have made to both, it is perhaps striking that the terms for "covenant" (Lat. *foedus*, Fr. *alliance*, Ger. *Bund*, and Dut. *verbond*) appear only at the margins of the defining standards of the Dutch Reformed tradition—and related terms for "pact" and "testament" hardly at all beyond references to the Old and New Testaments. *Covenant*, in other words, is not an obvious organizing principle for the system of doctrine outlined in the Three Forms of Unity.[1]

The scarcity of explicit covenant language does not imply the absence of the concept or its associated logic. Covenant theology was developing rapidly at the time these standards were being written, taking on the proportions of a doctrinal locus and becoming an increasingly important unifying theme.[2] This development is reflected in the

---

1. The Belgic Confession (1561), in French, uses the term *alliance* in the single reference to the covenant, which occurs in its discussion of baptism, and *testament* only when referring to the Old and New Testaments. The Heidelberg Catechism (1563), in German, uses both *Bund* (qq. 74; 82) and *Testament* (qq. 74; 79; and for the Old and New Testaments throughout), though the Latin translation uses *foedus*, not *testamentum*, even for the Old and New Testaments. The relative scarcity of references to "covenant" and its related terms in these two forms is not unusual for Reformed confessions and theological treatises of the era. Lyle D. Bierma, for example, offers similar observations about Heinrich Bullinger's *Summa Christlicher Religion* (1556) and the Second Helvetic Confession (1566). *The Covenant Theology of Caspar Olevianus* (1996; repr., Grand Rapids, MI: Reformation Heritage Books, 2005), 143; cf. Zacharias Ursinus's Larger Catechism and *Commentary on the Heidelberg Catechism*. In the Canons of Dort (1618–1619), "covenant" appears most often in the rejections of errors.

2. Lyle D. Bierma, *The Theology of the Heidelberg Catechism: A Reformation Synthesis*, CSRT (Louisville: Westminster John Knox, 2013), 90–100. See also Herman Bavinck, *Reformed Dogmatics*, vol. 2, *God and Creation*, ed. John Bolt, trans. John Vriend (Grand Rapids, MI: Baker Academic, 2004), 567–68. Contrary to views later advanced by Anthony Hoekema, John Stek, and John Murray, Bavinck argues that although the Three Forms of Unity "do not mention it in so many words," the covenant of works "is nevertheless embodied" in them "materially," and he cites Belgic Confession 14 and 15, Heidelberg Catechism 6–11, and Canons of Dort 3/4 as proof. See

writings, for example, of the German Reformed theologian and primary author of the Heidelberg Catechism, Zacharias Ursinus (1534–1583). Indeed, reading the Heidelberg Catechism in light of Ursinus's other writings leads Lyle Bierma to conclude that "for a document that employs the word covenant in only two of its 129 questions and answers," it "contains a remarkable amount of covenantal material—much more, certainly, than first meets the eye." This material includes, among other things, the "treatment of the believer as Christ's possession, the mediatorship of Christ, the definition of the gospel, and the sacraments"—the last notably featuring a "defense of infant baptism" that identifies both "the forgiveness of sin and the gift of the Holy Spirit as a twofold benefit of the covenant."[3]

Furthermore, the scarcity of explicit covenant language in the Three Forms of Unity does not accurately reflect the role *covenant* played in the development of Reformed theology in the Netherlands, which was already becoming evident by the Synod of Dort. The judgments of the Synod in the Canons of Dort on the points of doctrine disputed by the Remonstrants are shaped and richly informed by the concepts and associated logic of covenant theology, including a covenantal explanation of infant baptism (1.17), a covenantal framing of Christ's mediatorial work on behalf of the elect (2.8, errors 2, 4, 5), and the effective operation of God's grace in perseverance (5, error 1).

The relative scarcity of covenantal language and the muted treatment of covenant theology in the Three Forms of Unity do suggest, however, that the systematic elaboration of this teaching into a distinct doctrinal locus was largely the work of seventeenth-century theologians and their heirs. This chapter sketches a bit of the distinctly Dutch elaboration of this teaching into a well-rounded covenant theology and doctrinal locus, noting some of its sources and continuities with federal theology across the Continent while highlighting significant Dutch developments. While Dutch covenant theology reflects the rich diversity found in Reformed covenant theology more broadly—and teasing out the concrete expressions of that diversity within the Dutch Reformed tradition is beyond the scope of this chapter—it is important to recognize that this diversity is bounded, constrained by Scripture and the understanding of Scripture codified in the standards of the Reformed churches. As such, the story sketched here displays diversity against a deeper and broader theological continuity across generations and cultures.

Reassessing Dutch Covenant Theology

This deeper and broader continuity has not always been appreciated. Indeed, odd tales are sometimes told: differences in nuance and emphasis are exaggerated into tensions

---

Anthony Hoekema, *Created in God's Image* (Grand Rapids, MI: Eerdmans, 1986), 117–21; John Stek, "'Covenant' Overload in Reformed Theology," *CTJ* 29 (1994): 12–41; John Murray, "The Adamic Administration," in *Collected Writings of John Murray*, vol. 2, *Select Lectures in Systematic Theology* (Carlisle, PA: Banner of Truth, 1977), 47–59. See also Michael Brown, "The Covenantal Foundation of the Heidelberg Catechism," *PRJ* 7, no. 1 (2015): 88–102. An even stronger case can be made for the covenant of grace, of course.

3. Bierma, *Heidelberg Catechism*, 100.

and divisions; organic developments and elaborations are misunderstood as doctrinal innovations and deviations. Along the way, the deep biblical roots of this theological vine have been overlooked or even obscured.

Some have suggested that the Reformed tradition was already divided into two contrary covenant camps by the time the Dutch masters wrote. Heinrich Heppe, for example, proposes that the covenant idea that developed in Heidelberg was taken over from Philipp Melanchthon (later altered to Zurich's independently developed federalism) and represents a German innovation intended to soften the severe strains of Geneva's strict teaching on predestination.[4] After Heppe, "a series of writers," Richard Muller observes, "assume two divergent trends in covenant theology."[5] J. Wayne Baker even claims that the differences between Zurich and Geneva constitute two conflicting Reformed traditions: an original bilateral, conditional, federal tradition arising in Zurich and a unilateral, testamentary tradition arising in Geneva—supposedly correlated to different views on predestination.[6]

The suggestion that the Reformed tradition is somehow divided and that covenant theology is entangled in this conflict has proved attractive to many writers.[7] There is little agreement among them, however, about which covenant theologian belongs to which side, but the contributions of the Dutch are frequently interpreted in this frame. Some argue that Dutch covenant theology was a late, scholastic, and legalistic or commercial development that diverged rather sharply from the Reformers. Michael McGiffert, Holmes Rolston III, James Torrance, Thomas Torrance, and David Poole generally follow Barth's critique of this development as obscuring the Reformers' priority on grace.[8] Perry Miller,

---

4. For his earlier assessment, see Heinrich Heppe, *Dogmatik des Deutschen Protestantismus im sechzehnten Jahrhundert*, 3 vols. (Gotha: Friedrich Andreas Perthes, 1857), 1:139–204. For his later reflection, see Heppe, *Geschichte des Pietismus und der Mystik in der Reformirten Kirche, Namentlich der Niederlande* (Leiden: Brill, 1879), 205–16. Cf. Geerhardus Vos, "The Doctrine of the Covenant in Reformed Theology," in *Redemptive History and Biblical Interpretation: The Shorter Writings of Geerhardus Vos*, ed. Richard B. Gaffin Jr. (Phillipsburg, NJ: Presbyterian and Reformed, 1980), 234–35; Herman Bavinck, *Reformed Dogmatics*, vol. 3, *Sin and Salvation in Christ*, ed. John Bolt, trans. John Vriend (Grand Rapids, MI: Baker Academic, 2006), 209–12. Both theologians summarily dismiss Heppe's argument.

5. Richard A. Muller, "The Covenant of Works and the Stability of Divine Law in Seventeenth-Century Reformed Orthodoxy: A Study in the Theology of Herman Witsius and Wilhelmus à Brakel," in *After Calvin: Studies in the Development of a Theological Tradition*, OSHT (Oxford: Oxford University Press, 2003), 176. Muller cites Leonard J. Trinterud, "The Origins of Puritanism," *CH* 20, no. 1 (1951): 37–57; Jens Møller, "The Beginnings of Puritan Covenant Theology," *JEH* 14 (1963): 46–67; Richard Greaves, "The Origins and Early Development of English Covenant Thought," *Historian* 31, no. 1 (1968): 21–35; J. Wayne Baker, *Heinrich Bullinger and the Covenant: The Other Reformed Tradition* (Athens: Ohio University Press, 1980). See also Andrew A. Woolsey, *Unity and Continuity in Covenantal Thought: A Study in the Reformed Tradition to the Westminster Assembly* (Grand Rapids, MI: Reformation Heritage Books, 2012), 80–158.

6. Baker, *Bullinger and the Covenant*; Baker, "Heinrich Bullinger, the Covenant, and the Reformed Tradition in Retrospect," *SCJ* 29, no. 2 (1998): 359–76; see also Charles S. McCoy and J. Wayne Baker, *Fountainhead of Federalism: Heinrich Bullinger and the Covenantal Tradition; With a Translation of "De testamento seu foedere Dei unico et aeterno" (1534)* (Louisville: Westminster John Knox, 1991), 11–43.

7. Besides those named above, Bierma identifies W. A. Brown, Perry Miller, Gottlob Schrenk, and Jürgen Moltmann as arguing that Olevianus's covenant theology was an attempt to "soften" or even "counterattack" the "stricter . . . predestinarianism" of Geneva. *Olevianus*, 23–25. See also Bierma, "Federal Theology in the Sixteenth Century: Two Traditions?," *WTJ* 45, no. 2 (1983): 304–21.

8. Michael McGiffert, "Grace and Works: the Rise and Division of Covenant Divinity in Elizabethan Puritanism," *HTR* 75, no. 4 (1982): 463–502; McGiffert, "From Moses to Adam: The Making of the Covenant of

however, sees federal theology as a creative modification that accommodated a "spiritual commercialism" enabling believers to find assurance of election in their works.[9]

The various interpretations of the Dutch theologian Johannes Cocceius (1603–1669) are illuminating. Miller presents him as the founder of the federal school of theology just described; he was neither the first nor the last to suggest that Cocceius was a revolutionary federalist within the Reformed tradition. Dutch historian Anneus Ypey advanced a version of this view by the end of the eighteenth century.[10] Karl Hagenbach, Wilhelm Gaß, Ludwig Diestel, Isaak A. Dorner, Gottlob Schrenk, Grete Möller, and A. F. Stolzenburg all offer variations on the same basic theme: that in Cocceius's covenant theology we see a break with scholastic approaches and "the beginning of a development that culminates in the historicism of the mid-nineteenth century."[11] After Miller, assessments vary: some see Cocceius's theology as the pass into a lamentable rationalism, while others admire his theological breakthrough. Karl Barth and Jürgen Moltmann tend toward the former, and Charles McCoy and Heiner Faulenbach toward the latter.[12]

Scholarly attention to covenant theology since the mid-nineteenth century is occupied largely with discovering the origins of the idea and causes of its seventeenth-century development. Curiously, Brian Lee notes that "a pattern of scholarship" has emerged that is "almost entirely focused upon demonstrating dogmatic causality in an exegetical vacuum."[13] From this perspective, federal theology often seems to leap onto the theological scene as something new and practically unprecedented, sparked by "disputes about predestination and theodicy, the rising influence of either Ramism or Aristotelianism, or

Works," *SCJ* 19, no. 2 (1988): 131–55; Holmes Rolston III, *John Calvin versus the Westminster Confession* (Richmond, VA: John Knox, 1972); James B. Torrance, "Strengths and Weaknesses of the Westminster Theology," in *The Westminster Confession in the Church Today*, ed. Alasdair I. C. Heron (Edinburgh: Saint Andrew Press, 1982), 40–53; T. F. Torrance, *The School of Faith: The Catechisms of the Reformed Church* (London: James Clark, 1959), xii–cxxvi; David N. J. Poole, *The History of the Covenant Concept from the Bible to Johannes Cloppenburg, "De Foedere Dei"* (San Fransisco: Mellen Research University Press, 1992); Karl Barth, *Church Dogmatics*, ed. G. W. Bromiley and T. F. Torrance (Edinburgh: T&T Clark, 1956), 4.1:54–66.

9. Perry Miller, *The New England Mind: The Seventeenth Century* (Cambridge, MA: Harvard University Press, 1939), 395, 502–4; see also Miller, "The Marrow of Puritan Divinity," in *Errand into the Wilderness* (Cambridge, MA: Harvard University Press, 1956), 48–98.

10. Annaeus Ypey, *Beknopte Letterkundige Geschiedenis der Systematische Godgeleerdheid*, 3 vols. (Haarlem: C. Plaat, 1793–1798), 2:70–79; cf. Bavinck, *Reformed Dogmatics*, 3:209–12.

11. Willem J. van Asselt, *The Federal Theology of Johannes Cocceius (1603–1669)*, SHCT 100 (Leiden: Brill, 2001), 3. See Karl Hagenbach, *Compendium of the History of Doctrine*, trans. Carl W. Buch, 2 vols., (Edinburgh: T&T Clark, 1852), 2:183; Wilhelm Gaß, *Geschichte der Protestantischen Dogmatik* (Berlin: Georg Reimer, 1857), 253–300; Ludwig Diestel, "Studien zur," *JDT* 10 (1865): 209–76; Isaak A. Dorner, *History of Protestant Theology: Particularly in Germany*, trans. George Robson and Sophia Taylor, 2 vols. (Edinburgh: T&T Clark, 1871), 2:9, 35–41; Gottlob Schrenk, *Gottesreich und Bund im Älteren Protestantismus, Vornehmlich bei Johannes Cocceius* (Gütersloh: Bertelsmann, 1923); Grete Möller, "Föderalismus und Geschichtsbetrachtung im XVII. und XVIII. Jahrhundert," *ZKG* 50, no. 3 (1931): 393–440; A. F. Stolzenburg, *Die Theologie des Jo. Franc. Buddeus und des Chr. Matth. Pfaff* (Berlin: Trowitzsch, 1926).

12. Van Asselt, *Federal Theology*, 9–16. See Barth, *Church Dogmatics*, 4.1:54–66, who admires the dynamism of Cocceius's view of revelation but rejects the place he allots to the covenant of works and the inevitable slide into rationalism he thought this entailed; Jürgen Moltmann, "Geschichtstheologie und Pietistisches Menschenbild bei J. Cocceius und Th. Undereyck," *EvT* 19, no. 8 (1959): 343–63; Charles S. McCoy, "The Covenant Theology of Johannes Cocceius" (PhD diss., Yale University, 1956); Heiner Faulenbach, *Weg und Ziel der Erkenntnis Christi: Eine untersuchung zur Theologie des Johannes Cocceius* (Neukirchen-Vluyn: Neukirchen Verlag, 1973).

13. Brian J. Lee, *Johannes Cocceius and the Exegetical Roots of Federal Theology: Reformation Developments in the Interpretation of Hebrews 7–10*, RHT 7 (Göttingen: Vandenhoeck & Ruprecht, 2009), 15.

the growing influence of scholasticism and/or legalism." What "was taken for granted" by covenant theologians of the era, Lee concludes, "has been largely overlooked by modern historians," leading to "dogmatic explanations for the rise and import of covenant doctrine [that] are at best insufficient, at worst wholly misleading."[14]

The current reassessment of Dutch covenant theology is a small piece of a larger reassessment of the sources and development of covenant theology in general. Contributors include Richard Muller, Lyle Bierma, Peter Lillback, Willem J. van Asselt, R. Scott Clark, Andrew Woolsey, and Brian Lee. This reassessment acknowledges diversity and development but also takes account of strong continuities across the various stages of the formation of the Reformed tradition, extending back into the medieval era. It is now clear that, in Lee's words, "the concept of covenant itself was not new in the sixteenth century; rather, the novel aspect was the development of a new, distinct locus '*de foedere*' in the system, and over time, the further use of covenant as an ordering principle for the system itself."[15] Dutch theologians made important contributions to this doctrinal development.

Early Dutch Covenant Theology

"From the Reformed Churches of Switzerland and Germany," Louis Berkhof observes, "federal theology passed over to the Netherlands."[16] This happened quickly and tracked closely with developments in covenant theology across the Continent. We already "find the main ideas of Federalism," Vos notes, among the earliest Dutch theologians, including Gellius Snecanus, Franciscus Junius, Franciscus Gomarus, Lucas Trelcatius Sr., Lucas Trelcatius Jr., Henricus Nerdenus, Sibrandus Lubbertus, and Jacob Ravensperger.[17]

In the survey that follows, four factors stand out in the early and rather easy reception of covenant teachings in the Netherlands. First, Dutch Reformed theologians fully embraced the humanist call to *ad fontes* scholarship. This compelled them to grapple with the variations in covenant terminology between Hebrew (בְּרִית), Greek (διαθήκη), and Latin (*foedus, testamentum, pactum, dispositio, dispensatio,* etc.) and with the fact that Scripture is divided into two Testaments or covenants. These linguistic and structural elements demanded an account of the biblical concept of God's covenants with humanity developed from Scripture. This, in turn, drove interest in those places in Scripture that most directly address God's covenants with humanity and the relation of the Old and New Testaments.

Second, many of the same questions and controversies compelling Reformed theologians elsewhere on the Continent to develop Scripture's covenant theology were also at work in the Netherlands. Snecanus (1540–ca. 1596), for example, follows Huldrych

14. Lee, *Cocceius*, 14, 17; cf. D. A. Weir, who concludes that covenant theology "seems to stem from systematic, dogmatic thinking, not from exegetical study of Scripture." *The Origins of the Federal Theology in Sixteenth-Century Reformation Thought* (Oxford: Clarendon, 1990), 158.

15. Lee, *Cocceius*, 17.

16. Louis Berkhof, *Systematic Theology* (1938; repr., Grand Rapids, MI: Eerdmans, 1996), 2:212.

17. Vos, "Covenant," 234; the list offered here is enlarged.

Zwingli and Heinrich Bullinger when writing against Anabaptists in Friesland. The substantial pressures exerted on Dutch Reformed theology by Roman Catholic polemicists (especially Robert Bellarmine), Socinians, and Remonstrants intensified interest in covenant theology. Even disputes with Lutherans and intramural debates over Christ's satisfaction, justification, sanctification, ecclesiology, and sacraments all involved covenant theology.

Third, from the beginning, Reformed theology was an international movement scattered across Europe. A growing body of confessed doctrines, shared ideas, and reorganized institutions connected these communities. Reformed works passed freely from one region to another, and Reformed folk often moved about the Continent pursuing education and ministry opportunities or fleeing oppression. In this sense, while early Dutch theology was clearly Dutch, it was the Dutch front of an international movement.

Finally, the early Dutch theologians not only read earlier Protestant thinkers like Martin Luther, Philipp Melanchthon, Martin Bucer, Johannes Oecolampadius, Huldrych Zwingli, Heinrich Bullinger, Peter Martyr Vermigli, John Calvin, and Theodore Beza, all of whom more or less consciously shaped the emerging doctrinal locus, but many of them also studied under or served alongside leading pioneers of covenant theology in their generation. Members of the Reformed faculty of Heidelberg were especially influential on the formation of Dutch covenant theology.

Junius

Franciscus Junius (1545–1602) embodies these factors. Joining a humanist commitment to *ad fontes* scholarship with scholastic rigor, Junius addressed many of the most pressing theological questions of his day. A native of France, he studied under Calvin and Beza in Geneva before devoting most of his life to serving the people of the Netherlands— as pastor of the Walloon Reformed church in Antwerp (where he revised, disseminated, and oversaw the synod's adoption of Guido de Bres's Belgic Confession), as pastor briefly in Limburg, then as pastor to Walloon refugees in Palatinate Schönau, and eventually as professor at Leiden.

The few years Junius was not directly serving these communities, he labored alongside members of the Heidelberg faculty. Most notably, from 1573 to 1578, Junius worked closely with the Heidelberg Hebraist Immanuel Tremellius on a fresh Latin translation of the Bible, which became a standard reference in Reformed circles for the next two centuries. Then, in 1578, he and Ursinus became founding members of the Casimirianum faculty in Neustadt an der Haardt. In 1583, Junius returned to Heidelberg as professor of theology and later, in 1592, assumed the same post at Leiden, Holland, where he remained till his death in 1602.

Broadly, Junius taught what could already be described as a traditional Reformed understanding of a covenant of works (or nature) and the substantial unity of the covenant of grace across redemptive history.[18] His close work with the text of Scripture, as both a translator and an exegete, compelled him to pay particular attention to the relation of the biblical concept(s) of covenant to the many terms used in Scripture and tradition. To be clear, the terminological question predates the Reformation. Nevertheless, the nuances of his view would prove important to subsequent Dutch developments.

The terminological problem turns chiefly on the New Testament's consistent use of διαθήκη, a term ordinarily used for wills or testaments, instead of the expected συνθήκη, with its suggestion of mutually agreed conditions. This curiosity was already raised by Jerome and addressed by Augustine—and most provocatively by Erasmus on the eve of the Reformation.[19] It was carried into the Vulgate, which uses *foedus* and *pactum* for the Hebrew בְּרִית throughout the Old Testament but only *testamentum* for διαθήκη in the New.

Jerome, Augustine, Erasmus, Luther, Bullinger, Calvin, and practically everyone else Junius would have read on this issue viewed διαθήκη and *testamentum* as, at best, loose equivalents of בְּרִית and *foedus*—though they sometimes used these terms interchangeably. Taking certain cues from Calvin, Beza denied that בְּרִית is properly translated by *testamentum* and, unwilling to suggest the same of διαθήκη, argued that the Greek term has two meanings in Scripture: a primary meaning best translated by *foedus* (which he later altered to *pactum*) and a secondary, testamentary meaning to which New Testament authors sometimes "allude," such as in Hebrews 9:16.[20]

Junius, Lee observes, disagreed with his teacher on two counts: he (1) "believes that בְּרִית is a broad term that can mean both *foedus* and *testamentum*" and (2) "sees the New Testament usage of διαθήκη as an intentional specification of covenant language, a determination of a generic Old Testament concept into a more narrow, testamental sense."[21] The two points are related: if בְּרִית is a broad term, as he believed, then it may well comprehend the sense specified by διαθήκη and thus *testamentum*; and if so, then the primary meaning of διαθήκη may have the sense of *testamentum*, which the New Testament authors intentionally drew out.

By all appearances, Junius did not adopt this view in order to support some doctrinal or philosophical difference with his teachers; he was not advancing a different or deviant covenant teaching here but attempting to solve a long-standing philological riddle. That said, his solution is suggestive, and although Junius is "not departing

---

18. See Junius's two orations *De Promissione et Federe Gratioso Dei cum Ecclesia* and *De Federe et Testamento Dei in Ecclesia Vetere* (vol. 1, cols. 13–30); *Sacrorum Parallelorem Libre Tres*, 1588 (vol. 1, cols. 1367–1654); *De Politia Mosis Observatione* (vol. 1, cols. 1862–1920); and his two theological theses, *De Foederibus et Testamentis Divinis* and *De Veteri et Novi Dei Foedere* (vol. 1, cols. 2048–56); as well as particular passages in his expositions—all of which are in Franciscus Junius, *Opera Theologica Francisci Junii Biturgis Sacrarum Literarum Professoris Eximii*, 2 vols. (Geneva: Crispinum, 1613).

19. See Augustine on Gen. 21:27; 26:28; Josh. 9:7; Pss. 82:6; 102:25; Rom. 11:27; and see Erasmus's annotations on Matt. 26:28; Rom. 9:4; 11:27; Heb. 9:16. References culled from Lee, *Cocceius*, 24, 28; Woolsey, *Unity and Continuity*, 182.

20. Lee, *Cocceius*, 44–49.

21. Lee, *Cocceius*, 50.

significantly from the standard Reformed view of continuity," his argument rests partly on a supposed historical progress at least "of revelation" and apparently also, Lee argues, "of *things*."[22]

We see this progress of things in two respects. First, Junius embraced a distinction that belongs to the theological structure of the *pactum salutis*. There are, he argues, "two distinct relations of Christ, 'a *foedus* of God in Christ,' and 'a *Testamentum* of Christ calling us into his *foedus*.'" With this distinction, "Junius seems to emphasize the legal relation between the Son and the Father and the Gospel relation between Christ and the church."[23] Although Herman Witsius does not include Junius in his list of divines who taught a *pactum salutis* prior to Cocceius,[24] Herman Bavinck does, finding the *pactum salutis* "briefly and materially" in Junius as well as in Caspar Olevianus before him and Gomarus alongside or just after him.[25]

Second, Junius formulates a progressive structure moving from *promissio* to *foedus* to *testamentum* across redemptive history, and he subdivides the latter between an "old, broken *testamentum* of Moses," which rested on "the condition of works," and "the New, certain one founded upon the merit of Christ," which rests on "a mere donation of grace" on the merit of Christ alone.[26] It is apparent, therefore, that on Junius's scheme *promissio, foedus*, and *testamentum* do not necessarily displace each other so much as build on each other, and a *testamentum* may be just as bilateral and conditional as a *foedus*. In other words, there appears to be a multilayered complexity that not only defies some simpler assessments in the secondary literature but would soon play a much more prominent role in the Dutch covenant theology.

Gomarus

Flemish theologian Franciscus Gomarus (1563–1641), on the other hand, adopted the more traditional line, if you will, in defining terms (à la Beza on διαθήκη) and emphasizing the substantial unity of the "one and eternal" covenant of grace (à la Bullinger), though he studied under Junius (as well as Ursinus, Girolamo Zanchius, and other Palatinate professors) at Neustadt and Heidelberg.[27] Like Junius, Gomarus's education and ministry exemplify the international character of the Reformed movement. A native

---

22. Lee, *Cocceius*, 51.

23. Lee, *Cocceius*, 51.

24. Herman Witsius, *The Economy of the Covenants between God and Man: Comprehending a Complete Body of Divinity*, 2 vols. (Grand Rapids, MI: Reformation Heritage Books, 2010), 1:176–77; on his list, Witsius also identifies William Ames, James Arminius, Johannes Cloppenburg, Gisbertus Voetius, Andreas Essenius, John Owen, and even, among Roman Catholics, Jacobus Tirinus.

25. Bavinck, *Reformed Dogmatics*, 3:213. Bavinck cites the theological theses included in the first volume of Abraham Kuyper's *Bibliotheca Reformata* series (1882).

26. Lee, *Cocceius*, 52, citing Junius, *De Federe et Testamento Dei in Ecclesia Vetere*, in Junius, *Opera*, vol. 1, cols. 25–26.

27. See Franciscus Gomarus's oratio *De Foedere Dei* (1594), which appears as the "Prolegomena" to his *Omnia* (1.1 [unnumbered pages]), and particular passages in his expositions (cf. his disputation *De Adami Primi et Secundi Collatione*, 1.3:55–58)—all of which are in Franciscus Gomarus, *Opera Theologica Omnia*, 2 vols. (Amsterdam: Joannis Janssonii, 1664).

of Flanders, he grew up in exile in the Palatinate and in Strasbourg. Between his studies at Neustadt and Heidelberg, he spent time with John Rainolds at Oxford and William Whitaker at Cambridge, where he graduated in 1584. After this he served as a pastor to Low Country refugees in Frankfurt (1587–1593) before eventually joining Junius on the faculty at Leiden in 1594.

Gomarus is best known for his opposition to the teachings of James Arminius. Arminius followed Junius to Leiden in 1603 and remained there till his death in 1609. After that, Leiden installed Remonstrant-approved and Socinian-inclined Conrad Vorstius over Gomarus's opposition. Gomarus left Leiden in 1611, and after spending a few years in Middelburg, Zeeland, and the French Academy of Saumur, he settled at Groningen, the year the Synod of Dort convened (1618), and lived out his life there.

Gomarus is also known, however, as an early expositor of the covenant of works, though he styled it *foedus naturale* ("natural covenant"). The notion of a prelapsarian covenant between God and Adam already appeared in the works of his teachers Ursinus, Olevianus, and Junius, as well as in Wolfgang Musculus, Andreas Hyperius, and, arguably, Calvin, Bullinger, and Melanchthon.[28] Ursinus also referred to this covenant as *foedus naturale* but contrasted it to the *foedus gratia* ("covenant of grace"); Gomarus, however, contrasted it to a *foedus supernaturale* ("supernatural covenant").[29]

Later Reformed theologians distanced themselves from the term *foedus naturale*, with its connotations of a natural relation between the required obedience and the promised eternal life. Over time they also tended to drop the less problematic terms *foedus naturae* ("covenant of nature") and *foedus creationis* ("covenant of creation," preferred by Olevianus). Bavinck's comments on the point reflect the general concern:

> The matter itself is certain. After creating men and women after his own image, God showed them their destiny and the only way in which they could reach it. Human beings could know the moral law without special revelation since it was written in their hearts. But the probationary command is positive; it is not a given of human nature as such but could only be made known to human beings if God communicated it to them. Nor was it self-evident that keeping that command would yield eternal life. In that [narrow] sense the "covenant of works" is not a "covenant of nature."[30]

Bavinck then adds this gentle critique of Gomarus:

> Initially, the church did not yet clearly understand this, but gradually it became obvious—and was taught as such—that God was in no way obligated to grant heavenly blessedness and eternal life to those who kept his law and thereby did not do

---

28. Muller, "Covenant of Works," 181–82. See also Peter A. Lillback, "Ursinus' Development of the Covenant of Creation: A Debt to Melanchthon or Calvin?," *WTJ* 43, no. 1 (1981): 247–88.

29. Gomarus, *De Foedere Dei*. See also van Asselt, *Federal Theology*, 254–57.

30. Bavinck, *Reformed Dogmatics*, 2:571.

anything other than what they were obligated to do. There is no natural connection here between work and reward.[31]

Though Bavinck identifies Gomarus only in a footnote, he also cites Johannes Cloppenburg, Cocceius, and Witsius, among others, against him on this narrow point, even though each also elaborated Gomarus's broader points of a prelapsarian covenant between God and Adam and a natural knowledge of the moral law written on the hearts of divine image bearers.

Gomarus also makes Witsius's list of "greatest divines" who "have sometimes made mention of" the *pactum salutis*—a list that includes Arminius (with qualification), William Ames, Cloppenburg, Gisbertus Voetius, and John Owen, among others. Admittedly, Gomarus offers us little more than an occasional mention of "this covenant" in his exegetical works, but he does explicitly teach a "covenant between God and Christ" in which the Father promises to "be his God, and the bestower of salvation," and in which Christ "was bound to perform obedience from a principle of perpetual gratitude." It is clear from what little Gomarus does write on this point that he has a working concept of what will be termed the *pactum salutis*, which he develops from an array of texts from both Testaments.[32]

Finally, while Reformed theologians of the era consistently affirmed a continuity of substance across the various administrative forms of the covenant of grace, there was some diversity of emphasis, terminology, and apparently views on the relation of the old (Mosaic) and new administrations. Bullinger had quickly realized that the continuity of substance was a fundamental difference between Reformed theology and Anabaptist teachings in Zurich, and Gomarus emphasized a unity in language that echoed Bullinger. While Calvin and Beza arguably distinguished a bit more sharply between Old and New, they restricted the contrast to a matter of form, not substance. Nevertheless, this formal distinction was strongly framed in terms of law and gospel, which Calvin likely drew from Melanchthon. Beza could even speak of "two covenants."[33] Thus, the old/Mosaic covenant was styled a *foedus legalis*, and the new a *foedus evangelicum*. Junius's strong contrast between the "old, broken *testamentum* of Moses" and "the New, certain one founded upon the merit of Christ" should be read against this background, and the brokenness of the Mosaic covenant should probably be taken as a reference to the weakness of the law to save, owing to fallen humanity's spiritual inability.[34]

---

31. Bavinck, *Reformed Dogmatics*, 2:571.

32. Witsius cites Gomarus on Matt. 3:13; 5:17; Luke 2:21; John 6:38; and cites his disputation *De Merito Christi* (in Gomarus, *Opera*, 1.3:70–72). Witsius, *Economy*, 1:176–77. Gomarus also directs readers to Gen. 17:7; Gal. 3:16; Ps. 45:7; Heb. 1:9. Interestingly, Gomarus interprets Jesus's circumcision and baptism each as "a sign and seal of the covenant between God and Christ."

33. Lee, *Cocceius*, 88, For Melanchthon as background to Calvin and thus Beza, see Richard A. Muller, *Unaccommodated Calvin: Studies in the Foundation of a Theological Tradition*, OSHT (Oxford: Oxford University Press, 2000), 126–27.

34. Lee, *Cocceius*, 52, citing Junius, *De Federe et Testamento Dei in Ecclesia Vetere*, in *Opera*, vol. 1, cols. 25–26.

Gomarus also adopted the law-gospel distinction and the corresponding two-covenant framework of a *foedus legalis* and a *foedus evangelicum* in his comments on Hebrews 8. While the two covenants are founded on the same promised blessing and involve the same moral law (albeit in different ways), they differ in terms of the condition: the *foedus legalis* offers eternal communion with God on the condition of works, whereas the *foedus evangelicum* offers the same on the condition of Christ's merits. That said, the Mosaic administration is not just a *foedus operum*; it also presents Christ and the better promises of the new covenant—namely, Calvin's *duplex gratia* of justification and sanctification. As such, the gospel was preached to the people of Israel through the old covenant under the various types and shadows of its worship, and the one who believed was saved by grace under the *foedus evangelicum*.[35]

Behind the two-covenant framework, then, were the two (theoretical) ways one could be justified before God: either by works or by faith.[36] The former properly belongs to the *foedus operum* and the latter to the *foedus gratia*. Gomarus was as clear as Calvin that no sinner can attain justification by works of the law and that there is therefore no possibility of salvation under either the *foedus operum* or the Mosaic covenant as a *foedus legalis* strictly considered. Even though the *foedus legalis* embodies the condition of works, the elect were still justified under this administration through faith in the promises of the coming *foedus evangelicum*, and in this sense the Mosaic covenant can also be considered a promissory administration of the *foedus gratia*. With the arrival of the substance of the *foedus evangelicum* in Christ, the *foedus legalis*, with its ceremonial types and shadows, was abrogated.

Space does not permit similar discussions on the covenant teachings of Lucas Trelcatius Sr., Lucas Trelcatius Jr., Henricus Nerdenus, Sibrandus Lubbertus, or Jacob Ravensperger. Nor have I touched on the significant positive influence of William Ames or the largely negative influences of Remonstrant and Socinian writers. This brief review of Junius and Gomarus is sufficient, however, to demonstrate that although the material was perhaps widely scattered and unformed, covenant theology was clearly in the DNA of Dutch Reformed theology from the inception of this distinguished strand of the Reformed tradition.

High Dutch Covenant Theology

Covenant theology blossomed in the seventeenth century as the *Nadere Reformatie* gained energy in the Netherlands, especially under the influence of Gomarus's student Gisbertus Voetius (1589–1676). Voetius exemplified an Ames-like combination of scholastic rigor, Reformed orthodoxy, and practical piety and was the great Reformed

35. Lee, *Cocceius*, 90–91.
36. John Calvin, *Institutes of the Christian Religion*, ed. John T. McNeill, trans. Ford Lewis Battles, LCC 20–21 (Philadelphia: Westminster, 1960), 3.11.2.

systematician of seventeenth-century Dutch Reformed theology. Nevertheless, Cocceius attracts far more attention on what became the controversial topic of covenant theology.

Berkhof notes that Cocceius

> is often mistakenly called "the father of federal theology," and Johannes Cloppenburg (1592–1652) his "forerunner." The real distinction of Cocceius lies, at least partly, in the fact that he sought to substitute for the usual scholastic method of studying theology, which was rather common in his day, what he considered a more Scriptural method.[37]

This carefully worded assessment hints at several common yet misleading characterizations of Cocceius's contributions to covenant theology.

Most glaringly, "Covenant theology is not the brainchild of Cocceius," as Bavinck bluntly puts it. "Long before Cloppenburg or Cocceius," he continues, "the doctrine of the covenants was native to Reformed theology."[38] While Zwingli stressed the unity of the Old and New Testaments in his polemic with the Anabaptists, subsequent Reformed theologians from Bullinger on significantly developed this insight. As they did, however, the question of diversity also demanded attention: at first to do justice to the Bible's contrasting of the new with the old (Jer. 31; 2 Cor. 3; Heb. 8; et al.) but then also to combat the neonomian thrust of Socinian soteriology, which was making inroads in the Netherlands by 1610.[39]

By this time, Dutch Reformed theology had developed a robust covenant teaching that included a standard discussion of terms (בְּרִית, διαθήκη, *foedus*, *pactum*, *testamentum*, etc.); a distinction between one eternal substance and the diversity of forms (or dispensations); the distinct concepts, at least materially, of a *pactum salutis*, *foedus operum*, and *foedus gratia*; a distinction between *foedus legalis* and *foedus evangelicum*; a notion of historical progression both in revelation and in things; and even a sense of multilayered complexity in relating the law-gospel distinction to the principles of works and grace in the Old Testament. Although a diversity of terms and views on many questions existed, much of the exegetical underpinning and systematic framework and most of the content of a distinct theological locus was already in place by the time Cloppenburg and Cocceius applied their considerable learning to that task.

Cloppenburg

Johannes Cloppenburg's contributions should not be reduced to mere prelude. He was a student of Gomarus, briefly a colleague, and he formed a lifelong friendship with

---

37. Berkhof, *Systematic Theology*, 212.
38. Bavinck, *Reformed Dogmatics*, 3:209–10.
39. See Earl Morse Wilbur, *A History of Unitarianism*, vol. 1, *Socinianism and Its Antecedents* (Cambridge, MA: Beacon, 1945), 573–87; Andrew Cooper Fix, *Prophecy and Reason: The Dutch Collegiants in the Early Enlightenment* (1990; repr., Princeton, NJ: Princeton University Press, 2016), 135–61.

Voetius while at Heusden around the time of Dort.[40] Cloppenburg also, however, served with Cocceius at Franeker for seven years (1643–1650) and is one of the few men highly commended by Cocceius.[41] Dutch theologians from Witsius to Bavinck cite him favorably, including his contributions to the development of the *pactum salutis*, covenant of works, and covenant of grace. Bavinck also, however, links Cloppenburg and Cocceius in their method and criticizes the "basic change" their approach produced.[42]

Yet Cloppenburg's covenant theology mostly follows what were already well-worn paths. His *Disputationes de Foedere Dei et Testamento Veteri et Novo* consists of eleven disputations mostly on the standard body of questions. In it he teaches a prelapsarian covenant of works that promised eternal life on condition of perfect obedience to God's law. Adam's failure to satisfy this condition resulted in "the annulment of the old covenant of works" and the promise of a new covenant of grace with Jesus Christ as its sponsor, founded on an eternal agreement between the Father and the Son. He maintains the unity of substance (the Old Testament church shares in the same salvation through the same faith in Christ as the New Testament church) and a progression of dispensations (with the New surpassing the antiquated Old in various ways). He then wraps up his disputations on covenant theology with a discussion of the "mediatorial offices" of Christ under the New Testament.[43]

This is, however, the longest organized discussion of the topic to that point in the Dutch tradition (1642–1643), and we can discern in its order the general structure and even place this emerging locus would assume in Reformed systems: (1) the covenant of works follows the creation of Adam and Eve and increasingly frames Reformed hamartiology, especially the point of original sin; (2) the turn to Christology opens with discussions of the covenant of grace and the *pactum salutis* as its ground (though the latter was sometimes introduced after election); and (3) the discussion of the covenant of grace typically includes its substantial unity and various dispensations, usually consisting in a comparison of the Old and New in terms of the law-gospel, promise-fulfillment, and type-substance dynamics of progress. In *Disputationes de Foedere Dei et Testamento Veteri et Novo*, Reformed teaching on the covenant begins to acquire the shape of a new doctrinal locus.[44]

---

40. Van Asselt, *Federal Theology*, 29. Voetius once referred to Cloppenburg as his "*alter ipse.*"

41. Johannes Cocceius, *The Doctrine of the Covenant and Testament of God*, trans. Casey Carmichael, CRT 3 (Grand Rapids, MI: Reformation Heritage Books, 2016), 229; see also van Asselt, *Federal Theology*, 25.

42. See, e.g., Bavinck, *Reformed Dogmatics*, 2:567; 3:210, 213.

43. Johannes Cloppenburg, *Disputationes de Foedere Dei et Testamento Veteri et Novo*, in *Theologica Opera Omnia*, 2 vols. (Amsterdam: Gerardus Borstius, 1684), 1:487–570.

44. Cf. Westminster Confession of Faith and Francis Turretin, *Institutes of Elenctic Theology*, trans. George Musgrave Giger, ed. James T. Dennison Jr., 3 vols. (Phillipsburg, NJ: P&R, 1992–1997). A minority of theologians place the covenant of grace between Christology and soteriology, including Foppe M. Ten Hoor, *Compendium der Gereformeerde Dogmatiek* (Holland, MI: A. Ten Hoor, 1922); William Heyns, *Manual of Reformed Doctrine* (Grand Rapids, MI: Eerdmans, 1926); J. van Genderen and W. H. Velema, *Concise Reformed Dogmatics*, trans. Gerrit Bilkes and Ed M. van der Maas (Phillipsburg, NJ: P&R, 2008), 539–40. See also Anthony A. Hoekema, "The Christian Reformed Church and the Covenant," in *Perspectives on the Christian Reformed Church:*

Cocceius and Voetius

Cloppenburg also, however, developed a distinction between πάρεσις ("passing over") and ἄφεσις ("remission") out of Romans 3:25–26.[45] Both he and Cocceius traced this distinction back to Beza and argued that prior to the New Testament, a full remission of sin was not possible because God's justice had not yet been satisfied, since animal sacrifices were powerless to propitiate for sin. Under the Old Testament, Cocceius explained, the sins of the elect were merely passed over by God, like a creditor who willingly overlooks collecting on a debt without forgiving the debt in full.[46]

Cocceius used the πάρεσις-ἄφεσις distinction in his comparison of the Old and New Testaments. The soteriological point overshadowing this discussion, however, is justification. Although Scripture contrasts the New with the Old and pronounces the latter in some sense abrogated (Heb. 8:13), it also insists that sinners have been and can only be justified by grace and through faith, and it argues the point from the Law (Gen. 15), the Prophets (Hab. 2), and the Writings (Ps. 32). For this reason, the πάρεσις-ἄφεσις distinction, while largely overlooked in Cloppenburg, became a lightning rod of criticism once Cocceius took it up and set it in his elaborate redemptive-historical scheme.[47]

Cocceius structured his covenant theology around a five-stage abrogation or antiquation of the covenant of works. Each abrogation is effected by a corresponding eschatological realization of the covenant of grace in a process that begins with Adam's fall. This gives his covenant theology a decidedly historical cast that many modern writers anachronistically associate with biblical theology.[48] The five successive stages are shown in table 18.1.

For Cocceius, there are just two covenants: one of works and another of grace, though he also has a highly developed *pactum salutis*. The latter covenant displaces the former in a series of advances. Under the covenant of grace, however, there are also two distinct Testaments: the Old Testament with its economy of types and the New with its economy of fulfillment, so to speak.

It is in this context that Cocceius develops his πάρεσις-ἄφεσις distinction. Since both Testaments are economies of the covenant of grace, there is no sense in which the elect under the Old were justified by works: there is just one "perpetual object of justifying and saving faith," he insists, but "differences follow, which happen to faith and the

---

Studies in Its History, Theology, and Ecumenicity, ed. Peter De Klerk and Richard R. De Ridder (Grand Rapids, MI: Baker, 1983), 185–201.

45. Cloppenburg, *Disputationes de Foedere Dei*, in *Opera Omnia*, 1:528–31.

46. Cocceius, *Covenant*, 227–30, 245–47; van Asselt, *Federal Theology*, 28–30, 280–84. Cf. WCF 7.5: "under the law . . . they had full remission of sins."

47. Lee describes this as Cocceius's "most controversial teaching (for both his contemporaries and modern readers)." *Cocceius*, 156.

48. While Cocceius's emphasis on historical progression departs from scholastic approaches of his day, the scholastic structure evident in Cloppenburg is also evident in Cocceius.

faithful by reason of the diversity οἰκονομιῶν, of the economies, and καιρῶν, of the time periods."[49] So believers prior to the death of Christ

> did not hear the word of the gospel about sins having been expiated and reconciliation having been made. There was a certain darkness that accompanied the time. . . . There was anxiety, desire, and searching for things to be given not to them but to their posterity. . . . For transgression was remaining until Christ took it away and was threatening wrath[—a] . . . terror by which the godly were continually disturbed in this life.[50]

For this reason, "that time was also partly called ἀνοχὴ τοῦ θεοῦ, the tolerance of God, on account of the delay of judgment in which God would . . . condemn sin in Christ." As such, "*forgiveness of sins*, in that time when accusing sin was not yet condemned and it was impossible for the law to condemn it, is called πάρεσις, omission or disregarding, rather than δικαίωσις, justification (Rom 3:25–26)."[51]

Although Cocceius insists that saving faith, ever since the fall, is faith in the mediator of the covenant of grace and that all who have such faith are justified under that covenant, he also insists that the experience of justification differs significantly before and after Christ's death because of the redemptive-historical progress both of the revelation of the gospel and the eschatological realization of the covenant of grace in time. "Christ," he contends, "is *Mediator of a better testament* . . . from which flows the promise of ἀφέσεως, of remission, and of righteousness without accusation of guilt."[52]

Table 18.1 Cocceius's Five-Stage Covenant Theology Structure*

Abrogation of Covenant of Works		Realization of Covenant of Grace	
Abrogation of	1. the promise of life on condition of perfect obedience	*through*	1. Adam's sin
	2. the condemnation		2. faith in the promise of a new covenant
	3. terror and bondage		3. the promulgation of the New Testament under the typology of the Old
	4. the struggle against sin		4. the death of the body
	5. all remaining effects of the covenant of works		5. the resurrection of the body

* Cocceius, *Covenant*, 7–12.

49. Cocceius, *Covenant*, 192.
50. Cocceius, *Covenant*, 192.
51. Cocceius, *Covenant*, 192–93; emphasis original; see also 226–30.
52. Cocceius, *Covenant*, 227. See also Lee, *Cocceius*, 156–65.

Cocceius's πάρεσις-ἄφεσις distinction is intended to display the redemptive-historical significance and necessity of Christ's death; Voetius was unconvinced—and troubled. This distinction (together with Cocceius's lax views on the Sabbath)[53] raised questions about his views on justification, the suretyship of Christ, and even his theological method: "In the summer of 1665 Voetius took up Cocceius's theses regarding ἄφεσις and πάρεσις."[54] In the exchange that followed, both men doubled down, and the Dutch Reformed community was deeply divided into the eighteenth century, though the church managed not to split.

Scripture clearly teaches that justification includes the full remission of sins, Voetians argued, and believers under both Testaments enjoyed this blessing. Any suggestion to the contrary not only undermines the argument for justification by faith from the Old Testament but also appears to open a door to purgatory and a possible appropriation of Roman Catholic soteriology, since believers at that time were not fully forgiven in this life. It also seems to divide Christ's suretyship. In the *pactum salutis*, the Son has agreed from eternity to take the sins of his people on himself and stand as surety on their behalf before divine justice. To suggest that believers under the Old Testament did not have the full benefit of Christ's suretyship implies that he was not, in substance, their surety—that his suretyship was somehow not absolute and strict but complex and variegated.

Cocceians responded to this last point by distinguishing between two kinds of suretyship found in Roman law. A *fideiussor* agrees to pay another's debt but as long as the debt is unpaid, it is still charged against the debtor's account, not the sponsor's; an *expromissor*, however, agrees to pay another's debt, and that debt is immediately charged to the sponsor's account, where it remains until paid in full. Cocceius used this kind of analogy to explain the πάρεσις-ἄφεσις distinction in his *Summa Theologiae*, and Cocceians followed his lead by asserting that Christ is more like a *fideiussor* than an *expromissor*.[55] Voetians disagreed, asserting that Christ's surety is absolute and rejecting the πάρεσις-ἄφεσις distinction.[56]

The structure of Cocceius's covenant theology, van Asselt muses, "must have sounded quite revolutionary in the era of orthodoxy." Though we may "discern an initial impetus" for Cocceius's scheme in Cloppenburg, nothing quite like it appears before or since in Dutch Reformed theology, with the single exception of Franciscus Burmannus (1628–1679).[57]

53. See Cocceius, *Covenant*, 226. The controversy over the Sabbath in Leiden was so heated that the States of Holland banned further debate on the matter in 1659, just before the publication of Cocceius's *Covenant*.

54. Van Asselt, *Federal Theology*, 282. Cocceius responded with *Moreh Nabochim* (1665) and Voetius with *Problemata de Justificatione* (1666–1667).

55. See Cocceius, *Summa Theologiae ex Scripturis Repetita* (Geneva: Sumptibus Samuelis Chouët, 1665), 51§11.

56. See W. J. van Asselt, "Voetius en Coccejus over de Rechtvaardiging," in *De Onbekende Voetius: Voordrachten Wetenschappelijk Symposium 1989*, ed. J. van Oort et al. (Kampen: Kok, 1989), 32–47; van Asselt, "*Expromissio* or *Fideiussio*? A Seventeenth-Century Theological Debate between Voetians and Cocceians about the Nature of Christ's Suretyship in Salvation History," *MJT* 14 (2003): 37–57.

57. Van Asselt, *Federal Theology*, 275, 281; cf. Johannes à Marck's regret over his grandfather's contribution to this distinction in the preface of Cloppenburg's *Opera Omnia*, vol. 1, fourth page of preface (pages unnumbered).

Cocceians did not, however, just fade away. Cocceius's emphasis on historical progress in his theological method influenced the subsequent development of this locus.
While some Cocceians—Abraham Heidanus, Burmannus, Christophorus Wittichius,
Henricus Groenewegen—embraced Cartesian philosophy to one degree or another,
others—Campegius Vitringa Sr., Friedrich Adolph Lampe—pursued a more pietistic
path that permitted some rapprochement with piety-minded Voetians. Still, nearly all
the most prominent orthodox theologians of the continuing *Nadere Reformatie* belong
to the Voetian side: Petrus van Mastricht, Herman Witsius, Wilhelmus à Brakel, and
Johannes à Marck, to name a few.

Witsius and Brakel

Remarkably, the erudite and irenic minister and scholar Herman Witsius (1636–1708)
produced what has arguably become the standard treatment of covenant theology in
Reformed theology—certainly, at least, in the Dutch tradition—in an attempt to bring
Voetians and Cocceians closer together. His monumental *The Economy of the Covenants
between God and Man* embodies the classic structure of the topic as it had emerged prior
to the Cocceian controversy and is filled with Voetian theology—if understood as the
continuing development of Reformed orthodoxy by *Nadere Reformatie* theologians. It is
also marked, however, by certain Cocceian accents, emphases, and caveats.

In standard form, Witsius opens his book with a careful discussion of covenant
terminology and divine covenants with humans in general—which he argues are always
unilateral in initiative and bilateral in administration—before launching into a discussion of the covenant of works (book 1). He then turns to the covenant of grace, grounding it in the eternal *pactum salutis* (book 2). Next, he affirms the substantial unity of
the covenant of grace, which he further elucidates by working through the *ordo salutis*
(book 3), and finally, he distinguishes this from the diversity of dispensations throughout redemptive history (book 4).

Reflecting the impact of the controversy with Cocceians, as well as those with Remonstrants and Socinians, Witsius devotes the bulk of his discussion of the *pactum
salutis* to the suretyship and satisfaction of Christ. Much to the chagrin of Cocceians,
he rejects the πάρεσις-ἄφεσις distinction. While using carefully qualified *fideiussor*
language in places,[58] Witsius also insists that Christ's suretyship secures the blessings of
"justification, spiritual peace, adoption, and, in a word, all the particulars" of the *ordo
salutis* "promised by the covenant of grace." This is true for all the elect who have come
to faith, because "the Old Testament is nothing but the covenant of grace, as it was
dispensed before Christ came in the flesh." These blessings, he conceded, "are much
more eminent under the New Testament, yet all of them, as to their substance, were

---

58. See his reply to James Altingius: Witsius, *Economy*, 2:345–47; see also van Asselt, "*Expromissio* or *Fideiussio?*," 50.

conferred even under the Old."[59] Though Witsius apparently gleaned exegetical support for the *pactum salutis* from Cocceius (and Cloppenburg, among others),[60] he adopted a non-Cocceian (or Voetian) position on this hotly contested point about the mode and experience of salvation prior to Christ.

Indeed, there is nothing just like Cocceius's scheme of abrogations in Witsius. He identifies a single "*abrogation* of the Old Testament," dispensing with "those things superadded to the covenant of grace, as shadows, types, and symbols of the Messiah to come."[61] Yet as van Asselt observes, Cocceius's theology is characterized more by the attention he pays to the application of the *ordo salutis* in time across various redemptive-historical economies than the five abrogations as such, and these features are on full display in Witsius from the title of his *magnum opus* to his descriptions of numerous dispensations to his nine-phase transition from the Old Testament ecnomy to the New.[62] Witsius also devotes about a third of his work to the *ordo salutis* "in time" and approximately two-fifths to the diversity of dispensations (pre-Noahic, Noahic, Abrahamic, Mosaic, and new) throughout redemptive history.

The *Nadere Reformatie* development of this locus continued to the end of the century, arguably culminating with the publication of *The Christian's Reasonable Service* by Witsius's good friend and younger colleague, Wilhelmus à Brakel (1635–1711). By this time, covenant theology was approaching two centuries of exegetical and systematic development by an international cast of Reformed scholars, and the expectation of theological literacy and desire for personal holiness reflected in Brakel's work—intended for the education and edification of the laity rather than use in schools—is striking. One example, of curiously modern relevance, should suffice.

The *pactum salutis* asserts an agreement between the Father and the Son in eternity and an appointment of the Son to deadly obedience as the surety of the elect. This raises a challenging question about the unity of the divine being. Brakel confronts it directly: "Since the Father and the Son are one in essence and thus have one will and one objective, how can there possibly be a covenant transaction between the two, as such a transaction requires the mutual involvement of two wills?"[63] To the thinking Dutch layman (or the twentieth-century theologian),[64] the *pactum salutis* might imply tritheism.

Following the lead of others, Brakel distinguishes between the essential unity of the divine will and the distinct mode of each person's manner of willing.[65] "The one

---

59. Witsius, *Economy*, 2:316; see also 1:308, 310–13.

60. Richard A. Muller, "Toward the *Pactum Salutis*: Locating the Origins of a Concept," *MJT* 18 (2007): 11–65.

61. Witsius, *Economy*, 2:378; emphasis original.

62. Witsius, *Economy*, 1:315–17.

63. Wilhelmus à Brakel, *The Christian's Reasonable Service*, trans. Bartel Elshout, ed. Joel R. Beeke, 4 vols. (Grand Rapids, MI: Reformation Heritage Books, 1992–1995), 1:252.

64. See Barth, *Church Dogmatics*, 4.1:65.

65. See, e.g., John Owen's Exercitation 28.13 (1674), in *An Exposition of the Epistle to the Hebrews with Preliminary Exercitations*, ed. W. H. Goold, vol. 2 (Grand Rapids, MI: Baker, 1980), 87–88. See also van Asselt, *Federal Theology*, 219–47; Muller, "Toward the *Pactum Salutis*," 63; Scott R. Swain, "Covenant of Redemption," in *Christian Dogmatics: Reformed Theology for the Church Catholic*, ed. Michael Allen and Scott R. Swain (Grand Rapids, MI: Baker Academic, 2016), 121–22.

divine will can be viewed from a twofold perspective," he reasons. "It is the Father's will to redeem by the agency of the second Person as Surety, and it is the will of the Son to redeem by His own agency as Surety."[66] There is just one divine will, but there is also a manner of willing that corresponds to each divine person's distinct mode of subsistence (*modus subsistendi*) and working (*modus agendi*).

This question is vital to the successful dogmatic formulation of the *pactum salutis*, which Brakel insists is important for Christians "to understand and to make use of . . . continually." To illustrate his point, he offers readers five "practical observations concerning the covenant of redemption." One of them is that "this covenant reveals a love which is unparalleled, exceeding all comprehension. How blessed and what a wonder it is . . . to have been the object of the eternal mutual delight of the Father and the Son to save you!"[67]

Far from illustrating the speculative excesses of a legalistic precisionism, *Nadere Reformatie* theologians found the *pactum salutis*, and indeed the whole locus of covenant theology, to be a window into the unspeakable love of God for the elect in Jesus Christ, and therefore of enormous practical benefit to pilgrims of faith in a fallen world.

Late Dutch Covenant Theology

Such was the advanced state of theological development and refinement of covenant theology under *Nadere Reformatie* divines in the post-Dort era. Yet despite this extraordinary theological achievement, by "about the middle of the eighteenth century," Berkhof laments, "the doctrine of the covenant in the Netherlands had all but passed into oblivion."[68] The *pactum salutis* was already attacked as an innovation by the time Witsius wrote, and Bavinck notes that it was openly "opposed by Deurhof, Wesselius, and others" in the early eighteenth century and eventually "banished from dogmatics altogether."[69]

The covenant of works hardly fared better. Some Dutch divines continued to bring the covenant of works forward in their theology—among them, anti-*tolerantie* subscriptionists Nicolaus Holtius (1693–1773) and Alexander Comrie (1706–1774), who are often considered the last *Nadere Reformatie* theologians. It may not have been as neglected among the *Afscheiding* churches in the Netherlands (Christelijke Gereformeerde Kerken, 1837) and the United States (Christian Reformed Church, 1857), but "even such conservative scholars as Doedes and Van Oosterzee," Berkhof notes, "rejected it."[70]

---

66. Brakel, *Reasonable Service*, 1:252.
67. Brakel, *Reasonable Service*, 1:263.
68. Berkhof, *Systematic Theology*, 212.
69. Bavinck, *Reformed Dogmatics*, 2:213.
70. I.e., Utrecht professors Jacob Isaak Doedes (1817–1897) and Jan Jacob van Oosterzee (1817–1882). Berkhof, *Systematic Theology*, 212. The *Afscheiding* (Secession) of 1834 was a split within the Dutch Reformed Church sparked by Hendrik de Cock's objections to perceived theological liberalism within the state church and fueled by the church's attempt to quiet his protests and restrain his followers. These events led to a secession of churches from the state church and the founding of the Christelijke Gereformeerde Kerken in 1837.

Despite this general neglect, targeted criticism, and partial rejection of the orthodox doctrine, a broadly covenantal view of redemptive history continued to shape Reformed thought, especially in its more confessional strands. This, in turn, also distinguished a distinctly Reformed conception of redemptive history from more rationalistic, actualistic, and evolutionary outlooks.[71] Reformed theology cannot do without covenant theology without losing its identity, and insofar as the Reformed tradition is a theologically determined tradition, it must find its identity at least partly in covenant theology.

Retrieval of Orthodoxy

"In the Netherlands," Berkhof could write by 1938, "there has been a revival of interest in federal theology."[72] He attributes this to the influence of Abraham Kuyper (1837–1920) and Herman Bavinck (1854–1921). This revival of interest, though perhaps instigated among the *Doleantie* (those who sought to reform the Dutch Reformed Church but finally separated from it), was evident on both sides of the Atlantic.[73] In North America, theologians working (and sometimes walking) out of the Christian Reformed Church, such as Geerhardus Vos, Foppe Ten Hoor, William Heyns, Herman Hoeksema, and Louis Berkhof, among others, all prominently featured covenant theology in their theology.

The outstanding achievement of this revival for covenant theology was the retrieval of the doctrinal formulation achieved in seventeenth-century orthodoxy. This is clearly seen in Bavinck's magisterial *Reformed Dogmatics*, which retraces the contours of the old form, recovering its structure, placement, and content. Although willing to criticize the early formation of the *pactum salutis* as "defective," Bavinck consistently defends orthodox formulas, corrects misleading historiographies of its origin and development, makes extensive use of sixteenth- and especially seventeenth-century sources, and even takes the Voetian side in the Cocceian controversy. Breaking with many of his contemporaries (and channeling *Nadere Reformatie* divines), Bavinck contends that "for dogmatics as well as for the practice of the Christian life, the doctrine of the covenant is of the greatest importance."[74]

Differences and Divisions

Though Bavinck, Vos, Berkhof, and others were largely engaged in the task of retrieving and restating the covenant theology of Late Orthodoxy, differences emerged over various

---

71. For this typology, see van Asselt, *Federal Theology*, 295–96.

72. Berkhof, *Systematic Theology*, 213.

73. The *Doleantie* ("Sorrowful"), who included Kuyper and Bavinck, grieved the perceived theological liberalism permeating the Dutch Reformed Church and seceded from that church in 1886, eventually uniting with the *Afscheiding* church, Christelijke Gereformeerde Kerken, in 1892.

74. Bavinck, *Reformed Dogmatics*, 3:212. The same point could be illustrated from Vos (1862–1949) or Berkhof (1873–1957); cf. G. C. Berkouwer (1903–1996), who accepts Barth's critique of covenant theology, and Hendrikus Berkhof (1914–1995), who finds little use for the doctrine.

Kuyperian emphases, sometimes splitting Reformed churches. In North America, for example, Herman Hoeksema (1886–1965) took strong exception to Kuyperian notions of common grace, rejected the covenant of works, and advanced an unconditional view of the covenant of grace. He and a few like-minded ministers were deposed and then left the Christian Reformed Church to form the Protestant Reformed Churches in 1924, which embodies these distinctive views while continuing to confess the Three Forms of Unity.

In the Netherlands, Kuyper's emphasis on common grace and eternal justification and perhaps especially his suggestion that infants are baptized on the presumption of regeneration proved at least as controversial as in North America, even though, among those theologians discussed above, Junius, Cloppenburg, Voetius, and Witsius each affirmed some notion of the presumptive regeneration of covenant children. They differed over when regeneration is assumed to occur, and most Reformed theologians who permitted such an assumption objectively grounded it in the promise of God and the infant's membership in the (external) covenant of grace. Kuyper did not, though later Kuyperians embraced a modified view of the matter.[75]

Both the influential Kampen professor and Liberation leader Klaas Schilder (1890–1952) and the founder of the Netherlands Reformed Congregations, Gerrit Hendrik Kersten (1882–1948), objected to Kuyper's formulations. Schilder believed the priority of God's word was discredited in Kuyper's view and, in response, advocated a single gracious yet conditional covenant between God and humanity both before and after the fall and stressed the necessity of faith to appropriate its benefits. Kersten, on the other hand, maintained the clear distinction between the covenants of works and grace but viewed the *pactum salutis* as just "the Covenant of Grace from eternity" and strongly criticized Schilder, among others, for drawing "an *essential* difference" between the two.[76]

Conclusion

The Dutch Reformed development of covenant theology through the era of orthodoxy was driven largely by a combination of meticulous *ad fontes* scholarship and scholastic argumentation, as Dutch Reformed theologians tackled common and sometimes ancient philological, exegetical, and theological questions. They did so, thoroughly aware that they belonged to an international Reformed movement, which they often personally embodied. Covenant theology is neither a Dutch innovation nor a reaction to prior developments in Reformed theology. While Dutch divines made substantial contributions to this emerging doctrinal locus and displayed a rich diversity of views, they also operated under a robust confessional commitment to Reformed orthodoxy, which constantly framed the terms of their debates.

---

75. Bavinck, *Reformed Dogmatics*, 56–58; Vos, "Covenant," 65–67; et al.
76. G. H. Kersten, *Reformed Dogmatics*, 2 vols. (Grand Rapids, MI: Netherlands Reformed Book and Publishing Committee, 1980), 1:144, 234–35.

Covenant theology, however, is largely a post- and to some degree subconfessional development in the Dutch tradition. The Three Forms of Unity assume and employ covenant logic, they impinge on covenant theology in profound ways, and they even embody an early stage of its development, but they do not contain a distinct doctrinal locus or the kind of explicit formulations one finds in the Westminster Standards (1647) or the Helvetic Consensus (1675). This obviously did not hinder the Dutch Reformed from achieving a doctrinal formulation of this locus as impressive as any other branch of the Reformed tradition; neither has it diminished the role this doctrine plays in Dutch Reformed identity. Although covenant theology has been a source of much debate and division among the Dutch Reformed churches since its late nineteenth-century retrieval, interest in the orthodox achievement remains strong, and thus the task of retrieval and reassessment continues.

19

Covenant Theology in Barth
and the Torrances

Mark I. McDowell

The theology of Karl Barth has played a considerable role in recent reception of and reflection on covenant theology. Barth's influence, in terms of both his material exposition of the covenant and his critical assessment of covenant theology, has shaped the discussion in significant ways. As one of the commanding theological figures of Protestant theology in the twentieth century, Barth captured the theological attention and imagination of many in Europe. One of these figures was H. R. Mackintosh, who taught systematic theology at New College, Edinburgh.[1] One of Mackintosh's students, Thomas Forsyth Torrance, was encouraged to pursue further studies, and with the help of a fellowship, Torrance made arrangements to go to Basel to study under Karl Barth. Torrance would become the primary channel through which Barth's theology would reach the English-speaking world. Torrance's theology bears many of the hallmarks found in the work of Barth and, along with his younger brother James B. Torrance, extends Barth's theological ideas and commitments in further directions. These three theologians operate out of a Reformed theological position and, taken together, form the most serious challenge to an account of covenant theology as it is articulated by the federal divines and taught in the post-Reformation tradition.

Barth's account of the covenant differs in form and structure from that seen in the work of both T. F. and J. B. Torrance. His teaching on the covenant is so expansive that

---

1. Not incidentally, Mackintosh would spend time in Germany under the dynamic and deeply influential teaching of Wilhelm Herrmann, a professor who also happened to leave a tremendous theological impact on another student, Karl Barth.

it can be found throughout *Church Dogmatics*.[2] The doctrine itself was so central to his thinking that he had contemplated giving volume 4 of *Church Dogmatics* the title *The Doctrine of the Covenant*, but he decided to keep the traditional title, *The Doctrine of Reconciliation*.[3] Neither T. F. nor J. B. Torrance offer anything like a systematic theology of the covenant. What we find are recurring reflections on the covenant adjoined to a persistent critique of federal theology. J. B. Torrance, in particular, devotes considerable space to pointing out what he considers to be the flawed trajectory of this stream of Reformed theology as well as its many dogmatic deficiencies. Given the size, scope, and substance of Barth's elaboration of the covenant, his engagement with federal theology's handling of the covenant, and his influence on the Torrances, we proceed by giving immediate attention to how Barth expounds the covenant and then move to his engagement with federal theology. This is then followed by an analysis and assessment of the positions of T. F. and J. B. Torrance, respectively, looking at their dependence on Barth but also the course their own concerns take.

Karl Barth and the Covenant

John Webster has said that "Barth's theology was unified around a two-fold concern: for God and humanity, agents in covenant, bound together in the mutuality of grace and gratitude."[4] Barth's is a theology that seeks to explore what it means to say that "God is with us." The scope and range of material dedicated to unfolding this central organizing theme is far too broad to give a comprehensive evaluation here, so our attention in this section looks briefly at four theological loci in which the idea of covenant plays a considerable role. The decision for doing so is because Barth's teaching on the covenant cannot be understood as a freestanding concept in isolation from other coordinating dogmatic loci but only as it is situated in its broader theological context. Taking this approach helps shed light on how Barth understands the covenant as well as why he chooses to depart from some of the key teachings on the covenant as evidenced in federal theology. First, then, we turn our attention to Barth's understanding of the covenant as it arises from his doctrine of God.

Covenant and God

As is the case with many aspects of Barth's theology, one discovers that it is stamped with remarkable innovation. One of the enduring convictions of Barth's theology is his deep concern that God not be co-opted for our own purposes and agendas. He describes this later in life as the "nostrification" of God, but the idea is evident from the very beginning

---

2. Karl Barth, *Church Dogmatics*, ed. G. W. Bromiley and T. F. Torrance (Edinburgh: T&T Clark, 1956–1975).
3. Eberhard Busch, *Karl Barth: His Life from Letters and Autobiographical Texts*, trans. John Bowden (Grand Rapids, MI: Eerdmans, 1994), 377.
4. John Webster, "Introduction," in *Cambridge Companion to Karl Barth*, ed. John Webster (Cambridge: Cambridge University Press, 2000), 14.

of his career.[5] In his commentary on Romans, he states that "God is God," a tautological claim that prohibits any explanation of God that is not provided by God.[6] In *Church Dogmatics* 2.1, Barth extends this line of thought by defining "God is" as "God is who He is in His works."[7]

Barth wants to draw together as closely as possible the being of God and the acts of God. In other words, by positively affirming that the being of God is God's being in act, how God reveals himself is identical with who God is.[8] This means that God's eternal existence as God (*ad intra*) is disclosed in God's external existence as God to us (*ad extra*).

The identity of God is understood and only understood through the activity of God. This activity of God's self-disclosure to us is funneled with concrete particularity in the person of Jesus Christ. "What God is as God . . . is something which we shall encounter either at the place where God deals with us as Lord and Savior, or not at all."[9] In the person of Jesus Christ, we encounter God as God truly is. Barth strongly resists any theology that constructs its understanding of the being of God independent of the person of Jesus Christ, because he worries that such a theology teaches a "hidden God," a *Deus absconditus*, who elects with an "inscrutable decree," a *decretum absolutum*. As one might imagine, this point factors in a crucial way in his doctrine of election, which we will look at shortly. Barth's point here is to secure the claim that Christ discloses the identity of God.

God is a revealing God who reveals himself wholly in the person of Jesus Christ. Christ reveals God's purpose to draw us into covenant with God. The phrase "God is" enlarges to include the teaching that "God is He who, without having to do so, seeks and creates fellowship between Himself and us."[10] Significantly, when Barth describes God's activity of seeking and creating fellowship between himself and us, he insists that this movement discloses the character and being of God. God is a covenant-making God, but because God is who he is on the basis of his works, God's covenant-making activity in time reflects God's covenantal character in eternity. In the person of Jesus Christ, we see God's eternal determination to make humanity his covenant partner.[11]

---

5. Karl Barth, *The Christian Life*, trans. Geoffrey Bromiley (Grand Rapids, MI: Eerdmans, 1981), 130.

6. Karl Barth, *Commentary on Romans*, 342. To learn more of how this statement functions in Barth's theology, see Eberhard Busch, "God Is God: The Meaning of a Controversial Formula and the Fundamental Problem of Speaking about God," *Princeton Seminary Bulletin* 7 (1986): 101–13.

7. Barth, *Church Dogmatics*, 2.1:260.

8. The question of how to read Barth properly has been the subject of vigorous debate, much of which concerns Barth's commitment to an actualistic ontology and how this structures and informs his doctrines of the Trinity and Christology in particular. A helpful place to enter this discussion is the set of essays in Michael T. Dempsey, ed., *Trinity and Election in Contemporary Theology* (Grand Rapids, MI: Eerdmans, 2011).

9. Barth, *Church Dogmatics*, 2.1:261.

10. Barth, *Church Dogmatics*, 2.1:273.

11. Bruce McCormack recommends a strong actualistic reading of Barth:

The eternal act of establishing a covenant of grace is an act of Self-determination by means of which God determines to be God, from everlasting to everlasting, in a covenantal relationship with human beings and to be God in no other way. This is not a decision for mere role-play; it is a decision which has ontological significance. What Barth is suggesting is that election is the event in God's life in which he assigns to himself the being he will have for all eternity.

As can be recognized from this brief sketch, Barth's doctrine of the covenant is rooted in the heart of Barth's doctrine of God. God is understood not abstractly but only in light of his act, his work, his divine movement toward us in the person of Jesus Christ. This theme is given further depth as he expounds the doctrine of election.

Covenant and Election

Barth's treatment of election adds to our understanding of his doctrine of covenant. If covenant characterizes God's eternal being in movement to us for the purpose of creating gracious fellowship with us, election is God's eternal decision to enter into this fellowship.

Barth's worry over the ordering and content of the doctrine of election that he finds in Reformed orthodoxy is flagged early in his theological career. In his *Göttingen Dogmatics*, compiled from lectures given in the 1920s, Barth expresses his concern that election, when articulated with a division between the elect and the reprobate, is "the worm in the timbers of Reformed orthodoxy."[12] Orthodoxy, represented in this instance by J. H. Heidegger (and drawn from Heinrich Heppe), claims a category of "fixed men" or "certain people." This kind of decretal theology, Barth posits, commits the Reformed to the same theological errors of their semi-Pelagian opponents, that is, the "old Remonstrants."[13] In effect, the Reformers proceeded by "eliminating the element of the mysterious, the lofty, the majestic, and the free," constraining God to our knowledge and trapping his agency in an ossified fate.[14]

Furthermore, Barth calls the Reformed account a "secular error," by which he means that unless "God's free sovereignty" includes the notion that God is Lord over all humanity in a distinctly gracious way, it is susceptible to the possibility that there remains a sphere of autonomous human agency where God's freedom "does not triumph," where humanity is not determined by God's gracious and loving being.[15]

In his mature account on election, Barth advances his critique with a more finely drawn Christological emphasis. This focus, reaffirming what was presented in his doctrine of God, is now fully centered on Jesus Christ. The most significant outcome of this move is to make sure that the "good news" Christ offers is not only for "fixed men"

"Grace and Being: The Role of God's Gracious Election in Karl Barth's Theological Ontology," in Webster, *Cambridge Companion to Karl Barth*, 98.

12. Karl Barth, *Göttingen Dogmatics: Instruction in the Christian Religion*, trans. Geoffrey Bromiley (Grand Rapids: MI, Eerdmans, 1991), 1:455.

13. In addition to theological abstraction, Barth holds that both parties put forward a teaching that

anthropologizes or psychologizes a thought which strictly makes sense only as a concept of the knowledge of God. It mechanizes a truth which has its basis precisely in the inexhaustible life of God. It isolates an event in time from the event in the divine eternity instead of relating it to it. It stabilizes the divine either-or which is posted for us and which, precisely because it is the divine, inescapable, and serious either-or, must always be thought of as fluid.

Barth, *Göttingen Dogmatics*, 454.

14. Barth, *Göttingen Dogmatics*, 455.

15. Barth, *Göttingen Dogmatics*, 454.

or "certain people" but for all humanity. To achieve this, Barth has to reconfigure the theological content of the doctrine to begin with Jesus Christ and has to orient the outworking of the doctrine "under this name." By doing so, Barth sets forth Christ as "both the electing God and the elected man in One,"[16] which means that Christ is both the subject of election and the object of election.[17]

The "Christological simultaneity" of electing God and elected human in Jesus Christ indicates the distance Barth's doctrine has traveled from that of his Reformed forebears not only in arrangement but also in substance.[18] To say that Christ is the electing God means that "He himself executes the decision in the establishment of the covenant between God and man; that He too, with the Father and the Holy Spirit, is the electing God."[19] By considering Christ as the subject of election, as "the electing God," Barth expands Christ's role to include Christ's active and eternally decisive commitment to be man's covenant partner.[20]

This move includes a clutch of theological implications. First, election is constitutive of who God is.[21] Because election is the eternal activity of Christ to be the covenantal companion of the creature, election functions as an eternal moment in the life of God and as such determines the identity of God. Second, election discloses who God is. Because election is defined with an "irreducible specificity" in and through the person of Jesus Christ, election governs what can be said about God. This is of utmost importance for Barth because he wants to ensure that what we know of God we learn exclusively through Christ. Because Christ eternally elects to be in covenant with humanity, God can be known only as the Lord of the covenant, and never otherwise.[22] In other words, election attempts to safeguard any claim that there exists a different and inscrutable God "behind the back" of Jesus Christ. Third, because Christ eternally self-elects to bind himself to humankind for the sake of covenantal fellowship, God is not bound to the kind of blind decree that Barth sees in the theology of the Reformers or their epigones. Taken together, it might be said that these final two points further emphasize Barth's persistent effort to avoid any account that posits a *Deus absconditus* and a *decretum absolutum*.

---

16. Barth, *Church Dogmatics*, 2.2:3.

17. While Barth explores the idea that Christ is both elect and reprobate under his doctrine of God, it is in his doctrine of reconciliation, in *Church Dogmatics* 4.1, that Barth tries to explain in a more narratively rich way how Christ fulfills the covenant as the Judge and the one judged for us.

18. Tom Greggs, *Barth, Origen, and Universal Salvation: Restoring Particularity* (Oxford: Oxford University Press, 2009), 23.

19. Barth, *Church Dogmatics*, 2.2:105.

20. Barth puts it this way, "We maintain of God that in Himself, in the primal and basic decision in which He wills to be and actually is God, in the mystery of what takes place from and to all eternity within Himself, within His triune being, God is none other than the One who in His Son or Word elects Himself, and in and with Himself elects His people." *Church Dogmatics*, 2.2:76.

21. The pitch of Barth's claim is increased by McCormack to yield the following rendering: "What Barth is suggesting is that election is the event in God's life in which he assigns himself the being he will have for all eternity." "Grace and Being," 35.

22. Barth explains that God cannot be God without the covenant; thus, the "divine electing" is "the eternal electing in which and in virtue of which God does not will to be God, and is not God, apart from those who are His, apart from His people." *Church Dogmatics*, 2.2:77.

As elected human, Christ chooses to be rejected.[23] As the object of election, therefore, Christ stands in the place of sinful humanity and bears their reprobation. Given Barth's insistence that Christ is the electing God and that election is the primal act of God, there is, as Tom Greggs points out, "no room for a prior decision of God to create, or elect and condemn before the decision to elect Jesus Christ."[24] What emerges is an innovative reenvisioning of John Calvin's idea of *mirifica commutatio*, of a wonderful exchange that occurs between God and us: Christ assumes both our rejection and our election. To wit, just as all humanity is elect in Christ, so all humanity is reprobate in Christ.

What are we to make of Barth's account? The picture of the covenant in Barth's theology is decisively shaped by his teaching on election. Election shows us who God is and how God has moved to draw humanity into fellowship with God. Election displays two things in particular: first, it reveals that God is a covenantal God who is for us, and second, it shows how God enacts his covenant with us. Barth's account departs from the Reformed presentation in a number of significant ways. Most obviously, the traditional Reformed account of two peoples, those who are elected to the covenant and those who are rejected from the covenant, is now reconceived Christologically so that all humanity is embraced in the singular covenant of grace. We turn our attention to what the covenant looks like when addressed in the locus of creation.

Covenant and Creation

Under the banner of his broader project to articulate a theology of "God with us," Barth's doctrine of creation not only attempts to explain how this covenantal community is brought into a distinct existence by its Creator but also endeavors to show how this community was sought, formed, and desired by its Creator. God creates a people with whom he will share covenantal fellowship.

The bulk of Barth's teaching on creation in *Church Dogmatics* 3.1 unfolds under two dialectically related claims, the first, "creation as the external basis of the covenant" (treating Gen. 1:1–2:4a),[25] and the second, "the covenant as the internal basis of creation" (treating Gen. 2:4b–25).[26] Barth's point is clear from the beginning: creation and covenant are integrally related, such that the purpose and meaning of creation "is to make possible the history of God's covenant with man."[27] As God's first work, "creation sets the stage for the story of the covenant of grace."[28] This means that creation is directed toward and exists for the covenant, or, as Barth puts it, "The covenant is the goal of creation and the creation the way to the covenant."[29] Creation is the historical sphere

---

23. Cf. Barth, *Church Dogmatics*, 2.2:166, 353.
24. Greggs, *Universal Salvation*, 25.
25. Barth, *Church Dogmatics*, 3.1:94–228.
26. Barth, *Church Dogmatics*, 3.1:228–329.
27. Barth, *Church Dogmatics*, 3.1:42.
28. Barth, *Church Dogmatics*, 3.1:44.
29. Barth, *Church Dogmatics*, 3.1:97.

in which God's covenant is realized, "the theatre and instrument of His acts."[30] In one sense, the covenant is given historical grounding in creation, but in another sense, one might worry that the goodness of creation is found not in the act of creation itself but only with the onset of the formation of the covenant community.[31]

When Barth turns to the second claim of his twofold thesis, covenant as the internal basis of creation, he explains, "The inner basis of the covenant is simply the free love of God, or more precisely the eternal covenant which God has decreed in Himself as the covenant of the Father with His Son as the Lord and Bearer of human nature, and to that extent the Representative of all creation."[32] Leaving aside for the moment the fact that this statement strongly suggests that Barth appears to embrace a position that he will later criticize in volume 4, namely, the covenant of redemption, it is important to see at this stage that Barth is working out the claim that while the doctrine of creation has historical precedence, the doctrine of the covenant has material precedence.[33]

If creation marks the "road to the covenant"[34] and serves as its historical setting, then the content of the covenant has "its beginning, its center, and its culmination in Jesus Christ."[35] The creation of man and woman initiates God's covenantal life with humanity, a covenantal life that prefigures the formation of the people of Israel with whom God would have fellowship and that finds its culmination and fulfillment in the person of Jesus Christ. In Christ, all humanity is drawn into covenantal fellowship with God. The covenantal fellowship that began with two people in the garden expands into a communion with the specific people of Israel and climaxes in a relationship that finds all humanity becoming God's covenantal partners.

Covenant and Reconciliation

As we move into the last stretch of our doctrinal analysis of Barth's depiction of the covenant, we look at what he has to say about this topic in the largest and most mature expression of the *Church Dogmatics*, that is, the doctrine of reconciliation. In the three parts of volume 4, Barth reaches the point in his theological project that deals with what was anticipated from the beginning, namely, the confirmation of the covenant in the person of Jesus Christ. In earlier volumes, Barth had set out to explain the relationship between God and humanity—"God with us"—by way of the covenant. Now, in his doctrine of reconciliation, Barth announces that we have arrived at the heart of the Christian message, which, he explains, is "the covenant fulfilled in the work of reconciliation."[36]

---

30. Barth, *Church Dogmatics*, 3.1:102.

31. Edwin Chr. van Driel makes this criticism in *Incarnation Anyway: Arguments for Supralapsarian Christology* (Oxford: Oxford University Press, 2008), 80–81. Andrew K. Gabriel responds to similar criticisms in *Barth's Doctrine of Creation: Creation, Nature, Jesus, and the Trinity* (Eugene, OR: Cascade, 2014), 51–60.

32. Barth, *Church Dogmatics*, 3.1:97.

33. Cf. Barth, *Church Dogmatics*, 3.1:232.

34. Barth, *Church Dogmatics*, 3.1:231.

35. Barth, *Church Dogmatics*, 3.1:42.

36. Barth, *Church Dogmatics*, 4.1:3.

While Barth headlines this volume with the claim that "reconciliation is the fulfilment of the covenant between God and man,"[37] his explanation of how the covenant is fulfilled takes on a different complexion from what is typically recognized in most accounts of Reformed theology. For starters, his doctrine of reconciliation, which spans three part volumes, embraces the themes of Christology, hamartiology, soteriology, pneumatology, ecclesiology, and ethics. Furthermore, Barth's revision of the Reformed tradition is further applied through his refusal to "develop a christology independent of a soteriology."[38] Barth forges the firmest connection between Christology and soteriology by coordinating the twofold states of Christ (humiliation and exaltation) and the threefold office of Christ (prophet, priest, and king).

Barth's doctrine of reconciliation is the outworking of his doctrine of the covenant. Reconciliation builds on theological claims already established in his doctrine of God, election, and creation. God eternally determines to be humanity's covenantal companion. Creation is the concrete reality in which God enters into fellowship with his people, first with Adam and Eve and more comprehensively with the children of Israel. God's eternal ordination to be for humanity reaches its most intensely specified and fulfilled character in the incarnation of Jesus Christ.[39]

God in Christ enters our existence, and his history reconciles us to God. The history of Christ includes a set of reconciliatory events, such as his life, death, and resurrection, that brings God's covenant with humanity to fulfillment and, by doing so, completes the purpose of election. The history of reconciliation effected by Christ is so intimately bound to the person of Christ, thus achieving the closest proximity between Christology and soteriology, that Barth can even claim that "Christ is reconciliation."[40] For Barth, then, God's elective determination to be for us is realized in Christ's reconciliatory life to be God with us.

The scope of God's reconciling work is also expanded to include all humanity. This is a move already accomplished in his doctrine of creation, but it is amplified here. Barth continues, "He is the eschatological realization of the will of God for Israel and therefore for the whole race." In his capacity as mediator, Christ "reveals that the particular covenant with Israel was concluded for their sake too, that in that wider circle it also encloses them."[41] How can this be? Barth's radical notion of election, wherein Christ operates as

---

37. Barth, *Church Dogmatics*, 4.1:22.

38. Busch, *Karl Barth*, 378. Robert W. Jenson claims that Barth "carries out what had heretofore been only an unfulfilled postulate of Reformed theology: that Christology and soteriology be identical." "Karl Barth," in *The Modern Theologians: An Introduction to Christian Theology in the Twentieth Century*, ed. David F. Ford, 2nd ed. (Oxford: Blackwell, 2001), 30.

39. Indeed, Barth not only builds on claims already made, but he extends them. God's covenant with the people of Israel is the context from which the Word "became Jewish flesh." *Church Dogmatics*, 4.1:166. Seeking to avoid theological abstraction and Christological reflection untethered to the Old Testament, Barth emphasizes that what must be said must always relate "to a man who is seen to be not a man in general, a neutral man, but the conclusion and sum of the history of God with the people of Israel, the One who fulfils the covenant made by God with this people." *Church Dogmatics*, 4.1:166.

40. Barth, *Church Dogmatics*, 4.1:136.

41. Barth, *Church Dogmatics*, 4.1:35.

both the "electing God" and the "elected human," is unpacked in such a way that the unique and irreducible history of Jesus Christ discloses the fulfillment of the covenant, the concrete enactment of election. In Jesus Christ, God is represented to humanity, and in Jesus Christ, humanity is represented to God.

Barth and Covenant Theology

Having looked at Barth's doctrinal description of the covenant, we turn our attention to how this account runs up against that of federal theology. Barth begins his extended excursus on federal theology early in *Church Dogmatics* 4.1, under the heading "The Covenant as the Presupposition of Reconciliation." He begins by stating, "In the older Reformed Church there was a theology in which the concept of the covenant played so decisive a role that it came to be known as Federal theology."[42] While Barth acknowledges that the concept of the covenant was neither novel nor restricted to any one theologian of this tradition, he singles out Johannes Cocceius as the figure not only in whose work this theology finds its "classical and systematic form"[43] but whom Barth considers to be federal theology's "most perfect . . . [and] ripest and strongest and most impressive" representative.[44]

Barth's next move is to examine the achievements of federal theology. First, federal theology advanced beyond both medieval and Protestant scholasticism an understanding of the "work and Word of God attested in Holy Scripture dynamically and not statically, as an event and not as a system of objective and self-contained truths."[45] Barth sees in Cocceius and Calvin a theology of God with us that is characterized as a dynamic and living history, less constrained by a series of "self-contained" and static loci and more of an account guided by the singular divine movement of God to humanity. Barth claims that the federal theologians "saw excellently that the Bible tells us about an event," but they were not able to follow through with the full implications of this insight.[46] Instead of seeing God's commerce with man as the outflowing of God's eternal determination to be God for us in Christ, their hermeneutic broke up the one dynamic and living history of God and man and fell prey to historicizing the biblical covenants. It did this by isolating discrete biblical moments and then putting forward a biblical history that rendered the "irreducibly particular identity" of Jesus Christ as one more "stage" among others. In short, the followers of Calvin flattened biblical history and made Christ one part of the whole.

Second, Barth approaches Huldrych Zwingli and Heinrich Bullinger on the topic with some initial warmth, but his evaluation becomes less favorable as he considers some

42. Barth, *Church Dogmatics*, 4.1:54.
43. Barth, *Church Dogmatics*, 4.1:54.
44. Barth, *Church Dogmatics*, 4.1:60.
45. Barth, *Church Dogmatics*, 4.1:55.
46. Barth, *Church Dogmatics*, 4.1:56.

of the directions their theology would eventually take. He finds that their teaching of the covenant led into a "blind alley" when they, and other figures from this tradition, held to the "grim doctrine" of double predestination.[47] As we have already observed, Barth resists any statement that divides the history of the covenant into two histories, one that pertains to the elect and the other that pertains to the reprobate. We recall that to do so, according to Barth, is to downgrade the universally gracious character of the covenant enacted and fulfilled in Christ.

In Barth's third point, he fine-tunes his appraisal by asking, "What is the meaning and character of the covenant according to this theology?"[48] He argues that the federal theologians introduced into the Reformed tradition a division of the covenant into a twofold schema, creating "an established dualism" that would eventually be given confessional status in the Westminster Confession. He offers a brief historical sketch to show how this development occurred, beginning with a contrast of theological perspectives.

On the one side, he places the theology of Zwingli, Bullinger, and Calvin, who together hold to a position on the covenant that appears very close to Barth's own position, namely, the covenant described "uniformly, unequivocally and exclusively as the covenant of grace."[49] On the other side is the theology that flows from the mature thought of Philipp Melanchthon and is adopted by Zacharias Ursinus. The influence of the former on the latter led to the introduction of a twofold understanding that consisted of a general covenant (*foedus generale*) and a special covenant (*foedus speciale*). The former is a temporal covenant that was "contracted with man at creation and is therefore known to man by nature. It promises eternal life to those who obey, but threatens eternal punishment to those who disobey."[50] The latter is an eternal covenant, a covenant of grace (*foedus gratiae*), "which is not known by nature. This is the fulfilling of the Law accomplished by Christ, our restoration by His Spirit, the free promise of the gift of eternal life to those who believe in Him."[51]

Barth's concern with the twofold covenantal schema is that it is framed too symmetrically, so that "nature and grace are both on the same historical level, and confront one another as the principles of individual covenants."[52] Barth identifies Amandus Polanus and Johannes Wollebius as theologians who followed the two-covenant path of Ursinus and who adjusted the inherited structure by replacing the covenant of nature with a covenant of works. This theological trajectory found a fuller expression in the theology of Cocceius, which Barth believes continued to trade on a faulty conception of the covenant that was "alien to the Reformers."[53] Barth sees Cocceius's covenant theol-

47. Barth, *Church Dogmatics*, 4.1:58, 57.
48. Barth, *Church Dogmatics*, 4.1:58.
49. Barth, *Church Dogmatics*, 4.1:59.
50. Barth, *Church Dogmatics*, 4.1:59.
51. Barth, *Church Dogmatics*, 4.1:59.
52. Barth, *Church Dogmatics*, 4.1:59.
53. Barth, *Church Dogmatics*, 4.1:61.

ogy troubled by the priority given to the covenant of works, which he believes not only guides and informs the covenant of grace but, because it does so, also subordinates it, making grace dependent on the law.[54] We do well to note that the Torrances assumed this feature in their theology and applied it with vigor.

To condense Barth's critique further, he deems Cocceius's position to betray that of the Reformers because the original form of the covenant in this scheme focuses too much on Adam and Adam's agency in paradise, such that the concrete character of grace that Barth attaches to Jesus Christ is found to be absent. What is put forward instead is a portrayal of the relationship between God and Adam defined as *do ut des* ("I give [to you] that you may give [to me]"), which suggests a more contractually defined arrangement. When the covenant of works serves as the starting point for understanding the covenant of grace, the former orients the latter such that the relationship between God and man is characterized by "the unfortunate preoccupation of man with himself and his works," in which the consideration of rewards for Adam's obedience and of punishments for his disobedience occupies too much room.[55] Framed this way, Barth senses that this federal iteration aggravates in the believer a constant state of insecurity and anxiety about where one stands in relation to God.

The fourth concern Barth flags relates to the covenant of redemption. This piece of federal teaching presents the notion that an eternal intra-Trinitarian agreement was reached between the Father and the Son pertaining to the salvation of the elect and the enacting of the covenant of grace, otherwise known as the *pactum salutis*.[56] Barth rehearses a familiar refrain in his criticism of this aspect of federal theology. He states that its proponents failed to engage in a "loyal hearing of the Gospel and a strict looking to Jesus Christ as the full and final revelation of the being of God."[57] Close to the core of Barth's complaint is his suspicion that this theology is parsed with inadequate reference to Jesus Christ. He objects that because God's gracious being in Christ is not allowed to orient God's redemptive dealings with humanity, this account ends up veering dangerously close to portraying God in an indeterminate way. This has the effect of suggesting that the God who redeems can be defined in terms other than those governed by the self-revelation of Jesus Christ. In other words, we are back to his concern about a theology of God defined in abstraction.

Barth protests that the *pactum salutis* suggests that God's righteousness and mercy "are secretly and at bottom two separate things," such that behind the covenant of grace,

---

54. Barth, *Church Dogmatics*, 4.1:62.

55. Barth, *Church Dogmatics*, 4.1:63.

56. For an in-depth examination of the theological provenance and pedigree of the *pactum salutis*, see J. Mark Beach, "The Doctrine of the *Pactum Salutis* in the Covenant Theology of Herman Witsius," *MJT* 13 (2002): 101–42; J. V. Fesko, *The Covenant of Redemption: Origins, Development, and Reception*, RHT 35 (Göttingen: Vandenhoeck & Ruprecht, 2016); Fesko, *The Trinity and the Covenant of Redemption* (Fearn, Ross-shire, Scotland: Mentor, 2016); Richard A. Muller, "Toward the *Pactum Salutis*: Locating the Origins of a Concept," *MJT* 18 (2007): 11–65.

57. Barth, *Church Dogmatics*, 4.1:65.

there is "some inner depth" to the being of God that may have seen God acting differently, which is to question the claim that God is absolutely and decisively for us.[58] As has already been shown, Barth refuses to loosen the connection between who God is and what God does. On this claim, then, Barth judges Cocceius's conception of the *pactum salutis* a failure because it does not sufficiently coordinate the plan of redemption and the being of God.

The second issue Barth has with the covenant of redemption concerns the consequences it has on the doctrine of the Trinity. Barth argues that it portrays the relationship between the Father and the Son as a "mythology," depicting two eternal yet discrete agents who broker a legal contract for the purpose of securing the salvation of the elect. Barth asks, "Can we really think of the first and second persons of the triune Godhead as two divine subjects and therefore as two legal subjects who can have dealings and enter into obligations with one another?"[59]

Barth is right to worry about this doctrine if it really does describe two, or possibly three, distinct wills in the Godhead. If so, then the possibility arises that the will of the Son could possibly contest with the will of the Father and vice versa. Barth is also surely correct to see that this reading would end up undermining and disordering the doctrine of divine simplicity. And while questions remain about the historical accuracy of Barth's interpretation of Cocceius and other theologians from this era who espouse this teaching,[60] we have to address the theological substance of his censure of them. We have to find out, in other words, if there is any cogency to Barth's claim that the *pactum salutis* rests on faulty Trinitarian theology. The answer is well beyond the scope of this chapter, but one of Barth's keenest interpreters, John Webster, points us in the right direction:

> There is no abstract divine will working behind the covenant of redemption, despite Barth's worries on that score, because the pact between the Father and Son repeats their eternal relations and personal properties. So the covenant of redemption is not, as Barth feared, a point at which some kind of amorphous deity takes shape. No, it derives from the antecedent identities of the triune persons and accords with the eternal order of God's own life.[61]

Before we leave the topic, we do well to look at one more aspect of Barth's criticism of the *pactum salutis*. The covenant of redemption attempts to give dogmatic expression to the eternal purpose of God for the elect as it arises out of the eternal life of God. The

58. Barth, *Church Dogmatics*, 4.1:65.

59. Barth, *Church Dogmatics*, 4.1:65.

60. For instance, Willem J. van Asselt argues that Barth has overlooked the role of the Holy Spirit in Cocceius's account, which attempts to emphasize God's friendship (*amicitia*) with humanity. See *The Federal Theology of Johannes Cocceius (1603–1669)*, SHCT 100 (Leiden: Brill, 2001). Also helpful on this point is Rinse H. Reeling Brouwer, *Karl Barth and Post-Reformation Orthodoxy*, BSS (Farnham, UK: Ashgate, 2015).

61. John Webster, "God's Perfect Life," lecture 2 of *Perfection and Presence: God with Us, according to the Christian Confession*, inaugural Kantzer Lectures (Carl F. H. Henry Center for Theological Understanding, Trinity Evangelical Divinity School, September 12, 2007), henrycenter.tiu.edu/resource/gods-perfect-life/.

theological purpose of the *pactum* strives to express what is found in Scripture. As it does so, it follows the instruction of revelation and tries to elucidate in a conceptual idiom the analogy of an eternal arrangement between the Father and the Son. The resources that the doctrine depends on as it strains to give a clear voice to this teaching include an analogy of the covenant that is closely governed and strictly shaped by Scripture but is also assisted by careful theological reasoning.[62] Scripture warrants this doctrine, but the distinction between Creator and creature chastens it.

A piece of later Protestant theology offers help here. Reformed orthodox theologians articulated the distinction between Creator and creature by way of the distinction between ectypal theology (humans' finite knowledge of God) and archetypal theology (God's infinite knowledge of himself).[63] The import of this distinction reminds us that our own theology remains in the sphere of the former, and while it reflects and represents the latter, it has a limited and restricted capacity. As Scripture speaks of the loving and personal ways in which the Father and the Son arrange and order our redemption, we must be careful that our ectypal theology does not transgress God's archetypal theology. In terms of theological reasoning, the analogy keeps us from pressing the logic of an eternal agreement between the Father and the Son too far, allowing it to drift free of Scripture and untethered from Trinitarian teaching. Perhaps Barth's protest against this doctrine would have been more restrained had his reading of the Calvinist divines been more attuned to their commitment to a sober analogical description that both acknowledges the limits of human reason and upholds the eternally rich relations of the inner-Trinitarian life.

In sum, the idea of the covenant is central to Barth's theology. It is his way of speaking of God's relationship with humanity, of God with us. When Barth deploys this doctrine, it can be said that it sits so centrally that it manages to unify all his theology. Yet as he expounds the covenant, it becomes clear that his rendering is drawn so differently from that of his federal interlocutors that one finds it difficult to position it alongside that of Reformed orthodoxy. His reading of the Reformed divines, while deep and appreciative at turns, ends up as a sharp challenge that is mistaken at many points. He finds that the two-covenant schema of federalism is set too symmetrically, which leads to it being articulated too anthropologically. Barth senses that Adam gets too much attention in the federal reading of the covenant of works. What ought to have caught attention, especially in the section on creation and covenant, is the conspicuous absence of Adam in Barth's reading. By removing the covenant of works, Barth's Christology appears to have absorbed the role traditionally occupied by Adam. This involves a number of serious consequences. For one, it elides central teachings of Scripture.

62. A fine treatment that explores both the biblical depth and dogmatic pedigree of this doctrine is Scott R. Swain, "Covenant of Redemption," in *Christian Dogmatics: Reformed Theology for the Church Catholic*, ed. Michael Allen and Scott R. Swain (Grand Rapids, MI: Baker Academic, 2016), 107–25.

63. See Willem J. van Asselt, "The Fundamental Meaning of Theology: Archetypal and Ectypal Theology in Seventeenth-Century Reformed Thought," *WTJ* 64, no. 2 (2002): 319–35.

Genesis and key passages in Romans 5 and 1 Corinthians 15, among others, lose their explanatory power when Adam falls from view. Consequently, as Adam is removed from Barth's account, so is the significance of what was lost in Adam and what was gained in Christ. What we find in Barth is a failure to appreciate the character and presence of a broader definition of grace than that which is merely tied to redemption. This restricted definition of grace sees Barth out of step with his Reformed predecessors on the matter. As Richard Muller explains,

> There was not only considerable agreement among Reformed theologians in the seventeenth century concerning the identity of the prelapsarian relationship between God and Adam as a covenant, virtually all of the Reformed theologians of the era recognized, albeit in varying degrees, that there could be no relationship between God and the finite, mutable creatures apart from grace.[64]

By excluding this aspect of Reformed theology, Barth gives himself the unfortunate (and wrongheaded) task of having to reconcile the God of the covenant of works with the God of the covenant of grace. The result, as we have seen, is to flatten out both covenants into a single covenant of grace and with it, somewhat ironically, a less textured portrayal of grace.

The Torrance brothers pick up Barth's charge, and we give it attention below. In fact, as we move into our study of the Torrances, we hear many theological resonances of Barth echo in their work. We also see how Barth's theology of the covenant and some of his criticisms of federal theology shape their own thinking on the topic, even though they move in different directions.

T. F. Torrance and Covenant Theology

What follows is an attempt to detail some of the key doctrinal commitments shared by the Torrance brothers that are inherited from Barth and make an impact on their exposition of covenant theology. This section looks at the pastoral concerns they have about covenant theology in a federal rendering; outlines T. F. Torrance's doctrine of God, out of which flows his strong reservations about two-covenant theology; and finally addresses some of the theological impressions that J. B. Torrance offers on the topic.

Not only did T. F. Torrance undertake doctoral studies under the supervision of Karl Barth, and introduce English readers to Barth's *Church Dogmatics* (alongside Geoffrey Bromiley), but later in life, Torrance acknowledged that Barth wanted him to be his successor at Basel and mentioned that one of his regrets in life was not accepting the in-

---

64. Richard A. Muller, *After Calvin: Studies in the Development of a Theological Tradition*, OSHT (New York: Oxford University Press, 2003), 183. Mark Jones and Joel Beeke demonstrate the presence of this notion in the works of Puritans like Anthony Burgess, William Ames, and Francis Roberts, among others. *A Puritan Theology: Doctrine for Life* (Grand Rapids, MI: Reformation Heritage Books, 2012), 229–32. As they note, "For the most part, then, grace was operative in both covenants, but the terms of its operation were different in each" (230).

vitation from the theology faculty to do so.[65] Torrance held Barth in high esteem, stating that he is "perhaps the most powerful theological mind we've had for many centuries" and going on to claim that Barth's "doctrine of God is simply the best thing of its kind"[66] and that he was "the one theological giant of the modern era."[67] Torrance saw Barth as building on and completing the theological achievement of Nicaea and the Reformation. The following quote shows this and indicates the path that Torrance would take:

> Thus if the Nicene Fathers had to lay their main emphasis on the *being* of God in his acts, the Reformers had to lay their main emphasis on the *acts* of God in his being. It belongs to the great merit of Karl Barth that he has brought those two emphases together in a doctrine of the dynamic being of God, particularly evident in his identification of the electing and revealing act of the eternal God with the incarnation of his beloved Son in space and time.[68]

More on this shortly, but for now it is important to point out that not only does the substance of Torrance's theology bear the imprint of Barth's influence, but also the historical framework out of which both Torrances work shows resemblances to Barth's. T. F. and J. B. Torrance participate in an interpretation of the post-Reformation tradition that sees it as a defection from the warmer and more pastoral and exegetically grounded theology of its pioneers. The divergence that is purported to have occurred between Calvin and the subsequent Calvinists consisted in an "imposition of a rigidly logicalized system of belief upon Reformed theology."[69] T. F. Torrance sums up his objections to federal theology as follows: "The change came about with the disastrous place given to the priority of God's eternal decree over the doctrines of the Trinity and the Incarnation."[70] Theodore Beza is identified as the theologian whose thinking struck out a course of theological decline that would eventually be given the structural expression found in William Perkins's charts outlining the order of causes of salvation and confessional expression found in the Westminster Confession and Catechisms.[71]

When we approach the Torrances' work, the first concern that catches our attention relates to the pastoral dimension of their theology. Both T. F. and J. B. Torrance

---

65. T. F. Torrance, "Thomas Torrance," interview in *Roundtable: Conversations with European Theologians*, ed. Michael Bauman (Grand Rapids, MI: Baker, 1990), 113.

66. Torrance, "Thomas Torrance," in *Roundtable*, 112.

67. T. F. Torrance, *God and Rationality* (Edinburgh: T&T Clark, 1997), viii.

68. T. F. Torrance, "The Distinctive Character of the Reformed Tradition," *RefR* 54, no. 1 (2000): 6.

69. T. F. Torrance, "Thomas Torrance Responds," in *The Promise of Trinitarian Theology: Theologians in Dialogue with T. F. Torrance*, ed. Elmer M. Colyer (Lanham, MD: Rowman and Littlefield, 2001), 306.

70. Torrance, "Thomas Torrance Responds," 307.

71. Torrance, "Thomas Torrance Responds," 307. Muller has provided the most detailed rebuttal of Torrance's charge against the Calvinist divines in *After Calvin*; see esp. chaps. 4–5. It is also important to recognize at this juncture that Barth's reading of Beza shows points of discontinuity from that of the Torrances. In *Church Dogmatics* 2.2, Barth notes that the idea of a "central dogma" in Reformed theology in which the doctrine of predestination operated as "a kind of speculative key—a basic tenet from which they could deduce of all other dogmas"—has no "historical justification." He goes on to add, "Not even the famous schema of T. Beza was intended in such a sense." *Church Dogmatics*, 2.2:77–78.

are convinced that the legacy of federal Calvinism afflicted Scottish theology and, by doing so, negatively shaped its church life. The list of complaints include the following:

- damage to the evangelical message for sinners
- the taking of joy out of public worship
- a slavish subscription to a system of belief rather than joyful commitment to Jesus Christ
- a moralizing effect on the life of the church
- a legalistic church climate
- an atmosphere in which a sense of gospel assurance in the hearts of believers was disturbed by anxious introspection instead of confident repose on Christ
- deep splits in the church

J. B. Torrance identifies a moment in Scottish church life when the Lord's Supper transitioned in meaning from a "converting ordinance," which carried with it a strong evangelistic opportunity, to an occasion in which the Supper came to symbolize a "badge of our conversion." This came about, according to J. B. Torrance, through an attack "by the Federal Calvinists of the seventeenth century," whose logic was underwritten by "the doctrine of a double decree and of a limited atonement."[72]

The second implication bound up with this shift is felt in the doctrine of God. T. F. Torrance argues that the theology represented by Perkins and particularly by the Westminster Confession failed to give adequate expression to the doctrine of the Trinity and neglected to give the doctrine primacy in ordering. Beginning with a description of "what God is (*quid sit Deus*)" instead of "what kind of God is he (*qualis sit Deus*), and who God is (*quis sit Deus*)," Westminster theology departed from the "classical theology of the Nicene Church" by substituting the Nicene account of God parsed according to the Trinitarian and personal relations with an account that was given decisive shape "by an abstract idea of the absolute sovereignty of God."[73] This move, Torrance warns, foreshortens the notion of "the Fatherhood, Sonship and Communion" that belong to the essential nature of who God is.[74] It does this by presenting an account of God as "omnipotent creator, lawgiver, and judge of all the earth."[75] Torrance laments that because the Confession did not allow its exposition of the doctrine of the Trinity to guide and inform its account of God as omnipotent Creator and Judge, it ended up detaching divine law from divine love.

---

72. James B. Torrance, "Some Theological Grounds for Admitting Children to the Lord's Table," *RefR* 40 (1987): 203. Torrance continues, "You cannot say to all indiscriminately, 'This is the body of Christ broken for you!' Christ died only for the elect. Therefore the sacrament of communion is only for the elect, and the 'evidence' of election is repentance, conversion. So people were taught to 'examine themselves' for 'evidences' of grace, and such evidences were in effect conditions required for worthy communicating" (203).

73. Thomas F. Torrance, *Scottish Theology: From John Knox to John McLeod Campbell* (Edinburgh: T&T Clark, 1996), 131.

74. Torrance, *Scottish Theology*, 131.

75. Torrance, *Scottish Theology*, 131.

This being so, only the redeemed can relate to God as Father, and only then after all the requirements of God's law are "rigorously satisfied and God himself is thus satisfied."[76] The primacy of the law to grace in Christ emerges as the key way that God is known in relation to us. Furthermore, the effect of relocating the doctrine of the Trinity to a position that follows rather than guides the doctrine of God opened the door to viewing God's relation to the world not through Christ but through the decree and election.[77] Torrance objects to the idea that there can be a decree of predestination that precedes grace or "goes behind the back of Jesus Christ, for that would be to split the act of God into two, and to divide Christ from God."[78]

Following in step with Barth, Torrance sees this problem exemplified in federalism's configuration of a covenant of works alongside the covenant of grace, with the former gravely altering the content of the latter. The introduction of the covenant of works destabilized a biblical understanding of the covenant and "built into the background of Westminster theology a concept of contractual law that gave a forensic and conditional slant even to the presentation of the truths of the gospel."[79] In addition to privileging law over gospel, this two-covenant theology also gave preference to nature over grace and to a notion of God in the abstract over one that highlights the radical particularity of God in Christ.

Torrance was further troubled by the bicovenantal schema because he sensed that it contained a soteriological weakness, namely, that there is a "lack of a mediator between God and humanity" in the covenant of works.[80] The newly minted federal framework held up a bifurcated structure: "a covenant of nature and works contracted by God with Adam and the covenant of grace contracted by God and Christ on behalf of the elect."[81] This means that while God is related providentially to all people through one covenant, God is, nevertheless, also related redemptively to an exclusive group of people through another covenant. The work of Christ is annexed to the covenant of grace, which strips redemption of its universal efficacy and treats the atoning work of Christ "as an organ of God's activity separated from the intrinsic nature and character of God as love."[82] In

---

76. Torrance, *Scottish Theology*, 133.

77. Muller is rather pointed in his assessment of this position: "From a purely historical perspective, no Reformed theology of the sixteenth or seventeenth century understood the decree as one of the *principia theologiae*, none ever set aside the *locus* method, and certainly none ever assumed that any single doctrine could be used as a central dogma or deductive principle." *After Calvin*, 95.

78. T. F. Torrance, "Universalism or Election?," *SJT* 2, no. 3 (1949): 315. In a lecture from 1988, Torrance makes a similar comment and claims his preference for Barth's position, stating that Calvinist theology runs the risk of Nestorianism in its "misguided attempts to construe the 'pre' in 'predestination' in a logical, causal or temporal way, and then to project it back into an absolute decree behind the back of Jesus and thus to introduce a division in the very person of Christ. It is one of Karl Barth's prime contributions to Reformed theology that he has decisively exposed and rejected such a damaging way of thought." "Distinctive Character," 7.

79. Thomas F. Torrance, "From John Knox to John McLeod Campbell: A Reading of Scottish Theology," in *Disruption to Diversity: Edinburgh Divinity, 1846–1996*, ed. David F. Wright and Gary D. Badcock (Edinburgh: T&T Clark, 1996), 10–11.

80. Torrance, "From John Knox," 5.

81. Torrance, "From John Knox," 7.

82. Torrance, *Scottish Theology*, 133.

effect, then, Christ becomes instrumental in the accomplishment of redemption for a few rather than effectively displaying the eternal love of God for all.

Torrance's proposal is highly reminiscent of what Barth does. By closing the gap between the covenant and Christ, the work of Christ and the range of redemption's recipients are no longer restricted. Torrance writes that "Christ is himself the covenant of grace."[83] The purpose of doing so is to guarantee "that there is an unbroken relation in being and act between what God is in himself and what he is toward us in Jesus Christ."[84] Torrance continues: "Jesus Christ is the election of God . . . [and] is wholly identical with God's action."[85] God's love is not demonstrated in a limited fashion and by means of a legal transaction but is understood as a person, and so, "the eternal election of God has become encounter, . . . a living act that enters time and confronts us face to face in Jesus Christ the living Word of God."[86] From the singular nature of God's being and act arises the corollary claim that salvation is also singular in scope. Inversely, one cannot limit the range of atoning redemption without also limiting the range of the being and love of the triune God.[87]

Torrance has fully embraced Barth's insistence that Christology sits at the center of one's theology, but he gives it a different accent. For Torrance, it is the doctrine of the incarnation that does most of the heavy lifting but with the same outcome. Instead of viewing humanity as separated into two distinct people groups, those related to Adam and those related to the new Adam, Torrance sees all humanity "ontologically bound" to Christ.[88] For Barth, the Christocentric nature of the covenant serves the purpose of encompassing all humanity, while for Torrance, the incarnation occupies this role. When Torrance brings Christ's person and work together as closely as he does, the incarnation takes on redemptive significance: "By God taking [fallen humanity] upon himself, he was redeeming. You see, the incarnation is already atoning, and not merely his death. It is an atoning incarnation. The atonement is not separate from the incarnation."[89] Torrance's criticism of federalism's soteriology is that it is limited in its reference to a particular people, is transacted in a legal framework, and is administered extrinsically. With a doctrine of the incarnation fashioned in dialogue with Barth and some strands of patristic theology, Torrance espouses a view of the incarnation that appears to assert a seamless ontological identity between Christ and all humanity.

---

83. Torrance, "From John Knox," 17.

84. Thomas F. Torrance, "The Atonement: The Singularity of Christ and the Finality of the Cross; The Atonement and the Moral Order," in *Universalism and the Doctrine of Hell*, ed. Nigel M. de S. Cameron, *SBET* 5 (Exeter, UK: Paternoster, 1992), 230.

85. Torrance, "Universalism or Election?," 315.

86. Torrance, "Universalism or Election?," 315.

87. Cf. Torrance, "Atonement," 244.

88. Torrance, "Atonement," 244.

89. Torrance, "Thomas Torrance," in *Roundtable*, 116. See, inter alia, Thomas F. Torrance, *Incarnation: The Person and Life of Christ*, ed. Robert T. Walker (Downers Grove, IL: IVP Academic, 2008), 193–96; Torrance, *The Mediation of Christ*, rev. ed. (Edinburgh: T&T Clark, 1992), 64–65.

J. B. Torrance and Covenant Theology

J. B. Torrance approaches the topic from the same historical and theological vantage point of his older brother, but he presses the criticism in a more pointed way. While a deep aversion to federal theology is inscribed onto the work of both Torrances, J. B. Torrance elevates his complaint against this stream of Reformed theology to the highest level. This derives from his claim that much of the Western theological tradition has been plagued by a profound confusion between a covenantal understanding of God's relation to humanity and a contractual understanding.[90] Along with T. F. Torrance, J. B. Torrance locates the pathology of this problem in a departure from authentic Reformation theology articulated early on in Calvin, John Knox, and the Scots Confession. After a period in which this theology is allegedly obscured, the heart of Calvin's thought is later salvaged in Thomas Boston, in Ebenezer and Ralph Erskine, and most emphatically in John McLeod Campbell.[91] But the damage wrought by this decline, J. B. Torrance asserts, has left an extensive and troubling legacy.

As J. B. Torrance recounts the move away from Calvin's thought by his later followers, he adds additional layers to the critique and points out that the early covenant theology that later shaded into one that bore a contractual guise was further aggravated by the attempt "to effect a synthesis between Christianity and culture in the interests of communication."[92] Torrance feels that the federal rendition of the covenant was exacerbated by the pressures exerted by the sociopolitical context of the seventeenth century. This was a time when trade unions, civil rights, settlement of wage disputes, and other factors introduced a vernacular that ended up being appropriated by theologians and ministers to explain how God relates to humanity. By doing so, the covenant was transposed out of its biblical and theological context into one more influenced by commerce and economics. The effect was a drastic modification of its original definition. The emergence of "social contract" theory and the writings of Jean-Jacques Rousseau, John Locke, and others cultivated a meaning of relationships in general that were alien to Scripture. These aggravating factors, in combination with a profound shift in theology, steered the central message of the Reformation far from its original course.

The task of this final section is to examine the complaint of J. B. Torrance, and to do this, we consider a set of prominent themes along two lines. First, we look at how he understands the covenant from the theological side, and second, we look at how he understands the covenant from the anthropological side.

---

90. As with many of J. B. Torrance's complaints, this one finds extensive circulation in his work.

91. J. B. Torrance paints in very broad historical strokes, aligning Calvin with Irenaeus, the "the great Greek Fathers, Athanasius, and the Cappadocian divines," John McLeod Campbell, the Erskine brothers, and Thomas Boston, rather than the "Latin Western Fathers," Augustine, Tertullian, Beza, the Westminster divines, Perkins, John Owen, and Jonathan Edwards. Inter alia, see James B. Torrance, "The Contribution of McLeod Campbell to Scottish Theology," *SJT* 26, no. 3 (1973): 295–311.

92. Torrance, "Covenant or Contract?," 54.

Theological Side of the Covenant

J. B. Torrance sees the determining issue as it relates to the covenant in the register of the doctrine of God. By declaring that "the God of the Bible is a Covenant-God and not a contract god," Torrance not only considers the covenant in terms of God's relation to humanity but also wants to push the discussion of the covenant back into the doctrine of God. As already shown, this approach echoes the theological intentions of Barth and T. F. Torrance. For J. B. Torrance, it means that when God relates to humanity, he does so according to his character, which is covenantal.[93] The shape of the covenant flows from a Trinitarian understanding of God, which emphasizes that "God is Love—he is Father, Son and Holy Spirit in his innermost being—and what he is in his innermost being, he is in all his works and ways,"[94] or as he puts it in another place, "What God is towards us, He is eternally and antecedently in himself."[95] Certainly, Torrance would be hard pressed to find those who subscribe to a federal interpretation objecting to this description. Yet he finds that the introduction of the covenant of works has the effect of altering the complexion of the covenant, which derives from a flawed doctrine of God.

Torrance stresses that because God is depicted in federal theology as the "contract god," then certain ontological implications inevitably arise from this.[96] With the onset of a covenant of works in the federal scheme, "a radical dichotomy between the sphere of Nature and the sphere of Grace" was forged, and by so doing, federal theology set forth two different ways in which God was understood to relate to humanity.[97] As Torrance puts it, "All men by nature stand related to God, the contracting Sovereign, as to a *Judge*, under natural law and exposed to the sanctions of the law. Only the elect are related to God through Christ as Mediator."[98] The inclusion of a covenant of works, therefore, yields a picture of God who either acts as Judge to one group of people and thus treats them according to the law or acts as Father to another group of people and treats them according to love.

Torrance argues that if God is not related to all people in love, then love becomes arbitrary to the very nature of God. In this telling, justice ends up as "the essential attribute" of God.[99] One of the most dangerous consequences of this perspective, Torrance warns, is that it can lead to "a new Sabellianism by implying that God is loving *toward* some men but not essentially *in his Being*."[100] The shift in the doctrine of God, there-

---

93. Torrance, "Covenant or Contract?," 55.

94. J. B. Torrance, "The Concept of Federal Theology—Was Calvin a Federal Theologian?," in *Calvinus Sacrae Scripturae Professor*, ed. Wilhelm H. Neuser (Grand Rapids, MI: Eerdmans, 1994), 35.

95. James B. Torrance, "Introduction," in J. McLeod Campbell, *The Nature of the Atonement* (Edinburgh: Handsel, 1996), 9.

96. In another place, Torrance puts the question more directly: "In the movement from Calvin to federal Calvinism, do we not see a basic shift in the doctrine of God, from a prime emphasis on God as triune to a Stoic concept of God as primarily the Lawgiver, the contract God, or to an Aristotelian concept of God in whom there are no unrealized potentialities?" "Concept of Federal Theology," 35.

97. Torrance, "Covenant or Contract?," 67.

98. Torrance, "Covenant or Contract?," 67.

99. James B. Torrance, "Strengths and Weaknesses of the Westminster Theology," in *The Westminster Confession in the Church Today*, ed. Alasdair I. C. Heron (Edinburgh: Saint Andrew Press, 1982), 48.

100. Torrance, "Strengths and Weaknesses," 50; emphasis original. The same line of reasoning is also found in "Concept of Federal Theology," 35.

fore, moves the accent from the biblical portrait of God as Father, Son, and Holy Spirit communing eternally in love to a portrayal of God as Creator, Judge, and Lawgiver. The greatest weakness of the doctrinal inheritance of federal theology, so his argument runs, is that it puts forward a picture of God who waits to be appeased, who demands that contractual conditions be met, and who is just before he is loving.

Anthropological Side of the Covenant

Torrance is right to insist that "what our doctrine of God is, that is our anthropology."[101] He maintains that federal theology has eclipsed a Trinitarian account because it advances a doctrine of God defined in terms of justice and law. The consequences of this move are felt in how humanity is viewed in the federal scheme. Torrance insists that because God is seen as the "contract god," then the manner of God's dealings with humanity will reflect this. God is the God "of legal justice who has created men and women for legal obedience."[102] He continues, "The counterpart of the contract God of the covenant of works is the individual with his/her legal rights—and a work ethic!"[103]

   This trajectory of seventeenth-century Reformed theology constitutes an aberration because it betrays the teaching of Calvin and Knox by prioritizing law over grace. This means that we relate to God in a depersonalized manner, exercising obedience to the law before we can enjoy forgiveness and mercy. Life in the covenant begins with meeting its conditions; therefrom one might achieve the favor of God. Torrance points out that the covenant of works ends up being underwritten by "a doctrine of conditional grace,"[104] which inverts the "evangelical order of grace and makes repentance prior to forgiveness."[105] If one repents, one receives grace; if one obeys, one receives God's love. In other words, Torrance charges that such a position does not allow for an evangelism that can begin with a declaration that God loves the world. Instead, Westminster theology reverted to a medieval *ordo salutis* that begins with man and moves to law, from which sin is exposed, repentance is made, and grace is then finally offered.[106] With a strange twist of irony, Torrance implies that the successors of Calvin are guilty of a kind of works-based righteousness. Expounded by Torrance, the followers of the Reformers fell back into a brand of legalism by emphasizing the imperatives of action over the indicatives of grace.[107]

---

101. Torrance, "Concept of Federal Theology," 35.
102. Torrance, "Concept of Federal Theology," 35.
103. Torrance, "Concept of Federal Theology," 35.
104. Torrance, "Contribution of John McLeod Campbell," 297.
105. Torrance, "Covenant or Contract?," 57.
106. Torrance, "Strengths and Weaknesses," 51. A frequent charge is that Westminster theology reverts to a medieval theology in its account of salvation and its understanding of the distinction between nature and grace. In "Covenant or Contract?," for instance, Torrance sees this separation as a return to "the medieval view that *grace presupposes nature and grace perfects nature*—a departure from the great emphasis of the Reformation that nothing is prior to grace" (66).
107. Torrance draws much purchase from this theological standpoint, bringing it to bear on the sociopolitical sphere as a way to pursue reconciliation and overcome the sectarianism he saw in the troubles of Northern

The legal character of Christian existence that is enshrined in Westminster overtook the filial character manifest in Calvin and the earlier Reformers. Once this occurred, the assurance that believers sought as they looked to the singular message of grace that characterizes all God's dealings as attested in Scripture was shrouded. Advocating the theology of Westminster breeds uncertainty that God is fully for us, that our sins are finally forgiven, and that reconciliation is entirely achieved. It fosters questions of doubt: "Am I one of the elect? Does God love me? Am I worthy enough to go to the sacrament? How can I know I am one of the elect?"[108] Beneath all these questions lurks the theological question, "Can I relate to God as my heavenly Father? Does the Father love me as a child of God?"[109]

In addition to the question of assurance that is supposed to haunt the legacy of federal theology, a soteriological implication also arises from this theology, namely, the doctrine of limited atonement. In his introductory essay to John McLeod Campbell's work on the atonement, Torrance teases out what a doctrine of the atonement looks like according to a theology of the contract god. He says that the doctrines of limited atonement and penal substitution as they are expounded by federalism invert the biblical order of the relationship between forgiveness and atonement. Accordingly, forgiveness can be made only for the sins of the elect and only after atonement has first been made.[110] He continues, "In other words, the Father had to be conditioned into being gracious by the obedience and the satisfaction of the Son."[111] The contract god brokers the redemption of the elect on the basis that Christ fulfills the necessary conditions.[112]

These two features of Torrance's covenantal theology, looked at from the theological and anthropological sides of his perspective on the covenant, lead him to conclude that a serious shortcoming of federal theology is that it is not furnished with an adequate Christology. Indebted to Barth, Torrance worries not only that Westminster theology gives precedence to the doctrine of decrees but also that the outworking of this doctrine occurs without much reference to Jesus Christ.[113] He objects that the covenant of works

---

Ireland and the apartheid of South Africa. See "The Ministry of Reconciliation Today: The Realism of Grace," in *Incarnational Ministry: The Presence of Christ in Church, Society, and Family; Essays in Honor of Ray S. Anderson*, ed. Christian D. Kettler and Todd Speidell (Colorado Springs: Helmers and Howard, 1990), 130–39.

108. Torrance, "Strengths and Weaknesses," 51.

109. Torrance points to the "*syllogismus practicus*" ("the practical syllogism") as a Puritan instance of this problem. See "Calvin and Puritanism in England and Scotland: Some Basic Concepts in the Development of Federal Theology," in *Calvinus Reformator: His Contribution to Theology, Church and Society* (Potchefstroom, South Africa: Potchefstroom University for Christian Higher Education, 1982), 275. Richard Muller addresses the "syllogism" in a more historically sober treatment in *Calvin and the Reformed Tradition: On the Work of Christ and the Order of Salvation* (Grand Rapids, MI: Baker Academic, 2012), chap. 8.

110. Torrance, "Introduction," in Campbell, *Atonement*, 9.

111. Torrance, "Introduction," in Campbell, *Atonement*, 9.

112. I tend to think that Sinclair B. Ferguson's comment is helpful here: "It bears repeating that unless one is a universalist, one's doctrine of the atonement is 'limited' wither in intention (Christ died to save his people) or in application (Christ died for all, yet all are not saved)." *The Whole Christ: Legalism, Antinomianism, and Gospel Assurance; Why the Marrow Controversy Still Matters* (Wheaton, IL: Crossway, 2016), 39n8.

113. J. B. Torrance elaborates on this point in his essay "The Vicarious Humanity of Christ," in *The Incarnation: Ecumenical Studies in the Nicene-Constantinopolitan Creed, A.D. 381*, ed. Thomas F. Torrance (Edinburgh: Handsel, 1981), 127–47.

strips Christ of his role as head over all creation as mediator, his solidarity with all humanity as the head of the race as established in the incarnation. We are back again to the familiar charge of contract theology with its judicial interpretation and its expectations that obedience precedes acceptance. Much preferred is a theology of union with Christ that conveys the unconditional love of the Father.[114]

Assessment of J. B. Torrance

How are we to assess Torrance's position? It is not a stretch to say that J. B. Torrance sees a widespread and wholesale impoverishment in the covenant theology of federalism. Two points need to be noted. First, from the theological vantage point, Torrance objects to federalism's doctrine of God because he believes it posits justice as an essential characteristic of God's being instead of God's love.[115] The cogency of this objection depends on whether God's justice is cast in such a way that it is mutually exclusive to God's love. If the theology of federalism does in fact pit these two attributes against each other, then it will be important to see if God's justice has a determining role in governing other aspects of federalism's instruction, especially as it is displayed in the teaching of Westminster. It would be important, in other words, to see if Torrance's accusation that the covenant of works implies a legalistic understanding of God holds water.

The first thing we need to point out is that the doctrine of God found in the Westminster Confession (chap. 2) has catholic pedigree. It makes clear that the attributes of God are not arbitrary properties of God but are creaturely attempts to indicate the reality of who God is in himself. In its formulation, Westminster rehearses a theology of God's absolute independence and freedom from creation, which itself secures God's loving relation to creation. God's external action in relation to the world is a repetition of God's internal identification in God's inner life as Father, Son, and Holy Spirit. We are in the theological provenance of divine simplicity that tries to uphold the teaching that God's identity, negatively, is not made up of the sum total of his parts but, positively, reflects God's "singular, infinite fullness, perfect integrity, and abundance of life."[116] This means that "God's essence and God's attributes coincide, . . . that the divine attributes are identical with the divine substance and with each other."[117] Not only does this teaching ensure that there is clear continuity between who God is and how God acts, but it also means that when we affirm that God's actions reflect God's undivided essence, we are

---

114. Torrance, "Introduction," in Campbell, *Atonement*, 7. A consequence of this is that "the whole focus of attention moves away from what Christ has done for us and for all men, to what we have to do IF we would be (or know that we are) in covenant with God." Torrance, "Covenant or Contract?," 69.

115. This is a criticism that Donald Macleod also makes. See Macleod, "Covenant Theology," in *Dictionary of Scottish Church History and Theology*, ed. Nigel M. de S. Cameron (Downers Grove, IL: InterVarsity Press, 1993), 217.

116. John Webster, "Divine Attributes," in *The Cambridge Dictionary of Christian Theology*, ed. Ian A. McFarland, David A. S. Fergusson, Karen Kilby, and Iain R. Torrance (Cambridge: Cambridge University Press, 2014), 47.

117. Webster, "Divine Attributes," 47.

also affirming that speaking about God's justice is also speaking about God's love. The Westminster Confession (2.1) communicates this teaching, affirming the self-sufficiency and plenitude of God, which is followed by a consideration of God's life in himself as the triune God. It would be unfair to say that the divines departed from a classical reading and allowed their locus of God to be filled out instead by abstract justice. If anything, the teaching of the confession is not only tightly indexed to the classical tradition but speaks to the filial nature of God. As Sinclair Ferguson points out, "There is a special emphasis in the Confession on the Fatherhood of God in a separate chapter devoted to the Christian's adoption into God's family (XII)."[118]

Second, from the anthropological vantage point, Torrance claims that the presence of a covenant of works in the federal scheme reflects a flawed account of who God is and how God interacts with us. He suggests that the contract god engages us contractually and conditionally. If we repent, we will be accepted by God. From a historical point of view, both Torrance brothers miss the point that for many theologians within the federal movement, the covenant of works was drafted to address soteriological concerns, particularly the relation of grace and nature prior to the fall.[119] According to the so-called codifier of this doctrine, Cocceius understood that the covenant of works points to the priority of grace seen in God's desire to have fellowship (*amicitia Dei*) with his creatures, which would appear to draw the sting out of claims that federal theologians tragically inverted the relationship of grace and law.

Furthermore, and contrary to J. B. Torrance's argument, the covenant of works does not spell out bilateral negotiations between two equal partners. God sovereignly and freely created a perfect paradise, lovingly formed Adam from the dust, graciously brought our first parents into communion with God, and lavishly provided all that was needed to attain happiness with God. Yet Eden also demonstrates that prior to the fall, Adam and Eve were to live out this relationship in perfect obedience to God with the clear injunction not to eat of a specific tree. The imperative flows out of the indicative. The charge that the covenant of works destabilized and consequently disordered the theology of grace of the early Reformers because it framed the original relationship between Creator and creature in terms of a contract appears to be wrongheaded. It is important to see that one's view of humanity derives from one's view of God, that one's anthropology is shaped by one's doctrine of God. If God truly does demand that we earn his favor prior to receiving his acceptance, then Torrance is right to reason that the contract god is a constituent feature in the teaching of Calvin's followers. Torrance, however, overlooks the filial character that was present to Adam and Eve even before they heard the prohibition that, if broken, would lead them away from friendship with God.

118. Sinclair B. Ferguson, "The Teaching of the Confession," in Heron, *Westminster Confession in the Church Today*, 30.
119. See van Asselt, *Federal Theology*, 265–68.

Conclusion

Karl Barth's relationship with Reformed theology and confessional orthodoxy is complicated. To pursue a deeper clarity and understanding, time would need to be devoted to his theological reading of tradition, his understanding of history, and what he views to be the task of historical theology.[120] Much attention would also have to be given to how Barth relates to his own theological heritage and his initial training in Reformed theology at Göttingen in the early 1920s, in which he tried to overcome his Protestant liberal background by engaging with an older tradition. As it stands, Barth's commitment to the theology of the later Protestant divines was similar to his commitment to the magisterial Reformers. He by no means repristinated their theologies but appropriated from the Reformed tradition theological instincts, sensibilities, categories, motifs, texts, and interlocutors that would enable him to pursue his broader theological project. This proves to be a point of frustration for many in the Reformed world, and understandably so. Barth's thinking resembles Reformed theology at so many points, but his reconstruction and revision of the tradition shows that his continuity with the tradition is equally matched, if not exceeded, by points of discontinuity. In the end, Barth's relationship with Reformed theology is idiosyncratic and independent, critical yet also appreciative. We have seen how he augments the doctrine of God, election, creation, and reconciliation with considerable consequences for his account of the covenant.

This chapter has also tried to demonstrate how Barth's theology set the foundation for both T. F. Torrance and his brother J. B. Torrance. Both took Barth's interpretation of the covenant and extended his reservations and criticisms in specific directions. Where Barth was perhaps less vexed by the theology of Calvin's post-Reformation heirs, T. F. and especially J. B. Torrance saw Westminster theology as the logical conclusion of a Reformation theology that betrayed its original intention and teaching. Aside from the lack of documentary evidence provided, the material criticism is that the introduction of a covenant of works by Calvin's successors not only stemmed from a flawed doctrine of God but promoted an equally flawed account of the relationship between God and humanity, and this claim flies in the face of what can be seen in the work of later Reformed thinkers. This chapter has tried to suggest that the theological complaints made by the Torrances rest on a series of theological missteps in their analysis of confessional orthodoxy. While their arguments do not prove convincing, they give much food for thought for those who value the key elements of the Reformed tradition to thoroughly understand and clearly articulate the historic development of covenantal thinking, as well as the exegetical and dogmatic underpinnings that delineate the covenant of works, the covenant of grace, and the intra-Trinitarian covenant of redemption.

---

120. For this topic, see John Webster, *Barth's Earlier Theology: Four Studies* (London: T&T Clark, 2005).

20

COVENANT IN RECENT THEOLOGY

Michael Allen

Covenant theology plays a rather small role in much contemporary theology. That's not to say something terribly notable about covenant, however, for recent theology has tended to diversify and broaden its reaches. A coherent center does not hold once one moves beyond the most simple reference points ("God" or "Jesus") in so much of what flies under the banner of Christian theology. Theology in the twentieth and twenty-first centuries has frequently taken such a revisionary impulse that it no longer simply modifies the way a given topic is addressed but also frequently shifts the very topics under discussion. Why talk covenant, then, when one can talk social constructivism or cosmopolitan community?

Lost in the Breadth

An example can be seen in observing a leading liberal or progressive theological project, the Workgroup on Constructive Christian Theology. This colloquial gathering has now produced four textbooks across the span of four decades, each of which involves significant figures in modern theology in the liberal key. The initial volume, *Christian Theology*, was edited by Peter Hodgson and Robert King and included the following chapters:[1]

- "Theological Method"
- "Scripture and Tradition"
- "God"
- "Revelation"

---

1. Peter C. Hodgson and Robert H. King, eds., *Christian Theology: An Introduction to Its Traditions and Tasks* (Philadelphia: Fortress, 1985).

- "Creation and Providence"
- "Human Being"
- "Sin and Evil"
- "Christ and Salvation"
- "Church"
- "Sacraments"
- "Spirit and Christian Life"
- "Kingdom of God and Life Everlasting"
- "The Religions"

Later publications turned to very different concerns, as noted by the chapter titles. For example, Rebecca Chopp and Mark Lewis Taylor edited *Reconstructing Christian Theology*, whose chapters include the following:[2]

- "God, Sexism, and Transformation"
- "God, Religious Pluralism, and Dialogic Encounter"
- "The Bible, the Global Context, and the Discipleship of Equals"
- "Creation, Environmental Crisis, and Ecological Justice"
- "Creation, Handicappism, and the Community of Differing Abilities"
- "Human Beings, Embodiment, and Our Home the Earth"
- "Human Beings, White Supremacy, and Racial Justice"
- "Militarism, Evil, and the Reign of God"
- "Sin, Addiction, and Freedom"
- "Christology, Anti-Semitism, and Christian-Jewish Bonding"
- "Christian Redemption between Colonialism and Pluralism"
- "The Church, Classism, and Ecclesial Community"
- "Eschatology, Ecology, and a Green Ecumenacy"
- "Eschatology, White Supremacy, and the Beloved Community"

More recent volumes vary a bit, tilting slightly more traditional or even more revisionary in tone.[3] The shift away from classical theological loci and toward conversational themes stands out jarringly, so it may not be notable that much liberal theology has avoided discussion of covenant, given that this is true of several other topics as well.

References to covenant theology in wider theological literature of a more systematic stripe remain meager. Germanic tomes of the last generation address the topic and term only in an occasional and somewhat happenstance manner (see, e.g., the second volume of Wolfhart Pannenberg's *Systematic Theology* or the dogmatics series of Jürgen Moltmann). In the English-speaking realm, many influential theologians operate without any

---

2. Rebecca S. Chopp and Mark Lewis Taylor, eds., *Reconstructing Christian Theology* (Minneapolis: Fortress, 1994).

3. See Serene Jones and Paul Lakeland, eds., *Constructive Theology: A Contemporary Approach to Classic Themes* (Minneapolis: Fortress, 2005); Laurel C. Schneider and Stephen G. Ray Jr., eds., *Awake to the Moment: An Introduction to Theology* (Louisville: Westminster John Knox, 2016).

reference to the idea, such as John Milbank, Robert Jenson, or Rowan Williams. Others address it at key junctures related to salvation or to the church, as does Kathryn Tanner in her small systematics, *Jesus, Humanity, and the Trinity*, and Veli-Matti Kärkkäinen in volume four of his *Constructive Christian Theology for the Pluralistic World*.[4] Two of the most significant current English-language systematics projects are not yet far enough along to adjudicate the place of covenant within them, though it is notable that this theme does not appear at all in the first volume by either Kate Sonderegger or Sarah Coakley. Frequently used textbooks by evangelical authors sometimes do (e.g., Wayne Grudem) and sometimes do not (e.g., Gerald Bray) include any lengthy discussion of the topic.[5]

Like the prophet, however, this volume on covenant theology is not the only one left standing (1 Kings 19:18). Reformed theologians—whether liberal or confessional, English-speaking or Dutch-speaking—remain far more likely to attend with regularity to the covenant. The Presbyterian Douglas Ottati's *Theology for Liberal Protestants* probably addresses covenant as much as anyone. In the last generation, Donald Bloesch regularly turned to address the significance of biblical language about the covenant in his Christian Foundations series. Douglas Kelly addresses the covenant of grace within the first volume of his systematics, and John Frame's one-volume textbook includes a chapter titled "The Lord's Covenants" in its first section.[6] Also, the recent textbook by Cornelis van der Kooi and Gijsbert van den Brink, *Christian Dogmatics*, engages with the topic both in a significant chapter ("Israel, the Raw Nerve in Christian Theology") and in a couple of excurses regarding church and election.[7]

The present volume witnesses to the fact that covenant theology remains a lively area of study and debate. Covenant theology has become a genre and a lens. Some texts focus on covenant theology at length, while others employ it as a lens through which various topics may be examined. In the remainder of this essay, I want to consider what has drawn attention away from the topic of covenant by looking at the development of the theme of participation in recent theology and then to consider two significant exemplars of a recent theology of the covenant, the late John Webster and Michael Horton.

Distracted by the Dominant Focus: On Participation in Recent Theology

The absence of covenant in much recent theology does not mean the abject void of every facet of the doctrine of the covenant. Douglas Knight's work illustrates a broader

4. Kathryn Tanner, *Jesus, Humanity, and the Trinity: A Brief Systematic Theology* (Minneapolis: Fortress, 2001), 44–46, 84–88; Veli-Matti Kärkkäinen, *Constructive Christian Theology for the Pluralistic World*, vol. 4, *Spirit and Salvation* (Grand Rapids, MI: Eerdmans, 2016), 246–55, 325–33.

5. Wayne Grudem, *Systematic Theology: An Introduction to Biblical Doctrine* (Grand Rapids, MI: Zondervan, 1995), 515–28; Gerald Bray, *God Is Love: A Biblical and Systematic Theology* (Wheaton, IL: Crossway, 2012).

6. Douglas F. Kelly, *Systematic Theology, Grounded in Holy Scripture and Understood in the Light of the Church*, vol. 1, *The God Who Is: The Holy Trinity* (Fearn, Ross-shire, Scotland: Mentor, 2008), 387–446; John M. Frame, *Systematic Theology: An Introduction to Christian Belief* (Phillipsburg, NJ: P&R, 2013), 55–86.

7. Cornelis van der Kooi and Gijsbert van den Brink, *Christian Dogmatics: An Introduction* (Grand Rapids, MI: Eerdmans, 2017), 338–80; see also 585–86, 706.

trend in that he tends to the way that God makes and gives and even spends time with his human creatures. Knight also repeatedly references biblical language regarding the covenant and its significance, occasionally with noteworthy perception.[8] And yet his overarching structural category is *oikonomia* ("economy"), as drawn from Ephesians 1:10, rather than covenant language. Even when referenced, then, covenant is relativized by another term.

The most significant topic in recent theology that overlaps with and regularly crowds out the doctrine of covenant is the theme of participation. Participation (*methexis*) has played an outsized role in the last few decades and can be identified as playing it in four settings.[9] First, Eastern versions of participation draw on the deep, Greek-speaking tradition of working on deification, or *theosis*. Norman Russell has traced the meandering movement whereby texts such as Psalm 82:6 and 2 Peter 1:4 took on focal significance for shaping the Eastern understanding of the work of Christ in drawing his own into partaking of the divine life.[10] Maximus the Confessor plays a crucial role in speaking of participation as transfiguration of created reality.[11] More recently, Eastern theologians have continued to employ this kind of language in potent ways and have influenced even Western scholars (such as the aforementioned Douglas Knight, who has drawn at length on the work of John Zizioulas, including his participatory metaphysics).

The Radical Orthodoxy movement of the late 1990s and early 2000s has emphasized the significance of *methexis*, or participation, as a necessary metaphysical category to help us avoid secularism. This claim played a key role in John Milbank's *Theology and Social Theory*, and it has marked the projects of a number of others working within this conversation.[12] In the introduction to the collaborative volume *Radical Orthodoxy: A New Theology*, the claim is found in this form: "The central theological framework of radical orthodoxy is 'participation' as developed by Plato and reworked by Christianity, because any alternative configuration perforce reserves a territory independent of God."[13] Critics have questioned the validity of Radical Orthodox readings of classical figures and expressions of participation, whether of

---

8. Douglas H. Knight, *The Eschatological Economy: Time and the Hospitality of God* (Grand Rapids, MI: Eerdmans, 2006), esp. 65–68, 164–65.

9. For a helpful sketch of the varied iterations of participation or deification, see Michael J. Christensen and Jeffery A. Wittung, eds., *Partakers of the Divine Nature: The History and Development of Deification in the Christian Traditions* (Grand Rapids, MI: Baker Academic, 2008).

10. Norman Russell, *The Doctrine of Deification in the Greek Patristic Tradition*, OECS (New York: Oxford University Press, 2006).

11. See especially Paul M. Blowers, *Maximus the Confessor: Jesus Christ and the Transfiguration of the World*, CTC (New York: Oxford University Press, 2016).

12. John Milbank, *Theology and Social Theory: Beyond Secular Reason* (Oxford: Blackwell, 1990), esp. 422–43 (where he works out a "counter-ontology" to liberalism). More recently, the theme has been developed with far greater rigor and nuance by Adrian Pabst, *Metaphysics: The Creation of Hierarchy* (Grand Rapids, MI: Eerdmans, 2012), 201–71.

13. John Milbank, Graham Ward, and Catherine Pickstock, "Suspending the Material: The Turn of Radical Orthodoxy," in *Radical Orthodoxy: A New Theology* (London: Routledge, 1999), 3.

Thomas Aquinas (deemed an ontological saint) or Duns Scotus (deemed a meta-physical sinner).[14]

But it is not just the Eastern churches and the Anglo-Catholic and Roman Catholic adherents of a Radical Orthodoxy who are turning to deification and participatory language. Even Lutherans have addressed the subject. Tuomo Mannermaa and his students at the University of Helsinki have focused on language used at times by Luther, *in ipsa fide Christus adest* ("Christ present in faith"), to speak of a participatory focus of the German Reformer's teaching.[15] This Finnish Lutheranism has certainly not won the day historically or dogmatically, and it continues to find notable critics who claim that it distorts and disorders Luther's theology. For instance, the recent *Oxford Handbook of Martin Luther's Theology* includes two chapters on this subject, one of which advances the Finnish emphasis on participation as central to the Reformer's vision and the other of which focuses more on forensic metaphors for grace.[16]

Calvin studies have also sought to bring out the participatory focus of the Genevan Reformer's work in a way that somewhat parallels the focus of the Finnish Lutherans. J. Todd Billings has responded to the challenge of John Milbank and Radical Orthodoxy, namely, that Calvin offers nothing by way of a participatory or realist vision of salvation. In so doing, Billings has helped point to the way Calvin weds the deifying and the justifying work of Christ without thereby collapsing either into the other (which often seems the result of the Finnish Lutheran approach, collapsing the forensic note into the more dominant participatory key).[17] Others who have sought to unpack the teaching of Calvin on union with Christ have sometimes neither made as much of his broadly participatory theology nor addressed union in such a way that justification and sanctification are rightly distinguished and connected.[18]

Participation need not conflict with covenant, but a number of its familiar iterations do. Kevin Vanhoozer has helpfully noted that participation language can occur at two levels—creational and salvific:

> We therefore have to distinguish two kinds of "being in" or participation in Christ: a general cosmological participation in the Son through whom all things were made

14. See especially Laurence Paul Hemming, ed., *Radical Orthodoxy? A Catholic Enquiry* (2000; repr., London: Routledge, 2017).

15. For a survey of the material (much of which is not available in English), see especially Veli-Matti Kärk-käinen, "Salvation as Justification and *Theosis*: The Contribution of the New Finnish Luther Interpretation to Our Ecumenical Future," *Di* 45, no. 1 (2006): 74–82. See also Carl E. Braaten and Robert W. Jenson, eds., *Union with Christ: The New Finnish Interpretation of Luther* (Grand Rapids, MI: Eerdmans, 1998). The most introductory primary text is Tuomo Mannermaa, *Christ Present in Faith: Luther's View of Justification*, ed. Kirsi I. Stjerna (Minneapolis: Fortress, 2005).

16. Risto Saarinen, "Justification by Faith: The View of the Mannermaa School," and Mark Mattes, "Luther on Justification as Forensic and Effective," chaps. 17 and 18, respectively, of *The Oxford Handbook of Martin Luther's Theology*, ed. Robert Kolb, Irene Dingel, and Ľubomír Batka (New York: Oxford University Press, 2014), 254–73.

17. J. Todd Billings, *Calvin, Participation, and the Gift: The Activity of Believers in Union with Christ*, CPSHT (New York: Oxford University Press, 2008).

18. Thomas Wenger has done some helpful work in surveying the terrain: "The New Perspective on Calvin: Responding to Recent Calvin Interpretations," *JETS* 50, no. 2 (2007): 311–28.

(Col. 1:16) and a more particular Christological abiding in the Son in whom there is reconciliation (2 Cor. 5:17). . . . Salvation involves more than relating to God generically as a creature; it involves relating to God covenantally "in Christ."[19]

It is not insignificant that Vanhoozer brings out covenantal relation to speak of this intensified participation, even as he rightly notes the presence of a wider ontological frame by which we affirm that all things "live and move and have [their] being" in Christ (Acts 17:28). In the remainder of this essay, we look to two accounts of covenant that address the theme while remaining alert to the increasing tendency to allow participation language to crowd out or even distort covenant theology. We see that John Webster's essays focused on covenant by going deep and sketching the metaphysical and economic principles of such a doctrine. Then we see Michael Horton ranging wide by drawing out the implications of covenant and eschatology as principles of all systematic theology.

Going Deep: John Webster on a Dogmatics for Covenant

The late John Webster called for a "theological theology" that assumed nothing and sought to take every thought and protocol "captive to obey Christ" (2 Cor. 10:5). When considering other contemporary theological projects, he warned against too quickly moving into the mode of conversation and thereby assuming that we already have the Christian matter down pat and are ready to talk about its relation to other discourses. Webster always pointed us to the significance of being unsettled again by the Christian distinction and the singularity of the perfect God.

As Webster developed not merely a set of principles for theological practice but also an increasing array of material studies on key themes, he attempted to plumb each topic to its depths. Over time, covenant was an increasingly significant focus of his work, albeit his fullest expressions regarding it remained unpublished at the time of his death in 2015. While we do not have his elaborated exegetical account as was hinted at in his 2007 Kantzer Lectures, *Perfection and Presence: God with Us according to the Christian Confession* (especially in lectures 3 and 4) or as would be elaborated in the third, fourth, and fifth volumes of his planned *Systematic Theology*, we can discern much from his many collected essays that were released during his lifetime. We want to explore how his approach to thinking through what he would regularly deem the architecture of Christian dogmatics implies for the doctrine of the covenant. What systemic connections provide its foundations? What were the walls and windows that mark out its facade?

First, Webster realized the significance of not skating past the intellectual and ethical calling to develop a theological ontology. When he was earlier doing work in exploring

---

19. Kevin J. Vanhoozer, *Remythologizing Theology: Divine Action, Passion, and Authorship*, CSCD 18 (Cambridge: Cambridge University Press, 2010), 281–82. Patristic precursors to this doubled account can be found in the work of Irenaeus, Origen, and Cyril of Alexandria (albeit not in Theodore of Mopsuestia and Diodore of Tarsus), according to Donald Fairbairn, *Grace and Christology in the Early Church*, OECS (New York: Oxford University Press, 2003), 21.

the theology of Karl Barth, he found a phrase from Charles Taylor to be important: "moral ontology."[20] The concept was meant to evoke the need for a metaphysical space within which ethics (Christian or otherwise) could be explored. Anything that fails to be ontological of one sort or another simply does not address the deepest needs. This was a noteworthy feature not only of his analysis of Barth (and of Eberhard Jüngel before him) but of his own anthropological and moral essays in the 1990s.[21]

Covenant plays a shaping role at times here, especially in his more mature work. In the third of his Kantzer Lectures delivered in 2007, Webster said,

> Covenant history is special history. But for the canon, it is the basic thread of human affairs, and in it God's relation to creatures is enacted. In all its particularity and contingency, it is this history which continues the history of Adam after Adam broke fellowship with God and fled from his maker's presence. In this respect, therefore, the history of the covenant is universal history, in one sense enclosed by, but in a far more important sense circumscribing, recapitulating, and bringing to fulfilment all other occurrence, above all in the climactic moment of God with us.[22]

Webster interpreted global history from the inside out, with God's revelatory presence among his people (Israel) and in Christ as the "circumscribing, recapitulating, and bringing to fulfillment all other occurrence."

So our ontology must be shaped by the revealed wisdom of God, not simply taken pell-mell from some other discipline or ideology. We dare not presume the forms of Plato nor assume their implosion by Martin Heidegger. We need a distinctly theological ontology. What doctrines govern and rule that metaphysics? Most central is Webster's expression of how God's being shapes all reality. Beginning with the unpublished Kantzer Lectures given in late 2007 (especially lectures 1 and 2) and then with a programmatic essay published in 2009,[23] the approach became ubiquitous in his work (although it had also been present in places prior to those writings). The development deserves greater care than can be given here, but Webster began with the concept of aseity, then spoke also of divine perfection (distinguished from divine presence), added the distinction between uncreated and created being, developed the use of the distinction between theology and economy, and finally adopted the Trinitarian categories of divine processions and divine missions. In each case, the Creator-creature distinction serves a governing role

---

20. Webster drew the language of "moral ontology" into his account of Barth's moral dogmatics from Charles Taylor, *Sources of the Self: The Making of the Modern Identity* (Cambridge, MA: Harvard University Press, 1989), 8; first employed by Webster in *Barth's Ethics of Reconciliation* (Cambridge: Cambridge University Press, 1995), 215.

21. John Webster, "Eschatology, Ontology, and Human Action," *TJT* 7, no. 1 (1991): 4–18; Webster, "Eschatology, Anthropology, and Postmodernity," *IJST* 2, no. 1 (2000): 13–28.

22. John Webster, "God Is Everywhere but Not Only Everywhere," lecture 3 of *Perfection and Presence: God with Us, according to the Christian Confession*, inaugural Kantzer Lectures (Carl F. H. Henry Center for Theological Understanding, Trinity Evangelical Divinity School, September 13, 2007), henrycenter.tiu.edu/resource/god-is-everywhere-but-not-only-everywhere/.

23. See John Webster, "Principles of Systematic Theology," *IJST* 11, no. 1 (2009): 56–71.

in defining metaphysical reality along the lines of a sharp and insurmountable distinction between created and uncreated being.

Second, Webster's theological ontology led him to express rather significant worries about the way that participatory language was employed in much modern theology:

> I remain uneasy with at least some uses of the idiom of participation in the theology of creation and salvation, chiefly because of its slender exegetical foundation, but also because of its sometimes hectoring and often drastically schematic history of Christian thought, and its apparent lack of concern with the hypertrophy or atrophy of some tracts of Christian teaching.[24]

Webster found the language of participation to occur only occasionally within the biblical witness, and (as with other topics, "image of God" and "body of Christ" being two instances) he thought our systematic usage needed to map more closely to the narrow biblical interest in a theme. He also found the historical accounts to be "drastically schematic," which is the British equivalent of a German or American saying it is undisciplined (one thinks perhaps especially of the Finnish Lutherans here).[25]

Admittedly, Webster at times showed a calm and patient interest in avoiding impulsive reaction to modern trends. In his essay "Perfection and Participation," he sought to listen to participationist theologies in a charitable vein:

> We may begin by observing that a prudent and modest Reformed dogmatics will feel no compelling need to rush to its own defense in these matters but will be open to learn from its interlocutors, however hostile or underinformed they sometimes prove to be. It is undoubtedly the case that some of what the Reformed tradition has had to say about the perfection of God and the supremacy of God's good pleasure has been unguarded and subject to distortion. Furthermore, Reformed dogmatics would do well to look for what is of value in the very different conceptions of its critics.[26]

Webster did not find participation to be obviously wrong in every potential way:

> There is nothing self-evidently pantheistic about theologies of participation, no obvious compromise of the distinction between the agenetic and the genetic orders of reality. God does not need to be protected from degradation by establishing a caesura between the divine and the creaturely; "uncreated" is not necessarily a counterpoint to "contingent": it may mean plenitude as source.[27]

---

24. John Webster, "Perfection and Participation," in *The Analogy of Being: Invention of the Antichrist or the Wisdom of God?*, ed. Thomas Joseph White (Grand Rapids, MI: Eerdmans, 2011), 380.

25. Webster challenges the historical depth of the Helsinki School and Mannermaa's reading of Luther in "Immanuel, God's Presence with Us," lecture 1 of *Perfection and Presence: God with Us, according to the Christian Confession*, inaugural Kantzer Lectures (Carl F. H. Henry Center for Theological Understanding, Trinity Evangelical Divinity School, September 11, 2007), henrycenter.tiu.edu/resource/immanuel-gods-presence-with-us/.

26. Webster, "Perfection and Participation," 387.

27. Webster, "Perfection and Participation," 387.

So participation (even the *analogia entis*) is not the fount of all ills: "At the same time, a fittingly confident Reformed dogmatics will not make hurried, impetuous adjustments to its construal of the gospel. . . . Simply to concede that one's tradition is trapped by philosophical defect is inadequate for reasons that are as much spiritual as intellectual" and actually may be "a diminishment of catholicity."[28] Not surprisingly, Webster regularly pushed back against what he took to be lush and undisciplined versions of participation and instead turned to other tools to express his approach to the relationship of God and creatures.

Third, Webster turned to the terminology of covenant fellowship to express the way that union with Christ draws the child of God into the adopted life with God. When posing the question of how a Reformed theologian considers the modern praise of participation, Webster frames a distinctly Reformed approach:

> The larger setting of a Reformed theology of participation has characteristically been a "dramatic" conception of the economy of divine grace, organized around two basic principles: (1) the history of God's dealings with creatures is "covenantal," that is, an ordered moral history between personal agents (the uncreated God and his creatures) and not a process of diffusion of being; (2) the course of this history is shaped by God's good pleasure.[29]

Covenant is of great significance and import here not only because it has exegetical pedigree and such deep canonical resonance but also because it accents the "ordered" nature of "moral history." Webster rightly brings out the fact that covenant orders a relationship and speaks not of some willy-nilly interaction but of a structured fellowship "between personal agents."

What remains notably underdeveloped is the historically varying order of this covenant fellowship. Webster does routinely speak of creation, fall, reconciliation, and redemption in his moral essays (and he was aiming to use these four phases of the divine economy as structuring principles of a major portion of his planned systematic theology). And he did regularly write on the doctrine of the "covenant of redemption" in addressing his Trinitarian approach to salvation and covenant.[30] Yet he did not in his published writings offer more specific exegesis of particular covenant passages (e.g., Noah, Abraham). His work remains structural rather than specific, though his structural emphases point to the shaping role of the specific. His Reformed reliance on the language of covenant fellowship (more so than, and even at times to the exclusion of, participation) led him more closely to align also with earlier catholic conceptions of the

---

28. Webster, "Perfection and Participation," 388.
29. Webster, "Perfection and Participation," 386.
30. John Webster, "'It Was the Will of the Lord to Bruise Him': Soteriology and the Doctrine of God," in *God of Salvation: Soteriology in Theological Perspective*, ed. Ivor Davidson and Murray Rae (Aldershot, UK: Ashgate, 2011), 15–34.

God-creature relation, such as Thomas Aquinas's claim that such relations are real on the side of the creature but only conceptual on the side of God.[31]

Fourth, this insistence on the Creator-creature distinction led not only to worry about participation but also, especially, toward a distinctly Reformed account of the hypostatic union. In a batch of essays as well as in his Kantzer Lectures, Webster sought to draw out the exegetical force of Chalcedonian and Reformed Christology especially over against more historicist approaches that blurred or elided the distinction of the two natures.[32] He defended the *extra Calvinisticum* and the Calvinist approach to the *communicatio idiomatum* as implications of his approach more generally to covenant fellowship rooted in divine perfection, that is, as always and everywhere (even in Christ's person) as bearing out the distinction of created and uncreated being.

Fifth, Webster's approach to covenant fellowship also shaped his depiction of communal church life and the individual's experience of salvific union in Christ. Here he interacted at some length with claims made by members of the ever-popular *nouvelle théologie*, which was significant for the Second Vatican Council and increasingly dominant in not only post–Vatican II Roman Catholicism but also more and more among Protestant devotees (such as Milbank).[33] Webster was not keen on claims that the church becomes the sacrament or that the church just is the body of Christ; such claims failed to maintain the right kind of externalism (but not utter extrinsicism) between the church and Christ.[34]

We might listen to his own summary of how divine perfection recasts many topics, with covenant right at the heart of them:

> I have come to think that the rather strictly drawn demarcations between Creator and creature in some classical Calvinist divinity—in its doctrine of God, its account of the hypostatic union, its doctrine of election and covenant fellowship, and the modesty of its theology of *unio* and *inhabitatio*—bring a good deal more to the table than is generally allowed.[35]

In Webster, we see a theologian suspicious of the overreach of participationist jargon and more impressed with the exegetical pedigree of covenantal categories. We see him

---

31. John Webster, "*Non Ex Aequo*: God's Relation to Creatures," in *God without Measure: Working Papers in Christian Doctrine*, vol. 1, *God and the Works of God* (London: T&T Clark, 2015), 115–26.

32. John Webster, "Incarnation," in *Word and Church: Essays in Christian Dogmatics* (Edinburgh: T&T Clark, 2001), 113–49; Webster, "Jesus in Modernity: Reflections on Jüngel's Christology," in *Word and Church*, 151–89; Webster, "Prolegomena to Christology: Four Theses," in *Confessing God: Essays in Christian Dogmatics II* (London: T&T Clark, 2005), 131–51; Webster, "Christology, Theology, Economy: The Place of Christology in Systematic Theology," in *God without Measure*, 1:43–58; Webster, "One Who Is Son," in *God without Measure*, 1:59–81.

33. John Webster, "Purity and Plenitude: Evangelical Reflections on Congar's *Tradition and Traditions*," in *God without Measure*, 1:195–210; and especially "He Will Be with Them," lecture 6 of *Perfection and Presence: God with Us, according to the Christian Confession*, inaugural Kantzer Lectures (Carl F. H. Henry Center for Theological Understanding, Trinity Evangelical Divinity School, September 18, 2007), henrycenter.tiu.edu/resource/he-will-be-with-them/.

34. See especially John Webster, "Christ, Church, and Reconciliation," in *Word and Church*, 211–30; Webster, "On Evangelical Ecclesiology," in *Confessing God*, 153–93.

35. Webster, "Perfection and Participation," 380.

highlighting its ordering function in shaping relations between God and creatures in not merely metaphysical but also moral manners. Finally, we see that this reliance on the language of covenant fellowship and insistence on expressing it in such a form that the distinction between created and uncreated being is always honored leads him to think about not merely communion but also Christology and ecclesiology in distinctly Reformed ways. While we may wish for greater specificity (especially perhaps regarding the different "administrations" of the covenant of grace, to take the language of WCF 7.5–6), we see in his work an attempt to reflect on the deep grammar of covenant in Reformed theology.

Ranging Wide: Michael Horton on Covenant for Dogmatics

We turn now to another theologian who has ranged widely with his consideration of covenant in a host of writings. Michael Horton has written an introductory textbook on covenant theology and a number of journal articles or essays that seek to examine and to commend classical federal theology. His most significant work, however, has been to unfold a four-volume dogmatics that is guided by structuring principles of covenant and eschatology. While he has written many other volumes, not least a one-volume systematic theology textbook,[36] this dogmatics series represents the crowning achievement of his written corpus.

Horton describes the series as "an attempt to integrate biblical theology and systematic theology on the basis of Scripture's own intrasystematic categories of covenant and eschatology."[37] He argues that methodological principles ought to be derived from Scripture's own teaching rather than imposed on theology from some other intellectual terrain. It will not do to govern theological inquiry by the rules of some other disciplinary domain; the unique object of theological study—the living and true God— demands a unique and specific pathway of reflection. He says briefly that both medieval and modern systems tend to move too quickly from "preexisting axioms of universal reason and experience from which ecclesiastical dogmas, or at least theories, could be extrapolated."[38] Over against such problematic presumptions, he turns to the post-Reformation Reformed scholastics as finally refining theological methodology on truly Christian theological grounds.

Horton, then, seeks to repristinate post-Reformation theology, and he suggests that the postmodern milieu, at least "the more that modern foundationalism is shaken off," might provide a context within which we find "greater openness to particular confessional theologies."[39] Fifteen years later, one probably should doubt whether a

---

36. Michael Horton, *The Christian Faith: A Systematic Theology for Pilgrims on the Way* (Grand Rapids, MI: Zondervan, 2011).

37. Michael S. Horton, *Covenant and Eschatology: The Divine Drama* (Louisville: Westminster John Knox, 2002), 1.

38. Horton, *Covenant and Eschatology*, 2.

39. Horton, *Covenant and Eschatology*, 4.

postmodern context—driven not just by opposition to modern foundationalism and a focus on context but also by critical theory and the privileging of identity politics—will be any more capacious or welcoming to particular confessional approaches such as that of covenant theology. Horton's assessment, however, was not uncommon in the early 2000s.

Substantively speaking, how does this repristination of post-Reformation Reformed theology and this desire to elaborate a truly theological methodology play out? Horton explains, "Taking advantage of advances in biblical theology, this work will argue that eschatology should be a lens and not merely a locus. In other words, it affects the way we see everything in Scripture rather than only serving as an appendix to the theological system."[40] Admittedly, the use of "appendix" is exaggerated; "finale" would more accurately describe eschatology in most systematic theologies, where it is typically viewed as the final topic rather than as an extraneous topic only to be covered after the main substance of the endeavor has been concluded. Nonetheless, Horton's point is well taken, namely, that teleology drives and thus marks all other matters of God's engagement with his creatures. Still further, Horton accents the significance of a particular sort of eschatology that affirms the "already–not yet dialectic."[41]

All subjects must be plotted on and analyzed within this divine drama, whereby God has acted and will bring things to an eschatological end and, still further, where the triune God continues to engage human history today. In so doing, we are outbidding the postmodern emphasis on context, realizing that our location in the divine drama is even more constitutive of our existence than matters of race, gender, or class. Horton explains, "God's covenant with his people, through the history of Israel and the church, is the stage on which the divine drama is performed. This is the primary sociocultural location of the play and its performers—rendering it this play and not another."[42] Because covenant is the chief biblical context for life in this drama, it gives shape and some coherence to the wider theological task (without thereby becoming a central dogma from which others are deduced).[43] Horton goes on to relate covenant as a structuring principle to Jesus as the center of Scripture in himself (e.g., Luke 24:27, 44–45). Jesus must be the center of all we know, "yet his centrality cannot be accounted for in the abstract. It requires a context, and that context seems to be shaped in scripture by the notion of covenant."[44]

If that vision marks the goal of the series, then the remainder of *Covenant and Eschatology*, the first volume in the series, seeks to show that covenant and eschatology help

---

40. Horton, *Covenant and Eschatology*, 5.

41. Horton, *Covenant and Eschatology*, 5. For a fleshing out of the historical progress of the two cities through this dialectic, which he terms "mercy-serving time," see Horton, *Covenant and Eschatology*, 273–76. He argues further that the Pauline two-age model must be contrasted with the Platonic two-world model. "Eschatology after Nietzsche," in Horton, *Covenant and Eschatology*, 20–45.

42. Horton, *Covenant and Eschatology*, 15.

43. Horton, *Covenant and Eschatology*, 17.

44. Horton, *Covenant and Eschatology*, 18.

frame a viable way—a biblically faithful and intellectually coherent way—of thinking about God's action in history and of God's speech to us. While he employs more recent tools such as speech-act theory along the way, Horton does provide his argument for divine engagement in human history by returning to proper theological themes (especially regarding the doctrine of providence) and the way that it speaks of dual agency, primary and secondary causality, and the like: "God's faithfulness to redemptive history, therefore, and not a fatalistic 'development' of history in terms of a noncontingent teleology, preserves the fragile bond between the contingent and particular on the one hand and the universal plan of redemption on the other."[45] When Horton turns to address divine speech, he foregrounds covenant and eschatology even more directly (as he relates canon, law, and prophecy to covenantal relations and order).[46] Thinking about the implications of the "covenantal treaty" of Holy Scripture provides a lens by which to speak of God—as other, who can be experienced analogically and thereby who can summon each self and each community.[47]

Three volumes follow to apply these methodological and intrasystematic principles to the subjects of Christ, salvation, and the church. Each deserves brief mention here. *Lord and Servant* refers back to covenant and eschatology as "frameworks," "lenses," and "motifs" to lend clarity to the topic of Christology.[48] Yet truth be told, the volume offers a good bit more than a Christology. It begins with a significant sketch of theology proper, focusing around the subject of divine lordship. Horton works with a typology to regulate how we speak of divine transcendence and immanence in a productive fashion, arguing that God is a stranger whom we do in fact meet. Though we do not comprehend or control him, we also do not lack any awareness of or relation to him. It is accurate to say that this early chapter fleshes out the metaphysical underpinnings of his affirmation of the principle of analogy in *Covenant and Eschatology*.[49] Crucial to this principle of analogy and of meeting a lordly stranger is both the need to affirm creation *ex nihilo*, so as to give creaturely being space, and the need to affirm that nature is not yet grace, so as to give creaturely being integrity.[50] One might suggest that this last concern need not— indeed, should not—follow; its absence would not undercut his broader argument here.

---

45. Horton, *Covenant and Eschatology*, 118.

46. See especially Horton, *Covenant and Eschatology*, 131–39.

47. Horton, *Covenant and Eschatology*, 193–206 (on the summoned self), 206–19 (on the summoned community).

48. Michael S. Horton, *Lord and Servant: A Covenant Christology* (Louisville: Westminster John Knox, 2005), vii ("hermeneutical guide," "architectonic scheme," "framework"), xii ("matrix," "motif," "lens").

49. Horton, *Lord and Servant*, 9–16, 86; the analogy principle appears in Horton, *Covenant and Eschatology*, 7–9.

50. Horton, *Lord and Servant*, 76–79 (see also 103). Here as elsewhere, Horton's reliance on the way Meredith Kline and Delbert Hillers have distinguished between conditional and unconditional covenant relationships (in the ancient near East and in the canon of Scripture) leads to some unnecessary and unsustainable binaries. See his programmatic reliance on Kline and Hillers in Horton, *Lord and Servant*, viii–x; and at much greater length in Horton, *Covenant and Salvation: Union with Christ* (Louisville: Westminster John Knox, 2007), 11–36; even later usage of the terminology of *unilateral* and *bilateral* can be too simple, as in *Covenant and Salvation*, 149–50. I have sought to engage more recent historiographical work (from Gary Knoppers and Jon Levenson) and to recast the issues of conditional and unconditional covenantal relations in Michael Allen, "Into the Family of God:

Then Horton turns to offer an analysis of biblical anthropology, with the theme of servant playing a leading role and the idea of the covenant of works providing the matrix for developing this servant aspect. He offers a lengthy analysis of Genesis 1–3 and of the Adamic vocation of humans in innocence. He states, "Covenant and eschatology do not exhaust the meaning of the human, but significantly contextualize and orient it"; indeed, perhaps the most significant contextualizing prompt is the question that frames his anthropology: "Adam, where are you?" (cf. Gen. 3:9).[51] Covenant plays a more significant role than nature, and it is directed toward a particular teleological end. One might wonder if image language must be related so directly to covenant or even to eschatology, but Horton surely shows how the topics work coinherently in a powerful fashion.[52] One might also ask if he tends to suggest a more functional reduction of image language than Genesis and the rest of the canon warrants, but he surely shows the usefulness of asking the "who" question ("Who am I?") and of not being satisfied with the "what" question ("What am I"?).[53]

Then and only then does it center on the Lord who becomes servant, that is, on the incarnate Son of God:

> Everyone is looking for the nexus between transcendence and immanence. In the pantheistic turn with Schelling, Hegel, and Schleiermacher, the key idea is God's ontological unity with the world and the self, and some contemporary theologies are often simply variations on this theme. But the covenant is the proper site.[54]

For Horton, covenant prompts us to find a way to confess both transcendent otherness and lordship as well as immanent presence and solidarity in the one person of the incarnate Son; hence, he pushes against the historicist, more vividly kenoticist, or hyper-Lutheran Christologies that have gained prestige in recent decades (e.g., Robert Jenson).[55] He also points to how recent interest in Irenaeus and recapitulation can be furthered and expanded by Reformed teaching on the active obedience of the Christ, who fulfills the covenant of creation on our behalf, thereby wedding a supposedly Greek emphasis on the life of Jesus with a purportedly forensic emphasis from the Latin West.[56] Finally, a Reformed Christology that avoids any confusion of the natures also creates space for affirming a healthy Spirit Christology, whereby the humanity of Jesus is empowered by the work of the Spirit.[57] One might wish a slightly less exclusive focus

---

Covenant and the Genesis of Life with God," *TJ* 39, no. 2 (2018): 181–98. See also J. Nicholas Reid, "Ancient Near Eastern Backgrounds to Covenants," chap. 21 in this volume.

51. Horton, *Lord and Servant*, 92, 120.
52. Horton, *Lord and Servant*, 104.
53. Horton, *Lord and Servant*, 105–13.
54. Horton, *Lord and Servant*, 84.
55. Horton, *Lord and Servant*, 160–77.
56. Horton, *Lord and Servant*, 173. Note that the forensic has roots in the Old Testament and that claims regarding the "Latin heresy" (whether from Dietrich Ritschl or Colin Gunton) have little historiographic force.
57. Horton, *Lord and Servant*, 176–77.

on the Spirit (rather than the Word) as the divine agent influencing the human nature; nonetheless, Horton's point in drawing out an orthodox Spirit Christology remains a needed development of a host of texts (particularly in Luke).

Lord and Servant concludes by briefly reflecting on atonement theology. Here covenant is employed to frame how we approach sacrificial language over against its many detractors and to flesh out the three offices of Christ, whereby his prophetic, priestly, and royal work ministers a multifaceted word of good news to his people.[58] Horton's third volume in the series, *Covenant and Salvation*, picks up where *Lord and Servant* ends, with the ways in which covenant and eschatology structure thought about the work of Christ. Following analysis of atonement and office, *Covenant and Salvation* turns to justification and participation, engaging in debates with the trend formerly known as the New Perspective(s) on Paul, on the one hand, and then with the Finnish Lutheran and Radical Orthodox versions of participation, on the other.

Elaboration of his covenant theology exegetically moves to the forefront in *Covenant and Salvation*, where Horton nuances his description of a bicovenantal approach. In the initial chapter, he seeks "to demonstrate that the basic lines of thought that underwrite the distinction between law and gospel and the specific types of covenants advocated in confessional Reformed theology can be sustained on exegetical grounds."[59] Again, one could raise questions about whether the architectonic breakdown of covenants of law and of promise fits either the ancient Near Eastern evidence or the Old Testament quite right. For instance, Horton says that "the Abrahamic covenant will not be realized in history if it is in any way dependent on the zeal of his sinful people. If the promise is going to become a reality, it is Yahweh himself who will have to make it happen."[60] While a surface reading may find this to be unobjectionable, a further probing would lead one to ask why human "zeal" is the contrast point to complete divine provision? Why not "faith"? And can we really speak of fulfillment, even here, apart from "faith"? While faith itself is not a cause in a material sense, that doesn't mean that in other causal senses fulfillment doesn't "depend" on human moral agency (e.g., Gen. 15:6).[61]

Horton navigates a host of soteriological debates in this volume: how justification relates to the project of the kingdom of God and the new creation,[62] how individual or personal salvation relates to corporate salvation,[63] how law as a covenant principle differs from law as a redemptive-historical epoch,[64] how *Christus victor* language is distinct

---

58. Horton, *Lord and Servant*, 178–207, 208–70, respectively.

59. Horton, *Covenant and Salvation*, 12.

60. Horton, *Covenant and Salvation*, 18.

61. Even Horton's own approach toward a republication thesis for the Mosaic covenant would be strengthened by engagement with Francis Watson, *Paul and the Hermeneutics of Faith* (London: T&T Clark, 2004). I would argue, however, that a host of texts (not least Rom. 9:30–32) would argue much more broadly against republication.

62. Horton, *Covenant and Salvation*, 35–36.

63. Horton, *Covenant and Salvation*, 55–64.

64. Horton, *Covenant and Salvation*, 87–101.

from yet integrated with forensic images,[65] how the eternal roots of salvation relate to its historical unfolding (via the *pactum salutis*),[66] how biblical language of "we in Christ" sits alongside the equally scriptural talk of "Christ in us,"[67] and the like. This last example illustrates the broader trend, inasmuch as the notion of "covenant mutuality" (where we really meet the stranger, to speak ontologically) helps make sense of union and of distinction, of the one and of the many, or a Christian identity that does not obliterate our specific persona. Here as well as in the subsections of part 2 of the book, where Horton addresses matters pertaining to sanctification and participation, he continues to draw out the heuristic significance of covenant and eschatology.

Horton's final volume in the series, *People and Place*, "highlights the inextricable connection between union with Christ (soteriology) and the communion of saints (ecclesiology)," "plotting ecclesiology on the map of the redemptive-historical economy" and then tracing "the source or origin of the church in proclamation and sacrament" and fleshing out "its consequent identity and mission."[68] Again, eschatology provides the melody line throughout, and covenantal order gives directorial notes along the way. The way includes turns into discussion of what it means to speak of the church as a listening or hearing church identified as the creature of the divine Word and then twists into Reformed eucharistic theology as well.[69] The book also includes a robust discussion of the Nicene notes of the church in a way that is marked historically by the church's place in redemptive history. Perhaps most significantly, Horton considers the central category of *totus Christus* (the "whole Christ" image drawn from Augustine) and pushes against tendencies to confuse Christ and his body or to contrast them.[70] He states, "In a covenantal model, the hypostatic union of deity and humanity in Christ is distinguished from the mystical union of the church with its head."[71]

Admittedly, parts of the series play out without much direct reference to the theme of covenant. For instance, perhaps the most fascinating and, to my mind, most compelling chapter of the whole project is "Real Absence, Real Presence: Ecclesiology and the Economy of Grace," which fixes heavily on redemptive history and eschatology but has rather little overt connection to covenant as such.[72] That is not a criticism of the chapter, however, for the force of Horton's series often comes in showing how post-Reformation Reformed scholasticism and modern Reformed redemptive-historical analyses can be shown to sit productively alongside wider and older catholic

---

65. Horton, *Covenant and Salvation*, 109–14.

66. Horton, *Covenant and Salvation*, 130–39.

67. Horton, *Covenant and Salvation*, 139–52.

68. Michael S. Horton, *People and Place: A Covenant Ecclesiology* (Louisville: Westminster John Knox, 2008), ix.

69. Horton, *People and Place*, 37–98, 124–52, respectively.

70. Horton, *People and Place*, 155–89.

71. Horton, *People and Place*, 187. He also warns of how too narrow of a focus on ecclesiology through the lens of the Eucharist can go awry and needs to be corrected, situated by an eschatological alertness to the church's place in redemptive history (188–89).

72. Horton, *People and Place*, 1–34.

theological themes (e.g., in that case, early Christian teaching on the ascension) to great effect.[73]

Like the varied writings of Webster, Horton's dogmatics represents one of the most sizable and fresh contributions to Christian, much less specifically Reformed, doctrine in recent decades. Even those who might wish for application to some other topic or a different exegetical tack on certain questions should appreciate the scope and consistency with which covenant serves a crucial role in commending the architecture of a confessionally Reformed theology that explicitly commends its scriptural roots. Not only do these projects bear a gravitas in their own right, but they also provide substantive counterproposals to the most influential contemporary alternatives to covenant theology (e.g., the various iterations of participationist theology).

Principles for Ongoing Theological Appropriation of Covenant Theology

What lessons might be learned from these two projects? Where might we fruitfully go from here? This chapter concludes with seven principles that might helpfully further our future theological defense and exposition regarding the ongoing appropriation of covenant theology for the work of Christian dogmatics. The principles are briefly stated, to be sure, but they warrant further elaboration as well as application in ongoing exegetical and dogmatic work regarding the covenants of the triune God.

1. Covenant has explanatory force precisely because it exists right at the nexus of the most fundamental theological tenets: divine identity and nature, human being, and all relations between the two.

2. Covenant theology serves not only as an analytic rubric for describing redemptive history and its moral-relational entailments (thus as a topic in its own right) but also as a synthetic lens through which we can appreciate the relationship of many or most theological doctrines and God's design to be with his people (and thus as a lens for viewing other topics well).

3. Covenant can help us appreciate the distinct integrity and yet intimate connection of time to its roots in divine eternity. For Reformed Christians, therefore, covenant can help us think more coherently about how divine election relates to the historical episodes in canonical history and cosmic experience.

4. Covenant theology may provide an ordered principle for moving beyond a few false binaries that continue to shape theological discussion: individual/communal, forensic/transformative, legal/filial, soteriological/cosmic, and the like.

5. Covenant theology ought to remain engaged with archaeological and comparative accounts of covenant language in the ancient Near East without lapsing

---

73. Horton also does well in seeking to engage historiographically with archaeologists (albeit sometimes with dated material: see note 50 above on his reliance on Hillers and Kline) and also with Jewish exegetical interlocutors such as Jon Levenson, which is a great strength—and again could only be enhanced by more recent analysis of volumes postdating Levenson's earlier *Sinai and Zion: An Entry into the Jewish Bible* (San Francisco: Harper and Row, 1985).

into reductive appropriation of scholarly constructs that too easily elide the thickness or complexity of the scriptural teaching, much less its distinctiveness at key points.

6. Covenant theology can and should be pursued in a nonreductive manner, which means attending to both its metaphysical foundations as well as its moral entailments, without thereby confusing the metaphysical and the moral.

7. Covenant theology ought to help us reorder our priorities and should alert us to the need for reordering our loves so as to match the emphases of Holy Scripture, rightly inclusive of the breadth of divine concern for all matters and yet fittingly focused on living communion with the triune God as the prize above all pearls.

PART 3

COLLATERAL AND
THEOLOGICAL STUDIES

21

Ancient Near Eastern
Backgrounds to Covenants

J. Nicholas Reid

While one might be tempted to move on to the next chapter of this volume, there are many reasons to wade through the complex material in this one.[1] I list but a few. One can hardly read a commentary on Deuteronomy without confronting issues related to the suzerain-vassal treaties of the ancient Near East (hereafter ANE). The ANE material is frequently cited to explain the structure and content and even determine the date of the composition of the book of Deuteronomy. Further, almost any work on covenant theology from the last fifty years, whether biblical theology or systematic theology, includes the categories of ANE land grants and suzerain-vassal treaties. While authors receive such scholarship in a variety of ways, the ANE evidence has come to shape not only the way we speak and write about covenants, but as seen below, the evidence has also come to inform and even at times shape interpretation.

Since the publication of George E. Mendenhall's book *Law and Covenant in Israel and the Ancient Near East*,[2] numerous comparisons have been drawn between the covenantal texts of the Old Testament and the related evidence from the rest of the ANE. Mendenhall's book appeared about a century after Akkadian cuneiform, a

---

1. I wish to thank the following readers for their helpful suggestions with respect to the ANE evidence: Caleb Howard, Matthew McAfee, Joshua Van Ee, and Noel Weeks. Michael Allen and Keith Mathison, two theologians, were kind enough to read this essay and offer comments. Finally, two students deserve mention for proofreading: Jesse Atkinson and Greg Gale. Of course, any errors that remain are my own.

2. George E. Mendenhall, *Law and Covenant in Israel and the Ancient Near East* (Pittsburgh: Biblical Colloquium, 1955).

Semitic language written in a system consisting of wedges, was officially considered deciphered. In AD 1857 a test was proposed to determine whether Akkadian cuneiform was actually understood by scholars. A long text had been recently dug up at Nimrud, and a copy of it was given to Henry Rawlinson, Edward Hincks, William Henry Fox Talbot, and Jules Oppert, who were each to decipher the text without consulting one another. After the Royal Asiatic Society in London received the four independent translations, it was determined that, despite some discrepancies together with the varying abilities and experience of the scholars, the correlation between their editions was significant enough for the society to declare decipherment achieved.[3] While most scripts of cuneiform have since been successfully deciphered, archaeologists are continuing to discover texts, and many more texts sit in collections around the world, waiting for scholars with the time and ability to read them. In this study of the ancient Near Eastern backgrounds to covenants, it seems important to make a basic observation related to the time at which cuneiform was deciphered: classical Reformed covenant theology was originally formed prior to our access to the Assyriological evidence. While the decipherment of cuneiform remains a significant development in scholarship, ancient Near Eastern evidence, in its current state, remains incapable of solving our key exegetical and theological debates about the nature of the biblical covenants. Put differently, the background, while informative, should not be made the foreground of covenant theology.

Many texts and text types from the ANE have been associated with the covenants found within the biblical record.[4] In the broadest of terms, covenants, which have a very long history in the ANE, may be divided into those that are between equals and those in which one party is superior.[5] A covenant can formalize that relationship, or it can even change the social dynamics either to return to parity or to establish supremacy

---

3. For a popular treatment of decipherment, see Dominique Charpin, *Reading and Writing in Babylon*, trans. Jane Marie Todd (Cambridge, MA: Harvard University Press, 2010), 2–6. See also Jean Bottéro, *La Mésopotamie: L'écriture, la raison et les dieux* (Paris: Folio, 1987), translated into English by Zainab Bahrani and Marc Van De Mieroop as *Mesopotamia: Writing, Reasoning, and the Gods* (Chicago: University of Chicago Press, 1992).

4. Kenneth A. Kitchen and Paul J. N. Lawrence have attempted to gather all the relevant comparative material into a multivolume work. *Treaty, Law and Covenant in the Ancient Near East*, 3 vols. (Wiesbaden: Harrassowitz, 2012). This ambitious work, however, still omits a number of relevant texts. The standard versions of the relevant texts should still have priority despite being published in multiple places, as these editions have fewer errors and less idiosyncratic interpretations than those found in Kitchen and Lawrence's work. For reviews of *Treaty, Law and Covenant in the Ancient Near East*, see Jacob Lauinger, "Approaching Ancient Near Eastern Treaties, Laws, and Covenants," *JAOS* 136, no. 1 (2016): 125–34; Eva Von Dassow, "Treaty, Law and Bible in Literalist Theory," *ANES* 53 (2016): 287–98.

5. Jon D. Levenson, *The Love of God: Divine Gift, Human Gratitude, and Mutual Faithfulness in Judaism*, LJI (Princeton, NJ: Princeton University Press, 2016), 7–8. See the discussion of "parity treaties," where involved parties are referred to as "brothers," and the discussion of "vassal treaties," where the relationship is described in terms of "father and son" or "master and slave," in Samuel Greengus, "Covenant and Treaty in the Hebrew Bible and in the Ancient Near East," in *Ancient Israel's History: An Introduction to Issues and Sources*, ed. Bill T. Arnold and Richard S. Hess (Grand Rapids, MI: Baker Academic, 2014), 98. On the use of the terms "brothers" and "fathers" in the Mesopotamian treaties, see Bertrand Lafont, "International Relations in the Ancient Near East: The Birth of a Complete Diplomatic System," *DS* 12, no. 1 (2001): 40–43.

formally.[6] The breadth of related material precludes an exhaustive treatment here. For this reason, the present essay focuses primarily on the ways in which scholars have used the laws, treaties, and land grants of the ancient Near East to contribute to our overall understanding of the biblical covenants. This chapter concludes with some basic observations about the prospects and limitations of such comparative projects.

At the outset it should be noted that one's assumptions or position about the authorship of a particular text and the nature of its composition has direct influence on how one understands the relationship between the covenants of the Bible and the ANE material. Those who hold to Mosaic authorship for the Pentateuch tend to emphasize connections that relate to that historical period.[7] Others, however, who think the text of Deuteronomy, for instance, was composed much later to support the reforms of Josiah, tend to see stronger connections with the texts of the neo-Assyrian period, which was the time when Josiah lived. This is not to suggest that all these arguments are purely circular or lacking attention to the evidence. In fact, proponents of the different views pay significant attention to the details of the texts under consideration. Nevertheless, it is inevitable that one's broader understanding of the situation contributes to how one accounts for and puts together the limited evidence. For instance, if one conceives of direct literary dependence rather than oral, traditional, and cultural influence, then one also needs to pinpoint plausible points of contact between the scribal cultures of the texts being compared. In other words, the scribe of text B must have access to and the ability to read text A if the scribe of text B is repurposing or borrowing directly from text A. If one text borrows directly from another, that restricts its composition to the plausible points of contact. All these issues should be kept in mind in the following survey, which discusses the main points of connections made in scholarship between the so-called laws, treaties, and land grants known from the rest of the ancient Near East.

Laws

The covenants of the Old Testament contain numerous laws that often touch on similar cases considered within other texts from the ANE. The most obvious example is the ox-goring laws found in the Laws of Ḥammurabi (LH) §§250–252 and Exodus 21:28–32 (see table 21.1).[8]

---

6. See the discussion of various redefinitions of social relationships in the Old Testament in Dominik Markl, "God's Covenants with Humanity and Israel," in *The Hebrew Bible: A Critical Companion*, ed. John Barton (Princeton, NJ: Princeton University Press, 2016), 316.

7. For a succinct and accessible overview of the differing perspectives, see John D. Currid, *Exodus*, vol. 1, *A Clear and Present Danger: A Commentary on Exodus 1–18*, EPSC (Darlington, UK: Evangelical Press, 2000), 27–32.

8. For a classic treatment of these passages, see Jacob J. Finkelstein, *The Ox That Gored*, TAPS, vol. 71, no. 2 (Philadelphia: American Philosophical Society, 1981). For a recent treatment and a survey of previous scholarship on the subject, see David P. Wright, *Inventing God's Law: How the Covenant Code of the Bible Used and Revised the Laws of Hammurabi* (Oxford: Oxford University Press, 2009), 7–24, 205–9. I avoid the preferable Amorite rendering "Ḥammurapi," since the name is more commonly rendered "Ḥammurabi."

Table 21.1   Exodus 21:28–32 and the Laws of Ḥammurabi Compared

Exodus 21:28–32	Laws of Ḥammurabi §§250–252*
21:28 When an ox gores a man or a woman to death, the ox shall be stoned, and its flesh shall not be eaten, but the owner of the ox shall not be liable.	§250 If an ox gores to death a man while it is passing through the streets, that case has no basis for a claim.
21:29 But if the ox has been accustomed to gore in the past, and its owner has been warned but has not kept it in, and it kills a man or a woman, the ox shall be stoned, and its owner also shall be put to death.	§251 If a man's ox is a known gorer, and the authorities of his city quarter notify him that it is a known gorer, but he does not blunt(?) its horns or control his ox, and that ox gores to death a member of the *awilu*-class, he (the owner) shall give 30 shekels of silver.
21:30 If a ransom is imposed on him, then he shall give for the redemption of his life whatever is imposed on him.	§252 If it is a man's slave (who is fatally gored), he shall give 20 shekels of silver.
21:31 If it gores a man's son or daughter, he shall be dealt with according to this same rule.	
21:32 If the ox gores a slave, male or female, the owner shall give to their master thirty shekels of silver, and the ox shall be stoned.	

* Translation from Martha Roth, *Law Collections from Mesopotamia and Asia Minor*, ed. Piotr Michalowski, 2nd ed., WAW (Atlanta: Scholars Press, 1997).

Even a cursory reading reveals a number of similarities between the two texts. Both texts deal with an ox that gores. Both texts also consider any possible negligence on behalf of the owner of an ox that gores. And both texts stipulate financial penalties for the death of a slave caused by a goring ox; the biblical text gives a penalty of thirty shekels of silver while the Laws of Ḥammurabi call for twenty shekels. Although the connections between these laws are apparent on a conceptual level, the explanation of the similarities situated in the broader legal traditions of the ANE is much more complicated. For this reason, other "law codes" from the ANE must be considered.

The earliest "law code" discovered from the ANE is the Laws of Ur-Namma (ca. 2100 BC).[9] While the classification of these "law codes" remains debated,[10] there is a long legal tradition of law collections spanning the late third to first millennium BC.[11] Even earlier texts, such

---

9. All dates are approximate and according to Middle Chronology. On chronology, see, e.g., Paul Aström, *High, Middle or Low? Acts of an International Colloquium on Absolute Chronology*, 3 vols., SMAL 56, 57, 80 (Gothenburg: University of Gothenburg, 1987–1989); F. H. Cryer, "Chronology: Issues and Problems," in *Civilizations of the Ancient Near East*, ed. Jack M. Sasson (New York: Hendrickson, 1995), 651–64; Michael Roaf, "The Fall of Babylon in 1499 NC or 1595 MC," *Akkadica* 133 (2012): 147–74.

10. On this issue and related matters, see J. Nicholas Reid, "The Children of Slaves in Early Mesopotamian Laws and Edicts," *RA* 111, no. 1 (2017): 9n3.

11. For transliterations, translations, and bibliography of the relevant primary sources, see Martha Roth, *Law Collections from Mesopotamia and Asia Minor*, ed. Piotr Michalowski, 2nd ed., WAW (Atlanta: Scholars Press, 1997). The primary edition for the "Laws of Ur-Namma" is the full edition with new textual information by Miguel Civil, "The Law Collection of Ur-Namma," in *Cuneiform Royal Inscriptions and Related Texts in the Schøyen*

as the Code of Enmetena and the Reforms of UruKAgina (ca. 2500–2300 BC),[12] include various edicts of reform that ideologically relate to the later law collections of Mesopotamia, demonstrating a very long history of legal writings in the ancient Near East.[13]

A number of theories have been offered to explain the similarities found in the laws of the Mosaic covenant and those from other cultures in the ANE. These theories often range from direct literary dependence to the concept of ANE "legal meta-traditions." Bruce Wells argues that the numerous similar laws spanning the ancient Near East are best explained as belonging to "legal meta-traditions," basically shared legal traditions that "pervaded legal thinking."[14] The most ambitious argument for direct literary dependence comes from David P. Wright. In his monograph *Inventing God's Law: How the Covenant Code of the Bible Used and Revised the Laws of Hammurabi*, Wright argues that the so-called Covenant Code, traditionally understood as Exodus 20:23–23:19, "is directly, primarily and throughout dependent upon LH."[15] To support a theory of direct literary dependence, one has to establish a plausible point of contact with the text of the Laws of Ḥammurabi by a person with some knowledge of cuneiform, the writing system used for the Laws of Ḥammurabi. For Wright, this contact took place during the neo-Assyrian period (ca. 740–640 BC), when both Assyria had influence over Israel and the Laws of Ḥammurabi were copied frequently as a canonical text. Christopher Hays's chart is very helpful for understanding the comparisons (see table 21.2).

While Wright has drawn a number of interesting points of connections, many of the comparisons are quite loose. For example, Wright compares Exodus 22:6–8 with the Laws of Ḥammurabi §§265–266, calling them laws of deposits (see table 21.3).

In this instance, the category is too generic to see any real connection. A rigorous methodology for comparison is wanting in Wright's book, leaving some alleged connections unconvincing.

While the blending of weaker connections with those that are much stronger arguably weakens Wright's position, thereby calling into question his overall proposal, other more substantial objections also exist. Bruce Wells, for instance, has argued that there was a legal "meta-tradition" in the ANE and that the "Covenant Code" can be connected to all

---

Collection, ed. A. R. George, CUSAS 17 (Bethesda, MD: CDL Press, 2011), 221–86. For a recent detailed analysis of the "Laws of Ur-Namma," see C. Wilcke, "Gesetze in sumerischer Sprache," in *Studies in Sumerian Language and Literature: Festschrift für Joachim Krecher*, ed. N. Koslova, E. Vizirova, and G. Zólyomi, BB 8 (Winona Lake, IN: Eisenbrauns, 2014), 455–612. For a history of the early developments of ANE law, see, in particular, Claus Wilcke, *Early Ancient Near Eastern Law: A History of Its Beginnings; The Early Dynastic and Sargonic Periods*, rev. ed. (Winona Lake, IN: Eisenbrauns, 2007).

12. For the standard editions and relevant bibliography, see Douglas R. Frayne, *Presargonic Period (2700–2350 B.C.)*, RIME 1 (Toronto: University of Toronto Press, 2008).

13. On the importance of justice to Mesopotamian kingship, Dominique Charpin states, "If there was one fundamental theme in kingship ideology of Mesopotamia during the three millennia of its history, it was truly that of justice." *Writing, Law, and Kingship in Old Babylonian Mesopotamia*, trans. Jane Marie Todd (Chicago: University of Chicago Press, 2010), 83. See also the discussion of these early edicts in Wilcke, *Early Ancient Near Eastern Law*, 21–25.

14. Bruce Wells, "The Covenant Code and Near Eastern Legal Traditions: A Response to David P. Wright," *Maarav* 13, no. 1 (2006): 116–18.

15. Wright, *Inventing God's Law*, 3.

the existing law collections from the Near East.[16] He demonstrates that parallels can also be drawn with other law collections, thereby undermining Wright's theory of direct dependence. Wells also criticizes Wright's lack of precision when it comes to points of comparison.

Table 21.2 Exodus 20–22 and the Laws of Ḥammurabi Compared, Based on Hays's Modified Summary of Wright*

Exodus 20–22		Laws of Ḥammurabi	
20:1–2	—	Prologue	—
21:2–6	Debt slavery of males, children of slaves, and master relations	§117 §175 §282	Son, father debt servant Children of slaves Master relations
21:7–11	Debt slavery of a daughter, including displeasure, law about daughters, taking second wife, and three means of support	§117 §§148–149 §§154–156 §178	Daughter debt servant, subsequent laws
21:12–14	Death from striking with intent	§207	Death from striking with intent
21:15–17	Child rebellion	§§192–193, 195	Child rebellion
21:18–19	Men fighting, injury, cure	§206	Men fighting, injury, cure
21:20–21	Killing one of lower class	§208	Killing one of lower class
21:22–23	Causing a miscarriage	§§209–214	Causing a miscarriage
21:23–25	—	§§196–197	—
21:23–27	Talion laws, injury to slaves	§§196–201	Talion laws, injury to slaves
21:28–32, 35–36	Goring ox	§§250–252	Goring ox
21:33–34	Negligence	§§229–230	Negligence
22:1, 4	Theft, animal theft	§§253–265	Animal theft
22:7–8	"Deposit"	§§265–266	"Deposit of animals"
22:9–12	"Injury and death of animals"	§§266–267	"Injury and death of animals"
22:13–14	"Animal rental"	§§268–271	"Animal rental"
22:20–31	—	Epilogue	—

* From Christopher B. Hays, *Hidden Riches: A Sourcebook for the Comparative Study of the Hebrew Bible and Ancient Near East* (Louisville: Westminster John Knox), 137–38.

---

16. Wells, "Covenant Code," 116–18.

Table 21.3　Exodus 22:6–8 and the Laws of Ḥammurabi Compared

Exodus 22:6–8	Laws of Ḥammurabi §§265–266*
22:6　If fire breaks out and catches in thorns so that the stacked grain or the standing grain or the field is consumed, he who started the fire shall make full restitution. 22:7　If a man gives to his neighbor money or goods to keep safe, and it is stolen from the man's house, then, if the thief is found, he shall pay double. 22:8　If the thief is not found, the owner of the house shall come near to God to show whether or not he has put his hand to his neighbor's property.	§265　If a shepherd, to whom cattle or sheep and goats were given for shepherding, acts criminally and alters the brand and sells them, they shall charge and convict him and he shall replace for their owner cattle or sheep and goats tenfold that which he stole. §266　If, in the enclosure, an epidemic should break out or a lion make a kill, the shepherd shall clear himself before the god, and the owner of the enclosure shall accept responsibility for him for the loss sustained in the enclosure.

* Translation from Martha Roth, *Law Collections from Mesopotamia and Asia Minor*, ed. Piotr Michalowski, 2nd ed., WAW (Atlanta: Scholars Press, 1997).

The diversity of the connections that can be drawn stretching throughout the legal tradition of the ANE presents challenges for pinpointing a period of direct literary influence from the "law codes," if such direct influence existed. If the "meta-tradition" proposal is correct, it is unclear exactly how such "meta-traditions" would have developed, perhaps orally. Nevertheless, the culture of the ANE was certainly more internationally connected through writing than some might assume. This reality becomes even more demonstrable in the following section, which deals with treaties.

Treaties

Treaties may be considered here in relation to covenants, but of course, much like the "laws" considered above, these two do not share a one-to-one correspondence. A treaty is usually a binding agreement between two or more parties that occurs in an international context. The Hebrew term בְּרִית, "covenant," is not restricted to international contexts but can be employed within them.[17] The extant treaties of the ANE belong predominately to four particular periods that demonstrate their very long history, and yet there were transitions in this history, particularly in relation to writing:[18]

- Texts from the early city-states of Mesopotamia, ca. 2400–2200 BC
- Amorite texts from Mari, ca. 1700–1600 BC
- Texts from the Hittites, ca. 1400–1200 BC
- Neo-Assyrian treaties, ca. 800–600 BC[19]

---

17. Gary Knoppers, "Ancient Near Eastern Royal Grants and the Davidic Covenant: A Parallel?," *JAOS* 116, no. 4 (1996): 670–97.

18. Lafont, "International Relations," 53–55.

19. The comparative project should consider not just compilations of these texts but also original and primary publications of the material by specialists. For convenience and brevity, the reader is pointed to one place where such extensive bibliography can be found: Greengus, "Covenant and Treaty," 96–97nn14–16.

While these are the main examples available to us, one must remember that at least a couple of mitigating circumstances may skew the evidence, as the state of Assyriology is very much a work in progress, with developments and discoveries happening all the time. First, textual finds are limited by the accidents of preservation and discovery. Other texts might have existed but have yet to be found. Others still may have been altogether destroyed in antiquity or otherwise unpreserved. Second, there is a common misconception that legal agreements and treaties had to be written down. Perhaps this perspective comes in part from assumptions relating to modern legal practices where written evidence is more concrete and legally binding. Indeed, attempts to pit the oral traditions, which are considered more subject to change, against writing have been abandoned by and large in the field of Assyriology, as it has become clear that agreements were typically written to preserve the details of the extraordinary cases and mitigating circumstances with numerous other details often assumed and omitted from the written texts.[20] In fact, not all these texts may be considered "treaties." That the oath was at the very least sometimes more important than the written texts themselves can be seen in the Amorite treaties of the seventeenth century, where the written sources merely served to enable the related parties to come to the terms of their agreements and facilitate the more important aspect of the agreement, which was the ceremony of taking an oath.[21] This is not to suggest that the written word was unimportant, but writing appears to have become more prominent in treaties to facilitate agreements when parties were separated by distance during the Amorite period.[22] Writing became even more significant in these agreements when the terms extended beyond the lifetime of the contracting parties. As writing becomes more important to the agreement itself, this is when we can speak of the development of treaties proper, where curses by the gods are threatened against anyone who alters the word of the treaty.[23] In short, while the most important evidence that we possess is archaeological and written, oral agreements and traditions, which were a common feature of life in the ANE, are no longer available to us.

A major debate exists about whether Deuteronomy has greater similarities to the Hittite treaties of the fourteenth and thirteenth centuries or the neo-Assyrian succession treaties of the eighth and seventh centuries. This debate has been rather significant, as the relation between the covenants of the ANE has often been used to argue for a particular date of the covenants. I survey these positions below, as they remain among the driving forces behind the comparative discussion. Table 21.4 illustrates the most common connections proposed and how they relate to Deuteronomy.

---

20. See Samuel Greengus, "The Old Babylonian Marriage Contract," *JAOS* 89, no. 3 (1969): 505–32; Charpin, *Writing, Law, and Kingship*, 48–49.
21. See Lafont, "International Relations," 54–55.
22. Charpin, *Reading and Writing in Babylon*, 165.
23. See the discussion of this "transformation of treaties from protocols of oaths to true contracts" in Charpin, *Reading and Writing in Babylon*, 166–68.

Table 21.4   Hittite, Deuteronomic, and Assyrian Treaties Compared*

Comparison:	Hittite	Deuteronomy	Assyrian
Covenant giver	§1	5:6	§§1, 4
Historical prologue	§§1–3	1:1–4:14	—
Stipulations	§§4–12	4:44–27:8	§§5–32
Divine witnesses	§§13–19	4:26 (31:28)	§§2–3
Curses	§20	28:15–68	§§37–56, 58–106
Blessings	§21	28:1–14	—
Oath taking	—	27:9–26	§57
Deposit/recital	—	31:10–13, 24–29	§§34–35

* Based on Christopher B. Hays, *Hidden Riches: A Sourcebook for the Comparative Study of the Hebrew Bible and Ancient Near East* (Louisville: Westminster John Knox), 179.

The first observation is that Deuteronomy shares common features with both extant Hittite and Assyrian treaties but that there are also points of divergence with each. The most significant point of comparison between Deuteronomy and the Hittite treaties is the historical prologue. The connections between the book of Deuteronomy and the Hittite treaties of the second millennium have been particularly popular among evangelical authors, since this affinity has been used to support Mosaic authorship for most of the book of Deuteronomy. Primary proponents of this view include Meredith Kline and Kenneth Kitchen.[24]

When seeking to draw parallels and points of similarity with the treaties of the ANE, other significant correlations between the curse sections of Deuteronomy with those found in, for example, Esarhaddon's succession treaty must be considered (see table 21.5).

The idea that there the book of Deuteronomy had direct literary dependence on Esarhaddon's succession treaty was seriously challenged, since all the known examples focused on Median lords (ancient Iran) with no examples found near Judah.[25] This all changed, however, with the discovery of another manuscript of Esarhaddon's succession treaty at Tell Tayinat, about three hundred miles north of Jerusalem, bringing Esarhaddon in much closer contact with the biblical world.[26]

24. See, e.g., Meredith G. Kline, *Treaty of the Great King: The Covenant Structure of Deuteronomy; Studies and Commentary* (Grand Rapids, MI: Eerdmans, 1963); Kline, *The Structure of Biblical Authority*, 2nd ed. (Eugene, OR: Wipf and Stock, 1997). The culmination of Kitchen's work on the subject is found in *Treaty, Law and Covenant*.

25. See the excellent survey of the main proponents in Laura Quick, *Deuteronomy 28 and the Aramaic Curse Tradition*, OTRM (Oxford: Oxford University Press, 2018), 41–67.

26. See Timothy P. Harrison and James F. Osborne, "Building XVI and the Neo-Assyrian Sacred Precinct at Tell Tayinat," *JCS* 64 (2012): 125–43; Jacob Lauinger, "Esarhaddon's Succession Treaty at Tell Tayinat: Text and Commentary," *JCS* 64 (2012): 87–123. See the discussion of the developing debate about the possibility of direct

Table 21.5   Deuteronomy 28:26–31 and Esarhaddon's Succession Treaty Compared*

Deuteronomy 28:26–31	Esarhaddon's Succession Treaty (by line number)
28:26 And your dead body shall be food for all birds of the air and for the beasts of the earth, and there shall be no one to frighten them away.	[Compare 427 below]
28:27 The Lord will strike you with the boils of Egypt, and with tumors and scabs and itch, of which you cannot be healed.	418 May Anu, king of the gods, let disease, exhaustion, malaria, sleeplessness, worries and ill health rain upon all your houses.
	419 May Sin, the brightness of heaven and earth,
	420 clothe you with leprosy . . .
28:28 The Lord will strike you with madness and blindness and confusion of mind,	422 May Šamaš, the light of heaven and earth,
28:29 and you shall grope at noonday, as the blind grope in darkness, and you shall not prosper in your ways. And you shall be only oppressed and robbed continually, and there shall be no one to help you.	423 not judge you justly. May he remove your eyesight.
	424 Walk about in darkness!
[Compare 28:26 above]	425 May Ninurta, the foremost among the gods, fell you with his fierce arrow;
	426 may he fill the plain with your blood
	427 and feed your flesh to the eagle and the vulture.
28:30 You shall betroth a wife, but another man shall ravish her.	428 May Venus, the brightest of the stars, before your eyes make your wives
	429 lie in the lap of your enemy.
You shall build a house, but you shall not dwell in it. You shall plant a vineyard, but you shall not enjoy its fruit.	May your sons
28:31 Your ox shall be slaughtered before your eyes, but you shall not eat any of it. Your donkey shall be seized before your face, but shall not be restored to you. Your sheep shall be given to your enemies, but there shall be no one to help you.	430 not take possession of your house, but a strange enemy divide your goods.

* See edition and comparisons in Quick, *Aramaic Curse Tradition*, 151–58.

literary dependence in Quick, *Aramaic Curse Tradition*, 25–36. For the very limited cuneiform finds in Judah and Samaria, see W. Horowitz, T. Oshima, and S. Sanders, "A Bibliographical List of Cuneiform Inscriptions from Canaan, Palestine/Philistia, and the Land of Israel," *JAOS* 122, no. 4 (2002): 753–66.

Table 21.6 Structural Parallels between Esarhaddon's Succession Treaty and Deuteronomy 13*

§	Esarhaddon's Succession Treaty	Deuteronomy 13	Verse†
4	Fidelity to the "word" of overlord (imposing the vassal treaty)	Fidelity to "word" of Moses (mediating legal corpus as treaty)	1
	A Double prohibition against alteration (merism) ⟍⟋ B Requirement for obedience	B' Requirement for obedience A' Double prohibition against alteration (merism)	
5	Obligation to protect heir‡	—	
6	Obligation to report opposition to succession within ruling family	Thematic overlap with §10, incorporated into 13:7–12	
7	Succession at Esarhaddon's untimely death	—	
8	Definition of loyalty	—	
9	Prohibition of disloyal conduct	—	
10	Sanctions against disloyalty; eliminate incitement even from	Sanctions against disloyalty; eliminate incitement even from	
	X Family member Y Prophet	Y' Prophet X' Family member	2–6 7–12

* From Bernard M. Levinson, "The Neo-Assyrian Origins of the Canon Formula in Deuteronomy 13:1," in *Scriptural Exegesis: The Shapes of Culture and the Religious Imagination; Essays in Honour of Michael Fishbane*, ed. Deborah A. Green and Laura S. Lieber (Oxford: Oxford University Press, 2009), 24–45 (chart on 34); Levinson, "Textual Criticism, Assyriology, and the History of Interpretation: Deuteronomy 13:7a as a Test Case in Method," *JBL* 120, no. 2 (2001): 211–43. See also Levinson, "'But You Shall Surely Kill Him!' The Text-Critical and Neo-Assyrian Evidence for MT Deuteronomy 13:10," in *Bundesdokument und Gesetz: Studien zum Deuteronomium*, ed. Georg Braulik, HBSt 4 (Freiberg: Herder, 1995), 37–63; Levinson, "Recovering the Lost Original Meaning of ולא תכסה עליו (Deuteronomy 13:9)," *JBL* 115, no. 4 (1996): 601–20; Levinson, "Esarhaddon's Succession Treaty as the Source for the Canon Formula in Deuteronomy 13:1," *JAOS* 130, no. 3 (2010): 337–47. The first three journal articles listed above have been reprinted and updated in Levinson, *The Right Chorale: Studies in Biblical Law and Interpretation*, FAT 54 (Tübingen: Mohr Siebeck, 2008), 112–94.

† Verse numbers in this chart follow Hebrew versification.

‡ The headings here for Esarhaddon's succession treaty §§5–9 follow Simo Parpola and Kazuko Watanabe, *Neo-Assyrian Treaties and Loyalty Oaths*, SAA 2 (Winona Lake, IN: Eisenbrauns, 2014), 31–33.

The curses are not the only proposed connections between Esarhaddon's succession treaty and Deuteronomy. The "canonical formula" found in Deuteronomy 12:32 (13:1 MT) forbids altering the text: "Everything that I command you, you shall be careful to do. You shall not add to it or take from it." In table 21.6, Bernard Levinson, who developed the table, argues for an extensive interaction with Esarhaddon's succession treaty in which textual borrowing is indicated by chiastic inversion. Levinson's view is more optimistic than some about cuneiform contact, since he sees direct literary contact, borrowing, and reworking.

Yet even those who see serious correlations between Esarhaddon's succession treaty and Deuteronomy, and who do not reject the possibility of access to the treaty, do not necessarily see direct literary dependence on cuneiform texts. For example, Laura Quick, who casts Esarhaddon's succession treaty as one of the "vectors" of influence on Deuteronomy, questions the idea that the Judean scribes possessed the multilingual and linguistic competence required to produce texts directly dependent on cuneiform texts.[27] Quick argues that oral and ritual contact with the content of cuneiform texts influenced the composition of Deuteronomy but that the greatest literary influence likely came from the texts of the Levant. Key to this position is her view that Aramaic should be viewed as an intermediary between the texts of the neo-Assyrian period and the biblical texts.[28] This position is among her conclusions achieved through her study of the Aramaic futility curse tradition in comparison with Deuteronomy 28. Futility curses are known from Aramaic texts in which one's effort becomes incapable of producing the desired result. In the above citation of Deuteronomy 28:30–31, there are a number of curses of futility. As examples, there is the wife that is enjoyed by another, the house one builds but cannot dwell in, the vineyard one plants but whose fruit one cannot enjoy, the ox slaughtered that one is unable to eat, and so on. Quick connects these to the Aramaic futility curses, arguing that they represent another vector of influence for the production of Deuteronomy (see table 21.7).

Table 21.7   Sampling of Aramaic Futility Curses*

KAI† 309:18–19	And may he sow but not harvest.
KAI 309:19	And may he sow one thousand measures, but take only a part from it.
KAI 309:20	And may one hundred ewes suckle a lamb, but let it not be satisfied.

 * From Laura Quick, *Deuteronomy 28 and the Aramaic Curse Tradition*, OTRM (Oxford: Oxford University Press, 2018), 75.
 † H. Donner and W. Röllig, *Kanaanäische und aramäische Inschriften* (Wiesbaden: Harrassowitz, 1962–1964).

For Quick, the nature of the outside influence on Deuteronomy is much more complex than the "direct dependence" claim, belonging to a dynamic context of orality and ritual rather than a scenario of inventive scribes merely copying and changing cuneiform texts.

Another important point of comparison is the theme of the love of God in Deuteronomy, which is similar both to the exclusive love required by the Hittite suzerain and to the oath of love that is to be sworn to Ashurbanipal during the neo-Assyrian period.[29] This exclusive devotion and love to God is expressed succinctly in the Shema.

While comparative projects relating the evidence to the Hittite or neo-Assyrian treaties represent the two significant camps that seek to date Deuteronomy on the basis of similarities of form and content, others have been suspicious about the extent to which one can use these similarities to establish a representative form that existed across cultures in the ANE at a single time. Noel Weeks, for example, questions the validity of

---

27. Quick, *Aramaic Curse Tradition*, 179–81.
28. Quick, *Aramaic Curse Tradition*, 181.
29. See, e.g., discussion in Levenson, *Love of God*, 9.

the perspective that covenant forms developed simultaneously across the ANE.[30] Weeks argues against the idea that Mesopotamian hegemony produced a single culture, which in his view would be requisite to sustain an argument for dating the Old Testament covenants on the basis of form alone. Instead, he sees that different people groups used and adapted covenants to fit their social, political, and theological contexts, which in turn explain the various manifestations. In his earlier work, Weeks perhaps overstates his case against the emergence of unified treaty forms by the international period during the middle of the second millennium BC. For instance, it is striking that in the fifteenth to thirteenth centuries, known as the Amarna period, there is significant documentation coming from a wider geopolitical context inclusive of Mesopotamia, Egypt, Syria, and Anatolia. As Bertrand Lafont observes,

> During the Amarnian period, although it is Egypt that dominates broadly the Near Eastern geopolitical scene, it is rather puzzling to see it acquiesce to the rules of a diplomatic game that it did not itself inspire, these rules having been created and used long before by its Asian neighbours, who are their true promoters. This adoption of external standards extends even to the recognition of a foreign Semitic language, Akkadian, as the international diplomatic language, adopted by kings as powerful and different as the Egyptian, the Babylonian, the Hurrian, the Hittite or the Elamite.[31]

This internationalization, however, is understandable despite being somewhat surprising. If there is a desire for binding agreements to be established in international contexts, the adoption of a single language will help facilitate such agreements. The adoption of a language such as Akkadian that was written in a complex writing system such as cuneiform had to be taught and learned. Scribal curriculum, which among other things was built on copying existing texts, lends itself to the development of certain expected forms. These expected forms can subsequently be adopted by the learned and used in other languages and political contexts. More recently, Weeks deals with this question and evidence more intentionally.[32] For Weeks, the spread of treaty forms related to two empirical periods, one that yields the Hittite treaties and a later one that yields the Assyrian treaties. The cleverness of Weeks's position can be seen in its ability to accommodate both the similarities and differences that emerge between comparative projects of texts across time and space in the ANE. Since covenants or treaties, as binding agreements, existed for a long period of time in both oral and written formats, it is natural that there would be numerous points of similarity discoverable in the texts across the ANE. These similarities do not necessarily have to be the result of direct influence or be

---

30. Noel Weeks, *Admonition and Curse: The Ancient Near Eastern Treaty/Covenant Form as a Problem in Inter-Cultural Relationships*, JSOTSup 407 (London: T&T Clark, 2004).

31. Lafont, "International Relations," 43.

32. See Noel Weeks, "The Disappearance of Cuneiform from the West and Elites in the Ancient Near East," in *Registers and Modes of Communication in the Ancient Near East: Getting the Message Across*, ed. Kyle H. Keimer and Gillan Davis (New York: Routledge, 2017), 25–42.

confined to a single period of time, as they belong to a longer, more complicated history. Instead, the more plausible explanation is that these similarities are best explained in the ways in which the authors of the treaties interacted with that larger tradition, whether oral or written, and adapted it for their own social, political, and theological context. On this point, Weeks is particularly helpful.

In short, the approaches of Kitchen and Levinson are unsustainable as clear indicators of the dating of Deuteronomy, since the evidence is too limited, both geographically and numerically, to establish firmly the chronological starting and ending points of the various constituent parts of the texts. Even if one assumes borrowing or intentional interaction with the traditions, using the texts to create a fixed point of date fails to account sufficiently for the complexities that arise from dynamic textual interaction, such as borrowing, adaptation, allusions, and intertextuality. Nevertheless, the ongoing project of analyzing the basic forms and parts of the various treaties has greater import for understanding biblical covenants. For example, the comparative project has resulted in increased knowledge about the ways in which the historical narratives, blessings, and curses serve to encourage fidelity. While this area has been fruitful, other results of the ongoing comparative project, such as land grants, have been more problematic.

Land Grants

In theological discussion about the nature of the Mosaic covenant, the distinction between land grants and suzerain-vassal treaties has been particularly important for the interpretation and explanation of the relationship and constituent parts of the covenants of the Old Testament. For instance, Kline used this sort of terminology quite frequently in his writings. If one does not comprehend his use and understanding of this terminology, one will struggle to grasp Kline's perspective on the covenants.[33] The undermining of these categories, however, would not undermine his theological system, which is best understood as developed through his exegesis but at points influenced or expressed by his understanding of the ANE covenants, rather than the opposite. In other words, to deal with Kline on his own terms, one must understand his use of these categories, yet his theological system can only be assessed at the exegetical and theological level. Exegesis was primary for Kline.[34]

---

33. Kline is more nuanced in his earlier treatment of the ANE background to the grant, *Treaty of the Great King*, 22–23. In his later works, Kline's focus is more theological, employing the categories with greater liberality to explain the typological and theological aspects of the grants. See, e.g., Kline, *Structure of Biblical Authority*, 230–41.

34. See also Michael Horton, *God of Promise: Introducing Covenant Theology* (Grand Rapids, MI: Baker, 2006). In his more recent writings, Horton holds these categories more loosely, while still viewing them as broadly representative of the exegetical and theological differences existing between the Abrahamic and Davidic covenants, which he views as promissory, and the Mosaic covenant, which he views as obligatory. See Horton, "Kingdom of God," in *Christian Dogmatics: Reformed Theology for the Church Catholic*, ed. Michael Allen and Scott R. Swain (Grand Rapids, MI: Baker Academic, 2016), 363–91. The same interpretive trend can be seen in Jon Levenson's use of the categories provided by Weinfeld to explain the differences; see *Sinai and Zion: An Entry into the Jewish Bible* (New York: HarperOne, 1985), and more recently, *Love of God*. Further, note Paul R. Williamson's use of

The distinction between "land grants" and "suzerain-vassal treaties" is traceable to the seminal article by Moshe Weinfeld, "The Covenant of Grant in the Old Testament and in the Ancient Near East," in 1970.[35] According to Weinfeld, Sinai was a treaty that focused on the threats against the people for unfaithfulness: "While the grant is a reward for loyalty and good deeds already performed, the treaty is an inducement for future loyalty."[36] For Weinfeld, the covenant of grant is a reward for past faithfulness that does not come with stipulations. Instead, the warnings are against those who might infringe on the enduring nature of the gift. For Weinfeld, this is how the Abrahamic and Davidic covenants need to be understood in relation to a typology of grant found in the ANE.[37] According to this view, both the Abrahamic and Davidic covenants represent gifts that were given as reward for loyalty and past faithfulness. Weinfeld writes, "Abraham is promised the land because he obeyed God and followed his mandate (Gen. XXVI, 5; cf. XXII, 16, 18) and similarly David was given the grace of dynasty because he served God with truth, righteousness and loyalty (I Kings III, 6; cf. IX, 4, XI, 4, 6, XIV, 8, XV, 3)."[38] In other words, according to this view, the suzerain-vassal treaties use historical narrative to impose obligations on a people in order to uphold the interests of the suzerain. The treaty focuses on the obligations of the vassal to the sovereign as an "obligatory covenant" and directs the curses toward that end.[39] Land grants, by contrast, are "promissory covenants" established on the basis of past faithfulness. With the land grant, the threats are directed at the one who might violate the rights of the recipient of the grant rather than addressing the recipient's future fidelity.

The significance of these categories relates to broader debates about the relationship between the Abrahamic, Mosaic, and Davidic covenants. Since these issues are dealt with more extensively elsewhere in this book, this chapter includes only a brief summary in order to contextualize the land grant versus suzerain-vassal distinction as it applies to the biblical covenants. If the Abrahamic covenant is viewed according to this system, Abra(ha)m is given a land inheritance in Genesis 15 for his faithfulness, in part for not accepting wealth from the alliance of kings in Genesis 14. The covenant in Genesis 15 rewards Abra(ha)m with an unconditional reward for his past faithfulness. This is confirmed further with his obedience in relation to Genesis 22: "because you have done

---

these categories to argue for two Abrahamic covenants. *Sealed with an Oath: Covenant in God's Unfolding Purpose*, NSBT 23 (Downers Grove, IL: InterVarsity Press, 2007), 86–91.

35. M. Weinfeld, "The Covenant of Grant in the Old Testament and in the Ancient Near East," *JAOS* 90, no. 2 (1970): 184–203.

36. Weinfeld, "Covenant of Grant," 185.

37. Weinfeld, "Covenant of Grant," 184.

38. Weinfeld, "Covenant of Grant," 185.

39. When Weinfeld discusses treaties, he is focused only on the disparate treaties of suzerains and vassals and does not treat parity treaties. See Viktor Korošec, *Hethitische Staatsverträge: Ein Beitrag zu ihrer Juristischen Wertung*, LRS 60 (Leipzig: T. Weicher, 1931), 5–11. See also Knoppers, "Ancient Near Eastern Royal Grants," 672n9. Knoppers rightly observes that Weinfeld's typology of covenants is undermined by his failure to consider agreements between equals.

this . . ." (22:16). Similarly, the Davidic covenant (2 Sam. 7; Ps. 89) is an unconditional promise of a dynasty for his past faithfulness to the Lord. Unlike these covenants, the Mosaic or Sinai covenant is understood to be a conditional gift of the land that focuses on blessing for faithfulness and cursing for unfaithfulness. With the promissory covenants to Abraham and David, their past faithfulness secured their reward. Among Reformed proponents of this view, this faithfulness is viewed as typological merit, not merit proper. That is, their typological merit points forward to the proper merit of Christ, who secured an eternal inheritance for his people. The Sinai covenant stipulates that while God brought the Israelites into the land because of his promises to Abraham, their continuation in the land is dependent on obedience.[40]

While one may debate whether these categories, as they relate to the covenants of the Old Testament, have exegetical and theological warrant, the ANE evidence does not fit the neat categories proposed by Weinfeld. The most significant criticism of Weinfeld's very influential view comes from Gary Knoppers.[41] Knoppers demonstrates that "the structure, form, and content of royal grants are much more complicated than Weinfeld's typology allows. . . . There is, moreover, significant evidence that land grants were predominately conditional in nature and function."[42] In fact, Knoppers observes, "Rather than merely rewarding diligent service, grants can redefine such service or induce further loyalty. An implicit conditionality can also be discerned in cases in which the king confiscates and disposes of property belonging to a guilty or disloyal party."[43] This point is key and goes back to earlier observations about the nature of writing in the ANE above. Land grants are clearly conditional in some instances and implicitly so in others. For example, the land grant from Ugarit (*PRU* 6, 30)[44] requires *pilku* service, a service performed for the crown from the person receiving the land.[45] In fact, in this text, the land is taken from one person and given to another. *PRU* 3, 15:z, however, explicitly states that the land is given to the recipient and their sons forever.[46] The land is confiscated from the previous owners by the king, and the future owners pay two hundred shekels of silver to the king. While there is some ambiguity about the nature of the transaction, what is clear is that the land has been confiscated from one person. This suggests implicit obligations. Further, the exchange of two hundred shekels sheds questionable light on the theory of rewards for past faithfulness without further obligations. In *PRU* 3, 16:153, the rather brief grant states only the benefits that the recipi-

---

40. See in particular Meredith G. Kline, *Kingdom Prologue: Genesis Foundations for a Covenantal Worldview* (Eugene, OR: Wipf and Stock, 2006), 236–39.

41. Knoppers, "Ancient Near Eastern Royal Grants," 670–97.

42. Knoppers, "Ancient Near Eastern Royal Grants," 673–74.

43. Knoppers, "Ancient Near Eastern Royal Grants," 688.

44. *PRU* refers to Claude F.-A. Schaeffer, ed., *Le palais royal d'Ugarit*, MRS (Paris: Imprimerie nationale, 1955–1970).

45. See the translation and references to other editions in William W. Hallo, ed., *The Context of Scripture* (Leiden: Brill, 2002), 3:107.

46. Hallo, *Context of Scripture*, 3:108.

ent gains, without any explicit mention of obligation. It is very unlikely, however, that such expectations, although unstated in the document itself, did not exist. LN-104, a cuneiform tablet from Emar, rewards a person with perpetual office as grave digger for an act of faithfulness.[47] Yet there is no mention of further obligation. Despite this, it seems illogical and contrary to the evidence to assume that a human king would reward someone for past faithfulness without any conditionality or expectation for continued service. In fact, the grant itself would anticipate and expect continued service in return. This expectation does not have to be expressly stated in the grant. Numerous other examples, of course, may be considered, but the foregoing discussion serves to illustrate the broader point that the grants cannot be categorized as neatly as Weinfeld suggests. Nevertheless, Weinfeld's view on the unconditionality of the Abrahamic and Davidic covenants stems in part from his views of source-critical theory. With the Abrahamic and Davidic covenants, Weinfeld argues that conditionality was added to the covenants by a redactor after the northern kingdom went into exile.[48] There is no need to posit this sort of development with the Abrahamic and Davidic covenants, since promise and obligation are compatible.[49] This more nuanced perspective on the covenants actually fits better with the land grants found elsewhere in the ANE, since land grants often have obligations attached to them.

On the basis of the actual textual evidence and on the basis of broader theoretical considerations, Weinfeld's typology simply cannot stand up to the evidence. The debate about the relationship between the Mosaic covenant and other covenants, such as the Abrahamic and Davidic covenants, must be continued exegetically and theologically but without an inaccurate typology formulated on ANE forms that cannot be sustained by the evidence.[50] This is not to suggest that comparisons cannot be made. The recognition of conditionality, whether implicit or explicit, in the land grants of the ANE is at least comparable on some level to the Abrahamic and Davidic covenants, which detail promises made by God but also come with various expectations placed on the recipients (Gen. 17; 2 Sam. 7:14; 1 Kings 2:3–4). Yet such parallelism deviates from the original thesis by Weinfeld and the way that thesis was adopted into covenant theology.

Conclusions

The covenants of the Bible share numerous points of comparison with related texts and practices found more broadly in the ancient Near East. While comparative projects will continue to yield interesting results and insights related to the biblical covenants, a portion of their success will be directly related to the extent to which they are able to pay

---

47. See the recent edition in Yoram Cohen and Maurizio Viano, "A Land-Grant Document from Emar: A (Re-)Edition and Discussion of LN-104 (AKA GS-Kutscher 6)," *KASKAL* 13 (2016): 57–71.

48. Weinfeld, "Covenant of Grant," 195–96.

49. See, e.g., Kline, *Kingdom Prologue*, 318–20.

50. Michael Allen engages with Knoppers's article from a systematic theology viewpoint in "Into the Family of God: Covenant and the Genesis of Life with God," *TJ* 39, no. 2 (2018): 181–98.

the requisite attention to both the points of continuity and discontinuity between the various texts and textual traditions. As the above survey demonstrates, the strengths of these insights can be judged only over time, since many assumptions and theories about the Assyriological evidence have been tested and significantly changed as new texts have been published and as theories have been considered afresh against the evidence. For example, the existence of tidy categories such as land grants and suzerainty treaties has proved unable to stand up to the evidence, despite the prominence of such theories in biblical studies. If connections between texts spanning from the circa eighteenth to sixth centuries BC can be made with the biblical material, it seems that the best explanation is that the biblical material, as is to be expected, was written in the ANE by people who belonged to historical and social contexts that were shared with other people, who also wrote texts about justice, allegiance, religion, and other important human questions. A Reformed doctrine of Scripture can account for this, as God speaks to his people in human language, using forms they can understand. Further, it should be noted that sometimes the connections and similarities are overstated, or the comparative project can obscure other meaningful ways of studying the text under consideration. For example, it was not until recently that the structure of Esarhaddon's succession treaty was analyzed on its own terms and independent of Deuteronomy.[51] This merely serves the basic point that comparative projects should not be done at the expense of studying the relevant texts on their own terms as well. Although the ANE evidence is incapable of solving the key exegetical and theological problems often asked of it, this essay is not an attempt to dismiss such evidence for solidifying and informing biblical exegesis.

While parity covenants occur between Jacob and Laban as well as between David and Jonathan, the covenants of the Old Testament lack parity when one of the parties is the Lord. Unlike the parity language that makes reference to agreements between "brothers," Leviticus 25:42 describes the Lord as master over his people. In numerous other texts, he is a parent to a child (Deut. 32:6, 18, etc.).[52] The covenantal relationship, then, is defined by these categories and yet functions in fundamentally surprising ways. The rituals of oath taking with blessings and curses are known from other ANE covenants and treaties, and the suzerain-to-vassal relationship is reflected in that the Israelites take these oaths on themselves. Yet with the Abrahamic covenant, something unexpected occurs. Even in a parity covenant, obligations and threats seem to have fallen on both parties. Various ritual actions, such as the sacrificing of a donkey or the touching of the throat, occur in the treaties formed in the ANE and seem to be indicating that death should

---

51. Kazuko Watanabe writes, "There has been quite a long history of discussions on the similarities between the 'treaty' formulae of the Ancient Near East and the Covenant formulae of the Hebrew Bible. The structure or formula of the ESOD itself, however, has never been discussed in detail." "Innovations in Esarhaddon's Succession Oath Documents Considered from the Viewpoint of the Documents' Structure," *SAAB* 21 (2016): 174.

52. It should be noted that the participants in the biblical covenants are not always limited to the Lord and his people; for example, the Noahic covenant includes all flesh (Gen. 9).

come on the one who fails to uphold the terms of the treaty.[53] In disparate treaties, if only one party ritually binds himself, it is expected that the lesser party would do so. In parity treaties or even disparity treaties, then, at the very least one assumes that the lesser party or both parties would take on the binding oaths or rituals related to the performance of these agreements. But in Genesis 15, after Abraham has sacrificed the animals, a vision of the Lord occurs, and only the Suzerain, God himself, passes through, taking the covenantal obligations on himself. What seems to be the idea behind the rituals found in the ANE rituals outside the Old Testament is confirmed in Jeremiah 34:17–22:

> Therefore, thus says the LORD: You have not obeyed me by proclaiming liberty, every one to his brother and to his neighbor; behold, I proclaim to you liberty to the sword, to pestilence, and to famine, declares the LORD. I will make you a horror to all the kingdoms of the earth. And the men who transgressed my covenant and did not keep the terms of the covenant that they made before me, I will make them like the calf that they cut in two and passed between its parts—the officials of Judah, the officials of Jerusalem, the eunuchs, the priests, and all the people of the land who passed between the parts of the calf. And I will give them into the hand of their enemies and into the hand of those who seek their lives. Their dead bodies shall be food for the birds of the air and the beasts of the earth. And Zedekiah king of Judah and his officials I will give into the hand of their enemies and into the hand of those who seek their lives, into the hand of the army of the king of Babylon which has withdrawn from you. Behold, I will command, declares the LORD, and will bring them back to this city. And they will fight against it and take it and burn it with fire. I will make the cities of Judah a desolation without inhabitant.

In Genesis 15 the Lord is taking all the obligations on himself. May he be cursed; may he die if the covenant is violated. As the New Testament teaches, the unthinkable happened at Calvary, when God was cursed and died for his people (Acts 20:28).

---

53. For specific examples and synthesis, see the discussion in Charpin, *Writing, Law, and Kingship*, chap. 3; Charpin, *Reading and Writing in Babylon*, 156–60. On *lipit napištim* (touching the throat), see the collection of references to the expression from Mari and related commentary in Bertrand Lafont, "Relations internationales, alliances et diplomatie au temps des royaumes amorrites: Essai de synthèse," in *Mari, Ébla et les Hourrites: Dix ans de travaux; Actes du colloque international (Paris, mai 1993)*, part 2, *Amurru 2*, ed. Jean-Marie Durand and Dominique Charpin (Paris: Éditions Recherche sur les Civilisations, 2001), 213–328, esp. 271–76. The meaning of *napištum* is contested. Jean-Marie Durand has argued that the term refers to blood rather than throat. "Assyriologie," *ACF* (2000–2001): 693–705, esp. 700–701.

22

COVENANT AND SECOND
TEMPLE JUDAISM

Peter Y. Lee

The era of Second Temple Judaism is the historical period that began with the reconstruction of the temple of Solomon during the ministries of Ezra and Nehemiah (ca. 515 BC) and continued until its final destruction at the hands of the Roman Empire in AD 70.[1] In many ways, this period was not unlike the First Temple history, which began during the reign of Solomon. This period also came to a tragic end when another pagan ruler (the Babylonian king Nebuchadnezzar) rolled into Jerusalem with his military war machine and decimated the city and temple because of the consistent treaty violations of her Judean kings. The rise and development of a distinctive Jewish religion, society, and culture began once the Judean exiles were restored in 539/538 BC under the reign of the Persian king Cyrus the Great.[2] One thing that these early Jews did was to reflect on the biblical covenants of the Old Testament Scriptures and how they pertained to them. The purpose of this essay is to describe the biblical covenants as they are articulated within the various Jewish literatures of the Second Temple era.

Noahic Covenant

We begin with the covenant with Noah.[3] Since the first occurrence of the word "covenant" (בְּרִית) in the Old Testament is in the Noahic narratives (Gen. 6:18; 9:9, 11), it is not

---

1. For a helpful summary of the history of the Second Temple period, see James C. VanderKam, *An Introduction to Early Judaism* (Grand Rapids, MI: Eerdmans, 2001), 1–52.

2. For a brief description of the distinction between preexilic Israel and Second Temple Judaism, see Shaye J. D. Cohen, *From the Maccabees to the Mishnah*, 2nd ed. (Louisville: Westminster John Knox, 2006), 8–12.

3. Although the covenantal nature of God's relationship with Adam is debated among biblical scholars, there is no clear treatment of such a "covenant" within Second Temple literature. Yet Adam is a prominent figure within

surprising that Second Temple Jewish texts would address this covenantal arrangement. Although the biblical figure of Noah is prominent within numerous Jewish literary works, the actual covenant made with Noah is scantily mentioned and appears in only a few texts. The Qumran text 4Q370 1.7, taken from Genesis 9:13, mentions the rainbow as a sign of the covenant. The Genesis Apocryphon (1QapGen) 12.1 also mentions the sign of the rainbow (although the word "covenant" does not occur, owing to the fragmentary nature of the text). Sirach 44:18 refers to the Noahic covenant and the promise God made to him "that all flesh should never again be blotted out by a flood." Pseudo-Philo, in Biblical Antiquities 3.4, cites from Genesis 6:18 and the statement that God "will establish my covenant with you." Whereas the Genesis text implies that the purpose of this covenant is for the salvation of Noah and his family, it is interesting to note that the purpose of the covenant in Pseudo-Philo is "to destroy all those inhabiting the earth."[4]

The book of Jubilees provides an extensive treatment of this covenant.[5] This literary work is a retelling of the biblical narrative of Genesis 1 through Exodus 19, in which the author edited and modified select portions of the biblical text to express his own theological and religious convictions. In so doing, the overall effect was to present the early patriarchs in the book of Genesis as conforming to Mosaic legal requirements before those laws had been revealed.

We may make two noteworthy observations about the Noahic covenant. First, Jubilees 6.10–14 states that Noah and his sons swore that they would follow the command against blood consumption and thus made a covenant with the Lord. Whereas it is the Lord who makes a covenant with Noah and his sons in the biblical texts (Gen. 9:9–11, 15), in Jubilees this is reversed. Second, Noah celebrates the Mosaic Festival of Weeks (Jub. 6.15–22). Jubilees, therefore, gives the impression that the Sinaitic covenant is a renewal of the ancient Noahic covenant and that Noah and his children followed a legal tradition that revives itself in the Mosaic era. Since the source text in Genesis does not give that same impression, it would be more accurate to say that the author of Jubilees reanalyzes the Noahic covenant as the same type of covenant as the one the Lord made with Moses on Mount Sinai.

Abrahamic Covenant

The covenant God made with Abraham is mentioned in Genesis 15, where the Lord takes a maledictory oath on himself that he will fulfill the covenantal promise and bring

this era. For a summary of Adam (and Eve) in Second Temple literature, see Jon D. Levenson, "Adam and Eve," in *The Eerdmans Dictionary of Early Judaism*, ed. John J. Collins and Daniel C. Harlow (Grand Rapids, MI: Eerdmans, 2010), 300–302.

4. Translation from Daniel J. Harrington, "Pseudo-Philo," in *The Old Testament Pseudepigrapha*, ed. James H. Charlesworth (New York: Doubleday, 1985), 2:306.

5. The full version of Jubilees is available only in Ethiopic; see R. H. Charles, trans., *The Book of Jubilees: Translation of Early Jewish and Palestinian Texts* (London: Forgotten Books, 2007). The Ethiopic version is a translation of the original Hebrew, copies of which were discovered in Qumran. For detailed comments on the Hebrew text of the book of Jubilees in Qumran, see James C. VanderKam and J. T. Milik, "Jubilees," in *Qumran Cave 4 VIII: Parabiblical Texts Part I*, DJD 13 (Oxford: Clarendon, 1994), 1–140.

Abraham's numerous descendants into the land of Canaan, and in Genesis 17, where the Lord gives the covenantal sign of circumcision. This covenantal arrangement is extended and renewed with Abraham's descendants—with Isaac (Gen. 26), with Jacob (Gen. 35), and with all the children of Jacob (i.e., the nation of Israel). It is the election of Abraham that led God to make this covenant with him and to elect Israel as his people. Accordingly, the biblical text uses the Abrahamic covenant to show God as merciful and gracious, and several Second Temple texts do the same. Philo, in *De mutatione nominum* (*On the Change of Names*) 51–54, is one Jewish writer who identifies the Abrahamic covenant of Genesis 15 and 17 as a "symbol of grace which God has set between himself who proffers it and man who receives it" (*Mut.* 52).[6]

Although several nonbiblical Jewish texts demonstrate grace in the covenant with Abraham, several also emphasize covenantal *obedience*. The Damascus Document (CD)[7] mentions a "covenant of your forefathers" (CD 1.4–5; cf. 6.2), which is most likely a reference to the Abrahamic covenant. According to this passage, God preserved a "remnant" at the time of the destruction of the first Solomonic temple because of this covenant with the forefathers. In a similar passage, in CD 3.1–4, Abraham is mentioned as one who kept covenant precepts and passed them on to Isaac and Jacob. They in turn also kept them and became "friends of God" and "members of the covenant forever" (3.4).

This is not the only place where we witness an emphasis on the obedience of Abraham. Just as Jubilees reanalyzes the Noahic covenant as sharing similar features with the Sinaitic covenant, so it does with the Abrahamic covenant as well. Like Noah in Jubilees, Abraham renews the Festival of Weeks (Jub. 6.20). He is also concerned with idolatry (Jub. 12.1–14), which was a major Mosaic concern. In these ways, Abraham is portrayed as an orthodox follower of the Sinaitic covenant. See also Jubilees 22.11–23, where Abraham renews the covenant with Jacob using language reminiscent of the Sinaitic covenant (e.g., separation from Gentiles, cf. Ex. 23:32; Deut. 20:11–20; not intermarrying with Canaanites, cf. Deut. 7:1–3).

Jacqueline de Roo also mentions that Jubilees describes Abraham's obedience as beginning in his youth prior to the Lord making covenant with him, "thus suggesting that he was chosen, because he chose God."[8] In other words, the grounds of the Lord's electing

---

6. Philo, however, also stated earlier that a covenant is for those "who are worthy of the gift" (*Mut.* 51). Thus, it is not clear how a covenant is gracious while at the same time is something that one must be worthy of. Lester L. Grabbe also states that Philo's concept of "covenant" is closer to a testament than a contractual agreement. "Did All Jews Think Alike? 'Covenant' in Philo and Josephus in the Context of Second Temple Judaic Religion," in *The Concept of the Covenant in the Second Temple Period*, ed. Stanley E. Porter and Jacqueline C. R. de Roo, JSJSupp 71 (Leiden: Brill, 2003), 252–53.

7. The Damascus Document is abbreviated CD for "Cairo Damascus." Cairo refers to the location in which this document was discovered, the genizah of the Ezra Synagogue of Old Cairo in 1896 by Solomon Schechter. Damascus refers to the numerous references made to the city of Damascus, which may be a cryptic name for Babylon, within the document itself (CD 6.5, 19; 7.15, 19; 8.21; 19.34; 20.12). It has become apparent that the Dead Sea Scrolls community had two rulebooks, the Damascus Document (CD) and the Rule of the Community (1QS). Their relationship to each other is unclear.

8. Jacqueline C. R. de Roo, "God's Covenant with the Forefathers," in Porter and de Roo, *Concept of the Covenant*, 195–96.

Abraham was his obedience. To further support her claim, de Roo cites Sirach 44:19–21, where, according to de Roo, it is of high significance that Abraham's obedience to the law of God ("he kept the law of the Most-High") is the grounds on which the Lord chose him and thus made a covenant with him ("and was taken into covenant with him"). Therefore, Jubilees and Sirach are witnesses to a strand of Jewish tradition suggesting that the Lord did not elect Abraham on the basis of internal factors within his own sovereign will (cf. Deut. 7:6–7). Rather, God chose Abraham because Abraham first chose God. This differs from the New Testament, which does not interpret Abraham's acts of obedience as the grounds on which he received the covenant or any of its blessings. His obedience is a demonstration of the genuineness of his faith in the Lord, and thus, he was justified by a faith that validated itself by producing obedience (James 2:21–23).

Other Second Temple texts also emphasize an obedient Abraham. In Biblical Antiquities 6, Abraham (called Abram) is one of seven men who do not participate in the sacrilegious activities of the Tower of Babel (Gen. 11:1–9). As a result, the chiefs of the peoples order that these seven be thrown into a fiery blaze. In the midst of an attempted escape, Abram stays and states, "If there be any sin of mine so flagrant that I should be burned up, let the will of God be done" (Bib. Ant. 6.11). Implicitly, Abram affirms that the Lord will rescue him from his peril because of his covenantal fidelity, not because of any notion of divine grace. Later, as Abram is thrown into the fiery furnace, the Lord causes an earthquake that cracks the foundations of the furnace, resulting in the incineration of Abram's enemies while "there was not the least injury to Abram from the burning of the fire" (Bib. Ant. 6.17).

Abraham also appears in the Prayer of Manasseh. This text is a repentant prayer of a Jew (Pseudo-Manasseh) who appeals to God for the forgiveness of his sins. This penitent sinner admits that he is not like the "righteous ones," whom he identifies as the patriarchs "Abraham, Isaac, and Jacob." He says that God did not appoint grace for them because they "did not sin" and thus do not need repentance. In contrast to them, he confesses that he is indeed a sinner and in need of the grace of God (Pr. Man. 7–8). Daniel Falk states that this text "raises the prospect of sinlessness."[9]

In addition to the themes of grace and obedience in the Abrahamic covenant, Second Temple texts are also replete with descriptions of the practice of circumcision as the mark of the Jews. According to David Bernat, 1 Maccabees is the earliest Jewish text where the term "circumcision" is treated as a synonym with "covenant."[10] First Maccabees 1 describes the rise of Antiochus IV Epiphanes and his brutal Hellenization of the Jews. Among the many cruel requirements that he demanded was that the Jews remove "the marks of circumcision," perhaps alluding to an ancient form of epispasm (1 Macc. 1:15).

---

9. Daniel Falk, "Psalms and Prayers," in *Justification and Variegated Nomism*, vol. 1, *The Complexities of Second Temple Judaism*, ed. D. A. Carson, Peter T. O'Brien, and Mark A. Seifrid, WUNT, 2nd ser., no. 140 (Grand Rapids, MI: Baker Academic, 2001), 14.

10. David A. Bernat, "Circumcision," in Collins and Harlow, *Eerdmans Dictionary of Early Judaism*, 472.

By doing this, according to 1 Maccabees, they would be abandoning "the holy covenant." It was the outlawing of the practice of circumcision that triggered the rebellion of Mattathias (1 Macc. 1:48, 60–63; cf. Josephus, *Ant.* 12.253–56). Once the Hasmoneans reestablished control over Judea, they "forcibly circumcised all the uncircumcised boys that they found within the borders of Israel" (1 Macc. 2:46). This close association between "circumcision" and "covenant" became widespread among the subsequent Jewish literary works and, according to James D. G. Dunn and N. T. Wright, one of the prime "boundary markers" for Jews.[11]

The importance of circumcision can be discerned from several Second Temple texts. Damascus Document 16.6 says that Abraham "circumcised himself on the day of his knowledge." Biblical Antiquities 9.13–15, says that Moses was born circumcised. The angels, according to Jubilees 15.25–27, were even created circumcised. Since circumcision is often used as a metaphor in the Old Testament and Jewish texts, it is not always clear when these references to circumcision are to be understood as physical or figurative.

As mentioned above, the Old Testament makes references to a metaphorical circumcision, particularly to specific parts of the body: the heart (Deut. 10:16; 30:6), the lips (Ex. 6:12, 30), and the ears (Jer. 6:10).[12] For that reason, we also find such references within the Second Temple texts. Jubilees 1.22–24 speaks of the "circumcision of the heart," which would mark the restoration of Israel to God's favor after a period of apostasy and alienation.[13] In Qumran, the manual that describes the code by which this Jewish sect is to live, the Rule of the Community (1QS), says that the one who desires to join them must "circumcise the foreskin of his tendency and of his stiff neck in order to lay a foundation of truth for Israel, for the Community of the eternal covenant" (1QS 5.5–6). Those who are not circumcised, both physically and figuratively, have no part within the Qumran community. They have "uncircumcised lips and a weird tongue" (1QH[a] 10.14–15), meaning that they are "men of deceit" who warp the truthful instruction of the author (possibly the "Teacher of Righteousness"). The text 1QH[a] 14.20 mentions a "holy path" that the "uncircumcised, the unclean, and the vicious" cannot travel on. Not only are they barred from community membership; 4Q458 frag. 2.2.4 even states that the Lord "will consume all the uncircumcised ones." Such is also the description of the community's primary nemesis, the "Wicked Priest," who is described as one who "did not circumcise the foreskin of his heart" (1QpHab 11.13). According to these texts, external (physical) circumcision did not identify one as a Jew unless it was accompanied with an internal (metaphorical) circumcision.

---

11. James D. G. Dunn, "The New Perspective on Paul," *BJRL* 65, no. 2 (1983): 107, 117–21; N. T. Wright, *The New Testament and the People of God*, vol. 1 of *Christian Origins and the Question of God* (Minneapolis: Fortress, 1992), 238. According to Dunn and Wright, "boundary markers" for Jews include, in addition to circumcision, the observance of Sabbath and dietary laws.

12. Cf. Lev. 19:23–24, which describes the fruit of the trees of the land in the first three years of habitation as "uncircumcised" (ESV mg.) and thus as unable to be eaten.

13. See also 4Q434 1.1.4 and possibly 4Q504 frag. 4.11.

The biblical texts clearly view Abraham as one who was elect by God, and this election becomes the foundation of viewing the Abrahamic covenant as a covenant of grace. This is also evidenced within several Second Temple texts (e.g., Philo; see above). Within these Jewish texts, however, there is some tension to the gracious nature of the Abrahamic covenant since evidence also suggests that the foundation of Abraham's election was his faithfulness to the Lord (i.e., Sir. 44; Bib. Ant. 6). This strain within the Abrahamic covenant differs when compared with the New Testament, which does not interpret Abraham's faithfulness as the grounds on which he received the covenant or any of its blessings. His faithfulness is a demonstration of the genuineness of his faith in the Lord, and thus he is justified by a faith that validated itself by producing obedience (James 2:21–23). His faith, in turn, opens the door for justification for the Gentiles (Rom. 4:11–19).

Sinaitic Covenant

The Sinaitic covenant (Ex. 19–24) was one of the most significant covenantal administrations during the postexilic period in the history of Israel and Second Temple Judaism. A survey of various Jewish literatures during this time frequently refers to that covenant and supports its importance for the Jews and in the shaping of an emerging Jewish identity. Several of the literary works examined above confirm this notion. Recall that E. P. Sanders made a similar observation in his "covenantal nomism" scheme. According to Sanders, although one comes into the covenant by grace, one maintains one's status as a member within the covenantal community by obedience to the "nomos" (the law).[14] Thus, the Sinaitic covenant is the covenant *par excellence* of the Jewish community, and obedience to its laws is one of the highest of virtues.[15]

In cases where the *covenant* itself seems absent, the *laws* of the covenant remain, and thus obedience is still implied. For example, George Nickelsburg, in his comments on 1 Enoch, says that "the general category of covenant seems not to be important for these authors [of 1 Enoch]. At the very least, the word is rare."[16] According to Nickelsburg, 1 Enoch is more interested in wisdom than covenant, and he says that "law and its interpretation are embodied in the notion of revealed 'wisdom.'"[17] David R. Jackson describes

---

14. See Sanders, *Paul and Palestinian Judaism: A Comparison of Patterns of Religion*, 40th anniversary ed. (Minneapolis: Fortress, 2017), 544–45.

15. Having stated the importance of obedience to the law in Second Temple Judaism, D. A. Carson insightfully comments that both aspects of covenantal nomism ("getting in" and "staying in") need clearer articulation. After surveying the study of several scholars on various Second Temple texts and concepts, he concludes that the first principle of "getting in" is the more stable of the two and that the concept of "staying in" is more problematic and "infinitely flexible." "Summaries and Conclusions," in Carson, O'Brien, and Seifrid, *Justification and Variegated Nomism*, 1:545. Thus, what it means to obey and for what purpose one obeys varies from text to text.

16. George Nickelsburg, *1 Enoch*, vol. 1, *Chapters 1–36*, Hermeneia (Minneapolis: Fortress, 2001), 50–52. Although the complete version of 1 Enoch is available only in Ethiopic, which dates beyond the parameters of Second Temple Judaism as defined above, the original text was written in Aramaic, numerous copies of which were discovered among manuscripts in Qumran. Although there is evidence to suggest that the Aramaic version differs from the Ethiopic text (e.g., Aramaic Enoch includes the "Book of the Giants" but not the "Similitudes of Enoch"), the observation regarding the covenant remains the same. For further comments regarding the Aramaic copies, see J. T. Milik, ed., *The Books of Enoch: Aramaic Fragments of Qumran Cave 4* (Oxford: Clarendon, 1976).

17. Nickelsburg, *1 Enoch*, 1:50.

the rise of an Enochic tradition within the Qumran literature and its acceptance as authoritative within the sect.[18] Although the Qumran community was consciously mindful of the covenant, there seems to have been at the time another stratum of religious thought (i.e., Enochic) that was not as focused on the covenant yet was still interested in law in the form of wise teachings.[19]

David M. Hay says something similar concerning the works of Philo. According to Hay, Philo rarely used the term "covenant," and his religious worldview was less interested in matters soteriological and more on the "pilgrimage of the soul to God."[20] Yet Hay still acknowledges that Philo wrote "as though every Jew in the world were dedicated to studying and living by *the law of Moses.*"[21]

Although it seems that the concept of the covenant is less prominent than wisdom in the Enochic literature, it would be a misstep to say that all wisdom literature is also less covenantally aware. For example, consider the wisdom instruction in Sirach, where the covenant is a vitally rich topos. In Sirach 24, wisdom is given a first-person voice and calls for Israel to follow her wise standards because "all this is the book of the covenant of the Most High God, the law that Moses commanded us as an inheritance for the congregations of Jacob" (Sir. 24:23; cf. 28:7). To follow the wisdom instruction of Sirach is also to obey the law commandments of Sinai. Observing this correlation between wisdom and covenant in Sirach, E. P. Sanders says,

> The variation between admonitions of a very general tone [i.e., wisdom] and explicit mention of obeying commandments given by Moses [i.e., covenant] is to be explained by the fact that Ben Sirach was intentionally defining the values of the well-established wisdom tradition in terms of the Mosaic covenant: that wisdom which is universally sought is in fact truly represented by and particularized in the Torah given by God through Moses.[22]

Even the book of Proverbs, which finds its final canonical form in the postexilic era, has motifs and language similar to the Mosaic book of Deuteronomy.[23]

---

18. David R. Jackson, *Enochic Judaism: Three Defining Paradigm Exemplars*, LSTS 49 (London: T&T Clark, 2004).

19. This is not to say that 1 Enoch is wisdom literature. Scholars have identified it as an early example of a Jewish apocalypse. Some suggest that wisdom literature is the origins of the apocalyptic genre; see Benjamin G. Wright III and Lawrence Wills, eds., *Conflicted Boundaries in Wisdom and Apocalypticism*, SBLSS 35 (Atlanta: SBL, 2005). See also James C. VanderKam, who says that mantic wisdom (e.g., dream interpretation) could be the source of the apocalypse. *Enoch and the Growth of an Apocalyptic Tradition*, CBQMS 16 (Washington, DC: Catholic Biblical Association of America, 1984), 3–8, 172–74. In opposition to this and defending prophecy as the origins of the apocalypse, see Stephen L. Cook, *Prophecy and Apocalypticism: The Postexilic Social Setting* (Minneapolis: Fortress, 1995).

20. David M. Hay, "Philo of Alexandria," in Carson, O'Brien, and Seifrid, *Justification and Variegated Nomism*, 1:365.

21. Hay, "Philo of Alexandria," 370; emphasis added. Because of these factors, Hay suggests that "covenantal nomism," as E. P. Sanders defines it, is an inaccurate way to understand Philo. He lacks the "covenant" part of covenantal nomism. See similar comments by Paul Spilsbury regarding Josephus's work *The Jewish Antiquities* in "Josephus," in Carson, O'Brien, and Seifrid, *Justification and Variegated Nomism*, 1:248–52.

22. Sanders, *Paul and Palestinian Judaism*, 331.

23. See Daniel J. Estes, "Wisdom and Biblical Theology," in *Dictionary of the Old Testament: Wisdom, Poetry, and Writings*, ed. Tremper Longman III and Peter Enns (Downers Grove, IL: IVP Academic, 2008), 853–58;

A specific instance of covenantal obedience is found within the Jewish sect at Qumran, where, according to Lawrence Schiffman, "the Sinai covenant is the central referent of the term ברית."[24] For example, consider the opening section of the preamble of 1QS 1.1–3, which lists several purpose statements of the manual, including these: "in order to seek God with [all (one's) heart and] with a[ll (one's) soul;] in order to do what is good and just in his presence, as he was commanded by the hand of Moses and by the hand of all his servants the Prophets."

The required obedience, however, has a sectarian specificity. The leadership of the sect are "the Sons of Zadok, the priests who guard [God's] covenant and . . . the majority of the men of the community who hold fast to the covenant" (1QS 5.2–3, 21–22), and it is their interpretation of the covenant that current and new initiates must conform to. Although most of their teachings pertain to common features of Judaism (e.g., purity laws, Sabbath, sacrifice), their application of them disagrees with the temple leadership in Jerusalem. In that sense, the Qumranic view of being in the covenant is much more restrictive regarding covenant obedience and thus membership, and it limits it to only those who conform to the covenantal peculiarities of that community, even if this means alienating fellow Jews. Thus, Markus Bockmuehl says that this covenantal identification of the Qumran sect "is no longer sufficiently defined as God's pact of grace with Abraham and his descendants or with all Israel at Sinai, but has become more particularly the sect's own exclusive alliance devoted to Torah observance."[25] Those who attain the required level of obedience/repentance are brought into the community, which is called the "covenant of mercy" (ברית חסד) in 1QS 1.8, the "covenant of an everlasting Community" in 3.11–12, and the "covenant of God" in 2.26.[26]

Although the general purpose of 1QS was intended to teach what is required of those within the sect (1.1–15), it also outlines how to receive others into the community (1.16–2.18). Anyone interested in joining this community begins a long, extensive process of "enter[ing] the covenant of God,"[27] which ultimately requires that they swear by oath to "revert to the law of Moses" as the Qumranic leadership interprets it (1QS 5.8–10;

Tremper Longman III, *The Fear of the Lord Is Wisdom: A Theological Introduction to Wisdom in Israel* (Grand Rapids, MI: Baker Academic, 2017), 172–75.

24. Lawrence H. Schiffman, *Qumran and Jerusalem: Studies in the Dead Sea Scrolls and the History of Judaism* (Grand Rapids, MI: Eerdmans, 2010), 247.

25. Markus Bockmuehl, "1QS and Salvation at Qumran," in Carson, O'Brien, and Seifrid, *Justification and Variegated Nomism*, 1:389. See also 1QH 12[=4]:7–20, which describes a similar description of restricted membership.

26. According to Bockmuehl, there are some sectarian texts (see CD 1.1–4; 16.1–2; 1QM 10.9–10; 12.13–14, along with other nonsectarian liturgical documents) that appear to call for a general obedience and repentance, nothing specific to sectarian orthodoxy. Bockmuehl says these texts "seem to take for granted a universal call to repentance as well as the election and eventual salvation of ethnic Israel as the holy covenantal people of God." "1QS," 388–89.

27. 1QS 2.12, 18; CD 2.2; 3.10; 6.11; 1QHᵃ 13.23; 21.9. Cf. 1QS 1.16, 18, 20, 24; 2.10, which describe joining the community as "crossing over into the covenant before God" (cf. CD 1.20; 16.12). Craig A. Evans suggests that this imagery of "entering" and "crossing over" is an allusion to Israel crossing the Jordan and entering the promised land of Canaan. "Covenant in the Qumran Literature," in Porter and de Roo, *Concept of the Covenant*, 63.

20.6.15; 1QSa 1.2–3). Once confirmed as members, they are considered "sons of the covenant" (1QM 17.8). For those "not in the covenant" (i.e., not in the community),[28] they walk on a wicked path and will ultimately suffer the "curses of the covenant . . . for everlasting annihilation" (1QS 5.10–13; cf. 2.25–3.12; 1QH[a] 6.19–22).

Just as in 1QS, the theme of the covenant plays a significant role also in the War Scroll (1QM). The opening section (1QM 1.1–3) sets the covenantal tone of the text. It calls members of the sect "sons of light" who will wage war against "the sons of darkness, the army of Belial." These "sons of darkness" include various Gentile nations (e.g., Edom, Moab, Ammon). Supporting these foreign enemies are "those who have violated the covenant"; these are fellow Jews who have rejected the sectarian instructions. In contrast to this unholy alliance are members of the sect, "the sons of light." Later in the text, they are called "the holy people of the covenant" (1QM 10.10), who have not been "led astray from [God's] covenant" (1QM 14.10).

Another important sectarian document worth noting is 4QMMT. It appears to be a letter sent by the leadership of the Qumran sect to the priestly officer(s)[29] in Jerusalem, a letter that explains the views of the sect, their disagreement with the teachings of the Jerusalem priesthood regarding the law, and their reasons for forming their separate community. It is divided into three sections: section A deals with calendrical concerns, section B lists approximately twenty grievances the sect has against the temple leadership in Jerusalem pertaining to their views on the law,[30] and section C is made up of hortatory material.

Much has been written on 4QMMT, and more can be said about it than this brief essay allows. Our interest is in one particular phrase that occurs in section C, מקצת מעשה התורה, "some of the works of the law."[31] After the sectarian view of the law is explained (sec. B), the letter goes on to say that these legal differences are why they had to "segregate [them]selves from the multitude of the peoples" (C.7–8). According to the writer of this document, the laws in section B are "some of the works of the law" (מקצת מעשי התורה, C.27) that exemplify the differences between the two groups. Thus, the legal setting of section B is the literary context of section C. The writer alludes to Solomon (C.17–18), Jeroboam and Zedekiah (C.18–21), and David (C.25–26) as those who demonstrate that proper obedience to the Mosaic law brought blessing (Solomon and David) and that

---

28. 1QM 1.2 calls them "violators of the covenant"; cf. 4Q387 3.6–8; 4Q171 1–10.3.12.

29. The letter refers to the addressees both in the singular and the plural. Schiffman suggests that this interplay between the singular and plural supports the notion that the letter was written with two audiences in view: one is the group of priests who remained in Jerusalem in support of the temple cult (plural), and the other is the high priest himself, who is referred to in the sectarian literature as the "Wicked Priest" (singular). *Qumran and Jerusalem*, 117.

30. The list of grievances has an affinity with the Temple Scroll (11QT[a]). For a more detailed description of the similarities between sec. B of 4QMMT and 11QT[a], see Lawrence H. Schiffman, "*Miqsat Ma'aseh ha-Torah* and the *Temple Scroll*," *RevQ* 14, no. 3 (1990): 435–57.

31. Scholars have named this manuscript based on the Hebrew of this phrase (miqṣat maʿaśê hattôrāʰ, hence MMT).

disobedience brought curse (Jeroboam and Zedekiah). The purpose of this letter is clear: to call the Jerusalem leadership to adjust their ways and follow the rules of the sect.[32]

The phrase "works of the law" is particularly noteworthy since the same phrase in Greek (ἔργων νόμου) occurs in several key Pauline texts in the New Testament (Rom. 3:20, 28; Gal. 2:16; 3:10). How one interprets this phrase affects our understanding of both the covenant and, more narrowly, Paul's doctrine of justification. Both 4QMMT and Paul use the phrase similarly. Whereas 4QMMT teaches that a proper standing before the Lord is based on obedience to these "works of the law," Paul stresses that righteousness before God comes by faith and not by "works of the law." In other words, both Qumran and Paul understand the phrase as a legal term that demonstrates the way that one comes into good standing with God. One (4QMMT) embraces the term, the other (Paul) rejects it. As Martin Abegg states so succinctly, "Paul and the author of 4QMMT are in a virtual theological face-off."[33]

Curiously, outside the biblical occurrences, this phrase is found only here in 4QMMT in all the Second Temple texts.[34] It would be a bold claim to suggest that Paul knew of 4QMMT specifically, although it cannot be ruled out. The scarcity of the phrase within extant Jewish literature invites comparative study. We should note that Paul uses the phrase to summarize the views of the "Judaizers" with whom he was engaged in theological-soteriological combat, not necessarily the views of the sectarian Jews in Qumran. So we cannot conclude simply that both 4QMMT and Paul mean the same thing when referring to the "works of the law." Whether Paul was aware of the text or not, what seems more significant is the fact that the two attested occurrences of the phrase place it within a context in which covenant obedience is a prerequisite for being "reckoned righteous" (C.31; Gal. 3:6) before God. Abegg gives a helpful comment: "All that need be said is that the concept of 'works of the law' is quite agile and allows for any number of strictures, the only condition being that they find their source in Torah and are concerned with practice which defines relationship to God in a particular sort of Judaism."[35]

According to several scholars, the phrase "works of the law" is not a forensic term for Paul but rather refers to boundary markers that distinguish Judaism from other pagan religions. We mentioned earlier James Dunn, who pioneered and championed this view. He sees a striking similarity between the historical and religious context of both 4QMMT and Paul in Romans and Galatians. He says the phrase "works of the law" in 4QMMT represents boundary markers, just as it does for Paul. In 4QMMT, however, the sectarian Jews in Qumran are distinguishing themselves from other Jews, not Gentiles. This is unlike Paul, for whom, according to Dunn, "the issue was of sepa-

---

32. A helpful summary of sec. C can be found in Schiffman, *Qumran and Jerusalem*, 115–17.

33. Martin G. Abegg Jr., "4QMMT C 27, 31 and 'Works Righteousness,'" *DSD* 6, no. 2 (1999): 139.

34. There are similar phrases in Qumran: e.g., "his works in the law" in 1QS 5.21; 6.18; "doers of the law" in 1QpHab 7.11; 8.1; 12.4.

35. Abegg, "4QMMT," 141.

ration between Jew and Gentile." Thus, both texts have that common understanding of "works of the law" as "defining a boundary which marks out those of faith/faithfulness from others."[36]

In an extensive treatment of "works of the law," N. T. Wright also adopts Dunn's position.[37] He complements Dunn's analysis by saying that the phrase occurs in an explicitly covenantal and eschatological context. According to Wright, in section C the writer is interested in the opening verses of Deuteronomy 30 and interprets it as prophetic history that was fulfilled partly in Old Testament history and also in the present days of the sect.[38] Wright says section C of 4QMMT provides a historical sequence of blessing (fulfilled in Solomon, C.17–18), then curse (fulfilled in Jeroboam and the exile with Zedekiah, C.19–21), followed by restored blessing in the last days. This leads the writer to see his own days eschatologically, as the "latter days" of Deuteronomy 30,[39] when blessing will be restored to the sect as a remnant of Israel.

Wright stresses that the references to the Judean kings mentioned in 4QMMT, section C, are not "merely examples of good or evil persons who as individuals, reaped blessing or curse as a result." They do not exemplify "a timeless blessing and a timeless curse to anyone, anywhere, who keeps or does not keep Torah," nor are they "ahistorical moral examples, or isolated examples of a merit-and-reward system."[40] Rather, he says they are "historical markers, showing the times when the Deuteronomic prophecy (first blessing, then curse) was fulfilled."[41] Thus, the phrase "works of the law," according to Wright, "*mark[s] them out in the present time as the true, returned-from-exile, covenant people of Israel.*"[42]

A closer examination of the text, however, suggests otherwise. In 4QMMT C.23–24, the writer calls his readers to "remember [imperative] the kings of Israe[l] and reflect on their deeds, how whoever of them was respecting [the . . . Law] was freed from affliction; and they were the se[ek]ers of the Law." The writer seems to imply the opposite of Wright's conclusions, that the ancient kings were not exemplars for the community to follow. He, in fact, appears to encourage the readers to "reflect" on these kings and "their deeds" (מעשיהמה). Of particular interest for the writer are the righteous kings, whom he calls "seekers of the Law." In 4QMMT C.25–26, the writer once again calls on the readers to "remember [imperative] David, who was a man of the pious ones, [and] he,

---

36. James D. G. Dunn, "4QMMT and Galatians," *NTS* 43, no. 1 (1997): 151. Dunn spends the bulk of this article discussing the similarities between Paul in Galatians and 4QMMT and simply states the "boundary marker" view without defending it. The brevity of the article suggests that Dunn presumed the reader was familiar with his "boundary marker" theory, which he defends in his other writings; see, e.g., James D. G. Dunn, *The Theology of Paul the Apostle* (Grand Rapids, MI: Eerdmans, 1998), 359–66.

37. N. T. Wright, "4QMMT and Paul: Justification, 'Works' and Eschatology," in *Pauline Perspectives: Essays on Paul, 1978–2013* (Minneapolis: Fortress, 2013), 332–55.

38. Wright, "4QMMT and Paul," 339–42.

39. The phrase "latter days" is not in Deut. 30 but in a similar passage, Deut. 4:30–31.

40. Wright, "4QMMT and Paul," 339–41.

41. Wright, "4QMMT and Paul," 340–41.

42. Wright, "4QMMT and Paul," 341; emphasis original.

too, [was] freed from many afflictions and was forgiven." Why would the writer encourage his readers to "remember" the ancient kings, particularly David, if they were nothing more than markers of prophetic history? More important, why would he encourage them to "reflect" on the fact that they were "freed from affliction" (C.24, 26) because they were "seekers of the Law" (C.24) and were "of the pious ones" (C.26)? Wright correctly observes that the writer interprets Deuteronomy 30 as prophetic history, but this view does not preclude the fact that he also uses the ancient kings as examples of covenant fidelity, suggesting that his readers would do well to heed their example.[43] Therefore, the "works of the law" are not merely religious boundary markers but are indeed legal requirements that need to be fulfilled for one to be "reckoned righteous" (C.31). In fact, we can say that the "works of the law" are boundary markers (of a religious, not an ethnic, sort) *because* they are legal requirements that need to be followed; the former is a by-product and result of the latter.[44] This was the case for righteous kings (Solomon, David), whereas wicked kings suffered the curse of the covenant (Jeroboam, Zedekiah).[45]

To further support his claim, Wright states that 4QMMT is not about how someone comes to be a member of the sect but rather how one stays in the sect. Concerning the notion of being "reckoned as righteous" in C.31, he says that this is "not about how someone comes to be a member of the sect. It is the recognition . . . that one is already a member. It is what marks someone out as having already made the transition from outsider to insider, from (in the sect's eyes) renegade Jew to member of the eschatological people."[46] Wright refers to E. P. Sanders's distinction of "getting in" and "staying in" and says that 4QMMT is about the latter. This is a rather perplexing conclusion. His comments here are similar to his definition of "works of the law" as described earlier. If, in fact, being "reckoned righteous" and "works of the law" are the distinguishing marks of the Qumran community, in distinction to other Jews, and if the intent of 4QMMT is to persuade them to join their community (something Wright acknowledges), then isn't the purpose of the letter to "get them in," not just for them to "stay in"? Wouldn't the "works of the law" function more as *requirements* for community membership than *markers* of it?

In summary, it is obvious that the Sinai covenant plays a major role in Second Temple Judaism. Whether the covenant is explicitly mentioned or not (i.e., Enoch, Philo), whether it takes a more restrictive form or not (i.e., Qumran), the legal tradition of the covenant is present within the literature. N. T. Wright suggests that the concept behind "works of the law" in 4QMMT "in a broad sense . . . characterized sectarian

---

43. Unfortunately, neither Dunn nor Wright comments on C.23–26 and the writer's use of the imperatives "remember" and "reflect."

44. Therefore, I suggest that 4QMMT supports a traditional Pauline understanding of the phrase "works of the law," in the sense that it is a forensic term (not merely boundary markers) and thus is antithetical to faith as the instrumentality of justification.

45. Wright does not deny this forensic view, what he refers to as the "metaphor of the lawcourt"; rather, he says that it must be understood within its "proper context." "4QMMT and Paul," 354. For a description of this proper context, see Wright, "4QMMT and Paul," 343–46.

46. Wright, "4QMMT and Paul," 342.

Judaisms of various sorts, and perhaps mainstream Judaism (insofar as there was such a thing) as well."[47]

Covenant of Eternal Priesthood

One text in Qumran refers to an eternal priestly covenant, namely, the War Scroll (1QM) 17.2–3. It refers to judgment against Nadab and Abihu and exhorts people to avoid their offering of "strange fire" (Lev. 10:1 ESV mg.). Instead, the Lord says that he has bestowed on Eleazar and Ithamar "an eternal covenant of priesthood." The promise of a perpetual line of priests leads logically to the expectation of a *priestly messiah*[48] as the realization of this covenantal promise. This messianic expectation is referred to in several places within the texts in Qumran. It is not clear, however, how significant it was outside this community.

According to the Qumran texts, this promise of an eternal priesthood is seen in the lines of both Levi and Aaron. In this way, these texts apparently saw a preexisting priesthood in Levi, prior to the establishment of the actual priesthood in Aaron. So Jubilees 30.17–19 alludes to Genesis 34 and praises the slaughtering of the Shechemites by Simeon and Levi as performing "righteousness and uprightness and vengeance upon sinners" (Jub. 30.18, 23). For this reason, Levi and his seed were chosen for the priesthood. In Jubilees 32.1–3, Jacob is with Levi at Bethel, where Levi dreams that he and his sons were appointed to be priests of the Most High God. Levitical priests also play a significant role in the so-called Aramaic Levi Document, which praises Levi's passion for the purity of the Lord and his people, his establishment and rise in the priesthood, and his wise instruction to his sons.

The sectarians in Qumran saw the priestly line not only originating in Levi but also continuing through Aaron. They apparently saw themselves as a priestly community, where the community itself was frequently called an "everlasting plantation," "a holy house," even "the holy of holies" (1QS 8.5–6; cf. 9.6; 5.1–7), all for the sake of Aaron. The text 4Q419 1.1–3 refers to the members of the community as the "sons of Aaron," because they maintain the covenant of God. The myriad references to "the sons of Aaron" within the sectarian texts of Qumran supports the lofty position of Aaron and their close connection to him.

Interestingly, the prominence of Aaron was not isolated to the Qumran community. To validate Hasmonean claims to the priesthood, 1 Maccabees traces the ancestry of the Jewish hero Mattathias to Aaron by describing his zeal for the purity of Israel as equivalent to Phinehas, the grandson of Aaron (1 Macc. 2:26, 54; cf. Num. 25:6–13).

---

47. Wright, "4QMMT and Paul," 353.

48. The term "messiah" simply means "anointed one" (מָשִׁיחַ), referring to the practice of anointing individuals with oil when they began their official duties. It is used in the Old Testament predominantly for the royal office (2 Sam. 23:1; Ps. 2:2) but also for the priestly office (Lev. 4:3; cf. Ex. 28:41; 30:30). On one occasion, it is used for the prophetic office (Ps. 105:15), although the actual act of "anointing" was rarely performed on prophets (1 Kings 19:16; possibly Isa. 61:1).

It is interesting to note how the Jews in both Jerusalem and Qumran attempt to support the legitimacy of their respective priestly ministry by connecting them to Aaron. In fact, there is evidence to suggest that Qumran Jews saw the priesthood in Jerusalem and their high priest, a figure referred to in the sectarian texts as "the Wicked Priest" (1QpHab [Pesher Habakkuk] 8.8; 9.9; 11.4), as the adversary of their leader, the "Teacher of Righteousness."

The Zadokite priesthood is mentioned prominently in Qumran. In the Rule of Blessings (1QSb) 3.22–30, they are blessed and identified as the ones "whom God has chosen to strengthen his covenant" (3.23) and also with whom the Lord "renews the covenant of eternal priesthood" (3.26). It is clear from these sectarian texts that the Jews in Qumran believed that the Zadokite priests were covenantally established as priests by the Lord and thus that only they would have been considered legitimate priests (contra the Hasmonean line). Therefore, proper and legitimate priesthood developed from Levi to Aaron to the Zadokites to the Qumran community.

Davidic Covenant

The promise of a royal messiah, which was based on the covenant made with David in 2 Samuel 7, was well attested within Jewish literature. In that chapter, the Lord promised David that his descendants would eternally be seated on the throne of Israel. Just as we saw above with the priestly covenant, so the promise of 2 Samuel 7 developed the expectation of a coming, royal messianic son of David. Second Temple writers often allude to several other key Old Testament passages associated with 2 Samuel 7: Genesis 49:8–12; Numbers 24:17; Psalms 2; 89; 110; 132; and Isaiah 11, to name a few. This Davidic messiah is a prominent figure in Qumran and is given various titles: "the branch of David" (4QpIsa[a] [4Q161] 7–10.3.22; 4QFlor. [Florilegium, or 4Q174] 1.1–13; 4Q285 [Sefer Hamilḥamah] frag. 5.3–4) and the "prince of the congregation" (1QSb 5.20–29; CD 7.18–21; 4QpIsa[a] [4Q161] 2–6.2.19).

One of the more vivid portrayals of this Davidic messiah is found in the Psalms of Solomon. This is the response of a small, devout group of Jews to the capture of Jerusalem by the Roman general Pompey in the first century BC. Having found Jerusalem under the control of a foreign power, these Jews prayed for a royal messiah who would lead a revolt against their oppressors. Psalms of Solomon 17 is a hymnic praise of that expected coming son of David, who is specifically designated as "messiah." Several references are made to the covenant of David of 2 Samuel 7; Psalms 2; 89; and Isaiah 11. When this messiah arrives, the poem describes his regathering of the dispersed Jews, the removal of pagans in the land, and the establishment of a messianic reign over Israel and the nations.[49]

---

49. Although Pss. Sol. 17 is the outstanding description of the expected messiah and his saving activities within Second Temple literature, other Jewish texts provide accounts similar to Pss. Sol. 17: see also 4 Ezra 11.1–12.3; T. Jud. 21.4–6 in the Testament of the Twelve Patriarchs; and numerous texts within Qumran.

From the evidence above, it becomes self-evident that in Qumran at least two messiahs were expected: the royal messiah and the priestly messiah. The most notable reference to this dual messiahship is found in 1QS 9.9–11, which anticipates the coming of "the Messiahs [plural] of Aaron and Israel [משיחי אהרון וישראל]." A similar phrase occurs in CD with one major difference: 1QS explicitly refers to two messiahs (משיחי), whereas CD appears to refer to one (משיח [no final yod] in CD 12.23–13.1; 14.19; 19.10–11; 20.1). Although earlier scholarship believed the "messiah" in CD to be a single figure, the current consensus is that משיח is a singular construct noun "with each of two (or more) absolutes."[50]

According to these texts, these sectarian Jews are called to live by the rules of their community during "the era of wickedness" (CD 12.23). This will continue "until the prophet comes, and the Messiahs [plural] of Aaron and Israel" (1QS 9.11; cf. CD 12.23–13.1). When these messianic figures appear on the scene, obedient Jews will "escape in the time of punishment," while the enemies of Israel "will be handed over to the sword" (CD 19.10–11). This will also be the time when the iniquity of the Jews will "be atoned for" (CD 14.19), presumably by the messianic priest.

Other texts in Qumran describe with greater clarity another curious feature in this dual messianism implied in 1QM: the subordination of the royal messiah to the priestly messiah. In the pesher on Isaiah, 4QpIsa[a] (4Q161), 8.1–10.3.29 (esp. 10.3.22–29), it appears that the royal messiah ("the Branch of David") will submit to the direction of the priest. This is also the scenario in 4Q285 frag. 5.1–6, where the "branch of David" is victorious over his enemies, executes the leader of the enemy forces, and judges the nations. His judgments, however, are done at the behest of the messianic priest. Thus, this Davidic son, who possesses formidable strength and power, is limited in the exercise of his duties and must conform to the standards set on him by the messianic priest. See also 1QSa 2.11–22, where the "priest" (also called the "head of the entire congregation of Israel" in 2.12) enters into the eschatological banquet and partakes of the grand meal prior to the royal messiah entering.

New Covenant

The biblical prophets often prophesied about the days of the restoration. Jeremiah 31:31–34, one of the most prominent prophecies, foretold that after the days of the exile, the Lord would make a "new covenant" with the house of Israel and Judah. Since the beginning of the restoration saw a resurgence of interest in Mosaic themes, even a renewal ceremony of the Sinaitic covenant in Nehemiah 8–9, the Judean returnees did not see this period as the inauguration of the "new covenant" of Jeremiah 31. Rather, the major covenantal administration was still the old covenant of Sinai.

---

50. James VanderKam, "Messianism in the Scrolls," in *The Community of the Renewed Covenant: The Notre Dame Symposium on the Dead Sea Scrolls*, ed. Eugene Ulrich and James VanderKam, CJA 10 (Notre Dame, IN: University of Notre Dame Press, 1994), 230.

It remains unclear, therefore, what the understanding of the "new covenant" prophecy was for the Jews in the Second Temple period. One group of Jews who did have a clear understanding of the new covenant was the Qumran community. According to their sectarian texts, they undoubtedly saw themselves as the community of the new covenant that was mentioned in the prophecy of Jeremiah 31.[51] In two places in CD, they identify themselves as the "community of those who entered into the new covenant" (יחד באי הברית החדשה in CD 6.19; אשר באו הברית החדשה in CD 8.29). According to the pesher on Habakkuk, those who reject the teaching of their movement have in fact "rejected the sure covenant that they made in the land of Damascus, that is the new covenant" (1QpHab. 2.6; cf. CD 6.19; 8.21; 19.33; 20.12). Although the identity of "Damascus" is unclear, what is clear is that this community believed that they were fulfilling the "new covenant."

Another section in CD reveals more information on this Jewish community's understanding of the new covenant. According to CD 15.7–10, when new initiates are brought forward to be interviewed for membership, they are to be registered by the "oath of the covenant that Moses made with Israel," a clear reference to the Sinaitic covenant. This covenant by which the initiate is to swear is also described with terms associated with the new covenant. It is referred to as "the covenant to return to the Law of Moses with a whole heart, and to return with a whole spirit." The two phrases "whole heart" (Jer. 31:33; 32:39, 40; cf. Deut. 30:6; Ezek. 11:19; 36:26) and "whole spirit" (cf. Ezek. 11:19; 36:26–27) are references to the new covenant (cf. Jer. 32:39 with Ezek. 11:19; 36:26–27). This suggests that for the Qumran community the covenant to which all their members swear is actually the "new covenant" of Jeremiah 31. They interpret the word "new" to mean "renewed" and recognize this covenant as a "renewed covenant" of the original Sinaitic administration.

Conclusion

E. P. Sanders has argued for a "basic consistency in the underlying pattern of religion" with his proposal of "covenantal nomism."[52] According to Sanders, one "gets in" the covenant by divine grace, while one "stays in" by obedience to the law.[53] From the literary evidence, we can see some truth to this notion within several Jewish texts mentioned above (e.g., Jubilees).[54] We also see, however, that this does not fit with the way Abraham

---

51. See Shemaryahu Talmon, "The Community of the Renewed Covenant: Between Judaism and Christianity," in Ulrich and VanderKam, *Community of the Renewed Covenant*, 3–26.

52. Sanders's definition of "covenantal nomism" is found in Sanders, *Paul and Palestinian Judaism*, 422–23.

53. See Sanders, *Paul and Palestinian Judaism*, 544–45.

54. For example, according to Sanders, the book of Jubilees stresses the importance of election. *Paul and Palestinian Judaism*, 362–64. Peter Enns offers a helpful critique of the view of Sanders regarding Jubilees. Although Enns acknowledges that this Jewish text fits the mold of covenantal nomism, it is not without problems. He challenges the categories of "getting in" and "staying in" and says that this dichotomy is not the most accurate way to understand the message in Jubilees. "Expansions of Scripture," in Carson, O'Brien, and Seifrid, *Justification and Variegated Nomism*, 1:92–97. D. A. Carson, summarizing Enns's view, says, "If 'salvation' is by grace, how precisely is 'staying saved' a matter of obedience? If obedience is an absolute condition of 'preserving' salvation, in precisely what sense

is described in other Jewish texts. Recall that according to the Prayer of Manasseh 8, he did not need the grace of God because he "did not sin." In fact, according to Sirach 44, Abraham "got in" by his obedience, which was the basis of his election. Even in Pseudo-Philo, Abraham's salvation from a fiery fate is brought on by his sinlessness. At best, it would seem that the concept of "covenantal nomism" reflects one tradition of Jewish understanding of the covenant, though it does not apply to all.

In fact, if it is true that there is no "uniformity of systematic theology"[55] among the Second Temple materials, then we cannot ignore the evaluation of Friedrich Avemarie, who suggests that Sanders, in his attempt to correct the cold works-righteousness conclusions of the previous generation of scholars, has overly emphasized election and grace within the Jewish literature. Avemarie says that there may have existed several competing religious systems and that we cannot disregard the literary evidence suggesting that deeds are determinative in matters of final salvation.[56]

This has an enormous impact on our understandings of the covenants as expounded within the New Testament. It has been alleged that the Reformers of the sixteenth and seventeenth centuries falsely interpreted Paul in light of the Protestant-Romanist polemic of their day and that a forensic understanding of justification (and thus the covenants) is an inaccurate reflection of the theology of the church in her conflict with early Judaism. Although it is true that it is overly simplistic to say that a basic works righteousness was characteristic of the Judaism of Paul's day, the presence of such a view cannot be ruled out. At best, early Judaism can be categorized as semi-Pelagian; at worst, as pure Pelagian. This confirms that the theological battle that Paul fought in his day is similar to that of the early Reformers, who also attempted to rid the church of any notion of merit-based righteousness before the Lord.

The literary evidence in Qumran is also helpful in providing a better understanding of the covenant of eternal priesthood and the royal covenant with David. With the promise of eternal officers comes messianic expectations, and this is what is found within Qumran. According to these texts, the call to obey the Mosaic code would continue until the arrival of two messianic figures, a priest and a king. Their appearance would come in the last days, which appears to mark the war against the "sons of darkness" (1QM 1.1), the final defeat of their enemies, and judgment against the nations.

This dual messianic expectation is not surprising, given the path of the Old Testament regarding the royal and priestly offices. It differs, however, from New Testament

---

may we speak, with Sanders, of salvation depending on the grace of God?" "Summaries and Conclusions," 509. Although Carson's statement is specifically about Jubilees, it applies to the concept of covenantal nomism as a whole.

55. Sanders, *Paul and Palestinian Judaism*, 423.

56. Friedrich Avemarie, *Tora und Leben: Untersuchungen zur Heilsbedeutung der Tora in der frühen rabbinischen Literatur*, TSAJ 55 (Tübingen: Mohr Siebeck, 1996). Avemarie's examination focuses on Rabbinic literature, not the texts of the Second Temple era as defined in this chapter.

messianic expectations. Whereas the Jewish hermeneutic seems to interpret the Old Testament texts as anticipating the coming of multiple messiahs, the New Testament anticipates one in whom both the priestly and royal offices are united (Heb. 5:5; Rev. 5:1–14). Such a messianic identification fits the New Testament claims of Jesus of Nazareth.

23

COVENANT IN CONTEMPORARY
NEW TESTAMENT SCHOLARSHIP

Benjamin L. Gladd

Surveying New Testament scholarship on the issue of covenant is a lot like scrawling the Sistine Chapel on a napkin. Perhaps we can get the broad outline, but there is no way to recreate its dazzling color and intricate depth. In what follows, we attempt to appreciate how scholars have understood the nature of the covenant in the New Testament in the last five or so decades. This is a tricky endeavor because we run the risk of speaking in such broad generalities that we fail to appreciate how scholars have admired the full beauty of God's formal relationship with his people. A full exploration of covenant in New Testament scholarship is obviously beyond the scope of this essay, so we confine ourselves to two areas: the Gospels and Paul's letters.

For us to appreciate the present, we should learn a bit about the past. In the early twentieth century, New Testament scholars (especially Pauline specialists) argued that the New Testament documents must be read primarily in light of their Greco-Roman background. These scholars found purported evidence of pagan mystery religions and Gnosticism under every nook and cranny of the New Testament. But this rereading came crashing down with the discovery of the Dead Sea Scrolls in the mid-twentieth century. In addition, the last three decades also witnessed a surge of attention on the use of the Old Testament in the New. Scholars soon realized that the New Testament must be read primarily in light of the Old Testament and Second Temple Judaism (530 BC–AD 70). So when scholars have attempted to articulate the nature of covenant in the New Testament in recent years, they have done so in light of the New Testament's relationship to the Old Testament and Second Temple Judaism.

Covenant in the Gospels

Discussion of the covenant in the four Gospels is a tricky matter. We have four different yet complementary Gospels that accent varied aspects of the covenant. This is not
to say that they are contradictory in their presentation of the covenant, but there are
some measured differences. In addition to the four distinct presentations, the whole
issue of Jesus's personal relationship to the covenant comes to the surface as we probe
inside the Gospels, and the complex discussion of the historical Jesus inevitably results.

To maintain the brevity and scope of this essay, we evaluate the role of the covenant
in the Gospels in a twofold manner: first, we examine the Last Supper as presented in
the Synoptics, and second, we sketch how various scholars understand Jesus's relationship to the covenant as a whole.

New Covenant and the Last Supper in the Synoptics

Since Jesus explicitly mentions the "new covenant" at the Last Supper, most discussions
of covenant focus their attention on the precise wording of Jesus:

> And he took a cup, and when he had given thanks he gave it to them, saying, "Drink
> of it, all of you, for this is *my blood of the covenant*, which is poured out for many for
> the forgiveness of sins." (Matt. 26:27–28)

> And he said to them, "This is *my blood of the covenant*, which is poured out for
> many." (Mark 14:24)

> And likewise the cup after they had eaten, saying, "This cup that is poured out for
> you is *the new covenant in my blood*." (Luke 22:20)

Scholars are quick to underscore the considerable role of the Old Testament in this
saying. Old Testament texts such as Exodus 24:8; Isaiah 52:13–53:12; Jeremiah 31:31,
34; and Zechariah 9:11 are some of the more prominent ones commentators highlight.

For the most part, the main historical-critical issue here is the unique nature of the
Last Supper and its timing with the Passover celebration.[1] Religious meals were common
in the ancient world, both in a Greco-Roman and Jewish environment.[2] But what makes
this meal so unique is Jesus's identification with the elements. He *is* the meal. Moreover,
three interrelated concepts are found in the saying: blood, covenant, and forgiveness. In

---

1. Scholars debate the timing of the Last Supper and its relationship to the Passover celebration. Was the Last
Supper a Passover meal? Was it held in advance, or were two calendars in play? Do the Synoptics and John present
conflicting narratives? These are tricky questions, and commentators offer different theories. A good case can be
made that Jesus did indeed celebrate a Passover meal a day early. Technically, the Passover celebration at the Last
Supper would still fall on Nisan 14, though, as required in the law. The Jewish day *began* after sundown. So in
anticipation of his atoning sacrifice, Jesus may have celebrated Passover at the Last Supper but without a lamb
(the lambs were slaughtered at noon on the following day at the temple). For a wise discussion of this complex
issue, see Eckhard J. Schnabel, *Jesus in Jerusalem: The Last Days* (Grand Rapids, MI: Eerdmans, 2018), 202–4.

2. See Craig S. Keener, *The Gospel of Matthew: A Socio-Rhetorical Commentary* (Grand Rapids, MI: Eerdmans,
2009), 627–29.

Matthew's account, the term "covenant" is nestled between "blood" and "forgiveness," giving us some clues about the meaning of Jesus's words.

The Last Supper celebrated the annual Passover meal. The institution of Passover finds its roots in Exodus 12. Each year, an Israelite family must find a perfect male lamb and slaughter it at twilight. It is an atoning sacrifice. Then the families are to eat it a certain way and dress accordingly. They are to take blood from the lamb and apply it to the doorframes of their houses (Ex. 12:1–50). The Passover lies deep within the heart of the Jewish nation, symbolizing God's redemption and deliverance. It recalls God vanquishing Pharaoh and the Egyptians and anticipates what God will do in the future. Remarkably, Jesus identifies himself as the ultimate Passover Lamb. He is also the Lord who promised to liberate Israel from slavery. In other words, Jesus is *both* the sacrificial Lamb and Israel's God in the flesh. Speaking of Matthew 26:28, R. T. France rightly exclaims,

> Here . . . is the fulfillment of the new exodus typology which we have noted in Matthew's application to Jesus of exodus-related texts especially in 2:15 and 4:1–11, but now with the addition of a shocking new dimension: Jesus is not only the new Israel, the focus of the restored people of God, but himself also the sacrifice by which it is to be achieved.[3]

France's comments bring us to an important point—the nature of Christ's fulfillment of the expectations of the old covenant. But a key question remains: Did the Passover itself anticipate the coming of Christ in its original context, or did the meal predict the coming of Christ only from the vantage point of the New Testament? To put it another way, can we discern a typology only from this side of the cross? Or is typology embedded, at least to some degree, within Exodus 12? Is the Passover celebration forward looking in its original context? Scholars vigorously debate the nature of typology, and some of that disagreement is found here in the event of the Last Supper.

Modern commentaries on the Synoptics tend to speak in generalities concerning the nature of Christ's fulfillment of the Passover celebration. David Garland, representative of many commentators, explains the connection between Jesus and the Passover meal in Luke 22 as follows:

> The past is never merely the past but is relived in the present. As the Passover remembers God's deliverance of Israel from the bondage of Egypt (Ex. 12:14; 13:3, 8; Deut. 16:3), so the re-presentation of this meal remembers God's deliverance of all believers through the cross of Jesus, giving them salvation.[4]

Garland is ambiguous here. Is the Passover meal simply analogous to the Last Supper? Is it typological? The crucial connection between the two Testaments and Jesus's relationship with the Old Testament is left somewhat vague.

---

3. R. T. France, *The Gospel of Matthew*, NICNT (Grand Rapids, MI: Eerdmans, 2007), 988.
4. David E. Garland, *Luke*, ZECNT 3 (Grand Rapids, MI: Zondervan, 2011), 856.

One of the most important books on the use of the Old Testament in the four Gospels is Richard Hays's *Echoes of Scripture in the Gospels*.[5] When he explores the Last Supper in Matthew's narrative in light of the Old Testament, he makes a number of wonderful observations. Hays points out that Jesus's discussion of the "blood of the covenant" recalls Exodus 24:8: "Moses took the blood and threw it on the people and said, '*Behold the blood of the covenant* that the LORD has made with you.'" Hays then goes on to connect the Last Supper with the meal that Moses ate with the seventy elders of Israel in Exodus 24:9–11 and with Israel's obligation to the covenant in Exodus 24:7. Hays labels these connections "figural correspondences" that trigger Matthew's readers to return to the Old Testament and look for further connections to the Last Supper.[6]

Richard Hays advocates a "rereading," or a "retrospective reading," of the Old Testament, in which the authors of the Gospels (and the church) reexamine Old Testament passages in light of Christ and discover new or "latent" or "unsuspected" meaning.[7] This conviction comes to the fore at the end of the book when he claims that "the 'meaning' of the Old Testament texts was not confined to the human author's original historical setting or to the meaning that could have been grasped by the original readers."[8] It appears that Hays advances a hermeneutical theory that denies the authorial awareness of how a particular Old Testament passage would later be used in the New Testament. For Hays and others, meaning thus tends to be retrospective. To be fair, he claims that once the Old Testament has been "reread," it can then inform the meaning of the New Testament—a prospective reading of sorts. But it is precisely at this point that Hays and others are vague. He is uncomfortable with "typology" at times, and in the case of Luke, he prefers "analogy." It is therefore unclear how a rereading of Old Testament passages informs the New Testament.

It appears that the institution of Passover in Exodus 12 was itself forward looking within its historical and original context. Embedded within each dimension of the celebration was an anticipating that the Passover would be climactically fulfilled in a coming redeemer, who would liberate Israel from "Egypt" once and for all at the end of history. Though Old Testament authors probably did not understand how a good many of their anticipations would eventually be fulfilled with great precision, they did understand the trajectory of them.[9] It may not be a stretch, therefore, to claim that the Passover meal was eschatological from the very beginning.

---

5. Richard B. Hays, *Echoes of Scripture in the Gospels* (Waco, TX: Baylor University Press, 2016).

6. Hays, *Echoes*, 134.

7. Richard B. Hays, *Reading Backwards: Figural Christology and the Fourfold Gospel Witness* (Waco, TX: Baylor University Press, 2014), 15. See also my review of this volume in *RFP* 1, no. 1 (2016): 72–78.

8. Hays, *Echoes*, 358.

9. For further elaboration of this difficult issue, see G. K. Beale and Benjamin L. Gladd, *Hidden but Now Revealed: A Biblical Theology of Mystery* (Downers Grove, IL: InterVarsity Press, 2014), 328–64. Hays argues that "staunch evangelical apologists . . . contend desperately that the authors of the Old Testament's narratives and poems actually did intentionally forecast the details of Jesus's life." *Echoes*, 359. I am not advocating the position that the Old Testament authors knew the "details" of Christ's life with great precision, but I am arguing for the idea that Old Testament authors *broadly* anticipated Christ's life, death, and resurrection.

The Law of Moses and Jesus

Our second area of concern is how Jesus's earthly ministry, death, and resurrection relate to Israel's covenant as a whole. Did Jesus fulfill the Mosaic covenant? Did he partially fulfill it? Did he abrogate it? These are complex issues. In fact, they are so difficult that few monographs on the historical Jesus are dedicated to this topic. For example, in the second edition of *Dictionary of Jesus and the Gospels*, there is no essay on "covenant," but there is one on "law."[10] Jesus's relationship to Israel's covenant is generally discussed in essays or restricted to a chapter or two in a single volume.[11]

The point of entry into this discussion is to take a step back and examine the question from a more fundamental and systematic level. We must examine how Jesus relates to the Mosaic law as a whole. As one can imagine, every conceivable option has been advocated, but we will restrict ourselves to the three most common views among evangelical scholars. Law and covenant are not synonymous; law regulates the covenant. Nevertheless, the goal in this section is to give a range of the options among contemporary scholars. Keep in mind that these three views operate on a spectrum and that the debate rests on matters of degree. This debate is also tied to a much bigger and fundamental issue—the relationship between Israel in the Old Testament and the church in the New.

Often among those in the Baptist and Lutheran traditions, we find a disjunction between Israel in the Old Testament and the church in the New. Dispensationalists argue that Israel and the church are separate entities, so they naturally see little under the Mosaic covenant that carries over into the new covenant.[12] Jesus's death and resurrection inaugurated a new people group—the church—and their relationship to the Mosaic law is quite indirect. Only the basic moral substructure of the law is applicable for the new covenant believer. On the other hand, those within the Lutheran tradition accent the Mosaic law's fulfillment in Christ. In contrast to dispensationalists, these scholars operate on a redemptive-historical plane. They view the church as true Israel, at least at some level, yet still argue for a strong separation of the old and new covenants.[13] Christ

---

10. Joel B. Green, Scot McKnight, and I. Howard Marshall, eds., *Dictionary of Jesus and the Gospels: A Compendium of Contemporary Biblical Scholarship*, 2nd ed. (Downers Grove, IL: InterVarsity Press, 2013).

11. See, though, Tom Holmén, *Jesus and Jewish Covenant Thinking*, BibInt 55 (Leiden: Brill, 2001); Kim Huat Tan, "Community, Kingdom and Cross: Jesus's View of Covenant," in *The God of Covenant: Biblical, Theological, and Contemporary Perspectives*, ed. Jamie A. Grant and Alistair I. Wilson (Leicester, UK: Apollos, 2005), 122–55. Perhaps the most audacious attempt to understand Jesus's relationship to Israel's covenant in recent memory is N. T. Wright, *Jesus and the Victory of God*, vol. 2 of *Christian Origins and the Question of God* (Minneapolis: Fortress, 1996). Wright forcefully argues that the portrayal of Jesus in the Gospels resonates with Second Temple Judaism and that Jesus came to renew God's covenant with Israel through his death and resurrection and to deliver his people from spiritual exile (127, 133, 172, 194, etc.). Wright insists that the new covenant would be marked by faith in Jesus and his kingdom message and not by externals that previously demarcated Israel from her pagan neighbors (286).

12. See Wayne G. Strickland, "The Inauguration of the Law of Christ with the Gospel of Christ: A Dispensational View," in *Five Views on Law and Gospel*, ed. Wayne G. Strickland (Grand Rapids, MI: Zondervan, 1996), 229–79.

13. One of the most prominent proponents of this view is Douglas J. Moo, who nicely summarizes his view of the Mosaic law's role in the church in "The Law of Christ as the Fulfillment of the Law of Moses: A Modified Lutheran View," in Strickland, *Five Views on Law and Gospel*, 319–76.

fulfills the Mosaic law and establishes a new administration in the New Testament era. The "law of Christ"—that is, the teaching of Christ and the apostles—is what regulates life in the church.

On the opposite end of the spectrum, some within the Reformed tradition contend for the continuance of much of the Mosaic law into the new covenant era.[14] Though the Old Testament looks forward to the coming of Jesus, the civil and moral laws of Moses are not abrogated in him. Christ came to deal with sin and empower God's people to obey the moral commands. The civil laws he gave to Israel at Sinai should also be enforced by civil magistrates. This view, once popular in some Reformed circles, has diminished to some degree in recent decades. It argues that the ceremonial laws are no longer required but that the civil and moral are still in force in the new covenant age.[15]

The third and final view is a bit of a balancing act between the two views above. This view is dominant within the Reformed tradition.[16] On the one hand, these scholars argue that the civil and the ceremonial laws have been fulfilled in Christ and are no longer in effect in the new covenant community (discontinuity). What remains in effect, though, is the moral law (continuity). Keep in mind that within Reformed circles there is flexibility here. Reformed scholars are not in complete agreement on what Mosaic laws carry over (and *how* they apply) in the new covenant age (e.g., the role of the Sabbath commandment).

Critical to this debate is whether the church is true Israel and stands in continuity with the people of God throughout the history of redemption. If so, then we would assume that new covenant believers have much in common with the Old Testament saints who enjoyed fellowship with God. Another key to this complex discussion (and building on the previous point) is the role of the Old Testament in the New. If the old covenant has little bearing on the lives of new covenant believers, then we would expect Paul rarely quoting or alluding to the Mosaic law.

What we find, though, in the writings of the New Testament is frequent citation of the Mosaic law. From one angle, all the Old Testament—its laws, institutions, patterns, and so on—point to Christ (Luke 24:27). But is the Old Testament *fully* fulfilled in him, and does it, consequently, have little bearing for new covenant believers? It does not appear so. The New Testament writers—most notably Luke, Paul, and Peter (whose audiences were largely Gentile)—often applied passages from the Old Testament, even from the law of Moses, to the church. For example, Paul argues in Galatians that the law should not regulate the life of new covenant believers the same way it did for the Israelites under the old covenant. But he does not throw the nomistic baby out with

14. One of the most articulate defenses of theonomy is Greg L. Bahnsen, *Theonomy in Christian Ethics* (Nutley, NJ: Craig Press, 1977).

15. See the critique of theonomy by Meredith Kline, "Comments on an Old-New Error," *WTJ* 41, no. 1 (1978): 172–79.

16. See, e.g., John Murray, *The Covenant of Grace: A Biblico-Theological Study* (London: Tyndale Press, 1954); O. Palmer Robertson, *The Christ of the Covenants* (Phillipsburg, NJ: Presbyterian and Reformed, 1980).

the bathwater. If obeying the Torah does not regulate the Christian life in the new age, then what does? Paul answers this pressing question, "The only thing that counts is faith expressing itself through love" (Gal. 5:6 NIV).

Faith in Christ is always accompanied by works, specifically, love toward God and one's neighbor (James 2:14–26). Galatians 5:14 explicitly claims that "the entire law is fulfilled in keeping this one command: 'Love your neighbor as yourself'" (NIV). Paul quotes Leviticus 19:18 here to reaffirm a central commandment contained within the Torah itself. Loving God and loving one another are concretely expressed in the Ten Commandments (Ex. 20:1–17; Deut. 5:6–21). Jesus himself says that loving God and loving one another are the greatest commandments (Mark 12:28–31 par.). Jesus quotes two Old Testament texts from the Torah in support of this claim: Deuteronomy 6:4–5 and Leviticus 19:18. Though the covenant community is not required to keep the civil and cultic portions of the Mosaic law that preserved Israel's identity in the new age, Christians are still obligated to obey the moral commandments of God's law, those commands that began in the garden of Eden and pass through the Mosaic covenant.

Covenant in Paul

For the past few decades, several scholars have argued for an overhaul of the traditional understanding of Paul, particularly Galatians and Romans. This reappraisal, known as the New Perspective, begins with a reevaluation of God's relationship to Israel in the Old Testament. Israel, the New Perspective argues, understood itself to be elected graciously by God at Sinai. Israel did nothing to "get into" the covenant. The Israelites did not attempt to "earn" salvation but performed law-sanctioned works in order to preserve and maintain their covenantal relationship with God. Judaism in the first century, they argue, was not works based, as has been traditionally understood. The New Perspective claims that scholars have been in the wrong for centuries in their misreading of the literature of the Jewish people, particularly the Pauline Epistles. The history of the New Perspective has been well documented. Indeed, entire books are dedicated to tracing the nuances of the debate.[17] We find ourselves nearly four decades into the New Perspective, and its proponents are still refining their views, even distancing themselves from other New Perspectivists. At the risk of oversimplifying the matter, our very brief overview examines only its three major pioneers—E. P. Sanders, James D. G. Dunn, and N. T. Wright.

Charting the New Perspective

In the late 1970s, Sanders published his seminal work, *Paul and Palestinian Judaism*, a book that continues to affect New Testament studies today. In it, Sanders sets out to

---

17. E.g., Stephen Westerholm, *Perspectives Old and New on Paul: The "Lutheran" Paul and His Critics* (Grand Rapids, MI: Eerdmans, 2004).

detect what he calls "patterns of religion," to discover how religious members perceive "getting in and staying in." After evaluating an enormous amount of Jewish literature, Sanders concludes that a notion he labeled "covenantal nomism" existed in the first century. This "pattern" is roughly defined as follows: Israel understood itself to be elected graciously by God at Sinai. Israel did nothing to "get into" the covenant. God sovereignly chose Israel. Also, God gave Israel his law, in order that they *maintain* their relationship with God. Therefore, in Judaism the people did not try to "earn" salvation; rather, they performed law-sanctioned works to preserve their covenantal relationship with God. Succinctly, Sanders attempted to demonstrate that Judaism was not works based. Christianity, both liberal and conservative, has been in the wrong for centuries by promoting such a skewed assessment of Judaism. Scholars who propounded such a view of Judaism used late Jewish sources (AD 300–1000) and thus anachronistically labeled Judaism a religion of works. In first-century Judaism, no sector of Judaism thought this way. Sanders argues,

> The "pattern" or "structure" of covenantal nomism is this: (1) God has chosen Israel and (2) given the law. The law implies both (3) God's promise to maintain the election and (4) the requirement to obey. (5) God rewards obedience and punishes transgression. (6) The law provides for means of atonement, and atonement results in (7) maintenance or re-establishment of the covenantal relationship. (8) All those who are maintained in the covenant by obedience, atonement and God's mercy belong to the group which will be saved.[18]

Such a conclusion on the nature of Israel's relationship to the covenant set the tone for studies on Paul for decades to come. The ink of *Paul and Palestinian Judaism* barely dried before James D. G. Dunn capitalized on Sanders's fundamental insights. Dunn crystallized Sanders's view in a number of ways. A prodigious New Testament scholar in the Methodist stream, Dunn attempted to remain indebted to the traditional Protestant view of justification. Though he often talks of the role of faith and God's grace in the covenant, his views differ from traditional Protestant thinking in several key ways, for he wholly subscribes to Sanders's model of "covenantal nomism." Dunn's contribution lies in a more thorough application of covenantal nomism in Paul than Sanders himself first understood. Dunn makes the following statements in two separate works:

> The most surprising feature of Sanders' writing . . . is that he himself had failed to take the opportunity his own mould-breaking work offered. Instead of trying to explore how far Paul's theology could be explicated in relation to Judaism's "covenantal nomism," he remained impressed at the difference between Paul's pattern of

---

18. E. P. Sanders, *Paul and Palestinian Judaism: A Comparison of Patterns of Religions* (Minneapolis: Fortress, 1977), 422.

religious thought and that of first-century Judaism. He quickly, too quickly in my view, concluded that Paul's religion could be understood only as a basically different system from that of his fellow Jews.[19]

Now Sanders has given us an unrivalled opportunity to look at Paul afresh, to shift our perspective back from the 16th century to the first century, to do what all true exegetes want to do—that is, . . . to let Paul be himself.[20]

Sanders surmised that Paul's problem with Judaism was simply that its adherents did not locate salvation in Christ, whereas Dunn contends that Paul's problem with Judaism was that its adherents not only lacked belief in Christ (Sanders) but also had a pervasive problem with nationalism. The problem with the law, therefore, was that it kept Gentiles at a distance, striking at the heart of Paul's mission to the nations. As a result, justification is much more horizontally oriented (Jew and Gentile) than vertically oriented (*coram Deo*).[21] The "works of the law" that Paul finds so offensive are not works that Jews perform in order to be "saved"; rather, "works of the law" refers to Jewish national "badges" that demarcate Israel from her pagan neighbors, such as circumcision, food laws, and Sabbath obedience. The problem with boasting in "works of the law" was that it did not allow Gentiles to become part of God's people, Israel.

We now turn to our final and most well-known candidate—N. T. Wright. It would not be a stretch to say that Wright, situated within the Anglican tradition, is one of the most published New Testament scholars of the last hundred years or so. His writings are voluminous, well crafted, and even at times entertaining. His lectures and sermons are no less captivating. What makes engaging Wright so difficult is the sheer breadth of his work. Though the quantity of Wright's work is astounding, we can get a handle on his thought by examining one of his earliest works on the subject on Paul and the law, *What Saint Paul Really Said*.[22] Though less than two hundred pages, this seminal work is where we discover the heart of Wright's thinking.

N. T. Wright tends to give more weight than Sanders and Dunn do to the broad story of Israel and the process of God redeeming his people. According to Wright, God covenanted with Israel in order to undo the fall. Israel would be sin's antidote! God also

---

19. James D. G. Dunn, *Jesus, Paul, and the Law: Studies in Mark and Galatians* (Louisville: Westminster John Knox, 1990), 100.

20. James D. G. Dunn, "The New Perspective on Paul," *BJRL* 65, no. 2 (1983): 100.

21. It should be noted that Dunn's most recent work attempts to soften some of what he argued in the 1980s and 1990s. He now claims that much of the traditional view of justification is primary and that he only seeks to point out a secondary problem with the law (the relationship between Jews and Gentiles). Dunn states, "The point I am trying to make is simply that there is another dimension (or other dimensions) of the biblical doctrine of God's justice and of Paul's teaching on justification which have been overlooked and neglected, and that it is important to recover these aspects and to think them through afresh in the changing circumstances of today's world." *The New Perspective on Paul*, rev. ed. (Grand Rapids, MI: Eerdmans, 2008), 23. It is hard to square Dunn's recent attitude with his previous writings, though, as he originally advocated an overhaul of our conception of Paul's view of justification.

22. N. T. Wright, *What Saint Paul Really Said: Was Paul of Tarsus the Real Founder of Christianity?* (Grand Rapids, MI: Eerdmans, 1997).

charged Israel to evangelize the nations and bring Gentiles into the covenant community. All the nations of the earth are to join with Israel in their worship of God.

Keeping in step with Dunn, Wright depends on Sanders's conclusion that "covenantal nomism" existed during Paul's day. He also, similar to Dunn, emphasizes a horizontal view of the law and highlights the Jewish badges, such as circumcision, food laws, and Sabbath. Paul's problem with the law was not that Jews were trying to "earn" their way to heaven; rather, Jews were keeping Gentiles out by boasting in their national identity through, for example, their observance of circumcision. These "works of the law" are not intrinsically bad, but now that Christ has come, faith in Christ is the only appropriate boundary marker.

Unfortunately, Israel, instead of being a light to the nations, boasted in its temple, circumcision, and Sabbath, thereby committing idolatry and refusing to integrate Gentiles. As a penalty, God sent the nation into exile in Babylon, but even though they returned to their land sometime thereafter, Israel did not, in reality, return spiritually. In the Gospels, Jesus leads his people out of spiritual exile. He judges Israel for their disobedience and welcomes Gentiles into the covenant community. The problem with the law, therefore, is that it divides Jews and Gentiles, not primarily that it exposes humanity's sin.

For Wright, God uses the covenant to deal with sin and its effects: "The covenant was there to put the world to rights, to deal with evil and to restore God's justice and order to the cosmos."[23] Justification is, therefore, the believer's identification with Israel. In short, justification is a declaration that an individual is part of the covenant community, and it is based on an individual's faith and "faithfulness" (i.e., "works"). Wright states,

> Justification in this setting, then, is not a matter of how someone enters the community of the true people of God, but of how you tell who belongs to that community. . . . "Justification" in the first century was not about how someone might establish a relationship with God. It was about God's eschatological definition, both future and present, of who was, in fact, a member of his people.[24]

In other words, justification is primarily concerned with God acknowledging that an individual is part of true Israel.

In keeping with his preoccupation with the covenant, Wright claims that the overwhelming majority of the time, righteousness language is bound up with faithfulness to the covenant. Righteousness is not an abstract quality but a concrete expression of either God's or an individual's faithfulness to the covenant. Wright argues,

> If and when God does act to vindicate his people, his people will then, metaphorically speaking, have the status of "righteousness." . . . But the righteousness they

---

23. Wright, *What Saint Paul Really Said*, 117.
24. Wright, *What Saint Paul Really Said*, 119.

have will not be God's own righteousness. That makes no sense at all. God's own righteousness is his covenant faithfulness, because of which he will (Israel hopes) vindicate her, and bestow upon her the status of "righteous," as the vindicated or acquitted defendant. But God's righteousness remains, so to speak, God's own property. It is the reason for his acting to vindicate his people. It is not the status he bestows upon them in so doing.[25]

Reconfiguring the notion of righteousness and justification inevitably leads to a reconfiguration of the gospel. The gospel, according to Wright, is not about how people "receive Christ" or "get saved from their sins"; rather, it is largely concerned with an individual's identification with the covenant community and the declaration that Jesus is cosmic King: "It [the gospel] is not, then, a system of how people get saved. The announcement of the gospel results in people being saved. . . . But 'the gospel' itself, strictly speaking, is the narrative proclamation of King Jesus."[26]

(Re)interpreting Paul

According to the New Perspective, when we turn to Paul's letters, we discover that the apostle Paul was not objecting to the Gentiles' legalistic understanding of the law. The Gentiles were not trying to earn their way to heaven by embracing the requirements of the Mosaic law. Instead, Paul was attempting to overturn the Gentiles' obedience to certain particulars of the Torah because the Gentiles were embracing specific Mosaic legislation that physically demarcated Gentiles from Jews (circumcision, dietary laws, and Sabbath observance). Now that Christ has come and ushered in a new age, Jews and Gentiles constitute one entity, and obeying such external requirements of the old covenant unravels what Christ has done on the cross. The New Perspective argues that the doctrine of justification is tied not so much to how an individual relates to God but to how an individual identifies with true Israel. Justification is not about how a person "enters" into the true community of faith but about how a person continues to be identified with that community through faithfulness (faith plus good works). When God "justifies" a person, he is declaring that person to be one who is persevering as an ongoing part of the end-time covenant community.

At the heart of the dispute between the traditional understanding of Paul and the New Perspective is whether Paul is primarily concerned for the individual's posture before an almighty God. Before the advent of the New Perspective, the majority of scholars understood Paul's conception of justification as entailing a sinner's stance before a just and righteous God. That is, those who trust in Christ's work on the cross are "declared righteous" from their sin and guilt before God's tribunal. But New Perspective scholars are convinced that Paul's gospel is primarily concerned with the social dimension of

25. Wright, *What Saint Paul Really Said*, 99.
26. Wright, *What Saint Paul Really Said*, 45.

the covenant community. They ask, How can believing Jews and Gentiles be unified? Such unity comes by believing in and giving allegiance to Jesus Christ as the greatest revelation of God, a revelation to which the Old Testament law pointed. Therefore, the New Perspective argues that one should give ultimate allegiance not to the nationalistic distinctives of the law (circumcision, dietary laws, etc.) as God's final revelation but to Christ as God's eschatological revelation.

Appraising the New Perspective

Now that we have a bit of a handle on how we got here and the high stakes of the debate, we can briefly give four responses to the New Perspective. We could list many more, but we will restrict ourselves to only these four.[27]

Second Temple Judaism and Legalism

A key plank of the New Perspective involves the relation between Jews in the first century and the law of Moses. Are they trying to pull themselves up by their own moral bootstraps and curry God's favor? Or are they consciously doing the law by God's grace, knowing that they are already in a covenant relationship with him? D. A. Carson, Peter T. O'Brien, and Mark A. Seifrid edited the volume *Justification and Variegated Nomism* to answer this question.[28] Their conclusion: it depends. There are strands within Second Temple Judaism that did indeed view their relationship to the law as an expression of God's grace and were not trying to earn his favor. On the other hand, we do have relevant passages that highlight a works-based or legalistic worldview. In the final chapter of the volume, Carson surmises, "One conclusion to be drawn, then, is not that Sanders is wrong everywhere, but he is wrong when he tries to establish that his category is right everywhere."[29] What we have, then, is indeed legalism in the first century, and Paul's language of justification, works, righteousness, and the law can be read in light of it.

The Protestant Canon

The New Perspective argues that legalism is not found anywhere in the Second Temple period, so if that is indeed the case, then the bulk of the New Testament should reflect this worldview and not only what we find in Paul's chief writings (or the *Hauptbriefe*): Romans, 1–2 Corinthians, and Galatians. Much, if not all, of the New Testament should be brought to bear on this debate. What we find, though, does not fit squarely with

---

27. For one of the most substantive critiques of N. T. Wright on his view of Second Temple Judaism, Paul's relationship to it, and Paul's internal logic, see the excellent essay by J. M. G. Barclay, "Paul and the Faithfulness of God," *SJT* 68, no. 2 (2015): 235–43.

28. D. A. Carson, Peter T. O'Brien, and Mark A. Seifrid, eds., *Justification and Variegated Nomism*, vol. 1, *The Complexities of Second Temple Judaism*, WUNT, 2nd ser., no. 140 (Grand Rapids, MI: Baker Academic, 2001).

29. D. A. Carson, "Summaries and Conclusions," in Carson, O'Brien, and Seifrid, *Justification and Variegated Nomism*, 1:543. See also Robert J. Cara, *Cracking the Foundation of the New Perspective on Paul: Covenantal Nomism versus Reformed Covenantal Theology*, REDS (Fearn, Ross-shire, Scotland: Mentor, 2017).

what the New Perspective argues. In the Gospels, is Jesus's main critique of the Pharisees that they are simply keeping Gentiles out of the covenant community? Certainly, he takes up that issue at key junctures in his ministry (e.g., Mark 11:17 par.), but there is something more going on. In the woe oracles against the Jewish leaders in Matthew 23, for example, Jesus is clearly targeting their lack of Torah obedience: "The scribes and the Pharisees sit on Moses' seat, so do and observe whatever they tell you, but not the works they do. *For they preach, but do not practice*" (Matt. 23:2–3). What about the book of Hebrews? Many scholars argue that Hebrews is written before the fall of the Jerusalem temple in AD 70. What we find in the book is quite interesting. According to the author of Hebrews, the Mosaic law is fundamentally flawed not because it kept Gentiles at a distance but because it was unable to "perfect the conscience of the worshiper" (Heb. 9:9). Forgiveness of sin and cleansing can be found only in Christ's work. The point of bringing up Matthew and Hebrews is that we have many perspectives in the New Testament regarding the nature of the Mosaic law, and they do not fit with what the New Perspectivists propose—that the exclusive problem with the Mosaic law is its separation of Jews and Gentiles.

The History of Redemption

In light of the previous point, another weakness of the New Perspective is its lack of integrating Paul (and other New Testament authors) into the grand storyline of the Bible. Paul's message must be understood as it relates to the arc of the biblical story. The Bible's story begins with the creation of Adam and Eve, their fall, and God's promise to overcome their failure (Gen. 3:15). Adam and Eve's failure in the garden profoundly affected the story of the cosmos, Israel, and all humanity.

At the most basic level, all humanity, whether Jew or Gentile, is tethered to either Adam and Eve's failure in the garden or to the success of the last Adam on the cross. Richard Gaffin puts his finger on a critical point when he argues,

> The sweep of Paul's covenant-historical outlook, the overarching hierarchy of his concern here [i.e., 1 Cor. 15], is such that no one comes into consideration but Adam and Christ—not David, not Moses and the law given at Sinai, not even Abraham as the promise-holder, not Noah, nor anyone else. . . . As Paul is looking at things in this passage, no one between them "counts."[30]

Possessing faith in Christ is the means by which a person is identified with the last Adam (Rom. 5:12–21; 1 Cor. 15:45–57). Focusing on how one continues to be identified with the covenant community puts the cart before the horse. Our identity with the first or last Adam must remain primary. If one believes in the last Adam's justifying work,

30. Richard B. Gaffin Jr., *By Faith, Not by Sight: Paul and the Order of Salvation* (Colorado Springs: Paternoster, 2006), 47.

then that individual's guilty and sinful identity with the first Adam has been dealt with. That person subsequently enters into the true covenant community and continues to be identified with the community by faith, inevitably producing good works.

Faith in Christ is the means by which God "justifies" an individual (Rom. 4:1–25; Gal. 2:15–16; Eph. 2:8–9). When an individual is declared "right" in God's sight, that person is admitted into true Israel. Becoming part of Israel is the effect or the result of being justified in God's sight. The two are not synonymous, and the vertical dimension of the gospel, that is, an individual's stance before a holy and just God, remains paramount.

Though the New Perspective is inherently flawed, it has refocused our attention on the social dimension of the Mosaic law and how aspects of the Mosaic law stood as a barrier between Jews and Gentiles. This is a good thing when properly understood. In the past, Pauline scholars often overlooked some of the social implications of Paul's gospel in his writings. The New Perspective is wrong, though, to collapse the horizontal implications of the gospel with the vertical dimensions of the gospel itself.

When we turn to the book of Galatians, we learn that the Galatian Gentiles were indeed trying to gain entrance into true Israel by adhering to particular national aspects of Mosaic law. These national laws are social and political in orientation. But these national laws that pertain to the nation of Israel are a *subset* of the entire law of Moses, and the law of Moses is a *subset* of "law" in general. Any form of human works that precedes faith stands in opposition to faith in Christ.

The Galatians were wrong on two counts. First, they failed to realize that by preserving the national laws of Moses, they were promoting obedience to all the Torah (Gal. 2:15–16) and the law in general, which no one can perfectly obey (Gal. 5:3; so also James 2:10). Faith plus works, in this errant framework, is seen as justifying. But that is an incorrect understanding of justification, as Paul argues. Faith in Christ, not through works, justifies. The Galatians were jeopardizing their vertical relationship with God, because they were not living a life that is first and foremost characterized by faith in Christ. Second, the Gentile Galatians were wrong in their appraisal of the Mosaic law in light of the new age. Now that Christ had come and had begun to establish the new creation, the old covenant as an administrative entity was no longer in force, and certain aspects of the Mosaic law were fulfilled. Christ is the true circumcision, the true temple, and all are ritually pure in him. The Old Testament laws about circumcision, the temple, and cleansing are no longer required in the new age, since they are fulfilled in Christ. The Galatians were attempting to obey laws that were, quite simply, out of date.

What Is "Legalism"?

One of the most confusing yet critical dimensions of the debate is the nature of "legalism" and "maintaining" the Mosaic covenant. Centrally problematic to Sanders's view is the notion of "staying in." He claims that Israel's works are done in order to maintain their covenantal status. At the end of the day, therefore, an individual does "works" or righteous acts in order to stay in the covenant. How does this proposal differ significantly from merit theology? Instead of placing merit theology at the entry point, Sanders simply moves it to another location. In other words, Jews must perform righteous works in order for them to be eventually saved. This conclusion still falls within the boundary of what has traditionally been termed "legalism."[31]

Crucially, Sanders fails to maintain a distinction between Pelagianism and semi-Pelagianism. Pelagianism is the doctrine whereby original sin is not passed on to the individual, and thus we are able to choose good or evil without God intervening. Individuals have the capacity to obey God fully and merit salvation. Semi-Pelagianism is a middle ground between Augustine and the heresy of Pelagianism. Though it does not deny the effects of original sin (human nature remains "injured"), this position argues that man still possesses a free will and can cooperate with God in salvation. The balm of God's "prevenient grace" heals the individual's incapacity to do good, so God and the individual combine their efforts for salvation (synergism). Those within the Reformed tradition have, for good reason, rejected this position time and again. Surely, persevering works are important, even the condition for salvation (that is, genuine works are a by-product of the Spirit), but they are never the *causal grounds* for salvation. The causal ground of the believers' salvation is solely Christ's work.

Apocalypticism and Paul's Understanding of Law and Covenant

Though apocalypticism has not replaced the fervor of the New Perspective, a few scholars are carefully studying its role in Second Temple Judaism and the New Testament. Traditionally, the book of Revelation was considered the main source of apocalypticism in the New Testament, but scholars are now rethinking that belief. The apostle Paul's relationship to apocalypticism has become the focus of much scholarly inquiry in the past few decades.[32] What if key elements of Paul are indebted to apocalyptic thought? What are the implications of Paul's conception of law and covenant? Central to apocalypticism is the contrast between a vertical dimension (heaven vs. earth) and a temporal dimension (this age vs. the age to come). Chief aspects of apocalypticism are its conception of revelation, the arrival of the eschatological kingdom of God, the in-breaking of the new age, and so on.

Those who argue for a reappraisal of Paul's view of law and justification contend that justification entails not primarily a forensic idea (one's legal status before God) but God's "unconditional saving action . . . in Christ."[33] Whereas Paul's understanding has

---

31. Carson, "Summaries and Conclusions," 544–45. See also Guy Prentiss Waters, *Justification and the New Perspectives on Paul: A Review and Response* (Phillipsburg, NJ: P&R, 2004), 185–87.

32. See, e.g., the recent volume by Ben C. Blackwell, John K. Goodrich, and Jason Maston, eds., *Paul and the Apocalyptic Imagination* (Minneapolis: Fortress, 2016).

33. Douglas A. Campbell, *The Deliverance of God: An Apocalyptic Rereading of Justification in Paul* (Grand Rapids, MI: Eerdmans, 2009), 190.

traditionally been framed in light of how an individual stands before an almighty and holy God, this newly assembled apocalyptic Paul is more concerned with God's end-time deliverance of humanity. The personal faith of believers is minimized, and God's deliverance of humanity is maximized. The apocalyptic approach appears to be working from the top down and not the bottom up.

A few scholars in this field, such as Ernst Käsemann, J.-C. Beker, J. Louis Martyn, and Douglas Campbell are arguing for a general overhaul of how Paul has been tradition-ally understood. While I do think that apocalypticism can sharpen our understanding of Paul's letters (indeed, I have argued this for his understanding of "mystery"[34]), there is simply not enough evidence to warrant a full-blown rereading of Paul.[35] Personal trust in Christ's work is a dominant theme in Paul, and it should not be swept under an apocalyptic rug.

Final Reflections

My task here is to conclude with a few brief reflections on the current state of affairs. Fifteen years ago, the New Perspective dominated nearly every aspect of New Testament studies. Countless dissertations were written from every conceivable angle, and mono-graph after monograph on Paul and the Mosaic law rolled off the presses. Now, though, interest has waned. There is a line in the sand, and both sides are staying put. Perhaps we are living in what may be called a post–New Perspective era. Certainly, the majority of scholars in the wider academy have embraced the main tenets of the New Perspective, but the chief advocates of the New Perspective are continuing to refine their views and are pointing out the differences between them. It may even be wise to call this stream of interpretation the New Perspective(s) on Paul.

While the number of books on Paul and the law are by no means in short supply, there are only a handful of biblical-theological treatments on law and covenant. This is certainly due to the historical-critical convictions of most scholars within the field, who are unconvinced of the unity and inspiration of Scripture. But even within evangelical-ism, there remains a surprising dearth of publications on a biblical theology of law and covenant. There are a handful of treatments,[36] but I am hopeful that scholars will fill this lacuna with robust biblical-theological monographs. The New Perspective has forced

---

34. Benjamin L. Gladd, *Revealing the* Mysterion*: The Use of Mystery in Daniel and Second Temple Judaism with Its Bearing on First Corinthians*, BZNW 160 (Berlin: de Gruyter, 2008).

35. For a substantial critique of Campbell's attempt to reinterpret Romans, see Douglas J. Moo, "The De-liverance of God: An Apocalyptic Rereading of Justification in Paul by Douglas A. Campbell," *JETS* 53, no. 1 (2010): 143–50.

36. See, e.g., Mark A. Seifrid, *Christ Our Righteousness: Paul's Theology of Justification*, NSBT 9 (Downers Grove, IL: InterVarsity Press, 2000); Bradley G. Green, *Covenant and Commandment: Works, Obedience, and Faithfulness in the Christian Life*, NSBT 33 (Downers Grove, IL: InterVarsity Press, 2014); Jeffrey J. Niehaus, *Biblical Theology*, vol. 1, *The Common Grace Covenants* (Wooster, OH: Weaver, 2014); Niehaus, *Biblical Theology*, vol. 2, *Special Grace Covenants: Old Testament* (Wooster, OH: Weaver, 2017); Niehaus, *Biblical Theology*, vol. 3, *Special Grace Covenants: New Testament* (Wooster, OH: Weaver, 2017); Thomas R. Schreiner, *Covenant and God's Purpose for the World*, SSBT (Wheaton, IL: Crossway, 2017); Scott W. Hahn, *Kinship by Covenant: A Canonical Approach to the Fulfillment of God's Saving Promises* (New Haven, CT: Yale University Press, 2009).

evangelicals to refine and reflect on the nature of justification. This is a good thing, and we need to make the most of it.

Dispensationalism, once very popular among evangelicals, probably peaked with Tim LaHaye and Jerry Jenkins's *Left Behind* series. Given the new interest in Calvinism and Reformed theology among a younger generation, it may not be a stretch to conclude that dispensationalism is waning. Baptists, who were traditionally dispensationalists, are now looking for an alternative. On the one hand, they are hesitant to embrace all Reformed theology, especially its emphasis on the continuity between the covenants. On the other hand, they desire to see *more* continuity between the people of God in the Old Testament and the New than what dispensationalism offers. So, caught between a theological rock and a hermeneutical hard place, Peter Gentry and Stephen Wellum have constructed what they label "progressive covenantalism," an attempt to chart a middle course.[37] It remains to be seen if this framework will last, but at the very least, it demonstrates the growing frustration of those within the Baptist tradition with dispensationalism and the desire to read the Bible as a whole.[38]

Regarding contemporary trends within the Reformed tradition, covenant theology has traditionally synthesized and nuanced the precise relationship between the various covenants. Most contemporary discussions within the Reformed tradition are generally consumed with the relationship between the covenant of works, the Mosaic law, and the new covenant at a systematic level.[39] A few prominent Reformed scholars[40] are even reluctant to view the covenant of works in a purely meritorious framework like Kline proposed decades ago.[41] The time is ripe, still, for biblical theologians to strengthen and refine the Reformed view of covenant and law. It appears that more work needs to be done on the precise relationship between Adam and Israel, between the covenant of works and the covenant at Sinai.

The Reformed tradition tends to highlight the negative command that God gave to Adam and Eve (Gen. 2:16–17) without sufficiently explaining the positive side of God's command in Genesis 1:28; 2:15; and 2:23–24. It is the divine commission that God gave Adam and Eve in Genesis 1–2 that is critical to how the history of redemption in large part hangs together.[42] Adam and Eve were created in God's image to be prophet,

---

37. Peter J. Gentry and Stephen J. Wellum, *Kingdom through Covenant: A Biblical-Theological Understanding of the Covenants*, 2nd ed. (Wheaton, IL: Crossway, 2018).

38. See Michael J. Glodo, "Dispensationalism," and Scott R. Swain, "New Covenant Theologies," chaps. 25 and 26, respectively, in this volume.

39. See Bryan D. Estelle, J. V. Fesko, and David VanDrunen, eds., *The Law Is Not of Faith: Essays on Works and Grace in the Mosaic Covenant* (Phillipsburg, NJ: P&R, 2009); Cornelis P. Venema, *Christ and Covenant Theology: Essays on Election, Republication, and the Covenants* (Phillipsburg, NJ: P&R, 2017).

40. E.g., Henri Blocher, "Old Covenant, New Covenant," in *Always Reforming: Explorations in Systematic Theology*, ed. A. T. B. McGowan (Downers Grove, IL: InterVarsity Press, 2006), 240–70. Francis Turretin nuances the term "merit" in that he argues that God's grace operated in Adam before the fall, so that any work or "merit" of Adam still flows from God in some way. See Francis Turretin, *Institutes of Elenctic Theology*, trans. George Musgrave Giger, ed. James T. Dennison Jr. (Phillipsburg, NJ: P&R, 1992–1997), 9.7.14–17.

41. Meredith G. Kline, "Covenant Theology under Attack," *New Horizons in the Orthodox Presbyterian Church* 15 (February 1994): 3–5.

42. Genesis 1:28 is central to G. K. Beale's argument in his massive volume, *A New Testament Biblical Theology: The Unfolding of the Old Testament in the New* (Grand Rapids, MI: Baker, 2011).

priest, and king, so that the earth would be filled with the veritable glory of God. So what is the precise relationship between the biblical covenants and the divine commission given to Adam and Eve? What is the relationship between New Testament believers and the divine commission? These are the sorts of questions that systematic and biblical theologians within the Reformed tradition may explore in the coming decades.

24

Israel and the Nations in God's Covenants

O. Palmer Robertson

Clearly, Israel is in God's covenants.[1] Paul the apostle expressly affirms this relationship when he identifies the "Israelites" as the special objects for whom he stands prepared to suffer God's anathema:

> To them belong the adoption as God's sons, and the Glory, *and the covenants*. (Rom. 9:4)[2]

But what about all the other nations of the world? Are they included in God's covenants? Or are they excluded? Are the divine covenants the personalized property of Israel? Or are some of God's covenants distinctly for Israel, while others include the nations? These questions are critical for determining the way the gospel of Christianity should be communicated, for the gospel is a covenantal thing.

To determine a proper biblical answer to these questions, we must examine the various covenants initiated by God across the ages. The covenants themselves must define their specific role in relation to Israel and the nations. With this perspective in mind, we now explore God's covenants in sequence.

---

1. This chapter was first presented as a lecture at a Tyndale House conference in Cambridge, England, on June 26, 2018.

2. All biblical translations in this chapter are my own unless otherwise indicated. Also, quite interesting is the textual variant in Rom. 9:4, with strong witnesses supporting both "covenants" and "covenant." Several ancient and reliable manuscripts support a reading in the plural: "the covenants." Equally strong manuscript readings favor the singular "the covenant." Significant theological conclusions would follow from the singular reading, which would suggest that Paul perceived all the various redemptive covenants of the Old Testament as being embraced in a singular divine "covenant."

God's Covenant at Creation

It has been argued that no such thing as a "covenant" existed at creation, particularly since the word "covenant" (בְּרִית) does not appear in the opening chapters of Genesis. Three factors, however, give us pause:

1. Some passages later in the Old Testament refer to the original relation between God and humanity in terms of a "covenant":

> [The Israelites], *like Adam*, have *broken the covenant*. (Hos. 6:7)

> If you can *break my covenant with the day and my covenant with the night* . . . (Jer. 33:20; cf. 33:25)

> The earth mourns and withers,
>> the world languishes and withers; . . .
> for they [the peoples of the world] have transgressed the laws,
>> violated the statutes,
>> *broken the everlasting covenant.* (Isa. 24:4–5)[3]

These verses support the presence of a divine covenant with humanity from the point of creation.

2. The use of the term "covenant" is not essential for the existence of a covenantal relationship. When the Lord made his formal commitment to David (2 Sam. 7:1–17; 1 Chron. 17:1–15), the term "covenant" did not appear. Yet this relationship clearly was covenantal in its essence, as later Scripture indicates (Ps. 89:3–4, 28, 34, 39; Isa. 55:3). God's relationship to Adam may be regarded as covenantal in nature, even though the term "covenant" does not appear in the Genesis narrative.

3. All the elements essential to a covenant are present in the original relationship established by God between himself and humanity. If a "covenant" may be defined as a "bond of life and death sovereignly administered," then the relationship between God and the original man is "covenantal" in its essence.[4] A "bond of life and death" was established with Adam when God in his sovereignty declared, "In the day you eat of it, you shall surely die" (Gen. 2:17).

This covenant established by God at creation includes the totality of humanity. Paul stresses the unity of the human race in its relation to the Creator when he declares to the Athenians, "[God] made from one [blood] every nation of humanity" (Acts 17:26). The various elements of the creational covenant are intended to direct the lifestyle of all peoples, nations, and tribes, even until today. God's covenantal command to "subdue the earth" and "fill it" applies equally to all descendants of the first man and woman (Gen. 1:28). The sanctification of one day in seven by the Lord of the covenant (Gen. 2:3)

---

3. For a fuller discussion of the relevance of these passages as confirming a covenant at creation, see O. Palmer Robertson, *The Christ of the Covenants* (Phillipsburg, NJ: Presbyterian and Reformed, 1980), 17–25.
4. For a discussion of this definition for "covenant," see Robertson, *Christ of the Covenants*, 3–17.

determines the work-and-rest pattern of the whole human race. Even the more specific commandment not to eat of the tree of the knowledge of good and evil (Gen. 2:17) serves as a basis for accountability for each and every descendant of Adam. For "by the one man's disobedience the many were made sinners" (Rom. 5:19), and "sin came into the world through one man . . . because all sinned" (Rom. 5:12).

Long before "Israel" existed, all human beings lived out their lives within the framework of God's creation covenant. Well worth remembering is this basic fact, for in the "last days," the reality of a universal covenant that embraces peoples from all nations, including Israel, will become clearly manifest once more. For "as in Adam all die, so also all in Christ shall be made alive" (1 Cor. 15:22).

Genealogies in God's Covenants

Genealogies in Scripture represent a "reality check." That is, the concrete binding of covenantal progression across generations underscores the reality of the history of God's redeeming a people to himself. Genealogies defy mythology. Indeed, myths may speak of "sons of the gods." But the impossibility of a systematic tracing of mythological figures across identifiable human history cuts against the grain of mythology's reality.

Contrariwise, concrete human genealogies affirm reality. Early on in the Bible, the "book of the generations of Adam" inaugurates the record of reality for humanity (Gen. 5:1). Stretching from Adam, the first representative man in covenant, to Noah, the second representative man in covenant, this earliest and ancient genealogy in Genesis affirms continuous covenantal connection (Gen. 5:1–32).[5] The evident gaps in this first and other subsequent genealogies do not disturb the reality of the continuity of God's covenants. For the historical connection remains intact even when as few as three generations span centuries of human history from Abraham to David to Jesus (Matt. 1:1). The connection is real, a solid linkage across two thousand years from Abraham to Jesus.

More than once, the significance of covenantal generations emerges as a principal factor in redemptive history. The faith of the fathers cannot be relegated to the realm of the irrelevant, for the fathers' internal faith transmits to succeeding generations, as do the external characteristics of their faith. As the Covenant LORD promises,

> "As for me, this is my covenant with them," says the LORD: "My Spirit that is upon you, and my words that I have put in your mouth, shall not depart out of your mouth, or out of the mouth of your offspring, or out of the mouth of your children's offspring," says the LORD, "from this time forth and forevermore." (Isa. 59:21 ESV)

---

5. Adam's role as representative man in covenant is, of course, significantly different from Noah's role as representative man in covenant. By God's appointment, Adam represented the whole of his descendancy in the original fall into sin, as indicated by Paul (Rom. 5:12–19). In contrast, Noah represented humanity more generally in God's covenantal commitment to preserve the earth so that his redemptive purposes might be accomplished.

This generational aspect of the covenant is not limited to the old covenant era. For according to the language of the New Testament, the promise of the covenant is "for you and for your descendants, and for those who are far off, even for as many as the Lord our God will call" (Acts 2:39). Of the ten instances of the application of the covenantal seal of baptism under the new covenant, two involve cases of single men (the Ethiopian eunuch and Paul, Acts 8:38–39; 9:18). Of the remaining eight instances of new covenant baptisms, six of the eight include or imply the inclusion of the succeeding generations (Acts 2:38–39; 10:1–2, 47; 16:15; 16:31–34; 18:8; 1 Cor. 1:16). At the same time, it should be recognized that blessings of the covenant do not flow automatically to the next generation. For life in the covenant threatens curses as well as offering blessings. Each new generation must claim for itself the promises of the covenant.

Quite striking is the generational role of the Table of Nations that follows immediately after the establishment of God's covenant with Noah and his sons. Genesis 10 records "the generations of the sons of Noah" (Gen. 10:1). This record of the rebirth of humanity after the flood describes the "sons of Noah, according to their genealogies, in their nations, and from these the nations spread abroad on the earth after the flood" (Gen. 10:32). Only after this genealogical record of the expansion of all the nations of humanity had been recorded in their connection with God's covenant with Noah does the scriptural record introduce Abraham and the covenant that God initiated with him and his descendants (Gen. 11:27–12:3).

The scriptural linkage from God's covenant with Noah to God's covenant with Abraham through the recorded generation of Noah's son Shem concludes with a totally unexpected statement to climax a genealogical record: "Now Sarai [the wife of Abraham] was barren; she had no child!" (Gen. 11:30). Yet this startling statement provides the perfect preparation for an insistence on supernatural divine intervention as the only way to realize the goal of redemption by a designated seed of the covenant. At the same time, this simple statement regarding Sarah's barrenness in the genealogical record underscores the impossibility of realizing the blessings of the covenant as the product of human resources. God himself must supernaturally intervene if the promise is to be fulfilled.

The consequence of the unbroken character of covenantal genealogies from Adam through Noah to Abraham is the inevitable inclusion of all nations of the world in God's covenants alongside the Israel of God. Not surprisingly, God's first words to Abraham underscore the all-inclusive element of this covenant: "In you all the families of the earth shall be blessed" (Gen. 12:3).[6] The unity of all nations with the patriarchal father of Israel through the blessings of the covenant may be captured by the phrase "Not by race but by grace"—grace as it manifests itself in the inclusion of peoples both from all nations and from Israel.

---

6. Both the Septuagint and Gal. 3:8 underscore the unity of all nations with Abraham as the way of covenantal blessing by duplicating the "in" factor in the verb and preposition: ἐνευλογηθήσονται ἐν σοὶ ("[all nations] shall be in-blessed in you").

The two genealogies of the New Testament complete the covenantal line from Adam to Christ. Luke's genealogy makes this point specifically by beginning with Jesus and working backward to Adam, the "son of God" (Luke 3:23–38). Matthew's genealogy specifies four women in the genealogical line leading to Jesus. Three of these women are descended from peoples of other nations: Tamar (apparently Canaanite), Rahab (Canaanite), and Ruth (Moabite) (Matt. 1:3, 5).

In sum, this genealogical aspect of the covenants underscores both the reality of redemptive history and the inclusion of peoples from all nations alongside Israel in God's covenants. These two principles play a significant role in God's saving work for his people.

Noah and the Nations

Noah was not an Israelite. He was not even a Shemite, seeing he was the father of Shem, who in turn was the father of Abraham the Shemite. Noah lived before any distinction existed between "the nations" and "Israel." For "Israel" did not exist in Noah's day.

Yet God entered into a covenant with Noah and his children:

> God said to Noah *and to his sons* with him, "Behold, I establish my covenant with you [plural] and your [plural] offspring after you [plural]." (Gen. 9:8–9)

In this passage, the covenant is explicitly declared to extend across at least three generations: Noah, his children, and the children of Noah's children.

Because the whole of humanity ultimately must trace their ancestry through these descendants of Noah, all nations are included in God's covenant with Noah. This covenant with Noah, his sons, and his son's sons provided a foundation for God's covenant with Abraham and his descendants. As descendants of Shem, Abraham's offspring were graciously included in the covenant that God had previously established with Noah. Once more, it becomes clear that through Noah and his sons, God's covenants embrace all nations, including Israel. For the rainbow as the sign of the covenant (Gen. 9:12–17) could hardly be claimed as the exclusive possession of any particular tribe or nation. Indeed, it may be that certain aspects of some of God's covenants have distinctive application to Israel. But the inclusion of all nations in God's covenant with Noah through Noah's sons is a factor that must not be overlooked.

The aftermath of the covenant with Noah anticipates a long history of God's redemptive dealings with humanity. Ham shames himself and his father Noah by "looking on his father's nakedness." This expression may very well serve as a circumlocution for "have sexual relations with" (Gen. 9:22; cf. Lev. 20:17–19).[7] Yet the curse is pronounced over Ham's son Canaan rather than Ham himself, which communicates God's grace in a

---

7. Cf. O. Palmer Robertson, "Current Critical Questions concerning the 'Curse of Ham,'" *JETS* 41, no. 2 (1998): 177–88.

context of extreme human depravity. Not all the sons of Ham experience this judgmental curse, and God's grace is ultimately extended even to the sons of Canaan.

Noah's covenantal blessing falls specifically on Shem, father of the Shemites. Through this genealogical line come Abraham, Israel, David, and Jesus, the promised Messiah. But what about Japheth, the third son of Noah, and his descendants?

It must be remembered that a prophetic utterance like the one given by Noah (Gen. 9:24–27) speaks in the broadest possible terms. Preciseness of definition cannot be insisted on. It is always safe to remember that more questions may be asked of a biblical text than the text is prepared to answer. Yet in broadest strokes it may be said that Noah's blessing on the Shemites means that ultimately the promised "seed of the woman" (see Gen. 3:15) would descend from the line of Shem. When the prophetic utterance declares that the Japhethites shall "dwell in the tents of Shem" (Gen. 9:27; cf. 1 Chron. 5:10), it indicates that the broader community of nations embodied in Japheth's descendants will also participate in redemptive blessings coming through Shem.

Once more, it becomes clear that peoples from all nations (descendants of Japheth) will share with Israel (descendants of Shem) in its redemptive blessings. God's covenant with Noah anticipates distinctive blessings for Israel, yet all nations will share in those same blessings.

But what about Ham and his descendants, the Canaanites? Hopefully it is clear that the curse on Ham is nonexistent, since it was Canaan, not Ham, who was cursed. The descendants of "Canaan" may be traced to the "Canaanites," including those peoples living in the region of Sodom and Gomorrah who were ultimately consumed in God's wrath for their sexual immorality (Gen. 10:19; 18:20; 19:24–25). Yet despite this curse, Rahab the harlot, a "Canaanite" woman, enters the tents of "Shem" and receives the blessings of redemption both for herself and her family (Josh. 6:22–23). In the processes of redemptive history, Rahab appears in the line of the promised Messiah (Matt. 1:5). All nations, even the cursed "Canaanites," share with the Shemites the blessings of covenantal redemption.

Abraham, the Father of Israel

Clearly, Abraham was the father of Israel. But was Abraham a "Jew"?

The answer to this question may appear obvious. As the father of the Israelite nation, it may be assumed that he must have been a "Jew." If the topic of this chapter is "Israel and the Nations in God's Covenants," and God made a covenant with Israel or with the "Jews" through Abraham, then the question whether Abraham was a "Jew" has critical significance for the matter currently under consideration. For this reason, it is tempting to quickly conclude, "Of course Abraham was a 'Jew'! In fact, he should be regarded as the 'first' of the 'Jews.'"

But the answer to the question is not quite so simple. For clearly, Abraham did not begin life as a "Jew." Instead, Abraham along with his father Terah "served other gods" on the other side of the Euphrates River (Josh. 24:2).

So what made Abraham a "Jew"?

Two things: (1) the call of God and (2) the response of faith (Gen. 12:1–5; cf. Heb. 11:8). These two elements turned Abraham the worshiper of idols into a "Jew," the recipient of God's covenantal promises. It was not a matter of race but of faith. Indeed, Abraham was a Shemite, a descendant of the genealogical line of covenantal promise. But there were many Shemites. Abraham was distinctive among the Shemites in that he received God's call. Abraham responded in faith to God's call. Abraham enjoyed the blessings of God's covenant. Following the identical pattern, idol-worshiping people from all nations are "*called* . . . in the grace of Christ*" (Gal. 1:6) "in order that the blessing given to Abraham might come to the nations through Christ Jesus, so that *by faith* we might receive the promise of the Spirit" (Gal. 3:14).

But a further question arises alongside the question whether Abraham was a "Jew," a question of some significance. Where did the term "Jew" arise, and what is its significance for a proper understanding of covenantal history?[8] This question is so broad that a full answer goes beyond the scope of the current chapter. Yet a few observations may be offered.

The designation "Jew" is actually a translator's gloss for "Judean." The term rendered "Jew" in the English Bible, in both Hebrew (יְהוּדִי [*yehudi*]) and Greek (Ἰουδαῖος [*ioudaios*]), is always "Judean."[9]

So what is a "Judean" in biblical usage? This term has multiple meanings. Consider the following aspects of the term "Judean":

1. From a tribal perspective, a "Judean" is a descendant of Judah, a member of the tribe of Judah.
2. From a geographical perspective, a "Judean" is an inhabitant of the territory assigned to the tribe of Judah.
3. From the perspective of international history, a "Judean" is a person who derives his identity from a connection with the Persian province of Judah.
4. From an ethnic-political-religious perspective, a "Judean" is a person identified with the community of Israel.

---

8. In terms of English Bible translations, "Jewe" and "Jewes" appear in the Bibles of both Wycliffe and Tyndale.

9. For an introduction to the intense discussion of this topic, see Steve Mason, "Jews, Judaeans, Judaizing, Judaism: Problems of Categorization in Ancient History," *JSJ* 38, nos. 4–5 (2007): 457–512. Mason strongly supports the rendering "Judaeans." In favor of the rendering "Jew," see Adele Reinhartz, "The Vanishing Jews of Antiquity," *Marginalia: Los Angeles Review of Books*, June 24, 2014. Reinhartz acknowledges that reading "Judean" would lessen the prejudice aroused by the term "Jew." But she nonetheless favors the rendering "Jew," particularly in the Gospel of John, as a way of exposing the prejudice of Christians against "Jews." Extensive materials on this subject may be found in three articles by David M. Miller, who explores the larger concepts of ethnicity and religion as they relate to the question of the translation of Ἰουδαῖος. David M. Miller, "The Meaning of *Ioudaios* and Its Relationship to Other Group Labels in Ancient 'Judaism,'" *CurBR* 9, no. 1 (2010): 98–126; Miller, "Ethnicity Comes of Age: An Overview of Twentieth-Century Terms for *Ioudaios*," *CurBR* 10, no. 2 (2012): 293–311; Miller, "Ethnicity, Religion and the Meaning of *Ioudaios* in Ancient 'Judaism,'" *CurBR* 12, no. 2 (2014): 216–65. Miller introduces his conclusion in the third article by citing another scholar: determining the meaning of *Ioudaios* is like "herding cats or participating in a greased pig contest." He concludes by stating that if forced to choose, contemporary concerns tilt the balance in favor of "Jew" rather than "Judean." Miller, "Ethnicity, Religion," 259.

All these various dimensions contribute to the identity of a "Judean." But one aspect of the identity of "Judean" appears to be altogether absent from recent discussions, which is the redemptive-historical perspective. From the perspective of the history of God's working redemption among humanity, a "Judean" is *a survivor of Israel's exile, a trophy of God's grace.*

When the Assyrians conquered the northern kingdom of Israel in 722 BC, they carried into exile the ten tribes of the North. The conquest strategy of the Assyrians was to keep conquered nations in meek subjection by decimating their family structures and scattering the peoples throughout their various territories. As a consequence, the tribes of the North became the "ten lost tribes" of Israel. For they indeed effectively "lost" their distinctive tribal identity.[10] Only through a few individuals here and there, such as Anna of the tribe of Asher (Luke 2:36), did the ten tribes of the North retain any semblance of identity. Scattered rumors of the "finding" of the ten lost tribes surface now and then. According to one unsubstantiated rumor, a tribe deep in the Amazon jungle of South America was discovered speaking "pure Hebrew." In another case, a wordplay supplies the basis for identifying the English peoples as the ten lost tribes of Israel, which would lend support to the theory of "British Israelism."[11] The Hebrew word for "covenant" is *berith* (בְּרִית), and the Hebrew word for "man" is *ish* (אִישׁ). Put the two together, and you have *Berit-ish*, "British"! But as a matter of fact, the ten tribes of the northern kingdom of Israel are truly lost, nonexistent in terms of ongoing tribal identity.

God in his redemptive grace preserved the single tribe of the southern kingdom, the tribe of Judah. He preserved this particular tribe, in part because the prophetic Scriptures declared that Messiah must come from the tribe of Judah (Gen. 49:10). He preserved them from Sennacherib, the invading Assyrian king who devastated the ten tribes of the North (see Isa. 37:1–38). But the Lord did not spare the "Judeans" from the judgment brought on them by King Nebuchadnezzar of Babylon 140 years later. The conquests of Judah in 605, 596, and 586 BC led to their wholesale exile from their homeland (2 Kings 24:1, 10–12; 25:1–4, 11; Dan. 1:1–2).

Only by the grace of God did a remnant of "Judean" exiles survive and then return to their land seventy years later, just as Jeremiah had predicted (Jer. 29:10; Dan. 9:1–3). They, too, deserved to be "lost" in terms of national identity because of their apostasy. But by the grace of God, they survived the exile and returned to the land

10. The actual "lostness" of the ten tribes of the North could be debated. For a review of the evidence for the "lostness" of the ten tribes, see "Ten Lost Tribes of Israel," *Encyclopaedia Britannica*, accessed December 18, 2019, www.britannica.com/topic/Ten-Lost-Tribes-of-Israel. The lost tribes named are Asher, Dan, Ephraim, Gad, Issachar, Manasseh, Naphtali, Reuben, Simeon, and Zebulun. The issue surrounds the question of tribal rather than individual identity. The strongest biblical case for a continuation of some of the ten lost tribes may be found in 2 Chron. 30:1, 10, 11, which mentions people of Ephraim, Manasseh, Zebulun, and Asher in the days of Hezekiah's reform, some years after the exile of the northern kingdom. Indeed, individuals of these tribes survived, but through the Assyrian dispersion, they lost their tribal identity.

11. Cf. Colonel Garnier, *Israel in Britain. A Brief Statement of the Evidences in Proof of the Israelitish Origin of the British Race* (London: Robert Banks and Son, 1890).

despite their continuing sinfulness, as the confessional prayer of Daniel indicates (Dan. 9:1–19).

These survivors of the exile, these trophies of God's grace, were called "Judeans." Even before their return from exile, they were designated "Judeans." For they consisted of the surviving members of the tribe of "Judah."

Chronologically speaking, the oldest historical reference to "the Judeans" (הַיְהוּדִים; τοὺς Ιουδαίους) in Scripture records the occasion in which King Rezin of Syria drove "the Judeans" from the port of Elath (2 Kings 16:6). The representation of "Judeans" as "Jews" in the English Bible occurs in the King James rendering of this same verse.[12] The word "Judean" ("Jew" in the Old Testament portion of the English Bible) is essentially restricted to the time of Judah's conquest, exile to Babylon, and return from exile. Never is Abraham called a "Judean"/"Jew" in the English Bible. The same fact is true of David and Moses. They are never designated in their biblical histories as "Judeans"/"Jews."

The bulk of references to "the Judeans" in the Old Testament occurs in three books that record Israel's exilic and postexilic periods (Ezra, Nehemiah, Esther). As previously noted, this designation "Judeans"/"Jews" for the descendants of Abraham derives from the fact that in contrast to the ten "lost" tribes of the North, the tribe of "Judah" retained its tribal identity.[13] These early references to "Judean" in the exilic and postexilic books of Ezra, Nehemiah, and Esther deserve further consideration.

The book of Ezra contains six references to "the Judeans." The designation is translated in various English versions as "the Jews" throughout Ezra, with a single exception (Ezra 4:12; 5:1; 6:7 [2x], 8, 14; cf. ESV, KJV, NASB, NIV [1984], NKJV).[14]

The opening verses of Nehemiah provide a distinctive dimension in identifying "the Judeans." Nehemiah inquired of returnees from Judah concerning "*the Judeans* who had escaped, who had *survived the exile*" (Neh. 1:2). These returnees from Judah to Babylon responded by describing the sad condition of "the survivors who had survived the exile" (Neh. 1:3). By the repetition of this phrase, the book of Nehemiah has identified "the Judeans" as a very specific people. They are "the survivors of the exile." In this very early appearance of the term "Judean," people with this designation are described as "survivors who had survived the exile."

This definition may not suit every occasion that "the Judeans" appears in Scripture. But it provides a distinctive dimension of the term that should regularly be kept in mind. Once the exile of the southern kingdom of Judah has occurred, and the ten tribes of the northern kingdom have been swallowed up into the vast world of many nations, a "Judean" should be perceived as "a survivor of the exile." Possibly some of these "Judeans"

---

12. Other versions render the word in this verse as "the men of Judah" (ESV, NKJV), "the people of Judah" (NIV), or "the Judahites" (NAB).

13. The tribe of Benjamin and the priestly tribe of Levi were not included among the ten tribes of the North.

14. The single exception is Ezra 4:12 in the NIV, which reads "the people." Otherwise, "the Jews" is the favored rendering throughout Ezra in the NIV. The NIV 1984 reads "Jews" in all six cases in Ezra.

in Nehemiah's day had never been dragged into Babylonian exile. But they still could be identified properly as "survivors of the exile."

The initial introduction of Mordecai in the book of Esther supports this perspective. Mordecai is described as "a 'Judean' . . . a Benjaminite" (Est. 2:5). But how could Mordecai both be identified as belonging to the tribe of Benjamin and also be denoted as a "Judean"? He could be identified as both only because "Judean" had come to mean something other than a member of the tribe of Judah. From the perspective of redemptive history, a "Judean" was "a survivor of Judah's exile."

This concept of a "Judean" experiences significant expansion in the subsequent narrative of Esther. Haman plotted to destroy "all the Judeans" in the Persian kingdom, which embraced a population scattered from India to Ethiopia (Est. 1:1; 3:6). In this context, "Judean" would appear to have largely lost its geographical significance in favor of its redemptive-historical significance. Whether in Asia, Africa, India, or the Middle East, all these people were known as "Judeans." At some points, racial concerns may enter into the definition of a "Judean" (see Est. 3:4). A "Judean" could refer at times to a person's connection with the Persian province of Judah or with the community of Israel viewed from an ethnic-political perspective. But from a redemptive-historical perspective, the overarching focus of identity for "Judeans" was that, though scattered across the nations, they had survived Israel's exile.[15]

A further note must not be overlooked in these early appearances of the term "Judean." As the narrative of Esther climaxes, a startling statement emerges: "Many peoples of the land turned themselves into Judeans" (מִתְיַהֲדִים, Est. 8:17). Or as the Greek version renders the text, "Many (peoples) of the nations were circumcised and judaized" (πολλοὶ τῶν ἐθνῶν περιετέμοντο καὶ ἰουδάιζον, Est. 8:17). In this context, these peoples from the various nations had chosen to identify themselves among the covenant community of Israel. By this step of faith, they were not changing their racial identity. They were not primarily connecting themselves with a geographical locale in Palestine. Instead, they were uniting themselves to the God of Mordecai and Esther, the God of the covenant who had preserved his people in the past through the historical trauma of Judah's exile and who had preserved them once more in the face of threats of annihilation.

It is just at this point that the prevailing and persistent English representation of "Judean" as "Jew" manifests a serious shortfall. As has been previously noted, the designation "Jew" never occurs in either the Hebrew or Greek versions of the Old Testament. Neither does it appear in the Greek version of the New Testament. Always the designation in the original languages of both Testaments is "Judean." By using the term "Jew" for "Judean," the English Bible lost a significant clue to this biblical-theological identity of the Israelites. For the term "Jew" does not communicate the same thing as the term "Judean."

---

15. An interesting parallel to this identity of disbursed Israelites as "Judeans" may be found in the New Testament record of peoples assembled in Jerusalem on the day of Pentecost: "Now there were dwelling in Jerusalem *Judeans*, devout men *from every nation under heaven*" (Acts 2:5).

"Jew" regularly identifies a race of people—not a pure race but a race. But "Judean" in the context of redemptive history identifies a "survivor of Israel's exile," a trophy of God's grace. At the same time, the term "Jew" quite possibly has contributed to the sometimes-negative attitude toward the "Jew" in the history of English-speaking cultures.

The history of the "Jew" within English-speaking cultures has not always been a pleasant one.[16] Strong negative rumors regarding "Jews" developed in the twelfth century. "Jews" were reported as kidnapping Christian children and offering their blood as sacrifice.[17] The Jewish badge was required by law to be worn by every "Jewish" man and woman. This requirement was first put into effect in 1218. According to this law, "every Jew, at all times, in the city or outside it, walking or riding, should wear upon his outer garment a piece of white cloth or parchment whereby he might be distinguished from Christians."[18] In 1275, Edward I stipulated that every "Jew" above seven years of age must wear the Jewish badge, which was to be yellow in color, six fingers long and three wide, in the shape of the two tables of the law.[19] Climactically, all "Jews" were expelled from England from the year 1290 until they were allowed to return under Cromwell and Charles II some four hundred years later.[20] Shakespeare's Shylock, with knife readied in hand, demanding a "pound of flesh" from a debtor who could not pay in *The Merchant of Venice*, epitomized the widespread attitude of English-speaking people toward the "Jews" for several centuries. Sir Walter Scott's popular novel *Ivanhoe* (1820), written some three hundred years after Shakespeare, presented the same perspective on the "Jew," even as his novel created a "Jewish" heroine.

Worth serious consideration is the evaluation of the negative effect of the English rendering "Jew" for "Judean" in the premier Greek-English lexicon of the New Testament:

> Incalculable harm has been caused by simply glossing Ἰ[ουδαῖος] with "Jew," for many readers or auditors of Bible translations do not practice the historical judgment necessary to distinguish between circumstances and events of an ancient time and contemporary ethnic-religious-social realities, *with the result that anti-Judaism in the modern sense of the term is needlessly fostered through biblical texts.*[21]

---

16. Cf. Cecil Roth, *A History of the Jews in England*, 3rd ed. (Oxford: Clarendon, 1964).

17. Diarmaid MacCulloch, *The Reformation: A History* (New York: Penguin, 2005), 9.

18. Roth, *History*, 95.

19. Roth, *History*, 96.

20. MacCulloch, *Reformation*, 527. Roth notes that England was the first country to expel all "Jews" from their land. He notes the consequences:

> The final tragedy of 1290 was the first general expulsion of the Jews from any country in the medieval period. Local precedents only had been known before. But it was Edward I who set the example for the wholesale banishment of the Jews, which was followed with such deadly effect in France sixteen years after . . . , and two centuries later by Ferdinand and Isabel of Spain, in the culminating tragedy of medieval Jewish history.

History, 90. Roth subsequently describes in detail the tortuous trail of the readmission of the "Jews" under Oliver Cromwell and Charles II. *History*, 158–72.

21. "Ἰουδαῖος," in Walter Bauer, William F. Arndt, F. Wilbur Gingrich, and F. W. Danker, *A Greek-English Lexicon of the New Testament and Other Early Christian Literature* (Chicago: University of Chicago Press, 2000); emphasis added.

From this perspective, the term "Jew" would be perceived as a misnomer in English Bibles that communicated a negative perspective on the descendants of Abraham. The term might better have been represented in English as "Judean" or "Judeans," identified in Nehemiah as "survivors of the exile," trophies of God's grace.

Could the rendering "Judean" rather than "Jew" have made a difference across the past five centuries since the first complete English translation of the Bible? Suppose every time an English-speaking Christian saw an Israelite, he thought, "This person is a *Judean,*' a 'survivor of Israel's exile,' a trophy of God's grace." Instead of thinking "Jew," which focuses on race, the thought would have been "Judean," focusing on this person as a product of God's special grace. Being differently perceived, these people might have been differently treated.

A full appreciation of the impact of the translation "Jew" instead of "Judean" in English Bibles may be realized only when its translation partner "Gentile" is considered. The words regularly rendered "Gentile" in the English Bible actually have the more basic meaning "nation" or "people" (גּוֹי, ἔθνος) rather than "Gentile."

But what is a "Gentile." How is the word "Gentile" to be defined?

According to *Webster's New Collegiate Dictionary*, the word "Gentile" may be defined as follows:

> 1. As used by the Jews, *one of non-Jewish faith or race*; as used by the Christians, one *not a Jew*; esp., a Christian *as distinguished from a Jew*; formerly, as used by Christians, a heathen.   2. Among the Mormons, a non-Mormon.[22]

In English parlance, a "Gentile" is a negative factor. A "Gentile" is a "non-Jew." By using the designation "Gentile," English Bibles have described 99.9 percent of the world's population negatively. Still further, if "Jews" are regarded as a people in some sense especially favored by God, then "Gentiles" as "non-Jews" must be regarded as not especially favored by God in whatever sense "Jews" are especially favored by God. If the term "Jew" represents a misnomer, the term "Gentile" represents a negation of a misnomer.

The words regularly rendered "Gentile" in the English Bible (גּוֹי; ἔθνος) might be better rendered consistently as "nation" or "people." The translation "nation" provides a positive dimension when all the various peoples of the world are being considered. The term for "nation," "nations," or "all nations" is altogether expansive in its significance. The root concept in the Bible refers to all the various nations of the world, frequently treated as the distinctive objects of God's saving grace, which lies at the very heart of the Christian gospel. All the nations of the world are recipients of the offer of God's grace. "Go and make disciples of *all the Gentiles*" simply could not capture the outward thrust of the new covenant gospel, but "Go therefore and make disciples of *all nations*"

---

22. *Webster's New Collegiate Dictionary*, 6th ed. (1956), s.v. "Gentile"; emphasis added.

(Matt. 28:19) summarizes the purpose of the suffering Savior's sacrifice and the risen Savior's expectation.

In many passages of the New Testament, ἔθνος simply cannot be translated "Gentiles" and do justice to the point of the text. A few sample passages in which the translation "Gentiles" is inserted for ἔθνος may serve to underscore the inadequacy of this rendering:

"This gospel shall be preached . . . to all *Gentiles*." (Matt. 24:14)

"My house shall be called a house of prayer for all *Gentiles*." (Mark 11:17)

"God shows no partiality, but accepts every *Gentile* fearing him." (Acts 10:34, 35)

"Just and true are your ways,
   O King of the *Gentiles*!" (Rev. 15:3)

Substitute "nation" or "nations" for "Gentile" or "Gentiles" in these passages, and the universal, all-embracive character of the Christian gospel shines forth brilliantly. In numerous other passages, the reading "nations" rather than "Gentiles" has the same enlarging effect. The arrest of John the Baptist serves as a sign to Jesus of the way the Israelite nation will eventually treat him. So he leaves Judah and goes to Capernaum, located on the international highway connecting three continents. This location is prophetically called by Isaiah "the way of the sea . . . Galilee of the *nations*" (Isa. 9:1; cf. Matt. 4:15).[23] At that critical crossroads, Jesus begins his public ministry declaring, "Repent, for the kingdom of *heaven* [not the kingdom of the 'Jews'] is at hand" (Matt. 4:17). In a similar way, Paul identifies himself as "an apostle to the *nations*" (Rom. 11:13), which defines more expansively his commission than "an apostle to the *Gentiles*." In these and many other cases, the positive, expansive character of "nations" contrasts with the negative, racial, restrictive character of "Gentiles."

The root ἔθνος occurs 162 times in the Greek New Testament. In various English translations, this term is represented as "Gentiles" 91 or 92 times, or more than half its occurrences. A sampling of these instances may indicate that in many cases the translation "nation" or "nations" could serve the expansive perspective of the New Testament far better:[24]

---

23. The term גּוֹי occurs over 500 times in the Old Testament, and the term עַם occurs over 600 times. In terms of the Old Testament, the English rendering "Gentile" appears 30 times in the KJV, 50 times in the NKJV, 3 times in the NIV, and 0 times in the ESV. In terms of the New Testament, all these versions read "Gentile" between 91 and 92 times. An interesting case in point is the English Bible rendering of Isa. 9:1. The phrase in Hebrew reads גְּלִיל הַגּוֹיִם. In Greek it is Γαλιλαία τῶν ἐθνῶν. Most English translations render the phrase "Galilee of the *nations*" (ESV, KJV, NAB, NIV). Only the NIV (1984) and the NKJV render it "Galilee of the *Gentiles*." But then in the New Testament quotation of this same phrase in Matt. 4:15, all the various consulted translations read "Galilee of the *Gentiles*" (ESV, KJV, NAB, NIV, NIV [1984], NKJV).

24. In four of the five quotations from the Old Testament presented in these texts, various English versions read "nations" in the Old Testament passage but "Gentiles" in the New Testament passage that is quoting the same passage from the Old Testament.

The land of Zebulun and the land of Naphtali, the way of the sea, beyond the Jordan, Galilee of the ~~Gentiles~~ *nations*. (Matt. 4:15 ESV; also KJV, NAB, NIV, NKJV)

I will put my Spirit upon him, and he will proclaim justice to the ~~Gentiles~~ *nations*. (Matt. 12:18 ESV; also KJV, NAB, NKJV)

In his name the ~~Gentiles~~ *nations* will hope. (Matt. 12:21 ESV; also KJV, NAB, NKJV)

For my eyes have seen your salvation, . . .
a light for revelation to the ~~Gentiles~~ *nations*,
    and for glory to your people Israel. (Luke 2:30, 32 ESV; also KJV, NAB, NIV, NKJV)

Why did the ~~Gentiles~~ *nations* rage,
    and the peoples plot in vain? (Acts 4:25 ESV; also NAB)

The gift of the Holy Spirit was poured out even on the ~~Gentiles~~ *nations*. (Acts 10:45 ESV; also KJV, NAB, NIV, NKJV)

Go, for I will send you far away to the ~~Gentiles~~ *nations*. (Acts 22:21 ESV; also KJV, NAB, NIV, NKJV)

The root of Jesse will come,
    even he who arises to rule the ~~Gentiles~~ *nations*;
in him will the ~~Gentiles~~ *nations* hope. (Rom. 15:12 ESV; also KJV, NAB, NKJV)

[God] was pleased to reveal his Son to me, in order that I might preach him among the ~~Gentiles~~ *nations*. (Gal. 1:16 ESV; also NAB, NIV, NKJV)

Substituting "nations" or "all nations" or "peoples from all nations" for "Gentiles" provides a much more illuminating reading appropriate to the expansive perspective of the Christian gospel. Indeed, some passages would present a translation challenge. But the consistent substitution of "nations" for "Gentiles" throughout the New Testament could have a significant impact on the communication of the universalistic character of the new covenant gospel and could provide a powerful impetus for evangelism and missionary endeavors.

The book of Revelation climaxes the biblical concept of "nations" and "peoples." Seven times over, Revelation joins together references to every tribe, tongue, people, and *nation* as those who share the blessings of the redeemed by Christ (Rev. 5:9; 7:9; 10:11; 11:9; 13:7; 14:6; 17:15). How out of place it would sound to substitute "Gentile" for "nation" in these climactic contexts. "Every tribe, tongue, people, *and Gentile*" shall praise him?

In this context, we can now properly evaluate the initial promise of the covenant to Abraham. The covenant with Adam included all nations of the world, though the nations were yet to be formed. The covenant with Noah is also clearly universalistic in character, embracing all nations and peoples of the world. God's first covenantal word to Abraham expresses the same expansive perspective: "In you *all the peoples of the earth* will be blessed" (Gen. 12:3). The Septuagint translation of this passage makes the universal scope of this covenantal commitment of God even clearer: "They shall be IN-blessed IN you all the tribes of the earth" (ἐνευλογηθήσονται ἐν σοὶ πᾶσαι αἱ φυλαὶ τῆς γῆς (Gen. 12:3).[25] Clearly all physical descendants of Abraham may be perceived as being "in" Abraham. But how are all nations of the world to be perceived as being "in" Abraham and so receive the blessings of the covenant? Paul personifies Scripture to provide a straightforward answer to this question as he quotes the identical words spoken to Abraham:

> The Scripture, having foreseen that *by faith* God justifies *the nations*, preached the gospel in advance to Abraham: "They shall be IN-blessed IN you *all the nations*." (Gal. 3:8)

It might be assumed that the same word appearing twice in the same verse of Scripture would be translated the same way, though that may not always be the case. Particularly when one of the occurrences of the word appears in an Old Testament quotation, it would be assumed that the same word appearing in the interpreting half of the verse would be rendered in the same way as the word in the quotation. But in this case, English Bible translations render τὰ ἔθνη uniformly as "the Gentiles" in the first half of Galatians 3:8, while the same phrase is rendered "the nations" in the second half of the verse, which is quoting the Old Testament (ESV, NAB, NIV, NKJV; the KJV translates it "heathen . . . all nations").

From God's initial pronouncement of the blessings of the Abrahamic covenant, all nations of the world were included. By faith they were *in* Abraham, in union with him. It may even be proposed that the "union with Christ" concept that permeates Paul's theology found its initial anticipation in the strongly stressed "in Abraham" concept. By faith the nations are "in" Abraham, and so they are "in" Christ. As such, the various nations of the world are clearly participants in the Abrahamic covenant.

The application of the covenantal seal to people from all nations of the world reinforces this concept. From the moment of its initiation, "all nations" were integrated into the Abrahamic covenant by the universal application of the covenantal seal of circumcision (Gen. 17:12–13). Nothing could establish more solidly the equal standing in the Abrahamic covenant of peoples from any and all nations of the world than the approved application of the covenantal seal to non-Israelites. Any suggestion that the Abrahamic covenant departed from the universalistic core of God's covenants would have to totally overlook this objective reality. Not merely in some vague spiritualistic manner but in the

---

25. The NIV reading "through you" stands counter to the most natural reading of the Hebrew text (בְּךָ), the Septuagint, and all other major English translations.

objective application of the covenantal seal, all nations participate in God's covenant with Abraham. How fitting, then, to the unbroken flow of covenantal redemption is the Lord's final admonition to his first disciples: "Go and make disciples of *all nations, baptizing them . . .*" (Matt. 28:19). That is, "Bring all nations into the bond of the covenant by applying to them the initiatory seal of the new covenant, just as it was indicated that they could appropriately receive the covenantal seal of the old covenant."

The Mosaic Covenant

If any covenant in Scripture might be read as including only Israelites, the bond of God at Sinai would appear to be that kind of covenant. Moses led the descendants of Jacob out of Egypt into the barren desert of Sinai. There, in isolation from all other nations of the world, God instituted his covenant through Moses. It would appear that the people of Israel and only the people of Israel were the human parties of this covenant. Several matters, however, must be considered before this conclusion is reached.

First, what is the relation of the Mosaic covenant to the Abrahamic covenant? If an integral connection exists between the Abrahamic and the Mosaic covenants, and if the Abrahamic covenant provided redemptive blessings to all nations, then the Mosaic covenant also must provide redemptive blessings to the nations.

Long, arduous, and unbroken have been the discussions and debates regarding the relation of the Mosaic covenant of law to the Abrahamic covenant of promise—even until today.[26] Suffice it to say that both in the structure of redemptive history and in the focal theme of all the redemptive covenants, a unity binds the covenants of Abraham and Moses despite their God-intended diversity.[27] This unity includes the embracing of peoples, tongues, and tribes of all nations. The most concrete indicator of the inclusion of the nations in the Mosaic covenant appears in the administration of the covenantal sacraments of circumcision and Passover. By being circumcised and professing the God of Israel, any non-Israelite from any other nation of the world could share in the highest privilege of the covenant nation, which was the Passover meal (Ex. 12:48–49). As a "Jewish" commentator on Genesis observes, "Every stranger who submits to [circumcision] receives Abraham as his father and becomes an Israelite. . . . Circumcision turned a man of foreign origin into an Israelite (Ex. 12:48)."[28] So peoples from all nations are welcomed participants in the Mosaic covenant.

---

26. See, for example, the following collection of essays favoring the "republication" of the original covenant of works in the Mosaic covenant, which has the effect of essentially separating the promise covenant of Abraham from the law covenant of Moses: Bryan D. Estelle, J. V. Fesko, and David VanDrunen, eds., *The Law Is Not of Faith: Essays on Works and Grace in the Mosaic Covenant* (Phillipsburg, NJ: P&R, 2009).

27. Note the fuller discussion in Robertson, *Christ of the Covenants*, 28–52. It would be very difficult to establish that the Mosaic covenant is void of redemptive grace and so disjointed from the Abrahamic covenant. For what means the Passover lamb, the cleansing of circumcision, the sacrificial system, the serpent on the pole, the Day of Atonement, and the promise of the land given to Moses?

28. Benno Jacob, *The First Book of the Bible: Genesis* (New York: Ktav, 1974), 115, 233.

Second, Israel's historical relationship to the Mosaic covenant did not end with the death of Moses. Joshua claimed the covenantal promise of the land under the auspices of God's promise to Moses. As the Lord said to Joshua, "Every place that the sole of your foot will tread upon I have given to you, *just as I promised to Moses*" (Josh. 1:3).

Subsequently, five hundred years of successive kings in Israel were judged by God on the basis of God's law given at Sinai. The nation's exile and restoration occurred according to the provisions of the Mosaic covenant (Deut. 30:1–4). During the thousand-year period from Moses to the exile, non-Israelite foreigners continued to be enfolded into the nation. Consider Rahab the Canaanite and Ruth the Moabite, who served Israel well as mothers of the messianic line leading through David to Jesus Christ. Quite clearly, non-Israelites were included among the covenant people of God under the auspices of the Mosaic covenant.

Third, the prophets of Israel regularly included the nations in the promises of the Mosaic covenant. They fulfilled their high calling as mouthpieces of God across the centuries as applicatory heralds of the Mosaic covenant. Constantly law and covenant provided the foundation for the ministry of the prophets. Notice just one sampling of their inclusion of non-Israelite nations in God's redemptive plan, as seen repeatedly through Isaiah's picture of the ministry of the servant of the Lord:

> Behold my servant; . . .
>> he will bring forth justice *to the nations*. . . .
> He will not grow faint or be discouraged
>> till he has established justice *in the earth*. (Isa. 42:1, 4)

> [God] says [to his servant]: . . .
> "I will make you as a *light for the nations*,
>> That my salvation may reach to the *end of the earth*." (Isa. 49:6)

> Behold, my servant. . . .
> so he shall sprinkle *many nations*;
>> *Kings* shall shut their mouths because of him. (Isa. 52:13, 15)

All three of these Servant Songs of Isaiah depict the ministry of the Lord's servant to the nations in terms of the provisions of the covenant law of Moses. Justice (according to the law of Moses), light (from the law of Moses), and sprinkling (according to the cleansing provided by the law of Moses) comprehend the specific ministry of this designated servant of the Lord.

A prophecy of Hosea as interpreted in the new covenant Scriptures underscores the inclusion of peoples from all nations as the people of God under the auspices of the Mosaic covenant, the violation of which brought about the judgment of Israel's exile. Hosea is instructed to name his children "No Mercy" and "Not My People," since God will show Israel "no mercy" and since they are "not his people" (Hos. 1:6, 9).

But subsequently the Lord declares, "I will have mercy on 'No Mercy,' and I will say to 'Not My People,' 'You are my people'" (Hos. 2:23). In applying this passage in a new covenant context, Paul gives full strength to both the negative and the positive aspects of this prophecy (Rom. 9:24–26). The northern kingdom of Israel actually became "Not My People" by their dispersal across the vast realm of the kingdom of Assyria. They lost their identity as God's people. The nations swallowed them up. Paul underscores this point by indicating that the fulfillment of Hosea's prophecy occurred when God summoned a people to salvation "not from the 'Judeans' only but also *from the nations*" (Rom. 9:24). That is, Israel had truly become "Not My People," indistinguishable from the peoples of other nations. They had reverted to their original condition before God called Abraham, as just one more element of the conglomerate of nations.

So when God calls people from the various nations of the world to be his people, he is fulfilling the prophecy of Hosea that God will transform "Not My People" into the people of the living God. As a consequence, the nations, including Israel, participate in God's covenant made with Moses as proclaimed by the prophets.[29]

The Davidic Covenant

Sometimes it is proposed that the sequence of covenants alternates from unconditional to conditional to unconditional: unconditional covenant with Abraham, conditional covenant with Moses, unconditional covenant with David. But a rudimentary analysis of the various covenants should dismiss this perspective regarding the sequence of God's redemptive covenants. Contrary to being unconditional, God set the bar quite high for Abraham. The patriarch must be *blameless*; only then would the Lord confirm his covenant with him (Gen. 17:1–2). Abraham must circumcise every male; otherwise, he would be cut off from God's people, since he would have broken the covenant (Gen. 17:10, 14). Clearly, conditions are an integral part of the Abrahamic covenant.

The same may be said of the Davidic covenant. In his deathbed charge to Solomon as his princely successor and covenant mediator, David says, "Keep the charge of the LORD your God, walking in his ways and keeping his statutes, his commandments, his rules, and his testimonies, *as it is written in the Law of Moses*, . . . that the LORD may establish his word that he spoke concerning me" (1 Kings 2:3–4). Without question, the Davidic covenant contains conditions as well as possessing promises.

All God's covenants have conditions and promises. At the same time, the various covenants of redemption have the absolute certainty that all the conditions will be met. They will be met by the Lord Christ, who has come to save his people from their sins by fulfilling in himself all the conditions of the covenant.

---

29. For a helpful analysis of Paul's use of Hosea's prophecy, see Jason A. Staples, "What Do the Gentiles Have to Do with 'All Israel'? A Fresh Look at Romans 11:25–27," *JBL* 130, no. 2 (2011): 380–83.

From another perspective, it is sometimes proposed that the Abrahamic covenant is international in scope, the Mosaic covenant is nationalistic, involving only the nation of Israel, while the Davidic covenant once more is international in its participants. Already it has been shown that the Mosaic covenant is also international in scope, welcoming as equal participants anyone from any nationality who will confess the God of Israel and receive circumcision as the sign of the covenant. It is now necessary only to confirm the international character of the Davidic covenant. Both the Prophets and the Psalms affirm this international character of God's covenant with David. A few sample passages should suffice to confirm the place of all nations in God's redemptive working throughout the world under the auspices of the Davidic covenant.

Quite striking is Isaiah's anticipation of the respective roles of the nations of Egypt, Assyria, and Israel in the Lord's redemptive purpose of blessing the earth:

> In that day Israel will be the third with Egypt and Assyria, a blessing in the midst of the earth, whom the LORD of hosts has blessed, saying, "Blessed be Egypt my people, and Assyria the work of my hands, and Israel my inheritance." (Isa. 19:24–25 ESV; cf. the blessing of Gen. 12:2–3)

Quite astounding is this prophetic perspective on these two greatest international threats to the ongoing existence of the nation of Israel. Those ancient enemies, Egypt to the south and Assyria to the north, are ranked alongside Israel (if not higher than Israel) in experiencing the redemptive blessings of the Lord.

At the very end of old covenant prophecy, Zechariah anticipates the day in which nations throughout the world will submit to David's successor as he rules from Mount Zion in Jerusalem:

> Rejoice greatly, O daughter of Zion!
>   Shout aloud, O daughter of Jerusalem!
> Behold, your king is coming to you;
>   righteous and having salvation is he,
> humble and mounted on a donkey,
>   on a colt, the foal of a donkey. . . .
>   He shall speak peace *to the nations*;
> his rule shall be *from sea to sea*,
>   and from the River *to the ends of the earth*. (Zech. 9:9–10 ESV)

This particular passage from Zechariah echoes the triumphant psalm that concludes book 2 of the Psalter. In the worshipful celebrations of Israel, the universal expansion of the Davidic kingdom served as a regular theme:

> May he have dominion *from sea to sea*,
>   and from the River *to the ends of the earth*!

> May desert tribes bow down before him,
>   and his enemies lick the dust!
> May the *kings* of Tarshish and of the coastlands
>   render him tribute;
> may the *kings* of Sheba and Seba
>   bring gifts!
> May *all kings* fall down before him,
>   *all nations* serve him! (Ps. 72:8–11 ESV)

This celebration of the international dominion of the Davidic messiah also appears in the second psalm, which sets the tone of the whole Psalter:

> The LORD said to me, "You are my Son;
>   today I have begotten you.
> Ask of me, and I will make *the nations* your heritage,
>   and *the ends of the earth* your possession." (Ps. 2:7–8 ESV)

Clearly, the prophets and psalmists delighted in celebrating the worldwide character of the Davidic messiah's rule over all nations.

The New Covenant

Does the new covenant embrace "the nations" as well as Israelites? Some interpreters have noted that Jeremiah's prophecy says that the new covenant will be made with the "house of Israel" and the "house of Judah" (Jer. 31:31). Do not these phrases imply that the new covenant is God's specific arrangement with the Israelite people, instead of including all nations of the world?

One critical moment among many in new covenant redemptive history underscores the place of non-Israelites among the new covenant "people of God," namely, the apostolic council's decision regarding the inclusion of individuals from all nations within the people of God (Acts 15:14–17).

The debate at Jerusalem among the apostles and elders regarding the inclusion of peoples from all the various nations within the covenant people of God answers this question. The Jerusalem Council reaches its critical point with the quotation of the Old Testament by James, the leader of the Jerusalem church.[30] James prefaces his quotation from Amos by capitalizing on the redemptive-historical setting of the moment. The language is loaded with significant implications for the relation between Israel and the nations in God's covenants. God has "made a visitation" (an old covenant concept

---

30. The quotation from Amos by James has many challenges in terms of its representation of the Old Testament text, as well as the interpretation of the passage in the context of Acts. For a fuller treatment, see O. Palmer Robertson, "Hermeneutics of Continuity," in John S. Feinberg, ed., *Continuity and Discontinuity: Perspectives on the Relationship Between the Old and New Testaments; Essays in Honor of S. Lewis Johnson Jr.* (Westchester, IL: Crossway, 1988), 89–108.

depicting the mighty acts of God in working redemption for his people) "to take *from the nations a people for his name*" (ἐξ ἐθνῶν λαὸν τῷ ὀνόματι αὐτοῦ, Acts 15:14). He then cites the prophetic words of Amos, and applies them to the present moment. God is rebuilding the fallen tent of David. He is restoring the Davidic dynasty for a specific purpose:

> that the surviving remnant of *humanity* may seek the Lord,
>> even *all the nations* [πάντα τὰ ἔθνη] *who have my name called upon them.* (Acts 15:17)

The relevance of the quotation from Amos is made clear by its impact on the final decision of the Jerusalem Council. God is assembling from all the various nations of the world "a people for his name." This phrase, "a people for his name," is equivalent to the chosen, the elect, the covenant people of God. In addition, these elect covenant people must not be perceived as a separate entity alongside Israel. For they are represented by James through his Old Testament quotation as an integral part of the rebuilding of the fallen booth of David, which represents nothing less than the messianic kingdom of the Christ.

This newly constituted entity that envelops equally Israelites and elect people from all nations of the world is God's covenant people. Just as Israel was God's treasured possession, so now this new conglomerate of peoples is equally his treasured possession (Ex. 19:6; 1 Pet. 2:9).

So do individuals from all the various peoples of the world have a place alongside Israel among God's new covenant people? By all means they do. Redeemed people from Israel along with redeemed peoples from all nations of the world join together to constitute the new covenant people of God.

Indeed, it may be affirmed without question that descendants of Abraham, by faith in Jesus as the Christ, are included among the blessed recipients of the new covenant. But their inclusion does not automatically exclude people from various nations as also being embraced in the fellowship of the new covenant. Once more, participation in the covenantal sacraments provides the key for measuring the extent of participation in the new covenant. Under the Abrahamic covenant, any individual from any nation of the world could participate fully in the covenantal sacrament of circumcision. As has been previously noted, circumcision turned a person of foreign origin into an Israelite.

So now with baptism replacing circumcision as the sacrament of entrance into the new covenant (Col. 2:11–12), the resurrected Christ commands, "Make disciples of *all nations, baptizing them* . . ." (Matt. 28:19). In the congregation of Corinth, with its many problems originating largely from its multinational character, all members of the church except those under discipline are expected to participate in the Lord's Supper, the covenantal sacrament of continuing in the covenant (1 Cor. 11:23–32).

The apostle Paul takes the inclusion of people from all nations in God's covenant of redemption to a higher level. The mystery long hidden but now revealed is not simply *participation* of the nations with Israel in God's covenant of redemption; it is the *equality* of peoples from every other nation in their participation with Israel in God's covenants that Paul stresses. As the "apostle to the nations" says, this mystery is that people from all the various nations are "fellow heirs, fellow members, and fellow participants" in the promise in Christ Jesus through the gospel (Eph. 3:6). Three times over, Paul underscores the equality of the peoples from all the various nations with believing Israelites in God's covenants.

Conclusion

Intentionally, the title chosen for this chapter is "Israel and the Nations in God's Covenants," rather than "Jew and Gentile in God's Covenants." Hopefully the reader can appreciate the reason for this choice of title. The terms "Jew" and "Gentile" simply do not manifest adequately the enlargement of God's grace in his covenants. All nations of the world are included in all God's gracious covenants, while Israel is not excluded.

Oh, the depth of the riches of God's grace in the covenants. May he ever enlarge our horizons as we gaze on a corrupt and immoral humanity, while always viewing them as potential participants in the riches of God's covenant grace.

25

Dispensationalism

Michael J. Glodo

Many Christians today do not see the Old Testament as particularly relevant. Some might even find it objectionable. It is often assumed that the Old Testament law is irrelevant since we are now under grace. Obedience to God's commands is desirable but is not a requirement for Christians. Popular Bible teachers explain contemporary events in relation to a perceived biblical road map for the end times. It is taken for granted that the nation of Israel is a key part of end-time events, so that it is a Christian duty to support Israel's policies, particularly in relation to possessing the promised land. The appeal of these beliefs is that they seem on the surface to be simply biblical. In fact, it was the belief in being simply biblical—in reaction to the growing encroachments of modernism in biblical interpretation—that helped spawn a mid-nineteenth-century movement that for nearly two centuries has been one of the most widespread interpretive paradigms among Bible-believing Christians. Though dispensationalism has undergone significant change and holds less ground among evangelical scholars than it once did, elements of it continue to be ubiquitous among everyday Christians, even if they do not hold to the system as a whole.

In contrast to covenant theology, dispensationalism perceives a fundamental degree of discontinuity between the different periods of redemptive history (dispensations), not only between the Old and New Testaments but even between different epochs within each Testament. This discontinuity is reflected in the dispensationalist distinctives, most notably the claim that there are two peoples of God, Israel and the church, with their own distinctive programs for salvation;[1] the separation of earthly and spiritual promises

---

1. In the past, dispensationalism has been criticized for teaching that Israel was to seek justification through the law. While Scofield and subsequent clarifications have distanced dispensationalism from the "unfortunate"

in the Old Testament; the removal (rapture) of the church out of the world prior to a literal one-thousand-year earthly reign of Jesus Christ; and the reconstitution of national Israel in the land of Palestine during that millennial period in which the temple will be rebuilt and its worship will resume until the consummation of the ages in the new heavens and new earth. While these distinctives are a product of a system of reading the Bible, the chief hermeneutical principle dispensationalism professes is the "literal" or "plain" meaning of Scripture.

To the casual observer, the differences between these two ways of reading the Bible might seem like a preoccupation with minutiae, especially some of the detailed parsing of prophecies and end-time events. There are, however, profound implications involved. Is obedience to God's commands a necessary consequence of God's saving grace? What are God's commands for Christians today? Can we actually preach the gospel from the Old Testament? What shall we think and how shall we act regarding world conflicts, especially those involving the modern state of Israel? These and other issues bear ultimately on how we understand the most important issue: the nature of the gospel.[2]

In-depth treatments of dispensationalism abound, both pro and con, but for this essay, as part of a volume on covenant theology, a more selective overview of the historical development and prime tenets of dispensationalism is called for, so that a pastor or other church leader can recognize, understand, and provide guidance when encountering its various features.[3] Such an awareness is necessary because dispensationalism has been covenant theology's primary rival system, it has influenced many average Christians without their realizing it, it has significantly shaped the impressions of evangelical Christianity among those outside the church, and it even has a continuing influence on international relations in our day. Most important, the glories of the gospel of Jesus Christ through the one covenant of grace from their nascent Edenic origins to their consummation in the new heavens and new earth shine brighter when viewed in contrast to dispensationalism's alternatives. What follows highlights key historical developments in dispensationalism with its distinctives, influences, developments, and revisions, giving attention to strengths and weaknesses particularly vis-à-vis covenant theology. After those highlights comes an assessment of some of the most important distinctives.

Dispensationalism has undergone significant revisions since its appearance, as discussed below. Even among those who are self-described adherents today, there is

---

and "unguarded" statements that created this impression, Scofield and dispensationalism in general have affirmed that Israel and the church are saved by God's grace. See Anthony C. Garland, "Does Dispensationalism Teach Two Ways of Salvation?," *ConTJ* 7, no. 22 (March 2003): 40–63. While this clarifying trend has been helpful, even still, dispensationalism holds that God's program of grace is distinctive for Israel and the church.

2. By this I am not suggesting that dispensationalism teaches an alternative way of salvation or a false gospel; rather, dispensationalism poses questions such as whether the gospel by its very nature will and must transform the believer or whether obedience to God's commands is desirable but not inevitable for someone with saving faith.

3. A historical junction between classic dispensationalism and more contemporary forms is available in Charles Ryrie, *Dispensationalism Today*, rev. ed. (Chicago: Moody Press, 2007). An excellent, clear, straightforward, concise, yet thorough critique of dispensationalism from a covenant theology perspective is available in Keith A. Mathison, *Dispensationalism: Rightly Dividing the People of God?* (Phillipsburg, NJ: P&R, 1995).

disagreement as to what necessarily and truly constitutes dispensationalism. This means that no summary is fully acceptable to every dispensationalist. Not only does the variation of beliefs make a critique challenging, but so also does the way dispensationalism has become tightly integrated after nearly two centuries of development. As Vern Poythress notes,

> Many Evangelicals who believe that dispensationalism is wrong have discovered that it is not at all easy to *show* this to the satisfaction of dispensationalism. . . . Classic dispensationalism is a whole system of theology. It has a great deal of internal coherence. A system that is carefully and thoroughly elaborated, whether right *or* wrong, will almost certainly include answers to standard objections; and different parts of the system come to the aid of any part that is challenged. . . . However, generally speaking, it is less true of modified forms of dispensationalism.[4]

Only an extensive treatment could acknowledge and treat all the permutations and combinations of dispensationalism as a movement. What follows is provided to help recognize and engage key features of the system when encountered.

It is difficult even to get at the factors that led to the appearance and development of this tightly coherent system. The kind of literalism historically claimed by dispensationalism with its (properly) high view of Scripture almost presupposes an innate lack of self-awareness, which characterized modernist interpretation in general. Words are thought to mean what they mean simply because that's what they mean. As observed below, however, the dispensationalist challenge involves more metaphysical than exegetical issues. This would include the role of sociological influences such as Norman Cohn has identified in his association of millennialism with social upheaval.[5] The process of reconsideration often requires a brick-by-brick loosening of the facade rather than a decisive reversal.

An important starting point in this analysis is to acknowledge the positive contributions of dispensationalism to the larger cause of biblical religion. Dispensationalists are not wholly at odds with covenant theologians, sharing certain fundamental commitments with them such as the infallibility of Scripture and inerrancy of its original autographa; justification by grace alone through faith alone; and classical formulations of other fundamental Christian beliefs such as the person and work of Christ, his second coming, and the Trinity. In fact, even while maintaining serious and substantive disagreements with dispensationalists, covenant theologians can reflect on dispensationalist distinctives as an impetus to ensure that their own formulations and emphases are faithful to the Scriptures. For example, dispensationalists' historical sense of urgency about the Great Commission and resistance to cultural accommodation can remind covenant

---

4. Vern S. Poythress, *Understanding Dispensationalists* (Grand Rapids, MI: Zondervan, 1987), 52.

5. Norman Cohn, *The Pursuit of the Millennium: Revolutionary Messianism in Medieval and Reformation Europe and Its Bearing on Modern Totalitarian Movements* (New York: Harper and Row, 1961).

theologians that without vigilance, these commitments can easily flag. For these reasons and others considered below, a working understanding of dispensationalism can provide helpful reminders to a covenant theologian.

Such a comprehension is also important in order to understand dispensationalists, as the title of Vern Poythress's book *Understanding Dispensationalists* emphasizes in a timely and helpful way.[6] In addition to sharing many fundamental beliefs in common with covenant theologians, some dispensationalist theologians were among the most capable and ready cobelligerents in the "battle for the Bible" of the twentieth century. Dispensationalists also have been at the forefront of evangelism and missions. As O. Palmer Robertson has written,

> It should not be forgotten that covenant theologians and dispensationalists stand side-by-side in affirming the essentials of the Christian faith. Very often these two groups within Christendom stand alone in opposition to the inroads of modernism, neo-evangelicalism, and emotionalism. Covenant theologians and dispensationalists should hold in highest regard the scholarly and evangelical productivity of one another. It may be hoped that continuing interchange made be based on love and respect.[7]

For these reasons, we must regard dispensationalists as brothers- and sisters-in-arms even as we critique their views on specific matters.[8] It was, in fact, some of these shared convictions that birthed dispensationalism as a movement. As critical approaches were raising more and more doubts about the traditional and historical understanding of the Bible, dispensationalism responded with its insistence on literal interpretation. While the Bible's historicity was being challenged by critical scholars, dispensationalism put the Bible's relevance on the front page of the newspapers. With the social upheaval of the industrial age, the waning of postmillennial optimism, the transition from the colonial era to the new globalism, and the growing accommodation of traditional denominations to their cultural contexts, dispensationalism renewed hope in Christ's second coming with its rapture theology, lent urgency to the task of evangelism, and provided its eschatology as a roadmap for the average Christian to navigate the uncertainty of the tumultuous changes of modern times as part of God's plan. Covenant theologians have lessons to learn from dispensationalists about fervency for the Great Commission, hope in Christ's return, and being fixed on God's eternal city in order to resist worldliness.

---

6. Vern S. Poythress, *Understanding Dispensationalists*, 2nd ed. (Phillipsburg, NJ: P&R, 1993). Its first edition (1987), which coincided with the advent of progressive dispensationalism (see below) and the creation of the Evangelical Theological Society's Dispensational Study Group (1986), preceded by only a few years the less charitable, somewhat anachronistic, and less fruitful approach in John Gerstner's *Wrongly Dividing the Word of Truth: A Critique of Dispensationalism* (Brentwood, TN: Wolgemuth and Hyatt, 1991).

7. O. Palmer Robertson, *The Christ of the Covenants* (Phillipsburg, NJ: Presbyterian and Reformed, 1980), 201–2.

8. A model for such an approach is Poythress, *Understanding Dispensationalists*, 2nd ed., widely regarded by dispensationalists as fair yet challenging.

History

The word *dispensation* refers to the different epochs of redemptive history as witnessed in Scripture. This notion, however, does not provide a sufficient basis on which to distinguish dispensationalism and covenant theology. The Westminster Confession of Faith, for example, recognizes such historical periods when it states, "There are not therefore two covenants of grace differing in substance, but one and the same under various dispensations" (7.6). As Poythress notes, "Virtually all ages of the church and all branches of the church have believed that there are distinctive dispensations in God's government of the world. . . . The recognition of distinctions between different epochs is by no means unique to [dispensationalists]."[9] The material distinction of dispensationalism is in believing that there are different divine programs for humanity in each epoch, especially for Israel and the church, which is why Poythress refers to them as "D-theologians." It is the theology, not the dispensations themselves, that distinguishes them: "The salient points are what the D-theologians say about these dispensations, not that they exist."[10]

Darby

Dispensationalism as a system is identified first with John Nelson Darby (1800–1882). Attempts to demonstrate its ancient origins identify only those features that have been common to general Christian tradition.[11] And as Keith Mathison points out, if dispensationalism is nothing new, that leaves it as a system without a distinction.[12] He is correct when he says, "Historical arguments are not the final test for the truthfulness of any doctrine. Scripture is our sole authority for both doctrine and practice."[13] On that basis, it must be acknowledged that dispensationalism as a distinctive phenomenon is an innovation.

In the nineteenth century, modernist (critical) interpretation of the Bible and the social conditions of the maturing industrial age precipitated an embrace of literal interpretation of the Bible and a sense that the end of the age was near. Additionally, it was a time when many orthodox in theology were neglecting the historical and progressive character of revelation for the sake of systematic formulation.[14]

Darby was originally ordained in the Church of England but renounced those credentials when required to affirm allegiance to the crown, at which time he helped establish the Plymouth Brethren. A Calvinist soteriologically, Darby believed the kingdom of God was distinct from the church. At some point in the near future, the church would

---

9. Poythress, *Understanding Dispensationalists*, 2nd ed., 9–10.
10. Poythress, *Understanding Dispensationalists*, 2nd ed., 11.
11. See Charles Ryrie's effort to show this in "The Origins of Dispensationalism," chap. 4 in *Dispensationalism Today*.
12. Mathison, *Dispensationalism*, 12.
13. Mathison, *Dispensationalism*, 12.
14. Poythress, *Understanding Dispensationalists*, 2nd ed., 14.

be removed, or "raptured," from the earth at the start of the "Great Tribulation," a seven-year period of worldwide calamity to include intense persecution for anyone who would subsequently come to believe in Jesus Christ. At the end of that seven years, Jesus would return, the temple would be rebuilt, a large-scale mass of Jews would turn to Jesus, and the theocracy of Israel would be restored in the land for a thousand years. At that time the consummation of the ages would occur. Like many mid- to late twentieth-century dispensationalists, Darby saw advancing technology and the social upheaval of the industrial age as a sign that the end was near. His five trips to North America helped spread his influence across the Atlantic.

Inglis

James Inglis (1813–1872), editor of a popular prophecy periodical and contributor to the growth of the prophecy-conference movement in the United States, is particularly credited for spreading dispensationalism to and in the United States in the 1860s. He adamantly denied promoting Plymouth Brethren or Darbyite theology.[15] According to historian Ernest Sandeen, his denials of Darbyism were due more to his exception to its sectarianism and separatism, which would not have played well with denominationally minded Americans. Sandeen observes, "Although not willing to admit their affiliation with [Darby's] denominational views, Americans raided Darby's treasuries and carried off his teachings as their own."[16] Inglis pastored first in southeastern Michigan, then in Saint Louis, where, through Presbyterian minister James H. Brookes, the recently converted attorney Cyrus Ingerson "C. I." Scofield was schooled in his principles. Influential evangelist Dwight L. Moody also came to adopt dispensationalism, although Inglis was initially unimpressed with Moody because the latter lacked a Calvinistic soteriology. Moody's widespread influence—including through the Moody Bible Institute, established in 1886—was a significant source for the spread of dispensationalism.

Scofield

C. I. Scofield (1843–1921) was born in southeast Michigan but grew up in Tennessee, where he became initially a Confederate soldier and ultimately a deserter to the North. Scofield was a lawyer by training and practice. As a Kansas legislator and prosecutor, an ethical cloud developed over him concerning financial irregularities, and he was alienated from his family at the time he was converted in 1879. Although ultimately unable to salvage his marriage, he was mentored by Brookes and ordained to the ministry in a Congregational church in Dallas. He spent eight years in the northeastern United States before briefly returning to Dallas and eventually moving to New York City and joining

---

15. Ernest R. Sandeen, *The Roots of Fundamentalism: British and American Millenarianism, 1800–1930*, new ed., TBS (Grand Rapids, MI: Baker, 1978), 100.
16. Sandeen, *Roots of Fundamentalism*, 102.

the Southern Presbyterian Church.[17] During his northeastern years, he awarded himself the title of Doctor of Divinity and founded Philadelphia School of the Bible, which later became Philadelphia College of the Bible and is now Cairn University.

It was through *The Scofield Reference Bible* that dispensationalism spread most rapidly and was popularized among American fundamentalists.[18] In the first point of his introductory essay, "A Panoramic View of the Bible," Scofield articulates a number of interpretive principles with which the covenant theologian could agree in general: the unity of the Bible, the progressive unfolding of the biblical story, and the centrality of Christ.[19] Israel's purpose was to bear witness to God among the nations, to exhibit the "greater blessedness" of serving him, and to be stewards of divine revelation.[20] Yet the distinctives of the system begin to emerge in the delineations of seven successive "dispensations," which Scofield defines as "period[s] of time during which man is tested in respect of obedience to some *specific* revelation of the will of God."[21] These periods include innocency (Gen. 1:28), conscience (Gen. 3:23), human government (Gen. 8:20), promise (Gen. 12:1), law (Ex. 19:8), grace (John 1:17), and kingdom (Eph. 1:10).[22] Scofield distinguishes separately eight divine-human covenants: Edenic (Gen. 1:28), Adamic (Gen. 3:14), Noahic (Gen. 9:1), Abrahamic (Gen. 15:18), Mosaic (Ex. 19:25), Palestinian (Deut. 30:3), Davidic (2 Sam. 7:16), and new (Heb. 8:8).[23] The precise difference between dispensations and covenants is not always clear, but "dispensation" is intended to describe not only the period under consideration but more particularly the terms for the testing of man during that time: "The dispensation must be distinguished from the covenant. The former is a mode of testing; the latter is everlasting because unconditional."[24]

Charles Ryrie says similarly, "Dispensation and age are connected ideas, but the words are not exactly interchangeable; . . . a dispensation is primarily a stewardship arrangement and not a period of time."[25] Yet as Robertson observes, this seems to create within dispensationalism two structures to redemptive history, covenants and dispensations. He states, "It is not easy to determine which of these systems should actually be understood in the mind of the dispensationalist himself as the key to understanding the progress of redemptive history."[26]

Each dispensation involves a particular probationary test for mankind, which he fails in each case only to be met with divine mercy in the provision of a new arrangement

17. David Lutzweiler, *The Praise of Folly: The Enigmatic Life and Theology of C. I. Scofield* (Draper, VA: Apologetics Group Media, 2009).
18. *The Scofield Reference Bible* (London: Oxford University Press) was published in 1909 and revised in 1917 and 1945. References that follow are to the first edition unless indicated otherwise.
19. *Scofield Reference Bible*, v.
20. *Scofield Reference Bible*, vi.
21. *Scofield Reference Bible*, 5.
22. *Scofield Reference Bible*, 5. See also the study notes on the passages cited.
23. *Scofield Reference Bible*, 9.
24. *Scofield Reference Bible*, 20.
25. Ryrie, *Dispensationalism Today*, 27, 29.
26. Robertson, *Christ of the Covenants*, 202–3.

or dispensation. Thus, each dispensation involves new revelation of the divine will particular to it: "A dispensation is a period of time during which man is tested in respect of obedience to some *specific* revelation of the will of God. Seven such dispensations are distinguished in Scripture."[27] As Scofield explains elsewhere, "Each of the dispensations may be regarded as a new test of the natural man, and each ends in judgment—marking his failure."[28]

Dallas Theological Seminary: Chafer, Walvoord, Pentecost, et al.

Lewis Sperry Chafer (1871–1952), who aided Scofield in the founding of Philadelphia School of the Bible, went on to found Dallas Theological Seminary in 1924 and served as president until his death. At various times a Congregationalist and a Presbyterian, Chafer was the first in a succession of notable dispensationalist scholars at Dallas, which included John F. Walvoord (his successor), J. Dwight Pentecost, Charles Ryrie, Eugene Merrill, Merrill Unger, Daniel B. Wallace, and Bruce Waltke, the latter of whom notably went on to adopt covenant theology and to write and deliver a number of critiques of his former system of interpretation.[29] Some Dallas Seminary faculty members, most notably Darrell Bock and Craig Blaising, participated in the modification movement of progressive dispensationalism (see below).

From its beginnings until the middle of the twentieth century, dispensationalism grew rapidly in popularity and underwent several refinements. Perhaps most notable was the deletion in the second edition of *The Scofield Reference Bible* of the following comment on Genesis 12:1: "The dispensation of promise ended when Israel rashly accepted the law (Ex. 19. 8). Grace had prepared a deliverer (Moses), provided sacrifice for the guilty, and by divine power brought them out of bondage (Ex. 19. 4); but at Sinai they exchanged grace for law."[30] This statement understood the Mosaic covenant as a regression rather than an advance in the progress of redemption. The second edition removed that statement and instead stated that the law "was not given as a way of life . . . but as a rule of living for people already in the covenant of Abraham and covered by blood sacrifice."[31] And yet, as Robertson notes, the second edition still said at a later point, "To Abraham the promise preceded the requirement; at Sinai the requirement preceded the promise."[32] This still suggests a reversal of the relationship between grace and obedience. Moreover, since the new covenant is treated as a resumption of the Abrahamic covenant,

---

27. *Scofield Reference Bible*, 2nd ed., 5; emphasis added.

28. C. I. Scofield, *Rightly Dividing the Word of Truth* (Old Tappan, NJ: Fleming H. Revell, 1972), 13.

29. E.g., Bruce K. Waltke, "Kingdom Promises as Spiritual," in *Continuity and Discontinuity: Perspectives on the Relationship between the Old and New Testaments; Essays in Honor of S. Lewis Johnson Jr.*, ed. John S. Feinberg (Westchester, IL: Crossway, 1988), 263–87; Waltke, "A Response," in *Dispensationalism, Israel and the Church: The Search for Definition*, ed. Craig A. Blaising and Darrell L. Bock (Grand Rapids, MI: Zondervan, 1992), 347–59. See also Bruce K. Waltke, *An Old Testament Theology: An Exegetical, Canonical, and Thematic Approach*, with Charles Yu (Grand Rapids, MI: Zondervan, 2007), 42–43, 322–23.

30. *Scofield Reference Bible*, 20.

31. *Scofield Reference Bible*, 2nd ed., 94. See Robertson, *Christ of the Covenants*, 215–16.

32. Robertson, *Christ of the Covenants*, 216.

albeit only in spiritual and not earthly fulfillment, it gives the wrong impression that conditionality does not exist under the new covenant (see "Conditionality in a Gracious Covenant" section below). And as Robertson notes, the situation under the Mosaic law is confusing since the unconditional Abrahamic covenant and the conditional Mosaic covenant are both in force.

Yet Scofield's successors remained no less certain about the dissonance of the Abrahamic and Mosaic covenants. For example, Charles Fred Lincoln says,

> The testimony of the Scripture everywhere is clear and manifest that the Covenant of the Law, given on Mount Sinai through Moses, is a separate and distinct Covenant from that made by God with Abraham. The teachers of Covenantism arbitrarily deny this fact because to concede it would take the very foundation from their erroneous scheme of things. But numerous Scriptures establish this foundational truth beyond all possibility of question. Many illustrative passages might be given, but at this point reference will be made to only two or three. Galatians 4:19–31 sets forth the "two covenants" of Moses and Abraham in distinct contrast and shows that they are incompatible and cannot live together. The declaration that there are "two covenants" is conclusive evidence of the erroneousness of the scheme of the covenantists. The contrast is not between the ceremonies and animal sacrifices of the law and the sacrifice of Christ on the cross, as the theory lamely contends, but between two wholly contrary systems represented by Abraham and Moses; the whole burden of the argument clearly rests upon this fundamental difference.[33]

Regarding the lack of unity between the covenants, Chafer states,

> [Covenantism] is that form of theological speculation which attempts to unify God's entire program from Genesis to Revelation under one supposed Covenant of Grace. That no such covenant is either named or exhibited in the Bible and that the covenants which are set forth in the Bible are so varied and diverse that they preclude a one-covenant idea, evidently does not deter many sincere men from adherence to the one-covenant theory.[34]

Ryrie

Eventually the movement underwent material modification such that by the middle of the twentieth century, Charles Ryrie (1925–2016) laid out the parameters of "essentialist," or *sine qua non*, dispensationalism in his *Dispensationalism Today*.[35] The essential elements begin, according to Ryrie, with recognizing that God has distinguishably different economies in governing the affairs of the world. Going on to list Charles Hodge and Louis Berkhof among those who hold to such distinctions, he states, "In other words, a

---

33. Charles Fred Lincoln, "The Biblical Covenants" (part 2), *BSac* 100, no. 399 (1943): 442.
34. Lewis Sperry Chafer, "Dispensational Distinctions Challenged," *BSac* 100, no. 399 (1943): 338.
35. Charles C. Ryrie, *Dispensationalism Today* (Chicago: Moody Press, 1965), 43–47.

man can believe in dispensations, and even see them in relation to progressive revelation, without being a dispensationalist."[36] To suggest that these and others he named might be compatible with his system stretches credulity, if not credibility.

According to Ryrie, no set number of dispensations is essential, even though Scofield insisted on seven. It is the distinction between dispensations rather than their number that is fundamental: "Theoretically the *sine qua non* ought to lie in the recognition of the fact that God has distinguishably different economies in governing the affairs of the world."[37]

Ryrie also points out that simply being premillennial does not make one a dispensationalist since there are premillennialists who are not dispensationalists, although for Ryrie the millennial kingdom for nondispensational premillennialists (i.e., historic premillennialists) "loses much of its Jewish character. This is due to the slighting of the Old Testament promises concerning the kingdom" by "generally assign[ing] them to the Church."[38] Nevertheless, he does insist, conversely, that "being a dispensationalist makes one a premillennialist."[39]

Ryrie's dispensations are as follows: innocency, or freedom (before the fall); conscience, or self-determination (fall to flood); civil government (postflood to Abraham); promise, or patriarchal rule; Mosaic law; grace; millennium. His definitive answer as to what constitutes a dispensationalist is maintaining (1) a distinction between Israel and the church; (2) a system of literal—"normal" or "plain"—interpretation of the Scripture; and (3) that God's underlying purpose is his glory rather than salvation, as Ryrie says the covenant theologian insists.[40]

Regarding the distinction between Israel and the church, Ryrie accepts Daniel Fuller's description of dispensationalism as maintaining that distinction "throughout eternity."[41] While the nondispensationalist sees the merger of Israel and the church in the inaugurated kingdom beginning with Christ's earthly ministry as described by Paul in Ephesians 2:11–22, this would be the place for Ryrie to at least acknowledge their confluence in the new heavens and new earth. Yet he does not do so, because, in spite of the New Testament writers identifying the fulfillment of the Old Testament promises to Israel in Christ's inaugurated kingdom, his "plain" hermeneutic divides those promises into earthly and spiritual aspects. Thus, essentialist dispensationalism fails to properly relate Israel and the church as a relationship of organic outgrowth rather than as parallel destinies.

As to Ryrie's charge that covenant theology prioritizes salvation over God's glory, this is ironic given that one of the fundamental creedal statements of covenant theologians,

---

36. Ryrie, *Dispensationalism Today*, 44.
37. Ryrie, *Dispensationalism Today*, 43.
38. Ryrie, *Dispensationalism Today*, 44.
39. Ryrie, *Dispensationalism Today*, 44.
40. Ryrie, *Dispensationalism Today*, 44–47.
41. Ryrie, *Dispensationalism Today*, 44–45, citing Daniel P. Fuller, "The Hermeneutics of Dispensationalism" (ThD diss., Northern Baptist Theological Seminary, 1957).

the Westminster Shorter Catechism, begins with stating that man's *summum bonum* is God's glory. Although saying it is the highest good alone does not necessarily mean that covenant theology achieves that goal, covenant theology does ground God's saving action in his purposes for creation as the theater of his glory.[42] The covenant of grace fulfills the creation covenant, thereby uniting creation and redemption under Christ, the firstborn of creation and firstborn from the dead (Col. 1:15–20). Furthermore, the Bible puts forth God's saving actions as the greater manifestation of his glory in salvation, and this is epitomized in the incarnation as the full revelation of God's glory (John 1:14) and in the attainment of eternal glory through Christ and the church (Eph. 3:20–21).

At Home among the Presbyterians

Those familiar with twentieth-century American Presbyterianism may have noted that dispensationalism was more than tolerated in the Northern Presbyterian Church. Grove City College, which was officially Presbyterian at the time, was the site of the first of two weeklong conferences to discuss the first draft of *The Scofield Reference Bible* in 1908. The town of Princeton, New Jersey, was the site of the third, the home of recently arrived Charles R. Erdman, professor of practical theology at Princeton Theological Seminary and a participant in the conferences.[43]

It must be remembered that modernism made inroads into biblical interpretation in the North more rapidly than in the South, including in the theological schools. This won institutions like Moody Bible Institute, Philadelphia College of the Bible, and the prophecy-conference movement greater trust among Presbyterian evangelicals. Additionally, New School Presbyterian influences diminished the role of the confessional standards as dispensationalist sources such as Scofield's notes became more and more prominent. Conversely, in the South, where the doctrine of the church had a more pronounced history and place, Southern Presbyterians had greater concern about the ecclesiological implications of dispensationalism's distinction between Israel and the church. Consequently, though not without controversy, a study committee report of the Southern Presbyterian Church concluded that dispensationalism rejected the unity of God's people, the Bible's one way of salvation, the one destiny for all God's people, and the Bible as God's one revelation to his one people.[44] This latter conclusion references Chafer's teachings that only the Gospel of John, Acts, and the Epistles of the New Testament are addressed to the church and that even the Lord's Prayer and the Great Commission are addressed to Jews of the tribulation period. The report also pointed

42. For more on this, see Robertson, *Christ of the Covenants*, chap. 5, "The Covenant of Creation," 67–87.
43. Sandeen, *Roots of Fundamentalism*, 223.
44. "1944 PCUS Report on Dispensationalism," excerpt from *Minutes of the Eighty-Fourth General Assembly (1944) of the Presbyterian Church, US*, PCA Historical Center, accessed March 31, 2019, http://www.pcahistory.org/documents/pcus1944.html. For more on the relationship of Presbyterianism to dispensationalism, see Vern S. Poythress, "Presbyterianism and Dispensationalism," in *The Practical Calvinist: An Introduction to the Presbyterian and Reformed Heritage*, ed. Peter A. Lillback (Fearn, Ross-shire, Scotland: Mentor, 2002), 415–24.

out that dispensationalism minimized the kingly office of Christ since under its church-kingdom distinction, Christ is only *head* of the church now and is not exercising his *kingly office* of subduing his enemies in the present age.

Christian Zionism

An ironic and inconsistent development out of dispensationalism has been Christian Zionism—the support of evangelicals for the restoration of the state of Israel, the return of Jews to the Palestinian territory, and the belief that political support for Israel is a divine imperative. As James Jordan has pointed out, even though Christian Zionism arises out of dispensationalism, it is fundamentally inconsistent with it because the kingdom age (restoration of Israel) is to follow the rapture of the church. It cannot be argued that there are signs of the rapture being near, because it will come "like a thief in the night," unexpectedly.[45] While support for the modern state of Israel can be argued as just and necessary in the wake of the Holocaust and in light of contemporary Middle East geopolitics, it is a different matter to believe that the Bible requires such support based on a continuing national covenant between God and Israel. While the problems of Middle Eastern politics are intractable and from a human perspective might even seem irresolvable, unconditional support for the state of Israel cannot be required to the detriment of human rights and prudent statecraft.

Dispensationalism not only divides the church from Israel, but in our present day, it is also dividing Bible-believing evangelical Christians from one another on the global scene. Dispensationalists' unconditional support for the state of Israel has resulted at times in difficult conditions for Christians living in the Palestinian territories and has also inflamed relationships between Middle Eastern Christians in general and American dispensationalist evangelicals.[46] While debates continue about whether Islam is a religion of peace, a well-meaning, often naïve, but flawed reading of the Christian Scriptures has caused biblical faith to be a source of regional conflict under the assumption that a large-scale conflict between Israel and the surrounding nations is inevitable in God's plan. This misreading is ironic given that the land was given to Israel in the Old Testa-ment to be a place of refuge for strangers (e.g., Lev. 19:34; Deut. 10:19). Seeing the land promise fulfilled in a greater way (see "Land/Inheritance" section below) does not obligate modern Israel to capitulate to those who threaten its security, but for evangeli-

---

45. James B. Jordan, "Christian Zionism and Messianic Judaism," chap. 8 in *The Sociology of the Church: Essays in Reconstruction* (Tyler, TX: Geneva Ministries, 1986).

46. E.g., Edward Wong, "The Rapture and the Real World: Mike Pompeo Blends Beliefs and Policy," *New York Times*, March 30, 2019, https://www.nytimes.com/2019/03/30/us/politics/pompeo-christian-policy .html; Philip Bump, "Half of Evangelicals Support Israel Because They Believe It Is Important for Fulfill-ing End-Times Prophecy," *Washington Post*, May 14, 2018, https://www.washingtonpost.com/news/politics /wp/2018/05/14/half-of-evangelicals-support-israel-because-they-believe-it-is-important-for-fulfilling-end -times-prophecy; David D. Kirkpatrick, "For Evangelicals, Supporting Israel Is 'God's Foreign Policy,'" *New York Times*, November 14, 2006, https://www.nytimes.com/2006/11/14/washington/14israel.html; Richard Allen Greene, "Evangelical Christians Plead for Israel," *BBC News*, July 19, 2006, http://news.bbc.co.uk/2 /hi/americas/5193092.stm.

cal Christians, it should mean gauging matters along the lines of modern global affairs rather than Old Testament law. In light of the politicization of evangelical Christians influenced by Christian Zionism, this irony is all the greater given that Darbyism began as a reaction against the church being co-opted by the state.

Progressive Dispensationalism

Continued reflection on some of the difficulties of classic dispensationalism along with external developments in biblical scholarship has created new movements out of dispensationalism. As the principal movement of this type, progressive dispensationalism sees redemptive history more in terms of the continuous development or "progress" (hence "progressive") of redemption. The relationships of the biblical covenants is seen as one of progression rather than more fundamentally discontinuous biblical epochs.[47] In acknowledging that the people of God are one people and the plan of God is one plan, progressive dispensationalists are a major variant from historic dispensationalism, even to the point that Ryrie does not acknowledge them as dispensationalists.[48] Ryrie states, "A man who fails to distinguish Israel and the Church will inevitably not hold to dispensational distinctions."[49] While engagement with critics of dispensationalism doubtless helped shape the development of progressive dispensationalism, so also did mainstream biblical scholarship, which was moving past the preoccupations of higher criticism with its speculative reconstructions of Scripture toward literary analysis. Greater awareness of how the genres of Scripture function in their extrabiblical literary context, features of ancient Near Eastern historiography, the workings of intertextuality, and other literary qualities have introduced the possibility that the plain meaning of Scripture is often not the literal meaning. As Craig Blaising describes it,

> In the 1950s and '60s, other evangelicals [besides "revised," or "essentialist," dispensationalists] were also shying away from "spiritual hermeneutics" in favor of grammatical-historical interpretation. However, evangelical grammatical-historical interpretation was also broadening in the mid-twentieth century to include the developing field of biblical theology. Grammatical analysis expanded to include developments in literary study, particularly in the study of genre, or literary form, and rhetorical structure. Historical interpretation came to include a reference to the historical and cultural context of individual literary pieces for their overall interpretation. And by the late 1980s, evangelicals became more aware of the problem of the interpreter's historical context and traditional preunderstanding of the text being

---

47. For a full discussion, see Craig R. Blaising and Darrell L. Bock, *Progressive Dispensationalism: An Up-to-Date Handbook of Contemporary Dispensational Thought* (Wheaton, IL: Victor Books, 1993); Robert L. Saucy, *The Case for Progressive Dispensationalism: The Interface between Dispensational and Non-Dispensational Theology* (Grand Rapids, MI: Zondervan, 1993).

48. Charles C. Ryrie, "Update on Dispensationalism," in *Issues in Dispensationalism*, ed. Wesley R. Willis and John R. Master (Chicago: Moody Press, 1994), 20–21.

49. Ryrie, *Dispensationalism Today*, 45.

interpreted. These developments . . . have opened up new vistas for discussion which were not considered by earlier interpreters, including classical and many revised dispensationalists. These are developments which have led to what is now called "progressive dispensationalism."[50]

Blaising continues, "Literary interpretation has developed so that some things which earlier interpreters thought they 'clearly' saw in Scripture, are not 'clearly' seen today at all."[51] Yet this development in the hermeneutical approach of progressive dispensationalists has not completely eliminated the literal interpretation distinctive to dispensationalism. For example, while acknowledging the highly "representative" or figural nature of many details in apocalyptic literature, Bock includes the temple of Daniel 9:24–27 among those things that must be insisted on as literal.[52] Thus, in spite of the near break with classic dispensationalism, progressive dispensationalism still maintains the restoration of national Israel, the rebuilding of the temple, and the literal earthly thousand-year reign of Christ before the consummation.

In light of the finality and fullness of what Jesus Christ has done with respect to the Old Testament temple rituals, the progressive dispensationalist must answer the same question as the classic or essentialist dispensationalist. How, in light of the teaching of Hebrews, can temple worship be reestablished? In the oldest forms of dispensationalism, each dispensation involves new revelation that accompanies each dispensation. With its focus on man's stewardship responsibilities in each dispensation and his varied testings under them, the stewardship and the basis for testing is based on the revelation specific to that dispensation. In response to the question, the progressive dispensationalist scholar responds, "Well I have to think that if God will bring about the rebuilding of the temple at that time, then he will provide us the new revelation necessary to worship there in light of Christ." While emphasis on new revelation is normally more muted in dispensationalism, especially in light of heretical traditions such as Islam and Mormonism, which rest on later "revelation," it should nonetheless be a matter on which dispensationalism should be pressed. The finality with which Hebrews declares an end to the temple worship should give great pause to the notion that new revelation will guide the faithful on earth to its reestablishment (e.g., Heb. 8:13; 9:12, 26).

New Covenant Theology and Progressive Covenantalism

While traditional dispensationalists have dismissed progressive dispensationalism as not adhering to dispensationalism's fundamental principles, other hermeneutical frameworks have emerged that provide alternatives to the extreme discontinuity between the Old and New Testaments reflected in classic and essentialist dispensationalism. Most

---

50. Blaising and Bock, *Progressive Dispensationalism*, 35–36.
51. Blaising and Bock, *Progressive Dispensationalism*, 37.
52. Blaising and Bock, *Progressive Dispensationalism*, 93.

notable are new covenant theology, which itself has undergone significant change in its short lifespan, and progressive covenantalism, the most recent development. Scott Swain treats these paradigms more fully in chapter 26 of this volume. Here we can note simply that what they share in common is an attempt to concede something of the high degree of continuity between the Old and New Testaments held by covenant theologians while resisting its full implications. As one example, they insist that the membership of the church be limited to only adults who can credibly articulate saving faith. If progressive dispensationalism is a halfway step from classic dispensationalism to covenant theology, and if these new paradigms represent successive incremental steps, one wonders if Zeno's paradox might apply—that one can never reach a destination because after traveling halfway, there is always still halfway to go.[53]

Analysis

The preceding survey of the historical development of dispensationalism describes some of its principal features. Whatever a particular dispensationalist's set of views today, the potentiality of the influence of these roots must be discerned. It is only fair to acknowledge what Robertson states here:

> Dispensational theologians have been quite active during the past few decades in refining their system of biblical analysis. Certainly it would not be fair to treat the dispensationalist today as though his modes of expression were identical to those which characterize the "old" Scofield Bible as it first appeared in 1909. Yet at the same time, these early foundations cannot be ignored altogether. For the earlier dispensational theology continues to provide the basic motive approach for dispensationalism today.[54]

The following addresses some of classic dispensationalism's distinctive beliefs, which, in light of this development, may or may not be representative of any specific individual.

The Hermeneutical Question

As has been observed, dispensationalism's early impulses included a fervent belief in the Bible as God's word, including an insistence on the literal or plain meaning of Scripture as its true meaning. This hermeneutic properly acknowledges that there was at times spiritual or allegorical significance to particular passages. But as Poythress observes, "Scofield is not a pure literalist, but a literalist with respect to what pertains to Israel," and he regards prophecies as always literal.[55] Yet Poythress also notes that the literal

---

53. For the case defending continuity between the Abrahamic, Mosaic, and new covenants regarding the status of children, see Michael J. Glodo, "Covenant Sign and Seal," *RFP* 2, no. 2 (2017), accessed March 31, 2019, https://journal.rts.edu/article/covenant-sign-seal/.

54. Robertson, *Christ of the Covenants*, 203.

55. Poythress, *Understanding Dispensationalists*, 2nd ed., 24.

approach is selective and inconsistent when Old Testament prophecies clearly refer to the church in some way. In those cases Scofield claims a twofold meaning—literal and spiritual.[56] Poythress rightly concludes that this bifurcation is the result not of a plain-meaning hermeneutic but rather of an *a priori* determination of separate divine purposes for Israel and the church. This determination is based on the belief that the "mystery" (μυστήριον) of Ephesians 3:3 is the previously undisclosed church and not, for example, the manner in which Gentiles would be brought into a full share of God's covenant with Israel. Poythress goes on to cite other examples in which, without such an *a priori*, no spiritual versus literal meaning is otherwise discernible. For example, the promise of "showers of rain" in Zechariah 10:1 is interpreted with "both a physical and spiritual meaning: Rain as of old will be restored to Palestine, but also, there will be a mighty effusion of the Spirit upon restored Israel."[57] As Poythress points out, in Scofield's view, a double meaning is fine as long as the nonliteral does not apply to the church.

The fact that the New Testament writers frequently appropriate promises to and about the Old Testament people of God as being fulfilled in the New Testament presents no difficulty to the traditional dispensationalist since, ipso facto, there is conveniently a twofold meaning.

Ryrie attempts to improve on Scofield's formulation by preferring the term "normal usage" or "plain interpretation" since "literal" can be misunderstood to preclude clear figural meanings, such as imagery and metaphor.[58] Nonetheless, he defends the substance of Scofield's literal sense by asserting that all the prophecies that Jesus fulfilled were fulfilled literally.[59] Yet this does nothing to resolve the original difficulty.

When we encounter this bifurcation of the meaning of an Old Testament passage in interpretation, we must examine it to see if it is the product of the passage's plain meaning or the result of an *a priori* assumption based on something else. The "something else," according to Poythress, O. T. Allis, and Robertson, is that rather than being a hermeneutical issue, it is a metaphysical issue. That is, it is an *a priori* belief, based on a certain philosophical dualism, that all Old Testament promises must have their literal or earthly fulfillment in national Israel—except those that have a spiritual meaning because the New Testament writers apply them to the church.

While noting dispensationalism's insistence that this distinction arises from a literal interpretation of the Bible, Robertson continues,

> The dispensational distinction between the two purposes of God in history arises from a metaphysical rather than a hermeneutical presupposition . . . [because] basic to this distinction is a metaphysical or philosophical dichotomy between the material

---

56. Poythress, *Understanding Dispensationalists*, 2nd ed., 25.
57. Poythress, *Understanding Dispensationalists*, 2nd ed., 25; *Scofield Reference Bible*, 974.
58. Ryrie, *Dispensationalism Today*, 87.
59. Ryrie, *Dispensationalism Today*, 88.

and the spiritual realms. It is this distinction that actually lies at the root of the difference between dispensationalism and covenant theology. . . . Because covenant theology sees redemption from the perspective of creation, no dichotomy exists ultimately between redemption in the spiritual realm and redemption in the physical realm.[60]

Poythress alleges that, in reacting against "a dehistoricized understanding of the Bible" coming from critical and modernist approaches, dispensationalism fails to take full account of the differences between periods of redemptive history as progressive and organic.[61] In other words, as higher-critical approaches severed the organic connection of Old Testament history from the present experience of the church by questioning the Old Testament's historical veracity, Darby tried to uphold the veracity of that history yet account for the historical distance via a vertical dualism between the earthly and the spiritual. Covenant theology accounts for this historical distance by what it perceives as an organic progression within and between the epochs of redemptive history as history moves from promise to fulfillment. As Allis observed long ago, the contrast between the dispensations is one not of genus but of history.[62] And as Poythress reminds us, "Though present-day dispensationalists may differ from Darby here and there, the same appeal remains among them to this day."[63]

The Continuity of the Covenants

With regard to that progressive and organic relationship, Robertson thoroughly and exegetically demonstrates that each successive covenant of the Old Testament and the new covenant is explicitly described as an outworking of the previous covenants.[64] From the Abrahamic to the Mosaic (Ex. 2:24; 3:16–17; 6:4–8; 32:13–14; Pss. 105:8–12, 42–45; 106:45), from the Mosaic to the Davidic (Deut. 17; 2 Sam. 7:6, 23; 1 Kings 2:3; 1 Chron. 16:15–18), and from the Davidic to the new (Acts 13:34), each successive covenant claims continuity with the previous, and the new covenant claims continuity with them all. Scripture's testimony is of one unified purpose whose variety is the by-product of the progressive nature of the history of salvation. As Geerhardus Vos explains,

[Revelation] has not completed itself in one exhaustive act, but unfolded itself in a long series of successive acts . . . [because it] is inseparably attached to another activity of God, which we call *Redemption*. Now redemption could not be otherwise than historically successive, because it addresses itself to the generation of mankind coming into existence in the course of history.[65]

---

60. Robertson, *Christ of the Covenants*, 213.
61. Poythress, *Understanding Dispensationalists*, 2nd ed., 17.
62. Oswald T. Allis, "Modern Dispensationalism and the Law of God: An Examination of the Scofield Bible Teachings on the Dispensations," *EvQ* 8, no. 3 (July 1936): 272–89.
63. Poythress, *Understanding Dispensationalists*, 2nd ed., 16.
64. Robertson, *Christ of the Covenants*, chap. 3, "The Unity of the Divine Covenants," 27–63.
65. Geerhardus Vos, *Biblical Theology: Old and New Testaments* (Grand Rapids, MI: Eerdmans, 1948), 6–7.

In other words, redemptive history by necessity is progressive because it must take place in history, where redemption resolves the real effects of the fall.

Conditionality in a Gracious Covenant

A negative view of the law is also unwarranted given Scripture's covenant continuity. It is the law of Moses that will be written on the heart (Jer. 31:33) and that was confirmed and commended by Christ (Matt. 5:17). Dispensationalism has taught that the law imposed new conditions on Israel. Regarding Exodus 19:3, Scofield writes,

> Jehovah reminded the people that hitherto they had been the objects of His free grace; . . . the law was not *imposed* until it had been *proposed* and voluntarily accepted. . . . What, under law, was *condition*, is under grace, freely *given* to every believer. . . . The Abrahamic . . . and New . . . covenants minister salvation and assurance because they impose but one condition, faith.[66]

Such a view overlooks the conditionality present in the Abrahamic covenant. While it is correct to describe the dispensations of the covenant of grace as nonmeritorious, it is incorrect to describe them as unconditional. The dispensationalist and covenant theologian alike would agree that faith is a condition of covenant blessings. When Scofield, however, described the Abrahamic covenant as wholly gracious and unconditional, in the very next sentence he said, "The descendants of Abraham had but to abide in their own land to inherit every blessing."[67] He apparently sees the descent to Egypt during famine as an act of disobedience, one that causes the loss of covenant blessings.

The conditions for Abraham are much more than staying in the land. When renewing the promises with Isaac, God said, "And in your offspring all the nations of the earth shall be blessed, because Abraham obeyed my voice [בְּקֹלִי וַיִּשְׁמֹר] and kept my charge [מִשְׁמַרְתִּי], my commandments [מִצְוֺתַי], my statutes [חֻקּוֹתַי], and my laws [וְתוֹרֹתָי]" (Gen. 26:4–5). God not only makes it clear that the blessings of the covenant are conditioned on Abraham's obedience, but he uses a succession of terms that the original readers would closely associate with Mosaic legislation. Although the specific stipulations are not indicated beyond circumcision, Abraham had much of God's revealed will by which he was to walk. This obedience would result in blessings not only on Abraham's physical descendants but also on the nations.

This conditionality within God's gracious arrangement with Abraham harmonizes with Genesis 18:19 that the necessary condition of God fulfilling his covenant promises to Abraham was Abraham's obedience: "For I have chosen him, that [לְמַעַן] he may command his children and his household after him to keep the way of the LORD by doing righteousness and justice, so that [לְמַעַן] the LORD may bring to Abraham what

---

66. *Scofield Reference Bible*, 93; emphasis original.
67. *Scofield Reference Bible*, 20.

he has promised him." While faith, including Abraham's faith, is not a ground of legal merit, it is a necessary condition for the workings of God's covenants, particularly for experiencing covenant blessings.

Land/Inheritance

One of the material(!) elements of God's promise to Abraham and a crucial promise remaining to be fulfilled, according to dispensationalists, is the giving of the promised land to national Israel. What about the land promises from a covenant theology perspective? Anthony Hoekema has shown that for the covenant theologian, the land promises are not merely spiritualized in some dualistic way but rather are realized in history in the most expansive possible way in the new heavens and new earth, a corporeal, material existence in a redeemed, reconstituted, and consummated creation.[68] On this point Waltke issues a challenge to dispensationalists:

> The New Testament, though produced by Jewish Christians who lived in a time when the land was of constant concern for most Jews, shows no interest in it. If revised dispensationalism produced one passage in the entire New Testament that clearly presents the resettlement of national Israel in the land, I would join them. But I know of none![69]

Specifically, of the apostle Paul he notes in reference to Romans 4:13 that what had been promised to Abraham is not merely land, but the "world" (κοσμος): "Paul resignifies gē from 'land' in the Abrahamic covenant to 'earth.' This is more than an argument from silence." Along the same lines, the promised long life in the land (אֲדָמָה) given to Israel in the fifth commandment (Ex. 20:12; Deut. 5:16) becomes for Paul a promise to the Jewish-Gentile church in Ephesians 6:3. Reflecting on Jesus's promise that the Spirit would guide the apostles into all truth (John 16:13–14), Waltke asks, "Is it creditable that Jesus withheld from 'all things' and from 'what is yet to come' that his consummate, glorious kingdom will occur in a future millennium with a Jewish flavor?"[70] "In truth, none of the epistles . . . teach a future for national Israel in the land. The book of Hebrews denies it. The dispensationalist case from the New Testament rests chiefly on the symbolic imagery of the apocalypse, not on its clear letters and epistles."[71] If one takes seriously the great lengths to which the New Testament writers went to interpret the true meaning of the Old Testament Scriptures, such an omission is unimaginable.

What the New Testament writers do discuss explicitly is the inheritance that belongs to both Jewish and Gentile followers of Christ (Eph. 1:11, 14, 18). The נַחֲלָה

---

68. Anthony A. Hoekema, *The Bible and the Future* (Grand Rapids, MI: Eerdmans, 1979); see esp. chap. 20, "The New Earth," and chap. 15, "A Critique of Dispensational Premillennialism."
69. Waltke, "A Response," 357.
70. Waltke, "A Response," 357.
71. Waltke, "A Response," 358.

("inheritance")—which is so thoroughly woven into the Pentateuch (particularly Numbers and Deuteronomy) in reference to the land, rendered as κληρονομία or κλῆρος in the Greek Old Testament—refers in the New Testament to what belongs to the believer in Christ. Of particular note is the Greek terms' frequent usage in Ephesians and Hebrews (e.g., Heb. 9:15), the former emphasizing the oneness of Jew and Gentile and the latter appropriating the promises to Old Testament Israel to narrate salvation for the Christian. More than receiving a share in the new heavens and new earth, the saints' inheritance is God himself in the Spirit (Eph. 1:14)! To borrow an analogy, if a promise of one hundred dollars is paid by the gift of a million, it is hardly an unmet promise.

The Role of the Theocracy

Rather than seeing Old Testament Israel as having a literal earthly fulfillment, its earthliness should be attributed to its provisional typological purpose, only sufficient for a time to point forward to a future transcendent reality or antitype. National Israel in the Old Testament was incapable of being all that the law of God envisioned, principally because it lacked the efficient operation of God on their hearts (Deut. 29:4). If Old Testament Israel could not have become the consummated kingdom of God on earth prior to the work of Christ and the giving of the Spirit, what was its purpose? Vos answers,

> Here it cannot be denied that a real connection exists [between obedience and blessing]. . . . It belongs not to the legal sphere of merit, but to the symbolico-typical sphere of appropriateness of expression. As stated above, the abode of Israel in Canaan typified the heavenly, perfected state of God's people. Under these circumstances the ideal of absolute conformity to God's law of legal holiness had to be upheld. Even though they were not able to keep this law in the Pauline, spiritual sense, yea, even though they were unable to keep it externally and ritually, the requirement could not be lowered. When apostasy on a general scale took place, they could not remain in the promised land. When they disqualified themselves for typifying the state of holiness, they ipso facto disqualified themselves for typifying that of blessedness, and had to go into captivity.[72]

> The primary purpose of Israel's theocratic constitution was not to teach the world the principles of civil government, though undoubtedly in this respect also valuable lessons can be learned from it, but to reflect the eternal laws of religious intercourse between God and man as they will exist in the consummate life at the end.[73]

Similarly, Meredith Kline states,

---

72. Vos, *Biblical Theology*, 127.

73. Geerhardus Vos, *The Teaching of Jesus concerning the Kingdom of God and the Church* (Nutley, NJ: Presbyterian and Reformed, 1972), 50.

Although Israel's inheritance and continued enjoyment of the promises was not a matter of legal merit, there was a connection between the nation's corporate piety and prosperity. For the Old Testament theocratic kingdom prefigured the consummate kingdom of God, in which righteousness and glory are united. Accordingly, to keep the typical-prophetic picture clear God allowed the Israelites to enjoy the blessings of the typical kingdom only as they, and especially their official representatives, exhibited an appropriate measure of the righteousness of the kingdom. Since any righteousness that Israel possessed was a gift of grace from the God of their salvation, the principle which informs Deuteronomy 28 has no affinities with a religion of works-salvation.[74]

Rather than seeing national Israel as the end product of a preconsummative earthly program, we should see it as an imperfect, preconsummation approximation of a consummative fulfillment.

Replacement

Seeing the church as the flowering of God's promises to Israel is often met by the dispensationalist with the charge of "replacement theology," or "supersession." These terms are often brought forward as pejoratives to describe the covenant theologian's view that the church is the new Israel and heir to all the Old Testament promises.[75] The answer to this charge begins with looking to the Gospels, in which few people—a remnant of Israel and the odd Gentile here and there—received the good news of Jesus with joy, while the religious leaders and apparently the majority of the people rejected Jesus. Though tragic, this is not surprising since the history of Israel involved the regular refinement of a faithful remnant from out of wider apostasy. Additionally, the Latter Prophets had foretold a fourfold dynamic in the coming of the kingdom: salvation of repentant Israel, judgment on Israel's oppressors, judgment on hard-hearted Israel, and the gathering of a great number of Gentiles to Israel's God with the faithful remnant (Isa. 9:5; 55:5; 56:3).[76] Those Gentiles coming to Jesus in faith in the Gospels are signs of the kingdom's immanence. The Syrophoenician woman, just like the Gentile multitude who were fed in the wilderness, recognized that she was partaking in the blessings over which the descendants of Abraham had priority (Mark 7:24–30; 8:1–9). When the Greeks sought Jesus through Andrew, it marked the time for Jesus's hour of glorification because it was a sign that the kingdom had arrived (John 12:20–23).

The language of replacement or "supersession" should be avoided by the covenant theologian because it is not what covenant theology teaches, and covenant theology bears no association with anti-Semitic connotations that once accompanied the terms.

74. Meredith G. Kline, *Treaty of the Great King: The Covenant Structure of Deuteronomy; Studies and Commentary* (Grand Rapids, MI: Eerdmans, 1963), 124–25.
75. See, e.g., Michael J. Vlach, "Various Forms of Replacement Theology," *MSJ* 20, no. 1 (2009): 57–69.
76. Herman Ridderbos, *The Coming of the Kingdom* (Philadelphia: Presbyterian and Reformed, 1962), 5.

The church has not replaced Israel, but the faithful remnant of Israel is reaching its full flowering in the all-nations (including Israel) church until the consummation. If replacement is a concern, then it is the dispensationalist who should be concerned about a double-replacement system in which Israel is replaced by the church during the parenthesis age, which itself is replaced by national Israel. It removes from Israel its pride of place as being the missionary people who, scattered once again from Jerusalem as followers of Jesus, brought good news to the nations. Since dispensationalists believe that after the millennium the people of God in the new heavens and new earth will be a Jewish-Gentile people in the unmediated presence of God, who with the Lamb will be their temple (Rev. 21:22), it is counterintuitive that a separation should be introduced when the New Testament writers, Paul in particular, see the church as the flowering of Old Testament Israel. At the very least, the dispensationalist should produce explicit exegetical evidence to the contrary since the New Testament refers to followers of Christ using the semantic inventory that referred to Old Testament Israel (e.g., Ex. 19:5–6; 1 Pet. 2:9).

Rather than a hitherto undisclosed "mystery," the church age is precisely what Abraham might have imagined by faith on the night he looked at the stars in the greater light of God's promises—one day his descendants would be too numerous to count. It was just what Moses and Israel would have expected had the nation been faithful to their priestly mission of being a light to the nations and just what was promised to the royal Son of God when he was pledged the nations as an inheritance from God (Ps. 2:8). This is precisely the picture Paul paints in Romans 11:11–24: God grafted in wild branches (Gentiles) and cut off natural branches (unbelieving Israel), but there is nothing indicated there to limit the ratio of engrafted to natural branches. Zechariah had foretold that when God reestablished Jerusalem, it would be too numerous to be counted and too expansive for a stone wall to encompass it (Zech. 2:4–5).

Will natural branches be grafted back in? That is, will there be a large-scale ingathering of Jewish people back to God through Jesus Christ before the consummation? On this there are two views among covenant theologians, depending on one's understanding of Romans 11:26, "And in this way [οὕτως] all Israel will be saved." Robertson is among those who understand οὕτως to be used in a correlative sense to mean "in this way." The hardening of Israel mentioned in 11:25 is the mechanism by which "all Israel" will be saved—that is, Gentiles will come to Israel's Messiah by means of the hardening of Israel. Robertson argues, "Of the approximately 205 times in which the term occurs in the NT, the lexicon of Arndt and Gingrich does not cite a single instance to support the concept of a temporal significance."[77] This comes at the conclusion of a well-developed argument about the context and sequence Paul follows both in answering questions of

---

77. O. Palmer Robertson, "Is There a Distinctive Future for Ethnic Israel in Romans 11?," in *Perspectives on Evangelical Theology: Papers from the Thirtieth Annual Meeting of the Evangelical Theological Society*, ed. Kenneth S. Kantzer and Stanley N. Gundry (Grand Rapids, MI: Baker, 1979), 221.

Romans 11:1 ("Has God rejected his people?") and 11:11 ("Did they stumble in order that they might fall?"). Thus "all Israel" is the Jewish-Gentile community of Christ followers whom Paul elsewhere calls "the Israel of God" (Gal. 6:16).

Alternatively, John Murray believes that "Israel" in Romans 11:26 must be interpreted consistently with its usage throughout the chapter as it refers to ethnic Jews. Thus he takes the phrase temporally to mean "at that time all Israel will be saved," indicating that at a future time there will be a large ingathering of Jewish people to Christ, if for the present there is a hardening.[78]

Whichever the case, it should serve as a reminder to Gentile Christians, who constitute the vast majority of believers worldwide, of the need to be self-consciously grateful for the Jewish nation to whom the oracles of God were entrusted and for the Jewish followers of Jesus who were a light to the nations in their witness and works (Rom. 3:2). Although not due to any merit in themselves (Deut. 7:7), it was to Israel and through Israel that God gave the promise of an inheritance, and from them came not only the Messiah of Israel but the Savior of the whole world.

Regardless of which option is the better understanding of Romans 11:26, the covenant theologian's answer to whether God has rejected his people or whether Israel has stumbled so as to fall is the same as Paul's: "By no means!" (Rom. 3:4). According to Paul, a true Jew is the one who is inwardly a Jew by the operation of the Spirit of God (Rom. 2:29), because "if you are Christ's, then you are Abraham's offspring, heirs according to promise" (Gal. 3:29). This is the "Israel of God" (Gal. 6:16); these are the citizens of "the Jerusalem above" (Gal. 4:26).[79]

Israel and the Church

Thus it remains that the central issue and the material disagreement between dispensationalists and covenant theologians is the relationship between Israel and the church. And Scofield certainly understood that this issue was crucial:

> I believe that the failure of the Church to see that she is a separated, a called-out Body in the purposes of God, charged with a definite mission limited in its purpose and scope, and the endeavor to take from Israel her promises of earthly glory, and appropriate them over into this Church dispensation, has done more to swerve the Church from the appointed course than all other influences put together.
>
> It is not so much wealth, luxury, power, pomp, and pride that have served to deflect the Church from her appointed course, as the notion, founded upon Israelitish Old Testament promises, that the Church is of the world, and that therefore, her mission is to improve the world. Promises which were given to Israel alone are

---

78. John Murray, *The Epistle to the Romans*, NICNT (Grand Rapids, MI: Eerdmans, 1968), 2:96–97.

79. A more thorough treatment of this perspective on the relationship of Israel and the church is available in Hans K. LaRondelle, *The Israel of God in Prophecy: Principles of Prophetic Interpretation*, AUMSR 13 (Berrien Springs, MI: Andrews University Press, 1983), esp. chaps. 6–9.

quoted as justifying what we see all about us today. The Church, therefore, has failed to follow her appointed pathway of separation, holiness, heavenliness and testimony to an absent but coming Christ; she has turned aside from that purpose to the work of civilizing the world, building magnificent temples, and acquiring earthly power and wealth, and in this way, has ceased to follow in the footsteps of Him who had not where to lay His head. Did you ever put side by side the promises given to the Church, and to Israel, and see how absolutely in contrast they are? It is impossible to mingle them.[80]

Scofield saw the church's mission as fundamentally otherworldly and viewed it as compromised if it was overinvested in the affairs of this world, similar to Darby when he resigned his Anglican credentials.

The church of Jesus Christ is the flowering of God's Old Testament promises to Israel.[81] The ἐκκλησία of the New Testament draws on the semantic inventory of the קָהָל ("assembly") of the Old Testament. The New Testament writers seamlessly apply Old Testament references to Israel to the church of Jesus Christ (e.g., 1 Pet. 2:9; cf. Ex. 19:5). The most "Jewish" of New Testament books, the letter to the Hebrews, not only places followers of Christ immediately in the same shoes as the wilderness generation but presents the same prospects for not believing and falling short or believing until the end. As an impetus to reaching the promised land, Hebrews tells us that because Christ has entered in, "you have come to Mount Zion and to the city of the living God, the heavenly Jerusalem, and to innumerable angels in festal gathering, and to the assembly [ἐκκλησία] of the firstborn who are enrolled in heaven, and to God, the judge of all" (Heb. 12:22–23).

Under a "plain reading" of this passage, followers of Christ now dwell on the true Mount Zion, not a spiritualized noumenal one. This is because earthly Zion pointed not to itself but to the city that God would build through his Son. It exists now in the heavenly realm to be manifested historically on earth, not because it is a dualistic entity of the spiritual and the earthly but because it is a city of historical progression. For "we do not yet see everything in subjection to [Christ]" (Heb. 2:8), yet we will see this because what has been inaugurated in the heavens will be consummated on earth.

Temple

Though the Israel-church question is the most central, the question of the temple is a fitting place to conclude this examination of some of the most salient points of difference between covenant theologians and dispensationalists. Though for the dispensationalist the temple is a corollary of restored national Israel, it is of mutual

80. C. I. Scofield, *Prophecy Made Plain* (Greenville, SC: Gospel Hour, 1967), 52.

81. For a more detailed development of the church in the Old Testament, see Michael J. Glodo, "The Church in the Old Testament," *WSJ* 3 (Summer 2019): 63–80. See also D. A. Carson, "When Did the Church Begin?," *Themelios* 41, no. 1 (2016): 1–4.

interest to the covenant theologian since it epitomizes the great promise of God in its various forms, "I will be your God and you will be my people and I will dwell in your midst" (e.g., Lev. 26:12; Ezek. 37:26–27; Zech. 2:10–11; 2 Cor. 6:16; Rev. 21:3). It would be a mistake to think that the covenant theologian is not concerned with the temple. Has God promised a future, final temple? When we look to the consummation, we see that there is no longer a temple then and there (Rev. 21:11). Are dispensationalists right to expect that one will be rebuilt at a future time until then? Again, as with the land, the dispensationalist's expectations are too low. That temple has already been built in the resurrected Son of God. Not only is he described as such by John (John 2:21), but he presented himself to the Samaritan woman as the one in which Samaritan and Jew alike would worship in the dawning age of the Spirit (John 4:21–24). No longer would they be confined to their stone edifices that made for walls between their peoples, because a temple of the Spirit was coming that would unite every believer together in the resurrected and ascended Son; all nations would worship as one.[82] Specifically in reference to the competing temples, Edmund Clowney argues,

> Jesus does not direct the woman from Gerizim to Jerusalem, but from Gerizim to himself. . . . Salvation is of the Jews not because the temple is in Jerusalem but because the Messiah is in Sychar, sitting on the curbing of the well—"I that speak unto thee am he!"[83]

As to a future stone temple with a restored national Israel, Clowney concludes,

> If there is a way back to the ceremonial law, to the types and shadows of what has now become the bondage of legalism, then Paul labored and ran in vain—more than that, Christ died in vain. To promise to a people with the covenant name of Israel second-class citizenship in the kingdom of heaven by way of the restoration of an earthly economy with a temple of stone, that is surely to obscure the gospel that is the power of God to salvation to everyone that believes, Jew or Greek.[84]

The eschatology of Jesus and the apostles in general and with respect to the temple is to produce an ethical life born out of interest in living stones of the temple of the Spirit rather than a speculative futurism preoccupied with the dead stones of an earthly temple. This is the vision and mission of God for his final temple according to the ethical admonition of 1 Peter 2:4–5 and 9:

> As you come to him, a living stone rejected by men but in the sight of God chosen and precious, you yourselves like living stones are being built up as a spiritual

---

82. For the relevant case for seeing πνεῦμα as referring to the Holy Spirit, see Herman Ridderbos, *The Gospel of John: A Theological Commentary* (Grand Rapids, MI: Eerdmans, 1997), 163–64.
83. Edmund P. Clowney, "The Final Temple," *WTJ* 35, no. 2 (1973): 176.
84. Clowney, "Final Temple," 189.

house, to be a holy priesthood, to offer spiritual sacrifices acceptable to God through Jesus Christ. . . .

You are a chosen race, a royal priesthood, a holy nation, a people for his own possession, that you may proclaim the excellencies of him who called you out of darkness into his marvelous light.

Conclusion

Given the highly developed and self-coherent system of dispensationalism acknowledged at the start, the attempt has been made here to present a holistic alternative with deeper analysis at particular points. The Westminster Confession of Faith 7.5–6 summarizes this alternative system as follows:

> 5. This covenant [of grace] was differently administered in the time of the law, and in the time of the gospel: under the law, it was administered by promises, prophecies, sacrifices, circumcision, the paschal lamb, and other types and ordinances delivered to the people of the Jews, all fore-signifying Christ to come; which were for that time sufficient and efficacious, through the operation of the Spirit, to instruct and build up the elect in faith in the promised Messiah, by whom they had full remission of sins, and eternal salvation; and is called the Old Testament.
>
> 6. Under the gospel, when Christ the substance was exhibited, the ordinances in which this covenant is dispensed are the preaching of the word, and the adminis-tration of the sacraments of Baptism and the Lord's supper; which, though fewer in number, and administered with more simplicity and less outward glory, yet in them it is held forth in more fulness, evidence and spiritual efficacy, to all nations, both Jews and Gentiles; and is called the New Testament. There are not therefore two covenants of grace differing in substance, but one and the same under various dispensations.

The kingdom of God was not delayed but rather inaugurated in the life and ministry of Jesus Christ (Luke 11:20). The strong man has been bound (Mark 3:27). The ruler of this world has been cast down (John 12:31). The one who is greater than the temple has come, has died, and has been raised (Matt. 12:6; John 2:19). Heaven and earth have been reconciled in his humiliation and exaltation (Col. 1:15–20). This is the Christian hope of the "not yet," grounded in the "already." Let us look not to current events but to the sky for Christ's appearing again, in order to find grace to persevere in this "not yet" time in such a way that our ethical life manifests his "now" reign.

26

New Covenant Theologies

Scott R. Swain

Covenant is not the principal theme of Christian theology.[1] That distinction belongs to the doctrine of God alone. God is not only "the Alpha and the Omega" (Rev. 1:8) in the order of being, he is also the Alpha and Omega in the order of theological understanding. As the Leiden Synopsis observes, God is the "primary *locus* of theology from which all others flow forth, by which they are held together, and to which they should be directed."[2] "From him and through him and to him are all things. To him be glory forever" (Rom. 11:36). While the doctrine of God is the principal theme of Christian theology, it is not the only theme of Christian theology, and this follows because the God who exists in and of himself wills also that creatures should exist alongside himself. Because God is the Creator, Redeemer, and Consummator of all things, not only God but also creatures are objects of theological understanding. Christian theology is thus concerned with "God and all things in relation to God."[3]

Covenant becomes a topic of theological analysis and understanding when we turn our attention to the relation between God and the creature made in his image. As Creator and King, God exercises sovereign "dominion" over all he has made: "The LORD is a great God, and a great King above all gods" (Ps. 95:3). Because he made them, all creatures are "in his hand" (Ps. 95:4–5), possessed and moved by God according to his sovereign goodness, in accordance with their various natures, toward the various ends he has appointed for them (Gen. 1:1–2:3; Eph. 1:9–11). Whereas God exercises sovereign

---

1. I am grateful to Richard C. Barcellos, Robert J. Cara, Christina Mansfield, Andy Naselli, and Stephen J. Wellum for their helpful comments on an earlier draft of this chapter.
2. Dolf te Velde, ed., *Synopsis of a Purer Theology*, trans. Riemer A. Faber, SMRT 187 (Leiden: Brill, 2015), 6.1.
3. John Webster, *God without Measure: Working Papers in Theology*, vol. 1, *God and the Works of God* (London: T&T Clark, 2016), 117.

"dominion" over all creatures, God exercises sovereign "government" over creatures made in his image, creatures designed for a personal relationship with God characterized by mutual knowledge and love.[4] Here is where covenant comes into play, as an instrument of God's sovereign government, whereby he possesses and moves creatures made in his image toward the ends he has appointed for them. Within his covenant, the Lord addresses those who are "the people of his pasture, and the sheep of his hand" by means of his "voice" (Ps. 95:7): presenting himself to them as their God, instructing them in the way of life, and directing them to their ultimate beatitude in his presence, the "rest" he has appointed for them since the creation of the world (Ps. 95:11; Heb. 4:3–9). "I will be your God, and you will be my people" is the essence of the covenant promise and the ultimate end of the covenant bond (cf. Lev. 26:12; Rev. 21:3, 7).

God presents himself to us in Holy Scripture as one who makes and fulfills a "new" (Jer. 31:31) or "everlasting" covenant with his people (Isa. 55:3; Jer. 32:40; Ezek. 16:60), a covenant also described as a "covenant of peace" (Isa. 54:10; Ezek. 37:26). Though the new covenant is not the principal theme of Christian theology, Scripture presents the new covenant as the climactic covenantal act in the history of God with his people. In the new covenant, God's relationship with his people is forever secured, and God's dwelling among his people is fully enjoyed (Gen. 17:7–8; Lev. 26:12; Ezek. 36:28; 43:7, 9; 2 Cor. 6:16–18; Rev. 21:3, 7). In the new covenant, all God's prior covenant promises find their ultimate fulfillment, their ultimate "Yes" (2 Cor. 1:20).[5] Scripture, moreover, presents this covenant as finding its realization in and through Jesus Christ, the "mediator" of the new covenant (Heb. 9:15; 12:24). Jesus Christ is the ultimate recipient of all God's covenant promises and the one in and through whom those covenant promises are bestowed on God's people (Gen. 22:17–18; Luke 22:20, 29; John 1:14–18; Acts 2:33; Gal. 3:16, 26–29).[6] "In him" and "through him," all God's covenant promises find their "Yes" and "Amen" to the glory of God (2 Cor. 1:20).

According to Scripture, the new covenant not only represents the climactic, Christ-centered fulfillment of God's covenant promises, it also represents a change, in some sense, relative to the Mosaic, or "old," covenant. According to Jeremiah, the new covenant that God will make with the house of Israel and the house of Judah in coming days

---

4. On the distinction between God's sovereign "dominion" and "government," see Francis Turretin, *Institutes of Elenctic Theology*, trans. George Musgrave Giger, ed. James T. Dennison Jr. (Phillipsburg, NJ: P&R, 1992–1997), 1.3.22.

5. In Isa. 54–55, Paul R. Williamson observes a

piling up of covenant echoes: the Abrahamic covenant is alluded to in verses 1–3 (cf. Gen. 22:17); the Sinai covenant is picked up in verses 4–8; the Noahic covenant comes into focus in verses 9–10; and the Davidic covenant is introduced in Isaiah 55:3–4. Together this suggests that this "covenant of peace" (or in the case of the next chapter, the "everlasting covenant") constitutes the climactic covenant in which all the major divine-human covenants find their ultimate fulfilment.

Sealed with an Oath: Covenant in God's Unfolding Purpose, NSBT 23 (Downers Grove, IL: InterVarsity Press, 2007), 161.

6. David Gibson, "'Fathers of Faith, My Fathers Now!' On Abraham, Covenant, and the Theology of Paedobaptism," *Themelios* 40, no. 1 (2015): 14–34.

(Jer. 31:31) is "not like the covenant that I made with their fathers on the day when I took them by the hand to bring them out of the land of Egypt" (Jer. 31:32). Speaking of what Jesus Christ has accomplished "in one body through the cross" (Eph. 2:16), Paul says that Christ's new covenant work has "abolish[ed] the law of commandments expressed in ordinances" (Eph. 2:15), a clear allusion to Mosaic stipulations.[7] In similar fashion, Hebrews states that the priestly ministry of Jesus Christ brings about a "change in the priesthood" and therefore a "change in the law" relative to Mosaic legislation regarding the Levitical priesthood (Heb. 7:12). In what seems to be an even more sweeping claim, Hebrews elsewhere says that the new covenant has made the old covenant "obsolete" (Heb. 8:13).[8]

Though the Scriptures repeatedly contrast the new covenant with the old covenant, they also insist that the difference between these two covenants is relative, not absolute.[9] In 2 Corinthians 3, for example, Paul identifies a number of striking contrasts between the old and new covenants. He contrasts the agencies of the old and new covenants, the former operating by "the letter" and the latter operating by "the Spirit" (3:6). He also contrasts the effects and objects of old and new covenant agencies. Whereas the old covenant "kills," the new covenant "gives life" (3:6). Whereas the old covenant was written "on tablets of stone," the new covenant is written "on tablets of human hearts" (3:3). Nevertheless, the contrast Paul observes between old and new covenants is relative, not absolute. There was indeed "glory in the ministry of condemnation," the apostle affirms, albeit a glory that pales in comparison to that of the new covenant, which "must far exceed" the old covenant in glory (3:9). Here we are dealing with the difference between a puppy and a dog, not the difference between a dog and a cat. Though Paul can say that the old covenant "has come to have no glory at all" in the new covenant epoch (3:10), its lack of glory is not categorical but redemptive-historical, pertaining to the obsolescence of the old covenant *as a covenant* (Rom. 6:14; Gal. 5:18).[10] According to Paul, both old and new covenants may be categorized as ministries endowed with divine glory, the former by a glory that is temporary and fading, the latter by a glory that is eternal and enduring (2 Cor. 3:11).[11] In the new covenant, the yelp of the puppy has been replaced by the bark of the dog.

---

7. Brian S. Rosner, *Paul and the Law: Keeping the Commandments of God*, NSBT 31 (Downers Grove, IL: InterVarsity Press, 2013), 24.

8. On the theme of the "repudiation" and "replacement" of the law more broadly, see Rosner, *Paul and the Law*, chap. 2.

9. For a helpful survey of the diverse ways in which Paul relates to the Mosaic covenant, see Rosner, *Paul and the Law*, along with Guy Waters's excellent review of Rosner: "Paul and the Law," *Reformation21* (blog), December 17, 2013, http://www.reformation21.org/shelf-life/paul-and-the-law.php.

10. According to Rosner, the contrast between "letter" and "Spirit" in 2 Cor. 3 and other Pauline texts concerns "a contrast in terms of salvation history," with the Mosaic covenant being "an obsolete Jewish legal code, from which Christians are exempt." *Paul and the Law*, 98–100.

11. The rest of Scripture confirms this pattern. To highlight but one central example, though a superficial reading of the Bible might lead one to conclude that the work of Christ and the Spirit is a distinctive feature of the new covenant over against the old covenant, Scripture portrays Christ and the Spirit as operative within both covenants. The Spirit who leads us in the new exodus (Rom. 8:14) is the same Spirit who led Israel in the first

Accounting for the place of the new covenant as the climactic, Christ-centered fulfill-ment of all previous covenant administrations, while observing the relative contrast that obtains between God's work in the old covenant and his work in the new covenant, is one of the greatest challenges for biblical interpretation and theological understanding. For this reason, the new covenant remains a topic of controversy in Christian theology. Different understandings of the new covenant inform different understandings of the character of God's unfolding kingdom, the shape of the moral life, and the character of the church as the new covenant community. These different understandings of the new covenant are often, in turn, related to different approaches to biblical interpretation.

The purpose of the present chapter is to consider how recent "new covenant the-ologies" address the aforementioned challenge.[12] As we will see, these new covenant theologies are committed to the primacy of biblical theology as an interpretive method and to providing a consistent, systematic account of the place of the new covenant within the unfolding ways of God with his people. Though their interpretive conclu-sions differ in certain respects, they share a common desire to transcend the limitations they perceive in both dispensationalism and Reformed covenant theology.[13] The primary goal in considering these approaches is neither descriptive nor polemical. The aim of the present chapter is not to provide an exhaustive overview of recent new covenant theolo-gies. Nor is it to provide a point-by-point critique of their arguments. The primary goal in considering these proposals is both hermeneutical and theological: to gain a better sense of how we should approach biblical teaching on the new covenant in order that we may gain deeper theological understanding of the place of the new covenant within God's unfolding kingdom purpose.

Our discussion proceeds as follows. First, we consider some of the common features of recent new covenant theologies with the aim of clarifying the "state of the question" in the debate between new covenant theologies and Reformed covenant theology (sec-

---

exodus (Isa. 63:11). The Spirit who dwells in our midst by virtue of the new covenant (1 Cor. 3:16) is the same Spirit who dwelt in Israel's midst by virtue of the old covenant (Hag. 2:5). The Christ who spiritually nourishes us in the Lord's Supper is the same Christ who spiritually nourished "our fathers" in the wilderness (1 Cor. 10:1–4). Though the work of Christ and the Spirit in the new covenant far surpasses their work in the old covenant in terms of its immediacy and in terms of the freedom and confidence it effects for God's people (Rom. 8:15; Gal. 3:23–4:7; Heb. 10:19–25; 12:18–28), both old covenant saints and new covenant saints drink of one and the same Spirit from one and the same Christ (1 Cor. 10:4; 12:13). And indeed, this must be the case because the triune Lord of both old and new covenants is "one" (Deut. 6:4; 1 Cor. 8:4–6). The difference between the work of Christ and the Spirit within the old covenant and their work within the new covenant is relative, not absolute; redemptive-historical, not categorical.

12. Within the framework of its own confessions, Reformed theology exhibits a diverse range of approaches to addressing this challenge. These, however, are not the focus of the present chapter. For two recent forays into the debate within Reformed theology, see Bryan D. Estelle, J. V. Fesko, and David VanDrunen, eds., *The Law Is Not of Faith: Essays on Works and Grace in the Mosaic Covenant* (Phillipsburg, NJ: P&R, 2009); Cornelis P. Venema, *Christ and Covenant Theology: Essays on Election, Republication, and Covenants* (Phillipsburg, NJ: P&R, 2017).

13. It is important to note that the new covenant theologies considered in this chapter seek to transcend not only historic Reformed and Presbyterian accounts of covenant theology but also historic Baptist accounts as expressed, for example, in the Second London Baptist Confession (1689). The debate between covenant theol-ogy and new covenant theologies is therefore not a debate between Presbyterians and Baptists but between two competing approaches to the interpretation and application of Holy Scripture.

tion 1). Second, operating on the principle that positive theological description is often the best polemic, we consider how a Reformed understanding of the place of the new covenant within God's unfolding kingdom better accounts for scriptural teaching on significant points of disagreement with new covenant theologies while setting some of the positive contributions of new covenant theologies on a firmer theological and hermeneutical foundation (sections 2–4). A brief conclusion rounds out the discussion.

New Covenant Theologies: Clarifying the State of the Question

"New covenant theologies" as an umbrella category refers to recent theological proposals that seek to describe the significance of the new covenant for Christian theology and practice. New covenant theologies, as discussed here, include the proposals of certain Baptist/baptistic theologians who describe their approaches under the labels of *new covenant theology* (hereafter NCT)[14] and *progressive covenantalism* (hereafter PC).[15] These proposals are by no means monolithic.[16] But they do share a number of family resemblances when it comes to theological foundations, theological method, and theological conclusions that warrant their consideration under one broad category.

New covenant theologies share a common theological foundation in the biblical exegesis of New Testament scholars such as D. A. Carson, Douglas Moo, and Peter T. O'Brien, with Carson's exegesis of Matthew's Sermon on the Mount providing what is perhaps the cornerstone of this foundation.[17] New covenant theologies also share a common commitment to the primacy of biblical theology for theological method, convinced that biblical theology provides the best hermeneutical strategy for allowing Holy Scripture's distinctive literary forms and redemptive-historical shape to exercise supreme authority over the church's doctrine and life.[18] In keeping with this commitment, new covenant theologies are especially concerned with tracing the historical trajectory of biblical revelation across various covenant epochs to its climactic fulfillment in the

---

14. Much of the literature of new covenant theology is self-published and therefore difficult to access. Representative works include John G. Reisinger, *Tablets of Stone* (Southbridge, MA: Crowne, 1989); Tom Wells and Fred Zaspel, *New Covenant Theology: Description, Definition, Defense* (Frederick, MD: New Covenant Media, 2002); A. Blake White, *What Is New Covenant Theology? An Introduction* (Frederick, MD: New Covenant Media, 2012).

15. Peter J. Gentry and Stephen J. Wellum, *Kingdom through Covenant: A Biblical-Theological Understanding of the Covenants*, 2nd ed. (Wheaton, IL: Crossway, 2018) (hereafter *KTC*); Stephen J. Wellum and Brent E. Parker, eds., *Progressive Covenantalism: Charting a Course between Dispensational and Covenant Theologies* (Nashville: B&H Academic, 2016).

16. Though they share many family resemblances, NCT and PC are not identical. Peter J. Gentry and Stephen J. Wellum, two of the major proponents of PC, originally described their view as a "subset" of NCT. On further reflection, however, they have since distanced themselves from this description because of the various disagreements that characterize the two approaches. Those disagreements include the existence of a covenant between God and man in creation, the nature of Christ's active obedience and the imputation of Christ's righteousness to believers, the place of the law of Moses in the Christian life, and the presence of "conditions" in God's various covenant administrations. Wellum and Parker, *Progressive Covenantalism*, 2–3; *KTC*, 35. In many ways, PC is "NCT 2.0."

17. NB: Carson, Moo, and O'Brien do not seem to self-identify with any of the proposals that have built on their exegesis.

18. Wells and Zaspel, *New Covenant Theology*, 20–22; *KTC*, chap. 1.

gospel of Jesus Christ. And as is common in the foundational literature on which they build, new covenant theologies tend to be preoccupied with questions of "continuity" and "discontinuity" along the historical trajectory of revelation.[19]

Along with their common theological foundation and theological method, new covenant theologies also share a number of common theological conclusions, which may be summarized under three headings. First, like Reformed covenant theology, new covenant theologies perceive a deep unity within God's unfolding purpose in history. According to Tom Wells, a leading proponent of NCT, "God has a single purpose of redemption running throughout history. History proceeds toward a single goal of a re-deemed world populated by a redeemed people. More than that this goal comes to frui-tion by a single Redeemer."[20] Using language common to Reformed covenant theology, PC describes the unity of God's unfolding purpose under the categories of "kingdom" and "covenant." God the sovereign King of creation progressively realizes his kingdom purpose by means of successive covenant administrations, which form "the backbone of Scripture's metanarrative."[21] According to Stephen J. Wellum, "God's *one, eternal plan* unfolds in history through a *plurality* of interrelated covenants, starting with Adam and creation and culminating in Christ and the new covenant."[22] For both NCT and PC, Holy Scripture proclaims the message of one divine King working to fulfill one saving purpose that reaches its climax in Jesus Christ, the mediator of the new covenant.

Second, the fundamental unity of God's saving purpose across redemptive history leads new covenant theologies to view the contrast between old and new covenants as relative rather than absolute. Though NCT sees a more radical contrast between the two covenants than do other new covenant theologies, NCT insists that the "newness" of the new covenant is not an "absolute category."[23] Wells states, "Flowing as it does from the mind and heart of the single, self-consistent God, the New Covenant could not be novel in every respect. But within the constraints imposed by his own inner self-consistency, the Lord declares its substantive dissimilarity to the covenant that preceded it."[24]

Though he does not fall under the umbrella of new covenant theologies as described above, Brian Rosner's sophisticated account of the variety of ways in which Paul de-scribes the relationship between the old and new covenants deserves mention in this context, particularly because of its influence on PC. On the one hand, according to Rosner, Paul "repudiates" the old covenant *as a covenant administration*, arguing that the people of God are no longer bound to the old covenant, and "replaces" it with the

---

19. As Craig A. Blaising observes, this preoccupation is not entirely helpful since "continuity" and "discontinu-ity" are not categories pressed on us by the literary form and redemptive-historical shape of biblical revelation. "A Critique of Gentry and Wellum's *Kingdom through Covenant*: A Hermeneutical-Theological Response," *MSJ* 26, no. 1 (2015): 114–15. We return to this criticism below.
20. Wells and Zaspel, *New Covenant Theology*, 44.
21. *KTC*, 31.
22. Wells and Zaspel, *New Covenant Theology*, 9–14, 50, 52; *KTC*, 36.
23. Wells and Zaspel, *New Covenant Theology*, 46.
24. Wells and Zaspel, *New Covenant Theology*, 46.

new covenant. On the other hand, according to Rosner, Paul "reappropriates" the old covenant for the people of God living under the new covenant, and that in two ways. Paul reappropriates the old covenant "as prophecy" that bears witness to the gospel of Jesus Christ and "as wisdom" that guides the conduct of the people of God living under the new covenant.[25] In a manner similar to Rosner, PC argues that although the people of God are no longer under the old covenant *as a covenant administration*, the old covenant still holds relevance for the people of God *as Scripture*. According to PC, the old covenant anticipates the gospel of Jesus Christ typologically in its persons, events, and institutions. And the old covenant contains moral teaching that may be applied to the people of God within the context of the new covenant.[26]

When it comes to the abiding moral significance of the old covenant for the new covenant community, new covenant theologies draw two further conclusions that distinguish their approaches from that of Reformed covenant theology: (1) because they view the Mosaic covenant as an indivisible whole, they reject the traditional threefold division of Mosaic stipulations into moral, civil, and ceremonial laws; and (2) consistent with the previous judgment, new covenant theologies do not regard the Ten Commandments as the Mosaic expression of God's unchanging moral law for human beings at all times and all places.[27] This does not mean that new covenant theologies see no place for the Ten Commandments in the Christian life. Although the Ten Commandments no longer bind the new covenant community *as a covenant*, the Ten Commandments are instructive for the new covenant community *as Scripture*. Accordingly, in keeping with their biblical-theological method, new covenant theologies seek to discern the abiding relevance of the Ten Commandments by viewing them on a historical trajectory that begins with the revelation of God's moral will for humanity in creation and that is fulfilled with the revelation of God's moral will in Jesus Christ. On this trajectory, new covenant theologies discern various degrees of continuity and discontinuity with respect to God's moral will across various covenant administrations, concluding that certain commandments, notably the Sabbath command, no longer apply to God's people,[28] while other commandments continue to apply to God's people, albeit in a manner "transformed" and "advanced" by Christ within the context of the new covenant.[29]

---

25. For a summary of these moves, see Rosner, *Paul and the Law*, 39–41.

26. *KTC*, chap. 18 (see *KTC*, 788, where Wellum cites Rosner's proposal positively).

27. Reisinger, *Tablets of Stone*; Wells and Zaspel, *New Covenant Theology*, 149–56; *KTC*, 694, 696–97; cf. Rosner, *Paul and the Law*, 36–37, 43.

28. Wells and Zaspel, *New Covenant Theology*, chaps. 13–14; Thomas R. Schreiner, "Good-Bye and Hello: The Sabbath Command for New Covenant Believers," in Wellum and Parker, *Progressive Covenantalism*, 159–88. Compare Schreiner's conclusion with that of Wellum, who argues that the Sabbath command should be applied to God's people, albeit "in light of its fulfillment" in the new covenant, though he does not specify what such an application might look like. *KTC*, 797. A foundational text for the aforementioned views of the Sabbath is D. A. Carson, ed., *From Sabbath to Lord's Day: A Biblical, Historical, and Theological Investigation* (Grand Rapids, MI: Zondervan, 1982).

29. Wells and Zaspel, *New Covenant Theology*, chaps. 9–10; *KTC*, 788–98. Zaspel uses the language of "advance." Wells and Zaspel, *New Covenant Theology*, 118. Wellum uses the language of "transformation." *KTC*, 789, 797.

Third, along with the transformation of God's moral will, new covenant theologies contend that the new covenant brings about a transformation of God's people as a people. Among new covenant theologies, NCT posits the most radical distinction between the people of God under the old covenant and the people of God under the new covenant. For NCT, the coming of the new covenant brings a new people of God *into being*.[30] Israel and the church are thus different peoples formed on the basis of different covenants.

According to PC, the distinction between the people of God under the old covenant and the people of God under the new covenant is less radical. "God has *one* people," Wellum insists, "yet there is an Israel-church distinction due to their respective covenants."[31] By virtue of its "union with Christ, the church is God's *new* covenant people, in continuity with the elect in all ages but *different* from Israel in its nature and structure."[32] In terms of its nature, unlike the old covenant community, which was constituted as a "mixed" community of regenerate and unregenerate members, the new covenant community is constituted as an "unmixed" community of regenerate members.[33] In terms of its structure, while God related to his old covenant people in an indirect manner, by means of anointed prophets, priests, and kings, and by means of a "genealogical principle," whereby God's covenant promises belong to believers and their children, God relates to his new covenant people in a direct manner. Through union with Christ, the mediator of the new covenant, all God's people are anointed as prophets, priests, and kings. Moreover, PC argues, in the new covenant community, the genealogical principle no longer applies.[34]

In sum, new covenant theologies share a number of family resemblances. New covenant theologies share a common theological foundation in the biblical exegesis of several leading evangelical New Testament scholars. New covenant theologies share a common theological method, seeking to account for the place and purpose of the new covenant in Holy Scripture primarily by means of biblical-theological analysis.[35] And they share a number of common theological conclusions, which are useful for comparing and contrasting new covenant theologies with Reformed covenant theology.

Like Reformed covenant theology, new covenant theologies perceive a deep unity within God's unfolding purpose in redemptive history. Like Reformed covenant theology, new covenant theologies perceive old and new covenants as part of God's one saving plan in redemptive history, differing from each other in a relative rather than an absolute sense. Unlike Reformed covenant theology, however, new covenant theologies perceive

---

30. Wells and Zaspel, *New Covenant Theology*, 9–14, 50, 52, 57.
31. *KTC*, 36.
32. *KTC*, 36, 748–49, 801.
33. *KTC*, 802–3, 807–12.
34. *KTC*, 749–50, 807–12. Wellum states, "*All* those in the church know God in a direct and immediate fashion." *KTC*, 752. On the implications of PC for infant baptism, see *KTC*, 812–24.
35. The exceptions to this are Wellum's systematic-theological chapters in *KTC*.

both continuity and discontinuity when it comes to God's moral will for his people under the old and new covenants. Furthermore, unlike Reformed covenant theology, new covenant theologies perceive both continuity and discontinuity regarding the being, nature, and structure of God's people under the old and new covenants. Whereas NCT perceives two peoples of God existing under two covenants, old and new, PC perceives the existence of one people of God from Abraham to Jesus Christ that, under the new covenant, receives a new nature and a new structure.

Comparing and contrasting new covenant theologies with Reformed covenant theology enables us to define more clearly the state of the question regarding the place of the new covenant within God's unfolding kingdom. The question at stake between new covenant theologies and Reformed covenant theology is not about whether one and the same God initiates all covenant administrations with his people or about whether one and the same God pursues one saving purpose across various covenant administrations. Though new covenant theologies are reticent to describe God's unified saving purpose under the rubric of the "covenant of grace," they nevertheless perceive a fundamental unity in the plan of salvation that begins with God's promises to Adam and Eve in Genesis 3:15 and finds fulfillment in the gospel of Jesus Christ, "born of a woman, born under the law, to redeem . . ." (Gal. 4:4).

Differences between new covenant theologies and Reformed covenant theology come into play with respect to the moral and communal entailments of God's one saving purpose. On this topic, whereas Reformed covenant theology perceives a fundamental unity, new covenant theologies perceive varying degrees of continuity and discontinuity across the various covenants God makes with his people. When it comes to the meaning and significance of the new covenant within God's unfolding kingdom, the question at stake between new covenant theologies and Reformed covenant theology concerns the shape of the moral life and the character of the covenant community. The question does not concern theology proper and soteriology but sanctification and ecclesiology. And yet, though sanctification and ecclesiology are the presenting issues in the debate between Reformed covenant theology and new covenant theologies, deeper issues related to creation and anthropology, and also to biblical interpretation, underlie the debate as well.

The Place of the New Covenant in Reformed Covenant Theology: Jeremiah 31:31–34

The new covenant theologies surveyed above offer distinctive construals of the place of the new covenant within God's unfolding kingdom. Their proposals share common ground with Reformed covenant theology in perceiving one saving purpose of God across various covenant administrations. They differ from Reformed covenant theology in their contention that the new covenant transforms the shape of the moral life and the character of the covenant community. In the remainder of this chapter, we focus on how a Reformed understanding of the new covenant addresses these two fundamental points of dispute. We begin our discussion with a look at Jeremiah 31:31–34, a text that functions as a *crux interpretum* in the debate. Jeremiah 31:31–34 helpfully orients our discussion in two ways. First, this text affirms the climactic nature of the new covenant within the context of a relative contrast between the new covenant and the old covenant. Second, this text addresses the two areas of debate between Reformed covenant theology and new covenant theologies, namely, sanctification and ecclesiology.

Jeremiah 31:31–34 begins with the Lord's solemn declaration that, in coming days, he is going to "make a new covenant with the house of Israel and the house of Judah," a covenant "not like the covenant" he made with their fathers when he brought them out of Egypt, a covenant "that they broke" (31:31–32). In the new covenant, God promises to do four things. First, he promises to write his law on the hearts of his people (31:33). Second, he promises to renew the covenant bond between himself and his people, repeating the oft-cited covenant formula "I will be their God, and they shall be my people" (31:33). Third, he promises that just as the law will be internalized in the new covenant, so too will it be universalized: "No longer shall each one teach his neighbor and each his brother, saying, 'Know the Lord,' for they shall all know me, from the least of them to the greatest, declares the Lord" (31:34). Fourth, he promises full and final forgiveness of his people's sins: "I will forgive their iniquity, and I will remember their sin no more" (31:34).

As Paul R. Williamson observes, the new covenant as presented in Jeremiah 31:31– 34 exhibits three features common to the old covenant: "It encompasses the same people (Israel and Judah); it involves the same obligation (Yahweh's law); and it serves to secure the same objective (a divine-human relationship) expressed by the same covenant formula."[36] First, the new covenant concerns the "same people" as the old covenant. In the new covenant, God will not leave Israel and Judah behind and take another nation to be his covenant people, but as other new covenant texts make clear, he will extend his covenant with Israel and Judah to embrace other nations as well (Ezek. 16:59–63). Second, the new covenant concerns the "same obligation" as the old covenant. In the new covenant, God will not abandon "[his] law" that he previously set before his people and their fathers (Jer. 44:10), though Israel and Judah have repeatedly rejected and forsaken it (Jer. 6:19; 9:13; 16:11). Instead, he will write "[his] law" on their hearts (Jer. 31:33). Third, the new covenant concerns the "same objective" as the old covenant. In the new covenant, God will not rend the covenant bond that he made with Abraham and his offspring (Gen. 17:7–8), which he fulfilled when he delivered Israel from Egypt (Ex. 6:7) and came to dwell in their midst (Ex. 29:46). Though Israel and Judah have broken the covenant bond (Jer. 31:32), the Lord promises that he will so renew and perfect it that it will never be broken again (Jer. 31:35–37; Ezek. 16:59–63).[37]

---

36. Williamson, *Sealed with an Oath*, 153.
37. For this reading of Ezekiel 16, see *KTC*, chap. 14.

Herein lies the fundamental basis for Reformed theology's claim that there is one covenant of grace that unfolds across various covenant administrations. The covenant bond, expressed in the covenant formula "I will be your God, and you will be my people" undergirds each successive covenant administration from Abraham through Moses to the new covenant in Jesus Christ (Gen. 17:7–8; Lev. 26:12; 2 Sam. 7:14; 2 Cor. 6:16, 18; Rev. 21:3, 7). The "backbone" of the scriptural storyline is not merely God's sovereign *plan*; it is God's sovereign *promise*, his gracious self-commitment to be the God of this people—through the thick and thin of his faithfulness and their unfaithfulness—at the cost of his beloved Son, to the enrichment of his people and to the glory of his name.

How, then, will the new covenant transcend the old covenant? In what sense will it be *unlike* the covenant the Lord made with Israel when he brought them out of Egypt? Jeremiah 31:31–34 indicates two ways in which the new covenant will transcend the old covenant. First, the Lord's work of internalizing the law within the hearts of his people will be universal in scope. According to Williamson, "It is perhaps this, more than anything else, that constitutes the most radical distinctive of the new covenant."[38] As Williamson helpfully observes, the *internalization* of the law is not the most radical distinctive of the new covenant, for the internalization of the law was required in the old covenant as well (Deut. 10:16; 11:18), and prophets like Jeremiah repeatedly pronounced the curses of the old covenant on those who failed to internalize its instruction (Jer. 4:4; 9:25–26).[39] Moreover, within the context of the old covenant itself, God promised that he would write his law on the hearts of those who had fallen under the covenant curses (Deut. 30:6, 8), a promise that old covenant saints regularly pleaded (Pss. 19:12–14; 119).[40] The most radical distinctive of the new covenant is not the internalization of the law but the *universalization* of the law. According to Jeremiah 31, the internalization of the law will no longer characterize only "Israel's righteous remnant" but "everyone who belong[s] to the covenant community of the future."[41] And

---

38. Williamson, *Sealed with an Oath*, 154.

39. Williamson, *Sealed with an Oath*, 154. New covenant theologies appear to confuse the *constitution* of the people of God across various covenant administrations with the *condition* of the people of God across various covenant administrations. In terms of the former, there are no covenants in Scripture that do not constitutionally require its members to internalize the covenant promises and requirements (Deut. 10:16; 11:18; Jer. 4:4; 9:25–26). In terms of the latter, we do witness progress and development across various covenant administrations from a largely unregenerate condition of God's covenant people (Deut. 29:4) to a wholly regenerate condition of God's covenant people (Deut. 30:1–10; Jer. 31:34).

40. Interpreters sometimes miss this point because they read Deut. 30:6, 8, not as *promises*, which old covenant saints could claim by faith before, during, and after the exile, but as *predictions*, which old covenant saints were supposed to wait on until after the exile. On the difference between the two in interpreting biblical prophecy, see Richard L. Pratt Jr., "Historical Contingencies and Biblical Predictions," in *The Way of Wisdom: Essays in Honor of Bruce K. Waltke*, ed. J. I. Packer and Sven K. Soderlund (Grand Rapids, MI: Zondervan, 2000), 180–203.

41. Williamson, *Sealed with an Oath*, 154. Williamson draws similar conclusions regarding Ezekiel's teaching about the internalization of the law in the new covenant age: "Such an infusion of Yahweh's Spirit, prompting inner transformation (i.e., regeneration), was apparently neither a novel concept nor distinctly eschatological (as Jesus' rebuke of Nicodemus clearly shows). Rather, the problem for Ezekiel was 'ecclesiological—this transformation was not occurring on a national scale. The issue was one of scope.'" *Sealed with an Oath*, 172, citing Daniel Block.

this universal internalization of the law in turn explains why God's people will no longer need to teach one another to know the Lord: because all God's people will know the Lord, "from the least of them to the greatest" (Jer. 31:34). Second, the Lord promises "complete forgiveness" of sins, a promise that "anticipates the end of the sacrificial system of the Old Testament."[42] In keeping with a pattern we have already observed, while the new covenant promise of forgiveness, in one sense, brings the ministry of the old covenant to an end (Heb. 10:18), in another sense, it represents the fulfillment of what various old covenant institutions promised and, in some sense, delivered (1 Kings 8:30, 34, 36, 39, 50; Ps. 32:1–2).

To summarize the preceding two points, (1) it is not the internalization of the law that constitutes the newness of the new covenant but the universalization of the law's internalization, and (2) it is not the forgiveness of sins that constitutes the newness of the new covenant but the fullness and finality of that forgiveness, which obviates any ongoing need for old covenant institutions designed to deal with sin (Rom. 3:21–26; WCF 7.5–6).[43] Moreover, as both of these examples indicate, the new covenant transcends the old covenant in ways that simultaneously fulfill its deepest intention and purpose. The yelp of the puppy is *replaced by* the bark of the dog because puppies are *designed to become* dogs.

Our brief analysis of Jeremiah 31:31–34 puts us in a position to address the two fundamental points of debate between Reformed covenant theology and new covenant theologies. First, we discuss how Reformed theology understands Jeremiah's claim that in the new covenant, God will write his law on the hearts of his people. Here we address debates regarding the shape of the moral life under the new covenant (i.e., sanctification). Second, we discuss how Reformed covenant theology understands Jeremiah's claim that in the new covenant, God will write his law on the hearts of all God's people. Here we address debates regarding the character of the new covenant community (i.e., ecclesiology).

The Place of the New Covenant in Reformed Covenant Theology: The Shape of the Moral Life

According to Reformed covenant theology, *the same law*[44] published on tablets of stone at Sinai (i.e., the Ten Commandments) is written on the hearts of God's people in the

---

42. Williamson, *Sealed with an Oath*, 157.

43. Space forbids addressing the complex question of Christ's status as Redeemer of Old Testament saints, a question vigorously debated in the seventeenth century. See Willem J. van Asselt, "*Expromissio* or *Fideiussio*? A Seventeenth-Century Theological Debate between Voetians and Cocceians about the Nature of Christ's Suretyship in Salvation History," *MJT* 14 (2003): 37–57.

44. Williamson uses the terminology of the "same obligation." *Sealed with an Oath*, 153. It is important to note that while the Ten Commandments are the Mosaic expression of God's unchanging moral law, they are delivered in a form that is accommodated to specific circumstances of the Mosaic era, and therefore they exhibit features specific to that era as well. See Franciscus Junius, *The Mosaic Polity*, trans. Todd M. Rester, ed. Andrew M. McGinnis (Grand Rapids, MI: CLP Academic, 2015), chap. 8.

new covenant. Consequently, although the transition from the old covenant to the new covenant brings about a number of transformations in and for the people of God (see section 2 of this chapter), it does not bring about a fundamental transformation in the shape of their moral life. The Ten Commandments, along with their summary in Jesus's double-love command (itself derived from the Mosaic covenant: Lev. 19:18; Deut. 6:4–5), represent the essence of the moral life brought into being by God through Christ in the Spirit under the new covenant.[45] What is the basis for this claim? And how does this claim inform Reformed covenant theology's understanding of the place of the new covenant within God's unfolding kingdom purpose? A brief sketch of the argument is as follows.

The Reformed claim rests, in part, on the traditional threefold division of the Mosaic law into the categories of moral, ceremonial, and civil laws. According to this traditional division, the Ten Commandments are the Mosaic expression of God's unchanging moral will for all human beings at all times and in all places. As Patrick D. Miller observes, the Mosaic covenant itself sets the Ten Commandments apart from the rest of the stipulations of the Mosaic covenant in a number of ways that exhibit their unique and unchanging status as moral instruction:

- Unlike any other body of instruction in the Old Testament, the Ten Commandments are given *twice*, once in the narrative of the events at Sinai (Exod. 20) and again when Moses recalls those events as the people prepare to go into the land (Deut. 5).
- The Commandments are given by the Lord *directly* to the people ("face to face," Deut. 5:4), and this is the only time such direct speech to the whole people takes place. The rest of the statutes and ordinances are given to Moses to be taught to the people, differentiating them from the Commandments.
- They are the *first* piece of legal material and *separated* from the statutes and ordinances that follow in the rest of Exodus and Deuteronomy, as well as in Leviticus and Numbers. Those statutes and ordinances function as interpretive specification of the Commandments . . .
- The Commandments are written by the *finger of God* on *stone*, to make clear their source and endurance (Exod. 31:18; Deut. 4:13; 5:22; 9:10).
- They are placed within the ark of the covenant, the Lord's dwelling place in the midst of the people (Deut. 10:5), while the other legislation/instruction is written on a scroll and put beside the ark, not in it (Deut. 31:24–26).[46]

---

45. It is worth emphasizing here that PC comes to many of the same conclusions as Reformed covenant theology with respect to the *content* of the moral law. Moreover, PC agrees that, from the perspective of "archetypal theology" (i.e., God's own knowledge of himself and of all things in relation to himself), God's moral will is eternal and unchanging. PC differs with Reformed covenant theology, however, about how the moral law is *revealed* in history and therefore about how we may come to know the moral law. The disagreement, in other words, concerns "ectypal theology" (i.e., *our* knowledge of God and of all things in relation to God).

46. Patrick D. Miller, *The Ten Commandments*, Int (Louisville: Westminster John Knox, 2009), 3.

In a manner distinct from the Ten Commandments, the Mosaic covenant presents many of its stipulations in a manner that suggests the limited nature of their application. Consider, for example, Deuteronomy 4:13–14, which distinguishes between the Ten Commandments delivered by the Lord directly at Sinai and the commandments delivered by the Lord through Moses. As the text indicates, many of the latter commandments were focused on specific circumstances, that of governing Israel's life "in the land," that is, as a theocratic nation-state (see also Deut. 4:5; 5:31; 6:1; 12:1).[47] Consider also the instructions given by the Lord to Moses regarding the ministry of the tabernacle in Exodus 25. The giving of the tabernacle instructions according to the "pattern" revealed to Moses on the mountain (Ex. 25:9, 40) suggests to the author of Hebrews that the ministry of the earthly tabernacle "was provisional in character," intending to foreshadow Christ's ministry in the heavenly tabernacle.[48] As these examples suggest, there are subtle indications within the Mosaic covenant itself that, unlike the Ten Commandments, some of its instructions were intended for limited application to specific circumstances and specific redemptive-historical epochs.[49]

Reformed covenant theology's distinction between laws that are provisional in nature, tied to specific circumstances and specific redemptive-historical epochs, and laws that are permanent in nature, binding on all human beings at all times, rests in part on the traditional threefold division of the Mosaic law. This, however, is not the fundamental basis of Reformed covenant theology's claim that the same law written on tablets of stone at Sinai is written on the human heart in the new covenant.[50] The fundamental bases for this claim are creational and anthropological.[51]

Along with confessional Lutheran and Baptist theologies, Reformed covenant theology's understanding of the moral law is ultimately rooted in the doctrines of creation and humanity.[52] According to this understanding, the Ten Commandments delivered to Israel at Sinai are a republication of *the same moral law* originally written by God on the hearts of human beings in creation. As Paul argues in Romans 1–2, all human beings "by nature" (2:14) have the "work of the law . . . written on their hearts" (2:15).[53] For this reason, although Gentiles do not possess the law of Moses (2:14), they may

47. Philip S. Ross, *From the Finger of God: The Biblical and Theological Basis for the Threefold Division of the Law* (Fearn, Ross-Shire, Scotland: Mentor, 2010), 114.

48. Richard B. Hays, "'Here We Have No Lasting City': New Covenantalism in Hebrews," in *The Epistle to the Hebrews and Christian Theology*, ed. Richard Bauckham, Daniel R. Driver, Trevor A. Hart, and Nathan Mac-Donald (Grand Rapids, MI: Eerdmans, 2009), 159.

49. For a more thorough discussion of the issues, see Junius, *Mosaic Polity*; Ross, *Finger of God*.

50. Contra *KTC*, 785 et passim.

51. From the perspective of archetypal theology, the ultimate foundation of the moral law is *theological* insofar as what is written on the human heart in creation and republished in the Ten Commandments at Sinai expresses God's eternal and unchanging will regarding the conduct of creatures made in his image. Junius, *Mosaic Polity*, chap. 1.

52. *The Book of Concord: The Confessions of the Evangelical Lutheran Church*, ed. Robert Kolb and Timothy J. Wengert, trans. Charles Arand (Minneapolis: Fortress, 2001), 502.2; 588.5; Second London Baptist Confession 18; WCF 19.

53. For a defense of this interpretation of Rom. 1–2, see Mark A. Seifrid, "Natural Revelation and the Purpose of the Law in Romans," *TynBul* 49, no. 1 (1998): 115–29.

nevertheless be described as violating its precepts. Why is this the case? Because when Gentiles act in ways that are "contrary to nature" (1:26), they act contrary to the moral law that is written on their hearts by nature, the same law delivered to Israel at Sinai. Thus, for example, in describing Gentile idolatry in Romans 1:23, Paul echoes language used in Psalm 106:20 to describe Israel's violation of the second commandment at Sinai in combination with language used in Deuteronomy 4:16–18 to elaborate on what it means to violate the second commandment.[54] Even though they did not possess the second commandment in its Sinaitic form, Gentiles committed *the same sin* as Israel because they violated *the same law* as Israel, the law written on their hearts by nature.

On this understanding, the moral law, written on the hearts of human beings by nature and republished in the Ten Commandments at Sinai, represents the "imperatival force" of human *being*.[55] As such, the moral law corresponds to human nature as designed by God in the beginning and directs us to the fulfillment of human nature appointed by God in his eternal kingdom. The moral law, on this understanding, is more than a set of norms, more than a particular set of policies for a particular redemptive-historical setting. The moral law reflects the creational design plan within which human beings thrive to the glory of God (Ps. 19:7–11) or else against which human beings not only dishonor God (Rom. 3:23) but also diminish themselves (Ps. 32:9–10).

This understanding of the moral law, common to confessional Lutheran, Reformed, and Baptist theology, explains why it is a category mistake to say that the new covenant brings about an "advance" or "transformation" of the moral law.[56] The moral law is not one of the things that changes or develops along the trajectory of redemptive history. The moral law is the unchanging standard against which human progress or regress is measured along the trajectory of redemptive history.[57] The moral law, thus understood, provides the framework or setting within which we may appreciate the dramatic conflict and resolution of the larger biblical storyline from creation to redemption to consummation. What *the law of Moses*, delivered on tablets of stone, *could not do*, weakened as it was by sinful human nature's inability to fulfill it, *God did, by sending his own Son* in the likeness of sinful flesh to fulfill the precept of the law on our behalf and to bear the penalty of the law on our behalf, and *by endowing a redeemed and sanctified humanity with the Holy Spirit*, "in order that the righteous requirement of the law might be fulfilled

---

54. Craig S. Keener, *The Mind of the Spirit: Paul's Approach to Transformed Thinking* (Grand Rapids, MI: Baker Academic, 2016), 15.

55. John Webster, *God without Measure: Working Papers in Theology*, vol. 2, *Virtue and Intellect* (London: T&T Clark, 2016), 29.

56. See note 29 above. Though biblical theology is an essential component of a sound hermeneutic, the present point highlights the limitations of making biblical theology the primary mode of biblical interpretation. Biblical theology's emphasis on the historical trajectory of biblical revelation, when not tempered by an awareness that not all biblical realities are historical in nature, can tend toward "historicism," the attempt to account for all reality by means of historical categories. On the problems of "historicism" more generally, see Oliver O'Donovan, *Resurrection and Moral Order: An Outline for Evangelical Ethics*, 2nd ed. (Grand Rapids, MI: Eerdmans, 1994), chap. 3.

57. Consider, for example, the way Israel is measured in the narrative of Judges and the way various kings are measured in the narratives of 1–2 Kings and 1–2 Chronicles.

in us, who walk not according to the flesh but according to the Spirit" (Rom. 8:3–4; Gal. 3:13–14; 4:4–7).

God's redeeming and sanctifying work in the new covenant is not about enabling human beings to transcend the moral law expressed in the Ten Commandments—which would require us to transcend our nature as human beings! In the new covenant, God redeems a lawless humanity by his incarnate Son and sanctifies human nature by his indwelling Spirit, writing the moral law on our hearts and enabling us to walk in it. As David Yeago eloquently states, what God "proposes" on tablets of stone at Sinai, he graciously "bestows" in Christ by the Spirit under the new covenant.[58] In so doing, the grace of God does not destroy human nature; the grace of God restores and perfects human nature.[59]

This brief sketch of Reformed covenant theology's understanding of the place of the moral law within the new covenant suggests (1) that new covenant theologies have not fully addressed the hermeneutical and theological bases of the threefold division of the law of Moses,[60] (2) that new covenant theologies have misidentified the fundamental basis of Reformed covenant theology's understanding of the place of the moral law within the new covenant, and (3) that new covenant theologies' own observations regarding the creational and anthropological bases of Christian moral teaching might be placed on a firmer hermeneutical and theological foundation by adopting a more robust account of the moral law.[61] Addressing each of these issues would not only move forward the debate between new covenant theologies and confessional forms of Protestant theology, it might also strengthen the hermeneutical and theological foundations of new covenant theologies.

The Place of the New Covenant in Reformed Covenant Theology: The Character of the Covenant Community

In the previous section, we considered how Reformed covenant theology understands Jeremiah's promise that in the new covenant, God will write his law on the hearts of his people (Jer. 31:33). In the present section, we consider how Reformed covenant theology understands Jeremiah's promise that in the new covenant, God will write his law on the hearts of *all God's people* (Jer. 31:34). As we have already seen, new covenant theologies believe this promise entails a radical transformation of the nature and

58. David Yeago, "Grace and the Good Life: Why the God of the Gospel Cares How We Live," in *The Morally Divided Body: Ethical Disagreement and the Disunity of the Church*, ed. Michael Root and James J. Buckley, ProEcclSer 1 (Eugene, OR: Cascade, 2012), 89.

59. Junius, *Mosaic Polity*, 38.

60. Too often, the traditional threefold division of the law of Moses is dismissed as an *a priori* theological category that Reformed covenant theology imposes on the biblical text (e.g., *KTC*, 791) without actually attending to the historical, hermeneutical, and theological arguments in its favor. A helpful corrective of this tendency may be found in D. A. Carson, "The Tripartite Division of the Law: A Review of Philip Ross, *The Finger of God*," in *From Creation to New Creation: Biblical Theology and Exegesis; Essays in Honor of G. K. Beale*, ed. Daniel M. Gurtner and Benjamin L. Gladd (Peabody, MA: Hendrickson, 2013), chap. 12.

61. See, e.g., Wells and Zaspel, *New Covenant Theology*, 140, 143; *KTC*, 789, 793, 795–96.

structure of the new covenant community. According to PC, whereas the old covenant community was constituted as a "mixed" community of regenerate and unregenerate members, the new covenant community is constituted as an "unmixed" community of regenerate members.[62] Moreover, whereas God related to his old covenant people in an indirect manner, by means of anointed prophets, priests, and kings, and by means of a "genealogical principle" related to parents and children, God relates to his new covenant people in a direct manner.[63] As we will see below, Reformed covenant theology agrees with new covenant theologies that the new covenant brings about a radical transformation of the covenant community. More specifically, Reformed covenant theology agrees that, in the new covenant, God brings about the existence of a wholly regenerate covenant community that no longer requires human intermediaries—other than the incarnate mediator of the new covenant—between God and his covenant people.[64] It disagrees with new covenant theologies, however, regarding the *timing* of this transformation. Why is this the case? The answer, in short, is that Reformed covenant theology reads the promise of Jeremiah 31:34 within the broader context of scriptural teaching regarding the new covenant, which indicates that the new covenant community will only realize Jeremiah 31:34's promised ideal in the new heaven and new earth, when the triune God's dwelling among his people reaches its fullest and most transformative expression. Though space forbids a full statement of the scriptural argument in support of this claim, what follows summarizes the most relevant points.

First, both the Old and New Testaments are replete with teaching that emphasizes the ongoing role of both human intermediaries (e.g., pastors, teachers, elders) and the genealogical principle within the new covenant community. With respect to human intermediaries, while Ezekiel denounces Israel's unfaithful shepherds and promises a day when the Lord himself will shepherd his people, Isaiah 24:23 declares that the glory of God's future reign will shine in the presence of "his elders." Moreover, Ephesians 4:7–16 describes apostles, prophets, evangelists, pastors, and teachers as gifts of the ascended Christ, given to lead God's people into maturity in Christ. Furthermore, the Pastoral Epistles provide extensive instruction about how such persons are to lead the new covenant community (1 Tim. 3:1–13; Titus 1:5–9), and Hebrews commends God's people to their care (Heb. 13:7, 17). With respect to the genealogical principle, within the immediate context of Jeremiah 31:34, Jeremiah affirms God's ongoing faithfulness to the genealogical principle within the new covenant epoch: "I will give them one heart and one way, that they may fear me forever, for their own good and the good of their children after them" (Jer. 32:39). Looking to the broader prophetic context of Jeremiah, we see that Isaiah also affirms God's ongoing faithfulness to the genealogical principle within the new covenant epoch (Isa. 44:1–5; 59:21). Furthermore, on the day of Pentecost,

---

62. *KTC*, 802–3, 807–12.
63. *KTC*, 749–52, 807–24.
64. William Ames, *The Marrow of Theology* (Grand Rapids, MI: Baker, 1997), 214.

Peter restates the genealogical principle for a new covenant audience (Acts 2:37–41), while Paul appropriates old covenant teaching regarding the nurture of covenant children to instruct parents within the new covenant community (Eph. 6:1–4).

Second, the New Testament repeatedly warns against the danger of falling away from the new covenant community. This is not because one's salvation can be lost (John 6:37–40; Rom. 8:28–30) but because it is possible to be joined to the new covenant community in a merely "external" manner, apart from an "internal" embrace of the Lord Jesus Christ, the mediator of the new covenant, by faith (Heb. 4:2).[65] According to John 15, it is possible to have a "dead" connection to Jesus Christ the vine and thus to stand under the threat of divine judgment. According to 1 John 2:19, it is possible to be "in" the new covenant community but not "of" the new covenant community. Moreover, Hebrews, which provides the New Testament's most explicit discussion of the new covenant, repeatedly warns members of the new covenant community of the peril of falling under God's covenant curses (Heb. 6:4–8; 10:26–31): "The Lord will judge *his people*" (Heb. 10:30).[66]

Third, scriptural teaching regarding the ongoing role of ministers within the new covenant community, regarding God's ongoing faithfulness to the genealogical principle, and regarding the possibility of falling away can be reconciled with the teaching of Jeremiah 31:34 when we understand the latter text in light of the "inaugurated eschatology" of the New Testament. According to New Testament inaugurated eschatology, although the fulfillment of the new covenant has *dawned* in Jesus Christ, its fulfillment will be *consummated* only when Jesus Christ returns to establish a new heaven and new earth in which righteousness dwells.[67] As the promises of Jeremiah 31:38–40 regarding the holy city Jerusalem await their full realization in the new heaven and new earth, so too do the promises of Jeremiah 31:34 regarding a wholly regenerate community, which has no need for pastoral oversight or a genealogical principle and which exists beyond the possibility of apostasy. Until then (Eph. 4:13), pastors and parents remain God's external and ordinary means of transmitting his new covenant promises to his people through time, while warnings against falling away from the new covenant community remain a vital means of preserving God's elect children in the faith and, when necessary, of disciplining those whose lives and teaching contradict their profession of faith. The ministries of pastors and parents, of warnings and discipline, are new covenant *means* of directing God's people to new covenant *ends*.[68]

---

65. The language of "external" versus "internal" membership in the covenant community arises from Rom. 2:28–29. For a helpful survey and assessment of different Reformed views on the manner in which unbelievers may be said to be members of the new covenant community, see Geerhardus Vos, *Reformed Dogmatics*, vol. 2, *Anthropology*, trans. and ed. Richard B. Gaffin Jr. (Bellingham, WA: Lexham, 2012–2014), 97–112.

66. Michael Horton, *The Christian Faith: A Systematic Theology for Pilgrims on the Way* (Grand Rapids, MI: Zondervan, 2011), 682–84.

67. On the relevance of inaugurated eschatology for Jer. 31:31–34, see Richard L. Pratt Jr., "Infant Baptism in the New Covenant," chap. 8 in *The Case for Covenantal Infant Baptism*, ed. Gregg Strawbridge (Phillipsburg, NJ: P&R, 2003).

68. Herman Bavinck, *Reformed Dogmatics*, vol. 3, *Sin and Salvation in Christ*, ed. John Bolt, trans. John Vriend (Grand Rapids, MI: Baker Academic, 2006), 228–32.

The worry, then, from the perspective of Reformed covenant theology, is that new covenant theologies suffer from an "overrealized eschatology" when it comes to the communal implications of Jeremiah's new covenant promises. That is, new covenant theologies apply realities pertaining to the new covenant community *in the eternal kingdom* to the new covenant community *on its pilgrimage* to the eternal kingdom. Doing so, however, loses sight of the teaching of the whole counsel of God regarding the new covenant. Though we look with eager expectation for the day described in Jeremiah 31:34, until that day comes, we continue to look to the external and ordinary means that God has provided for transmitting, nurturing, and protecting the precious promises he has made to his new covenant people. "For now we see in a mirror dimly, but then"—and *only then*—will we see "face to face" (1 Cor. 13:12), without mediation.

Conclusion

Theological debate continues to be part of the pathos of theology in the present age, something we must endure as we await the full revelation of things now hidden to pilgrims and sojourners. Nevertheless, theological debate remains a sanctifying force for theology.[69] Debate can serve to clarify, correct, and improve our fluency in biblical interpretation and our following of biblical instruction. Debate, in other words, can help us become more faithful disciples of Jesus Christ. The preceding discussion has attempted to identify the main points of debate between new covenant theologies and Reformed covenant theology with respect to the place of the new covenant in God's unfolding kingdom. As we have seen, these approaches have much in common, but they also differ in key respects, particularly when it comes to the nature of sanctification and the church. For all our differences, however, we can agree that it is God and God alone—the supreme and central theme of Christian theology—who is able to fulfill his new covenant promises for us and in us. In agreement on this most fundamental point, and with confidence in divine assistance, we conclude our discussion of the new covenant with a prayer of John Calvin, composed in response to the teaching of Jeremiah 31:31–34:

> Grant, Almighty God, that as thou hast favoured us with so singular a benefit as to make through thy Son a covenant which has been ratified for our salvation— O grant, that we may become partakers of it, and know that thou so speakest with us, that thou not only shewest by thy Word what is right, but speakest also to us inwardly by thy Spirit, and thus renderest us teachable and obedient, that there may be an evidence of our adoption, and a proof that thou wilt govern and rule us, until we shall at length be really and fully united to thee through Christ our Lord. Amen.[70]

---

69. John Webster, "Theology and the Peace of the Church," chap. 8 in *The Domain of the Word: Scripture and Theological Reason* (London: T&T Clark, 2012).

70. John Calvin, *Commentaries on the Book of the Prophet Jeremiah and the Lamentations* (repr., Grand Rapids, MI: Baker, 1998), 3:134.

27

Covenant, Assurance,
and the Sacraments

Derek W. H. Thomas

Crucial in formulating a biblical theology of baptism and the Lord's Supper is to recognize their covenantal nature and the signal that all divine covenants in Scripture are accompanied by corroborating signs. The first recorded use of the word "covenant" in Scripture is with Noah in Genesis 6:18: "But I will establish my covenant with you, and you shall come into the ark, you, your sons, your wife, and your sons' wives with you." To this verbal promise is added a physical sign—a rainbow (Gen. 9:12–16). The rainbow functions anthropomorphically, first of all, as a sign to God himself. God sees the rainbow and recalls his promise to Noah. Additionally, Noah himself is reassured by the rainbow of God's faithful word of promise never again to impose such a catastrophic water ordeal of judgment (Gen. 9:14–15).

In Genesis 6:18, the verb "to establish," or "to cause to stand" (וַהֲקִמֹתִי), rather than the usual "to cut" (כָּרַת), suggests to some that a covenant already existed prior to the Noahic administration.[1] This covenant relationship is with Adam, as the first man and representative of the human race. In the garden of Eden, the Lord threatened death to Adam for violating the terms of the covenant—not to eat of the tree of the knowledge of good and evil (Gen. 2:17). By parity of reasoning, obedience to the stipulation of the Edenic covenant would issue in eternal life, thereby removing Adam's initial probationary status. The sign attending this covenant was the tree of life (Gen. 2:9).

---

1. See William J. Dumbrell, *Covenant and Creation* (Exeter, UK: Paternoster, 1984), 11–26; Dumbrell, "Creation, Covenant and Work," *ERT* 13, no. 2 (1989): 138. Dumbrell examines the usage of בְּרִית in the three secular instances that involve the relationship of Abraham, Isaac, and Jacob to others (Gen. 21:22–32; 26:26–33; 31:43–54). In each case he concludes that the covenant does not initiate the relationship (which already exists); rather, the covenant gives the relationship a quasi-legal backing and guarantees its continuance.

A pattern therefore develops of divine covenants and accompanying signs. The Abrahamic covenant was confirmed by the sign of circumcision (Gen. 17:11), the Mosaic covenant by the Sabbath day (Ex. 31:16–17), the Davidic covenant by the royal throne of David (Ps. 89:29), and the new covenant by not one but *two* signs, baptism and the Supper (an initiatory wash and a confirmatory meal). Each individual covenant in redemptive history anticipates its fulfillment in Christ. Sinclair Ferguson explains, "He is the true Noah in whose ark we are saved (1 Pet 3:20–22), the seed of Abraham in whom all the nations of the earth are blessed (Gal 3:13–22), the prophet-leader like Moses in whom the final Exodus took place (Deut 18:15; cf. Lk 9:31)."[2] The Greek word for "departure" in Luke 9:31 is ἔξοδον, literally "exodus."

It is these *signs* of the covenant that Reformed theology designates *sacraments*. A classic definition of a sacrament is that found in the Westminster Confession of Faith (1646):

holy signs and seals of the covenant of grace, immediately instituted by God, to represent Christ and his benefits; and to confirm our interest in him; as also to put a visible difference between those that belong unto the church and the rest of the world; and solemnly to engage them to the service of God in Christ, according to his Word. (27.1)

Of particular interest to the goal of this chapter are two issues: first, what precisely is meant by describing the sacraments as "holy signs and seals of the covenant of grace"? And second, how do the sacraments "confirm our interest in [Christ]"?

Signs and Seals

The phrase "signs and seals" is a direct borrow from Paul's description of circumcision in Romans 4:11: "He received the sign of circumcision as a seal of the righteousness that he had by faith while he was still uncircumcised." The fact that the Westminster Confession employs circumcision language to sacraments in general demonstrates the manner in which a covenant-shaped hermeneutic governs the understanding of redemptive history. Baptism and the Supper in the administration of the new covenant function in much the same way as circumcision and Passover did in the old covenant.[3] This has immediate and definitive implications for the subjects of both baptism and the Supper, as we shall see, but of more immediate import is the implication for continuity of meaning and purpose.

Sacramental "signs" function as "visible words."[4] They portray fundamental blessings (and curses) of the gospel. They do so both in an *exhibitive* manner (by pointing in the

---

2. See Sinclair Ferguson, "Infant Baptism View," in *Baptism: Three Views*, ed. David F. Wright (Downers Grove, IL: InterVarsity Press, 2009), 85.

3. The view that the Lord's Supper is concerned not as much with Passover as with the covenant meal in Ex. 24, a view held by Robert Letham, has gained little support. See Letham, *The Lord's Supper: Eternal Word in Broken Bread* (Phillipsburg, NJ: P&R, 2001).

4. The phrase "visible words" is taken from Augustine's *Contra Faustum*, book 19. See also Augustine, *Tractates of the Gospel of John* 50.3, in *A Select Library of the Nicene and Post-Nicene Fathers of the Christian Church*, 1st ser., ed. Philip Schaff, 14 vols. (1870–1894; repr., Peabody, MA: Hendrickson, 1994), 7:34.

direction of the sacrament's meaning and intent), and in a *communicative* manner (the sacraments are themselves a demonstration of gospel blessing). In this sense, Reformed theology has stressed that the sacraments are not merely "bare signs" (*nuda signa*).[5] As Geerhardus Vos explains,

> The sacraments are no *nuda signa*, "bare signs," no *signa theoretica*, "theoretical signs." They are also *signa practica*, "practical signs." When they are used in faith, the user receives, by the working of the Holy Spirit, the grace that they portray and seal.[6]

Thus, by way of example, Paul can say of the bread and wine in the Supper, "The cup of blessing that we bless, is it not a participation [κοινωνία] in the blood of Christ? The bread that we break, is it not a participation in the body of Christ?" (1 Cor. 10:16). And of the waters of baptism, Paul can say, "We were buried therefore with him by baptism into death" (Rom. 6:4). In both cases, the blessing is symbolized and *conveyed* to faith and not in some mechanical, *ex opere operato* fashion. Equally, where faith is absent, the sacraments are equally capable, by divine economy, to convey judgment. Thus the harsh warning to the Corinthians, that anyone who participates in the Supper in an "unworthy" manner, devoid of discernment, "eats and drinks judgment on himself" (1 Cor. 11:27, 29) and renders the communicant "guilty concerning the body and blood of the Lord."

A seal functions as a marker of authenticity, confirming that which it seals. Paul describes the Corinthians as the "seal" (σφραγίς) of his apostleship (1 Cor. 9:2). Their very existence as professing Christians was evidence (assurance) of Paul's apostolic credentials. Similarly, the indwelling of the Holy Spirit is the seal of our inheritance of all God's covenantal promises to us in the gospel (cf. 2 Cor. 1:22; Eph. 1:13; 4:30).[7]

What precisely do the sacraments *seal*? More precisely, is the sacrament a seal of the response of the participant—a seal of faith itself? Or is the sacrament a seal to God's word of promise (and threat) to the one who receives it by faith? Putting this another way, do the sacraments function as seals "of faith" (effectively confirming our response) or "to faith" (effectively confirming the gospel to be received by faith)?[8] Paul's answer in the case of baptism seems clear in Romans 4:11: "He received the sign of circumcision as a seal of the righteousness that he had by faith while he was still uncircumcised." Circumcision was a seal not of Abraham's faith but of the objective righteousness credited to him through faith. As God told Abraham, "You shall be circumcised in the flesh of

---

5. See G. C. Berkouwer, *The Sacraments* (Grand Rapids, MI: Eerdmans, 1969), 136. For John Calvin's dismissal of Zwinglian memorialism, see Brian A. Gerrish, *Grace and Gratitude: The Eucharistic Theology of John Calvin* (Edinburgh: T&T Clark, 1993), 157–90.

6. Geerhardus Vos, *Reformed Dogmatics*, vol. 5, *Ecclesiology, the Means of Grace, Eschatology*, trans. Richard B. Gaffin Jr. (Bellingham, WA: Lexham, 2016), 96.

7. Some have viewed the seal of the Spirit as something in addition to the presence and witness of the Spirit himself. For a discussion, see Donald MacLeod, *The Spirit of Promise* (Fearn, Ross-shire, Scotland: Christian Focus, 1986), 52; Sinclair Ferguson, *The Holy Spirit*, CCT (Downers Grove, IL: InterVarsity Press, 1996), 181.

8. See Ferguson, "Infant Baptism View," 93.

your foreskins, and it shall be a sign of the covenant between me and you" (Gen. 17:11). Circumcision served to point to the objective covenant, sovereignly initiated by God and received by faith. Circumcision sealed the promises of the covenant—the righteousness credited to Abraham's account, received by faith alone.

In viewing the sacraments this way, Reformed theology has distanced itself from two divergent perspectives. In contrast to Roman Catholicism, the sacraments do not effect what they symbolize *ex opere operato*—by a power inherent within the sacrament itself. Rather, they function *ex opere operantis*—to the believing heart. Thus, the Heidelberg Catechism 66 reads:

> Q. What are the sacraments?
>
> A. The sacraments are holy, visible signs and seals. They were instituted by God so that by their use He might the more fully declare and seal to us the promise of the gospel. And this is the promise: that God graciously grants us forgiveness of sins and everlasting life because of the one sacrifice of Christ accomplished on the cross.

The sacraments "seal the promise of the gospel" rather than our responsive faith in the gospel. It is hardly possible to have any real assurance if the basis of it is *our grasp of Christ*, which varies from day to day. Only as the objective promise of God in a promised salvation based on the finished work of Christ and the dutiful and meticulous application of the Holy Spirit (applying precisely what Jesus has accomplished) may assurance be entertained. By way of contrast, the Council of Trent suggested that it is the recipient of the sacrament that is sealed:

> If anyone says that in the three sacraments, to wit, Baptism, Confirmation and order, there is not imprinted in the soul a character, that is a certain spiritual and indelible sign, on account of which it cannot be repeated; let him be anathema.[9]

Reformed confessions and catechisms emphasized the opposite of Trent. It is not the recipient that is sealed but the gospel itself in its multidimensional nature of regeneration, new creation, justification, and glorification.

The Problem Posed by Latin

Reformed theology has been equally critical of a *subjectivist* understanding of the sacraments. In its extreme form, the sacraments are viewed as seals of "my personal faith." They confirm my response—its genuineness and validity. They therefore symbolize acts of obedience, marks of personal willingness to be a disciple in obedience to the call of Christ. The sacraments are witnesses to a new heart and a life of faith. And for obvi-

---

9. Council of Trent, session 7, "On the Sacraments in General," canon 9, in *The Creeds of Christendom with a History and Critical Notes*, ed. Philip Schaff, rev. David S. Schaff, 6th ed. (Grand Rapids, MI: Baker, 1996), 2:121.

ous reasons, baptism can never be applied to an infant who, by nature, is incapable of expressing faith.

The term *sacrament* has not been altogether helpful in this regard. *Sacramentum*, in its Latin etymology, signaled the oath of allegiance made by a soldier. J. I. Packer explains:

> *Sacramentum* was a word borrowed from the army, where it signified a soldier's solemn oath pledging full loyalty to the Roman emperor, under whose banner he was enlisting. When Christians took the word over, the analogy shifted; the oath was understood to be God's, a promise guaranteeing salvation to everyone who receives Jesus Christ as Savior and Lord, professes penitent faith, and commits to be fully faithful to God throughout life. This profession, though vital in itself, was seen as responsive and therefore derivative, and thus of secondary importance compared to God's own pledge.[10]

The subjective element is not altogether discounted in Reformed confessions. As we saw in the definition of a sacrament in the Westminster Standards, it gave attention to the way a sacrament may "confirm our interest in [Christ]." Similarly, article 25 of the sixteenth-century Anglican Thirty-Nine Articles says,

> Sacraments ordained of Christ be not only badges or tokens of Christian men's profession, but rather they are certain sure witnesses, and effectual signs of grace . . . by the which [God] doth work invisibly in us, and doth not only quicken but also strengthen and confirm our Faith in him.

The crucial word here is "rather." The primary manner by which sacraments function is in their objective testimony to God's word of covenant promise.

The Baptism of Infants

It is precisely on the grounds of covenant theology that an argument is made for the baptism of the children of those who believe. At its core lies the argument of covenantal *continuity* in the administration of the covenant of grace. Put simply, if children were included in the administration of the old covenant, then they should also be included in the new—and, after all, "more excellent" and "better"—covenant (Heb. 8:6). How can the new covenant be better if it fails to include any word of promise to my children?

It is vital to see that every administration of God's covenant includes children. The Adamic covenant had ramifications for Adam's seed: "As in Adam all die . . ." (1 Cor. 15:22; cf. Rom. 5:12–21). The curse that fell on Adam fell on the entirety of his progeny. "Me and my seed" is the basic principle that operates in Eden. The covenant with Noah is explicit in its reference to seed: "I establish my covenant with you and your offspring after you" (Gen. 9:9). Similarly, the Abrahamic covenant has a promise for Abraham's

---

10. J. I. Packer, *Taking God Seriously: Vital Things We Need to Know* (Wheaton, IL: Crossway, 2013), 130.

"offspring" (Gen. 15:18). Abraham was to be "the father of a multitude of nations" (Gen. 17:4). And when God establishes his covenant with Moses, it is by way of recalling the covenant he made with Abraham, Isaac, and Jacob (Ex. 2:24), which included "little ones" (Deut. 29:11). A similar connection with seed ("David and his offspring") lies at the heart of the Davidic covenant (2 Sam. 22:51; cf. 23:5; Ps. 89:3–4).

This repeating "seed principle" of the old covenant provides crucial significance to Peter's words on the day of Pentecost—words given at the turning point of the old and new covenant administration, spoken to thousands of Jewish believers whose default consideration would surely have been "me and my family." When Peter said, "The promise is for you and for your children" (Acts 2:39), what else could this possibly have meant except a pattern of continuity in covenantal administration?

True, there are significant differences announced at Pentecost, differences that exemplify why the new covenant is "better" and "superior" (Heb. 8:6 NIV). They include the ethnic broadening of focus to include "all flesh" (Acts 2:17; cf. Joel 2:28). Though some Gentiles were included within the scope of the old covenant, the middle wall of partition was destroyed at Pentecost (Eph. 2:14). The sexual distinction that meant only male children received the sign of the old covenant gave way in the new to both sons and daughters prophesying (Acts 2:17) and receiving the sign of baptism. Indeed, in Christ, there is "no male and female" (Gal. 3:28). More pertinently, there is an experiential advancement in the new covenant by which the Holy Spirit is "poured out." Just a few weeks earlier, Jesus told the disciples in the upper room, "He dwells with you and will be in you" (John 14:17), indicating an exponential increase in the personal ministry of the Holy Spirit as the "representative agent" (παράκλητος, John 14:16, 26; 15:26; 16:7) of Jesus.[11] These are crucial and important differences in covenantal administration, but the seed principle remains a principle of continuity. Otherwise, Pentecost would have become the greatest day of excommunication the church has ever witnessed. As Stephen Marshall wrote in 1644, "Except in relation to the Covenant there was no occasion to name their children; it had been sufficient to have said, 'a promise is made to as many as the Lord shall call.'"[12] And as John Murray so pointedly argues,

> If infants are excluded now, it cannot be too strongly emphasized that this change implies a complete reversal of the earlier divinely instituted practice. So we must ask: do we find any hint of intimation of such reversal in either the Old or the New Testament? More pointedly, does the New Testament revoke or does it provide any intimation of revoking so expressly authorized a principle as that of the inclusion of infants in the covenant and their participation in the covenant sign and seal? This practice had been followed, by divine authority, in the administration of the covenant

---

11. See Ferguson, *Holy Spirit*, 57–92; J. I. Packer, *Keep in Step with the Spirit* (Leicester, UK: Inter-Varsity Press, 1984), 55–92.

12. Stephen Marshall, *A Sermon of the Baptizing of Infants* (London, 1644), 17; cited in Ferguson, "Infant Baptism View," 103.

for two thousand years. Has it been discontinued? Our answer to these questions must be that we find no evidence of revocation. In view of the fact that the new covenant is based upon and is the unfolding of the Abrahamic covenant, in view of the basic identity of meaning attaching to circumcision and baptism, in view of the unity and continuity of the covenant of grace administered in both dispensations, we can affirm with confidence that evidence of revocation or repeal is mandatory if the practice or principle has been discontinued under the New Testament.[13]

Similarly, it is this presuppositional default that provides us with the intended meaning of Luke's repeated reference to household baptisms in the book of Acts (Acts 11:14; 16:15, 31, 34; 18:8; cf. 1 Cor. 1:16; 16:15). Apart from a momentum of Old Testament expectation, the term for "household" (οἶκός) has no baptismal significance. But given the weight of a millennium of seed inclusion in covenantal administrations, it seems natural to side with the interpretation that the "οἶκός formula" underlines covenantal continuity in the inclusion of children.

Likewise, the Savior speaks words to parents—not so much parents in general but parents with faith to bring their children specifically to Jesus so that he might bless them—"Let the little children come to me and do not hinder them, for to such belongs the kingdom of heaven" (Matt. 19:14; cf. Mark 10:14–15; Luke 18:15–17), and these words carry a similar expectation of covenantal inclusion. As John Murray points out, "All doubt, however, is removed by Luke 18:15, for there we are informed that the children were babes (βρέφη), that is to say, little infants."[14] Similarly, Paul's words about the child of one believing parent being considered "holy" can mean only one thing: that the children of believers enjoy a special privilege of covenant inclusion (1 Cor. 7:14).

These considerations collectively reveal the importance of a covenantal hermeneutic in answering the question concerning the subjects of baptism. A similarly applied covenantal implication for paedo-Communion does not follow, since there is no evidence at all that infants participated in the Passover meal. How could they?[15] Rather, the central liturgical aspect of Pesach is the question put by the youngest child, "Why is this night different from all other nights?" (מַה נִּשְׁתַּנָּה הַלַּיְלָה הַזֶּה מִכָּל הַלֵּילוֹת). The point is that the child is capable of speaking and therefore precludes the notion of infant participation in Passover. The age of the child is irrelevant to the discussion of infant participation in Communion if a preconsideration of an ability to speak is made. The question of how young a child can be for confirmation (communicant membership) is a legitimate question, but it is a *different* question than "Can infants participate at the Table?"

13. John Murray, *Christian Baptism* (Philadelphia: Presbyterian and Reformed, 1974), 52–53.
14. Murray, *Christian Baptism*, 62.
15. See Derek W. H. Thomas, "Not a Particle of Sound Brain: A Theological Response to Paedo-Communion," in *Children and the Lord's Supper*, ed. Guy Waters and Ligon Duncan (Fearn, Ross-shire, Scotland: Mentor, 2011), 97–118. A basic bibliography on paedo-Communion includes the following volumes: Cornelis Venema, *Children at the Lord's Table? Assessing the Case for Paedocommunion* (Grand Rapids, MI: Reformation Heritage, 2009).

"The New Covenant in My Blood"

In the case of the Supper, we have dominical confirmation of its covenantal nature. In particular, Jesus records the cup as being "the new covenant." There are nuanced differences in the way this is recorded in the Synoptic Gospels and Paul's Corinthian correspondence, warranting a closer examination:

> And he took a cup, and when he had given thanks he gave it to them, saying, "Drink of it, all of you, for this is my blood of the covenant, which is poured out for many for the forgiveness of sins. I tell you I will not drink again of this fruit of the vine until that day when I drink it new with you in my Father's kingdom." (Matt. 26:27–29)

> And he took a cup, and when he had given thanks he gave it to them, and they all drank of it. And he said to them, "This is my blood of the covenant, which is poured out for many. Truly, I say to you, I will not drink again of the fruit of the vine until that day when I drink it new in the kingdom of God." (Mark 14:23–25)

> And he took bread, and when he had given thanks, he broke it and gave it to them, saying, "This is my body, which is given for you. Do this in remembrance of me." And likewise the cup after they had eaten, saying, "This cup that is poured out for you is the new covenant in my blood." (Luke 22:19–20)[16]

> In the same way also he took the cup, after supper, saying, "This cup is the new covenant in my blood. Do this, as often as you drink it, in remembrance of me." For as often as you eat this bread and drink the cup, you proclaim the Lord's death until he comes. (1 Cor. 11:25–26)

Several issues are worth noting in relation to these three "cup words."[17] In the Matthew text, the phrase "this is my blood of the covenant" (τὸ αἷμά μου τῆς διαθήκης, Matt. 26:28) recalls the inauguration of the Mosaic covenant in the Septuagint translation of Exodus 24:8 (τὸ αἷμα τῆς διαθήκης). In what amounted to a covenant-ratification ceremony, Moses read from the covenant in the presence of the people and sprinkled the blood of slaughtered beasts on them, declaring it to be "the blood of the covenant." The only difference between the Exodus and Matthew texts is the addition of the possessive pronoun "my" in Matthew. Jesus understood his own blood as having covenant-ratification significance.[18] Since the Mosaic covenant is the only occasion that involves sprinkling of blood on the people present, Jesus's identification with it is all the

---

16. A textual issue arises with the Lucan cup word, some manuscripts omitting 22:19b–20. For a defense of the longer version, see I. Howard Marshall, *Last Supper and Lord's Supper* (Grand Rapids, MI: Eerdmans, 1980), 40. In the shorter form, the Passover cup in 22:17 becomes the Communion cup, adding a significant problem in reversing the order of the bread and cup words.

17. Joachim Jeremias, *The Eucharistic Words of Jesus*, trans. Arnold Ehrhardt (Oxford: Blackwell, 1955), 96–100.

18. Marshall, *Last Supper*, 91–93. Cf. Douglas Moo's comment, "The covenant sacrifice of Exodus 24:8 is a unique foundational event implying, perhaps, the taking away of sins as a necessary prelude to relationship with

more significant. It is not with just *any* covenant that he associates but with the Mosaic covenant and its law. The law keeper is taking the punishment of the lawless.

It is only in Matthew's account (26:28) that we find the extra words "for the forgiveness of sins" (εἰς ἄφεσιν ἁμαρτιῶν), and this seems to echo the prophetic word announcing the new covenant in Jeremiah 31:34, "For I will forgive their iniquity, and I will remember their sin no more." Again, the connection with covenant is uppermost.

Both Matthew and Mark employ the formula "poured out for many" (τὸ περὶ πολλῶν ἐκχυννόμενον, Matt. 26:28; τὸ ἐκχυννόμενον ὑπὲρ πολλῶν, Mark 14:24), reminiscent of the fourth Servant Song in Isaiah 53:12:

> Therefore I will divide him a portion with *the many*,
>   and he shall divide the spoil with the strong,
> because he poured out his soul to death
>   and was numbered with the transgressors;
> yet he bore the sin of *many*,
>   and makes intercession for the transgressors.[19]

The pouring out (ἐκχυννόμενον) suggests a separation of flesh and blood and is the language of sacrifice.[20]

In place of "for many" (Matthew and Mark), Luke has the more personal "for you" (τὸ ὑπὲρ ὑμῶν ἐκχυννόμενον). This point seems to underline the vicarious, substitutionary aspect of Christ's bloodshedding. He bears the covenant curse of death so that we might have eternal life.

Luke specifically identifies the cup with the "new covenant," as does Paul in the Corinthian correspondence. There is no need to see a tension between Matthew-Mark and Luke-Paul. The original Supper discourse may well have been longer, and each writer is recalling a part of it. Since Jesus spoke these words in Aramaic, and given the decades of oral transmission to which they were subjected, it is not surprising in the least that nuanced emphases are made by one tradition and not another. Significantly, all four sources allude to Jeremiah 31. Paul's Corinthian correspondence mimics Luke's account. If we take the use of "we" in Acts 16:11 as a reference to Luke joining Paul as they set sail from Troas, we have every reason to think that Luke had experienced the Corinthian church plant and discussed the Supper with Paul.[21]

By way of conclusion, the Supper takes place at Passover, and Jesus identifies himself with the Passover lamb. In Joachim Jeremias's words, "He is the eschatological Passover lamb representing the fulfilment of that which the Egyptian Passover lamb and all the

---

God, but emphasizing more strongly the establishment of fellowship." *The Old Testament in the Gospel Passion Narratives* (1983; repr., Eugene, OR: Wipf and Stock, 2007), 311.

19. See further J. Alec Motyer, *The Prophecy of Isaiah: An Introduction and Commentary* (Leicester, UK: Inter-Varsity Press, 1993), 442–43.

20. Jeremias, *Eucharistic Words*, 229.

21. N. T. Wright, *Paul: A Biography* (New York: HarperOne, 2018), 176–77.

subsequent sacrificial lambs were the prototype."[22] And even more specifically, Jeremias underlines the *covenantal* aspect of Jesus's death: "Jesus describes his death as this eschatological Passover sacrifice. His vicarious *huper*, vicarious death, brings into operation the final deliverance, the New Covenant of God."[23]

The Supper underlines a deep undercurrent of covenantal consciousness on the part of Jesus. He viewed his Messiahship as the fulfillment of the projected trajectory of covenantal allusions in the Old Testament. Jesus is Israel's God, just as Israel (the church) is his. He came to inaugurate and ratify the new covenant, prophesied by Jeremiah and elaborated on in 2 Corinthians 3:5–18 and more fully in Hebrews 8:1–10:18. The new covenant is, in effect, an upgrade, ending the need for continual sacrifices by the once-for-all sacrifice of Christ (ἅπαξ, ἐφάπαξ, Heb. 7:27; 9:12, 26) and aiding in the motivational and behavioral aspect of holiness by the promise of the Holy Spirit, the representative agent of the risen and ascended Jesus.

Bilateral Covenant

The sacraments are signs and seals of the covenant of grace—the grace that necessitates its unilateral nature. The question therefore arises whether the covenant of grace is to be viewed entirely unilaterally. And again, Reformed theology has given nuanced and careful attention to the way that the covenant of grace is to be viewed as *unilaterally established* but *bilaterally administered*. All covenants, by definition, involve *two* parties. But in the case of the covenant of grace—God's purposeful, inviolable intention to save the elect—Scripture gives no hint that it is a contract in which two parties have come to a mutual agreement. The covenant of grace is unilateral in the establishment of its terms and conditions. It is sovereignly initiated, its terms carefully and meticulously set out by a sovereign God. The plan is entirely the Lord's.[24] And in this sense (and in this sense *only*), the covenant of grace is unconditional.

But as Sinclair Ferguson observes, "This unconditional covenant operates in a carefully conditioned fashion since its grace carries in its wake obligations for the covenanted party."[25] In that sense, there is no such thing as an entirely unconditional covenant. A covenant has obligations and duties, involving expected (commanded!) trajectories of responsive behavior. Faith and repentance are covenantal *requirements*. There can be no salvation without faith or repentance. The demands of progressive sanctification are not unilaterally fulfilled. They are conditions: "Strive for peace with everyone, and for the

---

22. Jeremias, *Eucharistic Words*, 223.
23. Jeremias, *Eucharistic Words*, 226.
24. See John Murray, *The Covenant of Grace: A Biblico-Theological Study* (London: Tyndale Press, 1954), 10–12; Murray, "Covenant Theology," in *Collected Writings of John Murray*, 4 vols. (Edinburgh: Banner of Truth, 1982), 4:216–40.
25. Ferguson, "Infant Baptism View," 97; cf. Cornelis Venema, *Christ and Covenant Theology: Essays on Election, Republication, and the Covenants* (Phillipsburg, NJ: P&R, 2017), 187–88.

holiness without which no one will see the Lord" (Heb. 12:14). No observable holiness on the part of those who profess faith implies no assured salvation.

The dynamic of necessary, observable holiness as a mark of true faith is basic to the New Testament's understanding of the way salvation operates. Take, for example, the warnings against apostasy:

> And Jesus answered them, "See that no one leads you astray. For many will come in my name, saying, 'I am the Christ,' and they will lead many astray. . . .
>
> "And then many will fall away and betray one another and hate one another. And many false prophets will arise and lead many astray. And because lawlessness will be increased, the love of many will grow cold. But the one who endures to the end will be saved." (Matt. 24:4–5, 10–13)

> Now these things happened to them as an example, but they were written down for our instruction, on whom the end of the ages has come. Therefore let anyone who thinks that he stands take heed lest he fall. (1 Cor. 10:11–12)

> Therefore we must pay much closer attention to what we have heard, lest we drift away from it. (Heb. 2:1)

> Take care, brothers, lest there be in any of you an evil, unbelieving heart, leading you to fall away from the living God. But exhort one another every day, as long as it is called "today," that none of you may be hardened by the deceitfulness of sin. (Heb. 3:12–13)

Similar statements in the New Testament imply some conditionality on the assured status of our salvation in Christ:

> He has now reconciled [you] in his body of flesh by his death, in order to present you holy and blameless and above reproach before him, if indeed you continue in the faith, stable and steadfast, not shifting from the hope of the gospel that you heard, which has been proclaimed in all creation under heaven, and of which I, Paul, became a minister. (Col. 1:22–23)

> If we endure, we will also reign with him;
> if we deny him, he also will deny us. (2 Tim. 2:12)

> For we have come to share in Christ, if indeed we hold our original confidence firm to the end. (Heb. 3:14)

The point of these citations is to underline elements of conditionality. While the covenant of grace is unilaterally designed and initiated, it functions bilaterally. In no sense whatsoever can the believer remain passive in the outworking of salvation. That is why, in the case of infants who are baptized, believing parents make a solemn vow to bring up their covenant children "in the nurture and admonition of the Lord" (Eph. 6:4 KJV), with the expectation that God, in his own appointed time and manner, will bring the child to saving faith in Jesus Christ.

Equally, covenant children must, at some point, express their personal, lively faith in Jesus Christ, for there can be no salvation without it. Apart from repenting faith and faith*ful* repentance, the curse of the covenant remains. This is the pattern with Noah (Gen. 5:29; 6:13; 8:21), Abraham (Gen. 15:7–21), and Moses (Ex. 6:2–8; 34:10–28; Deut. 28–30). The very nature of the new covenant sacraments as bloodless rituals—water in place of the bloodletting ritual of circumcision, bread and wine in place of the slain Passover lamb—relate that Christ has drawn the sting of the curse "by becoming a curse for us" (Gal. 3:13). By receiving Christ, we receive the blessings of the covenant ("every spiritual blessing," Eph. 1:3), because he received its curses.

The covenantal association of the sacraments raises the issue of covenantal obligations. Christians promise allegiance and loyalty to the covenant, and failure to do so renders them liable to discipline (as the sharply worded threats of Paul's Corinthian correspondence with regard to the Supper indicate). All this is part of a greater dynamic—the relationship of grace and law within the Christian life. There are definitive and progressive aspects of sanctification, and the latter imply a conscious, strenuous *effort* on the part of God's children to obey the stipulations of the covenant. It is, after all, what Jesus told his disciples in the upper room: "If you love me, you will keep my commandments" (John 14:15). The fact that we are incapable of rendering that obedience perfectly, even with the indwelling of the Holy Spirit promised on the very occasion Jesus gave this command, is not to result in our passivity and resignation. Too often, in the interest of maintaining the grace of the gospel word, Christians draw the conclusion that effortful obedience on our part *by way of response to the gospel already received* somehow negates the grace of the gospel. Only a deeply warped reading of the New Testament would draw this conclusion.

In particular, four aspects of obedience on our part warrant attention.

Improving Our Baptism

The Westminster Larger Catechism 167 pointedly asks, "How is our baptism improved by us?" The answer is as follows:

> The needful but much neglected duty of improving our baptism, is to be performed by us all our life long, especially in the time of temptation, and when we are present at the administration of it to others; by serious and thankful consideration of the nature of it, and of the ends for which Christ instituted it, the privileges and benefits conferred and sealed thereby, and our solemn vow made therein; by being humbled for our sinful defilement, our falling short of, and walking contrary to, the grace of baptism, and our engagements; by growing up to assurance of pardon

of sin, and of all other blessings sealed to us in that sacrament; by drawing strength from the death and resurrection of Christ, into whom we are baptized, for the mortifying of sin, and quickening of grace; and by endeavoring to live by faith, to have our conversation in holiness and righteousness, as those that have therein given up their names to Christ; and to walk in brotherly love, as being baptized by the same Spirit into one body.

When tempted, Martin Luther would repeat the phrase *baptismus sum* ("I am a baptized man").[26] Though we may have no conscious memory of our own baptism (if we were infants when it occurred), we have seen many since then, and each one is a reminder of our own baptism. The promises of the covenant uttered then have been realized as we now exercise faith and believe the promises.

Baptism—*our own baptism*—is a reminder that, by faith alone in Jesus Christ alone, my sins are wholly forgiven, and I have peace with God. I need fear no condemnation, not now, not ever, for Christ has borne the curse of the law in my stead. When Satan tempts, I may say to him with confidence, "Christ has died! Rather, he has risen from the grave and has triumphed over the forces of darkness. Jesus has 'disarmed the rulers and authorities and put them to open shame, by triumphing over them'" (Col. 2:15). I may not believe what I am saying, of course, and it is often the cause of my downfall. We believe Satan's lies and fail to benefit from the power of the truth of the gospel.[27]

Unworthy Communion

The issue of unworthy participation at the Supper (*manducatio indignorum*) has seemingly been a troublesome one. It arises from a consideration of the need to "examine oneself" *before* participating at the Table, together with the prior warning: "Whoever, therefore, eats the bread or drinks the cup of the Lord in an unworthy manner will be guilty concerning the body and blood of the Lord" (1 Cor. 11:27). What precisely does eating and drinking "in an unworthy manner" mean? The fact that the Corinthian context in all likelihood bears virtually no resemblance to any celebration of the Supper we may have witnessed seems to have eluded the historical debate. What the church—more especially, the Reformed church—concluded from the toxic atmosphere of Corinth was the need to "fence the Table," insisting on weeks of preparatory repentance, with the

---

26. "The only way to drive away the Devil is through faith in Christ, by saying, 'I have been baptized. I am a Christian.'" Cited by Heiko A. Oberman, *Luther: Man between God and the Devil* (New Haven, CT: Yale University Press, 2006), 105. Cf. Luther's Larger Catechism, "On Baptism," section 44: "To appreciate and use Baptism aright, we must draw strength and comfort from it when our sins or conscience oppress us, and we must retort, 'But I am baptized! And if I am baptized, I have the promise that I shall be saved and have eternal life, both in soul and body.'" *The Large Catechism of Martin Luther*, trans. Robert H. Fischer (Philadelphia: Fortress, 1959), 86.

27. See Hughes Oliphant Old, *Worship: Reformed according to Scripture* (Louisville: Westminster John Knox, 2002), 20–21.

additional provision of dire threats of judgment in the case of noncompliance. This, sadly, has made an occasion of joy and celebration into one of fear and foreboding and, in its worst forms, an occasion that has turned the gospel on its head. For in every sense, no one is "worthy" of communing with Jesus. And that is the whole point of the Table. It is a sign and seal of grace to sinners.

The story is often told, and worth repeating here, of Dr. John "Rabbi" Duncan, the Scottish theologian and minister who once noticed a young lady in his Highland congregation so gripped by guilt over her sin that she hesitated to take the Lord's Supper. The minister's counsel to her is worth remembering every time we come to the Lord's Table: "Take it, Lass. It's *meant* for sinners."[28] The gospel shape of Communion ensures assurance, whereas the emphasis on achieving a "worthiness" always ends in misery and death.

The Supper as Remembrance

The phrase "in remembrance of me" has been the cause of innumerable controversies as to the meaning of the Lord's Supper. On the one hand, strict memorialists have seen it as justification to view the Supper as solely a ritual of "remembering"—as a photograph might help us recall a person long since deceased. That this is—*in part, at least*—the intention can be denied only at the expense of avoiding the surface meaning of the verb "to remember" and the covenantal command "to remember" (or the negative, "do not forget") that infuses the narrative of redemptive history (Deut. 9:7; 24:22; Josh. 1:13; etc.). Such an interpretation seems rather silly. Communicants should indeed try and remember what Jesus said and did by deliberately calling to mind the memory of the event as recorded in Scripture. Such purposeful contemplation should lead to joyful praise and worship and a renewal of vows made to deny oneself and follow Jesus wherever he calls us to go.

On the other hand, strict *realists*, who may speak of the "real presence" of Jesus in the Supper are also missing the point. "This is my body," "This is my blood"—these words, too, have been the cause of quite unnecessary dispute. The Latin *hoc est corpus meum* suggested to the Reformers some mischievous hocus-pocus, something akin to a wizard's trick and a Roman Catholic transubstantiation of the bread and wine (though nuanced in clerical thought, if not by the laity, with Aristotelian metaphysical distinctions between "forms" and "accidents"), and therefore, the Reformers flatly rejected it. But others, claiming at times to be defenders of John Calvin, have loosely spoken of the "real presence" of Christ in the Supper (a phrase that Calvin did not use and would not have used). A moment's reflection on the fact that when Jesus first used the words, he was either standing or sitting there in front of them. His physical presence could hardly be there in the upper room and "in" the bread and wine at the same time. The "is" must

---

28. William Barclay, *The Letters to the Corinthians* (Louisville: Westminster, 1956), 124.

mean "represents" or "symbolizes."[29] In this way, we "look back" during the Supper, to a point in time, a historical event and a geographical location where the drama of redemption was played out before the eyes of humanity.

The physical body of Jesus can occupy only one point of the space-time universe. If it contains a shred of ubiquity, it is no longer a human body, and Jesus is no longer our representative. It is not, therefore, out of accord to ask at the celebration of the Supper, "Where is the body of Jesus?" or more specifically, "Where is the body that, by baptism, I have been baptized into—into his death and resurrection?" (Rom. 6:1–4). The answer has to be, "In heaven." And if we ask further where that might be, we can surmise that it is "somewhere" in the created universe—"up there," "at the right hand of God," "in a fold in space"—somewhere that isn't *here*. The resurrection of Jesus is meant to be viewed as a prototype of our own resurrection ("firstfruits," 1 Cor. 15:20), and at the Supper, the trajectory of thought is upward rather than downward. We should think of Jesus's body and remind ourselves that we, too, will share a resurrected body in the new heavens and new earth when Jesus will drink the cup of celebration portrayed in the marriage supper that closes the Bible (Rev. 19:6–9).

The Supper word in Paul contains both a "now" and a "not yet" act of remembrance. By looking "up," we remember that we have a Savior who helps us in our current infirmities and provides us with his agent, the Holy Spirit, to aid us in the pilgrimage and fight. This is what Calvin so marvelously taught about what the Supper truly represents—spiritual/Spiritual communion with the ascended Christ by the help of the Holy Spirit.[30] That communion is here and now. But there is also a "not yet" aspect—"until he comes" (1 Cor. 11:26). There is a "looking ahead," an anticipation of glory and what will be in the new heavens and new earth. At the Supper, we should tell Jesus how much we are looking forward to seeing him "face to face" (1 Cor. 13:12).

It is in this way that the Supper serves as a conduit in which the grace of the gospel is experienced afresh. The frequency of the Supper has been a matter of much dispute, and simply placing it in the morning Sunday service may not fully meet all that is necessary for Christian growth and nurture. Mention is often made of Calvin's unfulfilled desire for a weekly Lord's Supper (an impossibility given the strict supervision he demanded of who may or may not participate). Given the fact that Geneva had two Sunday services and alternated every other week between daily lunchtime expositions Monday through Friday and a Wednesday noon service, it has to be remembered that the ratio of sermons to Supper was in the order of ten to one. If having a weekly Lord's Supper in a church that has only one service a week also reduces the length of the sermon, the balance of Word and sacrament seems askew.

---

29. The words of Jesus at the Capernaum synagogue in John 6 cannot be used to interpret the Supper, an event that had not yet taken place.

30. See Ferguson, *Holy Spirit*, 199–205; Ligon Duncan, "True Communion with Christ: Calvin, Westminster and Consensus on the Lord's Supper," in *The Westminster Confession into the 21st Century*, ed. Ligon Duncan (Fearn, Ross-shire, Scotland: Mentor, 2004), 2:429–76.

That said, the "visible word" of the sacraments has an important function in Christian growth and nurture. The Heidelberg Catechism 75 underlines the manner in which the Supper serves as a tool of assurance:

> Q. How does the Lord's Supper signify and seal to you that you share in Christ's one sacrifice on the cross and in all His gifts?
>
> A. In this way: Christ has commanded me and all believers to eat of this broken bread and drink of this cup in remembrance of Him. With this command He gave these promises: First, *as surely as I see with my eyes* the bread of the Lord broken for me and the cup given to me, so surely was His body offered for me and His blood poured out for me on the cross. Second, as surely as I receive from the hand of the minister and taste with my mouth the bread and the cup of the Lord as sure signs of Christ's body and blood, so surely does He Himself nourish and refresh my soul to everlasting life with His crucified body and shed blood.

"As surely as I see with my eyes" is a way of saying, "Seeing is believing—in other words, that contemplating and actually consuming the sign confirms confidence that one is sharing in the thing signified."[31]

The Supper as Koinonia

From one point of view, it is surprising that the Supper is mentioned only once in Paul's correspondence. That in itself should make us cautious about overemphasizing it. And furthermore, when mention is made of the Supper, it is in the context of an appalling mishandling of the sacrament. The Corinthians' loveless treatment of each other at the Supper (of all occasions to demonstrate selfishness!) drew from Paul some of his most vehement words of rebuke and warning. But it also occasioned one of the most pointed insights into the meaning of the Supper:

> The cup of blessing that we bless, is it not a participation in the blood of Christ? The bread that we break, is it not a participation in the body of Christ? Because there is one bread, we who are many are one body, for we all partake of the one bread. (1 Cor. 10:16–17)

The Supper implies a "participation" in all that Christ is and represents. The Greek word is κοινωνία. The Supper—*Communion*, as many Christians rightly refer to it—is a meal in which we "commune" with Jesus, and he with us. Literally, we "share in common with" Jesus our body-soul existence. And as we eat and drink this covenant meal, we are strengthened and nourished by the recollection that we are "one body"—one with Christ and one with one another as his church (1 Cor.

---

31. Packer, *Taking God Seriously*, 129.

6:17).[32] In the Supper we are drawn by the Holy Spirit to fellowship with Christ, and thereby we are assured of our privileges and blessings in the gospel. Here, in communion with Jesus, is the end of all doubt. Here, by the Holy Spirit's energy (Lat. *virtus*), we are in the safest place and condition of all.[33]

It is the covenant—the covenant *of grace*—that ensures this assurance. The sacraments, in the language of the Westminster Confession, "confirm our interest in Christ" (27.1) Augustus Toplady expresses this belief with great conviction:

A debtor to mercy alone,
Of *covenant* mercy I sing;
Nor fear, with Thy righteousness on,
My person and offering to bring.
The terrors of law and of God
With me can have nothing to do;
My Savior's obedience and blood
Hide all my transgressions from view.

The work which His goodness began,
The arm of His strength will complete;
His promise is yea and amen,
And never was forfeited yet.
Things future, nor things that are now,
Not all things below nor above
Can make Him His purpose forego,
Or sever my soul from His love.[34]

---

32. For an extended discussion of this theme, see Guilelmus Saldenus and Wilhelmus à Brakel, *In Remembrance of Him: Profiting from the Lord's Supper*, ed. James A. De Jong (Grand Rapids, MI: Reformation Heritage Books, 2012); Herman Witsius, *The Economy of the Covenants between God and Man: Comprehending a Complete Body of Divinity*, trans. William Crookshank, 2 vols. (Grand Rapids, MI: Reformation Heritage Books, 2010), 1:271–80.

33. Calvin's view of the Supper is sometimes referred to as *virtualism*. Calvin uses the term *virtutem* in describing the mysterious "power" (*virtus*), the power of the Holy Spirit, in the sacrament of the Lord's Supper. Interestingly, Calvin alludes to the mind's inability to comprehend the truths that lie behind the sacrament of the Lord's Supper in a later section in book 4 of the *Institutes*:

Even though it seems unbelievable that Christ's flesh, separated from us by such great distance, penetrates to us, so that it becomes our food, let us remember how far the secret power of the Holy Spirit towers above all our senses, and how foolish it is to wish to measure his immeasurableness by our measure. What then, our mind does not comprehend, let faith conceive: that the Spirit truly unites things separated in space.

John Calvin, *Institutes of the Christian Religion*, ed. John T. McNeill, trans. Ford Lewis Battles, LCC 20–21 (Philadelphia: Westminster, 1960), 4.17.10. See Gerrish, *Grace and Gratitude*, 177–78; Ronald S. Wallace, *Calvin's Doctrine of the Word and Sacrament* (Tyler, TX: Geneva Divinity School Press, 1982), 218–21.

34. Augustus Toplady (1740–1778), "A Debtor to Mercy Alone," 1771.

Afterword

Why Covenant Theology?

Kevin DeYoung

Many of us are familiar with the language of the covenant.[1] We hear terms like covenant membership or covenant baptism, and yet some of us may still be hard pressed to describe what we mean by covenant. Why is this theme is so important in Scripture? Why does it matter in the Christian life? If we are people of the covenant, then we must understand what covenant theology is all about and how we can explain it to others. Even though much has been written about covenant theology—and rightly so!—at its most basic level, covenant theology is simple enough to sketch on the back of a napkin.

A Simple Definition

In simplest terms, a covenant is a contract, an agreement between two or more parties. Marriage is the most familiar example in our culture, but almost anything that requires two signatures can be considered a kind of covenant—from buying a car to getting approved for a mortgage to signing up for a home security system. Whenever we have legally binding agreements, we have covenants.

Covenants in the Bible, however, are about more than contracts. They are about people. *A covenant is a commitment that establishes a relationship between two or more persons.* For our purposes, we are looking at those covenants that establish a relationship between God and his people, a covenant bond that establishes stipulations, makes promises, guarantees blessings, and threatens curses. Just as we must sign on the dotted line in our legally binding documents, so too did ancient covenants require some kind of oath ratification. Normally this involved blood as a sign and seal of the obligations

---

1. This afterword is a modified version of a sermon originally delivered at University Reformed Church, East Lansing, Michigan, on Sunday evening, January 10, 2016.

established, the blessings promised (upon obedience), and the curses threatened (upon disobedience).

If that's what a covenant is (in general terms), what does covenant theology look like? Well, get out your napkins and follow along, because I think understanding covenant theology can be as easy as one, two, three. Or actually, as easy as three, one, two. If we want to help our people grasp covenant theology—or if we need some helpful hooks in our own minds—we need to understand three different covenants, one covenant of grace, and two ways of existing in this one covenant.

Three Covenants

Let's start by talking about three different covenants in the Bible.

Covenant of Works

The first covenant we encounter in Scripture is the covenant of works. It is sometimes called the Adamic covenant because it was made with Adam in the garden. The Westminster Shorter Catechism 12 calls it the "covenant of life" because to obey the stipulations would have given life. This Edenic administration has also been called the covenant of nature or the covenant of creation, but most often theologians now refer to it as the covenant of works.

Here's what we read in the Westminster Confession of Faith:

> The distance between God and the creature is so great, that although reasonable creatures do owe obedience unto him as their Creator, yet they could never have any fruition of him as their blessedness and reward, but by some voluntary condescension on God's part, which he hath been pleased to express by way of covenant. (7.1)

That is a fancy way of saying that for God to enter into any kind of agreement with man—even one based on works—was an act of grace. The confession continues:

> The first covenant made with man was a covenant of works, wherein life was promised to Adam; and in him to his posterity, upon condition of perfect and personal obedience. (7.2)

That is a succinct definition of the covenant of works. Adam was a public person. He was the federal head for the whole human race, meaning he was the representative for all who would come after him. This is sometimes called federal theology or federalism, *foedus* being the Latin word for "covenant."

Famously, Genesis never calls this arrangement with Adam a covenant. But Hosea 6:7 says that "like Adam [Israel] transgressed the covenant," implying that Adam's relationship to God was covenantal in nature. The tree of the knowledge of good and evil was a probationary tree, testing Adam to see if he would keep God's covenant. Eternal life in paradise with God was promised to Adam and his posterity on the condition of obedience, while death was promised if Adam disobeyed.

Adam and Eve would be God's treasured people, in paradise, in his presence—if they kept the covenant. That's at the heart of each covenantal arrangement. We see it with Abraham as God promises to make him into a great nation (people) and give him a great land (paradise) and be with him as his God (presence).[2] We see the same three basic items in the new covenant as well. As the church, we are God's chosen people, enjoying the "already" (and awaiting the "not yet") of our heavenly inheritance of paradise, while we delight in the presence of God by union with his Son and by the indwelling of his Spirit.

All three gifts—people, paradise, presence—were squandered by Adam in the garden. And so we see curse instead of blessing. Adam and Eve are cursed with toil and pain (people), then the ground is cursed (paradise), and finally Adam and Eve are cut off from the presence of God as they are kicked out of Eden and their reentry is barred. Adam is a covenant breaker—and all of us with him. God still requires perfect obedience in order to receive the full blessings of the covenant. But on this side of the fall, none of us are capable of meeting these requirements, so now all who rely on the works of the law are under a curse (Gal. 3:10).

Some people object to any sort of covenant based on works. They argue that God only, and always, deals with human beings in grace. In one sense, that is certainly true. As we've already seen from the Westminster Confession, even God's arrangement with Adam was marked by a gracious condescension. And yet, we don't have to shy away from the language of works, because there is clearly a "do this and live" principle central to God's command surrounding the probationary tree. There is no grace as forgiveness of sin in the covenant with Adam. No deliverance is operative (though it is foretold) because at that point there is no human sin to infest God's perfect world. The blessings of God are promised on condition of works fulfilled.

Covenant of Grace

If the first covenant is a covenant of works, the second is a covenant of grace. The stipulations of the covenant of works are still on us, but they no longer possess the ability to bless because we are no longer capable of fulfilling those obligations. To gain salvation by works is now a moral and metaphysical impossibility.

Again, here's the Westminster Confession of Faith:

Man, by his fall, having made himself uncapable of life by that covenant, the Lord was pleased to make a second, commonly called the covenant of grace; wherein he

---

2. Jonty Rhodes uses these three *p*'s in *Covenants Made Simple: Understanding God's Unfolding Promises to His People* (Phillipsburg, NJ: P&R, 2013), 22. He also references Graeme Goldsworthy and Vaughan Roberts as using the same alliterative summary of God's blessings.

freely offereth unto sinners life and salvation by Jesus Christ; requiring of them faith in him, that they may be saved, and promising to give unto all those that are ordained unto eternal life his Holy Spirit, to make them willing, and able to believe. (7.3)

We say more about this covenant in our next section, but for now let me simply point out that this covenant of grace is one covenant that allows for different manifestations.[3] We see God's promise to Noah (and to the rest of humanity through him) in Genesis 8–9—a covenant of preservation whereby God graciously promises to maintain the orderly workings of his creation. We see God's promise to Abraham (and to the nations that will come from him) in Genesis 12—the paradigmatic example in the Old Testament of covenantal blessing. We see God's promises to Moses (and to the nation he was leading) in the Pentateuch—a covenantal arrangement full of law but also replete with a gracious sacrificial system and rich messianic foreshadowing. We see God's promise to David (and his royal descendants) in 2 Samuel 7—a covenant of kingdom guaranteeing that a king from the line of David would forever sit on the throne. And finally, we see the new covenant predicted in Jeremiah 31—a covenant of consummation, fulfilling all that was prefigured through Abraham. In other words, outside of a couple of chapters in Genesis and Revelation, the entire Bible shows the unfolding of God's plan and promise to bless his people through this one covenant of grace.

Covenant of Redemption

Besides the covenant of works and the covenant of grace, there is a third type of arrangement, usually called the covenant of redemption. Sometimes you see it referenced with the Latin phrase *pactum salutis*, a salvation pact. In simple terms, the covenant of redemption refers to the eternal agreement between the Father and the Son to save a people chosen in Christ before the ages began. In slightly more detail, Louis Berkhof describes the covenant of redemption as "the agreement between the Father, giving the Son as Head and Redeemer of the elect, and the Son, voluntarily taking the place of those whom the Father had given him."[4]

At first, this may seem like overeager theologizing by speculative systematicians. But actually, there is plenty of evidence in Scripture for a salvation pact between the Father and the Son. We know that the elect were chosen not out of thin air but *in Christ* before the foundations of the world. We know that promises were made to Christ that he would be given a people by the Father (John 6:38–40; cf. 5:30, 43; 17:4–12). We know that Christ, as the second Adam, is the covenant head of his people (Rom. 5:12–21; 1 Cor.

---

3. We could call these manifestations "dispensations" as long as we don't understand by that word all the contours of dispensational theology.

4. Louis Berkhof, *Systematic Theology*, combined ed. (Grand Rapids, MI: Eerdmans, 1996), 271. This combined edition also includes Berkhof's *Introductory Volume to Systematic Theology*. The page numbers I cite all come from the *Systematic Theology* itself.

15:22). And we know from a text like Psalm 2 that there was a decree whereby the eternally begotten Son was given the nations as his heritage and the ends of the earth as his possession (2:7–8). In other words, the Son was granted, by an eternal arrangement, a people to save and to redeem. This is why Jesus in John 5:36 says that he has come to do the works that the Father has given him to accomplish and why Jesus in Luke 22:29 speaks of the kingdom the Father has assigned to him. The covenant of grace in time is made possible by the covenant of redemption from all eternity.

One Covenant of Grace

We've looked at the three overarching covenants in Scripture. Now I want to go back to the covenant of grace and show in more detail how this one covenant stretches across the Bible from cover to cover. How we understand the covenant of grace goes a long way in setting our theological trajectory.

Once again, Berkhof provides a succinct definition. The covenant of grace, he says, is "that gracious agreement between the offended God and the offending but elect sinner, in which God promises salvation through faith in Christ, and the sinner accepts this believingly, promising a life of faith and obedience."[5] Right away, this definition raises an important question: Is the covenant of grace conditional or unconditional? And the answer is yes. It's both, depending on how you understand both terms. The covenant of grace is unconditional if you understand the condition to mean some sort of merit. There is nothing that we earn or come to deserve in the covenant of grace. It is, after all, not a covenant of works. But on the other hand, many Reformed theologians have not shied away from calling the covenant of grace a conditional covenant. Entrance into this covenant is free, *and* it is contingent on faith, a faith that is itself a gift from the Holy Spirit.

Many Reformed Christians have objected to the word "condition" being used in connection with the covenant of grace. But Berkhof argues, "This was largely due to a reaction against Arminianism, which employed the word 'condition' in an un-Scriptural sense, and therefore to a failure to discriminate properly."[6] We must distinguish between *meritorious conditions* and *necessary conditions*. If I were to say, "You need a ticket to enter Bank of America Stadium to attend a Carolina Panthers game," the ticket would be a condition. You cannot enter without it. But that does not tell you how one gets a ticket. Maybe you have to work really hard and save your money in order to purchase a ticket. That would be a meritorious condition. But perhaps the ticket was given to you as a gift, in which case it would be a necessary condition for entrance into the stadium but not a condition you have met by your earning or deserving. In the same way, faith is a necessary condition for truly possessing the blessings of the covenant of

---

5. Berkhof, *Systematic Theology*, 277.
6. Berkhof, *Systematic Theology*, 281.

grace, but it is not a meritorious condition. You cannot inherit the fullness of covenant blessings apart from faith, but this faith is itself a divine gift.[7]

It's important to recognize that faith has been the condition (in the necessary sense) of covenant blessing from east of Eden to the new Jerusalem. To be sure, the contours of this one covenant look different under different administrations, but the substance has been the same. The Westminster Confession explains:

> This covenant was differently administered in the time of the law, and in the time of the gospel; under the law it was administered by promises, prophecies, sacrifices, circumcision, the paschal lamb, and other types and ordinances delivered to the people of the Jews, all for signifying Christ to come, which were for that time sufficient and efficacious, through the operation of the Spirit, to instruct and build up the elect in faith in the promised Messiah. (7.5)

In other words, the different administrations of the covenant of grace are not uniform. And yet, they are held together by an underlying unity:

> Under the gospel, when Christ the substance was exhibited, the ordinances in which this covenant is dispensed are the preaching of the word, and the administration of the sacraments of Baptism and the Lord's Supper, which, though fewer in number, and administered with more simplicity and less outward glory, yet, in them it is held forth in more fulness, evidence, and spiritual efficacy, to all nations, both Jews and Gentiles; and is called the New Testament. There are not therefore two covenants of grace differing in substance, but one and the same under various dispensations. (7.6)

Of the three foundational covenant blessings—I will make you a people, I will give you a land, I will be with you—the most important is the last one, the promise of God's presence. We see this promise repeated throughout both Testaments:

- In Genesis 17:8, in instituting the sign of circumcision, God promises to Abraham and his offspring, "I will be their God."
- In Exodus 6:7, God says to Moses, as he sets him on his journey to become Israel's deliverer and lawgiver, "I am the LORD your God, who has brought you out from under the burdens of the Egyptians."
- And again in Exodus 20:2, at the outset of the Ten Commandments, God reiterates, "I am the LORD your God, who brought you out of the land of Egypt, out of the house of slavery."
- Likewise, in Deuteronomy 29:13, as the covenant is renewed at Moab, we read that God will establish his people "that he may be your God, as he promised you, and as he swore to your fathers, to Abraham, to Isaac, and to Jacob."
- We see the same fundamental promise in 2 Samuel 7:14, where God promises to David's heir, "I will be to him a father, and he shall be to me a son."

---

7. Jonty Rhodes uses a similar illustration in *Covenants Made Simple*, 61–62.

- Again, Jeremiah 7:23 says, "Obey my voice, and I will be your God, and you shall be my people." The same promise is repeated several times in Jeremiah and again in Ezekiel 36.
- Jumping to the end of the Bible, we find that the heart of God's gracious covenant is still beating for people: "The one who conquers will have this heritage, and I will be his God and he will be my son" (Rev. 21:7).

Covenant theology is the Bible's story from the first page to the last. The promise of God's presence was given to childless Abraham, reiterated at the giving of the law on Mount Sinai, repeated at the renewal of the covenant on Moab, declared again to David and then to Jeremiah and Ezekiel, and finally fulfilled in the New Testament and brought to its culmination in the new heavens and new earth.

The covenant of grace, though it appears in different dispensations or administrations, is one covenant. Here is what Paul says in Galatians 3:17–18: "The law, which came 430 years afterward, does not annul a covenant previously ratified by God, so as to make the promise void. For if the inheritance comes by the law, it no longer comes by promise; but God gave it to Abraham by a promise."

Make no mistake, there are elements of previous administrations that fade away. There is, after all, an *old* covenant and a *new* covenant. But what was old and passing away was not the covenant of grace itself but a particular expression of that covenant under Moses. Paul makes clear in Galatians 3 that the giving of the law did not set aside that covenant of grace established with Abraham. God's covenant of grace—exemplified most distinctly in God's promise to Abraham—is still in effect.

Before we move to the final section, we need to say more about the new covenant replacing the old. This was the great promise made in Jeremiah 31, which finds its clearest fulfillment in Hebrews 8. Many people say, "I can see that covenant is an important concept in the Bible. I can even see how certain covenant promises are consistent in both Testaments. But I don't think you've paid enough attention to the *discontinuity* between the old and the new covenant. The new covenant introduces a new kind of relationship between God and his people—one that is based on a religion of the heart instead of mere national obligation. This is why Jeremiah 31 and Hebrews 8 say that in the new covenant the law will be written on the heart and no one will have to tell his brother to know the Lord. The covenant has moved from external to internal." It's this line of reasoning that leads Baptists to insist that the covenant sign of baptism can be applied *only* to professing believers.

These are plausible arguments, and there are many people I respect who understand the covenants in this way. But here's why I disagree: the new covenant is not as new as they think. That is, the new covenant is new in comparison to the ceremonies of the Mosaic law, but it is nothing more (and nothing less!) than the full embodiment of all that was promised to the patriarchs, to Moses, and to David.

Think of it this way. What are we promised in the new covenant in Jeremiah 31 and Hebrews 8? R. Scott Clark has helpfully summarized the new covenant as promising four things: an immutable covenant, an interior piety, an immediate knowledge, and iniquity forgiven.[8]

If the new covenant is *immutable*, so was the Abrahamic covenant, which Galatians 3 says was never annulled or abolished.

If the new covenant boasts of an *interior piety*, so does the covenant throughout the Old Testament, where God promises to circumcise the hearts of his people (Deut. 30:6) and where the psalmist often speaks of the law on his heart (Psalm 1; 19; 119). There is nothing new about an internal religion of the heart.

So what about *immediate knowledge*? Isn't it true that in the new covenant we won't have to teach each other anymore, for everyone will know God from the least to the greatest (Heb. 8:11)? Isn't that an undeniable sign that we have moved from a national religion based on birth to a spiritual religion based on new birth? To be sure, there is something wonderfully new described in this verse, but let's be careful that we don't claim too much for Hebrews 8:11. Do we really want to suggest that in the new covenant there is no teaching and there are no teachers? No pastors? No elders? No parental instruction? Surely that's not what the prophecy means. The point is not that we've moved from a national faith to a personal faith. The point, rather, is that we have no need for a mediator like Moses or for a Levitical class and an Aaronic line of priests.

And finally, we come to the promise of *iniquity forgiven* in Hebrews 8:12. Surely this is not a new promise. One only has to look at Psalm 32 (or a hundred other texts) to realize that God's people in the Old Testament enjoyed the blessing of having their trespasses atoned for and their sins pardoned.

In short, the prophecy in Jeremiah is about the removal of the Mosaic covenant, in particular the cultic rites and ceremonies. In moving from the old covenant to the new, we move from typology to fulfillment, from shadow to substance. What's new is the clarity of the covenant of grace, not its underlying content.

Two Ways of Existing in This One Covenant

We've looked at three covenants and the one covenant of grace. In this last section, we examine two ways of existing in this one covenant.

The covenant expressed in the Old Testament was always meant to be spiritual in nature. Circumcision of the flesh was supposed to have its counterpart in the circumcision of the heart (Lev. 26:40–42; Deut. 10:16; 30:6; Jer. 4:4; 6:10; 9:25). Paul makes this point forcefully in Romans 4:11, where circumcision is called a sign and seal given to Abraham of the righteousness that comes by faith. In other words, circumcision was, from its very inception, a sign of spiritual realities. And keep in mind, God commanded

8. R. Scott Clark, "On the New Covenant," January 1, 2011, https://rscottclark.org/2011/01/on-the-new-covenant/.

this sign, with all its spiritual import, to be applied to eight-day-old sons who could not yet appropriate its significance for themselves.

That may seem a strange arrangement, until we realize that it was (and still is) possible to be connected externally to the covenant without personally owning all the internal realities. This is why Romans 2:25–29 talks about Jews who are circumcised but not really circumcised, and why Romans 9:6–8 talks about children of Abraham who are not really children of Abraham. In the church, we might say, there are some who are baptized who have not really been baptized. This same reality—of being externally connected to the covenant sign without having the internal substance—is a possibility even in the new covenant.

This may sound strange, but it's the situation described in Hebrews 10:26–29:

> If we go on sinning deliberately after receiving the knowledge of the truth, there no longer remains a sacrifice for sins, but a fearful expectation of judgment, and a fury of fire that will consume the adversaries. Anyone who has set aside the law of Moses dies without mercy on the evidence of two or three witnesses. How much worse punishment, do you think, will be deserved by the one who has trampled underfoot the Son of God, and has profaned the blood of the covenant by which he was sanctified [i.e., "set apart"], and has outraged the Spirit of grace?

How do we make sense of a passage like this (and other similar verses in Hebrews)? If our understanding of the new covenant doesn't have an external and an internal dimension, we'll end up saying people can lose their salvation or Christians can become unjustified. Surely, that's not what the author means by trampling the Son of God and profaning the blood of the covenant. A better explanation is to understand that there always have been (and still are) two ways of existing in the one covenant of grace, even in its new covenant economy. Hebrews 10 describes those who are connected to the blood of the covenant and yet prove to be covenant breakers.

There are different ways to talk about this external-internal distinction. Some theologians refer to the administration of the covenant and the essence of the covenant, or the conditional covenant and the absolute covenant, or the covenant as a legal relationship and the covenant as a communion of life. That last phrase is how Berkhof describes the two ways of existing in the covenant:

> In discussing membership in the covenant as a legal relationship it should be borne in mind that the covenant in this sense is not merely a system of demands and promises, demands that ought to be met and promises that ought to be realized; but that it also includes a reasonable expectation that the external legal relationship will carry with it the weight of the glorious reality of a life in intimate communion with the covenant God. This is the only way in which the idea of the covenant is fully realized.[9]

---

9. Berkhof, *Systematic Theology*, 287.

The point is that in both the Old Testament and the New Testament, there is an objective and a subjective element to the covenant. We belong to the covenant community externally by family but belong internally by faith. In broad strokes, then, a Reformed Christian might say that credobaptists pay too little attention to the objective elements of the covenant, while Federal Vision proponents, Lutherans, and Catholics pay too little attention to the subjective elements. It is possible to have a legal relationship to the covenant without experiencing the communion of life, which is why children of believers ought to be baptized and why we pray for those children to make the baptismal promises their own.

I told you that covenant theology was as easy as one, two, three (or three, one, two, as the case may be).

A Relational Theology for Real People

I suppose the back of your napkin is pretty well full already, but we have to consider one last question, at least briefly. What difference does all this make? Let me suggest four reasons covenant theology matters.

First, covenant theology helps us see the grand sweep of salvation history. If you are a child of God, you are part of a long story that began in eternity past with the Father establishing a salvation pact with his Son. You can't have a longer story than this one.

Second, covenant theology means that God has entered into a relationship with you *and* with your children. God does not deal with us only as individuals; our God is a God of families.

Third, covenant theology reminds us that God wants to see faith in you and in your children. There is more to the covenant than external privileges and legal obligations. The things signified should become, by faith, the things internalized.

Finally, covenant theology gives us an important and necessary way of understanding God's revelation. The Bible is a book about covenants, and the central promise in God's covenantal arrangement is unimaginably glorious: that God will be our God and that we will be his people. What a difference pronouns can make! Anyone can believe in *a* God, but covenant theology teaches us that the true and living God is *our* God. That was the promise to Abraham, the promise throughout the Old Testament, and the promise that finds its wonderful fulfillment at the end of the age (Rev. 21:7).

That's worth putting on your napkin and worth sharing with those whose napkins are not as full.

An Annotated Bibliography
of Reformed Reflection
on the Covenant

John R. Muether

The contributors to *Covenant Theology* are indebted to and build on a rich tradition of reflection on the biblical covenants in the Reformed tradition, and so it is fitting to conclude with a survey of some of that literature. Users of this bibliography should be mindful of its limits. It is restricted to major works in English on the rise of covenant theology and subsequent reflections on its developments. Bibliographical information generally refers to the most accessible of modern editions. There are many important figures and works in the development of covenant theology that are omitted from this selected list. Deep reflection on the biblical covenants can be found in sermons, commentaries, systematic theologies, and other works, but this list must content itself with specific works that focus on the topic of covenant theology.

Within contemporary Reformed scholarship, "discussion of the covenant is anything but a 'peaceable kingdom,'" as one observer puts it.[1] The field of covenant theology, as the essays in this volume demonstrate, reveals exegetical challenges, theological disputes, and historiographical fault lines among those identifying with the Reformed tradition. Still, there is consensus that in the theology of the covenants, we find, in Andrew Woolsey's phrase, the "natural fruit of Reformed theology."[2]

---

1. Charles G. Dennison, "Thoughts on the Covenant," in *Pressing toward the Mark: Essays Commemorating Fifty Years of the Orthodox Presbyterian Church*, ed. Charles G. Dennison and Richard C. Gamble (Philadelphia: Committee for the Historian of the Orthodox Presbyterian Church, 1986), 18n2.

2. Andrew A. Woolsey, *Unity and Continuity in Covenantal Thought: A Study in the Reformed Tradition to the Westminster Assembly* (Grand Rapids, MI: Reformation Heritage Books, 2012), 98.

General Historical Surveys and Bibliographies

Woolsey, Andrew A. *Unity and Continuity in Covenantal Thought: A Study in the Reformed Tradition to the Westminster Assembly*. Grand Rapids, MI: Reformation Heritage Books, 2012.

The first place to go is this remarkably comprehensive study of the sources of the Reformed covenant tradition. Woolsey draws a picture of continuity and development in Reformed thinking on the covenant from an engagement with primary sources. A rich and extensive bibliography complements the historical analysis. (Users should be aware, however, that this 2012 imprint is the publication of a 1988 dissertation, so the book is more dated than it may appear.)

Golding, Peter. *Covenant Theology: The Key of Theology in Reformed Thought and Tradition*. Fearn, Ross-shire, Scotland: Mentor, 2004.

On a scale that is less thorough than Woolsey, Golding presents the history of covenant theology in three main historical sections: origins, the "golden age" of the seventeenth century, and modern interpretations. The value of this book as a reference tool is limited by the lack of an index.

Brown, W. Adams. "Covenant Theology." In *Encyclopedia of Religion and Ethics*, edited by James Hastings, 4:219–24. New York: Charles Scribner's Sons, 1912.

Murray, John. "Covenant Theology." In *The Encyclopedia of Christianity*, edited by Philip Edgcumbe Hughes, 3:199–216. Marshallton, DE: National Foundation for Christian Education, 1972.

Macleod, Donald. "Covenant Theology." In *Dictionary of Scottish Church History and Theology*, edited by Nigel M. de S. Cameron, 214–18. Downers Grove, IL: InterVarsity Press, 1993.

These three oft-cited and complementary surveys of covenant theology from the early, mid-, and late twentieth century each offer a succinct summary of major voices with accompanying bibliography. Though Murray's piece is the most obscure, it is reprinted in *Collected Writings of John Murray* (Edinburgh: Banner of Truth, 1982), 4:216–40.

Antecedents in the Early and Medieval Church

Ferguson, Everett. "The Covenant Idea in the Second Century." In *Texts and Testaments: Critical Essays on the Bible and Early Church Fathers*, edited by W. Eugene March, 135–62. San Antonio, TX: Trinity University Press, 1980.

Ferguson reviews major second-century sources such as the epistle of Barnabas, Justin Martyr, Tertullian, Clement of Alexandria, Melito of Sardis, and Origen, and he suggests that while covenant was less significant for the early church than it was in the Old Testament, it was employed especially in anti-Gnostic polemics.

Duncan, J. Ligon. *The Covenant Idea in Ante-Nicene Theology.* PhD diss., University of Edinburgh, 1995.

In his doctoral dissertation (summarized in his contribution to this volume), Duncan finds covenant logic implicit in early church fathers. His analysis extends from Clement of Rome to Novitian.

Gräbe, Petrus J. *New Covenant, New Community: The Significance of Biblical and Patristic Covenant Theology for Contemporary Understanding.* Milton Keynes, UK: Paternoster, 2006.

Gräbe, who teaches at Regent University, surveys the epistle of Barnabas, Justin Martyr, Irenaeus, and Clement of Alexandria.

Preus, James Samuel. *From Shadow to Promise: Old Testamental Interpretation from Augustine to the Young Luther.* Cambridge, MA: Harvard University Press, 1969.

This volume is useful as a study of the typology of salvation history in which God's covenant is central. Preus surveys the development of a promise-and-fulfillment hermeneutic in the Middle Ages that gave rise to Reformation theology.

Oberman, Heiko A. *The Harvest of Medieval Theology: Gabriel Biel and Late Medieval Nominalism.* Cambridge, MA: Harvard University Press, 1963.

———. *Forerunners of the Reformation: The Shape of Late Medieval Thought.* London: Lutterworth, 1967.

Oberman explores the "striking emphasis on the covenantal relationship between God and his people" that developed in late medieval theology (*Forerunners*, 24), in the nominalism of Thomas Bradwardine, Robert Holcot, Gabriel Biel, and others. Other scholars are unconvinced that a strong connection can be drawn from medieval nominalism to Reformed covenant theology.

Early Development in the Reformation Era

Recent scholarship points to the emergence of the covenant idea earlier in the Reformation movement than previous scholarship had suggested, and it has identified John Calvin as one of many sources on the covenant in the Reformed tradition.

Stoute, D. A. "The Origins and Early Development of the Reformed Idea of the Covenant." PhD diss., University of Cambridge, 1979.

Stoute's dissertation describes the evolution of the covenant ideal in the early church and Middle Ages and then proceeds to survey Huldrych Zwingli, Johannes Oecolampadius, Martin Bucer, Heinrich Bullinger, and John Calvin. It is noteworthy for arguing the essential continuity between Bullinger and Calvin on the covenant.

Strehle, Stephen. *Calvinism, Federalism, and Scholasticism: A Study of the Reformed Doctrine of Covenant.* Basler und Berner Studien zur historischen und systematischen Theologie 58. Bern: Peter Lang, 1988.

Strehle provides brief surveys of no fewer than forty-five theologians, from Thomas Aquinas to the High Reformed Orthodoxy of the seventeenth century. In establishing a connection between late medieval scholasticism and the Reformation voices on the concepts of "pact" and "covenant," Strehle's judgments are idiosyncratic, and he is hostile to the Reformed understanding of justification, dismissing it as "utter fiction."

Weir, D. A. *The Origins of the Federal Theology in Sixteenth-Century Reformation Thought.* Oxford: Clarendon, 1990.

In a prize-winning study, Weir distinguishes the "covenant idea" (which recognizes covenant forms in Scripture) from covenant theology (which sees the covenant as a basic biblical category) and federal theology (where the covenant holds together the details of a theological system). He proceeds with a detailed survey of the early history of covenant theology, focusing on John Calvin and Zacharias Ursinus, followed by representatives of the "federal school." The appendix is a valuable 35-page "Bibliography of the Federal Theology and the Covenant Idea before 1750."

Zurich: Huldrych Zwingli and Heinrich Bullinger

Who is the "father of covenant theology?" An internet search reveals at least eight candidates nominated for that title. Two common suggestions are the two leading Reformers from Zurich: Huldrych Zwingli and Heinrich Bullinger.

Cottrell, Jack W. "Covenant and Baptism in the Theology of Huldreich Zwingli." ThD diss., Princeton Theological Seminary, 1971.

Cottrell identifies Zwingli as a founder for his presentation of the organic unity of the covenant in the Old and New Testaments. Zwingli did this by way of defending infant baptism against the Anabaptists, in, for example, his *Refutation of the Tricks of the Anabaptists*. See Zwingli, *Selected Works*, ed. Samuel Macauley Jackson (Philadelphia: University of Pennsylvania Press, 1972), 123–258.

McCoy, Charles S. and J. Wayne Baker. *Fountainhead of Federalism: Heinrich Bullinger and the Covenant Tradition; With a Translation of "De testamento seu foedere Dei unico et aeterno" (1534).* Louisville: Westminster John Knox, 1991.

If the roots of federal theology are in Zwingli, the "fountainhead" is in the first treatise on the subject, penned by Bullinger in 1534. An English translation, *A Brief Exposition of the One and Eternal Testament or Covenant of God*, is included on 99–138.

Baker, J. Wayne. *Heinrich Bullinger and the Covenant: The Other Reformed Tradition.* Athens: Ohio University Press, 1980.

By stressing that Bullinger emphasized the covenant as a bilateral act, Baker argues that Bullinger downplayed John Calvin's decretal theology. The differences he finds between Zurich and Geneva form the basis of his "two traditions" theory of the origins of covenant theology.

Venema, Cornelis P. *Heinrich Bullinger and the Doctrine of Predestination: Author of "the Other Reformed Tradition"?* Texts and Studies in Reformation and Post-Reformation Thought. Grand Rapids, MI: Baker Academic, 2002.

In his challenge to Baker (above), Venema claims that, on the doctrine of predestination, Bullinger and Calvin are both firmly in the Augustinian tradition.

Geneva: John Calvin

Eenigenburg, Elton M. "The Place of the Covenant in Calvin's Thinking." *Reformed Review* 10 (1957): 1–20.

While conceding that covenant theology is under suspicion—"covenant theology simply does not 'fit' into modern man's Protestantism" (2)—Eenigenburg acknowledges that Calvin does discuss the covenant in some detail. He suggests that Calvin sees the covenant not as a "conceptual tool or instrument for the manipulation of other elements of Christian belief" but rather "as a constitutive, living component of the biblical expression of God's dealing with man," which is "precisely what it is in the Bible itself" (4).

Bruggink, Donald J. "Calvin and Federal Theology." *Reformed Review* 13 (1959): 15–22.

Bruggink's essay is perhaps the most polemical expression of the "Calvin versus the Calvinists" school. A covenant of works, Bruggink argues, is a "flat contradiction" to Calvin's theology and thus a "perversion of great seriousness" (16) that devalued a doctrine of the church and opened the door to Arminianism and Unitarianism.

Hoekema, Anthony A. "The Covenant of Grace in Calvin's Teaching." *Calvin Theological Journal* 2 (1967): 133–61.

Hoekema's conclusion is worth quoting: "Calvin's teaching on the covenant of grace helps us to see the great Reformer in a new light. As he unfolds various facets of the doctrine of the covenant, we see him insisting, not just on the sovereign grace of God, but also on the serious and urgent responsibility of man. Avoiding the extremes of fatalism on the one hand and Pelagianism on the other, Calvin pictures man as one who, though saved by grace alone, is saved not as a puppet but as a person" (161).

Osterhaven, M. Eugene. "Calvin on the Covenant." *Reformed Review* 33 (1980): 136–77.

Osterhaven identifies the heart of Calvin's covenant theology in his three main motifs: the foundation (in Christ), the historical realization, and the unity of the covenant.

Helm, Paul. "Calvin and the Covenant: Unity and Continuity." *Evangelical Quarterly* 55 (1983): 65–81.

Helm counters the "Calvin versus the Calvinists" argument by demonstrating that Calvin's theology implicitly bears all the main features of the covenant theology that would come to expression in covenant theology a century later.

Lillback, Peter A. *The Binding of God: Calvin's Role in the Development of Covenant Theology.* Grand Rapids, MI: Baker Academic, 2001.

In this book, which is arguably the most comprehensive study of Calvin's work on the covenant, Lillback looks at the body of Calvin's work (mostly but not entirely in the *Institutes*) to support his claim that covenant functions as a significant feature in Calvin's theology. He finds continuity between Calvin and his contemporaries as well as the Reformed tradition that followed, challenging the "Calvin versus the Calvinists" theory. Lillback even suggests that a prefall covenant of works can be found in Calvin, though less than fully developed.

Rhineland: Zacharias Ursinus and Caspar Olevianus

Lillback, Peter A. "Ursinus' Development of the Covenant of Creation: A Debt to Melanchthon or Calvin?" *Westminster Theological Journal* 43, no. 1 (1981): 247–88.

Though Ursinus was a pupil of Philipp Melanchthon, Lillback disputes the then-prevailing consensus that his covenant of works was "Melanchthonian" in origin and distinguished from John Calvin. He offers evidence of direct influence from Calvin instead.

Visser, Derk. "The Covenant in Zacharias Ursinus." *Sixteenth Century Journal* 18, no. 4 (1987): 531–44.

Visser analyzes the concept of the covenant in Ursinus, arguing against finding in him the origins of the doctrine of the covenant of works.

Bierma, Lyle D. "Law and Grace in Ursinus' Doctrine of the Natural Covenant: A Reappraisal." In *Protestant Scholasticism: Essays in Reassessment*, edited by Carl R. Trueman and R. Scott Clark, 96–110. Studies in Christian History and Thought. Carlisle, UK: Paternoster, 1999.

Bierma joins Lillback in denying that Ursinus's development of the covenant of works represented any departure from the teaching of John Calvin.

Olevianus, Caspar. *An Exposition of the Apostles' Creed: or, The Articles of the Faith, in Which the Main Points of the Gracious Eternal Covenant between God and Believers Are Briefly and Clearly Treated.* Translated by Lyle D. Bierma. Classic Reformed Theology 2. Grand Rapids, MI: Reformation Heritage Books, 2009.

Caspar Olevianus (1536–1587) is one of many who have been credited with being the "father of covenant theology." The role of the covenant as an organizing principle is displayed in this series of sermons on the basic articles of the Christian faith, originally published in 1576.

Bierma, Lyle D. *German Calvinism in the Confessional Age: The Covenant Theology of Caspar Olevianus*. Grand Rapids, MI: Baker, 1996. Reprinted as *The Covenant Theology of Caspar Olevianus*. Reformed Historical-Theological Studies. Grand Rapids, MI: Reformation Heritage Books, 2005.

Bierma does not portray the German Reformer as the originator of covenant theology but acknowledges him "as a key intermediary figure in its development" in that he drew distinctions between the substance and administration of the covenant and between the promise (which is unilateral) and the agreement (which is bilateral).

Clark, R. Scott. *Caspar Olevian and the Substance of the Covenant: The Double Benefit of Christ*. Reformed Historical-Theological Studies. Grand Rapids, MI: Reformation Heritage Books, 2008.

Building on Bierma's work, Clark underscores the connection that Olevianus draws between covenant theology and the doctrines of justification and sanctification.

Letham, Robert. "The *Foedus Operum*: Some Factors Accounting for Its Development." *Sixteenth Century Journal* 14, no. 4 (1983): 457–67.

Letham proposes that the influence of Ursinus and the pervasive adoption of Ramist philosophy were among the most significant of factors in the development of the covenant of works that would find expression beginning with Dudley Fenner (ca. 1558–1587) and Robert Rollock (1555–1599).

Rollock, Robert. *Some Questions and Answers about God's Covenant and the Sacrament That Is a Seal of God's Covenant: With Related Texts*. Translated by Aaron Clay Denlinger. 1597. Reprint, Eugene, OR: Pickwick, 2016.

An important work toward the end of the sixteenth century was Robert Rollock's catechism on the covenant, with a series of 102 questions and answers, wherein, according to Denlinger, the covenant of works emerges as a "foil" for the covenant of grace.

Development and Refinement in the Seventeenth Century

Blair Smith and Bruce Baugus describe this rich period of English and Continental development of covenant theology in their essays. Here we are very selective.

English Puritanism

Beeke, Joel R., and Mark Jones. *A Puritan Theology: Doctrine for Life*. Grand Rapids, MI: Reformation Heritage Books, 2012.

Beeke and Jones team up to produce a remarkable composite "systematic theology" of the major voices of the Puritan era, from theology proper to theology in practice. A major section of the work, "Anthropology and Covenant Theology," includes six chapters on covenant theology.

McGiffert, Michael. "Grace and Works: The Rise and Division of Covenant Divinity in Elizabethan Puritanism." *Harvard Theological Review* 75, no. 4 (1982): 463–502.
———. "From Moses to Adam: The Making of the Covenant of Works." *Sixteenth Century Journal* 19, no. 2 (1988): 131–55.
———. "The Perkinsian Moment of Federal Theology." *Calvin Theological Journal* 29, no. 1 (1994): 117–48.

In these three works McGiffert traces the rise of a twofold covenant (works and grace) through four founders: Dudley Fenner, Josias Nichols, Thomas Cartwright, and, preeminently, William Perkins, whose presentation of the conditionality of the covenant avoided the narrow precisionism of Cartwright and Fenner. This led to what McGiffert termed the "Perkinsian Moment"—the first four decades of the seventeenth century—when federalism "took form, caught on, gained strength—and grew problematic."

Perkins, Harrison. "Reconsidering the Development of the Covenant of Works: A Study in Doctrinal Trajectory." *Calvin Theological Journal* 53, no. 2 (2018): 289–317.

This volume presents a survey of five figures in early English covenant theology: Dudley Fenner, Thomas Cartwright, William Perkins, Samuel Cooke, and Robert Rollock. The author underscores the exegetical work of these writers: "The Reformed tradition was active in exegetical and theological refinements over the course of several generations, . . . us[ing] the work of previous generations and contemporary writers to shape the ongoing trajectories of particular doctrines" (317).

John Owen

The literature on John Owen is vast. Here are three works that reflect significantly on his covenant theology.

Ferguson, Sinclair B. *John Owen on the Christian Life*. Carlisle, PA: Banner of Truth, 1987.

Chapter 2 ("The Plan of Salvation") outlines Owen's views on the covenant. Writes Ferguson, "The relevance of the development of covenant theology in the teaching of Owen may be summarized thus: during the sixteenth century covenant theology came to be regarded as a key to the interpretation of *Scripture* and, during the seventeenth century, a key to the interpretation of *Christian experience*" (20).

Trueman, Carl R. *John Owen: Reformed Catholic, Renaissance Man*. Burlington, VT: Ashgate, 2007.

In chapter 3, "Divine Covenants and Catholic Christology," Trueman shows Owen employing a covenant vocabulary to describe the economic relations of the Trinity. Trueman terms this a "critical traditionary" exercise: covenant theology in service of catholic Christology.

Tweeddale, John W. *John Owen and Hebrews: The Foundation of Biblical Interpretation*. T&T Clark Studies in English Theology. London: T&T Clark, 2019.

Tweeddale studies Owen's federal theology by focusing on his exegesis of Hebrews. He concludes, "In many ways, Owen's view of the Mosaic Covenant defies simple classification" (143).

Johannes Cocceius

Cocceius, Johannes. *The Doctrine of the Covenant and Testament of God*. Translated by Casey Carmichael. Classic Reformed Theology 3. Grand Rapids, MI: Reformation Heritage Books, 2016.

This volume is a translation of Johannes Cocceius's 1660 *Summa Doctrinae de Foedere et Testamento Dei*. Willem van Asselt explains in the introduction that Cocceius formed a covenant theory to account for the progressive character of redemptive history. This yielded his controversial formulation of five "abrogations" of the covenant of works. Gisbertus Voetius and his followers argued that Cocceius's notion of covenantal progression undercut the unity of the covenant of grace.

van Asselt, Willem J. *The Federal Theology of Johannes Cocceius (1603–1669)*. Translated by Raymond A. Blacketer. Studies in the History of Christian Thought 100. Leiden: Brill, 2001.

In this book, a brief biography of Cocceius is followed by a detailed exposition and evaluation of Cocceius's federalism. One ought not overlook appendix 1, "The Origins of Federal Theology," in which van Asselt assesses seven theories of origins.

Lee, Brian J. *Johannes Cocceius and the Exegetical Roots of Federal Theology: Reformation Developments in the Interpretation of Hebrews 7–10*. Reformed Historical Theology 7. Göttingen: Vandenhoeck & Ruprecht, 2009.

This study of the exegesis of διαθήκη in the book of Hebrews in the Reformed tradition culminates in a study of Cocceius, prompting Lee's conclusion that exegesis, not dogmatic theology, was foundational in the development of covenant theology.

Reformed Scholasticism

Lim, Won Taek. *The Covenant Theology of Francis Roberts*. Seoul: King & Kingdom, 2002.

In this book, originally a Calvin Theological Seminary PhD dissertation, Lim underscores the role that Francis Roberts (1609–1675) played in refining covenant theology after Westminster and in the dialogue between English Puritans and Continental Reformed covenant theologians.

Beach, J. Mark. *Christ and the Covenant: Francis Turretin's Federal Theology as a Defense of the Doctrine of Grace*. Reformed Historical Theology 1. Göttingen: Vandenhoeck & Ruprecht, 2007.

As he works through Francis Turretin's *Institutes of Elenctic Theology*, Beach underscores that Turretin's federalism, far from depicting a mere legal arrangement, was designed to "safeguard God's charitable and kindly relationship" to humanity (146).

Gwon, Gyeongcheol. *Christ and the Old Covenant: Francis Turretin (1623–1687) on Christ's Suretyship under the Old Testament*. Reformed Historical Theology 51. Göttingen: Vandenhoeck & Ruprecht, 2019.

In this revision of a Westminster Theological Seminary PhD dissertation, Gwon presents Turretin as a "moderate and peaceful Voetian" (12) amid the intra-Reformed controversy between Gisbertus Voetius and Johannes Cocceius.

Mastricht, Peter van. *Theoretical and Practical Theology*. Vol. 6, *Covenant Theology*. Translated by Todd M. Rester. Edited by Joel R. Beeke. Grand Rapids, MI: Reformation Heritage Books, forthcoming.

A student of Voetius and a major voice in the *Nadere Reformatie*, Peter (or Petrus) van Mastricht (1630–1706) sought to present Reformed theology in "its exegetical, doctrinal, elenctical, and practical parts" in his seven-volume magnum opus, now being released in English by Reformation Heritage Bools. Volume 6 will treat the covenant of grace.

Witsius, Herman. *The Economy of the Covenants between God and Man: Comprehending a Complete Body of Divinity*. 2 vols. Translated by William Crookshank. 1677. Reprint, Escondido, CA: den Dulk Christian Foundation, 1990.

This work is a well-established standard originally published in Latin in 1677 in four books (covering the covenant of works, the covenant of redemption, the covenant of grace, and the covenant ordinances in different administrations). Herman Witsius (1636–1708) subsumes the "the complete body of divinity" under the two covenants of works and grace. Not to be overlooked in the most recent edition is the introduction by J. I. Packer, itself a classic introduction on covenant theology.

Brakel, Wilhelmus à. *The Christian's Reasonable Service*. Translated by Bartel Elshout. Edited by Joel R. Beeke. 4 vols. Grand Rapids, MI: Reformation Heritage Books, 1992–1995.

Subtitled *In which Divine Truths concerning the Covenant of Grace Are Expounded, Defended against Opposing Parties, and Their Practice Advocated*, this work was originally published in Dutch in 1700. Brakel composes a systematic presentation of Bible doctrines that emphasizes the three covenants—redemption, works, and grace. Practical observations and exhortations to godliness complete each chapter.

Muller, Richard A. "The Covenant of Works and the Stability of Divine Law in Seventeenth-Century Reformed Orthodoxy: A Study in the Theology of Herman Witsius and Wilhelmus à Brakel." *Calvin Theological Journal* 29 (1994): 75–100.

What is at stake in the covenant of works? Muller explains that though it is a "consequent doctrine," failure to acknowledge the covenant of works undermines a right understanding of primary doctrines in Christology and soteriology, according to both Herman Witsius and Wilhelmus à Brakel.

Scottish Reflection on Covenant Theology

Fisher, Edward. *The Marrow of Modern Divinity*. Fearn, Ross-shire, Scotland: Christian Focus, 2009.

Fisher wrote *The Marrow of Modern Divinity* in 1645 with the imposing subtitle, "Touching Both the Covenant of Works, and the Covenant of Grace, with Their Use and End, Both in the Time of the Old Testament, and in the Time of the New." Consisting of a series of dialogues involving a young Christian, a pastor, a legalist, and an antinomian, it became the center of Scottish debate over covenant theology when Thomas Boston brought it into the "Marrow Controversy."

Henderson, G. D. "The Idea of the Covenant in Scotland." *Evangelical Quarterly* 27, no. 1 (1955): 2–14.

This brief historical survey includes a treatment of the National Covenant (1638), the Solemn League and Covenant (1643), and the major Scottish voices in covenant theology.

Lindsay, T. M. "The Covenant Theology." *British and Foreign Evangelical Review* 28 (1879): 521–37.

In this study of the development of federalism, T. M. Lindsay, church historian at the Free Church College in Glasgow, lauds the value of the covenant idea "in experimental theology and pious meditation." In Scotland, covenant theology became associated with "a richness and fulness of evangelical truth." But Lindsay warns that it could tend toward "metaphysical speculation" and has "lent itself readily to incipient rationalism."

MacLean, Donald John. "Missing, Presumed Misclassified: Hugh Binning (1627–1653), Lost Federal Theologian." *Westminster Theological Journal* 75, no. 2 (2013): 261–78,

MacLean challenges a prevailing view that Hugh Binning was an opponent of the federal theology of Westminster, and he offers him as a case study for understanding unity and diversity in Scottish theology after the Westminster Assembly.

Macleod, J. N. "Covenant Theology: The Need for a Reappraisal and Reaffirmation." *Monthly Record of the Free Church of Scotland* (July/August 1983): 147–55.

This is John N. Macleod's moderator address to the 1983 General Assembly of the Free Church of Scotland. He surveys the history of covenant theology and issues a challenge to the church: "I am persuaded that a renewed appreciation of . . . the riches of covenant theology and a reaffirmation of it in our church life may by the blessing of God be the means of turning the religious tide in our land" (147).

Martin, Hugh. *The Atonement in Its Relations to the Covenant, the Priesthood, and the Intercession of Our Lord.* 1870. Reprint, Greenville, SC: Reformed Academic Press, 1997.

Martin (1822–1885) draws a connection between the covenant of redemption and the atonement. Writes Donald Macleod in the introduction: "Never was the covenant concept handled with such a lightness of touch or applied so effectively to modern challenges" (vi).

McGowan, A. T. B. *The Federal Theology of Thomas Boston.* Edinburgh: Paternoster, 1997.

Thomas Boston (1676–1732) wrote two lengthy pieces on covenant theology, "A View of the Covenant of Grace from the Sacred Records" and "A View of the Covenant of Works from the Sacred Records" (both found in his *Complete Works*), and a covenant framework also shapes his study of theological anthropology, *Human Nature in Its Fourfold State.* McGowan's study of Boston, originally a dissertation at Aberdeen under James Torrance, begins with a chapter outlining Boston's covenant theology, and McGowan goes on to feature the imprint of federalism on his theology as a whole.

Myers, Stephen G. *Scottish Federalism and Covenantalism in Transition: The Theology of Ebenezer Erskine.* Cambridge: James Clarke, 2016.

Myers provides a study of Erskine's covenant theology in light of the Marrow Controversy and the Scottish development of "covenantalism" (the covenant responsibility of the state to God), which led to Erskine's leadership in the secession that formed the Associate Presbytery.

Trueman, Carl R. "From Calvin to Gillespie on Covenant: Mythological Excess or an Exercise in Doctrinal Development?" *International Journal of Systematic Theology* 11, no. 4 (2009): 378–97.

Patrick Gillespie (1617–1675), younger brother of Westminster commissioner George Gillespie, wrote on the covenants in *The Ark of the Testament* (1661) and *The Ark of the Covenant* (1677). Challenging Karl Barth's claim that the covenant of redemption in the

Reformed tradition was a "piece of mythology," Trueman uses Gillespie as a case study to demonstrate that the doctrine emerged from the connection of exegesis to doctrinal synthesis in the same style and pattern of the earlier Reformers.

New England Puritans

Miller, Perry. *The New England Mind: The Seventeenth Century.* Boston: Beacon, 1939.

Harvard historian Perry Miller (1905–1963) is largely credited with casting Puritanism in a positive light in his highly influential proposal that covenant theology was a Puritan invention to soften the hard edges of Calvinist predestination. Human responsibility for those in covenant with God freed them from the terrifying capriciousness of the decretal theology of Calvin (who had no covenant theology, according to Miller). Miller's revisionism became quickly established in scholarly circles.

Trinterud, Leonard J. "The Origins of Puritanism." *Church History* 20, no. 1 (1951): 37–57.

Following in the direction of Miller, Trinterud suggested that "the essential genius" of Puritan thought lay in the development of the "contract-covenant scheme" (55). The Miller-Trinterud thesis was largely an extension of the two-covenant theory that divided Rhineland (bicovenantal) and Genevan (monocovenantal) versions of covenant theology.

Bierma, Lyle D. "Federal Theology in the Sixteenth Century: Two Traditions?" *Westminster Theological Journal* 45, no. 2 (1983): 304–21.

Bierma challenges Trinterud's two-covenant approach as an incomplete reading of sources that yields a caricature of both Zurich and Geneva teaching on covenant theology.

von Rohr, John. *The Covenant of Grace in Puritan Thought.* Atlanta: Scholars Press, 1986.

A close reading of the Puritans (with an extensive bibliography) produces the strongest rebuttal of Perry Miller's project distinguishing Puritan conditionalism from the absolutism of Calvin. "Calvin cannot be portrayed in Miller's terms," von Rohr concludes, "nor can the Puritans be as radically differentiated from him as Miller proposes" (20).

De Jong, Peter Y. *The Covenant Idea in New England Theology, 1620–1847.* Grand Rapids, MI: Eerdmans, 1945.

Covenant theology did not fare well among New England Puritans, in the judgment of Peter Y. De Jong. Constant modifications (through expedients such as the Halfway Covenant) produced a steady decline to the point that it was largely forgotten or rejected in New England theology. Even though he opposed the Halfway Covenant, Jonathan Edwards was complicit, according to De Jong, because his emphasis on revivals diminished the "organic place in Christ's church" of the children of believers (136).

Bogue, Carl W. *Jonathan Edwards and the Covenant of Grace.* Cherry Hill, NJ: Mack, 1975.

An assessment contrary to Peter De Jong is offered by Carl Bogue. In *Jonathan Edwards and the Covenant of Grace* (originally a dissertation at the Free University under G. C. Berkouwer), Bogue examines Edwards's sermons and "Miscellanies" to conclude that his devotion to a federal model yielded a consistent Calvinism that accounted for divine sovereignty and human response in coming to faith.

Kelly, Douglas F. *The Emergence of Liberty in the Modern World: The Influence of Calvin on Five Governments from the 16th through 18th Centuries; Calvin's Geneva, Huguenot France, Knox's Scotland, Puritan England, Colonial America.* Phillipsburg, NJ: P&R, 1992.

Calvin's principle that kings and princes are bound by covenant to their subjects led to the development of national covenants. In works such as Samuel Rutherford's *Lex Rex*, the "crown rights" of Jesus over his church limited the power of the civil magistrate. In colonial New England, the covenant doctrine of the state sanctioned resistance to political tyranny through lesser magistrates and contributed to the rise of modern constitutionalism.

Elazar, Daniel J., and John Kincaid, eds. *The Covenant Connection: From Federal Theology to Modern Federalism.* Lanham, MD: Lexington Books, 2000.

Fourteen essays explore the emphasis on covenant theology in the American political tradition, especially the role of Puritans in Old and New England.

Weir, David A. *Early New England: A Covenanted Society.* Emory University Studies in Law and Religion. Grand Rapids, MI: Eerdmans, 2005.

In this exhaustive study, reflection on the covenant in colonial New England expanded into the establishment of "church covenants" and beyond, as the covenant motif became the basis for the reformation of the civil realm as well.

Contemporary Reformed Voices on the Biblical Covenants

Vos, Geerhardus. *Biblical Theology: Old and New Testaments.* 1948. Reprint, Carlisle, PA: Banner of Truth, 2014.

———. "The Doctrine of the Covenant in Reformed Theology." In *Redemptive History and Biblical Interpretation: The Shorter Writings of Geerhardus Vos,* edited by Richard B. Gaffin Jr., 234–67. Phillipsburg, NJ: Presbyterian and Reformed, 1980.

Geerhardus Vos (1862–1949) is generally recognized as the father of modern Reformed biblical theology. In his long tenure at Princeton Theological Seminary, he emphasized that revealed truth comes in the form of a covenant. *Biblical Theology: Old and New*

Testaments traces the progress of the covenant theme through redemptive history. Vos's "Doctrine of the Covenant" is a survey of the rise of covenant theology in the Reformed tradition, followed by an explanation of how salvation unfolds in Scripture in a particularly covenantal way.

Murray, John. *The Covenant of Grace: A Biblico-Theological Study*. London: Tyndale Press, 1954.

In this brief (32-page) "recasting" of covenant theology, Murray describes biblical covenants as exclusively administrations of grace. Though Murray rejects the language of "covenant of works," his preferred term, "Adamic Administration," maintains a two-Adam typology that comes to clear expression in his larger study, *The Imputation of Adam's Sin* (Grand Rapids, MI: Eerdmans, 1959). Both titles are still in print from P&R.

Kline, Meredith G. *Kingdom Prologue: Genesis Foundations for a Covenantal Worldview*. Eugene, OR: Wipf and Stock, 2006.

In what many regard as his "magnum opus," Kline provides a fresh exegetical defense for the classic approach to the theology of the covenants. The covenants of works and grace in Genesis serve as the basis for understanding how works and grace operate in the accomplishment and application of redemption.

Robertson, O. Palmer. "Current Reformed Thinking on the Nature of the Divine Covenants." *Westminster Theological Journal* 40, no. 1 (1977): 63–76.

While appreciatively acknowledging the "significant contributions to the biblical concept of the covenant" from John Murray and Meredith Kline, Robertson finds areas of agreement and disagreement, and he offers criticisms of their views.

———. *The Christ of the Covenants*. Phillipsburg, NJ: Presbyterian and Reformed, 1980.

Robertson's own book-length contribution pictures the organic unity of the covenants, while remaining sensitive to the diversity of covenant administrations. This has become a standard textbook at many Reformed and Presbyterian seminaries.

Dumbrell, William J. *Covenant and Creation: A Theology of the Old Testament Covenants*. Nashville: Thomas Nelson, 1984.

Dumbrell, from Moore Theological College in Australia, offers a theology of the Old Testament from a covenant theme. With extensive engagement with higher-critical authors, Dumbrell remains committed to the unity of the biblical covenants while devoting exegetical attention to specific texts. Dumbrell rejects the covenant of works and does not draw theological connections from covenant theology to imputation or justification.

McComiskey, Thomas Edward. *The Covenants of Promise: A Theology of the Old Testament Covenants*. Grand Rapids, MI: Baker, 1985.

McComiskey's approach focuses on the distinction between promissory and administrative covenants. In his scheme the two forms are not antithetical; rather, administrative covenants regulate the promises with appropriate patterns of holy living.

Beckwith, Roger T. "The Unity and Diversity of God's Covenants." *Tyndale Bulletin* 38 (1987): 93–118.

Beckwith's essay provides an overview of twentieth-century studies on the biblical covenants, with attention to Reformed approaches in the Vosian tradition, including John Murray, O. Palmer Robertson, William Dumbrell, and Thomas McComiskey.

Ward, Rowland S. *God and Adam: Reformed Theology and the Creation Covenant.* Wantirna, Australia: New Melbourne, 2003.

Focusing on the covenant of works, Ward offers a historical survey underscoring that the seventeenth century was a period of continuity and refinement of the covenant theme.

Jeon, Jeong Koo. *Covenant Theology: John Murray's and Meredith G. Kline's Response to the Historical Development of Federal Theology in Reformed Thought.* Lanham, MD: University Press of America, 2004.

As he compares the approaches of John Murray and Meredith Kline, Jeon commends both for expressing the foundational role of the covenant in distinguishing law and grace and in opposing legalism and antinomianism in the application of the work of Christ.

Williamson, Paul R. *Sealed with an Oath: Covenant in God's Unfolding Purpose.* New Studies in Biblical Theology 23. Downers Grove, IL: InterVarsity Press, 2007.

Williamson, from Moore Theological College in Australia, surveys the Hebrew and Greek words for "covenant" in their biblical contexts. Rejecting the covenant of works (because there is no oath of ratification), he surveys covenantal development from the Old Testament to new covenant inauguration and consummation.

McGowan, A. T. B. *Adam, Christ and Covenant: Exploring Headship Theology.* London: Apollos, 2016.

After reviewing several contemporary perspectives, including Karl Barth, John Murray, Meredith Kline, and the Federal Vision, McGowan presents an Adam-Christ typology that jettisons covenant language for what he terms "headship theology."

Comparative / Ancient Near Eastern Studies

Nicholas Reid offers an in-depth assessment of comparative methods in chapter 21 of this volume. Here are some noteworthy works on this subject.

Eichrodt, Walther. *Theology of the Old Testament.* Translated by J. A. Baker. 2 vols. 1933. Reprint, Philadelphia: Westminster, 1961–1967.

Eichrodt broke away from the prevailing consensus in higher criticism by arguing that covenant is the central unifying feature of the Old Testament. His book, along with significant archaeological discoveries, further stirred scholarly interest in biblical covenants.

Mendenhall, George E. *Law and Covenant in Israel and the Ancient Near East.* Pittsburgh: Biblical Colloquium, 1955.

Mendenhall's comparison of ancient Hittite treaties and biblical covenants pointed to an early (second-millennium BC) dating of the covenant idea in Israel, challenging higher-critical assumptions regarding the dating of the Pentateuch.

Kline, Meredith G. *Treaty of the Great King: The Covenant Structure of Deuteronomy; Studies and Commentary.* Grand Rapids, MI: Eerdmans, 1963.

A detailed study of the parallels between Deuteronomy and ancient Near Eastern treaties prompted Kline to argue that the book forms a cohesive literary unit with Mosaic authorship.

Weeks, Noel. *Admonition and Curse: The Ancient Near Eastern Treaty/Covenant Form as a Problem in Inter-Cultural Relationships.* Journal for the Study of the Old Testament Supplement Series 407. London: T&T Clark, 2004.

Weeks agrees with Kline that there are significant parallels between the Mosaic covenant and ancient Near Eastern treaties but sees law covenants and promise covenants more on a continuum than in sharp contrast.

Hahn, Scott W. *Kinship by Covenant: A Canonical Approach to the Fulfillment of God's Saving Promises.* New Haven, CT: Yale University Press, 2009.

A student of Meredith Kline, Hahn presents an overview of recent scholarship on covenants followed by a survey of kinship, treaty, and grant covenants in the Old Testament and a survey of New Testament perspectives on the covenant. Hahn concludes with theological reflections from a Roman Catholic perspective.

The Covenant of Redemption: Recent Studies

Beach, J. Mark. "The Doctrine of the *Pactum Salutis* in the Covenant Theology of Herman Witsius." *Mid-America Journal of Theology* 13 (2002): 101–42.

After a survey of twentieth-century criticism of the covenant of redemption, Beach employs Herman Witsius as a case study to demonstrate that the criticisms are unfounded.

Baugh, S. M. "Galatians 3:20 and the Covenant of Redemption." *Westminster Theological Journal* 66 (2004): 49–70.

Baugh's exegesis of a difficult passage sees the *pactum salutis* as the basis of Paul's argument in Galatians 3.

Muller, Richard A. "Toward the *Pactum Salutis*: Locating the Origins of a Concept."
  Mid-America Journal of Theology 18 (2007): 11–65.

Charging critics of the covenant of redemption with anachronistic reading of sources, Muller argues that extensive exegetical and theological development of the doctrine in the face of polemical challenges led to its gaining quick acceptance among the Reformed despite its "abbreviated pedigree."

Campbell, Iain D. "Re-Visiting the Covenant of Redemption." In *The People's Theologian: Writings in Honour of Donald Macleod*, edited by Iain D. Campbell and Malcolm MacLean, 173–94. Fearn, Ross-shire, Scotland: Mentor, 2011.

Campbell reviews recent literature and responds to some contemporary objections to the covenant of redemption.

Fesko, J. V. *The Covenant of Redemption: Origins, Development, and Reception*. Reformed Historical Theology 35. Göttingen: Vandenhoeck & Ruprecht, 2016.
———. *The Trinity and the Covenant of Redemption*. Fearn, Ross-shire, Scotland: Mentor, 2016.

The first book is a thorough study of the doctrine of the covenant of redemption from seventeenth-century origins to twentieth-century critics. The second book summarizes much of the research in the former and proceeds to systematic formulation of the covenant of redemption as the first of a three-volume set (the other volumes are to cover the covenant of works and the covenant of grace).

Covenant in Reformed Systematic Theologies

Every Reformed systematic theology covers the covenants but some only superficially. Here are a few that excel in their treatment.

Hodge, Charles. *Systematic Theology*. 3 vols. 1873. Reprint, Grand Rapids, MI: Eerdmans, 1952.

Hodge examines the covenant of works under anthropology (part 2, chap. 6) and the covenants of grace and redemption under soteriology (part 3, chap. 2).

Bavinck, Herman. *Reformed Dogmatics*. Edited by John Bolt. Translated by John Vriend. 4 vols. Grand Rapids, MI: Baker Academic, 2003–2008.

In this long-awaited English translation of *Gereformeerde Dogmatiek* (1895–1901), Bavinck treats the Adamic covenant in volume 2 and the covenant of grace (along with the *pactum salutis*) in volume 3. A helpful guide to Bavinck is Anthony Hoekema's ThD dissertation, "Herman Bavinck's Doctrine of the Covenant" (Princeton Theological Seminary, 1953).

Vos, Geerhardus. *Reformed Dogmatics*. Translated and edited by Richard B. Gaffin Jr. 5 vols. Bellingham, WA: Lexham, 2012–2016.

The doctrine of the covenants saturates Vos's systematics throughout (first released in Dutch in 1896), and it is the special focus of his anthropology section in volume 2.

Berkhof, Louis. *Systematic Theology*. Grand Rapids, MI: Eerdmans, 1938.

The long-time professor of theology at Calvin Theological Seminary devotes a chapter to man in the covenant of works and five chapters to man in the covenant of grace (the latter including the covenant of redemption).

Horton, Michael S. *Covenant and Eschatology: The Divine Drama*. Louisville: Westminster John Knox, 2002.
———. *Lord and Servant: A Covenant Christology*. Louisville: Westminster John Knox, 2005.
———. *Covenant and Salvation: Union with Christ*. Louisville: Westminster John Knox, 2007.
———. *People and Place: A Covenant Ecclesiology*. Louisville: Westminster John Knox, 2008.

These four volumes constitute an ambitious project that brings covenant theology into critical engagement with major voices and approaches in modern theology. Horton commends a covenantal approach (using the analogy of "meeting a stranger") that avoids both pantheism or panentheism ("overcoming estrangement") and deism or atheism ("the stranger we never met").

Letham, Robert. *Systematic Theology*. Wheaton, IL: Crossway, 2019.

A sustained treatment of the development of the covenant in the Reformed tradition is found in part 5, "The Covenant of God."

Modern Critics of Covenant Theology

Lincoln, Charles F. "The Development of the Covenant Theory." *Bibliotheca Sacra* 100 (1943): 134–63.

Lincoln's article is a dated and inaccurate history of the rise of covenant theology, but it is helpful as an example of standard dispensational criticism. Covenant theology emerges as a response to the rigidity of Calvinistic predestinarianism. Lincoln concludes, "The covenants only have a theoretical and not a Biblical existence," and "it is impossible to prove they were ever established by God with the connotations that covenant theory teachers have given them" (162–63).

Torrance, James B. "Covenant or Contract? A Study of the Theological Background of Worship in Seventeenth-Century Scotland." *Scottish Journal of Theology* 23, no. 1 (1970): 51–76.
———. "The Covenant Concept in Scottish Theology and Politics and Its Legacy." *Scottish Journal of Theology* 34, no. 3 (1981): 225–43.

In two surveys of Scottish theological and political developments, Torrance describes a "recasting" of Reformed theology into "federal Calvinism," where legalism turned biblical covenants into contracts.

Rolston, Holmes, III. *John Calvin versus the Westminster Confession*. Richmond, VA: John Knox, 1972.

Celebrating the Confession of 1967 as the "official end of the four-century Presbyterian venture into covenant theology," Rolston makes the provocative claim that Calvin "knew nothing" of covenant theology but that "these theological innovations were the work of his successors" (23).

Fuller, Daniel P. *Gospel and Law: Contrast or Continuum? The Hermeneutics of Dispensationalism and Covenant Theology*. Grand Rapids, MI: Eerdmans, 1980.

As the title suggests, Fuller rejects a law-gospel contrast in his reading of Paul and his study of the Reformers on grace and faith, and he offers an interpretive alternative to dispensationalism and covenant theology.

Miller, Allen O., ed. *A Covenant Challenge to Our Broken World*. Atlanta: Darby, 1982.

This collection of thirty-four essays—the work of the Committee on Theology of the Caribbean and North American Area Council of the World Alliance of Reformed Churches—seeks to expose "the dark side" of traditional Reformed formulations of the covenant, where elitist arrogance justifies "the exercise of imperial power in human society" (21). Instead, "God's covenant people today must be the bearers of *shalom* to a revolutionary age" (334).

Stek, John H. "'Covenant Overload' in Reformed Theology?" *Calvin Theological Journal* 29 (1994): 12–41.

Stek, professor of Old Testament at Calvin Theological Seminary for three decades, expresses his dissatisfaction with what he regards as the eccentric and unconvincing emphasis on covenant in twentieth-century Reformed circles, finding no warrant for "employing covenant . . . as the *central* theological category for synthetic construal of the God-humanity relationship" (25). Stek takes particular aim at Meredith Kline, O. Palmer Robertson, William Dumbrell, and Thomas McComiskey.

Walton, John H. *Covenant: God's Purpose, God's Plan*. Grand Rapids, MI: Zondervan, 1994.

Eschewing a model that is built on systematic theology, Walton outlines a covenant approach that accommodates a broad "evangelical consensus" (25). This yields a "revelatory" view of the covenants that is distinct from both covenant theology and dispensationalism, classic or progressive.

Gentry, Peter J., and Stephen J. Wellum. *Kingdom through Covenant: A Biblical-Theological Understanding of the Covenants.* 2nd ed. Wheaton, IL: Crossway, 2018.

Two professors at Southern Baptist Theological Seminary make the case for "progressive covenantalism," a school of thought in Reformed Baptist circles that finds middle ground between covenant theology and dispensationalism. See Scott Swain's treatment in chapter 26 of this volume.

Answering Critics of Covenant Theology

Defenders of covenant theology have been mindful of the voices of critics. Here are a few worth noting.

McWilliams, David B. "The Covenant Theology of the *Westminster Confession of Faith* and Recent Criticism." *Westminster Theological Journal* 53, no. 1 (1991): 109–24.

McWilliams engages both with critics of confessional federalism, such as Karl Barth, Holmes Rolston III, T. F. Torrance, and J. B. Torrance, and with "Reformed re-evaluations" that include Robert Letham, John Murray, G. C. Berkouwer, and Meredith Kline.

Kline, Meredith G. "Covenant Theology under Attack." *New Horizons in the Orthodox Presbyterian Church* 15 (February 1994): 1–4.

Kline presents a defense of the covenant of works against the criticisms of Daniel Fuller and Norman Shepherd.

Holwerda, David E. *Jesus and Israel: One Covenant or Two?* Grand Rapids, MI: Eerdmans, 1995.

Is covenant theology plausible in the shadow of the Holocaust, or does it bear an incipient anti-Semitism? Dual-covenant theology has caught interest among Protestant liberals (as well as among some dispensationalists), wary of a supersessionism that suggests God has abandoned his promises to the Jews and "replaced" them with the church as his new chosen people. Holwerda responds by defending a traditional Reformed theology of the covenants, demonstrating that the promises of the Old Testament find their fulfillment exclusively in Christ.

Bolt, John. "Why the Covenant of Works Is a Necessary Doctrine: Revisiting the Objections to a Venerable Reformed Doctrine." In *By Faith Alone: Answering the Challenges to the Doctrine of Justification*, edited by Gary L. W. Johnson and Guy P. Waters, 171–89. Wheaton, IL: Crossway, 2006.

Bolt from Calvin Seminary respectfully challenges former Calvin professors Anthony Hoekema and John Stek for their denial of the covenant of works and argues that the doctrine is founded on a complex set of biblical texts, opposition to which manifests a biblicism that denies the principle of good and necessary consequence.

Duncan, Ligon. "Recent Objections to Covenant Theology: A Description, Evaluation, and Response." In *The Westminster Confession into the 21st Century*, edited by Ligon Duncan, 3:467–500. 3 vols. Fearn, Ross-shire, Scotland: Mentor, 2009.

Beyond providing a catalog of covenant theology critics and revisionists (from Karl Barth to the Federal Vision), Duncan further examines its relative neglect in contemporary Reformed circles.

Contemporary Issues in Covenant Theology

Intramural debates among confessional Reformed theologians have brought to light a set of issues that have shaped the direction of covenant discussions.

Waters, Guy Prentiss. *Justification and the New Perspectives on Paul: A Review and Response*. Phillipsburg, NJ: P&R, 2004.

———. *The Federal Vision and Covenant Theology: A Comparative Analysis*. Phillipsburg, NJ: P&R, 2006.

The confusion between justification and sanctification and between justice and grace is clarified in these titles by Guy Waters that assess the New Perspective on Paul and the Federal Vision movements from a traditional covenant theology perspective. Further reflections by the author on the New Perspective on Paul can be found in Waters, "Covenant Theology and Recent Interpretation of Paul: Some Reflections," *Confessional Presbyterian* 6 (2010): 167–79.

Clark, R. Scott, ed. *Covenant, Justification, and Pastoral Ministry: Essays by the Faculty of Westminster Seminary California*. Phillipsburg, NJ: P&R, 2007.

Fourteen essays explore the New Perspective and the Federal Vision movements. As the title suggests, particular attention is devoted to the connection between covenant theology and justification by faith. A historical survey of the covenant of redemption is found on 169–79.

Estelle, Bryan D., J. V. Fesko, and David VanDrunen, eds. *The Law Is Not of Faith: Essays on Works and Grace in the Mosaic Covenant*. Phillipsburg, NJ: P&R, 2009.

This volume includes eleven essays on historical, biblical, and theological studies, most of which present the case for seeing the Adamic covenant "republished" in the covenant at Sinai.

Elam, Andrew M., Robert C. Van Kooten, and Randall A. Bergquist. *Merit and Moses: A Critique of the Klinean Doctrine of Republication*. Eugene, OR: Wipf and Stock, 2014.

This book is a response to Estelle, Fesko, and VanDrunen, *The Law Is Not of Faith* (above). The ensuing debate in the Orthodox Presbyterian Church (OPC) led to a study committee report presented to the 2016 General Assembly of the OPC (below).

"Report of the Committee to Study Republication." In *Minutes of the 83rd General Assembly of the Orthodox Presbyterian Church*, 332–445. Willow Grove, PA: Orthodox Presbyterian Church, 2016.

Given the mandate to examine whether "the concept of the Mosaic Covenant as a republication of the Adamic Covenant is consistent" with the doctrinal standards of the Orthodox Presbyterian Church (332), this report distinguishes between administrative and substantive republication, and it commends the former as consistent with the teaching of the Westminster Standards.

Karlberg, Mark W. *Covenant Theology in Reformed Perspective: Collected Essays and Book Reviews in Historical, Biblical, and Systematic Theology.* Eugene, OR: Wipf and Stock, 2000.

Beginning with his Westminster Theological Seminary doctoral dissertation, "The Mosaic Covenant and the Concept of Works in Reformed Hermeneutics" (1979), Mark W. Karlberg has written extensively on the history of covenant theology, and many such works of his are made available in this volume.

Pipa, Joseph, and C. N. Wilborn, eds. *The Covenant: God's Voluntary Condescension.* Taylors, SC: Presbyterian Press, 2005.

This book is a collection of the nine presentations of the 2004 Theology Conference at Greenville Presbyterian Theological Seminary, including addresses defending and critiquing paedo-Communion.

Venema, Cornelis. *Christ and Covenant Theology: Essays on Election, Republication, and the Covenants.* Phillipsburg, NJ: P&R, 2017.

Venema, of Mid-America Reformed Seminary, has written extensively on covenant-related themes. *Christ and Covenant Theology* is a collection of twelve previously published essays that focus on creation, election, and justification, with special application to contemporary debates such as Federal Vision, the New Perspective on Paul, and republication.

Popular Treatments of the Covenants

For readers interested in teaching covenant theology in popular contexts, several non-technical and introductory studies are worth commending.

De Graaf, S. G. *Promise and Deliverance.* Translated by H. Evan Runner and Elisabeth Wichers Runner. 4 vols. St. Catherines, ON: Paideia Press, 1977–1981.

Can covenant theology be made accessible to children in the church? De Graaf excels in presenting it in simple terms for the very young. (The original title in Dutch, *Verbondsgeschiedenis*, can be translated, "History of the covenant.") Designed for Sunday schools and Christian day schools, the work presents a panoramic picture of the unfolding of God's covenants through more than two hundred biblical stories.

Robertson, O. Palmer. *Covenants: God's Way with His People*. Philadelphia: Great Commission, 1987.

This popularization of Robertson's seminary-level textbook is designed for adult Sunday school classes. Each of the thirteen chapters concludes with a review and discussion questions.

Horton, Michael S. *God of Promise: Introducing Covenant Theology*. Grand Rapids, MI: Baker, 2006.

This volume is a more ambitious introduction to covenant theology that delves into technical matters such as ancient Near Eastern treaties. Following Meredith Kline, Horton divides biblical covenants into two kinds: the Abrahamic covenant exemplifies a royal grant, and the Mosaic covenant, with its legal stipulations, is patterned after suzerain treaties.

Rhodes, Jonty. *Covenants Made Simple: Understanding God's Unfolding Promises to His People*. Phillipsburg, NJ: P&R, 2014.

This very readable introduction explores, in eleven chapters, topics from the covenant of works to life in the covenant and is aided by several charts and diagrams.

Brown, Michael, and Zach Keele. *Sacred Bond: Covenant Theology Explored*. 2nd ed. Grandville, MI: Reformation Fellowship, 2017.

This popular survey of the eight covenants is particularly noteworthy for its stress on the way each finds expression in the Reformed confessional tradition and in the importance of the covenants for understanding the Christian life.

Schreiner, Thomas R. *Covenant and God's Purpose for the World*. Short Studies in Biblical Theology. Wheaton, IL: Crossway, 2017.

Schreiner takes a new Reformed Baptist approach in a survey of six biblical covenants, from the covenant of creation to the new covenant. He affirms regenerate covenant membership as a distinguishing characteristic of the new covenant.

G2R God's Promises: Teen Bible Studies [Sunday school curriculum]. Atlanta: Great Commission, 2019.

Great Commission Publications, the Christian education partnership of the Orthodox Presbyterian Church and the Presbyterian Church in America, positions the covenant as the capstone of its Sunday school scope and sequence. Its teenage curriculum surveys the unfolding of the covenant of grace from Genesis to Revelation in eight thirteen-week units.

CONTRIBUTORS

Michael Allen (PhD, Wheaton College) is the John Dyer Trimble Professor of Systematic Theology and academic dean at Reformed Theological Seminary, Orlando. He has written or edited numerous books, most recently *Grounded in Heaven: Recentering Christian Hope and Life in God* (Eerdmans, 2018) and *The Oxford Handbook of Reformed Theology* (with Scott Swain; Oxford University Press, 2020).

Bruce P. Baugus (PhD, Calvin Theological Seminary) is associate professor of philosophy and theology at Reformed Theological Seminary, Jackson, where he has served since 2008. Baugus is the author of several articles and chapters, including "The Eclipse of Justification: Justification during the Enlightenment and Post-Enlightenment Eras," in *The Doctrine on Which the Church Stands or Falls: Justification in Biblical, Theological, Historical, and Pastoral Perspective* (Crossway, 2019), and is the editor of *China's Reforming Churches: Mission, Polity, and Ministry in the Next Christendom* (Reformation Heritage Books, 2014).

Richard P. Belcher Jr. (PhD, Westminster Theological Seminary) is the John D. and Frances M. Gwin Professor of Old Testament and academic dean at Reformed Theological Seminary, Charlotte. Before he joined the faculty in 1995, he served as a pastor for ten years. Belcher has written *The Messiah and the Psalms: Preaching Christ from All the Psalms* (Mentor, 2006); *Prophet, Priest, and King: The Roles of Christ in the Bible and Our Roles Today* (P&R, 2016); and *Finding Favour in the Sight of God: A Theology of Wisdom Literature* (Apollos, 2018).

Robert J. Cara (PhD, Westminster Theological Seminary) is the provost and chief academic officer for all the Reformed Theological Seminary campuses and the Hugh and Sallie Reaves Professor of New Testament, Charlotte campus, where he has served since 1993. He is currently completing a commentary on the book of Hebrews. Among his other writing projects are *1 & 2 Thessalonians* (Evangelical Press, 2009) and *Cracking the Foundation of the New Perspective on Paul: Covenantal Nomism versus Reformed Covenantal Theology* (Mentor, 2017).

John D. Currid (PhD, University of Chicago) is the Chancellor's Professor of Old Testament at Reformed Theological Seminary. He is a trained archaeologist, having served on the staffs of the excavations of Carthage (Tunisia), Bethsaida, Tell el-Hesi, and the Lahav Grain Storage Project. He has authored numerous books, such as *The ESV Bible Atlas* (with David Barrett; Crossway, 2010) and *Against the Gods: The Polemical Theology of the Old Testament* (Crossway, 2013). He currently serves as pastor of teaching and preaching at Sovereign Grace Church (PCA) in Charlotte.

Kevin DeYoung (PhD, University of Leicester) is senior pastor of Christ Covenant Church in Matthews, North Carolina, as well as assistant professor of systematic theology at Reformed Theological Seminary, Charlotte. DeYoung is the author of more than a dozen books, including *The Hole in Our Holiness: Filling the Gap between Gospel Passion and the Pursuit of Godliness* (Crossway, 2012); *The Biggest Story: How the Snake Crusher Brings Us Back to the Garden* (Crossway, 2015); and *The Ten Commandments: What They Mean, Why They Matter, and Why We Should Obey Them* (Crossway, 2018).

Ligon Duncan (PhD, University of Edinburgh) is chancellor, CEO, and John E. Richards Professor of Systematic and Historical Theology at Reformed Theological Seminary, where he has taught since 1989. He served as the senior minister of First Presbyterian Church in Jackson, Mississippi, from 1996 until 2013, when he returned full time to RTS. He is a cofounder of Together for the Gospel and has served on numerous boards and councils, including the Gospel Coalition, and the Alliance of Confessing Evangelicals. Duncan has edited, written, or contributed to over three dozen books.

Benjamin L. Gladd (PhD, Wheaton College) is associate professor of New Testament at Reformed Theological Seminary, Jackson, and series editor for Essential Studies in Biblical Theology (InterVarsity Press). His publications include *Hidden but Now Revealed: A Biblical Theology of Mystery* (with G. K. Beale; InterVarsity Press, 2014); *From Adam and Israel to the Church: A Biblical Theology of the People of God* (InterVarsity Press, 2019); and *The Story Retold: A Biblical-Theological Introduction to the New Testament* (with G. K. Beale; InterVarsity Press, 2020).

Michael J. Glodo (ThM, Westminster Theological Seminary) is associate professor of pastoral theology and dean of the chapel at Reformed Theological Seminary, Orlando, where he has served from 1991 to 2000 and 2007 to the present. Glodo is the author of "Numbers" and "Judges," in *A Biblical-Theological Introduction to the Old Testament: The Gospel Promised* (Crossway, 2016), and a contributor to the *ESV Gospel Transformation Study Bible* (Crossway, 2013).

Howard Griffith (PhD, Westminster Theological Seminary) was academic dean and professor of systematic theology at Reformed Theological Seminary, Washington, DC, from 2007 until his death in 2019. Before coming to RTS, he pastored All Saints Presbyterian Church in Richmond, Virginia, for twenty-three years. He is the author of *Spreading the Feast: Instruction and Meditations for Ministry at the Lord's Table* (P&R, 2015).

Douglas F. Kelly (PhD, University of Edinburgh) is Richard Jordan Professor of Systematic Theology Emeritus at Reformed Theological Seminary, Charlotte, where he served from 1994 to 2016, after serving at RTS Jackson from 1983 to 1994. Some of his books include *If God Already Knows, Why Pray?* (Christian Focus, 1989); *The Emergence of Liberty in the Modern World* (P&R, 1992); *Preachers with Power: Four Stalwarts of the South* (Banner of Truth, 1992); *Revelation* (Mentor, 2012); and *Systematic Theology* (Mentor, 2008–2014).

Michael J. Kruger (PhD, University of Edinburgh) is president and the Samuel C. Patterson Professor of New Testament and Early Christianity at Reformed Theological Seminary, Charlotte, where he has served since 2002. He is the author of numerous books, most recently *Christianity at the Crossroads: How the Second Century Shaped the Future of the Church* (IVP Academic, 2018). Other publications include *Canon Revisited: Establishing the Origins and Authority of the New Testament Books* (Crossway, 2012) and *The Question of Canon: Challenging the Status Quo in the New Testament Debate* (InterVarsity Press, 2013).

Gregory R. Lanier (PhD, University of Cambridge) is associate professor of New Testament at Reformed Theological Seminary, Orlando, where he has served since 2016. He is the author or editor of *How We Got the Bible: Old and New Testament Canon and Text* (Christian Focus, 2018); *Septuaginta: A Reader's Edition* (with William Ross; Hendrickson, 2019); and *Is Jesus Truly God? How the Bible Teaches the Divinity of Christ* (Crossway, 2020). He also serves as associate pastor of River Oaks Church (PCA) in Lake Mary, Florida.

Peter Y. Lee (PhD, Catholic University of America) is professor of Old Testament at Reformed Theological Seminary, Washington, DC, where he has served since 2008. He is the author of *Aramaic Poetry in Qumran* (Scholars Press, 2012) and *Joy Unspeakable: Finding Joy in Christ-like Suffering* (Wipf and Stock, 2019).

Mark I. McDowell (PhD, University of Aberdeen) is executive director and assistant professor of systematic theology at Reformed Theological Seminary, Dallas, where he has served since 2017. McDowell's doctoral research looked at the influence of Reformed theology on Karl Barth's developing Christology in Göttingen, where he occupied the role of honorary professor of Reformed theology. McDowell completed his dissertation under the supervision of the late John Webster.

Michael G. McKelvey (PhD, University of Aberdeen) is associate professor of Old Testament at Reformed Theological Seminary, Jackson, where he has served since 2014. He is the author of *Moses, David and the High Kingship of Yahweh: A Canonical Study of*

Book IV of the Psalter (Gorgias, 2010) and *Amos*, ESV Expository Commentary (Crossway, 2018).

John R. Muether (MAR, Westminster Theological Seminary) is dean of libraries and professor of church history at Reformed Theological Seminary, Orlando, where he has served since 1989. He is the author of *Cornelius Van Til: Reformed Apologist and Churchman* (P&R, 2007) and has coauthored several books, including *Seeking a Better Country: 300 Years of American Presbyterianism* (with D. G. Hart; P&R, 2008).

John Scott Redd (PhD, Catholic University of America), is president and professor of Old Testament at Reformed Theological Seminary, Washington, DC. Prior to coming to RTS Washington he served at RTS Orlando from 2009 to 2012. Redd is the author of *Constituent Postponement in Biblical Hebrew Verse* (Harrassowitz, 2014) and *The Wholeness Imperative: How Christ Unifies Our Desires, Identity and Impact in the World* (Christian Focus, 2018).

J. Nicholas Reid (DPhil, University of Oxford) is associate professor of Old Testament and ancient Near Eastern studies at Reformed Theological Seminary, Orlando, where he has served since 2017. Reid has authored several articles on unpublished cuneiform tablets and topics of Mesopotamian social history in journals such as the *Journal of Ancient Near Eastern History*, *Journal of Near Eastern Studies*, *Journal of the Economic and Social History of the Orient*, and *Revue d'Assyriologie*. He is currently co-authoring a book on unpublished Old Babylonian letters for Oxford University Press.

Guy M. Richard (PhD, University of Edinburgh) is executive director and assistant professor of systematic theology at Reformed Theological Seminary, Atlanta. Richard is the author of *The Supremacy of God in the Theology of Samuel Rutherford* (Paternoster, 2008); *What Is Faith?* (P&R, 2012); *Baptism: Answers to Common Questions* (Reformation Trust, 2019), as well as many essays and articles dealing with the theology of the Reformation and post-Reformation periods.

O. Palmer Robertson (ThD, Union Theological Seminary, Virginia) is executive director of Consummation Ministries. He was previously director of African Bible University in Uganda and has served on the faculties of Reformed Theological Seminary, Westminster Theological Seminary, and Covenant Theological Seminary. His published books include *The Christ of the Covenants* (P&R, 1980); *The Christ of the Prophets* (P&R, 2004); *The Flow of the Psalms: Discovering Their Structure and Theology* (P&R, 2015); and *The Christ of Wisdom: A Redemptive-Historical Exploration of the Wisdom Books of the Old Testament* (P&R, 2017).

D. Blair Smith (PhD, Durham University) is assistant professor of systematic theology at Reformed Theological Seminary, Charlotte. Before coming to Charlotte in 2016, he served in pastoral ministry in Bethesda, Maryland, and South Bend, Indiana. He is the author of several essays and articles on the Trinity and Christology.

Scott R. Swain (PhD, Trinity Evangelical Divinity School) is president and James Woodrow Hassell Professor of Systematic Theology at Reformed Theological Seminary, Orlando, where he has served since 2006. Swain is the author or editor of several books, most recently *Reformed Catholicity: The Promise of Retrieval for Theology and Biblical Interpretation* (with Michael Allen; Baker Academic, 2015); *Retrieving Eternal Generation* (with Fred Sanders; Zondervan, 2017); *The Trinity: An Introduction* (Crossway, 2020); and *The Oxford Handbook of Reformed Theology* (with Michael Allen; Oxford University Press, 2020).

Derek W. H. Thomas (PhD, University of Wales) is the Chancellor's Professor of Systematic Theology at Reformed Theological Seminary and senior pastor at First Presbyterian Church in Columbia, South Carolina, having previously served at RTS Jackson (1996–2011) and RTS Atlanta (2012–2017). Thomas is the author or editor of twenty-five books, including *Ezra and Nehemiah* (P&R, 2016); *Heaven on Earth: What the Bible Teaches about the Life to Come* (Christian Focus, 2018); and *John Calvin: For a New Reformation* (with John W. Tweeddale; Crossway, 2019).

Miles V. Van Pelt (PhD, Southern Baptist Theological Seminary) is the Alan Hayes Belcher Jr. Professor of Old Testament and Biblical Languages and academic dean, as well as director of the Summer Institute for Biblical Languages, at Reformed Theological Seminary, Jackson, where he has served since 2003. Van Pelt is the author or editor of numerous books, including *Basics of Biblical Aramaic* (Zondervan, 2011); *A Biblical-Theological Introduction to the Old Testament: The Gospel Promised* (Crossway, 2016); and *Basics of Biblical Hebrew*, 3rd ed. (with Gary D. Pratico; Zondervan, 2019).

Guy Prentiss Waters (PhD, Duke University) is the James M. Baird Jr. Professor of New Testament at Reformed Theological Seminary, Jackson, where he has served since 2007, and academic dean of the Houston and Dallas campuses. Waters is the author or editor of ten books, including *Justification and the New Perspectives on Paul* (P&R, 2004); *The Federal Vision and Covenant Theology: A Comparative Analysis* (P&R, 2006); *Children and the Lord's Supper* (with Ligon Duncan; Mentor, 2011); and *The Acts of the Apostles* (Evangelical Press, 2015).

General Index

Aaronic priesthood, 256, 259, 260, 265, 479
Abegg, Martin, 476
Abijam, 185
Abraham
  faith and faithfulness of, 135, 137, 139, 252–53, 342, 472
  and land of Canaan, 137
  obedience of, 469–70, 483, 542
  offspring of, 218, 233, 252, 576
  promises to, 218–19, 253–54, 265
  response to God's call, 134, 509
  testing of, 143–44
Abrahamic covenant, 93, 120, 133–47, 203, 591
  and blessings to the nations, 133, 135, 147, 508–18
  in Book of Consolation, 104
  conditionality of, 142–43, 542–43
  covenant amendment, 141–43
  covenant confirmation, 143–44
  covenant introduction, 136–38
  and Davidic covenant, 183
  fulfilled in new covenant, 253
  in the Gospels, 218–19, 226
  in Hebrews, 248, 251–54, 265
  as land grant, 461
  and Mosaic covenant, 152
  in Paul, 232–34
  ratification of, 138–41
  in redemptive history, 144–47
  in Revelation, 275, 276
  in Second Temple Judaism, 468–72
  unconditionality of, 140–41
  in writings of early church, 302
active obedience of Christ, 166, 216, 370n75, 440
Adam
  Barth on, 413–14
  brought condemnation, 87, 229
  conditions in paradise for, 65
  as covenant breaker, 66–67, 229
  in covenant of works with God, 58, 89, 571
  federal obedience as meritorious for, 367–68
  given the law, 302, 307
  natural relationship to God, 67–68
  as public persons, 590

  as representative head, 28, 65–66, 70, 80, 81, 84–85, 86, 89, 228–29, 366–67, 505, 590
  in Second Temple Judaism, 467–68n3
  seed of, 575
  sin of, 66, 69, 85–88, 99–102
  as son of God, 58
Adam and Eve
  cursing of, 591
  divine commission of, 501
Adam-Christ typology, 24, 58, 64, 86, 228–30, 369
Adamic administration (Murray), 72–73, 364n57
ad fontes scholarship, 383, 399
Adonai Yahweh, 177
adoption, 183n56, 243, 424
Adversus Judaeos (Pseudo-Cyprian), 294
Afscheiding, 397
agreement, essential ingredient of all covenants, 46
Akkadian, 447–48, 459
Albertus Magnus, 314
Alexander, Loveday, 212
Alexander, T. Desmond, 133–34
Alexander of Hales, 314
alienation
  from eternal life, 102
  from God, 101
  from one another, 101
  from physical environment, 101–2
  solution to, 109
Allis, O. T., 540, 541
already and not yet, 196, 249, 438, 550, 585, 591
Altaner, Berthold, 302n34
Ames, William, 44, 355n20, 363n52, 388, 389, 414n64
Anabaptists
  on the Old Testament, 341, 342, 343
  rejection of infant baptism, 329–30, 333, 334
  Zwingli's dispute with, 327, 336–38
analogy, Richard Hays on, 488
ancient church, sources of Reformation-era covenant theology, 293
ancient Near East treaties, 138, 139–40, 443, 447–65
Anderson, A. A., 176n17
angels, sons of God as, 114
animals, blood of, 126
"anointed one," 187, 188, 273

Scripture Index